WHO
WON
WHAT
WHEN

WHO

The Record Book of Winners

WON

compiled by Sandra Lee Stuart

WHAT

LYLE STUART INC.   *Secaucus, N.J.*

WHEN

For Morris Sorkin

First edition
Copyright © 1977 by Sandra Lee Stuart
All rights reserved, including the right to reproduce
this book or any portion thereof in any form

Published by Lyle Stuart Inc.
120 Enterprise Ave., Secaucus, N.J.   07094
Published simultaneously in Canada by George J. McLeod Limited
73 Bathurst St., Toronto, Ont.

Address queries regarding rights and permissions
to Lyle Stuart Inc.

Manufactured in the United States of America

Library of Congress Cataloging in Publication Data
Stuart, Sandra Lee.
    Who won what when.
1. Rewards (Prizes, etc.) 2. Sports—Records.
I. Title.
AS8.S83   001   77-23924
ISBN 0-8184-0247-4

INTRODUCTION

Vince Lombardi, a great coach and a sometimes philosopher, once proclaimed that winning wasn't everything. It was the only thing.

In the United States, at least, he was right. Nothing is more American than winning, John Wayne, and apple pie. We are a competitive people, a nation of strivers and goal-getters. A country that measures success by what one does, what one accomplishes. No wonder the Beats of the Fifties and the Hippies of the Sixties were such an affront to our work-ethic mentality.

And no wonder we are a country that gets tickled red-white-and-blue over games, contests, prizes, and medals. Starting with those gold stars that teachers hand out in grade school, up to the Nobel prize, there is every kind of accolade for gung-ho strivers to work for and win.

Competitiveness is part of our cultural nature. (The Zuni Indians would find the "We're Number One" ravings very curious, since their culture isn't based on the every-man-for-himself concept.) Psychologists have spent many a lab hour showing that an American man or woman working alone will finish a task in a certain length of time. But put someone else to work in the room, and the race is on. The first man or woman will finish the task a lot faster.

Winning. Someone is winning something all the time. This book is an attempt to catalog who won what when. Within certain boundaries, of course.

The awards are limited to those awarded since 1900, except when a contest or prize began a few years before the turn of the century. It would have been silly to omit the first modern Olympics because they were held in 1896.

Second, the listings are primarily American. The exceptions being when Americans have taken home many of the foreign prizes or have participated on a large scale. The Nobel Prize, the Olympics, the Wimbledon games are some of these entries.

Most importantly, I've left out the losers, the runners-up, and the also-rans. It wasn't germane to this book that Mark Spitz took a silver medal in the 1968 Olympics for the 100-meter butterfly. The listings that counted were all those gold medals he swam to in 1972.

Almost all the awards are still being presented. Again, there are exceptions. Some Pulitzer listings were discontinued— the "telegraphic" awards for example—but it was more that the titles were changed than that the awards were actually dropped.

One last thing, before mutterings of discontent begin. I apologize for all major or favorite awards that didn't make these pages. Some "honors" were deliberately not included because of fickleness. Others were left out because of oversight or stupidity. There were some organizations, however— and may a poxy mildew fall on their files— that ignored all pleas and entreaties to send lists of their winners. Perhaps they will be cajoled into the next edition.

SANDRA LEE STUART

CONTENTS

CONTENTS

CONTENTS

CONTENTS

CONTENTS

CONTENTS

CONTENTS

CONTENTS

CONTENTS

CONTENTS

THE BIGGIES

THE NOBEL PRIZE

It's not an American prize, but the United States is well-represented among the winners. And in any case, a book of "winners" that excluded the world's most prestigious honor wouldn't be worth a place on any library shelf. Alfred Bernhard Nobel invented dynamite, at the time the world's most awesome, devastating means of destruction. When he died he left $9,000,000 stipulating that the interest should be distributed yearly as prizes to those who "have conferred the greatest benefit on mankind in the fields of physics, chemistry, physiology or medicine, literature and peace." The shares in 1976 were $160,000 each.

A sixth award, in economics, was added in 1969 through a donation by Sweden's national bank. All awards are decided by various Swedish institutions, except for the peace prize. For some reason Mr. Nobel thought the Norwegians better suited to choose that winner.

CHEMISTRY

1901
    Jacobus H. van't Hoff, Netherlands
1902
    Emil H. Fischer, Germany
1903
    Svante A. Arrhenius, Sweden

1904
    William Ramsay, Great Britain
1905
    Adolf von Baeyer, Germany
1906
    Henri Moissan, France
1907
    Eduard Buchner, Germany
1908
    Ernest Rutherford, Great Britain
1909
    Wilhelm Ostwald, Germany
1910
    Otto Wallach, Germany
1911
    Marie S. Curie, France
1912
    F. A. Victor Grignard, France
    Paul Sabatier, France
1913
    Alfred Werner, Switzerland
1914
    Theodore W. Richards, United States
1915
    Richard M. Willstatter, Germany
1916   no award
1917   no award
1918
    Fritz Haber, Germany
1919   no award
1920
    Walther Nernst, Germany
1921
    Frederick Soddy, Great Britain
1922
    Francis W. Aston, Great Britain
1923
    Fritz Pregl, Austria
1924   no award
1925
    Richard A. Zsigmondy, Germany
1926
    Theodor Svedberg, Sweden

1927
 Heinrich O. Wieland, Germany
1928
 Adolf O. R. Windaus, Germany
1929
 Sir Arthur Harden, Great Britain
 Hans von Euler-Chelpin, Sweden
1930
 Hans Fischer, Germany
1931
 Carl Bosch, Germany
 Friedrich Bergius, Germany
1932
 Irving Langmuir, United States
1933   no award
1934
 Harold C. Urey, United States
1935
 Frederic Joliot-Curie, France
 Irene Joliot-Curie, France
1936
 Peter J. W. Debye, United States
1937
 Walter N. Haworth, Great Britain
 Paul Karrer, Switzerland
1938
 Richard Kuhn, Austria
1939
 Adolf F. J. Butenandt, Germany
 Leopold Ruzicka, Switzerland
1940   no award
1941   no award
1942   no award
1943
 Georg von Hevesy, Hungary
1944
 Otto Hahn, Germany
1945
 Artturi I. Virtanen, Finland
1946
 James B. Sumner, United States
 John H. Northrop, United States
 Wendell M. Stanley, United States
1947
 Robert Robinson, Great Britain
1948
 Arne W. K. Tiselius, Sweden
1949
 William F. Giauque, United States
1950
 Otto P. H. Diels, Germany
 Kurt Alder, Germany
1951
 Edwin M. McMillan, United States
 Glenn T. Seaborg, United States

1952
 Archer J. P. Martin, Great Britain
 Richard L. M. Synge, Great Britain
1953
 Hermann Staudinger, Germany
1954
 Linus C. Pauling, United States
1955
 Vincent du Vigneaud, United States
1956
 Cyril N. Hinshelwood, Great Britain
 Nikolai N. Semenov, U.S.S.R.
1957
 Alexander R. Todd, Great Britain
1958
 Frederick Sanger, Great Britain
1959
 Jaroslav Heyrovsky, Czechoslovakia
1960
 Willard F. Libby, United States
1961
 Melvin Calvin, United States
1962
 Max F. Perutz, Great Britain
 John C. Kendrew, Great Britain
1963
 Karl Ziegler, Germany
 Giulio Natta, Italy
1964
 Dorothy C. Hodgkin, Great Britain
1965
 Robert B. Woodward, United States
1966
 Robert S. Mulliken, United States
1967
 Manfred Eigen, Germany
 Ronald G. W. Norrish, Great Britain
 George Porter, Great Britain
1968
 Lars Onsager, United States
1969
 Derek H. R. Barton, Great Britain
 Odd Hassel, Norway
1970
 Luis F. Leloir, Argentina
1971
 Gerhard Herzberg, Canada
1972
 Dr. Christian Boehmer Anfisen,
 United States
 Dr. Stanford Moore, United States
 Dr. William Howard Stein,
 United States
1973
 Ernst Otto Fischer, Germany

Geoffrey Wilkinson, Great Britain
1974
Paul J. Flory, United States
1975
John W. Cornforth, Great Britain
Vladimir Prelog, Switzerland
1976
William N. Lipscomb, United States

ECONOMIC SCIENCE

1969
Ragnar Frisch, Norway
Jan Tinbergen, Netherlands
1970
Paul Anthony Samuelson,
United States
1971
Simon Kuznets, United States
1972
Kenneth J. Arrow, United States
John R. Hicks, Great Britain
1973
Wassily Leontief, United States
1974
Gunnar Myrdal, Sweden
Friedrich A. von Hayek,
Great Britain
1975
Leonid V. Kantorovich, U.S.S.R.
Tjalling C. Koopmans, United States
1976
Milton Friedman, United States

LITERATURE

1901
Rene F. A. Sully-Prudhomme,
France
1902
Theodor Mommsen, Germany
1903
Bjornstjerne Bjornson, Norway
1904
Frederic Mistral, France
Jose Echegaray, Spain
1905
Henryk Sienkiewicz, Poland
1906
Giosue Carducci, Italy
1907
Rudyard Kipling, Great Britain
1908
Rudolf C. Eucken, Germany
1909
Selma Lagerlof, Sweden

1910
Paul J. L. Heyse, Germany
1911
Maurice Maeterlinck, Belgium
1912
Gerhart Hauptmann, Germany
1913
Rabindranath Tagore, India
1914   no award
1915
Romain Rolland, France
1916
Verner von Heidenstam, Sweden
1917
Karl A. Gjellerup, Denmark
Henrik Pontoppidan, Denmark
1918   no award
1919
Carl F. G. Spitteler, Switzerland
1920
Knut Hamsun, Norway
1921
Anatole France, France
1922
Jacinto Benavente y Martinez, Spain
1923
William Butler Yeats, Ireland
1924
Wladyslaw S. Reymont, Poland
1925
George Bernard Shaw, Great Britain
1926
Grazia Deledda, Italy
1927
Henri Bergson, France
1928
Sigrid Undset, Norway
1929
Thomas Mann, Germany
1930
Sinclair Lewis, United States
1931
Erik A. Karlfeldt, Sweden
1932
John Galsworthy, Great Britain
1933
Ivan A. Bunin, U.S.S.R.
1934
Luigi Pirandello, Italy
1935   no award
1936
Eugene O'Neill, United States
1937
Roger Martin du Gard, France

*1938 Nobel Prize winner for literature,
Pearl S. Buck. (Wide World Photos)*

1938
  Pearl S. Buck, United States
1939
  Frans E. Sillanpaa, Finland
1940   no award
1941   no award
1942   no award
1943   no award
1944
  Johannes V. Jensen, Denmark
1945
  Gabriela Mistral, Chile
1946
  Hermann Hesse, Switzerland
1947
  Andre Gide, France
1948
  T. S. Eliot, Great Britain
1949
  William Faulkner, United States
1950
  Bertrand A. W. Russell, Great Britain
1951
  Par F. Lagerkvist, Sweden
1952
  Francois Mauriac, France
1953
  Sir Winston Churchill, Great Britain

1954
  Ernest Hemingway, United States
1955
  Halldor K. Laxness, Iceland
1956
  Juan Ramon Jimenez, Spain
1957
  Albert Camus, France
1958
  Boris L. Pasternak (declined for
  political reasons), U.S.S.R.
1959
  Salvatore Quasimodo, Italy
1960
  Saint-John Perse, France
1961
  Ivo Andric, Yugoslavia
1962
  John Steinbeck, United States
1963
  Giorgos Seferis, Greece
1964
  Jean Paul Sartre (declined), France
1965
  Mikhail A. Sholokov, U.S.S.R.
1966
  Samuel Y. Agnon, Israel
  Nelly Sachs, Sweden

1967
Miguel Angel Asturias, Guatemala
1968
Yasunari Kawabata, Japan
1969
Samuel Beckett, Ireland
1970
Aleksandr Solzhenitsyn, U.S.S.R.
1971
Pablo Neruda, Chile
1972
Heinrich Boll, Germany
1973
Patrick White, Australia
1974
Eyvind Johnson, Sweden
Edmund Martinson, Sweden
1975
Eugenio Montale, Italy
1976
Saul Bellow, United States

MEDICINE or PHYSIOLOGY

1901
Emil A. von Behring, Germany
1902
Ronald Ross, Great Britain
1903
Niels R. Finsen, Denmark
1904
Ivan P. Pavlov, Russia
1905
Robert Koch, Germany
1906
Camillo Golgi, Italy
Santiago Ramon y Cajal, Spain
1907
Charles L. A. Laveran, France
1908
Paul Ehrlich, Germany
Elie Metchnikoff, Russia
1909
E. Theodor Kocher, Switzerland
1910
Albrecht Kossel, Germany
1911
Allvar Sullstrand, Sweden
1912
Alexis Carrel, United States
1913
Charles R. Richet, France
1914
Robert Barany, Austria
1915   no award

1916   no award
1917   no award
1918   no award
1919
Jules J. P. V. Bordet, Belgium
1920
S. August Krogh, Denmark
1921   no award
1922
Archibald V. Hill, Great Britain
Otto F. Meyerhof, United States
1923
Frederick G. Banting, Canada
John J. R. Macleod, Great Britain
1924
Willem Einthoven, Netherlands
1925   no award
1926
Johannes A. G. Fibiger, Denmark
1927
Julius Wagner-Jauregg, Austria
1928
Charles J. H. Nicolle, France
1929
Christiaan Eijkman, Netherlands
Frederick G. Hopkins, Great Britain
1930
Karl Landsteiner, United States
1931
Otto H. Warburg, Germany
1932
Edgar D. Adrian, Great Britain
Charles S. Sherrington, Great Britain
1933
Thomas H. Morgan, United States
1934
George R. Minot, United States
William P. Murphy, United States
George H. Whipple, United States
1935
Hans Spemann, Germany
1936
Henry H. Dale, Great Britain
Otto Loewi, United States
1937
Albert von Szent-Gyorgyi,
United States
1938
Corneille J. F. Heymans, Belgium
1939
Gerhard Domagk (declined under
political pressure, received prize in
1947), Germany
1940   no award
1941   no award

Dr. Francis H. C. Crick shared the 1962 Nobel Prize for medicine with two other scientists. (Wide World Photos)

1942   no award
1943
  C. P. Henrik Dam, Denmark
  Edward A. Doisy, United States
1944
  E. Joseph Erlanger, United States
  Herbert S. Gasser, United States
1945
  Alexander Fleming, Great Britain
  Howard W. Florey, Great Britain
  Ernst B. Chain, Great Britain
1946
  Hermann Joseph Muller,
  United States
1947
  Carl F. Cori, United States
  Gerty T. Cori, United States
  Bernardo A. Houssay, Argentina
1948
  Paul H. Muller, Switzerland
1949
  Walter R. Hess, Switzerland
  Antonio de Egas Moniz, Portugal
1950
  Philip S. Hench, United States
  Edward C. Kendall, United States
  Tadeus Reichstein, Switzerland
1951
  Max Theiler, United States

1952
  Selman A. Waksman, United States
1953
  Fritz A. Lipmann, United States
  Hans A. Krebs, Great Britain
1954
  John F. Enders, United States
  Thomas H. Weller, United States
  Frederick C. Robbins, United States
1955
  A. Hugo T. Theorell, Sweden
1956
  D. W. Richards, United States
  Andre F. Cournand, United States
  Werner Forssmann, Germany
1957
  Daniel Bovet, Italy
1958
  George W. Beadle, United States
  Edward L. Tatum, United States
  Joshua Lederberg, United States
1959
  Severo Ochoa, United States
  Arthur Kornberg, United States
1960
  F. Macfarlane Burnet, Australia
  Peter B. Medawar, Great Britain
1961
  Georg von Bekesy, United States

1962
Francis H. C. Crick, Great Britain
Maurice H. F. Wilkins, Great Britain
James D. Watson, United States
1963
Alan L. Hodgkin, Great Britain
Andrew F. Huxley, Great Britain
John C. Eccles, Australia
1964
Konrad E. Bloch, United States
Feodor Lynen, Germany
1965
Francois Jacob, France
Andre M. Lwoff, France
Jacques L. Monod, France
1966
Charles B. Huggins, United States
Francis P. Rous, United States
1967
Haldan K. Hartline, United States
George Wald, United States
Ragnar A. Granit, Sweden
1968
Robert W. Holley, United States
H. Gobind Khorana, United States
Marshall W. Nirenberg, United
States
1969
Max Delbruck, United States
Alfred D. Hershey, United States
Salvador E. Luria, United States
1970
Bernard Katz, Great Britain
Ulf von Euler, Sweden
Julius Axelrod, United States
1971
Earl W. Sutherland, United States
1972
Gerald M. Edelman, United States
Rodney R. Porter, Great Britain
1973
Konrad Lorenz, Austria
Nikolaas Tinbergen, Great Britain
Karl von Frisch, Germany
1974
Albert Claude, United States
Christian Rene de Duve, Belgium
George Emil Palade, United States
1975
David Baltimore, United States
Renato Dulbecco, United States
Howard M. Temin, United States
1976
Baruch S. Blumber, United States
D. Carleton Gajdusek, United States

PHYSICS

1901
Wilhelm C. Roentgen, Germany
1902
Hendrik A. Lorentz, Netherlands
Pieter Zeeman, Netherlands
1903
Antoine H. Becquerel, France
Pierre Curie, France
Marie S. Curie, France
1904
John W. S. Rayleigh, Great Britain
1905
Philipp E. A. Lenard, Germany
1906
Joseph J. Thomson, Great Britain
1907
Albert A. Michelson, United States
1908
Gabriel Lippmann, France
1909
Guglielmo Marconi, Italy
Karl F. Braun, Germany
1910
Johannes D. van der Waals,
Netherlands
1911
Wilhelm Wien, Germany
1912
Nils G. Dalen, Sweden
1913
Heike Kamerlingh-Onnes,
Netherlands
1914
Max von Laue, Germany
1915
William H. Bragg, Great Britain
Lawrence Bragg, Great Britain
1916   no award
1917
Charles G. Barkla, Great Britain
1918
Max K. E. L. Planck, Germany
1919
Johannes Stark, Germany
1920
Charles E. Guillaume, France
1921
Albert Einstein, United States
1922
Niels H. D. Bohr, Denmark
1923
Robert A. Millikan, United States

1924
  Karl M. G. Siegbahn, Sweden
1925
  James Franck, Germany
  Gustav Hertz, Germany
1926
  Jean B. Perrin, France
1927
  Arthur H. Compton, United States
  Charles T. R. Wilson, Great Britain
1928
  Owen W. Richardson, Great Britain
1929
  Louis-Victor de Broglie, France
1930
  Chandrasekhara V. Raman, India
1931   no award
1932
  Werner Heisenberg, Germany
1933
  Erwin Schrodinger, Austria
  Paul A. M. Dirac, Great Britain
1934   no award
1935
  James Chadwick, Great Britain
1936
  Victor F. Hess, United States
  Carl D. Anderson, United States
1937
  Clinton J. Davisson, United States
  George P. Thomson, Great Britain
1938
  Enrico Fermi, United States
1939
  Ernest O. Lawrence, United States
1940   no award
1941   no award
1942   no award
1943
  Otto Stern, United States
1944
  Isidor Isaac Rabi, United States
1945
  Wolfgang Pauli, United States
1946
  Percy Williams Bridgman,
  United States
1947
  Edward V. Appleton, Great Britain
1948
  Patrick M. S. Blackett, Great Britain
1949
  Hideki Yukawa, Japan
1950
  Cecil F. Powell, Great Britain

1951
  Sir John D. Cockcroft, Great Britain
  Ernest T. S. Walton, Ireland
1952
  Felix Bloch, United States
  Edward Purcell, United States
1953
  Frits Zernike, Netherlands
1954
  Max Born, Great Britain
  Walther Bothe, Germany
1955
  Willis E. Lamb, Jr., United States
  Polykarp Kusch, United States
1956
  John Bardeen, United States
  Walter H. Brattain, United States
  William B. Shockley, United States
1957
  Tsung-Dao Lee, United States
  Chen Ning Yang, United States
1958
  Pavel A. Cherenkov, U.S.S.R.
  Ilya M. Frank, U.S.S.R.
  Igor Y. Tamm, U.S.S.R.
1959
  Emilio G. Segre, United States
  Owen Chamberlain, United States
1960
  Donald A. Glaser, United States
1961
  Robert Hofstadter, United States
  Rudolf L. Moessbauer, Germany
1962
  Lev. D. Landau, U.S.S.R.
1963
  Eugene P. Wigner, United States
  Maria Goeppert-Mayer,
  United States
  J. Hans D. Jensen, Germany
1964
  Charles H. Townes, United States
  Nikolai G. Basov, U.S.S.R.
  Aleksander M. Prokhorov, U.S.S.R.
1965
  Richard P. Feynman, United States
  Julian S. Schwinger, United States
  Sin-itiro Tomonaga, Japan
1966
  Alfred Kastler, France
1967
  Hans A. Bethe, United States
1968
  Luis W. Alvarez, United States

1969
    Murray Gell-Mann, United States
1970
    Louis Neel, France
    Hannes Alfven, Sweden
1971
    Dennis Gabor, Great Britain
1972
    John Bardeen, United States
    Leon Cooper, United States
    John Robert Schrieffer, United States
1973
    Leo Esaki, Japan
    Ivar Giaever, United States
    Brian D. Josephson, Great Britain
1974
    Sir Martin Ryle, Great Britain
    Anthony Hewish, Great Britain
1975
    James Rainwater, United States
    Aage N. Bohr, Denmark
    Ben R. Mottelson, Denmark
1976
    Burton Richter, United States
    Samuel C. C. Ting, United States

PEACE

1901
    Jean H. Dunant, Switzerland
    Frederic Passy, France
1902
    Elie Ducommun, Switzerland
    Charles A. Gobat, Switzerland
1903
    William R. Cremer, Great Britain
1904   Institute of International Law
1905
    Bertha von Suttner, Austria
1906
    Theodore Roosevelt, United States
1907
    Ernesto T. Moneta, Italy
    Louis Renault, France
1908
    Klas P. Arnoldson, Sweden
1909
    August M. F. Beernaert, Belgium
    Paul H. Benjamin Estournelles de
    Constant, France
1910   International Peace Bureau
1911
    Tobia M. C. Asser, Netherlands
    Alfred H. Fried, Austria

1912
    Elihu Root, United States
1913
    Henri La Fontaine, Belgium
1914   no award
1915   no award
1916   no award
1917   International Red Cross
            Committee
1918   no award
1919
    Woodrow Wilson, United States
1920
    Leon Bourgeois, France
1921
    Hjalmar Branting, Sweden
    Christian L. Lange, Norway
1922
    Fridtjof Nansen, Norway
1923   no award
1924   no award
1925
    Sir J. Austen Chamberlain,
    Great Britain
    Charles G. Dawes, United States
1926
    Aristide Briand, France
    Gustav Stresemann, Germany
1927
    Ferdinand E. Buisson, France
    Ludwig Quidde, Germany
1928   no award
1929
    Frank B. Kellogg, United States
1930
    Nathan Soderblom, Sweden
1931
    Jane Addams, United States
    Nicholas Murray Butler,
    United States
1932   no award
1933
    Norman Angell, Great Britain
1934
    Arthur Henderson, Great Britain
1935
    Carl von Ossietzky, Germany
1936
    Carlos Saavedra Lamas, Argentina
1937
    E. A. R. Cecil, Great Britain
1938   Nansen International Office
            for Refugees
1939   no award
1940   no award

1941   no award
1942   no award
1943   no award
1944   International Red Cross
        Committee
1945
    Cordell Hull, United States
1946
    John R. Mott, United States
    Emily Balch, United States
1947
    Friends Service Council, Great
    Britain
    American Friends Service
    Committee, United States
1948   no award
1949
    Sir John Boyd Orr, Great Britain
1950
    Ralph J. Bunche, United States
1951
    Leon Jouhaux, France
1952
    Albert Schweitzer, Alsace
1953
    George C. Marshall, United States
1954   Office of the U. N. High
        Commissioner for Refugees
1955   no award
1956   no award
1957
    Lester B. Pearson, Canada
1958
    Father Georges H. Pire, Belgium
1959
    Philip J. Noel-Baker, Great Britain
1960
    Albert J. Luthuli, South Africa
1961
    Dag Hammarskjold, Sweden
1962
    Linus C. Pauling, United States
1963   International Red Cross
        Committee
        League of Red Cross Societies
1964
    Martin Luther King, Jr.,
    United States
1965   UNICEF (U. N. Children's
        Fund)
1966   no award
1967   no award
1968
    Rene Cassin, France

1969   International Labor
        Organization
1970
    Norman E. Borlaug, United States
1971
    Willy Brandt, Germany
1972   no award
1973
    Henry A. Kissinger, United States
    Le Duc Tho (declined), Vietnam
1974
    Eisaku Sato, Japan
    Sean McBride, Ireland
1975
    Andrei D. Sakharov, U.S.S.R.
1976   no award

OLYMPIC GAMES

SUMMER OLYMPICS

	Sites
1896	Athens, Greece
1900	Paris, France
1904	St. Louis, U.S.
1906	Athens, Greece
1908	London, England
1912	Stockholm, Sweden
1920	Antwerp, Belgium
1924	Paris, France
1928	Amsterdam, Netherlands
1932	Los Angeles, U.S.
1936	Berlin, Germany
1948	London, England
1952	Helsinki, Finland
1956	Melbourne, Australia
1960	Rome, Italy
1964	Tokyo, Japan
1968	Mexico City, Mexico
1972	Munich, West Germany
1976	Montreal, Canada

Archery

(Men)
1972
    John Williams, United States
1976
    Darrell Pace, United States

(Women)
1972
   Doreen Wilbur, United States
1976
   Luann Ryon, United States

Basketball

(Men)
1936	United States
1948	United States
1952	United States
1956	United States
1960	United States
1964	United States
1968	United States
1972	Russia
1976	United States

(Women)
| 1976 | Russia |

Boxing

LIGHT FLYWEIGHT
1968
   F. Rodriguez, Venezuela
1972
   Gyoergy Gedo, Hungary
1976
   Jorge Hernandez, Cuba

FLYWEIGHT
1904
   G. Finnegan, United States
1920
   Frank De Genaro, United States
1924
   Fidel La Barba, United States
1928
   Antal Kocsis, Hungary
1932
   Istvan Enekes, Hungary
1936
   Willi Kaiser, Germany
1948
   Pascual Perez, Argentina
1952
   Nathan Brooks, United States
1956
   Terence Spinks, Great Britain
1960
   Gyula Torok, Hungary

1964
   Fernando Atzori, Italy
1968
   Ricardo Delgado, Mexico
1972
   G. Kostadinov, Bulgaria
1976
   Leo Randolph, United States

BANTAMWEIGHT
1904
   O. L. Kirk, United States
1908
   A. Thomas, Great Britain
1920
   Clarence Walker, South Africa
1924
   William Smith, South Africa
1928
   V. Tamagnini, Italy
1932
   Horace Gwynne, Canada
1936
   Ulderico Sergo, Italy
1948
   Tibor Csik, Hungary
1952
   P. Hamalainen, Finland
1956
   W. Behrendt, Germany
1960
   Oleg Grigoryev, Russia
1964
   Takao Sakurai, Japan
1968
   Valery Sokolov, Russia
1972
   Orlando Martinez, Cuba
1976
   Yong Jo Gu, N. Korea

FEATHERWEIGHT
1904
   O. L. Kirk, United States
1908
   Richard Gunn, Great Britain
1920
   Paul Fritsch, France
1924
   John Fields, United States
1928
   B. van Klaveren, Netherlands
1932
   C. Robledo, Argentina

1936
  Oscar Casanovas, Argentina
1948
  E. Formenti, Italy
1952
  Jan Zachara, Czechoslovakia
1956
  V. Safronov, Russia
1960
  Francesco Musso, Italy
1964
  S. Stepashkin, Russia
1968
  Antonio Roldan, Mexico
1972
  Boris Kousnetsov, Russia
1976
  Angel Herrera, Cuba

LIGHTWEIGHT
1904
  H. J. Spanger, United States
1908
  Frederick Grace, Great Britain
1920
  Samuel Mosberg, United States
1924
  Hans Nielsen, Denmark
1928
  Carlo Orlandi, Italy
1932
  Lawrence Stevens, South Africa
1936
  Imre Harangi, Hungary
1948
  Gerald Dreyer, South Africa
1952
  A. Bolognesi, Italy
1956
  R. McTaggart, Great Britain
1960
  K. Pazdzior, Poland
1964
  Jozef Grudzien, Poland
1968
  Ronnie Harris, United States
1972
  Jan Szcepanski, Poland
1976
  Howard Davis, United States

LIGHT WELTERWEIGHT
1952
  Charles Adkins, United States

1956
  V. Jengibarian, Russia
1960
  B. Nemecek, Czechoslovakia
1964
  Jerzy Kulej, Poland
1968
  Jerzy Kulej, Poland
1972
  Ray Seales, United States
1976
  Ray Leonard, United States

WELTERWEIGHT
1904
  Albert Young, United States
1920
  T. Schneider, Canada
1924
  Jean Delarge, Belgium
1928
  Ed Morgan, New Zealand
1932
  Edward Flynn, United States
1936
  Sten Suvio, Finland
1948
  Julius Torma, Czechoslovakia
1952
  Z. Chychla, Poland
1956
  Nicolae Linca, Romania
1960
  G. Benvenuti, Italy
1964
  Marian Kasprzyk, Poland
1968
  Manfred Wolke, East Germany
1972
  Emilio Correa, Cuba
1976
  Jochen Bachfeld, East Germany

LIGHT MIDDLEWEIGHT
1952
  Laszlo Papp, Hungary
1956
  Laszlo Papp, Hungary
1960
  W. McClure, United States
1964
  Boris Lagutin, Russia
1968
  Boris Lagutin, Russia

1972
Dieter Kottysch, West Germany
1976
Jerzy Rybicki, Poland

MIDDLEWEIGHT
1904
Charles Mayer, United States
1908
John Douglas, Great Britain
1920
Harry Mallin, Great Britain
1924
Harry Mallin, Great Britain
1928
Piero Toscani, Italy
1932
Carmen Barth, United States
1936
Jean Despeaux, France
1948
Laszlo Papp, Hungary
1952
Floyd Patterson, United States
1956
Genadiy Schatkov, Russia
1960
Edward Crook, United States
1964
V. Popenchenko, Russia
1968
Chris Finnegan, Great Britain
1972
V. Lemechev, Russia
1976
Mike Spinks, United States

LIGHT HEAVYWEIGHT
1920
Eddie Eagen, United States
1924
Harry Mitchell, Great Britain
1928
V. Avendano, Argentina
1932
David Carstens, South Africa
1936
Roger Michelot, France
1948
George Hunter, South Africa
1952
Norvel Lee, United States
1956
James Boyd, United States
1960
Cassius Clay, United States

1964
Cosimo Pinto, Italy
1968
Dan Pozdiak, Russia
1972
Mate Pavlov, Yugoslavia
1976
Leon Spinks, United States

HEAVYWEIGHT
1904
Samuel Berger, United States
1908
A. L. Oldman, Great Britain
1920
Ronald Rawson, Great Britain
1924
Otto von Porath, Norway
1928
A. R. Jurado, Argentina
1932
A. Lowell, Argentina
1936
Herbert Runge, Germany
1948
Rafael Iglesias, Argentina
1952
Edward Sanders, United States
1956
Pete Rademacher, United States
1960
F. de Piccoli, Italy
1964
Joe Frazier, United States
1968
George Foreman, United States
1972
Teofilo Stevenson, Cuba
1976
Teofilo Stevenson, Cuba

Canoeing

KAYAK SINGLES—500 METERS
(MEN)
1976
Vasile Diba, Romania

KAYAK SINGLES—1000 METERS
(MEN)
1936
G. Hradetzky, Austria
1948
G. Frederiksson, Sweden
1952
G. Frederiksson, Sweden

1956
G. Frederiksson, Sweden
1960
Erik Hansen, Denmark
1964
Rolf Peterson, Sweden
1968
Mihaly Hesz, Hungary
1972
A. Shaporenko, Russia
1976
Rudiger Helm, East Germany

KAYAK DOUBLES—500 METERS (MEN)
1976   East Germany

KAYAK PAIRS—1000 METERS (MEN)
1936   Austria
1948   Sweden
1952   Finland
1956   Germany
1960   Sweden
1964   Sweden
1968   Russia
1972   Russia
1976   Russia

KAYAK FOURS—1000 METERS (MEN)
1964   Russia
1968   Norway
1972   Russia
1976   Russia

CANADIAN SINGLES (MEN)
1936
Francis Amyot, Canada
1948
Josef Holecek, Czechoslovakia
1952
Josef Holecek, Czechoslovakia
1956
Leon Rottman, Romania
1960
Janos Parti, Hungary
1964
J. Eschert, Germany
1968
Tibor Tatai, Hungary
1972
Ivan Patzaichin, Romania
1976
Aleksandr Rogov, Russia

CANADIAN PAIRS (MEN)
1936   Czechoslovakia
1948   Czechoslovakia
1952   Denmark
1956   Romania
1960   Russia
1964   Russia
1968   Romania
1972   Russia
1976   Russia

KAYAK SINGLES SLALOM (MEN)
1972
Siegbert Horn, East Germany

CANADIAN SINGLES SLALOM (MEN)
1972
Reinhard Eiben, East Germany
1976
Matija Ljubek, Yugoslavia

CANADIAN DOUBLES SLALOM (MEN)
1972   East Germany
1976   Russia

KAYAK SINGLES—500 METERS (WOMEN)
1948
Karen Hoff, Denmark
1952
Sylvi Saimo, Finland
1956
E. Dementyeva, Russia
1960
A. Seredina, Russia
1964
L. Khvedosink, Russia
1968
L. Pinayeva, Russia
1972
Y. Ryabchinskaya, Russia
1976
Carola Zirzow, East Germany

KAYAK PAIRS—500 METERS (WOMEN)
1960   Russia
1964   Germany
1968   Germany
1972   Russia
1976   Russia

CYCLING 15

KAYAK SINGLES SLALOM
(WOMEN)
1972
Angelika Bahmann, East Germany

Cycling

1000 METERS SPRINT
1900
G. Taillandier, France
1920
M. Peeters, Netherlands
1924
Lucien Michard, France
1928
R. Beaufrand, France
1932
J. van Egmond, Netherlands
1936
Toni Merkens, Germany
1948
Mario Ghella, Italy
1952
Enzo Sacchi, Italy
1956
Michel Rousseau, France
1960
Sante Gaiardoni, Italy
1964
G. Pettenella, Italy
1968
Daniel Morelon, France
1972
Daniel Morelon, France
1976
Anton Tkac, Czechoslovakia

1000 METERS TIME-TRIAL
1928
W. Flack-Hansen, Denmark
1932
Edgar Gray, Australia
1936
A. van Vliet, Netherlands
1948
Jacques Dupont, France
1952
R. Mockridge, Australia
1956
Leandro Faggin, Italy
1960
S. Gaiardoni, Italy
1964
Patrick Sercu, Belgium

1968
Pierre Trentin, France
1972
Niels Fredborg, Denmark
1976
Klaus-Jurgen Grunke, East Germany

2000 METERS TANDEM
1908	France
1920	Great Britain
1924	France
1928	Netherlands
1932	France
1936	Germany
1948	Italy
1952	Australia
1956	Australia
1960	Italy
1964	Italy
1968	France
1972	Russia

ROAD RACE
1896
A. Konstantinidis, Greece
1912
Rudolph Lewis, Africa
1920
Herry Stenquist, Sweden
1924
A. Blanchonnet, France
1928
Henry Hansen, Denmark
1932
Attilio Pavesi, Italy
1936
R. Charpentier, France
1948
Jose Beyaert, France
1952
Andre Noyelle, Belgium
1956
Ercole Baldini, Italy
1960
Viktor Kapitonov, Russia
1964
Mario Zanin, Italy
1968
Pier Vianelli, Italy
1972
Hennie Kuiper, Netherlands
1976
Brent Johansson, Sweden

ROAD RACE (TEAM)
1912   Sweden

1920	France
1924	France
1928	Denmark
1932	Italy
1936	France
1948	Belgium
1952	Belgium
1956	France

ROAD TEAM TIME–TRIAL

1960	Italy
1964	Netherlands
1968	Netherlands
1972	Russia
1976	Russia

4000 METERS INDIVIDUAL PURSUIT

1964
Jiri Daler, Czechoslovakia
1968
Daniel Rebillard, France
1972
Knut Knudsen, Norway
1976
Gregor Braun, West Germany

4000 METERS TEAM PURSUIT

1920	Italy
1924	Italy
1928	Italy
1932	Italy
1936	France
1948	France
1952	Italy
1956	Italy
1960	Italy
1964	Germany
1968	Denmark
1972	West Germany
1976	West Germany

Equestrian

GRAND PRIX (JUMPING)
1912
Jean Cariou, France
1920
Tommaso Liquio, Italy
1924
Alphons Gemuseus, Switzerland
1928
Frantisek Ventura, Czechslovakia
1932
Takeichi Nishi, Japan

1936
Kurt Hasse, Germany
1948
Humberto Mariles, Mexico
1952
Pierre d'Oriola, France
1956
H. G. Winkler, Germany
1960
Raimondo d'Inzeo, Italy
1964
Pierre d'Oriola, France
1968
Bill Steinkraus, United States
1972
G. Mancinelli, Italy
1976
A. Schockemoehle, West Germany

GRAND PRIX (JUMPING)—TEAM

1912	Sweden
1920	Sweden
1924	Sweden
1928	Spain
1936	Germany
1948	Mexico
1952	Great Britain
1956	Germany
1960	Germany
1964	Germany
1968	Canada
1972	West Germany
1976	France

GRAND PRIX (DRESSAGE)
1900
C. Haegeman, Belgium
1912
Carl Bonde, Sweden
1920
Janne Lundblad, Sweden
1924
E. von Linder, Sweden
1928
C. von Langen, Germany
1932
Xavier Lesage, France
1936
Heinz Pollay, Germany
1948
Hans Moser, Switzerland
1952
Henri St. Cyr, Sweden
1956
Henri St. Cyr, Sweden

1960
Sergey Filatov, Russia
1964
Henri Chammartin, Switzerland
1968
Ivan Kizimov, Russia
1972
L. Linsenhoff, West Germany
1976
C. Stueckelberger, Switzerland

GRAND PRIX (DRESSAGE)—TEAM
1928   Germany
1932   France
1936   Germany
1948   France
1952   Sweden
1956   Sweden
1964   Germany
1968   Germany
1972   Russia
1976   West Germany

THREE DAY EVENT
1912
Axel Nordlander, Sweden
1920
Helmer Morner, Sweden
1924
A. van Zijp, Netherlands
1928
F. de Mortanges, Netherlands
1932
F. de Mortanges, Netherlands
1936
L. Stubbendorff, Germany
1948
B. Chevallier, France
1952
V. Blixen-Finecke, Sweden
1956
Petrus Kastenman, Sweden
1960
L. Morgan, Australia
1964
Mauro Checcoli, Italy
1968
Jean Guyon, France
1972
Richard Meade, Great Britain
1976
Tad Coffin, United States

THREE DAY EVENT (TEAM)
1912   Sweden

1920   Sweden
1924   Netherlands
1928   Netherlands
1932   United States
1936   Germany
1948   United States
1952   Sweden
1956   Great Britain
1960   Australia
1964   Italy
1968   Great Britain
1972   Great Britain
1976   United States

Fencing

INDIVIDUAL FOIL (MEN)
1896
E. Gravelotte, France
1900
C. Coste, France
1904
Ramon Fonst, Cuba
1912
Nedo Nadi, Italy
1920
Nedo Nadi, Italy
1924
Roger Ducret, France
1928
Lucien Gaudin, France
1932
Gustavo Marzi, Italy
1936
Giulio Gaudini, Italy
1948
Jean Buhan, France
1952
C. d'Oriola, France
1956
C. d'Oriola, France
1960
V. Zhdanovich, Russia
1964
Egon Franke, Poland
1968
Ileana Drimba, Romania
1972
Witold Woyda, Poland
1976
Fabio Dal Zotto, Italy

INDIVIDUAL EPEE (MEN)
1900
Ramon Fonst, Cuba

1904
   Ramon Fonst, Cuba
1908
   Gaston Alibert, France
1912
   Paul Anspach, Belgium
1920
   Armand Massard, France
1924
   Charles Delporte, Belgium
1928
   Lucien Gaudin, France
1932
   Giancarlo Medici, Italy
1936
   Franco Riccardi, Italy
1948
   Luigi Cantone, Italy
1952
   E. Mangiarotti, Italy
1956
   Carlo Pavesi, Italy
1960
   Giuseppe Delfino, Italy
1964
   Grigory Kriss, Russia
1968
   Gyozo Kulcsar, Hungary
1972
   Csaba Fenyvesi, Hungary
1976
   Alexander Pusch, West Germany

INDIVIDUAL SABRE (MEN)
1896
   Jean Georgiadis, Greece
1900
   G. de la Falaise, France
1905
   Manuel Diaz, Cuba
1908
   Jeno Fuchs, Hungary
1912
   Jeno Fuchs, Hungary
1920
   Nedo Nadi, Italy
1924
   Sandor Posta, Hungary
1928
   O. Tersztyansky, Hungary
1932
   Gyorgy Piller, Hungary
1936
   Endre Kabos, Hungary

1948
   A. Gerevich, Hungary
1952
   Pal Kovacs, Hungary
1956
   R. Karpati, Hungary
1960
   R. Karpati, Hungary
1964
   Tibor Pezsa, Hungary
1968
   Jerzy Pawlowski, Poland
1972
   Victor Sidiak, Russia
1976
   V. Krovopovskov, Russia

TEAM FOIL (MEN)
1920   Italy
1924   France
1928   Italy
1932   France
1936   Italy
1948   France
1952   France
1956   Italy
1960   Russia
1964   Russia
1968   France
1972   Poland
1976   West Germany

TEAM EPEE (MEN)
1908   France
1912   Belgium
1922   Italy
1924   France
1928   Italy
1932   France
1936   Italy
1948   France
1952   Italy
1956   Italy
1960   Italy
1964   Hungary
1968   Hungary
1972   Hungary
1976   Sweden

TEAM SABRE (MEN)
1908   Hungary
1912   Hungary
1920   Italy
1924   Italy
1928   Hungary

1932	Hungary
1936	Hungary
1948	Hungary
1952	Hungary
1956	Hungary
1960	Hungary
1964	Russia
1968	Russia
1972	Italy
1976	Russia

INDIVIDUAL FOIL (WOMEN)
1924
Ellen Osiier, Denmark
1928
Helene Mayer, Germany
1932
Ellen Preis, Austria
1936
Ilona Elek, Hungary
1948
Ilona Elek, Hungary
1952
Irene Camber, Italy
1956
Gillian Sheen, Great Britain
1960
Heidi Schmid, Germany
1964
Ildiko Rejto, Hungary
1968
Elena Novikova, Russia
1972
Antonnella Ragno, Italy
1976
I. Schwarczenberger, Hungary

TEAM FOIL (WOMEN)

1960	Russia
1964	Hungary
1968	Russia
1972	Russia
1976	Russia

Field Hockey

1908	England
1920	Great Britain
1928	India
1932	India
1936	India
1948	India
1952	India
1956	India

1960	Pakistan
1964	India
1968	Pakistan
1972	West Germany
1976	New Zealand

Gymnastics

INDIVIDUAL COMBINED EXERCISES (MEN)
1900
Gustave Sandras, France
1904
Adolf Spinnler, Germany
1908
Alberto Braglia, Italy
1912
Alberto Braglia, Italy
1920
Giorgio Zampori, Italy
1924
Leon Skutelj, Yugoslavia
1928
Georges Miez, Switzerland
1932
Romeo Neri, Italy
1936
K. Schwarzmann, Germany
1948
Veikko Huhtanen, Finland
1952
Viktor Chukarin, Russia
1956
Viktor Chukarin, Russia
1960
Boris Shakhlin, Russia
1964
Yukio Endo, Japan
1968
Sawao Kato, Japan
1972
Sawao Kato, Japan
1976
Nikolai Andrianov, Russia

TEAM COMBINED EXERCISES (MEN)

1924	Italy
1928	Switzerland
1932	Italy
1936	Germany
1948	Finland
1952	Russia
1956	Russia

1960	Japan
1964	Japan
1968	Japan
1972	Japan
1976	Japan

FLOOR EXERCISES (MEN)
1932
Istvan Pelle, Hungary
1936
Georges Miez, Switzerland
1948
Ferenc Pataki, Hungary
1952
Karl Thoresson, Sweden
1956
Valentin Muratov, Russia
1960
N. Aihara, Japan
1964
Franco Menicelli, Italy
1968
Sawao Kato, Japan
1972
Nikolai Andrianov, Russia
1976
Nikolai Andrianov, Russia

SIDE HORSE (MEN)
1976
Zoltan Magyar, Hungary

HORIZONTAL BAR (MEN)
1896
H. Weingartner, Germany
1904
Anton Heida, United States
Edward Hennig, United States
1924
Leon Stukelj, Yugoslavia
1928
Georges Miez, Switzerland
1932
Dallas Bixler, United States
1936
A. Saarvala, Finland
1948
Josef Stalder, Switzerland
1952
Jack Gunthard, Switzerland
1956
Takashi Ono, Japan
1960
Takashi Ono, Japan

1964
Boris Shakhlin, Russia
1968
Mikhail Voronin, Russia
A. Nakayama, Japan
1972
Mitsuo Tsukahara, Japan
1976
Mitsuo Tsukahara, Japan

PARALLEL BARS (MEN)
1896
Alfred Flatow, Germany
1904
George Eyser, United States
1924
August Guttinger, Switzerland
1928
Ladislav Vacha, Czechoslovakia
1932
Romeo Neri, Italy
1936
Konrad Frey, Germany
1948
Michael Reusch, Switzerland
1952
Hans Eugster, Switzerland
1956
Viktor Chukarin, Russia
1960
Boris Shakhlin, Russia
1964
Yukio Endo, Japan
1968
A. Nakayama, Japan
1972
Sawao Kato, Japan
1976
Sawao Kato, Japan

POMMELLED HORSE (MEN)
1896
Louis Zutter, Switzerland
1904
Anton Heida, United States
1924
Josef Wilhelm, Switzerland
1928
Hermann Hanggi, Switzerland
1932
Istvan Pelle, Hungary
1936
Konrad Frey, Germany
1948
Paavo Aaltonen (tie), Finland
Veikko Hutanen (tie), Finland

Heikki Savolainen (tie), Finland
1952
Viktor Chukarin, Russia
1956
Boris Shakhlin, Russia
1960
Eugen Ekman, Finland
Boris Shakhlin, Russia
1964
Miroslav Cerar, Yugoslavia
1968
Miroslav Cerar, Yugoslavia
1972
Viktor Klimenko, Russia

LONG HORSE VAULT (MEN)
1896
Karl Schumann, Germany
1904
Anton Heida, United States
George Eyser, United States
1924
Frank Kriz, United States
1928
Eugen Mack, Switzerland
1932
S. Guglielmetti, Italy
1936
K. Schwarzmann, Germany
1948
Paavo Aaltonen, Finland
1952
Viktor Chukarin, Russia
1956
Helmuth Bantz, Germany
Valentin Muratov, Russia
1960
Takashi Ono, Japan
Boris Shakhlin, Russia
1964
H. Yamashita, Japan
1968
Mikhail Veronin, Russia
1972
Klaus Koeste, East Germany
1976
Nikolai Andrianov, Russia

RINGS (MEN)
1896
Jean Mitropoulos, Greece
1904
Herman Glass, United States
1924
Franco Martino, Italy

1928
Leon Skutelj, Yugoslavia
1932
George Gulack, United States
1936
Alois Hudec, Czechoslovakia
1948
Karl Frei, Switzerland
1952
Grant Shaginyan, Russia
1956
Albert Azaryan, Russia
1960
Albert Azaryan, Russia
1964
Takuji Hayata, Japan
1968
A. Nakayama, Japan
1972
A. Nakayama, Japan
1976
Nikolai Andrianov, Russia

INDIVIDUAL COMBINED EXERCISES (WOMEN)
1952
M. Gorokhovskaya, Russia
1956
Larisa Latynina, Russia
1960
Larisa Latynina, Russia
1964
Vera Caslavska, Czechoslovakia
1968
Vera Caslavska, Czechoslovakia
1972
Ludmila Turischeva, Russia
1976
Nadia Comaneci, Romania

TEAM COMBINED EXERCISES (WOMEN)
1928	Netherlands
1936	Germany
1948	Czechoslovakia
1952	Russia
1956	Russia
1960	Russia
1964	Russia
1968	Russia
1972	Russia
1976	Russia

BALANCE BEAM (WOMEN)
1952
Nina Bocharyova, Russia

1956
  Agnes Keleti, Hungary
1960
  Eva Bosakova, Czechoslovakia
1964
  Vera Caslavska, Czechoslovakia
1968
  N. Kunchinskaya, Russia
1972
  Olga Korbut, Russia
1976
  Nadia Comaneci, Romania

ASYMMETRIC BARS (WOMEN)
1952
  Margit Korondi, Hungary
1956
  Agnes Keleti, Hungary
1960
  Polina Astakhova, Russia
1964
  Polina Astakhova, Russia
1968
  Vera Caslavska, Czechoslovakia
1972
  Karin Janz, East Germany
1976
  Nadia Comaneci, Romania

HORSE VAULT (WOMEN)
1952
  Y. Kalinchuk, Russia
1956
  Larisa Latynina, Russia
1960
  M. Nikolayeva, Russia
1964
  Vera Caslavska, Czechoslovakia
1968
  Vera Caslavska, Czechoslovakia
1972
  Karin Janz, East Germany
1976
  Nelli Kim, Russia

FLOOR EXERCISES (WOMEN)
1952
  Agnes Keleti, Hungary
1956
  Larisa Latynina, Russia
  Agnes Keleti, Hungary
1960
  Larisa Latynina, Russia

1964
  Larisa Latynina, Russia
1968
  Larissa Petrik, Russia
1972
  Olga Korbut, Russia
1976
  Nelli Kim, Russia

Handball

(MEN)

1936	Germany
1972	Yugoslavia
1976	Russia

(WOMEN)

1976	Russia

Judo

LIGHTWEIGHT
1964
  Takehide Nakatani, Japan
1972
  Takao Kawaguchi, Japan
1976
  Hector Rodriguez, Cuba

WELTERWEIGHT
1972
  T. Nomura, Japan

LIGHT MIDDLEWEIGHT
1976
  Vladimir Nevzorov, Russia

MIDDLEWEIGHT
1964
  Isao Okano, Japan
1972
  Shinoku Sekine, Japan
1976
  Isamu Sonada, Japan

LIGHT HEAVYWEIGHT
1972
  S. Chochoshvili, Russia
1976
  Kazuhiro Ninomiya, Japan

HEAVYWEIGHT
1964
  Isao Inokuma, Japan
1972
  Wilhelm Ruska, Netherlands

1976
  Sergei Novikov, Russia

OPEN CLASS (NO WEIGHT LIMIT)
1964
  Antonius Geesink, Netherlands
1972
  Wilhelm Ruska, Netherlands
1976
  Haruki Vemura, Japan

Modern Pentathlon (Individual)

1912
  Gustaf Lilliehook, Sweden
1920
  Gustaf Dryssen, Sweden
1924
  Bo Lindman, Sweden
1928
  Sven Thofelt, Sweden
1932
  J. G. Oxenstierna, Sweden
1936
  G. Handrick, Germany
1948
  William Grut, Sweden
1952
  Lars Hall, Sweden
1956
  Lars Hall, Sweden
1960
  Ferenc Nemeth, Hungary
1964
  Ferenc Torok, Hungary
1968
  Bjorn Ferm, Sweden
1972
  Andras Balczo, Hungary
1976
  Janucz Pyciak, Poland

TEAM
1952   Hungary
1956   Russia
1960   Hungary
1964   Russia
1968   Hungary
1972   Russia
1976   Great Britain

Rowing (Men)

SINGLE SCULLS
1900
  Henri Barrelet, France

1904
  Frank Greer, United States
1908
  Harry Blackstaffe, Great Britain
1912
  William Kinnear, Great Britain
1920
  John Kelly Sr., United States
1924
  Jack Beresford, Great Britain
1928
  Henry Pearce, Australia
1932
  Henry Pearce, Australia
1936
  Gustav Schafer, Germany
1948
  Mervyn Wood, Australia
1952
  Yuri Tyukalov, Russia
1956
  Vyacheslav Ivanov, Russia
1960
  Vyacheslav Ivanov, Russia
1964
  Vyacheslav Ivanov, Russia
1968
  Henri Wienese, Netherlands
1972
  Yuri Malishev, Russia
1976
  Pectti Karppinen, Finland

DOUBLE SCULLS
1904   United States
1920   United States
1924   United States
1928   United States
1932   United States
1936   Great Britain
1948   Great Britain
1952   Argentina
1956   Russia
1960   Czechoslovakia
1964   Russia
1968   Russia
1972   Russia
1976   Norway

QUADRUPLE SCULLS WITHOUT
  COXSWAIN
1976   East Germany

PAIRS WITHOUT COXSWAIN
1900   Belgium

1904	United States	1936	Germany
1908	Great Britain	1948	United States
1920	Italy	1952	Czechoslovakia
1924	Netherlands	1956	Italy
1928	Germany	1960	Germany
1932	Great Britain	1964	Germany
1936	Germany	1968	New Zealand
1948	Great Britain	1972	West Germany
1952	United States	1976	Russia
1956	United States		
1960	Russia		

EIGHTS WITH COXSWAIN

1964	Canada
1968	East Germany
1972	East Germany
1976	East Germany

1900	United States
1904	United States
1908	Great Britain
1912	Great Britain
1920	United States

PAIRS WITH COXSWAIN

1900	Netherlands
1924	Switzerland
1928	Switzerland
1932	United States
1936	Germany
1948	Denmark
1952	France
1956	United States
1960	Germany
1964	United States
1968	Italy
1972	East Germany
1976	East Germany

1924	United States
1928	United States
1932	United States
1936	United States
1948	United States
1952	United States
1956	United States
1960	Germany
1964	United States
1968	West Germany
1972	New Zealand
1976	East Germany

Shooting

FOURS WITHOUT COXSWAIN

1900	France
1904	United States
1908	Great Britain
1924	Great Britain
1928	Great Britain
1932	Great Britain
1936	Germany
1948	Italy
1952	Yugoslavia
1956	Canada
1960	United States
1964	Denmark
1968	East Germany
1972	East Germany
1976	East Germany

FREE PISTOL (50 METERS)

1896
  Sumner Paine, United States
1900
  Karl Roderer, Switzerland
1912
  Alfred Lane, United States
1920
  Carl Frederick, United States
1936
  T. Ullmann, Sweden
1948
  Edwin Vazquez, Peru
1952
  Huelet Benner, United States
1956
  P. Linnosvuo, Finland
1960
  Aleksey Gushchin, Russia
1964
  Vaino Markkanen, Finland
1968
  Grigory Kosykh, Russia

FOUR WITH COXSWAIN

1900	Germany
1912	Germany
1920	Switzerland
1924	Switzerland
1928	Italy
1932	Germany

1972
Ragnar Skanaker, Sweden
1976
Uwe Potteck, East Germany

RAPID-FIRE PISTOL
1924
H. M. Bailey, United States
1932
Renzo Morigi, Italy
1936
C. van Oyen, Germany
1948
Karoly Takacs, Hungary
1952
Karoly Takacs, Hungary
1956
Stefan Petrescu, Romania
1960
William McMillan, United States
1964
P. Linnosvuo, Finland
1968
Josef Zapedzki, Poland
1972
Josef Zapedzki, Poland
1976
Norbert Klaar, East Germany

FREE RIFLE
1908
Albert Helgerud, Norway
1912
Paul Colas, France
1920
Morris Fisher, United States
1924
Morris Fisher, United States
1948
Emil Grunig, Switzerland
1952
A. Bogdanov, Russia
1956
Vasiliy Borisov, Russia
1960
Hubert Hammerer, Austria
1964
Gary Anderson, United States
1968
Gary Anderson, United States
1972
Lones Wigger, United States

MOVING TARGET
1972
Lakov Zhelezniak, Russia

1976
Alexandr Gazov, Russia

SMALL-BORE RIFLES (PRONE)
1908
A. A. Carnell, Great Britain
1912
Frederick Hird, United States
1920
L. Nuesslein, United States
1924
C. C. de Lisle, France
1932
Bartil Ronmark, Sweden
1936
Willy Rogeberg, Norway
1948
Arthur Cook, United States
1952
Iosif Sarbu, Romania
1956
Gerald Ouellette, Canada
1960
Peter Kohnke, Germany
1964
Lazlo Hammerl, Hungary
1968
Jan Kurka, Czechoslovakia
1972
Ho Jun Li, North Korea
1976
Karlheinz Smieszek, West Germany

SMALL-BORE RIFLES (THREE
    POSITIONS)
1952
E. Kongshaug, Norway
1956
A. Bogdanov, Russia
1960
Viktor Shamburkin, Russia
1964
Lones Wigger, United States
1968
Bernd Klingner, Germany
1972
John Writer, United States
1976
Lanny Basham, United States

TRAPSHOOTING (CLAY PIGEONS)
1900
Roger de Barbarin, France
1908
W. H. Ewing, Canada

1912
   James Graham, United States
1920
   Mark Arie, United States
1924
   Gyula Halasy, Hungary
1952
   George Genereux, Canada
1956
   Galliano Rossini, Italy
1960
   Ion Dumitrescu, Romania
1964
   Ennio Mattarelli, Italy
1968
   John Braithwaite, Great Britain
1972
   Angelo Scalzone, Italy
1976
   Don Haldeman, United States

SKEET SHOOTING
1968
   Evgeny Petrov, Russia
1972
   Konrad Wirnhier, West Germany
1976
   Josef Panacek, Czechoslovakia

Soccer

1908	Great Britain
1912	Great Britain
1920	Belgium
1924	Uruguay
1928	Uruguay
1936	Italy
1948	Sweden
1952	Hungary
1956	Russia
1960	Yugoslavia
1964	Hungary
1968	Hungary
1972	Poland
1976	East Germany

Swimming and Diving

100 METERS FREE-STYLE (MEN)
1896
   Alfred Hajos, Hungary
1904
   Zoltan Halmay, Hungary
1908
   Charles Daniels, United States

1912
   D. Kahanamoku, United States
1920
   D. Kahanamoku, United States
1924
   Johnny Weismuller, United States
1928
   Johnny Weismuller, United States
1932
   Yasuji Miyazaki, Japan
1936
   Ferenc Csik, Hungary
1948
   Walter Ris, United States
1952
   C. Clark Scholes, United States
1956
   Jon Henricks, Australia
1960
   John Devitt, Australia
1964
   Don Schollander, United States
1968
   Mike Wenden, Australia
1972
   Mark Spitz, United States
1976
   Jim Montgomery, United States

200 METERS FREE-STYLE (MEN)
1900
   Frederick Lane, Australia
1968
   Michael Wenden, Australia
1972
   Mark Spitz, United States
1976
   Bruce Furniss, United States

400 METERS FREE-STYLE (MEN)
1904
   Charles Daniels, United States
1908
   Henry Taylor, Great Britain
1912
   George Hodgson, Canada
1920
   Norman Ross, United States
1924
   Johnny Weismuller, United States
1928
   Albert Zorilla, Argentina
1932
   Buster Crabbe, United States

Gold medallist in the 1964 Olympic Games, Don Schollander. (Wide World Photos)

1936
  Jack Medica, United States
1948
  William Smith, United States
1952
  Jean Boiteux, France
1956
  Murray Rose, Australia
1960
  Murray Rose, Australia
1964
  Don Schollander, United States
1968
  Mike Burton, United States
1972
  Brad Cooper, Australia
1976
  Brian Goodell, United States

1500 METERS FREE-STYLE (MEN)
1904
  Emil Rausch, Germany
1908
  Henry Taylor, Great Britain
1912
  George Hodgson, Canada
1920
  Norman Ross, United States

1924
  Andy Charlton, Australia
1928
  Arne Borg, Sweden
1932
  Kusuo Kitamura, Japan
1936
  Norboru Terada, Japan
1948
  James McLane, United States
1952
  Ford Konno, United States
1956
  Murray Rose, Australia
1960
  Jon Konrads, Australia
1964
  Robert Windle, Australia
1968
  Mike Burton, United States
1972
  Mike Burton, United States
1976
  Brian Goodell, United States

100 METERS BACKSTROKE (MEN)
1908
  Arno Bieberstein, Germany

1912
Harry Hebner, United States
1920
Warren Kealoha, United States
1924
Warren Kealoha, United States
1928
George Kojac, United States
1932
M. Kiyokawa, Japan
1936
Adolf Kiefer, United States
1948
Allen Stack, United States
1952
Yoshio Oyakawa, United States
1956
David Thiele, Australia
1960
David Thiele, Australia
1968
Roland Matthes, East Germany
1972
Roland Matthes, East Germany
1976
John Naber, United States

200 METERS BACKSTROKE (MEN)
1900
Ernst Hoppenberg, Germany
1964
Jed Graef, United States
1968
Roland Matthes, East Germany
1972
Roland Matthes, East Germany
1976
John Naber, United States

100 METERS BREASTSTROKE
     (MEN)
1968
Don McKenzie, United States
1972
Nobutaka Taguchi, Japan
1976
John Hencken, United States

200 METERS BREASTSTROKE
     (MEN)
1908
Fred Holman, Great Britain
1912
Walter Bathe, Germany

1920
Haken Malmroth, Sweden
1924
Robert Skelton, United States
1928
Yoshiyuki Tsuruta, Japan
1932
Yoshiyuki Tsuruta, Japan
1936
Tetsuo Hamuro, Japan
1948
Joseph Verdeur, United States
1952
John Davies, Australia
1956
Masura Furukawa, Japan
1960
William Mulliken, United States
1964
Ian O'Brien, Australia
1968
Felipe Munox, Mexico
1972
John Hencken, United States
1976
Dave Wilkie, Great Britain

100 METERS BUTTERFLY (MEN)
1968
Doug Russell, United States
1972
Mark Spitz, United States
1976
Matt Vogel, United States

200 METERS BUTTERFLY (MEN)
1956
William Yorzyk, United States
1960
Michael Troy, United States
1964
Kevin Berry, Australia
1968
Carl Robie, United States
1972
Mark Spitz, United States
1976
Mike Bruner, United States

200 METERS INDIVIDUAL
     MEDLEY (MEN)
1968
Charles Hickcox, United States
1972
Gunnar Larsson, Sweden

400 METERS INDIVIDUAL MEDLEY (MEN)

1964
Richard Roth, United States
1968
Charles Hickcox, United States
1972
Gunnar Larsson, Sweden
1976
Rod Strachan, United States

4 × 100 METERS FREE-STYLE RELAY (MEN)

1964	United States
1968	United States
1972	United States

4 × 200 METERS FREE-STYLE RELAY (MEN)

1908	Great Britain
1912	Australia
1920	United States
1924	United States
1928	United States
1932	Japan
1936	Japan
1948	United States
1952	United States
1956	Australia
1960	United States
1964	United States
1968	United States
1972	United States
1976	United States

4 × 100 METERS MEDLEY RELAY (MEN)

1960	United States
1964	United States
1968	United States
1972	United States
1976	United States

PLATFORM DIVING (MEN)

1908
Hjalmar Johansson, Sweden
1912
Erik Adlerz, Sweden
1920
Clarence Pinkston, United States
1924
Albert White, United States
1928
Pete Desjardins, United States
1932
Harold Smith, United States
1936
Marshall Wayne, United States
1948
Sammy Lee, United States
1952
Sammy Lee, United States
1956
Joaquin Capilla, Mexico
1960
Robert Webster, United States
1964
Robert Webster, United States
1968
Klaus Dibiasi, Italy
1972
Klaus Dibiasi, Italy
1976
Klaus Dibiasi, Italy

SPRINGBOARD DIVING (MEN)

1908
Albert Zurner, Germany
1912
Paul Gunther, Germany
1920
Louis Kuehn, United States
1924
Albert White, United States
1928
Pete Desjardins, United States
1932
Michael Galitzen, United States
1936
Richard Degener, United States
1948
Bruce Harlan, United States
1952
David Browning, United States
1956
Robert Clotworthy, United States
1960
Gary Tobian, United States
1964
Ken Sitzberger, United States
1968
Bernard Wrightson, United States
1972
Vladimir Vasin, Russia
1976
Phil Boggs, United States

100 METERS FREE-STYLE (WOMEN)
1912
Fanny Durack, Australia
1920
Ethelda Bleibtrey, United States
1924
Ethel Lackie, United States
1928
Albina Osipowich, United States
1932
Helene Madison, United States
1936
H. Mastenbroek, Netherlands
1948
Greta Andersen, Denmark
1952
Katalin Szoke, Hungary
1956
Dawn Fraser, Australia
1960
Dawn Fraser, Australia
1964
Dawn Fraser, Australia
1968
Jane Henne, United States
1972
Sandra Neilson, United States
1976
Kornelia Ender, East Germany

200 METERS FREE-STYLE (WOMEN)
1968
Debbie Meyer, United States
1972
Shane Gould, Australia
1976
Kornelia Ender, East Germany

400 METERS FREE-STYLE (WOMEN)
1924
Martha Norelius, United States
1928
Martha Norelius, United States
1932
Helene Madison, United States
1936
H. Mastenbroek, Netherlands
1948
Ann Curtis, United States
1952
Valeria Gyenge, Hungary

1956
Lorraine Crapp, Australia
1960
Chris von Saltza, United States
1964
Virginia Duenkel, United States
1968
Debbie Meyer, United States
1972
Shane Gould, Australia
1976
Petra Thumer, East Germany

800 METERS FREE-STYLE (WOMEN)
1968
Debbie Meyer, United States
1972
Keena Rothhammer, United States
1976
Petra Thumer, East Germany

100 METERS BACKSTROKE (WOMEN)
1924
Sybil Bauer, United States
1928
Marie Braun, Netherlands
1932
Eleanor Holm, United States
1936
Dina Senff, Netherlands
1948
Karen Harup, Denmark
1952
Joan Harrison, South Africa
1956
Judy Grinham, Great Britain
1960
Lynn Burke, United States
1964
Cathy Ferguson, United States
1968
Kaye Hall, United States
1972
Melissa Belote, United States
1976
Ulrike Richter, East Germany

200 METERS BACKSTROKE (WOMEN)
1968
Pokey Watson, United States
1972
Melissa Belote, United States

1976
Ulrike Richter, East Germany

100 METERS BREASTSTROKE (WOMEN)
1968
D. Bjedov, Yugoslavia
1972
Cathy Carr, United States
1976
Hannelore Anke, East Germany

200 METERS BREASTSTROKE (WOMEN)
1924
Lucy Morton, Great Britain
1928
Hilde Schrader, Germany
1932
Clare Dennis, Australia
1936
Hideko Maehata, Japan
1948
P. van Vliet, Netherlands
1952
Eva Szekely, Hungary
1956
Ursula Happe, Germany
1960
Anita Lonsbrough, Great Britain
1964
G. Prozumenshikova, Russia
1968
Sharon Wichman, United States
1972
Bev Whitfield, Australia
1976
Marina Koshevaia, Russia

100 METERS BUTTERFLY (WOMEN)
1956
Shelly Mann, United States
1960
Carolyn Schuler, United States
1964
Sharon Stouder, United States
1968
Lynn McClements, Australia
1972
Mayumi Aoki, Japan
1976
Kornelia Ender, East Germany

200 METERS BUTTERFLY (WOMEN)
1968
Aagie Kok, Netherlands
1972
Karen Moe, United States
1976
Andrea Pollack, East Germany

200 METERS INDIVIDUAL MEDLEY (WOMEN)
1968
Claudia Kolb, United States
1972
Shane Gould, Australia

400 METERS INDIVIDUAL MEDLEY (WOMEN)
1964
Donna de Varona, United States
1968
Claudia Kolb, United States
1972
Gail Neall, Australia
1976
Ulrike Tauber, East Germany

4 × 100 METERS FREE-STYLE RELAY (WOMEN)
1912	Great Britain
1920	United States
1924	United States
1928	United States
1932	United States
1936	Netherlands
1948	United States
1952	Hungary
1956	Australia
1960	United States
1964	United States
1968	United States
1972	United States
1976	United States

4 × 100 METERS MEDLEY RELAY (WOMEN)
1960	United States
1964	United States
1968	United States
1972	United States
1976	East Germany

PLATFORM DIVING (WOMEN)
1912
Greta Johansson, Sweden

1920
  S. Fryland-Clausen, Denmark
1924
  Caroline Smith, United States
1928
  E. Pinkston, United States
1932
  Dorothy Poynton, United States
1936
  D. Poynton Hill, United States
1948
  Victoria Draves, United States
1952
  Pat McCormick, United States
1956
  Pat McCormick, United States
1960
  Ingrid Kramer, Germany
1964
  Lesley Bush, United States
1968
  Milena Duchkova, Czechoslovakia
1972
  Ulkike Knape, Sweden
1976
  E. Vaytshekkovskaia, Russia

SPRINGBOARD DIVING (WOMEN)
1920
  Aileen Riggin, United States
1924
  Elizabeth Becker, United States
1928
  Helen Meany, United States
1932
  Georgia Coleman, United States
1936
  Marjorie Gestring, United States
1948
  Victoria Draves, United States
1952
  Pat McCormick, United States
1956
  Pat McCormick, United States
1960
  Ingrid Kramer, Germany
1964
  Ingrid Engel, Germany
1968
  Sue Gossick, United States
1972
  Micki King, United States
1976
  Jenny Chandler, United States

Track and Field

100 METERS (MEN)
1896
  Thomas Burke, United States
1900
  Frank Jarvis, United States
1904
  Archie Hahn, United States
1908
  Reginald Walker, South Africa
1912
  Ralph Craig, United States
1920
  Charley Paddock, United States
1924
  Harold Abrahams, Great Britain
1928
  Percy Williams, Canada
1932
  Eddie Tolan, United States
1936
  Jesse Owens, United States
1948
  Harrison Dillard, United States
1952
  Lindy Remigino, United States
1956
  Bobby Morrow, United States
1960
  Armin Hary, Germany
1964
  Bob Hayes, United States
1968
  James Hines, United States
1972
  Valery Borzov, Russia
1976
  Hasely Crawford, Trinidad

200 METERS (MEN)
1900
  J. W. Tewksbury, United States
1904
  Archie Hahn, United States
1908
  Robert Kerr, Canada
1912
  Ralph Craig, United States
1920
  Allen Woodring, United States
1924
  Jackson Scholz, United States

1928
Percy Williams, Canada
1932
Eddie Tolan, United States
1936
Jessie Owens, United States
1948
Mel Patton, United States
1952
Andy Stanfield, United States
1956
Bobby Morrow, United States
1960
Livio Berruti, Italy
1964
Henry Carr, United States
1968
Tommie Smith, United States
1972
Valery Borzov, Russia
1976
Don Quarrie, Jamaica

400 METERS (MEN)
1896
Thomas Burke, United States
1900
Maxwell Long, United States
1904
Harry Hillman, United States
1908
W. Halswell, Great Britain
1912
Charles Reidpath, United States
1920
Bevil Rudd, South Africa
1924
Eric Liddell, Great Britain
1928
Ray Barbuti, United States
1932
William Carr, United States
1936
Archie Williams, United States
1948
Arthur Wint, Jamaica
1952
George Rhoden, Jamaica
1956
Charley Jenkins, United States
1960
Otis Davis, United States
1964
Mike Larrabee, United States

1968
Lee Evans, United States
1972
Vince Matthews, United States
1976
A. Juantorena, Cuba

800 METERS (MEN)
1896
Edwin Flack, Australia
1900
Alfred Tysoe, Great Britain
1904
James Lightbody, United States
1908
Mel Sheppard, United States
1912
James Meredith, United States
1920
Albert Hill, Great Britain
1924
Douglas Lowe, Great Britain
1928
Douglas Lowe, Great Britain
1932
Thomas Hampson, Great Britain
1936
John Woodruff, United States
1948
Mal Whitfield, United States
1952
Mal Whitfield, United States
1956
Tom Courtney, United States
1960
Peter Snell, New Zealand
1964
Peter Snell, New Zealand
1968
Ralph Doubell, Australia
1972
Dave Wottle, United States
1976
A. Juantorena, Cuba

1500 METERS (MEN)
1896
Edwin Flack, Australia
1900
Charles Bennett, Great Britain
1904
James Lightbody, United States
1908
Mel Sheppard, United States

1912
  Arnold Jackson, Great Britain
1920
  Albert Hill, Great Britain
1924
  Paavo Nurmi, Finland
1928
  Harri Larva, Finland
1932
  Luigi Beccali, Italy
1936
  Jack Lovelock, New Zealand
1948
  Henry Eriksson, Sweden
1952
  Josef Barthel, Luxemburg
1956
  Ron Delany, Eire
1960
  Herb Elliott, Australia
1964
  Peter Snell, New Zealand
1968
  Kipchoge Keino, Kenya
1972
  Pekka Vasala, Finland
1976
  John Walker, New Zealand

5000 METERS (MEN)
1912
  H. Kolehmainen, Finland
1920
  Joseph Guillemot, France
1924
  Paavo Nurmi, Finland
1928
  Ville Ritola, Finland
1932
  Lauri Lehtinen, Finland
1936
  Gunnar Hockert, Finland
1948
  Gaston Reiff, Belgium
1952
  Emil Zatopek, Czechoslovakia
1956
  Vladimir Kuts, Russia
1960
  Murray Halberg, New Zealand
1964
  Bob Schul, United States
1968
  M. Gammoudi, Tunisia

1972
  Lasse Viren, Finland
1976
  Lasse Viren, Finland

10,000 METERS (MEN)
1908
  Emil Voight, Great Britain
1912
  H. Kolehmainen, Finland
1920
  Paavo Nurmi, Finland
1924
  Ville Ritola, Finland
1928
  Paavo Nurmi, Finland
1932
  Janusz Kusocinski, Poland
1936
  Ilmari Salminen, Finland
1948
  Emil Zatopek, Czechoslovakia
1952
  Emil Zatopek, Czechoslovakia
1956
  Vladimir Kuts, Russia
1960
  Pyotr Bolotnikov, Russia
1964
  Billy Mills, United States
1968
  Naftali Temu, Kenya
1972
  Lasse Viren, Finland
1976
  Lasse Viren, Finland

MARATHON (MEN)
1896
  Spyridon Louis, Greece
1900
  Michel Theato, France
1904
  Thomas Hicks, United States
1908
  John Hayes, United States
1912
  K. McArthur, South Africa
1920
  H. Kolehmainen, Finland
1924
  Albin Stenroos, Finland
1928
  A. B. El Quafi, France

1932
Juan Zabala, Argentina
1936
Kitei Son, Japan
1948
Delfo Cabrera, Argentina
1952
Emil Zatopek, Czechoslovakia
1956
Alain Mimoun, France
1960
Abebe Bikila, Ethiopia
1964
Abebe Bikila, Ethiopia
1968
Mamo Wolde, Ethiopia
1972
Frank Shorter, United States
1976
W. Cierpinski, East Germany

110 METERS HURDLES (MEN)
1896
Thomas Curtis, United States
1900
Alvin Kraenzlein, United States
1904
Fred Schule, United States
1908
Forest Smithson, United States
1912
Fred Kelly, United States
1920
Earl Thompson, Canada
1924
Daniel Kinsey, United States
1928
Sydney Atkinson, South Africa
1932
George Saling, United States
1936
Forrest Towns, United States
1948
William Porter, United States
1952
Harrison Dillard, United States
1956
Lee Calhoun, United States
1960
Lee Calhoun, United States
1964
Hayes Jones, United States
1968
Willie Davenport, United States

1972
Rod Milburn, United States
1976
Guy Drut, France

400 METERS HURDLES (MEN)
1900
J. W. Tewksbury, United States
1904
Harry Hillman, United States
1908
Charles Bacon, United States
1920
Frank Loomis, United States
1924
F. Morgan Taylor, United States
1928
Lord Burghley, Great Britain
1932
Robert Tisdall, Eire
1936
Glenn Hardin, United States
1948
Roy Cochran, United States
1952
Charley Moore, United States
1956
Glenn Davis, United States
1960
Glenn Davis, United States
1964
Warren Cawley, United States
1968
Dave Hemery, Great Britain
1972
John Akii-Bua, Uganda
1976
Edwin Moses, United States

3000 METERS STEEPLECHASE
   (MEN)
1900 (2 separate races)
George Orton, United States
John Rimmer, Great Britain
1904
James Lightbody, United States
1908
Arthur Russell, Great Britain
1920
Percy Hodge, Great Britain
1924
Ville Ritola, Finland
1928
Toivo Loukola, Finland

1932
  V. Iso-Hollo, Finland
1936
  V. Iso-Hollo, Finland
1948
  Tore Sjostrand, Sweden
1952
  Horace Ashenfelter, United States
1956
  Chris Brasher, Great Britain
1960
  Z. Krzyszkowiak, Poland
1964
  Gaston Roelants, Belgium
1968
  Amos Biwott, Kenya
1972
  Kipchoge Keino, Kenya
1976
  Anders Gadrerud, Sweden

4 × 100 METERS RELAY (MEN)
1912   Great Britain
1920   United States
1924   United States
1928   United States
1932   United States
1936   United States
1948   United States
1952   United States
1956   United States
1960   West Germany
1964   United States
1968   United States
1972   United States
1976   United States

4 × 400 METERS RELAY (MEN)
1912   United States
1920   Great Britain
1924   United States
1928   United States
1932   United States
1936   Great Britain
1948   United States
1952   Jamaica
1956   United States
1960   United States
1964   United States
1968   United States
1972   Kenya
1976   United States

20,000 METERS WALK (MEN)
1956
  Leonid Spirin, Russia
1960
  V. Golubnichiy, Russia
1964
  Ken Matthews, Great Britain
1968
  V. Golubnichiy, Russia
1972
  Peter Frenkel, East Germany
1976
  Daniel Bautista, Mexico

50,000 METERS WALK (MEN)
1932
  Thomas Green, Great Britain
1936
  Harold Whitlock, Great Britain
1948
  John Ljunggren, Sweden
1952
  Giuseppe Dordoni, Italy
1956
  Norman Read, New Zealand
1960
  Don Thompson, Great Britain
1964
  Abdon Pamich, Italy
1968
  Christopf Hohne, East Germany
1972
  Bern Kannenberg, West Germany

HIGH JUMP (MEN)
1896
  Ellery Clark, United States
1900
  Irving Baxter, United States
1904
  Samuel Jones, United States
1908
  Harry Porter, United States
1912
  Alma Richards, United States
1920
  Richmond Landon, United States
1924
  Harold Osborn, United States
1928
  Robert King, United States
1932
  D. McNaughton, Canada
1936
  Cornelius Johnson, United States

1948
John Winter, Australia
1952
Walter Davis, United States
1956
Charles Dumas, United States
1960
R. Shavlakadze, Russia
1964
Valery Brumel, Russia
1968
Richard Fosbury, United States
1972
Yuri Tarmak, Russia
1976
Jacek Wszola, Poland

POLE VAULT (MEN)
1896
William Hoyt, United States
1900
Irving Baxter, United States
1904
Charles Dvorak, United States
1908
Albert Gilbert, United States
Edward Cook, United States
1912
Harry Babcock, United States
1920
Frank Foss, United States
1924
Lee Barnes, United States
1928
Sabin Carr, United States
1932
William Miller, United States
1936
Earle Meadows, United States
1948
O. Guinn Smith, United States
1952
Bob Richards, United States
1956
Bob Richards, United States
1960
Donald Bragg, United States
1964
Fred Hansen, United States
1968
Bob Seagren, United States
1972
Wolfgang Nordwig, East Germany
1976
Tadeusz Slusarski, Poland

LONG JUMP (MEN)
1896
Ellery Clark, United States
1900
Alvin Kraenzlein, United States
1904
Myer Prinstein, United States
1908
Frank Irons, United States
1912
Albert Gutterson, United States
1920
W. Pettersson, Sweden
1924
De Hart Hubbard, United States
1928
Edward Hamm, United States
1932
Edward Gordon, United States
1936
Jesse Owens, United States
1948
Willie Steele, United States
1952
Jerome Biffle, United States
1956
Gregory Bell, United States
1960
Ralph Boston, United States
1964
Lynn Davies, Great Britain
1968
Bob Beamon, United States
1972
Randy Williams, United States
1976
Archie Robinson, United States

TRIPLE JUMP (MEN)
1896
James Connolly, United States
1900
Myer Prinstein, United States
1904
Myer Prinstein, United States
1908
Timothy Ahearne, Great Britain
1912
Gustaf Lindblom, Sweden
1920
Vilho Tuulos, Finland
1924
A. Winter, Australia
1928
Mikio Oda, Japan

1932
 Chuhei Nambu, Japan
1936
 Naoto Tajima, Japan
1948
 Arne Ahman, Sweden
1952
 A. F. da Silva, Brazil
1956
 A. F. da Silva, Brazil
1960
 Jozef Schmidt, Poland
1964
 Jozef Schmidt, Poland
1968
 Viktor Saneyev, Russia
1972
 Viktor Saneyev, Russia
1976
 Viktor Saneyev, Russia

SHOT PUT (MEN)
1896
 Robert Garrett, United States
1900
 Richard Sheldon, United States
1904
 Ralph Rose, United States
1908
 Ralph Rose, United States
1912
 Patrick McDonald, United States
1920
 Ville Porhola, Finland
1924
 Clarence Houser, United States
1928
 John Kuck, United States
1932
 Leo Sexton, United States
1936
 Hans Wollke, Germany
1948
 Wilbur Thompson, United States
1952
 Parry O'Brien, United States
1956
 Parry O'Brien, United States
1960
 William Nieder, United States
1964
 Dallas Long, United States
1968
 Randy Matson, United States

1972
 Wladyslaw Komar, Poland
1976
 Udo Beyer, East Germany

DISCUS THROW (MEN)
1896
 Robert Garrett, United States
1900
 Rudolf Bauer, Hungary
1904
 Martin Sheridan, United States
1908
 Martin Sheridan, United States
1912
 Armas Taipale, Finland
1920
 Elmer Niklander, Finland
1924
 Clarence Houser, United States
1928
 Clarence Houser, United States
1932
 John Anderson, United States
1936
 Kenneth Carpenter, United States
1948
 Adolfo Consolini, Italy
1952
 Sim Iness, United States
1956
 Al Oerter, United States
1960
 Al Oerter, United States
1964
 Al Oerter, United States
1968
 Al Oerter, United States
1972
 Ludvik Danek, Czechoslovakia
1976
 Mac Wilkins, United States

HAMMER THROW (MEN)
1900
 John Flanagan, United States
1904
 John Flanagan, United States
1908
 John Flanagan, United States
1912
 Matt McGrath, United States
1920
 Patrick Ryan, United States

1924
Fred Tootell, United States
1928
P. O'Callaghan, Ireland
1932
P. O'Callaghan, Ireland
1936
Karl Hein, Germany
1948
Imre Nemeth, Hungary
1952
Jozsef Csermak, Hungary
1956
Harold Connolly, United States
1960
Vasily Rudenkov, Russia
1964
Romuald Klim, Russia
1968
Gyula Zsivotzky, Hungary
1972
A. Bondarchuk, Russia
1976
Yuri Syedekh, Russia

JAVELIN THROW (MEN)
1908
Erik Lemming, Sweden
1912
Erik Lemming, Sweden
1920
Jonni Myyra, Finland
1924
Jonni Myyra, Finland
1928
Erik Lundkust, Sweden
1932
Matti Jaervinen, Finland
1936
Gerhard Stock, Germany
1948
T. Rautavaara, Finland
1952
Cy Young, United States
1956
Egil Danielsen, Norway
1960
Viktor Tsibulenko, Russia
1964
Pauli Nevala, Finland
1968
Janis Lusis, Russia
1972
Klaus Wolferman, West Germany

1976
Miklos Nemeth, Hungary

DECATHLON (MEN)
1912
Hugo Wieslander, Sweden. (Won first by Jim Thorpe, United States, who was then disqualified for having played professional baseball)
1920
Helge Lovland, Norway
1924
Harold Osborn, United States
1928
Paavo Yrjola, Finland
1932
James Bausch, United States
1936
Glenn Morris, United States
1948
Bob Mathias, United States
1952
Bob Mathias, United States
1956
Milt Campbell, United States
1960
Rafer Johnson, United States
1964
Willi Holdorf, Germany
1968
Bill Toomey, United States
1972
Nikolai Avilov, Russia
1976
Bruce Jenner, United States

100 METERS (WOMEN)
1928
E. Robinson, United States
1932
S. Walasiewicz, Poland
1936
Helen Stephens, United States
1948
F. Blankers-Koen, Netherlands
1952
Marjorie Jackson, Australia
1956
Betty Cuthbert, Australia
1960
Wilma Rudolph, United States
1964
Wyomia Tyus, United States

1968
  Wyomia Tyus, United States
1972
  Renate Stecher, East Germany
1976
  Annegret Richter, West Germany

200 METERS (WOMEN)
1948
  F. Blankers-Koen, Netherlands
1952
  Marjorie Jackson, Australia
1956
  Betty Cuthbert, Australia
1960
  Wilma Rudolph, United States
1964
  Edith McGuire, United States
1968
  Irena Szewinska, Poland
1972
  Renate Stecher, East Germany
1976
  Baerbel Eckert, East Germany

400 METERS (WOMEN)
1964
  Betty Cuthbert, Australia
1968
  Colette Besson, France
1972
  Monika Zehrt, East Germany
1976
  Irena Szewinska, Poland

800 METERS (WOMEN)
1928
  Lina Radke, Germany
1960
  Ludmila Shevtsova, Russia
1964
  Ann Packer, Great Britain
1968
  Madeline Manning, United States
1972
  Hildegard Falck, West Germany
1976
  T. Kazankina, Russia

1500 METERS (WOMEN)
1972
  Ludmila Bragina, Russia
1976
  T. Kazankina, Russia

100 METERS HURDLES (WOMEN)
1972
  Annelie Ehrhardt, East Germany
1976
  Johnanna Schaller, East Germany

4 × 100 METERS RELAY (WOMEN)
1928   Canada
1932   United States
1936   United States
1948   Netherlands
1952   United States
1956   Australia
1960   United States
1964   Poland
1968   United States
1972   West Germany
1976   East Germany

4 × 400 METERS RELAY (WOMEN)
1972   East Germany
1976   East Germany

HIGH JUMP (WOMEN)
1928
  Ethel Catherwood, Canada
1932
  Jean Shiley, United States
1936
  Ibolya Csak, Hungary
1948
  Alice Coachman, United States
1952
  Esther Brand, South Africa
1956
  Mildred McDaniel, United States
1960
  Iolanda Balas, Romania
1964
  Iolanda Balas, Romania
1968
  M. Rezkova, Czechoslovakia
1972
  Ulrike Meyfarth, West Germany
1976
  R. Ackermann, East Germany

LONG JUMP (WOMEN)
1948
  Olga Gyarmati, Hungary
1952
  Y. Williams, New Zealand
1956
  E. Krzesinska, Poland

1960
Vyera Krepkina, Russia
1964
Mary Rand, Great Britain
1968
V. Viscopoleanu, Romania
1972
H. Rosendahl, West Germany
1976
Angela Voigt, East Germany

SHOT PUT (WOMEN)
1948
M. Ostermeyer, France
1952
Galina Zybina, Russia
1956
T. Tyshkyevich, Russia
1960
Tamara Press, Russia
1964
Tamara Press, Russia
1968
M. Gummel, East Germany
1972
Nadejda Chizhova, Russia
1976
Ivanka Khristova, Bulgaria

DISCUS THROW (WOMEN)
1928
H. Konopacka, Poland
1932
Lilian Copeland, United States
1936
G. Mauermayer, Germany
1948
M. Ostermeyer, France
1952
Nina Romashkova, Russia
1956
Olga Fikotova, Czechoslovakia
1960
Nina Ponomaryeva, Russia
1964
Tamara Press, Russia
1968
Lia Manoliu, Romania
1972
Faina Melnik, Russia
1976
Evelyn Schlaak, East Germany

JAVELIN THROW (WOMEN)
1932
Babe Didrikson, United States

1936
Tilly Fleischer, Germany
1948
Hermine Bauma, Austria
1952
Dana Zatopkova, Czechoslovakia
1956
Inese Jaunzeme, Russia
1960
Elvira Ozolina, Russia
1964
Mihaela Penes, Romania
1968
Angela Nemeth, Hungary
1972
Ruth Fuchs, East Germany
1976
Ruth Fuchs, East Germany

PENTATHLON (WOMEN)
1964
Irina Press, Russia
1968
Ingrid Becker, West Germany
1972
Mary Peters, Great Britain
1976
Sigrun Siegel, East Germany

Volleyball

MEN
1964	Russia
1968	Russia
1972	Japan
1976	Poland

WOMEN
1964	Japan
1968	Russia
1972	Russia
1976	Japan

Water Polo

1900	Great Britain
1904	United States
1908	Great Britain
1912	Great Britain
1920	Great Britain
1924	France
1928	Germany

1932	Hungary
1936	Hungary
1948	Italy
1952	Hungary
1956	Hungary
1960	Italy
1964	Hungary
1968	Yugoslavia
1972	Russia
1976	Hungary

Weight Lifting

FLYWEIGHT
1972
Z. Smalcerz, Poland
1976
A. Voronin, Russia

BANTAMWEIGHT
1948
Joseph de Pietro, United States
1952
Ivan Udodov, Russia
1956
Charles Vinci, United States
1960
Charles Vinci, United States
1964
Alexei Vakhonin, Russia
1968
M. Nassiri, Iran
1972
Imre Foldi, Hungary
1976
Norair Nurikian, Bulgaria

FEATHERWEIGHT
1920
L. de Haes, Belgium
1924
Pierino Gabetti, Italy
1928
Franz Andrysek, Austria
1932
Raymond Suvigny, France
1936
Anthony Terlazzo, United States
1948
Mahmoud Fayad, Egypt
1952
R. Chimishkyan, Russia
1956
Isaac Berger, United States

1960
E. Minayev, Russia
1964
Y. Miyake, Japan
1968
Y. Miyake, Japan
1972
Norair Nurikian, Bulgaria
1976
N. Kolesnikov, Russia

LIGHTWEIGHT
1920
Alfred Neyland, Estonia
1924
E. Decottignies, France
1928
Kurt Helbig, Germany
Hans Haas, Austria
1932
Rene Duverger, France
1936
Mohammed Mesbah, Egypt
Robert Fein, Austria
1948
Ibrahim Shams, Egypt
1952
Tommy Kono, United States
1956
Igor Rybak, Russia
1960
Viktor Bushuyev, Russia
1964
W. Baszanowski, Poland
1968
W. Baszanowski, Poland
1972
M. Kirshinov, Russia
1976
Z. Kaczmarek, Poland

MIDDLEWEIGHT
1920
Henri Gance, France
1924
Carlo Galimberti, Italy
1928
Francois Roger, France
1932
Rudolf Ismayr, Germany
1936
Khadr El Thouni, Egypt
1948
Frank Spellman, United States

1952
Peter George, United States
1956
F. Bogdanovsky, Russia
1960
A. Kurynov, Russia
1964
Hans Zdrazila, Czechoslovakia
1968
Viktor Kurentsov, Russia
1972
Yordan Bikov, Bulgaria
1976
Yordan Mitkov, Bulgaria

LIGHT-HEAVYWEIGHT
1920
Ernest Cadine, France
1924
Charles Rigoulot, France
1928
Said Nosseir, Egypt
1932
Louis Hostin, France
1936
Louis Hostin, France
1948
Stanley Stanczyk, United States
1952
Trofim Lomakin, Russia
1956
Tommy Kono, United States
1960
Ireneusz Palinski, Poland
1964
R. Plyukfeider, Russia
1968
Boris Selitsky, Russia
1972
Lief Jenssen, Norway
1976
Valery Shary, Russia

MIDDLE-HEAVYWEIGHT
1952
N. Schemansky, United States
1956
Arkadi Vorobyev, Russia
1960
Arkadi Vorobyev, Russia
1964
V. Golovanov, Russia
1968
K. Kangasniemi, Finland

1972
Andon Nikolov, Bulgaria
1976
David Rigert, Russia

HEAVYWEIGHT
1896
Viggo Jensen, Denmark
1904
Perikles Kakousis, Greece
1920
Filippo Bottino, Italy
1924
Giuseppe Tonani, Italy
1928
Josef Strassberger, Germany
1932
Jaroslav Skobia, Czechoslovakia
1936
Josef Manger, Austria
1948
John Davis, United States
1952
John Davis, United States
1956
Paul Anderson, United States
1960
Yuriy Vlasov, Russia
1964
L. Zhabotinsky, Russia
1968
L. Zhabotinsky, Russia
1972
Yan Talts, Russia
1976
Valentin Khristov, Russia

SUPER-HEAVYWEIGHT
1972
Vasily Alexeev, Russia
1976
Vasily Alexeev, Russia

Wrestling

FREE-STYLE—PAPERWEIGHT
1972
Roman Dmitriev, Russia
1976
Khassan Issaev, Bulgaria

FREE-STYLE—FLYWEIGHT
1904
Robert Curry, United States

1908
Lennart Viitala, Finland
1952
Hasan Gemici, Turkey
1956
M. Tsalkalamanidze, Russia
1960
Ahmet Bilek, Turkey
1964
Y. Yoshida, Japan
1968
Shigeo Nakata, Japan
1972
Kymoni Kato, Japan
1976
Yuji Takata, Japan

FREE-STYLE—BANTAMWEIGHT
1904
Isaac Niflot, United States
1908
George Mehnert, United States
1924
K. Pihlajamaki, Finland
1928
Kaarie Makinen, Finland
1932
Robert Pearce, United States
1936
Odon Zombori, Hungary
1948
Nasuk Akkar, Turkey
1952
Shohachi Ishii, Japan
1956
M. Dagistanli, Turkey
1960
Terrence McCann, United States
1964
Yojiro Uetake, Japan
1968
Yojiro Uetake, Japan
1972
Hideaki Yanagida, Japan
1976
Vladimir Umin, Russia

FREE-STYLE—FEATHERWEIGHT
1904
B. Bradshaw, United States
1908
George Dole, United States
1920
Charles Ackerley, United States

1924
Robin Reed, United States
1928
Allie Morrison, United States
1932
H. Pihlajamaki, Finland
1936
K. Pihlajamaki, Finland
1948
Gazanfer Bilge, Turkey
1952
Bayram Sit, Turkey
1956
Shozo Sasahara, Japan
1960
M. Dagistanli, Turkey
1964
Osamu Watanabe, Japan
1968
Masaaki Kaneko, Japan
1972
Z. Abdulbekov, Russia
1976
Jung-Mo Jang, South Korea

FREE-STYLE—LIGHTWEIGHT
1904
Otto Roehm, United States
1908
G. de Relwyskow, Great Britain
1920
Kalle Antilla, Finland
1924
Russel Vis, United States
1928
Osvald Kapp, Estonia
1932
Charles Pacome, France
1936
Karoly Karpati, Hungary
1948
Celal Atik, Turkey
1952
Olle Anderberg, Sweden
1956
Emamali Habibi, Iran
1960
Shelby Wilson, United States
1964
Enio Dimov, Bulgaria
1968
Abdollah Mohaved, Iran
1972
Dan Gable, United States

1976
  Pavel Pinigin, Russia

FREE-STYLE—WELTERWEIGHT
1904
  Charles Erickson, United States
1924
  Herman Gehri, Switzerland
1928
  Arve Haavisto, Finland
1932
  Jack van Bebber, United States
1936
  Frank Lewis, United States
1948
  Yasar Dogu, Turkey
1952
  William Smith, United States
1956
  Mitsuo Ikeda, Japan
1960
  Douglas Blubaugh, United States
1964
  Ismail Ogan, Turkey
1968
  Mahmut Atalay, Turkey
1972
  Wayne Wells, United States
1976
  Date Jiichiro, Japan

FREE-STYLE—MIDDLEWEIGHT
1908
  Stanley Bacon, Great Britain
1920
  Eino Leino, Finland
1924
  Fritz Haggman, Switzerland
1928
  Ernest Kyburz, Switzerland
1932
  Ivar Johansson, Sweden
1936
  Emile Poilvé, France
1948
  Glen Brand, United States
1952
  D. Tsimakuridze, Russia
1956
  Nikola Nikolov, Bulgaria
1960
  Hassan Gungor, Turkey
1964
  Prodan Gardjev, Bulgaria

1968
  Boris Gurevitch, Russia
1972
  L. Tediashvila, Russia
1976
  John Peterson, United States

FREE-STYLE—LIGHT-
    HEAVYWEIGHT
1920
  Anders Larsson, Sweden
1924
  John Spellman, United States
1928
  Thur Sjostedt, Sweden
1932
  Peter Mehringer, United States
1936
  Knut Fridell, Sweden
1948
  Henry Wittenberg, United States
1952
  Wiking Palm, Sweden
1956
  Ghalam Tahkti, Iran
1960
  Ismet Atli, Turkey
1964
  Alexandr Medved, Russia
1968
  Ahmet Ayik, Turkey
1972
  Ben Peterson, United States
1976
  Levan Tediashvili, Russia

FREE-STYLE—HEAVYWEIGHT
1896
  Karl Schumann, Germany
1904
  B. Hansen, United States
1908
  G. C. O'Kelly, Great Britain
1920
  Robert Rothe, Switzerland
1924
  Harry Steele, United States
1928
  Johan Richthoff, Sweden
1932
  Johan Richthoff, Sweden
1936
  K. Palusalu, Estonia

1948
  Gyula Bobis, Hungary
1952
  A. Mekokishvili, Russia
1956
  Hamit Kaplan, Turkey
1960
  W. Dietrich, Germany
1964
  Alexandr Ivanitsky, Russia
1968
  Alexandr Medved, Russia
1972
  Ivan Yarygin, Russia
1976
  Ivan Yarygin, Russia

FREE-STYLE—SUPER-
  HEAVYWEIGHT
1972
  Alexandr Medved, Russia
1976
  Soslan Andiev, Russia

GRECO-ROMAN—PAPERWEIGHT
1972
  Gheorghe Bereanu, Romania
1976
  Alexei Schumakov, Russia

GRECO-ROMAN—FLYWEIGHT
1948
  Pietro Lombardi, Italy
1952
  Boris Gurevich, Russia
1956
  Nikolai Solviev, Russia
1960
  D. Pirvulescu, Romania
1964
  T. Hanahara, Japan
1968
  Petar Kirov, Bulgaria
1972
  Petar Kirov, Bulgaria
1976
  V. Konstantinov, Russia

GRECO-ROMAN—
  BANTAMWEIGHT
1924
  Edvard Putsep, Estonia
1928
  Kurl Leucht, Germany
1932
  Jakob Brendel, Germany

1936
  Marton Lorinc, Hungary
1948
  Kurt Pettersson, Sweden
1952
  Imre Hodos, Hungary
1956
  K. Vyrupayev, Russia
1960
  Oleg Karavaev, Russia
1964
  M. Ichiguchi, Japan
1968
  Janos Varga, Hungary
1972
  Rustem Kazakov, Russia
1976
  Pentti Ukkola, Finland

GRECO-ROMAN—
  FEATHERWEIGHT
1912
  Kalle Koskelo, Finland
1920
  Oskari Friman, Finland
1924
  Kalle Anttila, Finland
1928
  Voldemar Vali, Estonia
1932
  Giovanni Gozzi, Italy
1936
  Yasar Erkan, Turkey
1948
  M. Oktav, Turkey
1952
  Yakov Punkin, Russia
1956
  Rauno Makinen, Finland
1960
  Muzahir Sille, Turkey
1964
  Imre Polyak, Hungary
1968
  Roman Rurua, Russia
1972
  Gheorghi Markov, Bulgaria
1976
  Kazimier Lipien, Poland

GRECO-ROMAN—LIGHTWEIGHT
1908
  Enrico Porro, Italy
1912
  Eemil Vare, Finland

1920
  Eemil Vare, Finland
1924
  Oskari Friman, Finland
1928
  Lajos Keresztes, Hungary
1932
  Erik Malmberg, Sweden
1936
  Lauri Koskela, Finland
1948
  Karl Freij, Sweden
1952
  Shazam Safin, Russia
1956
  Kyosti Lehtonen, Finland
1960
  Avtandil Koridze, Russia
1964
  Kazim Ayvaz, Turkey
1968
  Muneji Munemura, Japan
1972
  S. Khisamutdinov, Russia
1976
  Suren Nalbandy, Russia

GRECO-ROMAN—
    WELTERWEIGHT
1932
  Ivar Johansson, Sweden
1936
  Rudolf Svedberg, Sweden
1948
  Gosta Andersson, Sweden
1952
  Miklos Szilvasi, Hungary
1956
  Mithat Bayrak, Turkey
1960
  Mithat Bayrak, Turkey
1964
  Anatoly Koleslav, Russia
1968
  Rudolf Vesper, East Germany
1972
  Vitezslav Macha, Czechoslovakia
1976
  Anatoly Bykov, Russia

GRECO-ROMAN—
    MIDDLEWEIGHT
1908
  F. Martensson, Sweden

1912
  Claes Johansson, Sweden
1920
  Carl Westergren, Sweden
1924
  E. Westerlund, Finland
1928
  Vaino Kokkinen, Finland
1932
  Vaino Kokkinen, Finland
1936
  Ivar Johansson, Sweden
1948
  Axel Gronberg, Sweden
1952
  Axel Gronberg, Sweden
1956
  Guivi Kartozia, Russia
1960
  Dimitro Dobrev, Bulgaria
1964
  Branislav Simic, Yugoslavia
1968
  Lothar Metz, East Germany
1972
  Csaba Hegedus, Hungary
1976
  Momir Petkovic, Yugoslavia

GRECO-ROMAN—LIGHT-
    HEAVYWEIGHT
1908
  Verner Weckman, Finland
1912
  Anders Ahlgren, Sweden
  Ivar Bohling, Finland
1920
  Claes Johansson, Sweden
1924
  Carl Westergren, Sweden
1928
  I. Moustafa, Egypt
1932
  Rudolf Svensson, Sweden
1936
  Axel Cadier, Sweden
1948
  Karl Nilsson, Sweden
1952
  Kaelpo Grondahl, Finland
1956
  V. Nikolayev, Russia
1960
  Tevik Kis, Turkey

1964
  B. Alexandrov, Bulgaria
1968
  Boian Radev, Bulgaria
1972
  V. Rezantsev, Russia
1976
  Valery Kezantsev, Russia

GRECO-ROMAN—HEAVYWEIGHT
1908
  Richard Weisz, Hungary
1912
  Yrjo Saarela, Finland
1920
  Adolf Lindfors, Finland
1924
  Henri Deglane, France
1928
  Rudolf Svensson, Sweden
1932
  Carl Westergren, Sweden
1936
  K. Palusalu, Estonia
1948
  Ahmed Kirecci, Turkey
1952
  Johannes Kotkas, Russia
1956
  Anatoli Parfenyov, Russia
1960
  Ivan Bogdan, Russia
1964
  Istvan Kozma, Hungary
1968
  Istvan Kozma, Hungary
1972
  N. Martinescu, Romania
1976
  N. Bolboshin, Russia

GRECO-ROMAN—SUPER-
  HEAVYWEIGHT
1972
  Anatoly Roshin, Russia
1976
  A. Kotchinski, Russia

Yachting

SOLING CLASS
1972   United States
1976   Denmark

TEMPEST CLASS
1972   Russia
1976   Sweden

DRAGON CLASS
1948   Norway
1952   Norway
1956   Sweden
1960   Greece
1964   Denmark
1968   United States
1972   Australia

470 CLASS
1976   West Germany

STAR CLASS
1932   United States
1936   Germany
1948   United States
1952   Italy
1956   United States
1960   Russia
1964   Bahamas
1968   United States
1972   Australia

TORNADO CLASS
1976   Great Britain

FINN CLASS
1956   Denmark
1960   Denmark
1964   Germany
1968   Russia
1972   France
1976   East Germany

FLYING-DUTCHMAN CLASS
1960   Norway
1964   New Zealand
1968   Great Britain
1972   Great Britain
1976   West Germany

Rowing (Women)

SINGLE SCULLS
1976
  C. Scheiblich, East Germany

DOUBLE SCULLS
1976   Bulgaria

QUADRUPLE SCULLS WITH
  COXSWAIN
1976   East Germany

PAIRS WITHOUT COXSWAIN
1976   Bulgaria

FOURS WITH COXSWAIN
1976   East Germany

EIGHTS WITH COXSWAIN
1976   East Germany

WINTER OLYMPICS

Sites
1924	Chamonix-Mont Blanc, France
1928	St. Moritz, Switzerland
1932	Lake Placid, New York
1936	Garmisch-Partenkirchen, Germany
1948	St. Moritz, Switzerland
1952	Oslo, Norway
1956	Cortina, Italy
1960	Squaw Valley, California
1964	Innsbruck, Austria
1968	Grenoble, France
1972	Sapporo, Japan
1976	Innsbruck, Austria

Biathlon

1960
  Klas Lestander, Sweden
1964
  Vladimir Melyanin, Russia
1968
  Magnar Solberg, Norway
1972
  Magnar Solberg, Norway
1976
  Nikolai Kruglov, Russia

Biathlon Relay

1968	Russia
1972	Russia
1976	Russia

Bobsledding

4-MAN BOB
1924	Switzerland
1928	United States II
1932	United States I
1936	Switzerland II
1948	United States II
1952	Germany
1956	Switzerland I
1960	no competition
1964	Canada I
1968	Italy I
1972	Switzerland I
1976	East Germany

2-MAN BOB
1932	United States I
1936	United States I
1948	Switzerland II
1952	Germany I
1956	Italy I
1960	no competition
1964	Great Britain
1968	Italy I
1972	West Germany II
1976	East Germany

Ice Hockey

1920	Canada
1924	Canada
1928	Canada
1932	Canada
1936	Great Britain
1948	Canada
1952	Canada
1956	Russia
1960	United States
1964	Russia
1968	Russia
1972	Russia
1976	Russia

Luge

MEN'S SINGLES
1964
  Thomas Koehler, Germany
1968
  Manfred Schmid, Austria
1972
  Wolfgang Scheidel, East Germany
1976
  Detlef Guenther, East Germany

MEN'S DOUBLES
1964	Austria
1968	East Germany

1972	Italy
	East Germany
1976	East Germany

WOMEN'S SINGLES
1964
  Otrun Enderlein, Germany
1968
  Erica Lechner, Italy
1972
  Anna-Maria Muller, East Germany
1976
  Margit Schumann, East Germany

Figure Skating

MEN
1908
  Ulrich Sachow, Sweden
1920
  Gillis Grafstrom, Sweden
1924
  Gillis Grafstrom, Sweden
1928
  Gillis Grafstrom, Sweden
1932
  Karl Schafer, Austria
1936
  Karl Schafer, Austria
1948
  Dick Button, United States
1952
  Dick Button, United States
1956
  Hayes Alan Jenkins, United States
1960
  David Jenkins, United States
1964
  M. Schnelldorfer, Germany
1968
  Wolfgang Schwarz, Austria
1972
  Ondrej Nepela, Czechoslovakia
1976
  John Curry, Great Britain

WOMEN
1908
  Madge Syers, Great Britain
1920
  Magda Julin-Mauroy, Sweden
1924
  Herma Planck-Szabo, Austria
1928
  Sonja Henie, Norway

1932
  Sonja Henie, Norway
1936
  Sonja Henie, Norway
1948
  Barbara Scott, Canada
1952
  Jeanette Altwegg, Great Britain
1956
  Tenley Albright, United States
1960
  Carol Heiss, United States
1964
  Sjoukje Dijkstra, Netherlands
1968
  Peggy Fleming, United States
1972
  Beatrix Schuba, Austria
1976
  Dorothy Hamill, United States

PAIRS
1908
  Anna Hubler,
  Heinrich Burger, Germany
1920
  Ludovika Jakobsson,
  Walter Jakobsson, Finland
1924
  Helene Engelmann,
  Alfred Berger, Austria
1928
  Andree Joly,
  Pierre Brunet, France
1932
  Andree Brunet,
  Pierre Brunet, France
1936
  Maxi Herber,
  Ernst Baier, Germany
1948
  Micheline Lamoy,
  Pierre Baugniet, Belgium
1952
  Ria Falk,
  Paul Falk, Germany
1956
  Elisabeth Schwarz,
  Kurt Oppelt, Austria
1960
  Barbara Wagner,
  Robert Paul, Canada
1964
  Ludmilla Belousova,
  Oleg Protopopov, Russia

Figure skater Sonja Henie took home gold medals in 1928, 1932, and 1936. (Memory Shop)

1968
Ludmilla Belousova,
Oleg Protopopov, Russia
1972
Irina Rodnina,
Alexei Ulanov, Russia
1976
Irina Rodnina,
Alexander Zaitzev, Russia

ICE DANCE
1976
Ludmila Pakhomova,
A. Gorschkov, Russia

Speed Skating

500 METERS (MEN)
1924
Charles Jewtraw, United States
1928
Clas Thunberg, Finland
Bernt Evensen, Norway
1932
John Shea, United States
1936
Ivar Ballangrud, Norway

1948
Finn Helgesen, Norway
1952
Kenneth Henry, United States
1956
Yevgeniy Grischin, Russia
1960
Yevgeniy Grischin, Russia
1964
Richard McDermott, United States
1968
Erhard Keller, Germany
1972
Erhard Keller, Germany
1976
Evgeny Kulikov, Russia

1000 METERS (MEN)
1976
Peter Mueller, United States

1500 METERS (MEN)
1924
Clas Thunberg, Finland
1928
Clas Thunberg, Finland
1932
John Shea, United States

1936
Charles Mathiesen, Norway
1948
Sverre Farstad, Norway
1952
Hjalmar Andersen, Norway
1956
Yevgeniy Grischin, Russia
Yuriy Michailov, Russia
1960
Roald Aas, Norway
Yevgeniy Grischin, Russia
1964
Ants Antson, Russia
1968
Cornelis Verkerk, Netherlands
1972
Ard Schenk, Netherlands
1976
Jan Egil Storholt, Norway

5000 METERS (MEN)
1924
Clas Thunberg, Finland
1928
Ivar Ballangrud, Norway
1932
Irving Jaffe, United States
1936
Ivar Ballangrud, Norway
1948
Reidar Liaklev, Norway
1952
Hjalmar Andersen, Norway
1956
Boris Schilkov, Russia
1960
Viktor Kositschkin, Russia
1964
Knut Johannesen, Norway
1968
Anton Maier, Norway
1972
Ard Schenk, Netherlands
1976
Sten Stensen, Norway

10,000 METERS (MEN)
1924
Julius Skutnabb, Finland
1928   no competition
1932
Irving Jaffe, United States
1936
Ivar Ballangrud, Norway

1948
Ake Seyffarth, Sweden
1952
Hjalmar Andersen, Norway
1956
Sigvard Ericsson, Sweden
1960
Knut Johannesen, Norway
1964
Johnny Nilsson, Sweden
1968
Johnny Haeglin, Sweden
1972
Ard Schenk, Netherlands
1976
Piet Kleine, Netherlands

500 METERS (WOMEN)
1960
Helga Haase, Germany
1964
Lydia Skoblikova, Russia
1968
Ludmila Titova, Russia
1972
Anne Henning, United States
1976
Sheila Young, United States

1000 METERS (WOMEN)
1960
Klala Guseva, Russia
1964
Lydia Skoblikova, Russia
1968
Carolina Geijssen, Netherlands
1972
Manika Pflug, Germany
1976
Tatiana Averina, Russia

1500 METERS (WOMEN)
1960
Lydia Skoblikova, Russia
1964
Lydia Skoblikova, Russia
1968
Kaija Mustonen, Finland
1972
Dianne Holum, United States
1976
Galina Stepanskaya, Russia

3000 METERS (WOMEN)
1960
Lydia Skoblikova, Russia

1964
Lydia Skoblikova, Russia
1968
Johanna Schut, Netherlands
1972
Stein Baas-Kaiser, Netherlands
1976
Tatiana Averina, Russia

Alpine Skiing

MEN'S DOWNHILL
1948
Henri Oreiller, France
1952
Zeno Colo, Italy
1956
Anton Sailer, Austria
1960
Jean Vuarnet, France
1964
Egon Zimmermann, Austria
1968
Jean-Claude Killy, France
1972
Bernhard Russi, Switzerland
1976
Franz Klammer, Austria

MEN'S SLALOM
1948
Edi Reinalter, Switzerland
1952
Othmar Schneider, Austria
1956
Anton Sailer, Austria
1960
Ernst Hinterseer, Austria
1964
Josef Stiegler, Austria
1968
Jean-Claude Killy, France
1972
F. Fernandez Ochoa, Spain
1976
Piero Gros, Italy

MEN'S GIANT SLALOM
1952
Stein Eriksen, Norway
1956
Anton Sailer, Austria
1960
Roger Staub, Switzerland

1964
Francois Boulieu, France
1968
Jean-Claude Killy, France
1972
Gustavo Thoeni, Italy
1976
Heini Hemmi, Switzerland

WOMEN'S DOWNHILL
1948
Hedy Schlunegger, Switzerland
1952
T. Jochum-Beiser, Austria
1956
Madeleine Berthod, Switzerland
1960
Heidi Biebl, Germany
1964
Christl Haas, Austria
1968
Olga Pall, Austria
1972
Marie Nadig, Switzerland
1976
Rosi Mittermaier, West Germany

WOMEN'S SLALOM
1948
Gretchen Fraser, United States
1952
Andrea Lawrence, United States
1956
Renee Colliard Switzerland
1960
Anne Heggtveit, Canada
1964
C. Goitschel, France
1968
Marielle Goitschel, France
1972
Barbara Cochran, United States
1976
Rosi Mittermaier, West Germany

WOMEN'S GIANT SLALOM
1952
Andrea Lawrence, United States
1956
Ossi Reichert, Germany
1960
Yvonne Ruegg, Switzerland
1964
Marielle Goitschel, France

1968
Nancy Greene, Canada
1972
Marie Nadig, Switzerland
1976
Kathy Kreiner, Canada

Nordic Skiing

15 KILOMETERS CROSS-COUNTRY (MEN)
1924
Thorleif Haug, Norway
1928
J. Grottumsbraaten, Norway
1932
Sven Utterstrom, Sweden
1936
Erik Larsson, Sweden
1948
Martin Lundstrom, Sweden
1952
Hallgeir Brenden, Norway
1956
Hallgeir Brenden, Norway
1960
Haakon Brusveen, Norway
1964
Eero Mantyranta, Finland
1968
Harald Gronningen, Norway
1972
Sven-Ake Lundback, Sweden
1976
Nikolai Bajukov, Russia

30 KILOMETERS CROSS-COUNTRY (MEN)
1956
Veikko Hakulinen, Finland
1960
Sixten Jernberg, Sweden
1964
Eero Mantyranta, Finland
1968
Franco Nones, Italy
1972
Viaceslav Vedenine, Russia
1976
Sergei Savaliev, Russia

50 KILOMETERS CROSS-COUNTRY (MEN)
1924
Thorleif Haug, Norway

1928
Per Erik Hedlund, Sweden
1932
Veli Saarinen, Finland
1936
Elis Wiklund, Sweden
1940
Nils Karlsson, Sweden
1952
Veikko Hakulinen, Finland
1956
Sixten Jernberg, Sweden
1960
Kalevi Hamalainen, Finland
1964
Sixten Jernberg, Sweden
1968
Olle Ellefsaeter, Norway
1972
Paal Tyldrum, Norway
1976
Ivar Formo, Norway

40 KILOMETER CROSS-COUNTRY RELAY (MEN)
1936	Finland
1948	Sweden
1952	Finland
1956	Russia
1960	Finland
1964	Sweden
1968	Norway
1972	Russia
1976	Finland

90 METER SKI JUMPING (MEN)
1964
Toralf Engan, Norway
1968
Vladimir Beloussov, Russia
1972
Wojciech Fortuna, Poland
1976
Karl Schnabl, Austria

70 METER SKI JUMPING (MEN)
1964
Veikko Kankkonen, Finland
1968
Jiri Raska, Czechoslovakia
1972
Yukio Kasaya, Japan
1976
Hans Aschenbach, East Germany

COMBINED-15 KILOMETER
CROSS-COUNTRY AND
JUMPING (MEN)
1924
Thorleif Haug, Norway
1928
J. Grottumsbraaten, Norway
1932
J. Grottumsbraaten, Norway
1936
Oddbjorn Hagen, Norway
1948
Heikki Hasu, Finland
1952
Simon Slattvik, Norway
1956
Sverre Stenersen, Norway
1960
Georg Thoma, Germany
1964
Tormod Knutsen, Norway
1968
Frantz Keller, Germany
1972
Ulrich Wehling, East Germany
1976
Ulrich Wehling, East Germany

5 KILOMETERS CROSS-COUNTRY
(WOMEN)
1964
Klaudia Boyerskikh, Russia
1968
Toini Gustafsson, Sweden
1972
Galina Koulakova, Russia
1976
Helena Takalo, Finland

10 KILOMETERS CROSS-
COUNTRY (WOMEN)
1952
Lydia Eidemen, Finland
1956
Lyubov Kosyryeva, Russia
1960
Maria Gusakova, Russia
1964
Klaudia Boyerskikh, Russia
1968
Toini Gustafsson, Sweden
1972
Galina Koulakova, Russia
1976
Raisa Smetanina, Russia

15 KILOMETER CROSS-COUNTRY
RELAY (WOMEN)
1956   Finland
1960   Sweden
1964   Russia
1968   Norway
1972   Russia
1976   Russia

THE PULITZER PRIZE

Administered by Columbia University's School of Journalism
What is now an American biggie began as an afterthought. Newspaper publisher Joseph Pulitzer wanted to establish a journalism school, which he eventually did at Columbia. His prestigious prizes just sort of emerged from the discussions and planning of the school.
Established 1917.

JOURNALISM (Meritorious Public Service)

1917	no award
1918	*New York Times*
1919	*Milwaukee Journal*
1920	no award
1921	*Boston Post*
1922	*New York World*
1923	*Memphis Commercial Appeal*
1924	*New York World*
1925	no award
1926	*Columbus* (Ga.) *Enquirer Sun*
1927	*Canton* (Ohio), *Daily News*
1928	*Indianapolis Times*
1929	*New York Evening World*
1930	no award
1931	*Atlanta Constitution*
1932	*Indianapolis News*
1933	*New York World-Telegram*
1934	*Medford* (Oreg.) *Mail Tribune*
1935	*Sacramento Bee*

1936	*Cedar Rapids* (Iowa) *Gazette*
1937	*St. Louis Post-Dispatch*
1938	*Bismarck* (N.D.) *Tribune*
1939	*Miami News*
1940	*Waterbury* (Conn.) *Republican-American*
1941	*St. Louis Post-Dispatch*
1942	*Los Angeles Times*
1943	*Omaha World-Herald*
1944	*New York Times*
1945	*Detroit Free Press*
1946	*Scranton* (Pa.) *Times*
1947	*Baltimore Sun*
1948	*St. Louis Post-Dispatch*
1949	*Nebraska State Journal*
1950	*Chicago Daily News* and *St. Louis Post-Dispatch*
1951	*Miami Herald* and *Brooklyn Eagle*
1952	*St. Louis Post-Dispatch*
1953	*Whiteville* (N.C.) *News Reporter* and *Tabor City* (N.C.) *Tribune*
1954	*Newsday,* Garden City, N.Y.
1955	*Columbus* (Ga.) *Ledger* and *Sunday Ledger-Enquirer*
1956	*Watsonville* (Calif.) *Register-Pajaronian*
1957	*Chicago Daily News*
1958	*Arkansas Gazette,* Little Rock
1959	*Utica* (N.Y.) *Observer-Dispatch* and *Utica Daily Press*
1960	*Los Angeles Times*
1961	*Amarillo* (Tex.) *Globe-Times*
1962	*Panama City* (Fla.) *News-Herald*
1963	*Chicago Daily News*
1964	*St. Petersburg* (Fla.) *Times*
1965	*Hutchinson* (Kans.) *News*
1966	*Boston Globe*
1967	*Louisville Courier-Journal* and *Milwaukee Journal*
1968	*Riverside* (Calif.) *Press-Enterprise*
1969	*Los Angeles Times*
1970	*Newsday,* Garden City, N.Y.
1971	*Winston-Salem* (N.C.) *Journal & Sentinel*
1972	*New York Times*
1973	*Washington Post*
1974	*Newsday,* Garden City, N.Y.
1975	*Boston Globe*
1976	*Anchorage Daily News*
1977	*Lufkin* (Tex.) *News*

JOURNALISM (Reporting)

(This originally included local, national, and international)

1917
   Herbert Bayard Swope, *New York World*

1918
   Harold A. Littledale, *New York Evening Post*

1919   no award

1920
   John J. Leary Jr., *New York World*

1921
   Louis Seibold, *New York World*

1922
   Kirke L. Simpson, Associated Press

1923
   Alva Johnston, *New York Times*

1924
   Magner White, *San Diego Sun*

1925
   James W. Mulroy, *Chicago Daily News*
   Alvin H. Goldstein, *Chicago Daily News*

1926
   William Burke Miller, *Louisville Courier-Journal*

1927
   John T. Rogers, *St. Louis Post-Dispatch*

1928   no award

1929
   Paul Y. Anderson, *St. Louis Post-Dispatch*

1930
   Russell D. Owen, *New York Times*

1931
   A. B. MacDonald, *Kansas City Star*

1932
   W. C. Richards, *Detroit Free Press*
   D. D. Martin, *Detroit Free Press*
   J. S. Pooler, *Detroit Free Press*
   F. D. Webb, *Detroit Free Press*
   J. N. W. Sloan, *Detroit Free Press*

1933
   Francis A. Jamieson, Associated Press

1934
   Royce Brier, *San Francisco Chronicle*

1935
   William H. Taylor, *New York Herald Tribune*

1936
  Lauren D. Lyman, *New York Times*
1937
  John J. O'Neill, *New York Herald Tribune*
  William L. Laurence, *New York Times*
  Howard W. Blakeslee, Associated Press
  Gobind Behari Lal, Universal Service
  David Dietz, Scripps-Howard Newspapers
1938
  Raymond Sprigle, *Pittsburgh Post-Gazette*
1939
  Thomas L. Stokes, Scripps-Howard Newspapers
1940
  S. Burton Heath, *New York World-Telegram*
1941
  Westbrook Pegler, *New York World-Telegram*
1942
  Stanton Delaplane, *San Francisco Chronicle*
1943
  George Weller, *Chicago Daily News*
1944
  Paul Schoenstein and Associates, *New York Journal-American*
1945
  Jack S. McDowell, *San Francisco Call-Bulletin*
1946
  William L. Laurence, *New York Times*
1947
  Frederick Woltman, *New York World-Telegram*
1948
  George E. Goodwin, *Atlanta Journal*
1949
  Malcolm Johnson, *New York Sun*
1950
  Meyer Berger, *New York Times*
1951
  Edward S. Montgomery, *San Francisco Examiner*
1952
  George de Carvalho, *San Francisco Chronicle*

JOURNALISM (Local General Reporting)
1953   *Providence Journal-Bulletin*
1954   *Vicksburg* (Miss.) *Sunday Post-Herald*
1955
  Mrs. Caro Brown, *Alice* (Tex.) *Daily Echo*
1956
  Lee Hills, *Detroit Free Press*
1957   *Salt Lake Tribune*
1958   *Fargo* (N. Dak.) *Forum*
1959
  Mary Lou Werner, *Washington Star*
1960
  Jack Nelson, *Atlanta Constitution*
1961
  Sanche de Gramont, *New York Herald Tribune*
1962
  Robert D. Mullins, *Deseret News,* Salt Lake City
1963
  Sylvan Fox, *New York World-Telegram and Sun*
  Anthony Shannon, *New York World Telegram and Sun*
  William Longgood, *New York World-Telegram and Sun*
1964
  Norman C. Miller, *Wall Street Journal*
1965
  Melvin H. Ruder, *Hungry Horse News,* Columbia Falls, Mont.
1966   *Los Angeles Times*
1967
  Robert V. Cox, *Chambersburg* (Pa.) *Public Opinion*
1968   *Detroit Free Press*
1969
  John Fetterman, *Louisville Times & Courier-Journal*
1970
  Thomas Fitzpatrick, *Chicago Sun-Times*
1971   *Akron Beacon Journal*
1972
  Richard Cooper, *Rochester (N.Y.) Times-Union*
  John Machacek, *Rochester* (N.Y.) *Times-Union*
1973   *Chicago Tribune*
1974
  Arthur M. Petacque, *Chicago Sun-Times*

Hugh F. Hough, *Chicago Sun-Times*
1975   Xenia (Ohio) *Daily Gazette*
1976
Gene Miller, *Miami Herald*
1977
Margo Huston, *Milwaukee Journal*

JOURNALISM (Local Specialized and Investigative Reporting)
1953
Edward J. Mowery, *New York World-Telegram*
1954
Alvin Scott McCoy, *Kansas City Star*
1955
Roland Kenneth Towery, *Cuero (Tex.) Record*
1956
Arthur Daley, *New York Times*
1957
Wallace Turner, *Portland Oregonian*
William Lambert, *Portland Oregonian*
1958
George Beveridge, *Washington Evening Star*
1959
John Harold Brislin, *Scranton (Pa.) Tribune*
1960
Miriam Ottenberg, *Washington Evening Star*
1961
Edgar May, *Buffalo (N.Y.) Evening News*
1962
George Bliss, *Chicago Tribune*
1963
Oscar Griffin, Jr., *Pecos (Tex.) Independent and Enterprise*
1964
James V. Magee, *Philadelphia Bulletin*
Albert V. Gaudiosi, *Philadelphia Bulletin*
Frederick A. Meyer, *Philadelphia Bulletin*
1965
Gene Goltz, *Houston Post*
1966
John A. Frasca, *Tampa Tribune*
1967
Gene Miller, *Miami Herald*

1968
J. Anthony Lukas, *New York Times*
1969
Albert L. Delugach, *St.Louis Globe-Democrat*
Denny Walsh, *St. Louis Globe-Democrat*
1970
Harold E. Martin, *Montgomery Advertiser & Alabama Journal*
1971
William Jones, *Chicago Tribune*
1972
Timothy Leland, *Boston Globe*
Gerard M. O'Neill, *Boston Globe*
Stephen A. Kurkjian, *Boston Globe*
Ann DeSantis, *Boston Globe*
1973   Sun Newspapers of Omaha
1974
William Sherman, *New York Daily News*
1975   *Indianapolis Star*
1976   *Chicago Tribune*
1977
Wendell Rawls, Jr., *Philadelphia Inquirer*
Acel Moore, *Philadelphia Inquirer*

JOURNALISM (Correspondence)
1929
Paul Scott Mowrer, *Chicago Daily News*
1930
Leland Stowe, *New York Herald Tribune*
1931
H. R. Knickerbocker, *Philadelphia Public Ledger* and *New York Evening Post*
1932
Walter Duranty, *New York Times*
Charles G. Ross, *St. Louis Post-Dispatch*
1933
Edgar Ansel Mowrer, *Chicago Daily News*
1934
Frederick T. Birchall, *New York Times*
1935
Arthur Krock, *New York Times*
1936
Wilfred C. Barber, *Chicago Tribune*
1937
Anne O'Hare McCormick, *New York Times*

1938
Arthur Krock, *New York Times*
1939
Louis P. Lochner, Associated Press
1940
Otto D. Tolischus, *New York Times*
1941   Group award to American war
correspondents
1942
Carlos P. Romulo, *Philippines
Herald*
1943
Hanson W. Baldwin, *New York
Times*
1944
Ernest Taylor Pyle, Scripps-Howard
Newspapers
1945
Harold V. Boyle, Associated Press
1946
Arnaldo Cortesi, *New York Times*
1947
Brooks Atkinson, *New York Times*

JOURNALISM (National Telegraphic Reporting)
1942
Louis Stark, *New York Times*
1943   no award
1944
Dewey L. Fleming, *Baltimore Sun*
1945
James Reston, *New York Times*
1946
Edward A. Harris, *St. Louis Post-
Dispatch*
1947
Edward T. Folliard, *Washington
Post*

JOURNALISM (National Reporting)
1948
Bert Andrews, *New York Herald
Tribune*
Nat S. Finney, *Minneapolis Tribune*
1949
C. P. Trussell, *New York Times*
1950
Edwin O. Guthman, *Seattle Times*
1951   no award
1952
Anthony Leviero, *New York Times*
1953
Don Whitehead, Associated Press

1954
Richard Wilson, Cowles Newspapers
1955
Anthony Lewis, *Washington Daily
News*
1956
Charles L. Bartlett, *Chattanooga
Times*
1957
James Reston, *New York Times*
1958
Relman Morin, Associated Press
Clark Mollenhoff, *Des Moines
Register & Tribune*
1959
Howard Van Smith, *Miami News*
1960
Vance Trimble, Scripps Howard
Newspapers
1961
Edward R. Cony, *Wall Street Journal*
1962
Nathan G. Caldwell, *Nashville
Tennessean*
Gene S. Graham, *Nashville
Tennessean*
1963
Anthony Lewis, *New York Times*
1964
Merriman Smith, United Press
International
1965
Louis M. Kohlmeier, *Wall Street
Journal*
1966
Haynes Johnson, *Washington
Evening Star*
1967
Stanley Penn, *Wall Street Journal*
Monroe Karmin, *Wall Street Journal*
1968
Howard James, *Christian Science
Monitor*
Nathan K. Kotz, *Des Moines Register*
and *Minneapolis Tribune*
1969
Robert Cahn, *Christian Science
Monitor*
1970
William J. Eaton, *Chicago Daily
News*
1971
Lucinda Franks, United Press
International
Thomas Powers, United Press
International

1972
  Jack Anderson, syndicated columnist
1973
  Robert Boyd, Knight Newspapers
  Clark Hoyt, Knight Newspapers
1974
  James R. Polk, *Washington Star-News*
  Jack White, *Providence* (R.I.) *Journal-Bulletin*
1975
  Donald L. Barlett, *Philadelphia Inquirer*
  James B. Steele, *Philadelphia Inquirer*
1976
  James Risser, *Des Moines Register*
  Walter Mears, Associated Press

JOURNALISM (International Telegraphic Reporting)
1942
  Laurence Edmund Allen, Associated Press
1943
  Ira Wolfert, North American Newspaper Alliance
1944
  Daniel de Luce, Associated Press
1945
  Mark S. Watson, *Baltimore Sun*
1946
  Homer William Bigart, *New York Herald Tribune*
1947
  Eddy Gilmore, Associated Press

JOURNALISM (International Reporting)
1948
  Paul W. Ward, *Baltimore Sun*
1949
  Price Day, *Baltimore Sun*
1950
  Edmund Stevens, *Christian Science Monitor*
1951
  Keyes Beech, *Chicago Daily News*
  Fred Sparks, *Chicago Daily News*
  Marguerite Higgins, *New York Herald Tribune*
  Homer William Bigart, *New York Herald Tribune*
  Relman Morin, Associated Press

  Don Whitehead, Associated Press
1952
  John M. Hightower, Associated Press
1953
  Austin Wehrwein, *Milwaukee Journal*
1954
  Jim G. Lucas, Scripps Howard Newspapers
1955
  Harrison E. Salisbury, *New York Times*
1956
  William Randolph Hearst, Jr., International News Service
  Kingsbury Smith, International News Service
  Frank Conniff, International News Service
1957
  Russell Jones, United Press
1958   *New York Times*
1959
  Joseph Martin, *New York Daily News*
  Philip Santora, *New York Daily News*
1960
  A.M. Rosenthal, *New York Times*
1961
  Lynn Heinzerling, Associated Press
1962
  Walter Lippmann, *New York Herald Tribune*
1963
  Hal Hendrix, *Miami News*
1964
  Malcolm W. Browne, Associated Press
  David Halberstam, *New York Times*
1965
  J. A. Livingston, *Philadelphia Bulletin*
1966
  Peter Arnett, Associated Press
1967
  R. John Hughes, *Christian Science Monitor*
1968
  Alfred Friendly, *Washington Post*
1969
  William Tuohy, *Los Angeles Times*
1970
  Seymour M. Hersh, Dispatch News Service

Reporting on the fall of the Cambodian government won New York Times *reporter Sydney H. Schanberg a Pulitzer.*

1971
　Jimmie Lee Hoagland, *Washington Post*
1972
　Peter R. Kann, *Wall Street Journal*
1973
　Max Frankel, *New York Times*
1974
　Hedrick Smith, *New York Times*
1975
　William Mullen, *Chicago Tribune*
　Ovie Carter, *Chicago Tribune*
1976
　Sydney H. Schanberg, *New York Times*
1977　no award

JOURNALISM (Editorials)
1917　*New York Tribune*
1918
　Henry Watterson, *Louisville Courier-Journal*
1919　no award
1920
　Harvey E. Newbranch, *Omaha Evening World Herald*
1921　no award

1922
　Frank M. O'Brien, *New York Herald*
1923
　William Allen White, *Emporia (Kans.) Gazette*
1924
　Frank I. Cobb, *Boston Herald* and *New York World*
1925　Charleston (S.C.) *News and Courier*
1926
　Edward M. Kingsbury, *New York Times*
1927
　F. Lauriston Bullard, *Boston Herald*
1928
　Grover C. Hall, *Montgomery* (Ala.) *Advertiser*
1929
　Louis Isaac Jaffe, *Norfolk Virginian-Pilot*
1930　no award
1931
　Charles S. Ryckman, *Fremont* (Neb.) *Tribune*
1932　no award
1933　*Kansas City Star*

1934
 E. P. Chase, *Atlantic* (Iowa) *News-Telegraph*
1935   no award
1936
 Felix Morley, *Washington Post*
 George B. Parker, Scripps Howard Newspapers
1937
 John W. Owens, *Baltimore Sun*
1938
 William Wesley Waymack, *Des Moines Register & Tribune*
1939
 Ronald G. Callvert, *The Oregonian*, Portland, Oreg.
1940
 Bart Howard, *St. Louis Post-Dispatch*
1941
 Reuben Maury, *New York Daily News*
1942
 Geoffrey Parsons, *New York Herald Tribune*
1943
 Forrest W. Seymour, *Des Moines Register & Tribune*
1944
 Henry J. Haskell, *Kansas City Star*
1945
 George W. Potter, *Providence Journal-Bulletin*
1946
 Hodding Carter, *Delta Democrat-Times,* Greenville, Miss.
1947
 William H. Grimes, *Wall Street Journal*
1948
 Virginius Dabney, *Richmond Times Dispatch*
1949
 John H. Crider, *Boston Herald*
 Herbert Elliston, *Washington Post*
1950
 Carl M. Saunders, *Jackson* (Mich.) *Citizen Patriot*
1951
 William H. Fitzpatrick, *New Orleans States*
1952
 Louis LaCoss, *St. Louis Globe Democrat*

1953
 Vermont Connecticut Royster, *Wall Street Journal*
1954
 Don Murray, *Boston Herald*
1955
 Royce Howes, *Detroit Free Press*
1956
 Lauren K. Soth, *Des Moines Register & Tribune*
1957
 Buford Boone, *Tuscaloosa* (Ala.) *News*
1958
 Harry S. Ashmore, *Arkansas Gazette,* Little Rock
1959
 Ralph McGill, *Atlanta Constitution*
1960
 Lenoir Chambers, *Norfolk Virginian-Pilot*
1961
 William J. Dorvillier, *San Juan* (Puerto Rico) *Star*
1962
 Thomas M. Storke, *Santa Barbara* (Calif.) *News-Press*
1963
 Ira B. Harkey, Jr., *Pascagoula* (Miss.) *Chronicle*
1964
 Hazel Brannon Smith, *Lexington* (Miss.) *Advertiser*
1965
 John R. Harrison, *Gainesville* (Fla.) *Daily Sun*
1966
 Robert Lasch, *St. Louis Post-Dispatch*
1967
 Eugene Patterson, *Atlanta Constitution*
1968
 John S. Knight, Knight Newspapers
1969
 Paul Greenberg, *Pine Bluff* (Ark.) *Commercial*
1970
 Philip L. Geyelin, *Washington Post*
1971
 Horance G. Davis, Jr., *Gainesville* (Fla.) *Sun*
1972
 John Strohmeyer, *Bethlehem* (Pa.) *Globe-Times*

1973
Roger B. Linscott, *Berkshire Eagle,*
Pittsfield, Mass.
1974
F. Gilman Spencer, *The Trentonian,*
Trenton, N.J.
1975
John D. Maurice, *Charleston* (W. Va.)
Daily Mail
1976
Philip Kerby, *Los Angeles Times*
1977
Warren L. Lerude, *Reno Evening
Gazette* and *Nevada State Journal*
Foster Church, *Nevada State Journal*
Norman F. Cardoza, *Reno Evening
Gazette*

JOURNALISM (Editorial Cartoons)
1922   Rollin Kirby
1923   no award
1924
Jay N. Darling, *New York Tribune*
1925
Rollin Kirby, *New York World*
1926
D. R. Fitzpatrick, *St. Louis Post-
Dispatch*
1927
Nelson Harding, *Brooklyn Eagle*
1928
Nelson Harding, *Brooklyn Eagle*
1929
Rollin Kirby, *New York World*
1930
Charles R. Macauley, *Brooklyn
Eagle*
1931
Edmund Duffy, *Baltimore Sun*
1932
John T. McCutcheon, *Chicago
Tribune*
1933
H. M. Talburt, *Washington Daily
News*
1934
Edmund Duffy, *Baltimore Sun*
1935
Ross A. Lewis, *Milwaukee Journal*
1936   no award
1937
C. D. Batchelor, *New York Daily
News*
1938
Vaughn Shoemaker, *Chicago Daily
News*

1939
Charles G. Werner, *Oklahoma City
Daily Oklahoman*
1940
Edmund Duffy, *Baltimore Sun*
1941
Jacob Burck, *Chicago Times*
1942
Herbert Lawrence Block (Herblock),
NEA Service
1943
Jay N. Darling, *New York Herald
Tribune*
1944
Clifford K. Berryman, *Washington
Evening Star*
1945
Sgt. Bill Mauldin, United Feature
Syndicate
1946
Bruce A. Russell, *Los Angeles Times*
1947
Vaughn Shoemaker, *Chicago Daily
News*
1948
Reuben L. Goldberg, *New York Sun*
1949
Lute Pease, *Newark Evening News*
1950
James T. Berryman, *Washington
Evening Star*
1951
Reginald W. Manning, *Arizona
Republic*
1952
Fred L. Packer, *New York Mirror*
1953
Edward D. Kuckes, *Cleveland Plain
Dealer*
1954
Herbert L. Block (Herblock),
Washington Post & Times-Herald
1955
D. R. Fitzpatrick, *St. Louis Post-
Dispatch*
1956
Robert York, *Louisville Times*
1957
Tom Little, *Nashville Tennessean*
1958
Bruce M. Shanks, *Buffalo (N.Y.)
Evening News*
1959
William H. (Bill) Mauldin, *St. Louis
Post-Dispatch*

1960   no award
1961
Carey Orr, *Chicago Tribune*
1962
Edmund S. Valtman, *Hartford Times*
1963
Frank Miller, *Des Moines Register*
1964
Paul Conrad, *Denver Post*
1965   no award
1966
Don Wright, *Miami News*
1967
Patrick B. Oliphant, *Denver Post*
1968
Eugene Gray Payne, *Charlotte Observer*
1969
John Fischetti, *Chicago Daily News*
1970
Thomas F. Darcy, *Newsday*, Garden City, N.Y.
1971
Paul Conrad, *Los Angeles Times*
1972
Jeffrey K. MacNelly, *Richmond News Leader*
1973   no award
1974
Paul Szep, *Boston Globe*
1975
Gary Trudeau, Universal Press Syndicate
1976
Tony Auth, *Philadelphia Inquirer*
1977
Paul Szep, *Boston Globe*

JOURNALISM (Photography)
1942
Milton Brooks, *Detroit News*
1943
Frank Noel, Associated Press
1944
Frank Filan, Associated Press
Earle L. Bunker, *Omaha World-Herald*
1945
Joe Rosenthal, Associated Press
1946   no award
1947
Arnold Hardy, Atlanta, Ga.
1948
Frank Cushing, *Boston Traveler*

1949
Nathaniel Fein, *New York Herald Tribune*
1950
Bill Crouch, *Oakland Tribune*
1951
Max Desfor, Associated Press
1952
John Robinson, *Des Moines Register & Tribune*
Don Ultang, *Des Moines Register & Tribune*
1953
William M. Gallagher, *Flint* (Mich.) *Journal*
1954
Mrs. Walter M. Schau, San Anselmo, Calif.
1955
John L. Gaunt, Jr., *Los Angeles Times*
1956   *New York Daily News*
1957
Harry A. Trask, *Boston Traveler*
1958
William C. Beall, *Washington Daily News*
1959
William Seaman, *Minneapolis Star*
1960
Andrew Lopez, United Press International
1961
Yasushi Nagao, Tokyo, for UPI
Mainichi Shimbun, Tokyo, for UPI
1962
Paul Vathis, Associated Press
1963
Hector Rondon, La Republica of Caracas, for AP
1964
Robert H. Jackson, *Dallas Times-Herald*
1965
Horst Faas, Associated Press
1966
Kyoichi Sawada, UPI
1967
Jack R. Thornell, AP

JOURNALISM (Spot News Photography)
1968
Rocco Morabito, *Jacksonville Journal*

1969
Edward T. Adams, Associated Press
1970
Steve Starr, Associated Press
1971
John Paul Filo, *Valley Daily News,*
New Kensington, Pa.
1972
Horst Faas, Associated Press
Michel Laurent, Associated Press
1973
Huynh Cong Ut, Associated Press
1974
Anthony K. Roberts, Beverly Hills,
Calif.
1975
Gerald H. Gay, *Seattle Times*
1976
Stanley Forman, *Boston Herald
American*
1977
Neal Ulevich, Associated Press
Stanley Forman, *Boston Herald
American*

JOURNALISM (Feature Photography)
1968
Toshio Sakai, UPI
1969
Moneta Sleet, Jr., *Ebony*
1970
Dallas Kinney, *Palm Beach Post*
1971
Jack Dykinga, *Chicago Sun-Times*
1972
Dave Kennerly, UPI
1973
Brian Lanker, *Topeka Capital-
Journal*
1974
Slava Veder, Associated Press
1975
Matthew Lewis, *Washington Post*
1976　*Louisville Courier-Journal
Louisville Times*
1977
Robin Hood, *Chattanooga News-
Free Press*

JOURNALISM (Commentary)
1970
Marquis W. Childs, *St. Louis Post-
Dispatch*
1971
William A. Caldwell, *The Record,*
Hackensack, N.J.

1972
Mike Royko, *Chicago Daily News*
1973
David S. Broder, *Washington Post*
1974
Edwin A. Roberts, Jr., *National
Observer*
1975
Mary McGrory, *Washington Star*
1976
Walter (Red) Smith, *New York Times*
1977
George F. Will, *Washington Post
Writers Group*

JOURNALISM (Criticism)
1970
Ada Louise Huxtable, *New York
Times*
1971
Harold C. Schonberg, *New York
Times*
1972
Frank Peters, Jr., *St. Louis Post-
Dispatch*
1973
Ronald Powers, *Chicago Sun-Times*
1974
Emily Genauer, Newsday Syndicate
1975
Roger Ebert, *Chicago Sun Times*
1976
Alan M. Kriegsman, *Washington Post*
1977
William McPherson, *Washington
Post*

JOURNALISM (Newspaper History Award)
1918　Minna Lewinson
　　　Henry Beetle Hough

JOURNALISM (Special Citations)
1938　*Edmonton* (Alberta) *Journal*
1941　*New York Times* foreign news report
1944　Byron Price, director of Office of Censorship
　　　William Allen White
1945　American press cartographers
1947　Columbia University, its Graduate School of Journalism
　　　St. Louis Post-Dispatch marking the centennial of Joseph Pulitzer's birth

Sinclair Lewis won a Pulitzer Prize for his novel Arrowsmith. (Wide World Photos)

1948   Dr. Frank Diehl Fackenthal
1951
  C. L. Sulzberger, *New York Times*
  Arthur Krock, *New York Times*
1952
  Max Kase, *New York Journal-*
  American
  Kansas City Star
1953   *New York Times* Review of
  the Week
1958
  Walter Lippmann, *New York Herald*
  Tribune
1964   Gannett Newspapers

PULITZER PRIZES IN LETTERS

Novel

1917   no award
1918
  Ernest Poole, *His Family*
1919
  Booth Tarkington, *The Magnificent*
  Ambersons
1920   no award
1921
  Edith Wharton, *The Age of*
  Innocence

1922
  Booth Tarkington, *Alice Adams*
1923
  Willa Cather, *One of Ours*
1924
  Margaret Wilson, *The Able*
  McLaughlins
1925
  Edna Ferber, *So Big*
1926
  Sinclair Lewis, *Arrowsmith*
1927
  Louis Bromfield, *Early Autumn*
1928
  Thornton Wilder, *The Bridge of San*
  Luis Rey
1929
  Julia Peterkin, *Scarlet Sister Mary*
1930
  Oliver LaFarge, *Laughing Boy*
1931
  Margaret Ayer Barnes, *Years of*
  Grace
1932
  Pearl S. Buck, *The Good Earth*
1933
  T. S. Stribling, *The Store*

1934
Caroline Miller, *Lamb in His Bosom*
1935
Josephine Winslow Johnson, *Now in November*
1936
Harold L. Davis, *Honey in the Horn*
1937
Margaret Mitchell, *Gone With the Wind*
1938
John Phillips Marquand, *The Late George Apley*
1939
Marjorie Kinnan Rawlings, *The Yearling*
1940
John Steinbeck, *The Grapes of Wrath*
1941   no award
1942
Ellen Glasgow, *In This Our Life*
1943
Upton Sinclair, *Dragon's Teeth*
1944
Martin Flavin, *Journey in the Dark*
1945
John Hersey, *A Bell for Adano*
1946   no award
1947
Robert Penn Warren, *All the King's Men*

Fiction

1948
James A. Michener, *Tales of the South Pacific*
1949
James Gould Cozzens, *Guard of Honor*
1950
A. B. Guthrie, Jr., *The Way West*
1951
Conrad Richter, *The Town*
1952
Herman Wouk, *The Caine Mutiny*
1953
Ernest Hemingway, *The Old Man and the Sea*
1954   no award
1955
William Faulkner, *A Fable*
1956
MacKinlay Kantor, *Andersonville*

1957   no award
1958
James Agee, *A Death in the Family*
1959
Robert Lewis Taylor, *The Travels of Jaimie McPheeters*
1960
Allen Drury, *Advise and Consent*
1961
Harper Lee, *To Kill A Mockingbird*
1962
Edwin O'Connor, *The Edge of Sadness*
1963
William Faulkner, *The Reivers*
1964   no award
1965
Shirley Ann Grau, *The Keepers of the House*
1966
Katherine Anne Porter, *Collected Stories*
1967
Bernard Malamud, *The Fixer*
1968
William Styron, *The Confessions of Nat Turner*
1969
N. Scott Momaday, *House Made of Dawn*
1970
Jean Stafford, *Collected Stories*
1971   no award
1972
Wallace Stegner, *Angle of Repose*
1973
Eudora Welty, *The Optimist's Daughter*
1974   no award
1975
Michael Shaara, *The Killer Angels*
1976
Saul Bellow, *Humboldt's Gift*
1977   no award

Drama

1917   no award
1918
Jesse Lynch Williams, *Why Marry?*
1919   no award
1920
Eugene O'Neill, *Beyond the Horizon*
1921
Zona Gale, *Miss Lulu Bett*

1922
Eugene O'Neill, *Anna Christie*
1923
Owen Davis, *Icebound*
1924
Hatcher Hughes, *Hell-Bent Fer Heaven*
1925
Sidney Howard, *They Knew What They Wanted*
1926
George Kelly, *Craig's Wife*
1927
Paul Green, *In Abraham's Bosom*
1928
Eugene O'Neill, *Strange Interlude*
1929
Elmer L. Rice, *Street Scene*
1930
Marc Connelly, *The Green Pastures*
1931
Susan Glaspell, *Alison's House*
1932
George S. Kaufman, *Of Thee I Sing*
Morrie Ryskind, *Of Thee I Sing*
Ira Gershwin, *Of Thee I Sing*
1933
Maxwell Anderson, *Both Your Houses*
1934
Sidney Kingsley, *Men in White*
1935
Zoe Akins, *The Old Maid*
1936
Robert E. Sherwood, *Idiot's Delight*
1937
Moss Hart, *You Can't Take It With You*
George S. Kaufman, *You Can't Take It With You*
1938
Thornton Wilder, *Our Town*
1939
Robert E. Sherwood, *Abe Lincoln in Illinois*
1940
William Saroyan, *The Time of Your Life*
1941
Robert E. Sherwood, *There Shall Be No Night*
1942   no award
1943
Thornton Wilder, *The Skin of Our Teeth*

1944   no award
1945
Mary Chase, *Harvey*
1946
Russel Crouse, *State of the Union*
Howard Lindsay, *State of the Union*
1947   no award
1948
Tennessee Williams, *A Streetcar Named Desire*
1949
Arthur Miller, *Death of a Salesman*
1950
Richard Rodgers, *South Pacific*
Oscar Hammerstein, 2nd, *South Pacific*
Joshua Logan, *South Pacific*
1951   no award
1952
Joseph Kramm, *The Shrike*
1953
William Inge, *Picnic*
1954
John Patrick, *The Teahouse of the August Moon*
1955
Tennessee Williams, *Cat on A Hot Tin Roof*
1956
Albert Hackett, *Diary of Anne Frank*
Frances Goodrich, *Diary of Anne Frank*
1957
Eugene O'Neill, *Long Day's Journey Into Night*
1958
Ketti Frings, *Look Homeward, Angel*
1959
Archibald MacLeish, *J. B.*
1960
Jerome Weidman, *Fiorello!*
George Abbott, *Fiorello!*
Jerry Bock, *Fiorello!*, music
Sheldon Harnick, *Fiorello!*, lyrics
1961
Tad Mosel, *All The Way Home*
1962
Frank Loesser, *How To Succeed In Business Without Really Trying*
Abe Burrows, *How To Succeed In Business Without Really Trying*
1963   no award
1964   no award
1965
Frank D. Gilroy, *The Subject Was Roses*

1966   no award
1967
Edward Albee, *A Delicate Balance*
1968   no award
1969
Howard Sackler, *The Great White
Hope*
1970
Charles Gordone, *No Place To Be
Somebody*
1971
Paul Zindel, *The Effect of Gamma
Rays on Man-in-the-Moon Marigolds*
1972   no award
1973
Jason Miller, *That Championship
Season*
1974   no award
1975
Edward Albee, *Seascape*
1976
Michael Bennett, *A Chorus Line*
James Kirkwood, *A Chorus Line*
Nicholas Dante, *A Chorus Line*
Marvin Hamlisch, *A Chorus Line*
Edward Kleban, *A Chorus Line*
1977
Michael Cristofer, *The Shadow Box*

History

1917
His Excellency J. J. Jusserand,
Ambassador of France to the United
States, *With Americans of Past and
Present Days*
1918
James Ford Rhodes, *A History of the
Civil War, 1861–1865*
1919   no award
1920
Justin H. Smith, *A War With Mexico*,
2 vols.
1921
William Sowden Sims in
collaboration with Burton J.
Hendrick, *The Victory at Sea*
1922
James Truslow Adams, *The
Founding of New England*
1923
Charles Warren, *The Supreme Court
in United States History*

1924
Charles Howard Mellwain, *The
American Revolution—A
Constitutional Interpretation*
1925
Frederic L. Paxson, *A History of the
American Frontier*
1926
Edward Channing, *The History of
the United States*
1927
Samuel Flagg Bemis, *Pickney's
Treaty*
1928
Vernon Louis Parrington, *Main
Currents in American Thought*, 2
vols.
1929
Fred Albert Shannon, *The
Organization and Administration of
the Union Army, 1861-1865*
1930
Claude H. Van Tyne, *The War of
Independence*
1931
Bernadotte E. Schmitt, *The Coming
of the War: 1914*
1932
John J. Pershing, *My Experiences in
the World War*
1933
Frederick J. Turner, *The Significance
of Sections in American History*
1934
Herbert Agar, *The People's Choice*
1935
Charles McLean Andrews, *The
Colonial Period of American History*
1936
Andrew C. McLaughlin, *The
Constitutional History of the United
States*
1937
Van Wyck Brooks, *The Flowering of
New England*
1938
Paul Herman Buck, *The Road to
Reunion, 1865-1900*
1939
Frank Luther Mott, *A History of
American Magazines*
1940
Carl Sandburg, *Abraham Lincoln:
The War Years*

1941
Marcus Lee Hansen, *The Atlantic Migration, 1607–1860*
1942
Margaret Leech, *Reveille in Washington*
1943
Esther Forbes, *Paul Revere and the World He Lived In*
1944
Merle Curtie, *The Growth of American Thought*
1945
Stephen Bonsal, *Unfinished Business*
1946
Arthur Meier Schlesinger, Jr., *The Age of Jackson*
1947
James Phinney Baxter 3rd, *Scientists Against Time*
1948
Bernard DeVoto, *Across the Wide Missouri*
1949
Roy Franklin Nichols, *The Disruption of American Democracy*
1950
Oliver W. Larkin, *Art and Life in America*
1951
R. Carlyle Buley, *The Old Northwest, Pioneer Period 1815–1840*
1952
Oscar Handlin, *The Uprooted*
1953
George Dangerfield, *The Era of Good Feelings*
1954
Bruce Catton, *A Stillness At Appomattox*
1955
Paul Horgan, *Great River: The Rio Grande in North American History*
1956
Richard Hofstadter, *Age of Reform*
1957
George F. Kennan, *Russia Leaves the War: Soviet-American Relations, 1917–1920*
1958
Bray Hammond, *Banks and Politics in America*
1959
Leonard D. White (with assistance of Miss Jean Schneider), *The Republican Era: 1869–1901*
1960
Margaret Leech, *In the Days of McKinley*
1961
Herbert Feis, *Between War and Peace: The Potsdam Conference*
1962
Lawrence H. Gipson, *The Triumphant Empire, Thunder-Clouds in the West*
1963
Constance McLaughlin Green, *Washington, Village and Capital, 1800–1878*
1964
Sumner Chilton Powell, *Puritan Village: The Formation of a New England Town*
1965
Irwin Unger, *The Greenback Era*
1966
Perry Miller, *Life of the Mind in America*
1967
William H. Goetzmann, *Exploration and Empire: The Explorer and the Scientist in the Winning of the American West*
1968
Bernard Bailyn, *The Ideological Origins of the American Revolution*
1969
Leonard W. Levy, *Origins of the Fifth Amendment*
1970
Dean Acheson, *Present at the Creation: My Years in The State Department*
1971
James MacGregor Burns, *Roosevelt, The Soldier of Freedom*
1972
Carl N. Degler, *Neither Black Nor White*
1973
Michael Kammen, *People of Paradox: An Inquiry Concerning the Origins of American Civilization*
1974
Daneil J. Boorstin, *The Americans: The Democratic Experience*
1975
Dumas Malone, *Jefferson and His Time*

1976
Paul Horgan, *Lamy of Santa Fe*
1977
David M. Potter, *The Impending Crisis*

Biography or Autobiography

1917
Laura E. Richards, Maude Howe Elliott, (assisted by Florence Howe Hall), *Julia Ward Howe*
1918
William Cabell Bruce, *Benjamin Franklin, Self-Revealed*
1919
Henry Adams, *The Education of Henry Adams*
1920
Albert J. Beveridge, *The Life of John Marshall*, 4 vols.
1921
Edward Bok, *The Americanization of Edward Bok*
1922
Hamlin Garland, *A Daughter of the Middle Border*
1923
Burton J. Hendrick, *The Life and Letters of Walter Page*
1924
Michael Idvorsky Pupin, *From Immigrant to Inventor*
1925
M. A. DeWolfe Howe, *Barrett Wendell and His Letters*
1926
Harvey Cushing, *The Life of Sir William Osler*, 2 vols.
1927
Emory Holloway, *Whitman*
1928
Charles Edward Russell, *The American Orchestra and Theodore Thomas*
1929
Burton J. Hendrick, *The Training of an American, The Earlier Life and Letters of Walter H. Page*
1930
Marquis James, *The Raven*
1931
Henry James, *Charles W. Eliot*
1932
Henry F. Pringle, *Theodore Roosevelt*

1933
Allan Nevins, *Grover Cleveland*
1934
Tyler Dennett, *John Hay*
1935
Douglas S. Freeman, *R. E. Lee*
1936
Ralph Barton Perry, *The Thought and Character of William James*
1937
Allan Nevins, *Hamilton Fish*
1938
Odell Shepard, *Pedlar's Progress*
Marquis James, *Andrew Jackson*, 2 vols.
1939
Carl Van Doren, *Benjamin Franklin*
1940
Ray Stannard Baker, *Woodrow Wilson, Life and Letters, Vol. VII & VIII*
1941
Ola Elizabeth Winslow, *Jonathan Edwards*
1942
Forrest Wilson, *Crusader in Crinoline*
1943
Samuel Eliot Morison, *Admiral of the Ocean Sea*
1944
Carleton Mabee, *The American Leonardo: The Life of Samuel F. B. Morse*
1945
Russel Blaine Nye, *George Bancroft: Brahmin Rebel*
1946
Linnie Marsh Wolfe, *Son of the Wilderness*
1947   *The Autobiography of William Allen White*
1948
Margaret Clapp, *Forgotten First Citizen: John Bigelow*
1949
Robert E. Sherwood, *Roosevelt and Hopkins*
1950
Samuel Flagg Bemis, *John Quincy Adams and the Foundations of American Foreign Policy*
1951
Margaret Louise Coit, *John C. Calhoun: American Portrait*

1952
Merlo J. Pusey, *Charles Evans Hughes*
1953
David J. Mays, *Edmund Pendleton 1721–1803*
1954
Charles A. Lindbergh, *The Spirit of St. Louis*
1955
William S. White, *The Taft Story*
1956
Talbot Faulkner Hamlin, *Benjamin Henry Latrobe*
1957
John F. Kennedy, *Profiles in Courage*
1958
Douglas Southall Freeman, *George Washington*, Vols. I–VI
John Alexander Carroll and Mary Wells Ashworth (after Dr. Freeman's death in 1953), *George Washington*, Vols. VII
1959
Arthur Walworth, *Woodrow Wilson, American Prophet*
1960
Samuel Eliot Morison, *John Paul Jones*
1961
David Donald, *Charles Sumner and the Coming of the Civil War*
1962   no award
1963
Leon Edel, *Henry James*
1964
Walter Jackson Bate, *John Keats*
1965
Ernest Samuels, *Henry Adams*, 3 vols.
1966
Arthur M. Schlesinger, Jr., *A Thousand Days*
1967
Justin Kaplan, *Mr. Clemens and Mark Twain*
1968
George F. Kennan, *Memoirs*
1969
Benjamin Lawrence Reid, *The Man From New York: John Quinn and His Friends*
1970
T. Harry Williams, *Huey Long*

1971
Lawrance Thompson, *Robert Frost: The Years of Triumph*
1972
Joseph P. Lash, *Eleanor and Franklin, 1915-1938*
1973
W. A. Swanberg, *Luce and His Empire*
1974
Louis Sheaffer, *O'Neill, Son and Artist*
1975
Robert A. Caro, *The Power Broker: Robert Moses and The Fall of New York*
1976
R. W. B. Lewis, *Edith Wharton: A Biography*
1977
John E. Mack, *A Prince of Our Disorder*

Poetry

Until 1922, the following were awarded from gifts provided by the Poetry Society:
1918
Sara Teasdale, *Love Songs*
1919
Margaret Widdemer, *Old Road to Paradise*
Carl Sandburg, *Corn Huskers*
The Pulitzer prizes for poetry follow:
1922
Edwin Arlington Robinson, *Collected Poems*
1923
Edna St. Vincent Millay, *The Ballad of the Harp-Weaver; A Few Figs from Thistles;* eight sonnets in *American Poetry, 1922, A Miscellany*
1924
Robert Frost, *New Hampshire: A Poem With Notes and Grace Notes*
1925
Edwin Arlington Robinson, *The Man Who Died Twice*
1926
Amy Lowell, *What's O'Clock*
1927
Leonora Speyer, *Fiddler's Farewell*
1928
Edwin Arlington Robinson, *Tristram*

1929
Stephen Vincent Benet, *John Brown's Body*
1930
Conrad Aiken, *Selected Poems*
1931
Robert Frost, *Collected Poems*
1932
George Dillon, *The Flowering Stone*
1933
Archibald MacLeish, *Conquistador*
1934
Robert Hillyer, *Collected Verse*
1935
Audrey Wurdemann, *Bright Ambush*
1936
Robert P. Tristram Coffin, *Strange Holiness*
1937
Robert Frost, *A Further Range*
1938
Marya Zaturenska, *Cold Morning Sky*
1939
John Gould Fletcher, *Selected Poems*
1940
Mark Van Doren, *Collected Poems*
1941
Leonard Bacon, *Sunderland Capture*
1942
William Rose Benet, *The Dust Which is God*
1943
Robert Frost, *A Witness Tree*
1944
Stephen Vincent Benet, *Western Star*
1945
Karl Shapiro, *V-Letter and Other Poems*
1946   no award
1947
Robert Lowell, *Lord Weary's Castle*
1948
W. H. Auden, *The Age of Anxiety*
1949
Peter Viereck, *Terror and Decorum*
1950
Gwendolyn Brooks, *Annie Allen*
1951
Carl Sandburg, *Complete Poems*
1952
Marianne Moore, *Collected Poems*
1953
Archibald MacLeish, *Collected Poems 1917-1952*
1954
Theodore Roethke, *The Waking*
1955
Wallace Stevens, *Collected Poems*
1956
Elizabeth Bishop, *Poems—North & South*
1957
Richard Wilbur, *Things of This World*
1958
Robert Penn Warren, *Promises: Poems 1954-1956*
1959
Stanley Kunitz, *Selected Poems 1928-1958*
1960
W. D. Snodgrass, *Heart's Needle*
1961
Phyllis McGinley, *Times Three: Selected Verse From Three Decades*
1962
Alan Dugan, *Poems*
1963
William Carlos Williams, *Pictures from Breughel*
1964
Louis Simpson, *At the End Of The Open Road*
1965
John Berryman, *77 Dream Songs*
1966
Richard Eberhart, *Selected Poems*
1967
Anne Sexton, *Live or Die*
1968
Anthony Hecht, *The Hard Hours*
1969
George Oppen, *Of Being Numerous*
1970
Richard Howard, *Untitled Subjects*
1971
William S. Merwin, *The Carrier of Ladders*
1972
James Wright, *Collected Poems*
1973
Maxine Kumin, *Up Country*
1974
Robert Lowell, *The Dolphin*
1975
Gary Snyder, *Turtle Island*
1976
John Ashbery, *Self-Portrait in a*

Convex Mirror
1977
James Merrill, *Divine Comedies*

General Nonfiction

1962
Theodore H. White, *The Making of the President 1960*
1963
Barbara W. Tuchman, *The Guns of August*
1964
Richard Hofstadter, *Anti-Intellectualism in American Life*
1965
Howard Mumford Jones, *O Strange New World*
1966
Edwin Way Teale, *Wandering Through Winter*
1967
David Brion Davis, *The Problem of Slavery in Western Culture*
1968
Will and Ariel Durant, *Rousseau and Revolution*
1969
Rene Jules Dubos, *So Human an Animal*
Norman Mailer, *The Armies of the Night*
1970
Erik H. Erikson, *Gandhi's Truth*
1971
John Toland, *The Rising Sun*
1972
Barbara W. Tuchman, *Stilwell and the American Experience in China, 1911–1945*
1973
Robert Coles, *Children of Crisis,* Vols. II and III
Frances FitzGerald, *Fire in the Lake: The Vietnamese and the Americans in Vietnam*
1974
Ernest Becker, *The Denial of Death*
1975
Annie Dillard, *Pilgrim at Tinker Creek*
1976
Robert N. Butler, *Why Survive? Being Old in America*

1977
William W. Warner, *Beautiful Swimmers: Crabs & the Chesapeake Bay*

SPECIAL CITATIONS—LETTERS

1944   Richard Rodgers and Oscar Hammerstein, 2nd, *Oklahoma!*
1957   "A special citation is awarded to Kenneth Roberts for his historical novels which have long contributed to the creation of greater interest in our early American history."
1960   "A special citation is awarded to *The Armada* by Garrett Mattingly, published by Houghton, Mifflin. It is a first class history and a literary work of high order."
1961   "A special citation is given to *The American Heritage Picture History of the Civil War* as a distinguished example of American book publishing."
1973   "A special citation is awarded to *George Washington,* Vols. I-IV, by James Thomas Flexner."
1974   "A special citation is awarded to Roger Sessions for his life's work as a distinguished American composer."
1977   Alex Haley, *Roots*

MUSIC

1943   William Schuman for his *Secular Cantata No. 2, A Free Song,* performed by the Boston Symphony Orchestra and published by G. Schirmer, Inc., New York
1944   Howard Hanson for his *Symphony No. 4, Opus 34,* performed by the Boston Symphony Orchestra on December 3, 1943
1945   Aaron Copland for his *Appalachian Spring,* a ballet written for and presented by Martha Graham and group, commissioned by Mrs. E. S. Coolidge, first presented at the Library of Congress, Washington, D.C., October, 1944
1946   Leo Sowerby for *The Canticle of the Sun,* commissioned by the Alice M. Ditson Fund, first performed by the Schola Cantorum in New York, April, 1945

1947   Charles Ives for his *Symphony No. 3,* first performed by Lou Harrison and Chamber Orchestra in New York, April, 1946

1948   Walter Piston for his *Symphony No. 3,* first performed by the Boston Symphony Orchestra in Boston, January, 1948

1949   Virgil Thomson for his music for the film *Louisiana Story,* released in 1948 by Robert Flaherty Productions

1950   Gian-Carlo Menotti for his music in the *Consul,* produced at the Barrymore Theatre, New York

1951   Douglas S. Moore for his music in *Giants in the Earth,* produced by the Columbia Opera Workshop, March 28, 1951

1952   Gail Kubik for his *Symphony Concertante,* performed at Town Hall, January 7, 1952

1953   no award

1954   Quincy Porter for *Concerto For Two Pianos and Orchestra,* first performed by the Louisville Symphony Orchestra, March 17, 1954. This was one of the works commissioned under a grant of the Rockefeller Foundation for new American compositions for orchestra, or soloists and orchestra

1955   Gian-Carlo Menotti for *The Saint of Bleecker Street,* an opera first performed at the Broadway Theatre, New York, December 27, 1954

1956   Ernst Toch for *Symphony No. 3,* first performed by the Pittsburgh Symphony Orchestra, December 2, 1955

1957   Norman Dello Joio for his *Meditations on Ecclesiastes,* first performed at the Juilliard School of Music on April 20, 1956

1958   Samuel Barber for *Vanessa,* an opera in four acts. Libretto by Gian Carlo Menotti. First presented January 15, 1958, at the Metropolitan Opera House

1959   John LaMontaine for his *Concerto for Piano and Orchestra,* first performed in Washington, D.C., by the National Symphony Orchestra on November 25, 1958

1960   Elliott Carter, for *Second String Quartet,* first performed at the Juilliard School of Music, March 25, 1960

1961   Walter Piston, for his *Symphony No. 7,* first performed by the Philadelphia Orchestra on February 10, 1961, and commissioned by the Philadelphia Orchestra Association

1962   Robert Ward, for *The Crucible,* an opera in three acts. Libretto by Bernard Stambler, based on the play by Arthur Miller. First performed at New York City Center, on October 26, 1961, by the New York City Opera Company

1963   Samuel Barber for *Piano Concerto No. 1,* which had its world premiere with the Boston Symphony at Philharmonic Hall on September 24, 1962

1964   no award

1965   no award

1966   Leslie Bassett, *Variations for Orchestra*

1967   Leon Kirchner, *Quartet No. 3*

1968   George Crumb, *Echoes of Time and the River*

1969   Karel Husa, *String Quartet*

1970   Charles Wuorinen, *Time's Encomium*

1971   Mario Davidovsky, *Synchronisms No. 6 for Piano and Electronic Sound*

1972   Jacob Druckman, *Windows*

1973   Elliott Carter, *String Quartet No. 3*

1974   Donald Martino, *Notturno*

1975   Dominick Argento, *From the Diary of Virginia Woolf*

1976   Ned Rorem, *Air Music*

1977   Richard Wernick, *Visions of Terror and Wonder*

ACHIEVEMENT

See Architecture, Architecture Critic's Medal and Citation, The American Institute of Architects

See Books, Morton Dauwen Zabel Award, The National Institute of Arts and Letters

RALPH BUNCHE AWARD—University of California Los Angeles Alumni Association

Ralph Bunche was not only a Nobel Peace Prize winner and a U.N. diplomat, he was also a member of the class of '27 of UCLA. To honor one of its most noteworthy students, the Alumni Association established this award after Bunche's death in 1971 to be given "to a world citizen whose efforts for the betterment of mankind reflect the spirit of Ralph Bunche." One doesn't need to be a UCLA alumnus to apply.

Established 1971.

1972   U Thant

FRANK A. CHAMBERS AWARD—Air Pollution Control Association

This is for scientific and technical achievement in the control of air pollution.

Established 1954.

1955	Moyer D. Thomas
1956	Ward F. Davidson
1957	Walter A. Schmidt
1958	Arie Jan Haagen-Smit
1959	Robert E. Swain
1960	no award
1961	Philip A. Leighton
1962	Bert L. Richards
1963	no award
1964	Charles W. Gruber
1965	Morris A. Katz
1966	Louis C. McCabe
1967	no award
1968	Sir Oliver Graham Sutton
1969	W. C. L. Hemeon

1970	A. Paul Altshuller
1971	Harry J. White
1972	no award
1973	W. L. Faith
1974	James P. Lodge
1975	E. R. Hendrickson

THE GRENVILLE CLARK PRIZE—The Grenville Clark Fund at Dartmouth College

Who, some might ask, is Grenville Clark? According to one biographer, "He was a tall, strong-framed man, with a rugged face, jutting eyebrows, and a great square jaw. He was the personification of tenacity, but his eyes were known to twinkle and his measured voice often chuckled." He was also rich, a lawyer, and a Harvard graduate who advised presidents and was nominated several times for the Nobel Peace Prize. His namesake prize, which carries a hefty $15,000 along with the honor, "seeks to promote the ideas, character and concept of the obligation of a private citizen to fight for that which is right," primarily in the fields of civil liberties, academic freedom, civil rights, peace and "good government." To be awarded every three years until 1999.

Established 1973.

1975   Jean Monnet

THE GOLD MEDAL AWARDS—The American Academy of Arts and Letters and the National Institute of Arts and Letters

Given for achievement in criticism, painting, sculpture, music, the novel, biography, poetry, architecture (including landscape architecture), drama, and graphic art.

Established 1909.

1909	Augustus Saint-Gaudens, sculpture
1910	James Ford Rhodes, history

1911	James Whitcomb Riley, poetry		1951	James Earle Fraser, sculpture
1912	W. Rutherford Mead, architecture		1951	Igor Stravinsky, music
			1952	Thorton Wilder, fiction
1913	Augustus Thomas, drama		1952	Carl Sandburg, history and biography

1911   James Whitcomb Riley,
        poetry
1912   W. Rutherford Mead,
        architecture
1913   Augustus Thomas, drama
1914   John Singer Sargent, painting
1915   William D. Howells, fiction
1916   John Burroughs, essays and
        belles-lettres
1917   Daniel Chester French,
        sculpture
1918   William R. Thayer, history
        and biography
1919   Charles M. Loeffler, music
1921   Cass Gilbert, architecture
1922   Eugene G. O'Neill, drama
1923   Edwin H. Blashfield,
        painting
1924   Edith Wharton, fiction
1925   William C. Brownell, essays
        and belles-lettres
1926   Herbert Adams, sculpture
1927   William M. Sloane, history
        and biography
1928   George W. Chadwick, music
1929   Edwin A. Robinson, poetry
1930   Charles Adams Platt,
        architecture
1931   William Gillette, drama
1932   Gari Mechers, painting
1933   Booth Tarkington, fiction
1935   Agnes Repplier, essays and
        belles-lettres
1936   George G. Barnard, sculpture
1937   Charles M. Andrews, history
        and biography
1938   Walter Damrosch, music
1939   Robert Frost, poetry
1940   Williams Adams Delano,
        architecture
1941   Robert E. Sherwood, drama
1942   Cecilia Beaux, painting
1943   Stephen Vincent Benet,
        literature
1944   Willa Cather, fiction
1945   Paul Manship, sculpture
1946   Van Wyck Brooks, essays and
        criticism
1947   John Alden Carpenter, music
1948   Charles Austin Beard, history
        and biography
1949   Frederick Law Olmstead,
        architecture
1950   John Sloan, painting
1950   Henry L. Mencken, essays
        and criticism

1951   James Earle Fraser, sculpture
1951   Igor Stravinsky, music
1952   Thorton Wilder, fiction
1952   Carl Sandburg, history and
        biography
1953   Marianne Craig Moore,
        poetry
1953   Frank Lloyd Wright,
        architecture
1954   Maxwell Anderson, drama
1954   Reginald March, graphic art
1955   Edward Hopper, painting
1955   Edmund Wilson, essays and
        criticism
1956   Ivan Mestrovic, sculpture
1956   Aaron Copland, music
1957   John Dos Passos, fiction
1957   Allan Nevins, history and
        biography
1958   Conrad Aiken, poetry
1958   Henry R. Shepley,
        architecture
1959   Arthur Miller, drama
1959   George Grosz, graphic art
1960   Charles E. Burchfield,
        painting
1960   E. B. White, essays and
        criticism
1961   William Zorach, sculpture
1961   Roger Sessions, music
1962   William Faulkner, fiction
1962   Samuel Eliot Morison,
        history and biography
1963   William Carlos Williams,
        poetry
1963   Ludwig Mies van der Rohe,
        architecture
1964   Lillian Hellman, drama
1964   Ben Shahn, graphic art
1965   Andrew Wyeth, painting
1965   Walter Lippmann, essays and
        criticism
1966   Jacques Lipchitz, sculpture
1966   Virgil Thomson, music
1967   Katherine Anne Porter, fiction
1967   Arthur Schlesinger, Jr.,
        history and biography
1968   R. Buckminster Fuller,
        architecture
1968   Wystan Hugh Auden, poetry
1969   Tennessee Williams, drama
1969   Leonard Baskin, graphic art
1970   Lewis Mumford, belles-
        lettres

1970	Georgia O'Keefe, painting
1971	Elliott C. Carter, music
1971	Alexander Calder, sculpture
1972	Eudora Welty, the novel
1972	Henry Steele Commager, history
1973	Louis I. Kahn, architecture
1973	John Crowe Ransom, poetry
1974	Saul Steinberg, graphic art
1975	Kenneth Burke, belles-lettres
1975	Willem de Kooning, painting
1976	Leo Edel, biography
1976	Samuel Barber, music

GOLD MEDAL FOR DISTINGUISHED ARCHAEOLOGICAL ACHIEVEMENT—Archaeological Institute of America

The award is for exactly what its name says.

Established 1965.

1965
Carl William Blegen, excavator of Troy and the Palace of Nestor at Pylos. Professor emeritus of Classical Archaeology at the University of Cincinnati

1966
Hetty Goldman, professor emeritus at the Institute for Advanced Study in Princeton and one of the pioneering women excavators in Greece and the Near East

1967
William Foxwell Albright, professor emeritus of Near Eastern Studies (Semitic Languages) at the John Hopkins University

1968
Gisela Marie Augusta Richter, scholar and curator

1969
Oscar Theodore Broneer, discoverer of the site of the Isthmian Games and the Sanctuary of Poseidon at the Isthmus of Corinth
Rhys Carpenter, professor emeritus of Clasical Archaeology at Bryn Mawr College
William Bell Dinsmoor, author, past president of the Archaeological Institute of America

1970
George Emmanuel Mylonas, Washington University, directed archaeological excavation at Aghios Kosmos, Eleusis, and Mycenae

1971
Robert John Braidwood, archaeologist, anthropologist, author, and leader in the field of Near Eastern prehistory

1972
Homer Armstrong Thompson, leading authority on the topography and monuments of ancient Athens

1973
Gordon Randolph Willey, New World archaeologist

1974
Margarete Bieber, authority on the archaeology of the Greek and Roman theater, on ancient dress, and on the sculpture of the Hellenistic Age

1975
Eugene Vanderpool, authority on the antiquities and the topography of Hellas; American School of Classical Studies at Athens

1976
Lucy Shoe Meritt, scholar, editor, and teacher

S. SMITH GRISWOLD AWARD—Air Pollution Control Association

Named after the onetime chief air pollution control officer for the Los Angeles Air Pollution Control District—no marshmallow post—this award goes to someone on the staff of a governmental agency who has helped in the prevention and control of air pollution.

Established 1971.

1972	Robert L. Chass
1973	William H. Megonnell
1974	John A. Maga
1975	William A. Munroe

ALEXANDER HAMILTON MEDAL—Columbia College Alumni Association

To win this medal, one must either be an alumnus or on the faculty and have shown distinguished service in some field of endeavor. Since the college in question is Columbia, winners aren't hard to come by.

Established 1947.

| 1947 | Nicholas Murray Butler ('82) |
| 1948 | Frank Diehl Fackenthal ('06) |

Astronaut Donald K. Slayton was the 1976 "Heart of the Year."

1949	Vi Kyuin Willington Koo ('09)	1962	John Allen Krout
1950	William Joseph Donovan ('05)	1963	Dwight David Eisenhower
		1964	William Towson Taylor ('21)
1951	Harry James Carman	1965	Peter Grimm ('11)
1952	Carlton Joseph Huntley Hayes ('04)	1966	Alfred A. Knopf ('12)
		1967	Benjamin J. Buttenwieser ('19)
1953	Arthur Hays Sulzberger ('13)		
1954	Frank Smithwick Hogan ('24)	1968	Allan Nevins
1955	Frederick Coykendall ('95) Marcellus Hartley Dodge ('03)	1969	Arthur F. Burns ('25) Joseph Wood Krutch
		1970	Andrew W. Cordier
1956	Richard Rodgers ('23) Oscar Hammerstein 2nd ('16)	1971	(presented in 1972) Lionel Trilling ('25)
1957	Grayson Kirk	1973	Emanuel Celler ('10)
1958	Edmund Astley Prentis ('06)	1974	Nicholas McD. McKnight ('21)
1959	Mark Van Doren		
1960	Ward Melville ('09)	1975	Meyer Schapiro ('24)
1961	The Columbia College Nobel		

1961 The Columbia College Nobel
Laureates: Edward Charles
Kendall ('08)
Polykarp Kush
Willis Eugene Lamb, Jr.
Joshua Lederberg ('44)
Hermann Joseph Muller ('10)
John Howard Northrop ('12)
Isidor Isaac Rabi
Harold Clayton Urey

HEART OF THE YEAR AWARD—
American Heart Association
Well, it's not exactly for someone with the best heart, but rather for someone "whose faith and courage in meeting the personal challenge of heart disease has inspired people throughout the nation with confidence in the objectives and program of the American

Singer, actress, and beautiful lady, Lena Horne won a Mademoiselle Award in 1943. (Memory Shop)

Heart Association." Yes, but Richard Nixon?

Established 1959.

1959	Lyndon Johnson
1960	Mrs. Dwight Eisenhower
1961	Arthur Sulzberger
1962	Clarence Randall
1963	Gen. Lauris Norstad
1964	Adm. H. G. Rickover
1965	George Tebbets
1966	Hon. J. E. Fogarty
1967	Dwight D. Eisenhower
1968	Patricia Neal
1969	Dr. Irvine H. Page
1970	Owens Cheatham
1971	Carl Albert
1972	Pearl Bailey
1973	Richard M. Nixon
1974	John Hiller
1975	Henry Fonda
1976	Donald K. Slayton

THE LYNDON BAINES JOHNSON FOUNDATION AWARD—The Lyndon Baines Johnson Foundation (Formerly known as the Zale Award)

Named after a local Texas boy who made good in Washington, this honor goes to person or persons who contribute to "the betterment of mankind in his or her field." The fields change from award year to award year. The $25,000 however stays the same.

Established 1972.

1973
Roy Wilkins, executive director of the National Association for the Advancement of Colored People

1974
Ivan Allen, Jr., former mayor of Atlanta
Franklin A. Thomas, president of the Bedford Stuyvesant Restoration Corporation, Brooklyn, New York

1975
Dr. George O. G. Lof, solar energy researcher

THE PILLSBURY BAKE-OFF—The Pillsbury Company

If inflation has been bedeviling you, pause and consider that the Pillsbury

people happily pay $25,000 for a pound cake. That's the top prize in this bake-off.

Established 1949.

1949
Mrs. Ralph E. Smafield, Rockford, Ill., Water-Rising Twists (a nut sweet-roll)

1950
Mrs. Peter Wuebel, Menlo Park, Calif., Orange Kiss Me Cake (a loaf cake topped with orange juice and nuts)

1951
Mrs. Samuel P. Weston, La Jolla, Calif., Starlight Double Delight Cake (a chocolate cake with cream cheese frosting)

1952
Mrs. Peter Harlib, Chicago, Ill., Snappy Turtle Cookies (a brown-sugar cookie, shaped in a chocolate shell)

1953
Mrs. Bernard Kanago, Denver, Colo., My Inspiration Cake (a quick-mix white cake with a nut crust and chocolate between the layers)

1954
Mrs. Bernard A. Koteen, Washington, D.C., Open Sesame Pie (a pie with a toasted sesame-seed crust and a date chiffon filling)

1955
Mrs. Henry Jorgenson, Portland, Ore., Ring-a-Lings (a no-knead sweet roll with a nut filling and an orange glaze)

1956
Mrs. Hildreth H. Hatheway, Santa Barbara, Calif., California Casserole (a veal casserole topped with crumb-covered dumplings)

1957
Mrs. Gerda Roderer, Hayward, Calif., Accordion Treats (an Alsatian-type cookie baked in aluminum foil)

1958
Mrs. Donald DeVault, Delaware, Ohio, Spicy Apple Twists (an apple rollup)

1959
Mrs. Eunice Surles, Lake Charles, La., Mardi Gras Party Cake (a

Southern-style buttermilk cake with melted butterscotch morsels and a sea-foam icing)

1960
Mrs. Leona P. Schnuelle, Beatrice, Neb., Dilly Casserole Bread (a dinner bread made with cottage cheese and dill)

1961
Mrs. Vernon Resse, Minneapolis, Minn., Candy Bar Cookies (a shortbread wafer with a caramel filling and a chocolate topping)

1962
Mrs. Erwin J. Smogor, South Bend, Ind., Apple Pie '63 ("All-American pie" with apples, caramel, and cheese)

1963
Mrs. Roman Walitko, Detroit, Mich., Hungry Boys' Casserole (main dish with ground beef, chickpeas, and pinwheel biscuits)

1964
Janis (Boykin) Risley, Sarasota, Fla., Peacheesy Pie (peach-flavored-crust pie with peaches and cheesecake filling)

1965
Mrs. John Petrelli, Ely, Nev., Golden Gate Snack Bread (yeast bread flavored with cheese spread and onion soup mix)

1966
Mrs. Carlos Bullock, Spring City, Tenn., Muffin Mix Buffet Bread (cream of vegetable soup and corn muffin mix in a yeast bread)

1967
Mrs. Phyllis Lidert, Ft. Lauderdale, Fla., Buttercream Pound Cake (lemon-flavored cake with poppy-seed filling)

1968
Mrs. Edna Holmgren, Hopkins, Minn., Magic Marshmallow Crescent Puffs (hollow-centered sweet roll made with crescent dough and marshmallows)

1969
Mrs. Nan Robb, Huachuca City, Ariz., Onion Lover's Twist (a yeast onion bread)

1970
  Mrs. Pearl Hall, Snohomish, Wash.,
  Pecan Surprise Bars (caramel pecan
  pie in bar form)
1971
  Mrs. Gerald Collins, (refrigerated
  winner), Elk River, Minn., Quick 'n'
  Chewy Crescent Bars (crescent
  dough, frosting mix, condensed
  milk, butter)
  Mrs. Carl DeDominicis, (grocery
  winner), Verona, Pa., Streusel Spice
  Cake (a pound cake made from
  yellow cake mix with a spiced
  streusel filling and topping
1972
  Mrs. Jerome Flieller, Jr.,
  (refrigerated winner), Floresville,
  Tex., Quick Crescent Pecan Pie Bars
  (bars that taste like pecan pie)
  Mrs. Ronald L. Brooks, (grocery
  winner), Salisbury, Md., Banana
  Crunch Cake (a banana and sour
  cream flavored yellow cake with a
  crunchy coconut topping)
1973
  Mrs. James S. Castle, (refrigerated
  winner), River Forest, Ill., Savory
  Crescent Chicken Squares (a
  seasoned chicken filling in a baked
  crescent sandwich)
  Mrs. Emil Jerzak, (grocery winner),
  Porter, Minn., Chocolate Cherry
  Bars (a dessert square made with
  chocolate cake and cherry pie filling)
1974
  Mrs. Barbara Gibson, (refrigerated
  winner), Ft. Wayne, Ind., Easy
  Crescent Danish Rolls (large rolls
  filled with cream cheese and
  preserves)
  Mrs. Luella Maki, (grocery winner),
  Ely, Minn., Sour Cream Apple
  Squares (apples and cinnamon flavor
  a cake-like bar)
1975
  Mrs. Edward Smith, Harahan, La.,
  Whole Wheat Raisin Loaf
1976
  Mrs. Bert Groves, San Antonio, Tex.,
  Caramel Swirl Ring

THE MADEMOISELLE AWARD—
Mademoiselle magazine
  Just about the time Gloria Steinem
was discovering the mysteries of bras-
sieres, this between-puberty-and-moth-
erhood fashion magazine began giving
citations to women for achievements in
their respective fields. Back in the old
days, however, it was known at the Ma-
demoiselle Merit Award.
  Established 1944.
1943
  Betty Smith, writer
  Agnes de Mille, dancer
  Claire McCardell, designer
  Valentina Orlikova, Russian war
  relief ship assistant
  Vera Anderson, war worker
  Lena Horne, singer
  Jennie Tourel, singer
  Kathleen Harriman
  Nana Rae, WAC
  Pistol Packin Mama
1944
  Betsy Barton
  Eleanor Steber, singer
  Mary Fretch, war worker
  Jean Stafford, writer
  Ruth Clifton, young authority on
  juvenile delinquency
  Kathleen Dial, war heroine, army
  nurse, DFC
  Hilda Simms, actress
  Lauren Bacall, movie actress
  Nicola, French FFI heroine
  Lady, war dog
1945
  Dr. Leona Woods Marshall, atomic
  physicist
  Capt. Arlene Schiedenhelm, WAC
  commanding officer
  Barbara Bel Geddes, actress
  Emily Wilkens, designer
  Patricia Van Delden, organizer of
  Dutch resistance
  Gwendolyn Brooks, writer
  Ruth M. Leach, vice president of
  IBM
  Susie Reed, folksinger
  Blanche Thebom, singer
  U.S.S. Missouri
1946
  Dr. Chien-Shiung Wu, senior
  research scientist in nuclear physics,
  Columbia University
  Alicia Alonso, dancer
  Pauli Murray, lawyer
  Pauline Betz, tennis

Janis Boykin of Melbourne, Fla., was only seventeen when she won the Pillsbury Bake-Off with her "Peacheesy Pie."

Virginia MacWatters, singer
Judy Holliday, actress
Elizabeth Gray Vining, Japanese crown prince's tutor
Dorothy Wheeler, director of nursing service of VA
Dorothy Fosdick, 'statesman', Dumbarton, SF, UN
Ceil Chapman, designer
1947
Barbara Ann Scott, figure skater
Anshid Ajmian, violinist
Toni Owen, designer
Santha Rama Rau, writer
Elisabeth M. Ackermann, new plastic glue, Westinghouse research
Mildred L. Lillie, municipal judge, Los Angeles
Shirley Adelson Siegel, executive director of housing councils, New York City, Los Angeles, Calif.
Anne Waterman, American teacher, Warsaw University
Carson McCullers, writer
Eliane Whitelaw, director of women's activities of Polio foundation

1948
Louise Suggs, golfer
Phoebe M. Bailey, Quaker executive
Hortense Williams, social worker
Florence Kelley, attorney
Jade Snow Wong, craftsman–potter
Barbara Ward, political sicnetist
Dorris Varnum, designer
Dorothy Q. Noyes, shop, New Design
Valerie Bettis, dancer
Grandma Moses, artist
1949
Chee Armstrong, designer
Frances Bible, singer
O. Louise Replogle, county attorney
Felice N. Schwartz, National Scholarship Service and Fund for Negro students
Honore Sharrer, artist
Margot Fonteyn, dancer
Julie Harris, actress
Geraldine Funk, head of textile division of Puerto Rico Industrial Development Company
Jane Noble, Indiana state legislature
Mabel, robot

1950
   Marguerite Higgins, reporter
   Gladys L. Hobby, bacteriologist,
   antibiotics
   Emma Gamboa, Costa Rican
   educator
   Janet Collins, dancer
   Florence Chadwick, swam the
   English Channel
   Patricia Neway, singer
   Dorothy and Fred Friendly, TV
   news
   Anne Fogarty, designer
   Belva Jane Barnes, architect
   Mara, war orphan
1951
   Caro Bayley, aviation
   Helen Imrie, government
   Elsie Frankfurt, business
   Maureen Stapleton, theatre
   Marie Tallchief, dancer
   Jeanne Campbell, designer
   Shelley Winters, movies
   Maureen Connolly, athlete
   Ilse Lisle Novak, mathematics
   Poodle
1952
   Mrs. Alett Radzai, courage
   Beatice Hicks, engineer
   Andrea Mead Lawrence, sports
   Geraldine Page, theatre
   Melissa Hayden, dancer
   Dr. Jane Cooke Wright, medicine
   Helen Cacheris, dietetics
   Basila Neilan, social service
   Lotte Werner, fashion
   Ni Gusti Raka, symbol of East-West
   cultural exchange
1953
   Carmel Carrington Marr,
   government
   Dr. Eugenie Clark, science
   Tenley Albright, sports
   Lorraine Budny, fashion
   Rosalind Wiener, politics
   Ceevah M. Rosenthal, social work
   Ilona Karmel, literature
   Audrey Hepburn, movies and theatre
   Maria Callas, music
   Aphrodite, symbol of woman
   rediscovered
1954
   Carol Haney, theatre
   Eva Marie Saint, movies

Diana Adams, dance
Mattiwilda Dobbs, music
Genevieve de Galard-Terraube,
heroism
Irene Osborne, human relations
Anne Klein, fashion
Marilyn Bell, sports
Sally Liberman, mental health
The Dior Bra, form
1955
   Kim Stanley, theatre
   Jane Prizant Gilman, law
   Leontyne Price, music
   Dorris Zeller, geology
   Machiko Kyo, movies
   Jeanne Carr, fashion
   Francoise Sagan, writing
   Pat McCormick, sports
   Liane Brauch Russell, genetics
   Gloria Lockerman, an American
   idea: the accident of democracy
1956
   Jacqueline Hawkins, teaching
   Shirley Fry, sports
   Barbara Lekberg, sculpture
   Julie Andrews, theatre
   Diana Chang, writing
   Blanche Lemco, city planning
   Doris Day, movies
   Najmeh Najafi, social service
   Mary M. Douglass, fashion
   Louisville, gumption (symbol)
1957
   Dorothy Lundquist, science
   Barbara Romney, poetry
   Althea Gibson, sports
   Gisele MacKenzie, television
   Dr. Charlotte Friend, cancer research
   Jeanne Essig, fashion
   Grace Hartigan, art
   Toshiko Akiyoshi, jazz
   Carol Lawrence, theatre
   Judy Szekeres, courage
1958
   Pat Farrar, educational TV
   Bianca Van Orden, writing
   Rosalind Elias, opera
   Marcia Rogers, city planning
   Jane Addams, cultural exchange
   Betty Carol, fashion
   Anne Bancroft, theatre
   Natalie Carbone Mangini, atomic
   science
   Violette Verdy, ballet

Jessie Angelina Evans,
independence
1959
Ingrid Thulin, actress
Teresa Borganza, soprano
Maya Plisetskaya, prima ballerina
Shirley O'Neill, life saving
(Carniegie Medal for heroism)
Lorraine Hansberry, playwright
Elizabeth Marshall
Thomas,anthropology
Gael Greene, reporter
Penny Pitou, skier
Mona Roset, designer
Elizabeth Roemer, astronomer
1960
Jane Powell Rosenthal, assistant
curator, archaeology
Lee Bontecou, sculptress
Wilma Rudolph, sprinter
Elaine May, improvisational social
and political satire
Elizabeth Seal, actress
Susan Greenburg, photographer
Lynn Seymour, ballerina
Patricia Bath, cancer research
Julie Isles, designer
Helen Jean Rogers, producer
1961
Monica Vitti, cinema
Grace Bumbry, Wagnerian opera
singer
Carole Eisner, designer
Nanette Edmonds Wachter, fashion
director
Jean Alice Szymanski, WAVE
electronics technician
Laura M. Roth, physicist
Hope Murrow, co-director,
neighborhood group
Carla Fracci, prima ballerina
Joan Baez, singer
Chryssa, sculptress and painter
1962
Margaret Smith, tennis
Regina Safaty, mezzo-soprano
Barbara Harris, actress
Sidna Brower, editor
Staphanie Merton Russell,
psychiatric social work
Edna O'Brien, novelist, playwright
Maggy Reese, designer
Ann Eckels Bailie, space
mathematician

Joan Brown, painter
Charlayne Hunter, student
1963
Deanna Littell, designer
Valentina Tereshkova, cosmonaut
Janet Newton, teacher
Nancy Brown, state legislator
Leela Naidu, movie actress
Susan Sontag, novelist
Muriel Grossfeld, gymnast
Barbra Streisand, theatre
Reri Grist, soprano
Anna Maria Rappaport, insurance
actuary
1964
Donna de Varona, swimmer
Emmanuelle Khanh, designer
Elizabeth Montgomery, actress
Renata Alder, critic
Patricia McBride, principal dancer,
ballet
Shirley Knight, actress
Marilyn Horne, soprano
Lois Sherr, landscape architecture
Anne Pyne Cowley, astronomer
Mississippi Project group
achievement
1965
The Metropolitan Opera National
Company
Anne Tyler, novelist
Suzanne Farrell, principal dancer,
ballet
Marian Wright, civil-rights lawyer
Lesley Ann Warren, singer, dancer,
actress
1966
USAID Nurses in Vietnam
Jane Marsh, soprano
Sylvia Wilkinson, novelist
Jane Ellen Brody, science reporter
Betsey Johnson, designer
1967
White House Fellows
Bobbie Gentry, music
Cecelia Holland, literature
Kathleen Linane, finance
France FitzGerald, journalism
Faye Dunaway, fashion influence
1969
Carolyn Adams, dancer
Jane Alexander, actress
Patti Cappalli, designer
Kyung-wha Chung, violinist

Valerie Dickerson, reporter
Jacqueline Du Pre, cellist
Susan Epperson, lawyer
Louise Gluck, poet
Ann Hart, political worker
Catherine Jermany, welfare worker
Jane Kramer, writer
Kathy Kusner, jockey
Sondra Locke, actress
Gail McHenry, political worker
Debbie Meyer, swimmer
Sheila Murphy, social worker
Laura Nyro, singer-composer
Joyce Carol Oates, writer
Beverly Rich, actress
Jane Marla Robbins, actress
Lynda Sinay, founder of Los Angeles
ad agency
Trinette Singleton, dancer
Sara Smith, scientist
Francine Stein, family planning
Wyomia Tyus, athlete
Pamela Weir, designer
1970
Alison Bernstein, Vassar trustee
Cathy Burns, actress
Maria Canino, seat on New York City
Board of Higher Education
Rosalind Cash, actress
Judi Cornelius, indian welfare
Blythe Danner, actress
Bernadette Devlin, member of
British Parliament
Sylvia Drew, NAACP Legal Defense
Fund lawyer
Robin Foote, businesswoman
Marsha Fox, designer
Elsa Garmire, scientist
Marcia Haydee, dancer
Ali MacGraw, actress
Kay Mazzo, dancer
Stephanie Mills, planned
parenthood
Liza Minnelli, actress
Anne Moody, writer
Joan Murray, TV news
correspondent
Poppy Northcutt, engineer
Bernadette Peters, actress
Ellen Proctor, physicist
Gloria Rojas, TV news
correspondent
Urban Corps
Lucy Warner, writer

Ruth White, athlete
1971
Florette Angel, developer of artisans
Mary Breasted, journalist
Peggy Cooper, founder of
Workshops for Careers in the Arts
Marion Edey, founder, chairman,
and national coordinator of League
of Conservation Voters
Eva Jefferson, student spokeswoman
Bonnie Sherk, artist
Alice Tepper, financial analyst
1972
Alicia Bay Laurel, author-illustrator
Glenda Copes, community affair
worker
Marjorie Crow, inspirer, organizer,
editor
Susan Davis, editor-publisher
Pamela Gentry, environmentalist
Nikki Giovanni, poet
Sherri Winter Kaplan, co-founder of
HELP
1973
Cindi Buchanan, author
Suzy Chaffee, skier
Judy Chicago, artist-feminist
Micki Grant, lyricist-songwriter;
writer
Barbara Haskell, art curator
Elizabeth Holtzman, U.S.
Representative
Brenda Itta, Eskimo welfare worker
Bobbie Greene Kilberg, lawyer
National Theatre of the Deaf (special
award)
Lesley Oelsner, lawyer, reporter
Amalie R. Rothschild, photographer
1974
Kathryn Burkhart, author
Lisa Connolly, co-founder of
MOMMA
Sharon Curtin, author
Mary M. Emmons, co-founder of
Funding Services Clearinghouse,
Inc.
Anne Grant, feminist
Karol Hope, co-founder of MOMMA
Kathy Kahn, singer, author
Bette Midler, singer
Carol Ruckdeschel, environmentalist
Mary Beth Shea, co-founder of
Funding Services Clearinghouse,
Inc.

Claudia Weill, filmmaker
Laura X, feminist
Boston Women's Health Book
Collective for *Our Bodies, Ourselves*
(special award)
1975
Rachel Scott, author
Leslie Crocker Snyder, assistant
district attorney, New York
Thea Lammers, co-founder Cell
Block Theatre
Francine Prose, author
Sylvia Law, author
Karen Petersen, filmmaker
J. J. Wilson, filmmaker
Jill Godmilow, filmmaker
Judy Collins, singer and director
Donna Karan, fashion designer
Colleen Myers, divinity student
Carol Vittert, founded "Aid to
Victims of Crime"
1976
Ruth Welting, opera singer
Twyla Tharp, choreographer
Susan Brownmiller, author
Louise McAllister Merritt, director
of Historic Albany Foundation
Diana Nyad, swimmer
Gayl Jones, author
Pamela Zekman, investigative
reporter
The women who formed and
invested in the First Women's Bank
(special award)

RICHARD BEATTY MELLON AWARD—Air Pollution Control Association

This is a pat on the back for helping to clean up the foul, foul air through administrative, legislative, or judicial means. Although Mr. Mellon died in 1933 when smog was hardly a particle in the public's eye, he lead in beginning and sustaining the first modern investigation for ways of controlling muck in the atmosphere.
Established 1954.

1956   Edward R. Weidlein, Sr.
1957   Raymond R. Tucker
1958   no award
1959   John F. Barkley
1960   Robert A. Kehoe

1961   no award
1962   Richard K. Mellon
1963   R. L. Ireland
1964   no award
1965   Edmund S. Muskie
1966   Leslie Silverman
1967   Arnold Marsh
1968   no award
1969   Vernon G. Mackenzie
1970   Arthur C. Stern
1971   Allen D. Brandt
1972   John T. Middleton
1973   no award
1974   W. Brad Drowley
1975   Maurice F. Strong

See Movies, Life Achievement Award, The American Film Institute

NATIONAL TEACHER OF THE YEAR—The Council of State School Officers along with the Encyclopaedia Britannica, and *Ladies Home Journal* magazine

Winners not only get a tie clasp or brooch, a certificate and appointment to the Commission on Presidential Scholars, but they get all this at a White House ceremony. A combat medal for elementary and secondary school teachers.
Established 1952.

1952
Geraldine Jones, first grade, Hope Public School, Santa Barbara, Calif.
1953
Dorothy Hamilton, social studies, Milford High School, Milford, Conn.
1954
Willard Widerberg, seventh grade, DeKalb Jr. High School, DeKalb, Ill.
1955
Margaret Perry Teufel, fourth grade, Monmouth Elementary, Monmouth, Ore.
1956
Richard Nelson, science, Flathead County High School, Kalispell, Mont.
1957
(tie) Eugene G. Bizzell, speech, English, and debate, A. N.

McCallum High School, Austin, Tex.
Mary F. Schartz, third grade, Bristol
Elementary, Kansas City, Mo.
1958
Jean Listebarger Humphrey, second
grade, Edwards Elementary, Ames,
Ia.
1959
Edna Donley, mathematics and
speech, Alva High School, Alva,
Okla.
1960
Hazel B. Davenport, first grade,
Central Elementary, Beckley, W. Va.
1961
Helen Adams, kindergarten,
Cumberland Public School,
Cumberland, Wis.
1962
Marjorie French, mathematics,
Topeka High School, Topeka, Kans.
1963
Elmon Ousley, speech, American
government, and world problems,
Bellevue Sr. High School, Bellevue,
Wash.
1964
Lawana Trout, English, Charles
Page High School, Sand Springs,
Okla.
1965
Richard E. Klinck, sixth grade, Reed
Street Elementary, Wheat Ridge,
Colo.
1966
Mona Dayton, first grade, Walter
Douglas Elementary, Tucson, Ariz.
1967
Roger Tenney, music, Owatonna Jr.-
Sr. High, Owatonna, Minn.
1968
David E. Graf, vocational education
and industrial arts, Sandwich
Community High School, Sandwich,
Ill.
1969
Barbara Goleman, language arts,
Miami Jackson High School, Miami,
Fla.
1970
Johnnie T. Dennis, physics, math
analysis, Walla Walla High School,
Walla Walla, Wash.

1971
Martha M. Stringfellow, first grade,
Lewisville Elementary, Chester
County, S.C.
1972
James M. Rogers, American history
and Black studies, Durham High
School, Durham, N.C.
1973
John A. Ensworth, sixth grade,
Kenwood School, Bend, Ore.
1974
Vivian Tom, social studies, Lincoln
High School, Yonkers, N.Y.
1975
Robert G. Heyer, science, Johanna
Jr. High School, St. Paul, Minn.
1976
Ruby Murchison, social studies,
Washington Drive Jr. High School,
Fayetteville, N.C.
1977
Myrra Lee, social living, Helix High
School, La Mesa, Calif.

See Poetry, The Fellowship of the
Academy of American Poets, The
Academy of American Poets

**THE PRESIDENT'S AWARD FOR
DISTINGUISHED FEDERAL CI-
VILIAN SERVICE**—United States
Civil Service Commission
The highest honor for a federal ca-
reer employee.
Established 1957.
1958
Loy W. Henderson, deputy under
secretary of state for administration
Sterling B. Hendricks, chief chemist,
Agriculture's Pioneering Research
Laboratory for Mineral Nutrition of
Plants
John Edgar Hoover, director,
Federal Bureau of Investigation
Roger W. Jones, assistant director for
legislative reference, Bureau of the
Budget
William B. McLean, technical
director, U.S. Naval Ordnance Test
Station (China Lake,Calif.)
1959
James V. Bennett, director, Bureau of

Prisons, Department of Justice
Robert D. Murphy, deputy under
secretary of state for political affairs
Doyle L. Northrup, technical
director, Special Weapons Squadron,
Department of the Air Force
Hazel K. Stiebeling, director,
Institute of Home Economics,
Department of Agriculture
Wernher Von Braun, director,
Development Operations Division,
Army Ballistic Missile Agency

1960

Andrew Barr, chief accountant,
Securities and Exchange
Commission
Hugh L. Dryden, deputy
administrator, National Aeronautics
and Space Administration
William J. Hopkins, executive clerk,
White House Office
Dr. Winfred Overholser,
superintendent, Saint Elizabeth's
Hospital
Robert M. Page, director of research,
Naval Research Laboratory

1961

Bert B. Barnes, assistant postmaster
general, Bureau of Operations, Post
Office Department
Wilbur S. Hinman, Jr., technical
director, Diamond Ordnance Fuze
Laboratories, Department of the
Army
Frederick J. Lawton, commissioner,
U.S. Civil Service Commission
Richard E. McArdle, chief, Forest
Service, Department of Agriculture
William McCauley, director, Bureau
of Employee's Compensation,
Department of Labor

1962

J. Stanley Baughman, president,
Federal National Mortgage
Association, Housing and Home
Finance Agency
Robert R. Gilruth, director, Manned
Spacecraft Center, National
Aeronautics and Space
Administration (Houston, Tex.)
Dr. Donald E. Gregg, chief,
Department of Cardiorespiratory
Diseases, Walter Reed Army
Institute of Research

Waldo K. Lyon, head, Submarine
and Arctic Research Branch, U.S.
Navy Electronics Laboratory (San
Diego, Calif.)
Llewellyn E. Thompson, Jr.,
ambassador to the Union of Soviet
Socialist Republics, Department of
State

1963

Winthrop G. Brown, career minister,
Department of State
Alain C. Enthoven, deputy
comptroller for Systems Analysis,
Office of the Secretary of Defense
Sherman E. Johnson, deputy
administrator, Foreign Economics,
Economic Research Service,.
Department of Agriculture
David D. Thomas, director, Air
Traffic Service, Federal Aviation
Agency
Fred L. Whipple, director,
Smithsonian Institution
Astrophysical Observatory

1964

John Doar, first assistant to the
assistant attorney general, Civil
Rights Division, Department of
Justice
Herbert Friedman, superintendent,
Atmosphere and Astrophysics
Division, U.S. Naval Research
Laboratory, Department of the Navy
Lyman B. Kirkpatrick, Jr., executive
director-comptroller, Central
Intelligence Agency
Bromley K. Smith, executive
secretary, National Security Council

1965

Howard C. Grieves, assistant
director of the Bureau of the Census,
Department of Commerce
Homer E. Newell, associate
administrator for space science and
applications, National Aeronautics
and Space Administration
Frank B. Rowlett, special assistant to
the director, National Security
Agency, Department of Defense
Clyde A. Tolson, associate director
of the Federal Bureau of
Investigation, Department of Justice
Philip H. Trezise, deputy assistant
secretary for economic affairs,
Department of State

1966
Elson B. Helwig, pathologist, The Armed Forces Institute of Pathology
Robert E. Hollingsworth
H. Rex Lee, administrator, American Samoa
Thomas C. Mann
James A. Shannon, scientific administrator
1967
Myrl E. Alexander, director, Federal Bureau of Prisons, Department of Justice
Arthur E. Hess, deputy commissioner, Social Security Administration, Department of Health, Education, and Welfare
Sherman Kent, director of National Estimates and chairman of the board of National Estimates, Central Intelligence Agency
C. Payne Lucas, deputy director, Africa region, Peace Corps
William J. Porter, ambassador to the Republic of South Korea, Department of State
Carl F. Romney, seismologist, Department of the Air Force
1968
James J. Rowley
1971
Samuel M. Cohn, assistant director for budget review, Office of Management and Budget
U. Alexis Johnson, career ambassador, under secretary for political affairs, Department of State
Edward F. Knipling, director, Entomology Research Division, Agricultural Research Service, Department of Agriculture
Fred Leonard, scientific director, Army Medical Biomechanical Research Laboratory, Walter Reed Army Medical Center, Department of the Army
George H. Willis, deputy to the assistant secretary for international affairs, Department of the Treasury
1972   no award
1973   no award
1974   no award

1975   no award
1976
Dr. Ernest Ambler, acting director, National Bureau of Standards, Department of Commerce
Lawrence S. Eagleburger, deputy under secretary of state for management and executive assistant to the secretary, Department of State
Dr. Alfred J. Eggers, Jr., assistant director for research applications, National Science Foundation
E. Henry Knoche, deputy director of central intelligence, Central Intelligence Agency
Dale R. McOmber, assistant director for budget review, Office of Management and Budget
Barber Ringer, register of copyrights, Library of Congress

See Science, David Livingstone Centenary Medal, American Geographical Society

SPINGARN MEDAL—National Association for the Advancement of Colored People
A gold medal for "the highest or noblest achievement by an American Negro during the preceding year or years," this award is also meant to be "a stimulus to the ambition of colored youth." The Spingarns of the medal's name are a former chairman of the board of the NAACP, J. E., his wife, Amy, and his brother, Arthur B.
Established 1914.
1915
Professor Ernest E. Just, Howard University
1916
Major Charles Young, United States Army
1917
Harry T. Burleigh, composer, pianist, singer
1918
William Stanley Braithwaite, poet, literary critic, and editor
1919
Archibald H. Grimke, U.S. consul in

Santo Domingo; president, American
Negro Academy; author; and
president of the District of Columbia
branch of the NAACP.

1920
William E. Burghardt DuBois,
author, editor of *The Crisis*

1921
Charles S. Gilpin, actor

1922
Mary B. Talbert, former president of
the National Association of Colored
Women

1923
George Washington Carver,
Tuskegee Institute, Ala.

1924
Roland Hayes, singer

1925
James Weldon Johnson, former U. S.
consul in Venezuela and Nicaragua;
former editor, secretary, National
Association for the Advancement of
Colored People.

1926
Carter G. Woodson, historian

1927
Anthony Overton, businessman

1928
Charles W. Chesnutt, author

1929
Mordecai Wyatt Johnson, president
of Howard University

1930
Henry A. Hunt, principal of Fort
Valley High and Industrial School,
Fort Valley, Ga.

1931
Richard Berry Harrison, actor

1932
Robert Russa Moton, Tuskegee
Institute, Ala.

1933
Max Yergan, missionary

1934
William Taylor Burwell Williams,
Tuskegee Institute

1935
Mrs. Mary McLeod Bethune,
founder and president of Bethune-
Cookman College, Daytona Beach,
Fla.

1936
John Hope, Atlanta University

1937
Walter White, executive secretary of
the NAACP.

1938 no award

1939
Marian Anderson, contralto

1940
Louis T. Wright, surgeon

1941
Richard Wright, author

1942
A. Philip Randolph, labor leader

1943
William H. Hastie, jurist and
educator

1944
Charles R. Drew, scientist

1945
Paul Robeson, singer and actor

1946
Thurgood Marshall, lawyer

1947
Dr. Percy L. Julian, research chemist

1948
Channing H. Tobias, "in recognition
of his consistent role as a defender of
fundamental American liberties . . ."

1949
Ralph J. Bunche, international civil
servant

1950
Charles Hamilton Houston,
chairman, NAACP Legal Committee

1951
Mabel Keaton Staupers, National
Association of Colored Graduate
Nurses

1952
Harry T. Moore, NAACP leader in
the state of Florida.

1953
Paul R. Williams, architect

1954
Theodore K. Lawless, physician,
educator, and philanthropist

1955
Carl Murphy, editor and publisher

1956
Jack Roosevelt Robinson, athlete

1957
Martin Luther King, Jr., clergyman

1958
Mrs. Daisy Bates and the Little Rock
Nine

1959
Edward Kennedy (Duke) Ellington, composer and orchestra leader
1960
Langston Hughes, poet, author, and playwright
1961
Kenneth B. Clark, professor, College of the City of New York City
1962
Robert C. Weaver, administrator, Housing and Home Finance Agency
1963
Medgar Wiley Evers, NAACP Field Secretary for the State of Mississippi
1964
Roy Wilkins, executive director, NAACP
1965
Leontyne Price, Metropolitan Opera star
1966
John H. Johnson, founder and president of the Johnson Publishing Company of Chicago, Ill.
1967
Edward W. Brooke III, U. S. senator
1968
Sammy Davis, Jr., singer and actor
1969
Clarence M. Mitchell, Jr., director, Washington Bureau, NAACP, and civil rights lobbyist
1970
Jacob Lawrence, artist and teacher
1971
Leon Howard Sullivan, clergyman and activist
1972
Gordon Alexander Buchanan Parks, photographer, writer, filmmaker, and composer
1973
Wilson C. Riles, educator
1974
Damon J. Keith, jurist
1975
Henry Aaron, athlete

MARJORIE PEABODY WAITE AWARD—The National Institute of Arts and Letters

This is given annually to an older art-ist, composer, or writer for "continuing achievement and integrity in his art." Established 1956.

1956   Fred Nagler
1957   Theodore Ward Chanler
1958   Dorothy Parker
1959   Leon Hartl
1960   Louise Talma
1961   Edward McSorley
1962   Abraham Walkowitz
1963   Richard Donovan
1964   Dawn Powell
1965   Paul Burlin
1966   Harry Partch
1967   Stringfellow Barr
1968   Abraham Harriton
1969   Herbert Elwell
1970   Ramon Guthrie
1971   Ben Benn
1972   Vittorio Rieti
1973   A. Hyatt Mayor
1974   Ray Prohaska
1975   Leo Ornstein
1976   Rene Wellek

WOMEN OF THE YEAR—*Ladies Home Journal* magazine

Nothing wrong with a "ladies" award for achievement which so far has honored only two actresses—Katharine Hepburn and Helen Hayes—and which named Congressperson Barbara Jordan *before* she made her delegate-rousing speech at the Democratic national nominating convention in 1976.

Established 1973.

1973
Shirley Chisholm, public affairs
LaDonna Harris, human rights
Ellen Strous, voluntary action
Mary Lasker, quality of life
Katharine Graham, economy and business
Nikki Giovanni, youth leadership
Helen Hayes, arts and humanities
Dr. Virginia Apgas, science and medicine
1974
Martha W. Griffiths, public affairs
Dorothy L. Height, human rights
Barbara McDonald, community service

Katharine Hepburn made Ladies' Home Journal's Women of the Year list in 1974. (Memory Shop)

Patricia Roberts Harris, business and professions
Katharine Hepburn, creative arts
Barbara Walters, communications
Billie Jean King, sports
Dixie Lee Ray, science and research

1975
Lady Bird Johnson, quality of life
Lillian Hellman, creative arts
Joan Gauz Cooney, education
LaRue C. Diaforli, humanitarian and community service
Sylvia Porter, business and economics
Barbara Jordan, political life
Helen Thomas, communications

Jeanne M. Holm, government and diplomacy
1976
Betty Ford, inspirational leadership
Margaret Mead, science and research
Bettye Caldwell, humanitarian and community service
Beverly Sills, performing arts
Betty Furness, business and economics
Ella T. Grasso, political life
Annie Dodge Wauneka, educational leadership
Shirley Hufstedler, government and diplomacy
Maya Angelou, communications
Micki King, sports

ARCHITECTURE AND PLANNING

See Achievement, Gold Medal Awards, The American Academy of Arts and Letters

AIA MEDAL FOR RESEARCH—The American Institute of Architects Established 1972.

94   ARCHITECTURE AND PLANNING

1972	Professor Christopher Alexander
1973	Dr. Harold B. Gores, Hon. AIA
1974	Professor Ralph Knowles
1975	Environmental Research & Development Foundation

ALLIED PROFESSIONS MEDAL—
The American Institute of Architects

For an individual or a company that has had "an inspiring influence" on the field of architecture.
Established 1958.

1958	Fred N. Severud
1959	Robert Moses
1960	Williams Francis Gibbs
1961	no award
1962	O. H. Ammann & Charles Whitney
1963	R. Buckminster Fuller
1964	Lawrence Halprin
1965	Leonardo Zeevaert
1966	Alexander Girard
1967	Richard Kelly
1968	Le Messurier Associates, Inc.
1969	John Skilling
1970	Robert L. Van Nice
1971	Daniel U. Kiley
1972	Ian L. McHarg
1973	Hideo Sasaki
1974	Kevin Lynch
1975	Carl M. Sapers

ARCHITECTURAL FIRM AWARD—
The American Institute of Architects

For a company where the collaborative efforts have "been the principal force in consistently producing distinguished architecture."
Established 1962.

1962	Skidmore Owings & Merrill
1963	no award
1964	The Architects Collaborative
1965	Wurster, Bernardi & Emmons
1966	no award
1967	Hugh Stubbins & Associates
1968	I. M. Pei & Partners
1969	Jones & Emmons Architects
1970	Ernest J. Kump Associates
1971	Albert Kahn Associates, Inc.
1972	Caudill Rowlett Scott

1973	Shepley Bulfinch Richardson & Abbott
1974	Kevin Roche, John Dinkeloo
1975	Davis, Brody & Associates
1976	Mitchell/Giurgola, Architects

ARCHITECTURAL PHOTOGRAPHY MEDAL—The American Institute of Architects

Given to an individual for outstanding architectural photography.
No subjects smiling "cheese," here.
Established 1960.

1960	Roger Sturtevant
1961	Ezra Stoller
1962	Ernst Haas
1963	G. E. Kidder Smith, FAIA
1964	Balthazar Korab
1965	Robert Damora, AIA
1966	Morley Baer
1967	William C. Hedrich
1968	Ernest Braun
1969	Julius Shulman
1970	George Cserna
1971	Alexandre Georges
1972	no award
1973	Robert C. Lautman
1974	David L. Hirsch
1975	Yukio Futagawa

ARCHITECTURE CRITICS' MEDAL AND CITATION—The American Institute of Architects

The medal goes for career-long achievement; the citation for a single work.
Established 1968.

Architecture Critics' Medal

1968	Lewis Mumford
1969	Ada Louise Huxtable
1970	Henry-Russell Hitchcock
1971	Sibyl Moholy-Nagy
1972	Wolf Von Eckardt, Hon. AIA
1973	Robin Royd
1974	Walter McQuade, FAIA
1975	Peter Blake, FAIA

Architecture Critics' Citation

1968	George McCue, Hon. AIA
1969	no award
1970	"Cosmopolis," documentary

by American Broadcasting Co.
1971 "Perspecta" Yale Architectural Journal
1972 Peter Collins
1973 Alan Dunn
1974 Regional Planning Association
1975 Jane Jacobs

THE HENRY BACON MEDAL FOR MEMORIAL ARCHITECTURE—
The American Institute of Architects
No auditoriums or housing projects need apply. This award is given for structures built solely to "portray, promote or symbolize an idea of high spiritual concern."
Established 1966.
1966 Gateway Arch, St. Louis, Mo.
1967 no award
1968 no award
1969 Fosse Ardeatine Caves, Rome, Italy
1970 no award
1971 no award
1972 no award
1973 no award
1974 no award
1975 Le Memorial des Martyrs de la Deportation, Paris, France

ARNOLD W. BRUNNER MEMORIAL PRIZE IN ARCHITECTURE—
The National Institute of Arts and Letters
Given to an architect who has contributed to architecture as an art.
Established 1955.
1955 Gordon Bunshaft
Minoru Yamaski, Honorable Mention
1956 John Yeon
1957 John Carl Warnecke
1958 Paul Rudolph
1959 Edward Larrabee Barnes
1960 Louis I. Kahn
1961 Ieoh Ming Pei
1962 Ulrich Franzen
1963 Edward Charles Bassett
1964 Harry Weese
1965 Kevin Roche

1966 Romaldo Giurgola
1968 John M. Johansen
1969 Noel Michael McKinnell
1970 Charles Gwathmey
Richard Henderson
1971 John Andrews
1972 Richard Meier
1973 Robert Venturi
1974 Hugh Hardy
Norman Pfeiffer
Malcolm Holzman
1975 Lewis Davis
Samuel Brody
1976

CITATION OF AN ORGANIZATION
—The American Institute of Architects
This is bestowed upon an individual or organization for an outstanding single project.
Established 1947.
1947 Tennessee Valley Authority
1948 no award
1949 no award
1950 no award
1951 Steuben Glass Inc.
1952 no award
1953 no award
1954 no award
1955 Reinhold Publishing Corp.
Kohler Foundation, Inc.
1956 Society of Architectural Historians
1957 Office of Foreign Buildings, Department of State
1958 United States Steel Corp.
1959 General Services Administration
1960 Providence City Plan Commission
General Motors Corp.
International Business Machines
1961 The Philadelphia City Planning Commission
1962 The Museum of Modern Art
1963 American Craftsmen's Council
1964 Educational Facilities Laboratories
1965 Architectural League of New York
1966 The Museum of Modern Art, Phillips Gallery

1967	Boston Architectural Center
1968	The Graham Foundation
1969	State University Construction Fund
1970	National Park Service
1971	San Francisco Bay Commission
1972	New York State Dormitory Authority
1973	San Francisco Planning Commission
1974	New York State Urban Development Corp.
1975	Cummins Engine Foundation

COLLABORATIVE ACHIEVEMENT IN ARCHITECTURE AWARD—The American Institute of Architects

To win, the project must be exceptional in, at the minimum, three of the following aspects: engineering, murals, sculpture, landscape architecture, and craftsmanship.

Established 1964.

1964	The Seagram Building, its plaza, and the Four Seasons Restaurant, New York City
1965	no award
1966	Ghirardelli Square, San Francisco, Calif.
1967	no award
1968	no award
1969	no award
1970	no award
1971	no award
1972	Rochester Institute of Technology, Rochester, N.Y.
1973	Bay Area Rapid Transit (BART), San Francisco, Calif.
1974	no award
1975	no award

CRAFTSMANSHIP MEDAL—The American Institute of Architects

Furniture, weaving, stained glass, ceramics—an award for the talented craftsmen who contribute to architecture.

Established 1921.

1921	Henry Mercer, ceramics
1922	Samuel Yellin, iron works
1923	Frederic W. Goudy, typography
1924	no award
1925	Charles Jay Connick, stained glass
1926	V. F. Von Lossberg, metal work
1927	Frank J. Holmes, ceramics
1928	William D. Gates, ceramics
1929	Cheney Brothers, textiles
1930	John Kirchmayer, wood carving
1931	Leon V. Solon, terra cotta, faience
1932	no award
1933	no award
1934	Walter W. Kantack, metal and glass
1935	no award
1936	John J. Earley, masonry, concrete
1937	no award
1938	J. H. Dulles Allen, ceramics
1939	no award
1940	no award
1941	no award
1942	no award
1943	no award
1944	no award
1945	no award
1946	no award
1947	Dorothy Wright Leibes, textiles; Wilbur H. Burnham, stained and leaded glass
1948	no award
1949	no award
1950	J. G. Reynolds, Jr., stained glass
1951	no award
1952	George Nakashima, furniture
1953	Emil Frei, stained glass
1954	Maria M. Martinez, pottery

1955
   John H. Benson, calligraphy
1956
   Harry Bertoia, metal design
1957
   Charles Eames, furniture
1958
   Francois Lorin, stained glass
1959   no award
1960
   William L. De Matteo, silversmith
1961
   Anni Albers, art of weaving
1962
   Theodore Conrad, model making
1963
   Paolo Soleri, ceramics
1964
   Jan de Swart, stained glass
1965   no award
1966
   Harold Balazs, wood sculpture
1967
   Sister Mary Remy Revor, SSND,
   fabric design
1968
   Jack Lenor Larsen, fabric design
   Henry Easterwood, fabric design
1969   no award
1970
   Trude Guermonprez, textiles
1971
   Wharton Esherick, wood furniture
1972   no award
1973   no award
1974
   Helena Harnmarck, tapestries
   Sheila Hicks, tapestries

DISTINGUISHED SERVICE AWARD—American Institute of Planners

To win this honor, one must have made nationwide planning impact and contributions for 15 years or more in at least three of the following areas: planning research or education; planning theory or philosophy; planning techniques and practices; implementation or administration of plans or planning programs; advancement of planning as a profession, especially through contributions to the Institute.

Established 1953.
1953   Frederick Bigger
       Russell Van Nest Black
       Frederick Olmstead
1954   Tracy B. Augur
1955   Frederick J. Adams
       Harland Bartholomew
       Flavel Shurtleff
1956   Charles B. Bennett
1957   Walter H. Blucher
       Harold M. Lewis
       Ladislas Segoe
       Lawrence V. Sheridan
1958   Harold S. Buttenheim
       Clarence S. Stein
1959   Robert B. Mitchell
       Gordon Whitnall
1960   S. R. DeBoer
1961   Charles W. Eliot
       Lawrence M. Orton
1962   Henry S. Churchill
       Hugh R. Pomeroy
1963   John T. Howard
1964   Francis A. Pitkin
       Warren J. Vinton
1965   Dennis O'Harrow
       Max Wehrly
1966   Howard Menhinick
1967   no award
1968   F. Stuart Chapin, Jr.
1969   Hans Blumenfeld
1970   Charles Abrams
1971   Edmund Bacon
1972   C. McKim Norton
       Coleman Woodbury

FINE ARTS MEDAL—The American Institute of Architects

An honor for those successfully melding the fine arts—painting, sculpture, photography, literature—with architecture.

Established 1921.
1921
   Paul Manship, sculpture
1922   no award
1923
   Arthur F. Mathews, decorative painting
1924   no award
1925
   John Singer Sargent, mural painting

1926
Leopold Stokowski, music
1927
Lee Lawrie, sculpture
1928
H. Siddons Mowbray, mural
painting
1929
Diego Rivera, painting
1930
Adolph A. Weinman, sculpture
1931
Frederick Olmstead, landscape
architecture
1932   no award
1933   no award
1934
James H. Breasted, literature
1935   no award
1935   no award
1936
Robert E. Jones, theatre design
1937   no award
1938
Carl Milles, sculpture
1939   no award
1940   no award
1941   no award
1942   no award
1943   no award
1944   no award
1945
John Taylor Arms, etching
1946   no award
1947
Samuel Chamberlain, etching
1948
John Marin, painting
1949
Louis C. Rosenberg, etching
1950
Edward Steichen, photography
1951
Thomas Church, landscape
architecture
1952
Marshall Fredericks, sculpture
1953
Donal Hord, sculpture
1954
Julian Hoke Harris, sculpture
1955
Ivan Mestrovic, sculpture
1956
Hildreth Meiere, painting

1957
Mark Tobey, painting
1958
Viktor Schreckengost, sculpture
1959
Kenneth Hedrich, photography
1960
Thomas Hart Benton, painter and
muralist
1961
Alexander Calder, sculpture
1962
Stuart Davis, painting
1963
Isamu Noguchi, sculpture
1964
Henry Moore, sculpture
1965
R. Burle Marx, landscape
architecture
1966
Ben Shahn, artist
1967
Costantino Nivola, sculpture
1968
Gyorgy Kepes, artist
1969
Jacques Lipchitz, sculpture
1970
Richard Lippold, sculpture
1971
Anthony Smith, sculpture
1972
George Rickey, sculpture
1973
Harry Bertoia, sculpture
1974
Ruth Asawa Lanier, sculpture
1975
Josef Albers, artist

GOLD MEDAL—The American Institute of Architects
The organization's biggie. For an individual, it may be awarded posthumously.
Established 1907.
1907
Sir Aston Webb, R. A., London,
England
1908   no award
1909
Charles Follen McKim, New York
City

1910   no award
1911
George B. Post, New York City
1912   no award
1913   no award
1914
Jean Louis Pascal, Paris, France
1915   no award
1916   no award
1917   no award
1918   no award
1919   no award
1920   no award
1921   no award
1922
Victor Laloux, Paris, France
1923
Henry Bacon, New York City
1924   no award
1925
Sir Edwin Landseer Lutyens,
London, England
Bertram Grosvenor Goodhue, New
York City
1926   no award
1927
Howard Van Doren Shaw, Chicago,
Ill.
1928   no award
1929
Milton Bennett Medary,
Philadelphia, Pa.
1930   no award
1931   no award
1932   no award
1933   no award
1934
Ragnar Ostberg, Stockholm, Sweden
(1933)
1935   no award
1936   no award
1937   no award
1938
Paul Philippe Cret, Philadelphia, Pa.
1939   no award
1940   no award
1941   no award
1942   no award
1943   no award
1944   no award
1945   no award
1946
Louis Henry Sullivan, Chicago, Ill.

1947
Eliel Saarinen, Bloomfield Hills
1948
Charles Donagh Maginnis, Boston,
Mass.
1949
Frank Lloyd Wright, Spring Green,
Wis.
1950
Sir Patrick Abercrombie, London,
England
1951
Bernard Ralph Maybeck, San
Francisco, Calif.
1952
Auguste Perret, Paris, France
1953
William Adams Delano, New York
City
1954   no award
1955
Willem Marinus Dudok, Hilversum,
Holland
1956
Clarence S. Stein, New York City
1957
Ralph Walker (Centennial Medal
of Honor), New York City
Luis Skidmore, New York City
1958
John Wellborn Root, Chicago, Ill.
1959
Walter Gropius, Cambridge, Mass.
1960
Ludwig Mies van der Rohe, Chicago,
Ill.
1961
Le Corbusier (Charles Edouard
Jeanneret-Gris), Paris, France
1962
Eero Saarinen, Bloomfield Hills
1963
Alvar Aalto, Helsinki, Finland
1964
Pier Luigi Nervi, Rome, Italy
1965   no award
1966
Kenzo Tange, Tokyo, Japan
1967
Wallace K. Harrison, New York City
1968
Marcel Breuer, New York City
1969
William W. Wurster, San Francisco,
Calif.

1970
Richard Buckminster Fuller,
Carbondale, Ill.
1971
Louis I. Kahn, Philadelphia, Pa.
1972
Pietro Belluschi, Boston, Mass.
1973   no award
1974   no award
1975   no award

HONOR AWARDS—American Institute of Planners
1962   Fremont, Calif.
1963   Cincinnati, Ohio
1964   Rye, N.Y. (population under 50,000)
Pomona, Calif. (population 50,000–500,000)
Detroit, Mich. (population more than 500,000)
1965   Rockville, Md. (under 50,000)
New Haven, Conn. (50,000–500,000)
1966   Camden, N.J. (50,000–500,000)
Capital Region of Conn. (more than 500,000)
1968   City & County of Denver, Colo. (more than 500,000)

INDUSTRIAL ARTS MEDAL—The American Institute of Architects
There is a silent partner working with the recipients of this medal—a machine—for the honor is given in recognition of "design for or execution by a machine, in such fields as furniture, textiles, typography, building products and equipment, and consumers' products."
Established 1958.
1958   Merle Armitage
1959   no award
1960   no award
1961   Florence Schust Knoll
1962   Sundbert-Ferar Inc.
1963   no award
1964   George Nelson
1965   Eilot Noyes
1966   Gideon Kramer
1967   Chermayeff & Geismar
1968   Paul Grotz
1969   Carl Koch

1970   Barbara Stauffacher Solomon
1971   Edith Heath
1972   Charles Eames
1973   Lella and Massimo Vignelli
1974   Ing. C. Olivetti & C. S. p. A.
1975   Gemini G. E. L.

MERIT AWARDS—The American Institute of Planners
1968   "Planning for Balanced Growth in Connecticut"
1969   Bay Conservation and Development Commission Plan
Goals for Dallas Program
"Principles and Practice of Urban Planning"
1971   Education Program, Philadelphia Regional Chapter
Goals for Texas Program, State of Texas

MERITORIOUS PROGRAM AWARDS—The American Institute of Planners
1972   Baltimore Metro Center, Md.
Salt River Indian Community Planning Program, Ariz.
Twin Cities Area of Minneapolis-St. Paul and its Metropolitan Council

SPECIAL FIFTIETH ANNIVERSARY AWARDS (1967)—The American Institute of Planners
American Society of Planning Officials   For contribution to the public acceptance and technical effectiveness of planning as a part of the process of government in the United States.
City of Philadelphia   To honor a city, two of its distinguished mayors who brought it through some decisive years of change (Joseph S. Clark and Richardson Dilworth) and a planner inseparably identified with the transformation these years have wrought (Edmund N. Bacon).
National Resources Planning Board   The spiritual forerunner of contemporary planning in the United States.

ART

Regional Plan Association (New York-New Jersey-Connecticut Metropolitan Area) For achievement and contribution in metropolitan planning.

Tennessee Valley Authority "For achievement in carrying through a pioneering philosophy of resource use; in recognition of an uninterrupted line of inspired leadership from its board of Directors; to honor the contributions from its distinguished and innovative professionals."

Frederick Johnstone Adams For achievement and contribution in planning education.

Harland Bartholomew For achievement and contribution in planning practice.

Alfred Bettman For achievement and contribution in planning law.

Kevin Lynch For achievement and contribution in planning and design theory.

Martin Meyerson For achievement and contribution in planning theory and research.

Lewis Mumford For achievement and contribution in planning philosophy.

Ladislassegoe For achievement and contribution in planning practice.

Clarence S. Stein For achievement and contribution in planning design principles

Catherine Bauer Wurster For achievement and contribution in planning criticism.

THE WHITNEY M. YOUNG, JR. CITATION—The American Institute of Architects

For contributing to social conscience in the architectural profession.

Established 1972.

1972   Robert J. Nash, AIA
1973   Architects Workshop of Philadelphia
1974   Stephen Cram
1975   Van B. Bruner, Jr., AIA

See Achievement, Gold Medal Awards, The American Academy of Arts and letters

See Achievement, Marjorie Peabody Waite Award

See Architecture, Arnold W. Brunner Memorial Prize in Architecture, The National Institute of Arts and Letters

See Architecture, Collaborative Achievement In Architecture Award, The American Institute of Architects

See Architecture, Fine Arts Medal, The American Institute of Architects

ARTS AND LETTERS AWARDS—The National Institute of Arts and Letters

To help artists who are not members of the Institute continue their creative work, the award, a prize of $3,000.

Established 1941.

1941   Jon Corbino
       Arthur Lee
1942   Peggy Bacon
       Donal Hord
       Cathal B. O'Toole
1943   Isabel Bishop
       Hugh Ferris
       Gertrude K. Lathrop
       Bruce Moore
1944   Janet De Coux
       Charles Locke
       Berta Margoulies
       Eleanor Pratt
       Charles Rudy
       Esther Williams
1945   Peter Dalton
       Donald De Lue
       Vincent Glinsky
       Edward Laning
       Andree Ruellan
       Raphael Soyer

1946	Richmond Barthe		Antonio Frasoni
	Louis Gugliemi		David K. Rubins
	Robert Gwathmey	1955	George Beattie
	Rosella Hartman		Hazel Janicki
	Jack Levine		Julian Levi
	Harry Rosin		Zygmunt Menkes
	Concetta Scaravaglione		Mitchell Siporin
	Zoltan Sepeshy		Albert Stewart
1947	Peter Blume		Sahl Swarz
	Dorothea Greenbaum	1956	Henry Di Spirito
	Joseph Hirsch		Philip Evergood
	Victoria Hutson Huntley		Morris Graves
	Mitchell Jamieson		Chaim Gross
	Carl Schmitz		Barbara Lekberg
1948	Louis Bosa		Theodoros Stamos
	Robert H. Cook, Jr.	1957	John Heliker
	Stephen Csoka		Jonah Kinigstein
	Philip Guston		Kenzo Okada
	Oronzio Maldarelli		Anne Poor
	John W. Taylor		Hugo Robus
1949	Federico Castellon		Polygnotos Vagis
	Carl Hall	1958	Charles H. Alston
	Henry Kreis		David Aronson
	John McCrady		Al Blaustein
	William Pachner		Herbert Katzman
	Harry Wickey		Seymour Lipton
1950	Jean de Marco		Jack Zajac
	Lamar Dodd	1959	Jose de Rivera
	Sue Fuller		Frank Duncan
	Peter Hopkins		Ruth Gikow
	Bruno Mankowski		John Guerin
	Sol Wilson		Minna Harkavy
1951	Saul Baizerman		Nathaniel Kaz
	Lu Duble		James Kearns
	Joseph Floch	1960	Chen Chi
	Xavier Gonzalez		Marvin Cherney
	Peppino Mangravite		Eugene Ludins
	William Thon		Rhoda Sherbell
1952	Clara Fasano		George Tooker
	H. L. Kammerer		Harold Tovish
	Edward Melcarth		Walter Williams
	Doris Rosenthal	1961	Leonard Baskin
	Walter Stuempfig		Paul Cadmus
	Charles White		Kahlil Gibran
1953	Hyman Bloom		Philip Grausman
	Albino Cavallito		Walter Murch
	Jacob Lawrence		Gregorio Prestopino
	William Palmer		Joseph Solman
	Carl M. Schultheiss	1962	Robert M. Broderson
	Francis Speight		Nicolai Cikovsky
1954	Virginia Cuthbert		Richard Diebenkorn
	Koren Der Harootian		Seymour Drumlevitch
	Edwin Dickinson		Camilo Egas
	Hazard Durfree		Dimitri Hadzi

1963	Bernard Reder
	Harola Altman
	Wolfgang Behl
	Elmer Bischoff
	Jan Doubrava
	James McGarrell
	Raymond Saunders
	Karl Zerbe
1964	Thomas B. Cornell
	Edward J. Hill
	Reuben Kramer
	Michael Mazur
	Bernard Perlin
	Sarai Sherman
	Charles Wells
1965	Sigmund Abeles
	Lee Gatch
	David V. Hayes
	Richard Mayhew
	Elliott Offner
	Joyce Reopel
	Thomas Stearns
1966	Romare Bearden
	Lee Bontecou
	Carroll Cloar
	Ray Johnson
	Ezio Mantinelli
	Karl Schrag
	Richard Claude Ziemann
1967	Byron Burford
	Jared French
	Stephen Greene
	Leo Kenney
	Dennis Leon
	Hugh Townley
	Louis Tytell
1968	Robert A. Birmelin
	Kenneth Callahan
	Leon Goldin
	Joe Lasker
	Vincent D. Smith
	Elbert Weinberg
	Charles Wilson
1969	Lennart Anderson
	William Christopher
	Frank Gallo
	Leonel Gongora
	Red Grooms
	Sidney J. Hurwitz
	Ben Kamihira
	Alice Neel
1970	Leland Bell
	Charles F. Cajori
	Kenneth Campbell

	Giorgio Cavallon
	Ralston Crawford
	Allan D'Arcangelo
	Harvey Weiss
1971	Ilya Bolotowsky
	Robert Goodnough
	Alfred Leslie
	Norman Lewis
	Ludwig Sander
	Hedda Sterne
	Harold Tovish
1972	Richard Aakre
	Varujan Boghosian
	Lowry Burgess
	Mary Frank
	Maud F. Gatewood
	Herman Rose
	Anton Van Dalen
1973	Rudolf Baranik
	Leon Golub
	Robert Grosvenor
	Raoul Hague
	Michio Ihara
	Clement Meadmore
	Philip Pearlstein
1974	Perle Fine
	Richard Fleischner
	Marilynn Gelfman-Pereira
	George Griffin
	Nancy Grossman
	Ibram Lassaw
	Charlotte Park
1975	Barbara Falk
	Claus Hoie
	Leonid and Seymour Pearlstein
	Calvin Albert
	Harry Bertoia
	William Talbot
1976	Gregory Gillespie
	William Kienbusch
	Julio Fernandez Larraz
	Joseph Wolins
	Judith Brown
	Anthony Padovano
	Sidney Simon

See Books, Art Publishing Award, Art Libraries Society of North America

See Books, Award of Merit Medal, The American Academy of Arts and Letters and The National Institute of Arts and Letters

See Cowboys and Indians, Western Heritage Awards, The National Cowboy Hall of Fame and Western Heritage Center

RICHARD AND HINDA ROSENTHAL FOUNDATION AWARD, PAINTING—The National Institute of Arts and Letters

For a young American painter of distinction who hasn't made it big yet.

1960   Ann Steinbrocker
1961   Zubel Kachadoorian
1962   Robert Andrew Parker
1963   Karen Arden
1964   Gregory Gillespie
1965   Marcia Marcus
1966   Howard Hack
1967   Robert D'Arista
1968   Elizabeth Osborne
1969   Nicholas Sperakis
1970   George Schneeman
1971   Donald Perlis
1972   Barkley L. Hendricks
1973   Jim Sullivan
1974   Julie Curtis Reed
1975   Richard Merkin

See Service, Award of Merit, The Decalogue Society of Lawyers

See Service, Freer Medal, Smithsonian Institution

BOOKS

See Achievement, Gold Medal Awards, The American Academy of Arts and Letters

See Achievement, Marjorie Peabody Waite Award

See Architecture, Fine Arts Medal, The American Institute of Architects

NATIONAL BOOK AWARDS

A big publishing award fallen on hard times as it gets bounced from sponsor to sponsor.

*Special citation
**Dual winner
***Tri-winner

1950
Fiction, Nelson Algren, *The Man With the Golden Arm*
Nonfiction, Ralph L. Rusk, *Ralph Waldo Emerson*
Poetry, William Carlos Williams, *Paterson III* and *Selected Poems*

1951
Fiction, William Faulkner, *The Collected Stories*
Fiction, Brendan Gill*, *The Trouble of One House*
Nonfiction, Newton Arvin, *Herman Melville*
Poetry, Wallace Stevens, *The Auroras of Autumn*

1952
Fiction, James Jones, *From Here to Eternity*
Nonfiction, Rachel Carson, *The Sea Around Us*
Poetry, Marianne Moore, *Collected Poems*

1953
Fiction, Ralph Ellison, *Invisible Man*
Nonfiction, Bernard DeVoto, *The Course of Empire*
Poetry, Archibald MacLeish, *Collected Poems 1917-1952*

1954
Fiction, Saul Bellow, *The Adventures of Augie March*
Nonfiction, Bruce Catton, *A Stillness at Appomattox*
Poetry, Conrad Aiken, *Collected Poems*

1955
Fiction, William Faulkner, *A Fable*
Nonfiction, Joseph Wood Krutch, *The Measure of Man*
Poetry, e. e. cummings*, *Poems, 1923-1954*
Poetry, Wallace Stevens, *The Collected Poems*

1956
Fiction, John O'Hara, *Ten North Frederick*

Nonfiction, Herbert Kubly, *An
American in Italy*
Poetry, W. H. Auden, *The Shield of
Achilles*

1957
Fiction, Wright Morris, *The Field of
Vision*
Nonfiction, George F. Kennan, *Russia
Leaves the War*
Poetry, Richard Wilbur, *Things of This
World*

1958
Fiction, John Cheever, *The Wapshot
Chronicle*
Nonfiction, Catherine Drinker Bowen,
The Lion and the Throne
Poetry, Robert Penn Warren, *Promises:
Poems 1954-1956*

1959
Fiction, Bernard Malamud, *The Magic
Barrel*
Nonfiction, J. Christopher Herold,
Mistress to an Age
Poetry, Theodore Roethke, *Words for
the Wind*

1960
Fiction, Philip Roth, *Goodbye,
Columbus*
Nonfiction, Richard Ellmann, *James
Joyce*
Poetry, Robert Lowell, *Life Studies*

1961
Fiction, Conrad Richter, *The Waters of
Kronos*
Nonfiction, William L. Shirer, *The Rise
and Fall of the Third Reich*
Poetry, Randall Jarrell, *The Woman at
the Washington Zoo*

1962
Fiction, Walker Percy, *The Moviegoer*
Nonfiction, Lewis Mumford, *The City
in History*
Poetry, Alan Dugan, *Poems*

1963
Fiction, J. F. Powers, *Morte D'Urban*
Nonfiction, Leon Edel, *Henry James,
Vol. 2 and 3*
Poetry, William Stafford, *Traveling
Through the Dark*

1964
Fiction, John Updike, *The Centaur*
Poetry, John Crowe Ransom, *Selected
Poems*
History & Biography, William H.
McNeill, *The Rise of The West*
Science, Philosophy & Religion,
Christopher Tunnard & Boris
Pushkarev, *Man-Made America:
Chaos or Control*
Arts & Letters, Aileen Ward, *John
Keats: The Making of a Poet*

1965
Fiction, Saul Bellow, *Herzog*
Poetry, Theodore Roethke, *The Far
Field*
History & Biography, Louis Fischer,
The Life of Lenin
Science, Philosophy, & Religion,
Morton Wiener, *God and Golem,
Inc.*
Arts & Letters, Eleanor Clark, *Oysters
of Locmariaquer*

1966
Fiction, Katherine Anne Porter, *The
Collected Stories*
Poetry, James Dickey, *Buckdancer's
Choice*
History & Biography, Arthur M.
Schlesinger, Jr., *A Thousand Days*
Arts & Letters, Janet Flanner, *Paris
Journal, 1944-1965*

1967
Fiction, Bernard Malamud, *The Fixer*
Poetry, James Merrill, *Nights and Days*
History & Biography, Peter Gay, *The
Enlightenment: An Interpretation*
Science, Philosophy, & Religion, Oscar
Lewis, *La Vida*
Arts & Letters, Justin Kaplan, *Mr.
Clemens and Mark Twain*
Translation, Gregory Rabassa**,
Hopscotch—Julio Cortazar
Translation, Willard Trask**, *History
of My Life*—Giacomo Casanova

1968
Fiction, Thornton Wilder, *The Eighth
Day*
Poetry, Robert Bly, *The Light Around
the Body*
History & Biography, George F.
Kennan, *Memoirs*

Science, Philosophy, & Religion, Jonathan Kozol, *Death at an Early Age*

Arts & Letters, William Troy, *Selected Essays*

Translation, Howard & Edna Hong, *Søren Kierkegaard's Journals and Papers*

1969

Fiction, Jerzy Kosinski, *Steps*

Poetry, John Berryman, *His Toy, His Dream, His Rest*

History & Biography, Winthrop D. Jordan, *White Over Black: American Attitudes Toward the Negro, 1550-1812*

Sciences, Robert J. Lifton, *Death in Life: Survivors of Hiroshima*

Arts & Letters, Norman Mailer, *The Armies of the Night: History as a Novel, the Novel as History*

Translation, William Weaver, *Cosmicomics*—Italo Calvino

Children's Literature, Meindert DeJong, *Journey From Peppermint Street*

1970

Fiction, Joyce Carol Oates, *Them*

Poetry, Elizabeth Bishop, *The Complete Poems*

History & Biography, T. Harry Williams, *Huey Long*

Arts & Letters, Lillian Hellman, *The Unfinished Woman: A Memoir*

Translation, Ralph Manheim, *Castle to Castle*—Louis Ferdinand Celine

Children's Literature, Isaac Bashevis Singer, *A Day of Pleasure: Stories of a Boy Growing Up in Warsaw*

Philosophy & Religion, Erik H. Erikson, *Gandhi's Truth: On the Origins of Militant Nonviolence*

1971

Fiction, Saul Bellow, *Mr. Sammler's Planet*

Poetry, Mona Van Duyn, *To See, To Take*

History & Biography, James MacGregor Burns, *Roosevelt: The Soldier of Freedom*

Sciences, Raymond Phineas Stearns, *Science in the British Colonies of America*

Arts & Letters, Francis Steegmuller, *Cocteau*

Translation, Frank Jones**, *Saint Joan of the Stockyards*—Bertolt Brecht

Translation, Edward G. Seidensticker, *The Sound of the Mountain*—Yasunari Kawabata

Children's Books, Lloyd Alexander, *The Marvelous Misadventures of Sebastian*

1972

Fiction, Flannery O'Connor, *The Complete Stories*

Poetry, Frank O'Hara**, *The Collected Poems*

Poetry, Howard Moss**, *Selected Poems*

History, Allan Nevins, *Ordeal of the Union Series*, 2 Volumes, *The War for the Union: The Organized War, 1863-64, Vol. VII; The War for the Union: The Organized War to Victory, 1864-65, Vol. VIII*

Sciences, George L. Small, *The Blue Whale*

Biography, Joseph P. Lash, *Eleanor and Franklin: The Story of Their Relationship, Based on Eleanor Roosevelt's Private Papers*

Philosophy, Martin E. Marty, *Righteous Empire: The Protestant Experience in America*

Arts & Letters, Charles Rosen, *The Classical Style: Haydn, Mozart, Beethoven*

Translation, Austryn Wainhouse, *Chance and Necessity: An Essay on the Natural Philosophy of Modern Biology*—Jacques Monod

Children's Books, Donald Barthelme, *The Slightly Irregular Fire Engine or the Hithering Thithering Djinn*

Contemporary Affairs, Stewart Brand, ed., *The Last Whole Earth Catalog: Access to Tools*

1973

Fiction, John Barth**, *Chimera*

Fiction, John Williams**, *Augustus*

Poetry, A. R. Ammons, *Collected Poems: 1951-1971*

History, Robert Manson Myers**, *The Children of Pride: A True Story of Georgia and the Civil War*

History, Isaiah Trunk, *Judenrat: The Jewish Councils in Eastern Europe Under Nazi Occupation*

Sciences, George B. Schaller, *The Serengeti Lion: A Study of Predator-Prey Relations*

Biography, James Thomas Flexner, *George Washington: Anguish and Farewell (1793-1799)*

Arts & Letters, Arthur M. Wilson, *Diderot*

Translation, Allen Mandelbaum, *The Aeneid of Virgil*

Philosophy, Sydney E. Ahlstrom, *A Religious History of the American People*

Children's Books, Ursula Le Guin, *The Farthest Shore*

Contemporary Affairs, Frances FitzGerald, *Fire in the Lake: The Vietnamese and the Americans in Vietnam*

1974

Fiction, Thomas Pynchon°°, *Gravity's Rainbow*

Fiction, Isaac Bashevis Singer°°, *A Crown of Feathers and Other Stories*

Poetry, Allen Ginsburg°°, *The Fall of America: Poems of These States (1965-1971)*

Poetry, Adrienne Rich, *Diving Into the Wreck: Poems, 1971-72*

History, John Clive, *Macaulay: The Shaping of the Historian*

Biography, Douglas Day, *Malcolm Lowry: A Biography*

Sciences, S. E. Luria, *Life: The Unfinished Experiment*

Philosophy & Religion, Maurice Natanson, *Edmund Husserl: Philosopher of Infinite Tasks*

Arts & Letters, Pauline Kael, *Deeper Into Movies*

Translation, Karen Brazell, *The Confessions of Lady Nijo*

Translation, Helen R. Lane°°°, *Alternating Current*—Octavio Paz

Translation, Jackson Mathews°°°, *Monsieur Teste*—Paul Valery

Children's Books, Eleanor Cameron, *The Court of the Stone Children*

Contemporary Affairs, Murray Kempton, *The Briar Patch: The People of the State of New York v. Lumumba Shakur, et al.*

1975

Fiction, Robert Stone°°, *Dog Soldiers*

Fiction, Thomas Williams°°, *The Hair of Harold Roux*

Poetry, Marilyn Hacker, *Presentation Piece*

History, Bernard Bailyn, *The Ordeal of Thomas Hutchinson*

Biography, Richard B. Sewall, *The Life of Emily Dickinson*

Sciences, Silvano Arieti, *Interpretations of Schizophrenia*

Sciences, Lewis Thomas, *The Lives of a Cell: Notes of a Biology Watcher*

Philosophy & Religion, Robert Nozick, *Anarchy, State, & Utopia*

Arts & Letters, Roger Shattuck, *Marcel Proust*

Translation, Anthony Kerrigan, *The Agony of Christianity and Essays on Faith*—Miguel D. Unamuno

Children's Books, Virginia Hamilton, *M. C. Higgins the Great*

Contemporary, Theodore Rosengarten, *All God's Dangers: The Life of Nate Shaw*

1976

Fiction, William Gaddis, *JR*

Poetry, John Ashberg, *Self-Portrait in a Convex Mirror*

History, David Brian Davis, *The Problem of Slavery in the Age of Revolution: 1770-1823*

Arts & Letters, Paul Fussell, *The Great War and Modern Memory*

Children's Literature, Walter D. Edmonds, *Bert Breen's Barn*

Contemporary Affairs, Michael J. Arlen, *Passage to Ararat*

1977

Fiction, Wallace E. Stegner, *The Spectator Bird*

Poetry, Richard Eberhart, *Collected Poems, 1930-1976*

History, Irving Howe, *World of Our Fathers*°

Special Award, Alex Haley, *Roots*

Biography, W. A. Swanberg, *Norman Thomas: The Last Idealist*

Translation, Li-li Ch'en, *Master Tung's Western Chamber Romance: A Chinese Chantefable*
Children's Literature, Katherine W. Paterson, *The Master Puppeteer*
Contemporary Thought, Bruno Bettelheim, *The Uses of Enchantment: The Meaning and Importance of Fairy Tales*

ART PUBLISHING AWARD—Art Libraries Society of North America
For art books with exemplary design, layout, workmanship, materials, binding, fine illustrations, indexes, and bibliographies. Must be published in U.S. or Canada.
Established 1973.
1973
  Jonathan Green, editor *Camera Work: A Critical Anthology,* Aperture
  Coy Ludwig, *Maxfield Parrish,* Watson-Guptill
1974
  Lincoln Kirstein, *Elle Nadelman,* Eakins Foundation Press
  Pierpont Morgan Library, *Major Acquisitions of the Pierpont Morgan Library, 1924–1974,* The Library
1975
  Dan Burne Jones, *The Prints of Rockwell Kent,* University of Chicago Press

ARTS AND LETTERS AWARDS—
The National Institute of Arts and Letters
  To help writers who are not members of the Institute continue their creative work; prize of $3,000.
  Established 1941.
1941   Mary M. Colum
        Jesse Stuart
1942   Hermann Broch
        Norman Corwin
        Edgar Lee Masters
        Muriel Rukeyser
1943   Virgil Geddes
        Carson McCullers
        Jose Garcia Villa
        Joseph Wittlin
1944   Hugo Ignotus
        Jeremy Ingalls
        Thomas Sancton

        Karl Shapiro
        Eudora Welty
        Tennessee Williams
1945   Kenneth Fearing
        Feike Feikema
        Alexander Greendale
        Norman Rosten
        Jean Stafford
        Marguerite Young
1946   Gwendolyn Brooks
        Kenneth Burke
        Malcolm Cowley
        Peter DeVries
        Langston Hughes
        Arthur Laurents
        Marianne Craig Moore
        Arthur Schlesinger, Jr.
        Irwin Shaw
1947   Nelson Algren
        Eleanor Clark
        Lloyd Frankenberg
        Robert Lowell
        Elizabeth Parsons
        James Still
1948   Bertolt Brecht
        Dudley Fitts
        Harry Levin
        James F. Powers
        Genevieve Taggard
        Allen Tate
1949   Leonie Adams
        James Agee
        Joseph Campbell
        Alfred Kazin
        Vincent McHugh
        James Stern
1950   John Berryman
        Paul Bowles
        Maxwell David Geismar
        Caroline Gordon
        Shirley Graham
        Hyam Plutzik
1951   Newton Arvin
        Elizabeth Bishop
        Louise Bogan
        Brendan Gill
        Randall Jarrell
        Vladimir Nabokov
1952   Saul Bellow
        Alfred Hayes
        Theodore Roethke
        Elizabeth Spencer
        Peter Taylor
        Yvor Winters

1953	Eric Bentley		David McCord
	Isabel Bolton		Warren Miller
	Richard Chase		Brian Moore
	Francis Fergusson		Howard Nemerov
	Paul Goodman	1962	Daniel Fuchs
	Delmore Schwartz		John Hawkes
1954	Hannah Arendt		Gelway Kinnell
	Ray Bradbury		Edwin O'Connor
	Richmond Lattimore		Frank O'Connor
	David Riesman		Joan Williams
	Ruthven Todd		John A. Williams
	C. Vann Woodward	1963	Richard Bankowsky
1955	Richard Eberhart		William Gaddis
	Robert Horan		Joseph Heller
	Chester Kallman		John Hollander
	William Krasner		William Humphrey
	Milton Lott		Peter Matthiessen
	Morton D. Zabel		Richard Yates
1956	James Baldwin	1964	Lionel Abel
	John Cheever		Dorothy Baker
	Henry Russell Hitchcock		Norman Fruchter
	Joseph Kerman		Thom Gunn
	Josephine Miles		Eric Hoffer
	Priscilla Robertson		David Ignatow
	Frank Rooney		Kenneth Rexroth
1957	Leslie Fiedler	1965	Ben Belitt
	Robert Fitzgerald		Robert Bly
	Mary McCarthy		J. V. Cunningham
	W. S. Merwin		Denise Levertov
	Flannery O'Connor		Joseph Mitchell
	Robert Pack		P. M. Pasinetti
1958	Joseph Frank		Henry Roth
	Herbert Gold		Harvey Swados
	R. W. B. Lewis	1966	William Alfred
	William Maxwell		John Barth
	William Meredith		James Dickey
	James Purdy		Shirley Hazzard
	Francis Steegmuller		Josephine Herbst
1959	Truman Capote		Edwin Honig
	Leon Edel		Gary Snyder
	Charles Jackson		M. B. Tolson
	Stanley J. Kunitz	1967	Philip Booth
	Conrad Richter		Hortense Calisher
	Isaac Bashevis Singer		Daniel Hoffman
	James Wright		Bernard Knox
1960	Irving Howe		Stanley Edgar Hyman
	Norman Mailer		Walker Percy
	Wright Morris		David Wagoner
	Adrienne Rich	1968	John Malcom Brinnin
	Philip Roth		Fred Chappell
	W. D. Snodgrass		Reuel Denny
	May Swenson		Howard Moss
1961	Edward Dahlberg		John Frederick Nims
	Jean Garrigue		Julia Randall
	Mark Harris		Richard G. Stern

	Eleanor Ross Taylor
1969	John Ashbery
	George P. Elliott
	Allen Ginsberg
	Hugh Kenner
	L. E. Sissman
1970	Brewster Ghiselin
	Gordon S. Haight
	Richard Howard
	Pauline Kael
	Jerzy Kosinski
	James A. McPherson
	N. Scott Momaday
	Grace Paley
	F. D. Reeve
	Kurt Vonnegut, Jr.
1971	Wendell Berry
	Stanley Burnshaw
	Martin Duberman
	Ronald Fair
	Charles Gordone
	Barbara Howes
	Arthur Kopit
	Leonard Michaels
	Leonard Nathan
	Reynolds Price
	Wilfrid Sheed
1972	Harry Crews
	Peter Davison
	Paula Fox
	Penelope Gilliatt
	Pauline Hanson
	Michael S. Harper
	Israel Horovitz
	Walter Kerr
	Gilbert Rogin
	Ann Stanford
1973	Marius Bewley
	Maeve Brennan
	Irving Feldman
	Frances FitzGerald
	Dorothy Hughes
	Philip Levine
	Daniel P. Mannix
	Cynthia Ozick
	Jonathan Schell
	Austin Warren
1974	Ann Cornelisen
	Stanley Elkin
	Elizabeth Hardwick
	Josephine Johnson
	Donald Justice
	David Rabe
	Charles Rosen
	Sam Shepard

	James Tate
	Hanry Van Dyke
	Lanford Wilson
1975	William S. Burroughs
	J. P. Donleavy
	John Gardner
	William H. Gass
	Terrence McNally
	Tillie Olsen
	John Peck
	Mark Strand
	Colin Turnbull
1976	Robert Coover
	Robert Craft
	E. L. Doctorow
	Eugene D. Genovese
	Kenneth Koch
	Charles Simic
	John Simon
	Louis Simpson
	Susan Sontag
	Louis Zukofsky

AWARD OF MERIT MEDAL—The American Academy of Arts and Letters and the National Institute of Arts and Letters

Winners of this medal may not be members of the Institute, but must have done exceptional work in either painting, sculpture, the novel, poetry, or drama.

Established 1940.

1942	Charles E. Burchfield
1943	Carl Milles
1944	Theodore Dreiser
1945	Wystan Hugh Auden
1946	John van Druten
1947	Andrew Wyeth
1948	Donal Hord
1949	Thomas Mann
1950	St. John Perse
1951	Sidney Kingsley
1952	Rico Lebrun
1953	Ivan Mestrovic
1954	Ernest Hemingway
1955	Jorge Guillén
1956	Enid Bagnold
1957	Raphael Soyer
1958	Jean de Marco
1959	Aldous Huxley
1960	Hilda Doolittle
1961	Clifford Odets

1962	Charles Sheeler
1963	Chaim Gross
1964	John O'Hara
1965	no award
1966	no award
1967	John Heliker
1968	Joseph Cornell
1969	Vladimir Nabokov
1970	Reed Whittemore
1971	no award
1972	Clyfford Still
1973	Reuben Nakian
1974	Nelson Algren
1975	Galway Kinnell

MILDRED L. BATCHELDER
AWARD—American Library Association

Besides being "outstanding," to qualify for this award a children's book must have been first published outside of the United States. Established 1966.

1968	*The Little Man*, Erich Kastner, Alfred A. Knopf, Inc.
1969	*Don't Take Teddy*, Babbis Friis-Baastad, Charles S. Scribner's Sons
1970	*Wildcat Under Glass*, Aliki Zei, Holt, Rinehart & Winston, Inc.
1971	*In the Land of Ur: The Discovery of Ancient Mesopotamia*, Han Baumann, Pantheon Books
1972	*Friedrich*, Hans Peter Richter, Holt, Rinehart & Winston, Inc.
1973	*Pulga*, S. R. Van Iterson, William Morrow & Co.
1974	*Petros' War*, Aliki Zei, E. P. Dutton & Co.
1975	*An Old Tale Carved Out of Stone*, A. Linevski, Crown
1976	*The Cat and Mouse Who Shared a House*, Ruth Hurlimann, Henry Z. Walck

THE CALDECOTT MEDAL—American Library Association

Randolph J. Caldecott was a nineteenth-century English illustrator. It's therefore more than appropriate that his award is presented to the artist of the "most distinguished" American picture book for children. Established 1937.

1938	*Animals of the Bible*, Dorothy P. Lathrop, Lippincott
1939	*Mei Li*, Thomas Handforth, Doubleday
1940	*Abraham Lincoln*, Ingri and Edgar Parin d'Aulaire, Doubleday
1941	*They Were Strong and Good*, Robert Lawson, Viking
1942	*Make Way for Ducklings*, Robert McCloskey, Viking
1943	*The Little House*, Virginia Lee Burton, Houghton
1944	*Many Moons*, Louis Slobodkin, Harcourt
1945	*Prayer for a Child*, Elizabeth Orton Jones, Macmillan
1946	*The Rooster Crows*, Maude and Miska Petersham, Macmillan
1947	*The Little Island*, Leonard Weisgard, Doubleday
1948	*White Snow, Bright Snow*, Roger Duvoisin, Lothrop
1949	*The Big Snow*, Berta and Elmer Hader, Macmillan
1950	*Song of the Swallows*, Leo Politi, Scribner
1951	*The Egg Tree*, Katherine Milhous, Scribner
1952	*Finders Keepers*, Nicolas Mordvinoff, Harcourt
1953	*The Biggest Bear*, Lynd Ward, Houghton
1954	*Madeline's Rescue*, Ludwig Bemelmans, Viking
1955	*Cinderella*, Marcia Brown, Scribner
1956	*Frog Went A-Courtin'*, Feodor Rojankovsky, Harcourt
1957	*A Tree is Nice*, Marc Simont, Harper
1958	*Time of Wonder*, Robert McCloskey, Viking
1959	*Chanticleer and the Fox*, Barbara Cooney, Crowell
1960	*Nine Days to Christmas*, Marie Hall Ets and Aurora

Labastida, Viking

1961 *Baboushka and the Three Kings*, Nicolas Sidjakov, Parnassus

1962 *Once A Mouse*, Marcia Brown, Scribner

1963 *The Snowy Day*, Ezra Jack Keats, Viking

1964 *Where the Wild Things Are*, Maurice Sendak, Harper

1965 *May I Bring a Friend?*, Beni Montresor, Atheneum

1966 *Always Room for One More*, Nonny Hogrogian, Holt

1967 *Sam, Bangs & Moonshine*, Evaline Ness, Holt

1968 *Drummer Hoff*, Ed Emberly, Prentice-Hall

1969 *The Fool of the World and the Flying Ship*, Uri Shulevitz, Farrar

1970 *Sylvester and the Magic Pebble*, William Steig, Windmill Books

1971 *A Story A Story*, Gail E. Haley, Atheneum

1972 *One Fine Day*, Nonny Hogrogian, Macmillan

1973 *The Funny Little Woman*, Blair Lent, Dutton

1974 *Duffy and the Devil*, Margot Zemach, Farrar

1975 *Arrow To the Sun*, Gerald McDermott Viking

1976 *Why Mosquitoes Buzz in People's Ears*, Leo and Diane Dillon, Dial

CAREY-THOMAS AWARDS—Publishers Weekly

Why should writers get all the awards? The publishing houses that sweat and edit, produce and peddle the books deserve a little credit also. And this is it, an award for "creative book publishing . . . not editorial judgment alone, but the exceptional display of initiative, imagination, co-operation with author, appropriate manufacture, successful promotion and marketing."

Established 1942.

1942 Farrar & Rinehart, *The Rivers of America*

1943 University of Chicago Press, *A Dictionary of American English on Historical Principles*

1944 E. P. Dutton & Co., Inc., *The World of Washington Irving* by Van Wyck Brooks

1945 Alfred A. Knopf, Inc., *The American Language* by H. L. Mencken

1946 Duell, Sloan & Pearce, Inc., *The New World* by Stefan Lorant

1947 Oxford University Press, Inc., *A Study of History* by Arnold Toynbee

1948 William Sloane Associates, *The American Men of Letters Series*

1949 Rand McNally & Co., *Cosmopolitan World Atlas*

1950 Princeton University Press, *The Papers of Thomas Jefferson*

1951 Houghton Mifflin Co., *Life in America* by Marshall B. Davidson

1952 The Macmillan Co., *The Diary of George Templeton Strong, 1835-1875* by Allan Nevins and Milton H. Thomas

1953 Houghton Mifflin Co., *The Second World War* by Sir Winston Churchill

1954 Doubleday & Co., *Anchor Books Series*

1955 Belknap Press of Harvard University Press, *The Poems of Emily Dickinson*

1956 Doubleday & Co., *Mainstream of America Series*

1957 Frederick A. Praeger, Inc., *The New Class* by Milovan Djilas

1958 New York Graphic Society, *The Complete Letters of Vincent Van Gogh*

1959 Oxford University Press, *James Joyce* by Richard Ellmann

1960 Simon & Schuster, *The Rise and Fall of the Third Reich* by William L. Shirer

1961	Belknap Press of Harvard University Press, *The Adams Papers—Diary and Autobiography of John Adams*
1962	Shorewood Publishers Inc., *Great Drawings of All Time*
1963	Wesleyan University Press, *New York Landmarks*, edited by Alan Burnham, A.I.A.
1964	Sierra Club, *Sierra Club Exhibit Format Series*, edited by David Brower
1965	Doubleday & Co., *The Anchor Bible*, edited by W. F. Albright and D. N. Freedman
1966	George Braziller, Inc., *The Hours of Catherine of Cleves*, introduction and commentaries by John Plummer
1967	Holt, Rinehart & Winston, *Wilderness Kingdom: The Journals and Paintings of Father Nicolas Point,* translated and introduced by Joseph P. Donnelly, S. J.
1968	W. W. Norton & Co., *The Norton Facsimile: The First Folio of Shakespeare,* prepared by Professor Charlton Hinman
1969	Alfred A. Knopf, Inc., *Huey Long* by T. Harry Williams
1970	Random House, Inc., Maecenan Press Ltd., Chanticleer Press, Inc., *Picasso 347* Collected Drawings of Pablo Picasso
1971	Oxford University Press, *The Compact Edition of the Oxford English Dictionary: Complete Text Reproduced Micrographically*
1972	Yale University Press, *The Children of Pride: A True Story of Georgia and the Civil War,* edited by Robert Manson Myers
1973	Princeton University Press, *The Bollingen Series*
1974	McGraw-Hill Book Co., *Madrid Codices of Leonardo da Vinci, The Unknown Leonardo,* both edited by Ladislao Reti
1975	Morgan Library/David R. Godine, Publisher, *Early Children's Books and Their Illustration* by Gerald Gottlieb

See Cowboys and Indians, Western Heritage Awards, The National Cowboy Hall of Fame and Western Heritage Center

JEFFERSON DAVIS AWARD—AWARD OF MERIT—FOUNDERS AWARD—Confederate Memorial Literary Society

The three honors bestowed by CMLS, based, appropriately enough, in Richmond, Virginia, are for research and writing on the Civil War period or what the society refers to as the "period of the Confederate States of America." Established 1970.

JEFFERSON DAVIS AWARD

1970	Frank E. Vandiver, Rice University
1971	Thomas L. Connelly
1972	Thomas B. Alexander Richard E. Beringer
1973	Thomas L. Connelly Archer Jones
1974	William C. Davis, editor, *Civil War Times Illustrated*
1975	Dr. Bell I. Wiley

AWARD OF MERIT

1970	William J. Cooper, Jr.
1971	W. G. Bean
1972	Dr. Raimondo Luaraghi, University of Genoa
1973	Dr. Bell I. Wiley, Emory University
1974	Miss Willie T. Weathers
1975	David W. Gaddy

FOUNDERS AWARD

1970	Warren Ripley
1971	Haskell M. Monroe
1972	Robert Manson Myers
1973	no award
1974	John Hammond Moore, professor, Georgia State

University and Macquarie
University in Australia
1975   Ezra J. Warner
        W. Buck Yearns

E. M. FORSTER AWARD—The National Institute of Arts and Letters
English author E. M. Forster left the royalties from his book *Maurice* to finance American visits by young English writers.
1972   Frank Touhy
1973   Margaret Drabble
1974   Paul Bailey
1975   Seamus Heaney
1976   Jon Stallworthy

THE EMERSON-THOREAU MEDAL—American Academy of Arts and Sciences
This is awarded from the "arts" part of the academy for "total achievement" in literature, rather than for one specific work.
Established 1958.
1958   Robert Frost
1959   T. S. Eliot
1960   Henry Beston
1961   Samuel Eliot Morison
1962   Katherine Anne Porter
1963   Mark Van Doren
1964   no award
1965   Lewis Mumford
1966   Edmund Wilson
1967   Joseph Wood Krutch
1968   John Crowe Ransom
1969   Hannah Arendt
1970   I. A. Richards
1971   no award
1972   no award
1973   no award
1974   no award
1975   Robert Penn Warren

EVA L. GORDON AWARD—The American Nature Study Society
Presented annually for children's nature books with "high standards of accuracy, readability, sensitivity to in-

terrelationships, timeliness, and joyousness."
Established 1964.
1964   Millicent Selsam
1965   Edwin Way Teale
1966   Robert M. McClung
1967   no award
1968   no award
1969   no award
1970   Jean Craighead George
1971   Verne Rockcastle
1972   no award
1973   no award
1974   Phyllis Busch
1975   Jeanne Bendick
1976   Helen Ross Russell

See Motion Pictures, George Jean Nathan Award for Dramatic Criticism, George Jean Nathan Trust and Manufacturers Hanover Trust

See Motion Pictures, Mrs. Ann Radcliffe Award, The Count Dracula Society

HORN BOOK AWARDS—The *Boston Globe*
Any juvenile book published in the United States is eligible.
Established 1967.
1967
    Fiction, *The Little Fishes,* Erik Haugaard
    Illustration, *London Bridge is Falling Down,* Peter Spier
1968
    Fiction, *The Spring Rider,* John Lawson
    Illustration, *Tikki, Tikki, Tembo,* Arlene Mosel, Illus.-Blair Lent
1969
    Fiction, *A Wizard of Earthsea,* Ursula K. LeGuin
    Illustration, *The Adventures of Paddy Pork,* John S. Goodall
1970
    Fiction, *The Intruder,* John Rowe Townsend
    Illustration, *Hi, Cat!,* Ezra Jack Keats
1971
    Fiction, *A Room Made of Windows,*

Eleanor Cameron
Illustration, *If I Built A Village,*
Kazue Mizamura
1972
Fiction, *Tristan and Iseult,*
Rosemary Sutcliff
Illustration, *Mr. Gumpy's Outing,*
John Burningham
1973
Fiction, *The Dark is Rising,* Susan
Cooper
Illustration, *King Stork,* Howard
Pyle, Illus.-Trina Hyman
1974
Fiction, *M. C. Higgins, The Great,*
Virginia Hamilton
Illustration, *Jambo Means Hello:
Swahili Alphabet Book,* Muriel
Feelings, Illus.-Tom Feelings
1975
Fiction, *Transport 7-41-R,* T. Degens
Illustration, *Anno's Alphabet,*
Mitsumasa Anno
1976
Fiction, *Unleaving,* Jill Paton Walsh
Illustration, *Thirteen,* Remy Charlip
and Jerry Joyner
Nonfiction, *Voyaging to Cathay:
Americans in the China Trade,*
Alfred Tamarin and Shirley Glubok

**THE WILLIAM DEAN HOWELLS
MEDAL**—The American Academy of
Arts and Letters
Presented once every five years, the
WDH is for "the most distinguished
work of American fiction published
during that period." Mr. Howells was
president of the Academy from 1908 to
1920.
Established 1921.

1925	Mary E. Wilkins Freeman
1930	Willa Cather
1935	Pearl S. Buck
1940	Ellen Glasgow
1945	Booth Tarkington
1950	William Faulkner
1955	Eudora Welty
1960	James Gould Cozzens
1965	John Cheever
1970	William Styron
1975	Thomas Pynchon

HUGO AWARD—World Science Fiction Convention
This was originally called the
Science Fiction Achievement Award
before it picked up its nickname
"Hugo." The convention gives out a
whole number of awards, but we are
listing only those for the novel. Anyone
interested in a complete listing should
contact Howard DeVore, 4705 Weddell
Street, Dearborn, Michigan 48125.
Established 1953.

1953	*The Demolished Man,* Alfred Bester
1954	no award
1955	*They'd Rather Be Right,* Mark Clifton and Frank Riley
1956	*Double Star,* Robert A. Heinlein
1957	no award
1958	*The Big Time,* Fritz Leiber
1959	*A Case of Conscience,* James Blish
1960	*Starship Troopers,* Robert A. Heinlein
1961	*A Canticle for Leibowitz,* Walter M. Miller, Jr.
1962	*Stranger in a Strange Land,* Robert A. Heinlein
1963	*The Man in the High Castle,* Philip K. Dick
1964	*Here Gather the Stars,* Clifford D. Simak
1965	*The Wanderer,* Fritz Leiber
1966	*... And Call Me Conrad,* Roger Zelazny *Dune,* Frank Herbert
1967	*The Moon is a Harsh Mistress,* Robert A. Heinlein
1968	*Lord of Light,* Roger Zelazny
1969	*Stand on Zanzibar,* John Brunner
1970	*The Left Hand of Darkness,* Ursula K. LeGuin
1971	*Ringworld,* Larry Niven
1972	*To Your Scattered Bodies Go,* Philip Jose Farmer
1973	*The Gods Themselves,* Isaac Asimov
1974	*Rendezvous With Rama,* Arthur C. Clarke
1975	*The Dispossessed,* Ursula K. LeGuin
1976	*The Forever War,* Joe Haldeman

INTERRACIAL BOOKS FOR CHILDREN AWARD—Council on Interracial Books for Children

The award was established to encourage minority writers "to prepare manuscripts for children that portray the lives of minority groups without racist or sexist stereotypes." Established 1968.

1968–69
Walter D. Myers, *Where Does the Day Go*
Kristin Hunter, *The Soul Brothers & Sister Lou*

1970
Virginia Cox, *ABC: The Story of the Alphabet*
Saron Bell Mathis, *Sidewalk Story*
Margot S. Webb, *Letter From Uncle David: Underground Hero*

1971
Ray Anthony Shepard, *Sneakers*
Virginia Driving Hawk Sneve, *Jimmy Yellowhawk*
Juan Valenzuela, *I Am Magic*

1972
Minfong Ho, *Sing to the Dawn*
Florenz Webb Maxwell, *The Rock Cried Out*
Theodore Laguer-Franceschi, *The Unusual Puerto Rican*
Cruz Martel, *Yagua Days*

1973
Dorothy Tomiye Okamoto, *Eyak*
Mildred D. Taylor, *Song of the Trees*
Nanabah Chee Dodge, *Morning Arros*
Michele P. Robinson, *Grandfather's Bridge*
Jack Agueros, *El Pito De Plata De Pito (Willy's Silver Whistle)*

1974
Aishah Abdullah, *Midnight, Simba, Mweusi* (a trilogy)
Abelardo Delgado, *My Father Hijacked a Plane*
Antonia Hernandez, *Yari*

1975
Emily R. Moore, *Letters to a Friend on a Brown Paper Bag*

THE NEBULA AWARD—The Science Fiction Writers of America

For excellent science fiction. Established 1966.

1965
Best novel, *Dune*, Frank Herbert
Best novella, *He Who Shapes*, Roger Zelazny
Best novelette, *The Doors of His Face; Lamps of His Mouth*, Roger Zelazny
Best short story, "'Repent, Harlequin!' Said the Ticktockman," Harlan Ellison

1966
Best novel, *Babel 17*, Samuel Delany; *Flowers for Algernon*, Daniel Keyes
Best novella, *The Last Castle*, Jack Vance
Best novelette, *Call Him Lord*, Gordon Dickson
Best short story, "The Secret Place," Richard McKenna

1967
Best novel, *The Einstein Intersection*, Samuel Delany
Best novella, *Behold the Man*, Michael Moorcock
Best novelette, *Gonna Roll The Bones*, Fritz Leiber
Best short story, "Aye and Gomorrah," Samuel R. Delaney

1968
Best novel, *Rite of Passage*, Alexi Panshin
Best novella, *Dragon Rider*, Anne McCaffrey
Best novelette, *Mother to the World*, Richard Wilson
Best short story, "The Planners," Kate Wilhelm

1969
Best novel, *The Left Hand of Darkness*, Ursula LeGuin
Best novella, *A Boy and His Dog*, Harlan Ellison
Best novelette, *Time Considered as a Helix of Semi-Precious Stones*, Samuel R. Delany
Best short story, "Passengers," Robert Silverberg

1970
Best novel, *Ringworld*, Larry Niven
Best novella, *Ill Met in Lankhmar*, Fritz Leiber
Best novelette, *Slow Sculpture*, Theodore Sturgeon
Best short story, no award

Abelardo Delgado, author of
My Father Hijacked a Plane

1971

Best novel, *A Time of Changes,* Robert Silverberg
Best novella, *The Missing Man,* Katherine MacLean
Best novelette, *Queen of Air and Darkness,* Poul Anderson
Best short story, "Good News from the Vatican," Robert Silberberg

1972

Best novel, *The Gods Themselves,* Isaac Asimov
Best novella, *A Meeting With Medusa,* Arthur C. Clarke,
Best novelette, *Goat Song,* Poul Anderson
Best short story, "When It Changed," Joanna Russ

1973

Best novel, *Rendezvous With Rama,* Arthur C. Clarke
Best novella, *The Death of Doctor Island,* Gene Wolfe
Best novelette, *Of Mist, and Grass, and Sand,* Vonda N. McIntyre
Best short story, "Love Is the Plan,

The Plan Is Death," James Tiptree, Jr.
Best dramatic presentation, *Soylent Green,* Stanley R. Greenberg

1974

Best novel, *The Dispossessed,* Ursula K. LeGuin
Best novella, *Born with the Dead,* Robert Silverberg
Best novelette, *If the Stars Are Gods,* Gordon Eklund and Gregory Benford
Best short story, "The Day Before the Revolution," Ursula K. LeGuin
Best dramatic presentation, *Sleeper,* Woody Allen

1975

Best novel, *The Forever War,* Joe Haldeman
Best novella, *Home Is the Hangman,* Roger Zelazny
Best novelette, *San Diego Lightfoot Sue,* Tom Reamy
Best short story, "Catch That Zeppelin," Fritz Leiber
Best dramatic presentation, *Young*

Frankenstein, Mel Brooks, Gene Wilder, and Mary Wollstonecraft Shelley

NEWBERY MEDAL BOOKS—
American Library Association
This is awarded to the author whose book made a "distinguished contribution" to American children's literature. Established 1921.

1922
The Story of Mankind, Hendrik Van Loon, Liveright
1923
The Voyages of Doctor Doolittle, Hugh Lofting, Lippincott
1924
The Dark Frigate, Charles Hawes, Little, Brown
1925
Tales from Silver Lands, Charles Finger, Doubleday
1926
Shen of the Sea, Arthur Chrisman, Dutton
1927
Smoky, the Cowhorse, Will James, Scribner
1928
Gay Neck, the Story of a Pigeon, Dhan Mukerji, Dutton
1929
The Trumpeter of Krakow, Eric P. Kelly, Macmillan
1930
Hitty, Her First Hundred Years, Rachel Field, Macmillan
1931
The Cat Who Went to Heaven, Elizabeth Coatsworth, Macmillan
1932
Waterless Mountain, Laura Armer, Longmans
1933
Young Fu of the Upper Yangtze, Elizabeth Lewis, Winston
1934
Invincible Louisa, Cornelia Meigs, Little Brown
1935
Dobry, Monica Shannon, Viking
1936
Caddie Woodlawn, Carol Brink, Macmillan

1937
Roller Skates, Ruth Sawyer, Viking
1938
The White Stag, Kate Seredy, Viking
1939
Thimble Summer, Elizabeth Enright, Rinehart
1940
Daniel Boone, James Daugherty, Viking
1941
Call It Courage, Armstrong Sperry, Macmillan
1942
The Matchlock Gun, Walter Edmonds, Dodd
1943
Adam of the Road, Elizabeth Gray, Viking
1944
Johnny Tremain, Esther Forbes, Houghton
1945
Rabbit Hill, Robert Lawson, Viking
1946
Strawberry Girl, Lois Lenski, Lippincott
1947
Miss Hickory, Carolyn Bailey, Viking
1948
The Twenty-One Balloons, William Pène du Bois, Viking
1949
King of the Wind, Marguerite Henry, Rand McNally
1950
The Door in the Wall, Marguerite de Angeli, Doubleday
1951
Amos Fortune, Free Man, Elizabeth Yates, Aladdin
1952
Ginger Pye, Eleanor Estes, Harcourt
1953
Secret of the Andes, Ann Nolan Clark, Viking
1954
. . . And Now Miguel, Joseph Krumgold, Crowell
1955
The Wheel on the School, Meindert DeJong, Harper

1956
Carry on, Mr. Bowditch, Jean Lee
Latham, Houghton
1957
Miracles on Maple Hill, Virginia
Sorensen, Harcourt
1958
Rifles for Watie, Harold Keith,
Crowell
1959
The Witch of Blackbird Pond,
Elizabeth George Speare, Houghton
1960
Onion John, Joseph Krumgold,
Crowell
1961
Island of the Blue Dolphins, Scott
O'Dell, Houghton
1962
The Bronze Bow, Elizabeth George
Speare, Houghton
1963
A Wrinkle in Time, Madeleine
L'Engle, Farrar
1964
It's Like This, Cat, Emily Neville,
Harper
1965
Shadow of a Bull, Maia
Wojciechowska, Atheneum
1966
I, Juan de Pareja, Elizabeth Borton
de Trevino, Farrar
1967
Up a Road Slowly, Irene Hunt,
Follett
1968
*From the Mixed-Up Files of Mrs.
Basil E. Frankweiler,* E. L.
Konigsburg, Atheneum
1969
The High King, Lloyd Alexander,
Holt
1970
Sounder, William H. Armstrong,
Harper
1971
Summer of the Swans, Betsy Byars,
Viking
1972
Mrs. Frisby and the Rats of NIMH,
Robert C. O'Brien, Atheneum
1973
Julie of the Wolves, Jean Craighead
George, Harper

1974
The Slave Dancer, Paula Fox,
Bradbury
1975
M. C. Higgins, the Great, Virginia
Hamilton, Macmillan
1976
The Grey King, Susan Cooper,
Atheneum

See Nobel Prize

THE P.E.N. TRANSLATION PRIZE
—P.E.N.
1963
Archibald Colquhoun, *The Viceroys*
by Federico de Roberto
1964
Ralph Mannheim, *The Tin Drum* by
Gunter Grass
1965
Joseph Barnes, *The Story of a Life* by
Konstantin Paustovsky
1966
Geoffrey Skelton and Adrian
Mitchell, *The Persecution and
Assassination of Jean-Paul Marat, As
Performed by the Inmates of the
Asylum at Charenton, Under the
Direction of the Marquis de Sade,* a
play by Peter Weiss.
1967
Harriet de Onis, *Sagarana* by J.
Guimaraes Rosa
1968
Vladimir Markov and Merrill Sparks,
Modern Russian Poetry
1969
W. S. Merwin, *Selected Translations
1948–1968*
1970
Sidney Alexander, *The History of
Italy* by Francesco Guicciardini
1971
Max Hayward, *Hope Against Hope*
by Nadezhda Mandelstam
1972
Richard and Clara Winston, *Letters
of Thomas Mann*
1973
J. P. McCulloch, *The Poems of
Sextus Propertius*
1974
Hardie St. Martin and Leonard

Mades, *The Obscene Bird of Night*
by Jose Donoso
1975
Helen R. Lane, *Count Julian* by Juan
Goytisolo
1976
Richard Howard, *A Short History of
Decay* by E. M. Cioran

THE PILGRIM AWARD—Science
Fiction Research Association
Science fiction is far more than fanci-
ful silliness. The SFRA honors individuals who have contributed to the study
of the modern science fiction. The
"Pilgrim" of the award's name is taken
from the title of first award winner J. O.
Bailey's book, *Pilgrims Through Space
and Time.*
Established 1970.
1970   J. O. Bailey
1971   Marjorie Nicolson
1972   Julius Kagarlitski
1973   Jack Williamson
1974   I. F. Clarke
1975   Damon Knight
1976   James Gunn

See Pulitzer Prize

REMEMBRANCE AWARD—World
Federation of the Bergen Belsen Asso-
ciations
Given to an author of any race or reli-
gion who has written a work "inspired
by the Holocaust experience and the
existential adventure of the Jewish
people."
Established 1965.
1965
Elie Wiesel, *The Town Beyond the
Wall*
1966
Manes Sperber, *Than a Tear in the
Sea*
1967
Jean Cayrol, *Collected Poems*
1968
Jacob Presser, *The Destruction of the
Dutch Jews*
Yeshua Vigodsky, *Collected Works*

1969
Arthur Morse, *While The Six Million
Died*
Chaim Grade, *Seven Little Lanes*
1970
City of Jerusalem
1971
Abba Kovner, *Little Sister of Mine*
1972
Uri Zvi Greenberg, *Poems of the
Holocaust*
1973
I. S. L. Schneiderman, *When the
Vistula Spoke Yiddish*
Mordecai Zanin, *Collected Works on
Eastern European Jewry*
Leon Leneman, *The Tragedy of
Russian Jewry*
Abraham Sutzkever, *Poems from the
Sea of Death*
Leib Rochman, *In Your Blood You
Shall Live*
Leon Eitinger, *Psychological
Studies of the Survivors of the
Holocaust*
Mendel Mann, *Holocaust Trilogy*
Michel Borwicz, *Jewish Resistance
in Nazi Occupied Europe*
Daniel Stern, *Who Shall Live, Who
Shall Die*
Itzhak Meras, *Stalemate with Death*
1974
George Steiner, *In Bluebirds Castle*
1975
Andre Neher, *Collected
Philosophical Works*

**RICHARD AND HINDA ROSEN-
THAL FOUNDATION AWARD, FIC-
TION**—The National Institute of Arts
and Letters
For a good work of fiction that
flopped in the sales department.
Established 1957.
1957
Elizabeth Spencer, *The Voice at the
Back Door*
1958
Bernard Malamud, *The Assistant*
1959
Frederick Buechner, *The Return of
Ansel Gibbs*
1960
John Updike, *The Poorhouse Fair*

1961
  John Knowles, *A Separate Peace*
1962
  Paule Marshall, *Soul Clap Hands and Sing*
1963
  William Melvin Kelley, *A Different Drummer*
1964
  Ivan Gold, *Nickel Miseries*
1965
  Thomas Berger, *Little Big Man*
1966
  Tom Cole, *An End to Chivalry*
1967
  Thomas Pynchon, *The Crying of Lot 49*
1968
  Joyce Carol Oates, *A Garden of Earthly Delights*
1969
  Frederick Exley, *A Fan's Notes*
1970
  Jonathan Strong, *Tike and Five Stories*
1971
  Christopher Brookhouse, *Running Out*
1972
  Thomas McGuane, *The Bushwacked Piano*
1973
  Thomas Rogers, *The Confession of a Child of the Century*
1974
  Alice Walker, *In Love and Trouble*
1975
  William Gaddis, *JR*
1976
  Richard Yates, *Disturbing the Peace*
See Service, Award of Merit, The Decalogue Society of Lawyers

TASTEMAKER   AWARD—R.   T.
French Company
  The tastemakers, in this case, are cookbook authors.
  Established 1966.
1966
  Gloria Bley Miller, *The Thousand Recipe Chinese Cookbook*
1967
  Ann Seranne, editor, *America Cooks*

Jose Wilson, editor, *House and Garden's New Cook Book*
Elisabeth Lambert Ortiz, *The Complete Book of Mexican Cooking*
Helen McCully, *Nobody Ever Tells You These Things About Food and Drink*
Clementine Paddleford, *Clementine Paddleford's Cook Young*
1968
  Jean Hewitt, *New York Times Large Type Cookbook*
  Dale Brown and the editors of Time-Life Books, *American Cooking*
  Annemarie Huste, *Annemarie's Personal Cookbook*
  Better Homes and Gardens Cooking For Two
  The editors of Sunset Books and *Sunset* magazines, *Sunset Cook Book of Desserts*
1969
  Craig Claiborne, *Kitchen Primer*
  Jean Hewitt, *Main Dishes, Better Homes and Gardens Ground Meat Cook Book*
  Adi Boni, *Italian Regional Cooking*
1970
  Albert Stockli, *Splendid Fare*
  Jeanne Voltz, *California Cookbook, Sunset Oriental Cook Book*
  Michael Field, *All Manner of Food*
1971
  Craig Claiborne, *The New York Times International Cook Book*
  Jean Hewitt, *The New York Times Natural Foods Cookbook*
  Charlotte Adams, *The Four Seasons Cookbook*
  Helen Worth, *Hostess Without Help*
  Alan Hooker, *Herb Cookery*
1972
  James Beard, *American Cookery*
  Craig Claiborne and Virginia Lee, *The Chinese Cookbook*
  Beatrice Trum Hunter, *The Natural Foods Primer, Better Homes and Gardens Low-Calorie Desserts*
  Diana Kennedy, *The Cuisines of Mexico*
  Dorothy Ivens, *Pâtés & Other Marvelous Meat Loaves*
  Marian Burros and Lois Levine, *Summertime Cookbook*

Jean Anderson, author of The Doubleday Cookbook

Editors of Sunset Books and *Sunset* magazine, *Cooking With Wine*

1973

Perla Meyers, *The Seasonal Kitchen*

Marcella Hazan, *The Classic Italian Cookbook*

Diana Collier and Joan Wiener, *Bread: Making It the Natural Way*

Madeleine Kamman, *Dinner Against the Clock*

Ann Seranne, *Ann Seranne's Good Food Without Meat*

Paul Rubenstein, *Feasts for Two*

Editors of Sunset Books and *Sunset* magazine, *Sunset Ideas for Cooking Vegetables*

1974

Richard Olney, *Simple French Food*

Bernard Clayton, Jr., *The Complete Book of Breads*

Nika Hazelton, *I Cook as I Please*

Helen Corbitt Cooks for Company

Beryl M. Marton, *Diet for One, Dinner for All*

Daphne Metaxas, *Classic Greek Cooking*

1975

Jean Anderson and Elaine Hanna,

Doubleday Cookbook; Better Homes & Gardens Heritage Cook Book

Craig Claiborne, *Craig Claiborne's Favorites from The New York Times*

Jean Hewitt, *The New York Times Weekend Cookbook*

June Roth, *Salt-Free Cooking with Herbs and Spices*

Mable Hoffman, *Crockery Cookery*

Evan Jones, *American Food, The Gastronomic Story*

1976

Michel Guerard, *Cuisine Minceur*

Carol Cutler, *The Six Minute Soufflé and Other Culinary Delights*

Nika Hazelton, *The Unabridged Vegetable Cookbook*

Diana and Paul von Welanetz, *The Pleasure of Your Company*

Barbara Gibbons, *The Slim Gourmet*

Mabel Hoffman, *Crepe Cookery*

WILLIAM ALLEN WHITE CHILDREN'S BOOK AWARD—William Allen White Library, Kansas State Teachers College

A children's book award voted for by children!

Established 1952.

1953
Amos Fortune: Free Man, Elizabeth Yates

1954
Little Vic, Doris Gates

1955
Cherokee Bill: Oklahoma Pacer, Jean Bailey

1956
Brighty of the Grand Canyon, Marguerite Henry

1957
Daniel 'Coon, Phoebe Erickson

1958
White Falcon, Elliott Arnold

1959
Old Yeller, Fred Gipson

1960
Flaming Arrows, William O. Steele

1961
Henry Reed, Inc., Keith Robertson

1962
The Helen Keller Story, Catherine Owens Peare

1963
Island of the Blue Dolphins, Scott O'Dell

1964
The Incredible Journey, Sheila Burnford

1965
Bristle Face, Zachary Ball

1966
Rascal, Sterling North

1967
The Grizzle, Annabel and Edgar Johnson

1968
The Mouse and the Motorcycle, Beverly Cleary

1969
Henry Reed's Baby Sitting Service, Keith Robertson

1970
From the Mixed-Up Files of Mrs. Basil E. Frankweiler, Elaine Konigsburg

1971
Kavik, The Wolf Dog, Walter Morey

1972
Sasha, My Friend, Barbara Corcoran

1973
Trumpet of the Swan, E. B. White

1974
Mrs. Frisby and the Rats of NIMH, Robert O'Brien
The Headless Cupid, Zilpha K. Snyder

1975
Dominic, William Steig

1976
Socks, Beverly Cleary

See Women, Headliners, Women in Communications, Inc.

MORTON DAUWEN ZABEL AWARD—The National Institute of Arts and Letters
You can't just be good, you also have to be progressive, original, and experimental to win this award for poetry, fiction, or criticism.
Established 1966.

1970	George Steiner, criticism
1971	Charles Reznikoff, poetry
1972	Donald Barthelme, fiction
1973	Marjorie Hope Nicolson, criticism
1974	John Logan, poetry
1975	Charles Newman
1976	Harold Rosenberg, criticism

BROADCASTING—
Radio and Television

ACT ACHIEVEMENT AWARD—Action for Children's Television
For contributions to children's television.
Established 1971.
1976

ABC	Afterschool Specials "Multiplication Rock"
CBS	"Captain Kangaroo," "In the News," "Marshall Efron's Illustrated, Simplified and Painless Sunday School," "The CBS Children's Film Festival"
NBC	"Go-USA"
PBS	"Carrascolendas," "Hodge Podge Lodge," "Mr. Rogers' Neighborhood," "Sesame Street," "The Electric Company," "Villa Alegre," "ZOOM"
Instructional	"Bread and Butterflies," "Inside Out," "Ripples," "Self-Incorporated"
National Public Radio	"The Spider's Web"
Syndicated	"Big Blue Marble," "Call It Macroni," "Hot Fudge," "Kukla, Fran & Ollie"

See Cowboys and Indians, Western Heritage Awards, The National Cowboy Hall of Fame, and Western Heritage Center

ALFRED I. DUPONT—COLUMBIA UNIVERSITY AWARDS—Columbia University
For journalistic achievement in broadcasting.
Established 1942.

1942	Radio Station KGEI, San Francisco, Calif.
	Fulton Lewis, Jr.
1943	Radio Station WLW, Cincinnati, Ohio
	Radio Station WMAZ, Macon, Ga.
	Raymond Gram Swing
1944	Radio Station WJR, Detroit, Mich.
	Radio Station WTAG, Worcester, Mass.
	H. V. Kaltenborn
1945	Radio Station KDKA, Pittsburgh, Pa.
	Radio Station WNAX, Yanktown, S. Dak.
	Lowell Thomas
1946	Radio Station WHO, Des Moines, Iowa
	Radio Station WKY, Oklahoma City, Okla.
	Elmer Davis
1947	Radio Station WBBM, Chicago, Ill.
	Radio Station WFIL, Philadelphia, Pa.
	Edward R. Murrow
1948	Radio Station WLS, Chicago, Ill.
	Radio Station KLZ, Denver, Colo.
	Henry J. Taylor
1949	Radio Station KNOX, Knoxville, Tenn.
	Radio Station WWJ, Detroit, Mich.

Morgan Beatty
Television Station WPIX
(Special Television Award),
New York City
American Broadcasting Co.
and Association (Special
Program Award), New York
City
1950 Television Station WFIL,
Philadelphia, Pa.
Radio Station WAVZ, New
Haven, Conn.
John Cameron Swayze
1951 Stations WCAU and WCAU-
TV, Philadelphia, Pa.
Radio Station WEEI, Boston,
Mass.
Joseph C. Harsch
1952 Television Station WBNS,
Columbus, Ohio
Radio Station WMT, Cedar
Rapids, Iowa
Gerald W. Johnson
1953 Stations WBZ and WBZ-TV,
Boston, Mass.
Television Station WOI,
Ames, Iowa
Pauline Frederick
1954 Radio Station WHAS,
Louisville, Ky.
Radio Station KGAK, Gallup,
N. Mex.
Eric Sevareid
1955 Radio Station WTIC,
Hartford, Conn.
Radio Station WICC,
Bridgeport, Conn.
Howard K. Smith
1956 Television Station KNXT,
Los Angeles, Calif.
Radio Station WFMT,
Chicago, Ill.
Chet Huntley
1957 Television Station KRON,
San Francisco, Calif.
Television Station KARD,
Wichita, Kans.
Clifton Utley
1958 Television Station KLZ,
Denver, Colo.
Radio Station WSNY,
Schenectady, N.Y.
David Brinkley
1959 Television Station WNTA,
Newark, N.J.

Television Station KOLN,
Lincoln, Nebr.
David Schoenbrun
1960 Television Station KDKA,
Pittsburgh, Pa.
Radio Station WAZV, New
Haven, Conn.
Edward P. Morgan
1961 Television Station KING,
Seattle, Wash.
Radio Station KPFK, Los
Angeles, Calif.
Martin Agronsky
1962 Radio Station WFMT,
Chicago, Ill.
Television Station KVOA,
Tucson, Ariz.
Howard K. Smith
1963 Radio Station WFBM,
Indianapolis, Ind.
Television Station WJZ,
Baltimore, Md.
Louis M. Lyons
1964 Radio Station WFTV,
Orlando, Fla.
Television Station WRCV-
TV, Philadelphia, Pa.
1965 WBBM-TV, Chicago, Ill.
KTWO-TV, Casper, Wyo.
WCCO, Minneapolis, Minn.
WHCU, Ithaca, N.Y.
WRVR, New York City
Cecil Brown
WFBM-TV, Indianapolis,
Ind.
1966 no award
1967 no award
1968–1969 Dr. Everett Parker
KQED-TV, San
Francisco, Calif.
WRKL-Radio, Mount
Ivy-New City, N.Y.
NBC and "First
Tuesday"
Al Levin and the Public
Broadcast Laboratory
Don Widener and
KNBC-TV, Los
Angeles, Calif.
WSB-TV, Atlanta, Ga.
1969–1970 Kenneth A. Cox
Frederick Wiseman and
National Education
Television
John Laurence and CBS
Evening News

WCCO-TV,
Minneapolis, Minn.
Fred Freed and the
National
Broadcasting Co.
WOOD-TV, Grand
Rapids, Mich.

1970–1971   John Sharnik and CBS
News
NBC News and "First
Tuesday"
Martin Carr and NBC
News
Susan Garfield and
Group W
Geraldo Rivera and
WABC-TV, New
York, N.Y.
Diane Orr and KUTV-
TV, Salt Lake City,
Ut.

1971–1972   Fred Freed and NBC
News
Robert Markowitz and
CBS News
Group W
John Drimmer and
WNJT, Trenton, N.J.
WTVJ, Miami, Fla.
Tony Batten and
WNET/13, New York
City
Richard Thurston
Watkins and WABC-
TV, New York City
Mike Wallace
NPACT
KERA, Dallas, Tex.

1972–1973   Arthur Holch and ABC
News
Irv Drasnin and CBS
News
Robert Northshield and
NBC News
Dick Hubert and Group
W
WBBM-TV, Chicago,
Ill.
WTIC-TV, Hartford,
Conn.
KGW-TV, Portland,
Ore.
Elizabeth Drew and
NPACT

1973–1974   Av Westin and ABC
News
Don Hewitt and CBS
News
Fred Freed and NBC
News
National Public Affairs
Center for Television
KFWB Radio, Los
Angeles, Calif.
KNXT-TV, Los
Angeles, Calif.
WKY-TV, Oklahoma
City, Okla.
TVTV and WNET/13
Frederick Wiseman and
WNET/13
WPVI-TV,
Philadelphia, Pa.

1974–1975   National Public Radio
Tom Pettit and NBC
Nightly News
Don Harris and KNBC-
TV, Burbank, Calif.
WBTV, Charlotte, N.C.
WCCO-Radio,
Minneapolis, Minn.
David Moore and
WCCO-TV,
Minneapolis, Minn.
WGBH-TV, Boston,
Mass.
Warren Doremus and
WHEC-TV,
Rochester, N. Y.
Brian Ross and WKYC-
TV, Cleveland, Ohio
Clarence Jones and
WPLG-TV, Miami,
Fla.

EMMY WINNERS—The National
Academy of Television Arts and
Sciences
Television has had a difficult time
deciding on categories.
Established 1948.
1948
Most outstanding television
personality, "Shirley Dinsdale and
her puppet Judy Splinters" (KTLA)
Most popular television program.
"Pantomime Quiz Time," Mike
Stokey (KTLA)

Best film made for television, "The
Necklace"
Station award, KTLA for outstanding
overall achievement in 1948
1949
Best live show, "Ed Wynn" (KTTV)
Best kinescope show, "Texaco Star
Theatre" (KNBH, NBC)
Best children's show, "Time For
Beany" (ITLA)
Most outstanding live personality, Ed
Wynn (KTTV)
Best film made for and viewed on
television in 1949, "Life Of Riley"
(KNBH)
Most outstanding kinescoped
personality, Milton Berle (KNBH,
NBC)
Best public service, cultural or
educational program, "Crusade In
Europe" (KECA-TV and KTTV)
Best sports coverage, Wrestling
(KTLA)
1950
Best actor, Alan Young (KTTV, CBS)
Best actress, Gertrude Berg (KTTV,
CBS)
Most outstanding personality, Groucho
Marx (KNBH, NBC)
Best public service, "City at Night"
(KTLA)
Best cultural show, "Campus Chorus
and Orchestra" (KTSL)
Special events, "Departure of Marines
for Korea" (KFMB-TV San Diego
and KTLA)
Best sports program, "Rams Football"
(KNBH)
Best variety Show, "The Alan Young
Show" (KTTV, CBS)
Best educational show, "KFI-TV
University" (KFI-TV)
Best children's show, "Time For
Beany" (KTLA)
Best dramatic show, "Pulitzer Prize
Playhouse" (KECA-TV)
Best news program, "KTLA Newsreel"
Best games and audience participation
show, "Truth Or Consequences"
(KTTV, CBS)
1951
Best dramatic show, "Studio One"
(CBS)
Best comedy show, "Red Skelton
Show" (NBC)

Best variety show, "Your Show of
Shows" (NBC)
Best actor, Sid Caesar
Best actress, Imogene Coca
Best comedian or comedienne, Red
Skelton (NBC)
Special achievement awards, U.S.
Senator Estes Kefauver for
outstanding public service on
television
1952
Best dramatic program, "Robert
Montgomery Presents" (NBC)
Best variety program, "Your Show Of
Shows" (NBC)
Best public affairs program, "See It
Now" (CBS)
Best mystery, action or adventure
program, "Dragnet" (NBC)
Best situation comedy, "I Love Lucy"
(CBS)
Best audience participation, quiz, or
panel program, "What's My Line?"
(CBS)
Best children's program, "Time For
Beany" (KTLA)
Best actor, Thomas Mitchell
Best actress, Helen Hayes
Best comedian, Jimmy Durante (NBC)
Best comedienne, Lucille Ball (CBS)
Most outstanding personality, Bishop
Fulton J. Sheen (Dumont)
1953
Best dramatic program, "U.S. Steel
Hour" (ABC)
Best situation comedy, "I Love Lucy"
(CBS)
Best variety program, "Omnibus"
(CBS)
Best program of news or sports, "See It
Now" (CBS)
Best public affairs program, "Victory
At Sea" (NBC)
Best children's program, "Kukla, Fran
and Ollie" (NBC)
Best new program, "Make Room For
Daddy" (ABC); "U.S. Steel Hour"
(ABC)
Best male star of regular series, Donald
O'Connor ("Colgate Comedy Hour")
(NBC)
Best female star of regular series, Eve
Arden ("Our Miss Brooks") (CBS)
Best series supporting actor, Art
Carney ("Jackie Gleason Show")
(CBS)

Crazy comedienne Lucille Ball won her first of several Emmy awards in 1952. (Memory Shop)

Best series supporting actress, Vivian Vance ("I Love Lucy") (CBS)

Best mystery, action, or adventure program, "Dragnet" (NBC)

Best audience participation, quiz, or panel program, "This Is Your Life" (NBC); "What's My Line?" (CBS)

Most outstanding personality, Edward R. Murrow (CBS)

1954

Most outstanding new personality, George Gobel (NBC)

Best cultural, religious, or educational program, "Omnibus" (CBS)

Best sports program, "Gillette Cavalcade Of Sports" (NBC)

Best children's program, "Lassie" (CBS)

Best daytime program, "Art Linkletter's House Party" (CBS)

Best western or adventure series, "Stories of the Century" (syndicated)

Best news reporter or commentator, John Daly (ABC)

Best audience, guest participation or panel program, "This Is Your Life" (NBC)

Best actor in a single performance, Robert Cummings, "Twelve Angry Men" ("Studio One") (CBS)

Best actress in a single performance, Judith Anderson, "Macbeth" ("Hallmark Hall of Fame") (NBC)

Best male singer, Perry Como (CBS)

Best female singer, Dinah Shore (NBC)

Best supporting actor in a regular series, Art Carney ("Jackie Gleason Show") (CBS)

Best supporting actress in a regular series, Audrey Meadows ("Jackie Gleason Show") (CBS)

Best actor starring in a regular series, Danny Thomas ("Make Room For Daddy") (ABC)

Best actress starring in a regular series, Loretta Young ("Loretta Young Show") (NBC)

Best mystery or intrigue series, "Dragnet" (NBC)

Best variety series including musical varieties, "Disneyland" (ABC)

Best situation comedy series, "Make Room For Daddy" (ABC)

Best dramatic series, "United States Steel Hour" (ABC)

Best individual program of the year, "Operation Undersea" ("Disneyland") (ABC)

1955

Best children's series, "Lassie" (CBS)

Best contribution to daytime programming, "Matinee Theatre" (NBC)

Best special event or news program, "A-Bomb Coverage" (CBS)

Best documentary program (religious, informational, educational, or interview), "Omnibus" (CBS)

Best audience participation series (quiz, panel, etc.), "$64,000 Question" (CBS)

Best action or adventure series, "Disneyland" ("Davy Crockett" series, etc.) (ABC)

Best comedy series, "Phil Silvers" ("You'll Never Get Rich") (CBS)

Best variety series, "Ed Sullivan Show" (CBS)

Best music series, "Your Hit Parade" (NBC)

Best dramatic series, "Producers' Showcase" (NBC)

Best single program of the year, "Peter Pan," Mary Martin ("Producer's Showcase") (NBC)

Best actor—single performance, Lloyd Nolan as Capt. Queeg "Caine Mutiny Court Martial" ("Ford Star Jubilee") (CBS)

Best actress—single performance, Mary Martin as Peter "Peter Pan" ("Producers Showcase") (NBC)

Best actor—continuing performance, Phil Silvers as Sergeant Bilko ("Phil Silvers Show, You'll Never Get Rich") (CBS)

Best actress—continuing performance, Lucille Ball as Lucy Ricardo ("I Love Lucy") (CBS)

Best actor in supporting role, Art Carney as Ed Norton ("Honeymooners") (CBS)

Best actress in supporting role, Nanette Fabray, various roles ("Caesar's Hour") (NBC)

Best comedian, Phil Silvers (CBS)

Best comedienne, Nanette Fabray (NBC)

Best male singer, Perry Como (NBC)

Best female singer, Dinah Shore (NBC)

Best M.C. or program Host—male or female, Perry Como (NBC)

Best news commentator or reporter, Edward R. Murrow (CBS)

Best specialty act—single or group, Marcel Marceau (NBC)

1956

Best single program of the year, "Requiem For A Heavyweight" ("Playhouse 90") (CBS)

Best new program series, "Playhouse 90" (CBS)

Best series—half hour or less, "Phil Silvers Show" (CBS)

Best series—one hour or more, "Caesar's Hour" (NBC)

Best public service series, "See It Now" (CBS)

Best coverage of a newsworthy event, "Years of Crisis," Year-end report, Murrow and correspondents (CBS)

Best continuing performance by an actor in a dramatic series, Robert Young, ("Father Knows Best") (NBC)

Best continuing performance by an actress in a dramatic series, Loretta Young ("Loretta Young Show") (NBC)

Best continuing performance by a comedian in a series, Sid Caesar ("Caesar's Hour") (NBC)

Best continuing performance by a comedienne in a series, Nanette Fabray ("Caesar's Hour") (NBC)

Best single performance by an actor, Jack Palance as prizefighter "Requiem for a Heavyweight" ("Playhouse 90") (CBS)

Best single performance by an actress, Claire Trevor as Mrs. Dodsworth "Dodsworth" ("Producer's Showcase") (NBC)

Best supporting performance by an actor, Carl Reiner, various roles ("Caesar's Hour") (NBC)

Best supporting performance by an actress, Pat Carroll various roles ("Caesar's Hour") (NBC)

Best male personality—continuing performance, Perry Como (NBC)

Best female personality—continuing performance, Dinah Shore (NBC)

Best news commentator, Edward R. Murrow (CBS)

1957
Best single program of the year—
created originally or fully adapted
for television, "The Comedian"
("Playhouse 90") (CBS)
Best new program series of year,
"Seven Lively Arts" (CBS)
Best dramatic anthology series,
"Playhouse 90" (CBS)
Best dramatic series with continuing
characters, "Gunsmoke" (CBS)
Best comedy series, "Phil Silvers
Show" (CBS)
Best musical, variety, audience
participation, or quiz series, "Dinah
Shore Chevy Show" (NBC)
Best public service program or series,
"Omnibus" (ABC and NBC)
Best coverage of an unscheduled
newsworthy event, Coverage of the
Rikers Island New York plane crash
as presented on "World News
Roundup," Feb. 3 (CBS)
Best continuing performance by an
actor in a leading role, Robert Young
as Jim Anderson ("Father Knows
Best") (NBC)
Best continuing performance by an
actress in a leading role, Jane Wyatt
as Margaret Anderson ("Father
Knows Best") (NBC)
Best continuing performance (male) in
a series who essentially plays
himself, Jack Benny ("Jack Benny
Show") (CBS)
Best continuing performance (female)
in a series who essentially plays
herself, Dinah Shore ("Dinah Shore
Chevy Show") (NBC)
Best single performance—lead or
support—actor, Peter Ustinov as
Samuel Johnson "The Life of
Samuel Johnson" ("Omnibus")
(NBC)
Best single performance—lead or
support—actress, Polly Bergen as
Helen Morgan "Helen Morgan
Story" ("Playhouse 90") (CBS)
Best continuing supporting
performance by an actor, Carl Reiner
Various Roles ("Caesar's Hour")
(NBC)
Best continuing supporting
performance by an actress, Ann B.
Davis as Schultzy ("Bob Cummings

Show") (CBS and NBC)
Best news commentary, Edward R.
Murrow ("See It Now") (CBS)
1958–1959
Most outstanding single program of the
year, "An Evening With Fred
Astaire" (NBC)
Best dramatic series—one hour or
longer, "Playhouse 90" (CBS)
Best dramatic series—less than one
hour, "Alcoa-Goodyear Theatre"
(NBC)
Best comedy series, "Jack Benny
Show" (CBS)
Best musical or variety series, "Dinah
Shore Chevy Show" (NBC)
Best western series, "Maverick" (ABC)
Best public service program or series,
"Omnibus" (NBC)
Best news reporting series, "Huntley-
Brinkley Report" (NBC)
Best panel, quiz, or audience
participation series, "What's My
Line?" (CBS)
Best special dramatic program—one
hour or longer, "Little Moon Of
Alban" ("Hallmark Hall of Fame")
(NBC)
Best special musical or variety program
—one hour or longer, "An Evening
With Fred Astaire" (NBC)
Best special news program, "Face Of
Red China," Dec. 28, 1958 (CBS)
Best actor in a leading role (continuing
character) in a dramatic series,
Raymond Burr as Perry Mason
("Perry Mason") (CBS)
Best actress in a leading role
(continuing character) in a dramatic
series, Loretta Young as hostess
("Loretta Young Show") (NBC)
Best actor in a leading role (continuing
character) in a comedy series, Jack
Benny as himself ("Jack Benny
Show") (CBS)
Best actress in a leading role
(continuing character) in a comedy
series, Jane Wyatt as Margaret
Anderson ("Father Knows Best")
(CBS and NBC)
Best supporting actor (continuing
character) in a dramatic series,
Dennis Weaver as Chester
("Gunsmoke") (CBS)

Best supporting actress (continuing
character) in a dramatic series,
Barbara Hale as Della Street ("Perry
Mason") (CBS)

Best supporting actor (continuing
character) in a comedy series, Tom
Poston "Man In The Street," others
("Steve Allen Show") (NBC)

Best supporting actress (continuing
character) in a comedy series, Ann B.
Davis as Schultzy ("Bob Cummings
Show") (NBC)

Best performance by an actor
(continuing character) in a musical
or variety series, Perry Como ("Perry
Como Show") (NBC)

Best performance by an actress
(continuous character) in a musical
or variety series, Dinah Shore
("Dinah Shore Chevy Show") (NBC)

Best single performance by an actor,
Fred Astaire as Fred Astaire ("An
Evening with Fred Astaire") (NBC)

Best single performance by an actress,
Julie Harris as Brigid Mary "Little
Moon of Alban" ("Hallmark Hall of
Fame") (NBC)

Best news commentator or analyst,
Edward R. Murrow (CBS)

1959–1960

Outstanding program in the field of
humor, "Art Carney Special," Dec. 4,
1959 (NBC)

Outstanding program in the field of
drama, "Playhouse 90" (CBS)

Outstanding program in the field of
variety, "Fabulous Fifties," Jan. 31,
1960 (CBS)

Outstanding program in the field of
news, "Huntley-Brinkley Report"
(NBC)

Outstanding program in the field of
public affairs and education,
"Twentieth Century" (CBS)

Outstanding children's program,
"Huckleberry Hound" (syndicated)

Outstanding achievement in the field
of music, "Leonard Bernstein and
the New York Philharmonic" (CBS)

Outstanding single performance by an
actor, Laurence Olivier ("The Moon
and Sixpence,") Oct. 30, 1959 (NBC)

Outstanding single performance by an
actress, Ingrid Bergman "The Turn

of the Screw" ("Ford Startime"),
Oct. 20, 1959 (NBC)

Outstanding performance by an actor
in a series, Robert Stack ("The
Untouchables") (ABC)

Outstanding performance by an actress
in a series, Jane Wyatt ("Father
Knows Best") (CBS)

Outstanding performance in a variety
or musical program or series, Harry
Belafonte "Tonight with Belafonte"
("Revlon Revue"), Dec. 10, 1959
(CBS)

1960–1961

Outstanding program in the field of
humor, "Jack Benny Show" (CBS)

Outstanding program in the field of
drama, "Macbeth" ("Hallmark Hall
of Fame"), Nov. 20, 1960 (NBC)

Outstanding program in the field of
variety, "Astaire Time," Sept. 28,
1960 (NBC)

Outstanding program in the field of
news, "Huntley-Brinkley Report"
(NBC)

Outstanding program in the field of
public affairs and education, "The
Twentieth Century" (CBS)

Outstanding children's program,
"Young People's Concert" ("Aaron
Copland's Birthday Party"), Feb. 12,
1961 (CBS)

Outstanding single performance by an
actor in a leading role, Maurice
Evans "Macbeth" ("Hallmark Hall
of Fame"), Nov. 20, 1960 (NBC)

Outstanding single performance by an
actress in a leading role, Judith
Anderson "Macbeth" ("Hallmark
Hall of Fame"), Nov. 20, 1960 (NBC)

Outstanding performance by an actor
in a series (lead), Raymond Burr
("Perry Mason") (CBS)

Outstanding performance by an
Actress in a series (lead), Barbara
Stanwyck ("Barbara Stanwyck
Show") (NBC)

Outstanding performance in a
supporting role by an actor or actress
in a single program, Roddy
McDowall "Not Without Honor"
(Equitable's "American Heritage"),
Oct. 21, 1960 (NBC)

Outstanding performance in a
supporting role by an actor or actress

in a series, Don Knotts as Deputy Barney Fife ("Andy Griffith Show") (CBS)

Outstanding performance in a variety or musical program or series, Fred Astaire "Astaire Time," Sept. 28, 1960 (NBC)

The program of the year, "Macbeth" ("Hallmark Hall of Fame"), Nov. 20, 1960 (NBC)

1961–1962

Outstanding program in the field of humor, "Bob Newhart Show" (NBC)

Outstanding program in the field of drama, "The Defenders" (CBS)

Outstanding program in the fields of variety and music, "Garry Moore Show" (CBS)

"Leonard Bernstein and the New York Philharmonic In Japan," Feb. 6, 1962 (CBS)

Outstanding program in the field of news, "Huntley-Brinkley Report" (NBC)

Outstanding program in the field of educational and public affairs programming, "David Brinkley's Journal" (NBC)

Outstanding children's program, "New York Philharmonic Young People's Concerts" with Leonard Bernstein (CBS)

Outstanding single performance by an actor in a leading role, Peter Falk as truck driver "The Price of Tomatoes" ("Dick Powell Show"), Jan. 16, 1962 (NBC)

Outstanding single performance by an actress in a leading role, Julie Harris as Victoria "Victoria Regina" ("Hallmark Hall of Fame"), Nov. 30, 1961 (NBC)

Outstanding continued performance by an actor in a series (lead), E. G. Marshall as Lawrence Preston ("The Defenders") (CBS)

Outstanding continued performance by an actress in a series (lead), Shirley Booth as Hazel ("Hazel") (NBC)

Outstanding performance in a supporting role by an actor, Don Knotts as Deputy Barney Fife ("Andy Griffith Show") (CBS)

Outstanding performance in a supporting role by an actress, Pamela Brown as Duchess of Kent "Victoria Regina" ("Hallmark Hall of Fame"), Nov. 30, 1961 (NBC)

Outstanding performance in a variety or musical program or series, Carol Burnett ("Garry Moore Show") (CBS)

Outstanding daytime program, "Purex Specials For Women" (NBC)

Program of the year, "Victoria Regina" ("Hallmark Hall of Fame"), Nov. 30, 1961 (NBC)

1962–1963

Program of the year, "The Tunnel," Dec. 10, 1962 (NBC)

Outstanding program in humor, "The Dick Van Dyke Show" (CBS)

Outstanding program in drama, "The Defenders" (CBS)

Outstanding program in the field of music, "Julie and Carol at Carnegie Hall," June 11, 1962 (CBS)

Outstanding program in variety, "The Andy Williams Show" (NBC)

Outstanding program in panel, quiz, or audience participation, "G-E College Bowl" (CBS)

Outstanding children's program, "Walt Disney's Wonderful World of Color" (NBC)

Outstanding documentary program, "The Tunnel," Dec. 10, 1962 (NBC)

Outstanding program in news, "Huntley-Brinkley Report" (NBC)

Outstanding program in field of news commentary or public affairs, "David Brinkley's Journal" (NBC)

Outstanding international reporting or commentary, "Piers Anderton, Berlin Correspondent, NBC" for "The Tunnel," Dec. 10, 1962 (NBC)

Outstanding single performance by an actor in a leading role, Trevor Howard as Disraeli "The Invincible Mr. Disraeli" ("Hallmark Hall of Fame"), Apr. 4, 1963 (NBC)

Outstanding single performance by an actress in a leading role, Kim Stanley as Faith Parsons "A Cardinal Act of Mercy" ("Ben Casey"), Jan. 14 and 21, 1963 (ABC)

Outstanding continued performance by an actor in a series (lead), E. G.

Marshall as Lawrence Preston ("The Defenders") (CBS)

Outstanding continued performance by an actress in a series (lead), Shirley Booth as Hazel ("Hazel") (NBC)

Outstanding performance in a supporting role by an actor, Don Knotts as Deputy Barney Fife ("The Andy Griffith Show") (CBS)

Outstanding performance in a supporting role by an actress, Glenda Farrell as Martha Morrison ("A Cardinal Act of Mercy") ("Ben Casey"), Jan. 14 and 21, 1963 (ABC)

Outstanding performance in a variety or musical program or series, Carol Burnett "Julie and Carol at Carnegie Hall," June 11, 1962 (CBS); and "Carol and Company," Feb. 24, 1963 (CBS)

The international award, "War and Peace" (Granada TV Network Ltd. of England)

1963–1964

The program of the year, "The Making of the President 1960," Dec. 29, 1963 (ABC)

Outstanding program in comedy, "The Dick Van Dyke Show" (CBS)

Outstanding program in drama, "The Defenders" (CBS)

Outstanding program in music, "Bell Telephone Hour" (NBC)

Outstanding program in variety, "The Danny Kaye Show" (CBS)

Outstanding children's program, "Discovery '63–'64" (ABC)

Outstanding documentary program, "The Making of the President 1960," Dec. 29, 1963 (ABC)

Outstanding news report, "Huntley-Brinkley Report" (NBC)

Outstanding program in news commentary or public affairs, "Cuba: Parts I and II—The Bay of Pigs," Feb. 4, 1964; "The Missile Crisis," Feb. 9, 1964 ("NBC White Paper") (NBC)

Outstanding single performance by an actor in a leading role, Jack Klugman as Joe Larch "Blacklist" ("The Defenders"), Jan. 18, 1964 (CBS)

Outstanding single performance by an actress in a leading role, Shelley

Winters as Jenny Dworak "Two Is the Number" ("Bob Hope Presents The Chrysler Theatre"), Jan. 31, 1964 (NBC)

Outstanding continued performance by an actor in a series (lead), Dick Van Dyke as Rob Petrie ("The Dick Van Dyke Show") (CBS)

Outstanding continued performance by an actress in a series (lead), Mary Tyler Moore as Laura Petrie ("The Dick Van Dyke Show") (CBS)

Outstanding performance in a supporting role by an actor, Albert Paulsen as Lieutenant Volkovoi "One Day in the Life of Ivan Denisovich" ("Bob Hope Presents The Chrysler Theatre"), Nov. 8, 1963 (NBC)

Outstanding performance in a supporting role by an actress, Ruth White as Mrs. Mangan "Little Moon of Alban" ("Hallmark Hall of Fame"), Mar. 18, 1964 (NBC)

Outstanding performance in a variety or musical program or series, Danny Kaye ("The Danny Kaye Show") (CBS)

The international award, "Les Raisins Verts" ("Radiodiffusion Television Francais")

1964–1965

Outstanding programs in entertainment, "The Dick Van Dyke Show" (CBS); "The Magnificent Yankee" ("Hallmark Hall Of Fame"), Jan. 28, 1965 (NBC); "My Name Is Barbra," Apr. 28, 1965 (CBS); What Is Sonata Form?" ("New York Philharmonic Young People's Concerts" with Leonard Bernstein), Nov. 6, 1964 (CBS)

Outstanding individuals in entertainment (actors and performers), Leonard Bernstein ("New York Philharmonic Young People's Concerts" with Leonard Bernstein) (CBS); Lynn Fontanne as Fanny Dixwell Holmes, "The Magnificent Yankee" ("Hallmark Hall of Fame"), Jan. 28, 1965 (NBC); Alfred Lunt as Oliver Wendell Holmes, "The Magnificent Yankee" ("Hallmark Hall of Fame"), Jan. 28, 1965 (NBC); Barbra Streisand, "My

Name Is Barbra," April 28, 1965 (CBS); Dick Van Dyke as Rob Petrie ("The Dick Van Dyke Show") (CBS)

Outstanding information and sports programs, "I, Leonardo Da Vinci" ("Saga of Western Man") Feb. 23, 1965 (ABC); "The Louvre," Nov. 17, 1964 (NBC)

Outstanding individuals in news, documentaries, information, and sports (narrators), Richard Basehart, "Let My People Go," Apr. 8, 1965 (syndicated); Charles Boyer, "The Louvre," Nov. 17, 1964 (NBC)

The international award, "Le Barbier De Seville" (Canadian Broadcasting Corporation, Canada)

1965–1966

Outstanding comedy series, "The Dick Van Dyke Show" (CBS)

Outstanding variety series, "The Andy Williams Show" (NBC)

Outstanding variety special, "Chrysler Presents The Bob Hope Christmas Special," Jan. 19, 1966 (NBC)

Outstanding dramatic series, "The Fugitive" (ABC)

Outstanding dramatic program, "Ages Of Man," January 23 and 30, 1966 (CBS)

Outstanding musical program, "Frank Sinatra: A Man And His Music," Nov. 24, 1965 (NBC)

Outstanding children's program, "A Charlie Brown Christmas," Dec. 9, 1965 (CBS)

Outstanding single performance by an actor in a leading role in a drama, Cliff Robertson as Quincey Parker "The Game" ("Bob Hope Presents The Chrysler Theatre"), Sept. 15, 1965 (NBC)

Outstanding single performance by an actress in a leading role in a drama, Simone Signoret as Sara Lescaut, "A Small Rebellion" ("Bob Hope Presents The Chrysler Theatre"), Feb. 9, 1966 (NBC)

Outstanding continued performance by an actor in a leading role in a dramatic series, Bill Cosby as Alexander Scott ("I Spy") (NBC)

Outstanding continued performance by an actress in a leading role in a

dramatic series, Barbara Stanwyck as Victoria Barkley ("The Big Valley") (ABC)

Outstanding continued performance by an actor in a leading role in a comedy series, Dick Van Dyke as Rob Petrie ("The Dick Van Dyke Show") (CBS)

Outstanding continued performance by an actress in a leading role in a comedy series, Mary Tyler Moore as Laura Petrie ("The Dick Van Dyke Show") (CBS)

Outstanding performance by an actor in a supporting role in a drama, James Daly as Dr. O'Meara, "Eagle In A Cage" ("Hallmark Hall Of Fame"), Oct. 20, 1965 (NBC)

Outstanding performance by an actress in a supporting role in a drama, Lee Grant as Stella Chernak ("Peyton Place") (ABC)

Outstanding performance by an actor in a supporting role in a comedy, Don Knotts as Deputy Barney Fife, "The Return of Barney Fife" ("The Andy Griffith Show"), Jan. 10, 1966 (CBS)

Outstanding performance by an actress in a supporting role in a comedy, Alice Pearce as Gladys Kravitz ("Bewitched") (ABC)

Outstanding achievements in news and documentaries (programs), "American White Paper: United States Foreign Policy," Sept. 7, 1965 (NBC); "KKK—The Invisible Empire" ("CBS Reports"), Sept. 21, 1965 (CBS); "Senate Hearings On Vietnam," Feb. 1966 (NBC)

Outstanding daytime programs, "Camera Three" (CBS); "Mutual Of Omaha's Wild Kingdom" (NBC)

Outstanding sports programs, "ABC Wide World Of Sports" (ABC); "CBS Golf Classic" (CBS); "Shell's Wonderful World Of Golf" (NBC)

Outstanding educational television, Julia Child, instructor and hostess on "The French Chef" (NET)

The international award, "Wyvern At War—No. 2" "Breakout" (Westward Television Limited, Plymouth, England)

1966-1967
Outstanding comedy series, "The Monkees" (NBC)
Outstanding variety series, "The Andy Williams Show" (NBC)
Outstanding variety special, "The Sid Caesar, Imogene Coca, Carl Reiner, Howard Morris Special," Apr. 5, 1967 (CBS)
Oustanding dramatic series, "Mission: Impossible" (CBS)
Outstanding dramatic program, "Death of a Salesman," May 8, 1966 (CBS)
Outstanding musical program, "Brigadoon," Oct. 15, 1966 (ABC)
Outstanding children's program, "Jack And The Beanstalk," Feb. 26, 1967 (NBC)
Outstanding single performance by an actor in a leading role in a drama, "Peter Ustinov as Socrates, "Barefoot In Athens" ("Hallmark Hall of Fame"), Nov. 11, 1966 (NBC)
Outstanding single performance by an actress in a leading role in a drama, Geraldine Page as Sookie, "A Christmas Memory" ("ABC Stage 67"), Dec. 21, 1966 (ABC)
Outstanding continued performance by an actor in a leading role in a dramatic series, Bill Cosby as Alexander Scott ("I Spy") (NBC)
Outstanding continued performance by an actress in a leading role in a dramatic series, Barbara Bain as Cinnamon Carter ("Mission: Impossible") (CBS)
Outstanding continued performance by an actor in a leading role in a comedy series, Don Adams as Maxwell Smart ("Get Smart") (NBC)
Outstanding continued performance by an actress in a leading role in a comedy series, Lucille Ball as Lucy Carmichael ("The Lucy Show") (CBS)
Outstanding performance by an actor in a supporting role—drama, Eli Wallach as Locarno, "The Poppy Is Also A Flower" ("Xerox Special"), Apr. 22, 1966 (ABC)
Outstanding performance by an actress in a supporting role in a drama, Agnes Moorehead as Emma

Valentine, "Night of the Vicious Valentine" ("Wild, Wild, West"), Feb. 10, 1967 (CBS)
Outstanding performance by an actor in a supporting role—comedy, Don Knotts as Barney Fife, "Barney Comes To Mayberry" ("The Andy Griffith Show"), Jan. 23, 1967 (CBS)
Outstanding performance by an actress in a supporting role—comedy, Frances Bavier as Aunt Bee ("The Andy Griffith Show") (CBS)
Outstanding news and documentary programs, "China: The Roots Of Madness" (syndicated), Theodore H. White, writer; "Hall of Kings" Feb. 14, 1967 (ABC); "The Italians," Jan. 17, 1967 (CBS)
Outstanding daytime programming, "Mutual Of Omaha's Wild Kingdom" (NBC); Mike Douglas, master of ceremonies on "The Mike Douglas Show" (syndicated)
Outstanding sports program, "ABC'S Wide World Of Sports" (ABC)
The international award (documentary), "Big Deal At Gothenburg" (Tyne Tees Television Limited, Newcastle-upon-Tyne, England)
The international award (entertainment), "The Caretaker" (Rediffusion Television Limited, London, England)
1967-1968
Outstanding regular news programs, "Crisis In The Cities" (Public Broadcast Laboratory), Mar. 3, 1968 (NET); John Laurence and Keith Kay, CBS News correspondent and CBS news cameraman, respectively, for "First Cavalry," "Con Thien," and other segments ("CBS Evening News with Walter Cronkite"); Sept. 28, 1967, Oct. 26, 1967 and various dates of broadcast (CBS)
Outstanding coverage of special events, Frank McGee (for his commentary on satellite coverage of Adenauer's funeral, Apr. 25, 1967 (NBC)
Outstanding news documentaries, "Africa," Sept. 10, 1967 (NBC); "Summer '67: What We Learned,"

Sept. 15, 1967 (NBC); Harry Reasoner, writer of CBS reports, "What About Ronald Reagan?," Dec. 12, 1967 (CBS); Vo Huynh, cameraman on "Same Mud, Same Blood," Dec. 1, 1967 (NBC)

Outstanding achievement in cultural documentaries, CBS News Special: Eric Hoffer: "The Passionate State Of Mind" ("CBS News Hour"), Sept. 19, 1967 (CBS); "CBS News Special: Gauguin In Tahiti: The Search For Paradise" ("CBS News Hour"), Nov. 21, 1967 (CBS); John Steinbeck's "America And Americans," Dec. 3, 1967, (NBC); "Dylan Thomas: The World I Breathe" (NET Festival), Jan. 17, 1968 (NET)

Other news and documentary achievements, "The 21st Century" (various dates of broadcast) (CBS); "Science And Religion: Who Will Play God?" ("CBS News Special"), Jan. 21, 1968 (CBS)

Outstanding comedy series, "Get Smart" (NBC)

Outstanding dramatic series, "Mission Impossible" (CBS)

Outstanding dramatic program, "Elizabeth the Queen" ("Hallmark Hall Of Fame"), Jan. 31, 1968 (NBC)

Outstanding musical or variety series, "Rowan And Martin's Laugh-In" (NBC)

Outstanding musical or variety program, "Rowan And Martin's Laugh-In Special," Sept. 9, 1967 (NBC)

Outstanding single performance by an actor in leading role in drama, Melvin Douglas as Peter Schermann, "Do Not Go Gentle into That Good Night" ("CBS Playhouse"), Oct. 17, 1967 (CBS)

Outstanding single performance by an actress in leading role in drama, Maureen Stapleton as Mary O'Meaghan, "Among the Paths to Eden" ("Xerox Special"), Dec. 17, 1967 (ABC)

Outstanding continued performance by an actor in leading role in dramatic series, Bill Cosby as Alexander Scott ("I Spy") (NBC)

Outstanding continued performance by an actress in leading role in dramatic series, Barbara Bain as Cinnamon Carter ("Mission: Impossible") (CBS)

Outstanding continued performance by an actor in leading role in comedy series, Don Adams as Maxwell Smart ("Get Smart") (NBC)

Outstanding continued performance by an actress in leading role in comedy series, Lucille Ball as Lucy ("The Lucy Show") (CBS)

Outstanding performance by an actor in supporting role—drama, Milburn Stone as Doc ("Gunsmoke") (CBS)

Outstanding performance by an actress in supporting role—drama, Barbara Anderson as Officer Eve Whitfield ("Ironside") (NBC)

Outstanding performance by an actor in supporting role—comedy, Werner Klemperer as Col. Wilhelm Klink ("Hogan's Heroes") (CBS)

Outstanding performance by an actress in supporting role—comedy, Marion Lorne as Aunt Clara ("Bewitched") (ABC)

Outstanding daytime program, "Today" (NBC)

Outstanding sports programs, "ABC's Wide World of Sports" (ABC); Jim McKay, Sports Commentator on "ABC's Wide World of Sports" (ABC)

Special individual achievements, Art Carney for performances on "The Jackie Gleason Show" (CBS); Pat Paulsen for performances on "The Smothers Brothers Comedy Hour" (CBS)

The international award, "La Section Anderson" (Office de Radio-diffusion Television Francaise, O.R.T.F., Paris, France); "Call Me Daddy" ("Armchair Theatre") (ABC Television Limited, Middlesex, England)

1968-1969

Outstanding regular news programs, Coverage of hunger in the United States ("The Huntley-Brinkley Report"), Dec. 23, 1968, Feb. 17, 18–21, March 3–10, 11, 1969 (NBC);

Charles Kuralt, "On The Road" ("CBS Evening News with Walter Cronkite"), various dates of broadcast (CBS); John Laurence, correspondent for "Police After Chicago" ("CBS Evening News with Walter Cronkite"), various dates of broadcast (CBS)

Outstanding coverage of special event, coverage of Martin Luther King assassination and aftermath ("CBS News Special Reports and Special Broadcasts"), April 4–9, 1968 (CBS)

Outstanding news documentary, "CBS Reports: Hunger in America" ("CBS News Hour"), May 21, 1968 (CBS); "Law And Order," Mar. 2, 1969 ("Public Broadcast Laboratory"), (NET)

Outstanding cultural documentary, "Don't Count The Candles" ("CBS News Hour"), Mar. 26, 1968 (CBS); "Justice Black and The Bill Of Rights" ("CBS News Hour"), Dec. 3, 1968 (CBS); "Man Who Dances: Edward Villella" ("Bell Telephone Hour"), Mar. 8, 1968 (Drew Associates, Inc.) (NBC); "The Great American Novel" ("CBS News Hour"), Apr. 9, 1968 (CBS)

Outstanding comedy series, "Get Smart" (NBC)

Outstanding dramatic series, "Net Playhouse" (NET)

Outstanding dramatic program, "Teacher, Teacher" ("Hallmark Hall of Fame"), Feb. 5, 1969 (NBC)

Outstanding variety or musical series, "Rowan and Martin's Laugh-In" (NBC)

Outstanding variety or musical program, "The Bill Cosby Special," March 18, 1968 (NBC)

Outstanding single performance by actor in leading role, Paul Scofield, "Male of The Species" ("Prudential's On Stage"), Jan. 3, 1969 (NBC)

Outstanding single performance by actress in leading role, Geraldine Page ("The Thanksgiving Visitor"), Nov. 28, 1968 (ABC)

Outstanding continued performance by actor in leading role—dramatic series, Carl Betz ("Judd for the Defense") (ABC)

Outstanding continued performance by actress in leading role—dramatic series, Barbara Bain ("Mission: Impossible") (CBS)

Outstanding continued performance by actor in leading role—comedy series, Don Adams ("Get Smart") (NBC)

Outstanding continued performance by actress in leading role—comedy series, Hope Lange ("The Ghost and Mrs. Muir") (NBC)

Outstanding single performance by actress in supporting role, Anna Calder-Marshall, "Male Of The Species" ("Prudential's On Stage"), Jan. 3, 1969 (NBC)

Outstanding continued performance by actor in supporting role—series, Werner Klemperer ("Hogan's Heroes") (CBS)

Outstanding continued performance by actress in supporting role—series, Susan Saint James ("The Name Of The Game") (NBC)

Outstanding daytime program, "The Dick Cavett Show" series (ABC)

Outstanding sports program, "19th Summer Olympics Games," Oct. 12–27, 1968 (ABC)

Special classification programs, "Firing Line With William F. Buckley, Jr.," series (syndicated); "Mutual of Omaha's Wild Kingdom" series (NBC)

Special classification—individual, Arte Johnson for "Rowan And Martin's Laugh-In" series (NBC); Harvey Korman for "The Carol Burnett Show" series (CBS)

The international documentary award, "The Last Campaign Of Robert Kennedy" (Swiss Broadcasting and Television, Zurich, Switzerland)

The international entertainment award, "A Scent Of Flowers" (Canadian Broadcasting Corporation, Ontario, Canada)

1969–1970

Outstanding regular news programs, "An Investigation Of Teenage Drug Addiction—Odyssey House" ("The

Huntley-Brinkley Report"), Dec. 25–29, 1969 (NBC); "Can The World Be Saved?" ("CBS Evening News With Walter Cronkite"), various dates of broadcast (CBS)

Outstanding coverage of special events, "Apollo: A Journey To The Moon (Apollo X, XI, XII)"; May 18–26, 1969, July 14–Aug. 13, 1969, Nov. 14–27, 1969 (NBC); "Solar Eclipse: A Darkness At Noon," Mar. 7, 1970 (NBC); Walter Cronkite, reporter for "Man On The Moon: The Epic Journey Of Apollo XI," July 14–Aug. 17, 1969 (CBS)

Outstanding news documentary, "Hospital" ("NET Journal"), Feb. 2, 1970 (NET); "The Making of the President, 1968," Sept. 9, 1969 (Metromedia Producers Corporation) (CBS)

Outstanding achievement in magazine-type program, "Black Journal" series (NET)

Outstanding cultural documentary, "Arthur Rubinstein," Sept. 5, 1969 (NBC); "Fathers And Sons" ("CBS News Hour"), Aug. 12, 1969 (CBS); "The Japanese" ("CBS News Hour"), Apr. 23, 1969 (CBS)

Outstanding comedy series, "My World and Welcome to It" (NBC)

Outstanding dramatic series, "Marcus Welby, M.D." (ABC)

Outstanding dramatic program, "A Storm in Summer" (NBC) ("Hallmark Hall of Fame"), Feb. 6, 1970

Outstanding variety or musical series, "The David Frost Show" (syndicated)

Outstanding variety or musical program, "Annie, The Women in the Life of a Man" (CBS), Feb. 18, 1970; "Cinderella—National Ballet Of Canada" (NET) ("NET Festival"), Feb. 10, 1970

Outstanding new series, "Room 222" (ABC)

Outstanding single performance by actor in leading role, Peter Ustinov, "A Storm In Summer" ("Hallmark Hall of Fame"), Feb. 6, 1970 (NBC)

Outstanding single performance by actress in leading role, Patty Duke,

"My Sweet Charlie" ("World Premiere"), Jan. 20, 1970 (NBC)

Outstanding continued performance by actor in leading role—dramatic series, Robert Young ("Marcus Welby, M.D.") (ABC)

Outstanding continued performance by actress in leading role—dramatic series, Susan Hampshire ("The Forsyte Sage") (NET)

Outstanding continued performance by actor in leading role—comedy series, William Windom ("My World And Welcome To It") (NBC)

Outstanding continued performance by actress in leading role—comedy series, Hope Lange ("The Ghost And Mrs. Muir") (ABC)

Outstanding performance by actor in a supporting role—drama, James Brolin "(Marcus Welby, M.D." series) (ABC)

Outstanding performance by actress in a supporting role—drama, Gail Fisher ("Mannix" series) (CBS)

Outstanding performance by actor in a supporting role—comedy, Michael Constantine ("Rome 222" series) (ABC)

Outstanding performance by actress in a supporting role—comedy, Karen Valentine ("Room 222" series) (ABC)

Outstanding children's program, "Sesame Street" series (NET)

Outstanding daytime program, "Today" series (NBC)

Outstanding sports program, "The NFL Games" (Sept. 20, 1969–Dec. 21, 1969) (CBS)

1970–1971

Outstanding regular news program, "Five Part Investigation Of Welfare" (NBC Nightly News), Feb. 22–26, 1971 (NBC)

Outstanding coverage of special events, "CBS News Space Coverage for 1970–71," "Aquarius on the Moon: The Flight of Apollo 13," and "Ten Years Later: The Flight of Apollo 14," Apr. 11, 1970, Jan. 31–Feb. 9, 1971 (CBS)

Outstanding news documentary, "The Selling of the Pentagon" (CBS News), Feb. 23, 1971 (CBS); "The World of Charlie Company" (CBS

News), July 14, 1970 (CBS); "NBC White Paper: Pollution Is a Matter of Choice" (NBC News), Apr. 7, 1970 (NBC)

Outstanding magazine-type program, "Gulf Of Tonkin Segment" ("60 Minutes"), Mar. 16, 1971 (CBS); "The Great American Dream Machine" series (PBS)

Outstanding cultural documentary programs, "The Everglades" (NBC News), Feb. 16, 1971 (NBC); "The Making of 'Butch Cassidy and The Sundance Kid' ", Nov. 29, 1970 (NBC)

Cultural documentary programming, "Arthur Penn, 1922–: Themes And Variants", May 26, 1970 (PBS)

Outstanding series—comedy, "All in the Family" (CBS)

Outstanding series—drama, "The Senator—The Bold Ones" (NBC)

Outstanding single program—drama or comedy, "The Andersonville Trial" (Hollywood Television Theatre), May 17, 1970 (PBS)

Outstanding variety series—musical, "The Flip Wilson Show" (NBC)

Outstanding variety series—talk, "The David Frost Show" (syndicated)

Outstanding single program—variety or musical, "Singer Presents Burt Bacharach" (CBS), Mar. 14, 1971; "Leopold Stokowski" NET Festival," Apr. 28, 1970 (PBS)

Outstanding new series, "All in the Family" (CBS)

Outstanding single performance by an actor in leading role, George C. Scott, "The Price" ("Hallmark Hall of Fame"), Feb. 3, 1971 (NBC)

Outstanding single performance by an actress in leading role, Lee Grant, "The Neon Ceiling" ("World Premiere NBC Monday Night at the Movies"), Feb. 8, 1971 (NBC)

Outstanding continued performance by an actor in leading role—dramatic series, Hal Holbrook ("The Senator —The Bold Ones") (NBC)

Outstanding continued performance by an actress in leading role— dramatic series, Susan Hampshire, "The First Churchills" (Masterpiece Theatre) (PBS)

Outstanding continued performance by an actor in leading role—comedy series, Jack Klugman ("The Odd Couple") (ABC)

Outstanding continued performance by an actress in leading role— comedy series, Jean Stapleton ("All in the Family") (CBS)

Outstanding performance by actor in supporting role—drama, David Burns "The Price" ("Hallmark Hall of Fame"), Feb. 3, 1971 (NBC)

Outstanding performance by actress in supporting role—drama, Margaret Leighton, "Hamlet" ("Hallmark Hall of Fame"), Nov. 17, 1970 (NBC)

Outstanding performance by actor in supporting role—comedy, Edward Asner ("The Mary Tyler Moore Show" series) (CBS)

Outstanding performance by actress in supporting role—comedy, Valerie Harper ("The Mary Tyler Moore Show" series) (CBS)

Outstanding children's programs, "Sesame Street" series (PBS); Burr Tillstrom, performer ("Kukla, Fran And Ollie" series) (PBS)

Outstanding daytime programs, "Today" (series) (NBC)

Outstanding sports programs, "ABC'S Wide World Of Sports" series (ABC); Jim McKay, commentator "ABC'S Wide World of Sports" series (ABC); Don Meredith, commentator "NFL Monday Night Football" series (ABC)

1971–1972

Outstanding achievement within regularly scheduled news programs, "Defeat Of Dacca" ("NBC Nightly News"), Dec. 18, 1971 (NBC); Phil Brady, reporter "Defeat of Dacca" (NBC Nightly News); Bob Schieffer, Phil Jones, Don Webster, Bill Plante, correspondents "The Air War" ("CBS Evening News with Walter Cronkite"), Dec. 20–24, 1971 (CBS)

Outstanding achievement for regularly scheduled magazine-type programs, "Chronolog" series (NBC); "The Great American Dream Machine" series (PBS); Mike Wallace, correspondent "60 Minutes" series (CBS)

Outstanding coverage of special events, "The China Trip," Feb. 17–29, 1972 (ABC); "June 30, 1971, A Day for History: The Supreme Court and the Pentagon Papers," June 30, 1971 (NBC); "A Ride On The Moon: The Flight Of Apollo 15", July 16–Aug. 7, 1971 (CBS)

Outstanding documentary program, "A Night in Jail, A Day in Court" ("CBS Reports"), Jan. 27, 1972 (CBS); "This Child Is Rated X: An ABC News White Paper On Juvenile Justice," May 2, 1971 (NBC); "Hollywood: The Dream Factory" ("The Monday Night Special"); Jan. 10, 1972 (ABC); "A Sound Of Dolphins" ("The Undersea World of Jacques Cousteau"), Feb. 25, 1972 (ABC); "The Unsinkable Sea Otter" ("The Undersea World of Jacques Cousteau"), Sept. 26, 1971 (ABC)

Outstanding Series—Comedy, "All in the Family" (CBS)

Outstanding Series—Drama, "Elizabeth R" ("Masterpiece Theatre") (PBS)

Outstanding Single Program—drama or comedy, "Brian's Song" ("Movie of The Week"), Nov. 30, 1971 (ABC)

Outstanding variety series—musical, "The Carol Burnett Show" (CBS)

Outstanding variety series—talk, "The Dick Cavett Show" (ABC)

Outstanding variety or musical, "Jack Lemmon In 'S Wonderful, 'S Marvelous, 'S Gershwin" ("Bell System Family Theatre") (NBC); "Beethoven's Birthday: A Celebration In Vienna With Leonard Bernstein" (CBS)

Outstanding new series, "Elizabeth R" ("Masterpiece Theatre") (PBS)

Outstanding single performance by actor in leading role, Keith Michell "Catherine Howard" ("The Six Wives of Henry VIII"), Aug. 29, 1971 (CBS)

Outstanding single performance by actress in leading role, Glenda Jackson ("Shadow In The Sun") "Elizabeth R" ("Masterpiece Theatre"), Feb. 27, 1972 (PBS)

Outstanding continued performance by actor in leading role—dramatic series, Peter Falk "Colombo" ("NBC Mystery Movie") (NBC)

Outstanding continued performance by actress in leading role—dramatic series, Glenda Jackson, "Elizabeth R" ("Masterpiece Theatre") (PBS)

Outstanding continued performance by actor in leading role—comedy series, Carroll O'Connor "All in the Family" (CBS)

Outstanding continued performance by actress in leading role—comedy series, Jean Stapleton "All in the Family" (CBS)

Outstanding performance by actor in supporting role—drama, Jack Warden "Brian's Song" ("Movie Of The Week"), Nov. 30, 1971 (ABC)

Outstanding performance by actress in supporting role—drama, Jenny Agutter, "The Snow Goose" ("Hallmark Hall of Fame"), Nov. 15, 1971 (NBC)

Outstanding performance by actor in supporting role—comedy, Edward Asner ("The Mary Tyler Moore Show" series) (CBS)

Outstanding performance by actress in supporting role—comedy, Valerie Harper ("The Mary Tyler Moore Show" series) (CBS); Sally Struthers ("All in the Family" series) (CBS)

Outstanding achievement by a performer in music or variety, Harvey Korman ("The Carol Burnett Show" series) (CBS)

Special classification of outstanding program and individual achievement, "The Pentagon Papers" ("PBS Special"), June 21, 1971 (PBS); "The Search For The Nile—Parts I–VI," Jan. 25, Feb. 1, 15, 22 and 29, 1972 (NBC)

Outstanding sports programming, "ABC'S Wide World Of Sports" series (ABC)

Outstanding children's programming, "Sesame Street" series (PBS)

Outstanding daytime drama, "The Doctors" series (NBC)

1972–1973

Outstanding comedy series, "All in the Family" (CBS)

Outstanding drama series—
continuing, "The Waltons" (CBS)
Outstanding drama/comedy—limited
episodes, "Tom Brown's
Schooldays" ("Masterpiece Theatre;
Parts I Through V") (PBS)
Outstanding variety musical series,
"The Julie Andrews Hour" (ABC)
Outstanding single program—drama or
comedy, "A War Of Children" ("The
New CBS Tuesday Night Movies"),
Dec. 5, 1972 (CBS)
Outstanding single program—variety
and popular music, "Singer Presents
Liza With A 'Z' " Sept. 10, 1972
(NBC)
Outstanding single program—classical
music, "The Sleeping Beauty," Dec.
17, 1972 (PBS)
Outstanding new series, "America"
(NBC)
Outstanding daytime program,
"Dinah's Place" series (NBC)
Outstanding daytime drama, "The
Edge of Night" (CBS)
Outstanding single performance by
actor in leading role, Laurence
Olivier "Long Day's Journey Into
Night," Mar. 10, 1973 (ABC)
Outstanding single performance by
actress in leading role, Cloris
Leachman, "A Brand New Life,"
("Tuesday Movie Of The Week")
Feb. 20, 1973 (ABC)
Outstanding continued performance
by actor in leading role, Richard
Thomas ("The Waltons") (CBS);
Anthony Murphy, "Tom Brown's
Schooldays" ("Masterpiece Theatre;
Parts I Through V") (PBS)
Outstanding continued performance
by actress in leading role, Michael
Learned ("The Waltons") (CBS);
Susan Hampshire "Vanity Fair"
("Masterpiece Theatre; Parts I
Through V") (PBS)
Outstanding continued performance
by actor in leading role—comedy
series, Jack Klugman ("The Odd
Couple") (ABC)
Outstanding continued performance
by actress in leading role—comedy
series, Mary Tyler Moore ("The
Mary Tyler Moore Show") (CBS)

Outstanding performance by actor in
supporting role—drama, Scott
Jacoby, "That Certain Summer"
("Wednesday Movie Of The Week"),
Nov. 1, 1972 (ABC)
Outstanding performance by actress in
supporting role—drama, Ellen
Corby ("The Waltons" series) (CBS)
Outstanding performance by actor in
supporting role—comedy, Ted
Knight ("The Mary Tyler Moore
Show" series) (CBS)
Outstanding performance by actress in
supporting role—comedy, Valerie
Harper ("The Mary Tyler Moore
Show" series) (CBS)
Outstanding achievement by a
supporting performer—music or
variety, Tim Conway ("The Carol
Burnett Show") Feb. 17, 1973 (CBS)
Outstanding individual in daytime
program, Mary Fickett ("All My
Children" series) (ABC)
Outstanding children's programs,
"Sesame Street" series (PBS);
"Zoom" series (PBS); "Last Of The
Curlews" ("The ABC Afterschool
Special"), Oct. 4, 1972 (ABC)
Outstanding sports programs, "ABC'S
Wide World Of Sports" series (ABC);
"1972 Summer Olympic Games,"
Aug. 25–Sept. 11, 1972 (ABC)
Outstanding regular news program,
"The US/Soviet Wheat Deal: Is
There A Scandal?" ("CBS Evening
News with Walter Cronkite") Sept.
27–Oct. 6, 1972 (CBS)
Outstanding regular magazine-type
programs, "The Poppy Fields Of
Turkey—The Heroin Labs Of
Marseilles—The N.Y. Connection,"
Dec. 10, 1972 (CBS); "The Selling
Of Colonel Herbert," Feb. 4, 1973
(CBS); "60 Minutes" series (CBS)
Outstanding coverage of special
events, "Coverage Of The Munich
Olympic Tragedy," ("ABC
Special"), Sept. 5, 1972 (ABC); Jim
McKay, commentator "Coverage of
the Munich Olympic Tragedy"
(ABC)
Outstanding documentary program,
"The Blue Collar Trap" ("NBC
News White Paper"), June 27, 1972;
"The Mexican Connection" ("CBS

Reports"), June 25, 1972; "One Billion Dollar Weapon and Now the War Is Over—The American Military In The 70's" ("NBC Reports"), Feb. 20, 1973; "America," series (NBC); Alistair Cooke for "America" series (NBC) Hugo Van Lawick, director; "Jane Goodall And The World Of Animal Behavior," Jan. 22, 1973 (ABC)

Outstanding religious program, "Duty Bound," Mar. 11, 1973 (NBC)

1973-1974

Outstanding comedy series, "M°A°S°H" (CBS)

Outstanding drama series, "Upstairs, Downstairs" ("Masterpiece Theatre") (PBS)

Outstanding music-variety series, "The Carol Burnett Show" (CBS)

Outstanding limited series, "Columbo" ("NBC Sunday Mystery Movie") (NBC)

Outstanding special—comedy or drama, "The Autobiography Of Miss Jane Pittman," Jan. 31, 1974 (CBS)

Outstanding comedy-variety, variety, or music special, "Lily," Nov. 2, 1973 (CBS)

Outstanding children's special, "Marlo Thomas and Friends in Free To Be . . You And Me," Mar. 11, 1974 (ABC)

Best lead actor—comedy series, Alan Alda, ("M°A°S°H") (CBS)

Best lead actor—drama series, Telly Savalas, ("Kojak") (CBS)

Best lead actor—limited series, William Holden ("The Blue Knight") (NBC)

Best lead actor—drama, Hal Holbrook ("Pueblo") ("ABC Theatre"), Mar. 29, 1973 (ABC)

Actor of the year—series, Alan Alda ("M°A°S°H") (CBS)

Actor of the year—special, Hal Holbrook ("Pueblo") ("ABC Theatre"), Mar. 29, 1973

Best lead actress in comedy series, Mary Tyler Moore ("The Mary Tyler Moore Show") (CBS)

Best lead actress in drama series, Michael Learned ("The Waltons") (CBS)

Best lead actress in limited series, Mildred Natwick, "The Snoop Sisters" ("NBC Tuesday Mystery Movie") (NBC)

Best lead actress—drama, Cicely Tyson ("The Autobiography Of Miss Jane Pittman") Jan. 31, 1974 (CBS)

Actress of the year—series, Mary Tyler Moore ("The Mary Tyler Moore Show") (CBS)

Actress of the year—special, Cicely Tyson ("The Autobiography of Miss Jane Pittman") Jan. 31, 1974 (CBS)

Best supporting actor—comedy, Rob Reiner ("All in the Family" series) (CBS)

Best supporting actor—drama, Michael Moriarty ("The Glass Menagerie") Dec. 16, 1973 (ABC)

Best supporting actor—comedy-variety, variety, or music, Harvey Korman ("The Carol Burnett Show" series) (CBS)

Best supporting actor of the year, Michael Moriarty ("The Glass Menagerie") Dec. 16, 1973 (ABC)

Best supporting actress—comedy, Cloris Leachman, "The Lars Affair" ("The Mary Tyler Moore Show") Sept. 15, 1973 (CBS)

Best supporting actress—drama, Joanna Miles ("The Glass Menagerie") Dec. 16, 1973 (ABC)

Best supporting actress in comedy-variety, variety, or music, Brenda Vaccaro ("The Shape Of Things") Oct. 19, 1973 (CBS)

Best supporting actress of the year, Joanna Miles ("The Glass Menagerie") Dec. 16, 1973 (ABC)

Special classification of outstanding program and individual achievement, "The Dick Cavett Show" series (ABC); Tom Snyder, host, "Tomorrow" series (NBC)

Outstanding sports program, "ABC's Wide World Of Sports" series; Jim McKay, host, "ABC'S Wide World Of Sports" series

The international awards—nonfiction, "Horizon: The Making of a Natural History Film" (British Broadcasting Corporation, London, England)

The international awards—fiction, "La Cabina" (Television Espanola, Madrid, Spain)

Outstanding daytime drama series, "The Doctors" (NBC)

Outstanding daytime drama special, "The Other Woman" ("ABC Matinee Today"), Dec. 4, 1973.

Outstanding daytime game show, "Password" (ABC)

Outstanding daytime talk show service or variety series, "The Merv Griffin Show" (syndicated)

Outstanding daytime children's series, "Zoom," (PBS)

Outstanding daytime children's special, "Rookie of the Year" ("The ABC Afterschool Special"), Oct. 3, 1973

Best actor in daytime drama, Macdonald Carey ("Days Of Our Lives" series) (NBC); Pat O'Brien, "The Other Woman," ("ABC Matinee Today"), Dec. 4, 1973

Best daytime actor of the year, Pat O'Brien, "The Other Woman" ("ABC Matinee Today"); Dec. 4, 1973

Best actress in daytime drama, Elizabeth Hubbard ("The Doctors" series) (NBC); Cathleen Nesbitt, "The Mask Of Love" ("ABC Matinee Today"), Dec. 7, 1973

Best daytime actress of the year, Cathleen Nesbitt, "The Mask Of Love" ("ABC Matinee Today"), Dec. 7, 1973

Best daytime host or hostess in game show, Peter Marshall ("The Hollywood Squares" series) (NBC)

Best host or hostess in daytime talk, service, or variety series, Dinah Shore ("Dinah's Place") (NBC)

Best daytime host of the year, Peter Marshall ("The Hollywood Squares" series) (NBC)

Outstanding achievement within regularly scheduled news programs, "Coverage Of the October War From Israel's Northern Front" ("CBS Evening News With Walter Cronkite"), Oct. 1973; "The Agnew Resignation" ("CBS Evening News With Walter Cronkite"), Oct. 10, 1973; "The Key Biscayne Bank Charter Struggle" ("CBS Evening News With Walter Cronkite"), Oct. 15, 16, 18, 1973; "Reports On World Hunger" ("NBC Nightly News"), Mar. 1974–June 1974

Outstanding achievement for regularly scheduled magazine-type programs, "America's Nerve Gas Arsenal" ("First Tuesday"), June 5, 1973 (NBC); "The Adversaries" ("Behind The Lines"), Mar. 28, 1974 (PBS); "A Question Of Impeachment" ("Bill Moyers' Journal"), Jan. 22, 1974 (PBS)

Outstanding achievement in coverage of special events, "Watergate: The White House Transcripts," May 1, 1974 (CBS); "Watergate Coverage," May 17–November 15, 1973 (PBS)

Outstanding documentary program achievements, "Fire!" ("ABC News Close Up"), Nov. 26, 1973; "CBS News Special Report: The Senate and the Watergate Affair," May 13, 1973 (CBS)

Outstanding documentary program achievements, "Journey to the Outer Limits" ("National Geographic Society"), Jan. 10, 1974 (ABC); "The World At War" series (syndicated); "CBS Reports: The Rockefellers," Dec. 28, 1973

Outstanding interview program, "Solzhenitsyn" ("CBS News Special"), June 24, 1974 (CBS); "Henry Steele Commager," ("Bill Moyers' Journal") Mar. 26, 1974 (PBS)

Outstanding television news broadcasters, Harry Reasoner ("ABC News"), Mar. 19, 1973–June 30, 1974; Bill Moyers, "Essay on Watergate" ("Bill Moyers' Journal"), Oct. 31, 1973 (PBS)

Outstanding informational children's series, "Make a Wish" (ABC)

Outstanding informational children's special, "The Runaways," Mar. 27, 1974 (ABC)

Outstanding instructional children's program, "Inside/Out" series (syndicated)

1974-1975

Outstanding comedy series, "The Mary Tyler Moore Show" (CBS)

Outstanding drama series, "Upstairs, Downstairs" ("Masterpiece Theatre") (PBS)

Outstanding comedy-variety or music series, "The Carol Burnett Show" (CBS)

Outstanding limited series, "Benjamin Franklin" (CBS)

Outstanding special—drama or comedy, "The Law" ("NBC World Premiere Movie"), Oct. 22, 1974

Outstanding special—comedy-variety or music, "An Evening With John Denver," Mar. 10, 1975 (ABC)

Outstanding classical music program, "Profile In Music: Beverly Sills, Festival '75," Mar. 10, 1975 (PBS)

Outstanding lead actor—comedy series, Tony Randall ("The Odd Couple") (ABC)

Outstanding lead actor—drama series, Robert Blake ("Baretta") (ABC)

Outstanding lead actor—limited series, Peter Falk, "Columbo ("NBC Sunday Mystery Movie")

Outstanding lead actor in a special program—drama or comedy, Laurence Olivier, "Love Among The Ruins" ("ABC Theatre") Mar. 6, 1975

Outstanding lead actress—comedy series, Valerie Harper ("Rhoda") (CBS)

Outstanding lead actress—drama series, Jean Marsh, "Upstairs, Downstairs," ("Masterpiece Theatre") (PBS)

Outstanding lead actress in a limited series, Jessica Walter, "Amy Prentiss" ("NBC Sunday Mystery Movie") (NBC)

Outstanding lead actress in a special program—drama or comedy, Katharine Hepburn, "Love Among The Ruins," ("ABC Theatre"), Mar. 6, 1975

Outstanding continuing performance by a supporting actor—comedy series, Ed Asner ("The Mary Tyler Moore Show") (CBS)

Outstanding continuing performance by a supporting actor—drama series, Will Geer ("The Waltons") (CBS)

Outstanding continuing or single performance by supporting actor in variety or music, Jack Albertson ("Cher"), Mar. 2, 1975 (CBS)

Outstanding single performance by a supporting actor in a comedy or drama special, Anthony Quale, "QB VII—Parts 1 and 2" ("ABC Movie Special"), Apr. 29 and 30, 1974

Outstanding single performance by a supporting actor in a comedy or drama series, Patrick McGoohan, "By Dawn's Early Light, Columbo" ("NBC Sunday Mystery Movie"), Oct. 27, 1974

Outstanding continuing performance by a supporting actress—comedy series, Betty White, "The Mary Tyler Moore Show" (CBS)

Outstanding continuing performance by a supporting actress—drama series, Ellen Corby ("The Waltons") (CBS)

Outstanding continuing or single performance by a supporting actress —variety or music, Cloris Leachman ("Cher"), Mar. 2, 1975 (CBS)

Outstanding single performance by a supporting actress—comedy or drama special, Juliet Mills, "QB VII —Parts 1 and 2" ("ABC Movie Special"), Apr. 29 and 30, 1974

Outstanding single performance by a supporting actress in a comedy or drama series, Cloris Leachman, "Phyllis Whips Inflation" ("The Mary Tyler Moore Show") Jan. 18, 1975 (CBS); Zohra Lampert ("Queen of the Gypsies—Kojak") Jan. 19, 1975 (CBS)

Outstanding children's special, "Yes, Virginia, There Is a Santa Claus," Dec. 6, 1974 (ABC)

Outstanding sports event, "Jimmy Connors vs. Rod Laver Tennis Challenge," Feb. 2, 1975 (CBS)

Outstanding sports program, "Wide World Of Sports," Apr. 14, 1974 (ABC)

Outstanding sports broadcaster, Jim McKay ("Wide World Of Sports"), Apr. 14, 1974 (ABC)

Special classification of outstanding program and individual achievement, "The American Film Institute Salute To James Cagney," Mar. 18, 1974 (CBS); Alistair Cooke, host ("Masterpiece Theatre" series) (PBS)

The international awards—fiction

(1973–1974), "Mr. Axelford's Angel"
(Yorkshire Television Limited,
London, England)
The international awards-nonfiction
(1973–1974), "Aquarius: Hello
Dali!" (London Weekend Television,
London, England)
The international awards—fiction
(1974–1975), "The Evacuees"
(British Broadcasting Corp.,
London, England)
The international awards—nonfiction
(1974–1975), "Inside Story: Marek"
(British Broadcasting Corporation,
London, England)
Outstanding daytime drama series,
"The Young And The Restless"
(CBS)
Outstanding daytime drama special,
"The Girl Who Couldn't Lose"
("ABC Afternoon Playbreak"), Feb.
13, 1975
Outstanding game or audience
participation show, "Hollywood
Squares" (NBC)
Outstanding talk, service, or variety
series, "Dinah" (syndicated)
Outstanding entertainment children's
special, "Harlequin" ("The CBS
Festival Of Lively Arts For Young
People"), Apr. 10, 1974
Outstanding entertainment children's
series, "Star Trek" (NBC)
Outstanding actor in a daytime drama
series, MacDonald Carey ("Days Of
Our Lives") (NBC)
Outstanding actor in a daytime drama
special, Bradford Dillman, "The
Last Bride Of Salem" ("ABC
Afternoon Playbreak"), May 8, 1974
(ABC)
Outstanding actress in a daytime
drama series, Susan Flannery, "Days
Of Our Lives" (NBC)
Outstanding actress in a daytime
drama special, Kay Lenz, "Heart In
Hiding" ("ABC Afternoon
Playbreak"), Nov. 14, 1974
Outstanding host in a game or
audience participation show, Peter
Marshall ("The Hollywood
Squares") (NBC)
Outstanding host or hostess in a talk,
service, or variety series, Barbara
Walters ("Today") (NBC)

1975–1976
Outstanding comedy series, "The Mary
Tyler Moore Show" (CBS)
Outstanding drama series, "Police
Story" (NBC)
Outstanding comedy-variety or music
series, "NBC's Saturday Night"
(NBC)
Outstanding limited series, "Upstairs,
Downstairs" (PBS)
Outstanding special—drama or
comedy, "Eleanor And Franklin"
("ABC Theatre"), Jan. 11 and 12,
1976
Outstanding special—comedy/variety
or music, "Gypsy In My Soul," Jan.
20, 1976 (CBS)
Outstanding classical music program,
"Bernstein and the New York
Philharmonic," Nov. 26, 1975 (PBS)
Outstanding lead actor—comedy
series, Jack Albertson, "Chico and
the Man" (NBC)
Outstanding lead actor—drama series,
Peter Falk, "Columbo" ("NBC
Sunday Mystery Movie") (NBC)
Outstanding lead actor—limited series,
Hal Holbrook ("Sandburg's
Lincoln") (NBC)
Outstanding lead actor—drama or
comedy special, Anthony Hopkins,
"The Lindbergh Kidnapping Case"
("NBC World Premiere Movie"),
Feb. 26, 1976
Outstanding lead actor for a single
appearance in a drama or comedy
series, Edward Asner ("Rich Man,
Poor Man"), Feb. 1, 1976 (ABC)
Outstanding lead actress—comedy
series, Mary Tyler Moore ("The
Mary Tyler Moore Show") (CBS)
Outstanding lead actress—drama
series, Michael Learned ("The
Waltons") (CBS)
Outstanding lead actress—limited
series, Rosemary Harris, "Notorious
Woman" ("Masterpiece Theatre")
(PBS)
Outstanding lead actress in a drama or
comedy special, Susan Clark
("Babe"), Oct. 23, 1975 (CBS)
Outstanding lead actress for a single
appearance in a drama or comedy
series, Kathryn Walker ("John
Adams, Lawyer; The Adams

Chronicles"), Jan. 20, 1976 (PBS)

Outstanding continuing performance by a supporting actor—comedy series, Ted Knight ("The Mary Tyler Moore Show") (CBS)

Outstanding continuing performance by a supporting actor—drama series, Anthony Zerbe ("Harry O") (ABC)

Outstanding continuing or single performance by a supporting actor in variety or music, Chevy Chase ("NBC's Saturday Night"), Jan. 17, 1976

Outstanding single performance by a supporting actor in a comedy or drama special, Ed Flanders, "A Moon For The Misbegotten," (ABC Theatre"), May 27, 1975

Outstanding single performance by a supporting actor in a comedy or drama series, Gordon Jackson, "The Beastly Hun," "Upstairs, Downstairs" ("Masterpiece Theatre"), Jan. 18, 1976 (PBS)

Outstanding performance by a supporting actress in a comedy series, Betty White ("The Mary Tyler Moore Show") (CBS)

Outstanding continuing performance by a supporting actress in a drama series, Ellen Corby ("The Waltons") (CBS)

Outstanding continuing or single performance by a supporting actress in variety or music, Vicki Lawrence ("The Carol Burnett Show"), Feb. 7, 1976 (CBS)

Outstanding single performance by a supporting actress in a comedy or drama special, Rosemary Murphy, "Eleanor And Franklin" ("ABC Theatre"); Jan. 11 and 12, 1976 (ABC)

Outstanding single performance by a supporting actress in a comedy or drama series, Fionnuala Flanagan ("Rich Man, Poor Man"), Feb. 2, 1976 (ABC)

Outstanding children's special, "You're A Good Sport, Charlie Brown," Oct. 28, 1975 (CBS)

Outstanding live sports special, "1975 World Series," Oct. 11–12, 1975 (NBC)

Outstanding live sports series, "NFL

Monday Night Football," (ABC)

Outstanding sports personality, Jim McKay, "ABC's Wide World Of Sports, ABC's XII Winter Olympics"(ABC)

Special classification of outstanding program and individual achievement, "Bicentennial Minutes" (series) (ABC); "The Tonight Show Starring Johnny Carson" series (NBC)

Outstanding daytime drama series, "Another World" (NBC)

Outstanding daytime drama special, "First Ladies' Diaries: Edith Wilson," Jan. 20, 1976 (NBC)

Outstanding daytime game or audience participation show, "The $20,000 Pyramid" (ABC)

Outstanding daytime talk, service or variety series, "Dinah!" (syndicated)

Outstanding entertainment children's series, "Big Blue Marble" (syndicated)

Outstanding entertainment children's special, "Danny Kaye's Look-In at the Metropolitan Opera" ("The CBS Festival Of Lively Arts For Young People"); Apr. 27, 1975 (CBS)

Outstanding informational children's series, "GO" (NBC)

Outstanding informational children's special, "Happy Anniversary, Charlie Brown," Jan. 9, 1976 (CBS)

Outstanding instructional children's programming—series and specials, "Grammar Rock" (ABC)

Outstanding actor in a daytime drama series, Larry Haines, "Search For Tomorrow" (CBS)

Outstanding actor in a daytime drama special, Gerald Gordon ("First Ladies' Diaries: Rachel Jackson"), Apr. 18, 1975 (NBC); James Luisi ("First Ladies' Diaries: Martha Washington"), Oct. 23, 1975 (NBC)

Outstanding actress in a daytime drama series, Helen Gallagher ("Ryan's Hope") (ABC)

Outstanding actress in a daytime drama special, Elizabeth Hubbard ("First Ladies' Diaries: Edith Wilson"), Jan. 20, 1976 (NBC)

Outstanding host or hostess in a game or audience participation show,

Allen Ludden ("Password") (ABC)
Outstanding host or hostess in a talk,
service or variety series, Dinah Shore
("Dinah!") (syndicated)
Outstanding individual achievement
in a daytime program, Paul Lynde
("The Hollywood Squares") (NBC)
Outstanding individual achievement
in a children's program, The
Muppets ("Sesame Street") Apr. 25,
1975 (PBS)

See Journalism, Gavel Award, American Bar Association

See Journalism, Robert F. Kennedy
Journalism Awards, Robert F. Kennedy
Journalism Awards Committee

See Journalism, Murray Kramer
Award, Boston University

See Journalism, Sigma Delta Chi
Awards for Distinguished Service in
Journalism, The Society of Professional Journalists, Sigma Delta Chi

**THE LAUREL AWARD FOR TV
WRITING ACHIEVEMENT**-Writers Guild of America, West, Inc.
Same as the Laurel Award for Screen
Writing Achievement, except the
screen is smaller.
1976   Rod Serling
1977   James Fritzell and
        Everett Greenbaum

See Motion Pictures, Richard C. Craven Award, The American Humane
Association

See Motion Pictures, Patsy Awards,
The American Humane Association

See Motion Pictures, Mrs. Ann Radcliffe Award, The Count Dracula
Society

**THE GEORGE FOSTER PEABODY
BROADCASTING AWARDS**—University of Georgia
Banker George Foster Peabody (1852
–1938) didn't have much to do with
broadcasting, but he did come from
Georgia and got an honorary degree

from its university. His awards are
given in the following categories—
news (reporting, interpretation, and/or
commentary), entertainment, education, children's programs, "promotion
of international understanding," and
public service.
Established 1940.
1940
Public service by a network, CBS
Public service by a large station, Radio
Station WLW, Cincinnati, Ohio
Public service by a medium-sized
station, Radio Station WGAR,
Cleveland, Ohio
Public service by a small station, Radio
Station KRFU, Columbia, Mo.
Best reporting of the news, Elmer
Davis
1941
Outstanding reporting of the news,
Cecil Brown (CBS)
Outstanding entertainment in drama,
"Against the Storm" by Sandra
Michael and John Gibbs; "The Bill
of Rights" by Norman Corwin
Outstanding entertainment in music,
Alfred Wallenstein (Mutual)
Outstanding education program,
Chicago Round Table of the Air
(NBC)
Outstanding public service by stations,
"The International Shortwave
Broadcasters"
1942
Outstanding reporting of the news,
Charles Collingwood (CBS)
Outstanding entertainment in drama,
"The Man Behind the Gun" (CBS)
Outstanding entertainment in music,
The Standard Symphony (NBC
Pacific Coast Network)
Outstanding educational program,
"Afield with Ranger Mac," Radio
Station WHA, Madison, Wis.
Outstanding public service by a local
station, "Our Hidden Enemy—
Venereal Disease," Radio Station
KOAC, Corvalis, Ore. (Prepared by
Dr. Charles Baker for the University
of Kentucky)
Outstanding public service by a
regional station, "The Home Front,"
Radio Station WCHS, Charleston,
W.V.

1943

Outstanding community service by a regional station, "These Are American," Radio Station KNX, Los Angeles, Calif.

Outstanding community service by a local station, "Calling Longshoremen," Radio Station KYA, San Francisco, Calif.

Outstanding reporting of the news, Edward R. Murrow (CBS)

Outstanding entertainment in drama, "Lux Radio Theatre," CBS; "An Open Letter to the American People" (CBS)

Outstanding entertainment in music, "Music and The Spoken Word" (Salt Lake City Tabernacle Choir), Radio Station KSL, Salt Lake City, Ut.

Outstanding education program, "American Town Meeting," The Blue Network

Outstanding children's program, "Let's Pretend" (CBS)

Outstanding news commentary, Raymond Gram Swing (Blue Network-ABC)

Outstanding reporting of news, WLW, Cincinnati, Ohio

Outstanding entertainment in drama, "Cavalcade of America," (NBC)

Special award, "For Comedy unexcelled over a period of twelve years," Fred Allen (CBS)

Outstanding entertainment in music, "Telephone Hour," (NBC)

Outstanding education program, "Human Adventure," (Mutual)

Outstanding program for youth, "Philharmonic Young Artists Series," KFI, Los Angeles, Calif. (for outstanding development of young musicians)

Special award, "For brilliant adaptation of radio to the requirements of the armed forces and the homefront—American ingenuity on a global scale," Col. Edward M. Kirby, Chief, Radio Branch, War Department, Washington, D.C.

Outstanding public service by a regional station, "Worcester and the World," WTAG, Worcester, Mass.

Outstanding public service by a local station, Station WNYC, New York

City, and Mayor Fiorello LaGuardia; Station WIBX, Utica, N.Y., for "Cross-Roads"

1945

Outstanding reporting of the news, CBS and Paul White

Outstanding entertainment in drama, Edgar Bergen (NBC); Arch Oboler (Mutual)

Outstanding entertainment in music, "NBC Symphony of the Air" and Dr. Howard Hanson, Eastman School of Music; Station WHAM, Rochester, N.Y.

Outstanding educational program, "America's Town Meeting of the Air" (ABC) and George V. Denny, Jr.

Outstanding children's program, "We March With Faith," Station KUWH, Omaha, Neb.

Outstanding regional public service, Station KFWB, Hollywood, Calif. for its program series "Toward A Better World"

Outstanding local public service, Station KOMA, Oklahoma City, Okla. for the series "Save A Life"

1946

Outstanding public service by a regional station, Station WOW, Omaha, Nebraska for "Operation Big Muddy"

Outstanding public service by a local station, Station WELL, Battle Creek, Michigan for "Our Town"

Outstanding reporting and interpretation of the news, William L. Shirer and CBS

Outstanding entertainment in drama, "The Columbia Workshop"

Outstanding entertainment in music, The NBC "Orchestras of the Nation"

Outstanding educational program, Radio Station WMCA, New York City

1947

Outstanding public service by a regional station, Station WBBM, Chicago for "Report Uncensored"

Outstanding public service by a local station, Station KNAR, Hope, Ark. for "Disaster Broadcast from Cotton Valley"

Outstanding reporting and interpretation of the news, "CBS

Views the Press"; Elmer Davis (ABC)

Outstanding entertainment in drama, "Theatre Guild on the Air" (ABC)

Outstanding entertainment in music, The Boston Symphony Orchestra (ABC)

Outstanding educational program, CBS Documentary Unit Series

Special citation, United Nations Network for Peace for "United Nations Today"

1948

Outstanding public service by a regional station, Station KNBC, San Francisco, Calif. for "Forests Aflame"

Outstanding public service by a local station, Station WDAR, Savannah, Ga. for "You and Youth"

Outstanding reporting and interpretation of the news, Edward R. Murrow (CBS)

Outstanding entertainment in drama, "NBC University Theatre"; "The Groucho Marx Show" (ABC)

Outstanding entertainment in music, NBC for its overall contribution to the broadcasting of good music with special reference to "The NBC Symphony," "The Orchestras of the Nation," "The First Piano Quartet," and "The Boston Symphony Rehearsals"

Outstanding education program, "Communism-U.S. Brand" (ABC)

Outstanding program in the promotion of international understanding, CBS for its overall contribution with special reference to Larry LeSueur, "Memo From Lake Success," "Between the Dark and Daylight," "UN in Action," "Crusade for Children," "As Others See Us," and "An American Abroad"

Outstanding children's program, "Howdy Doody" (NBC)

Outstanding contribution to the art of television, "Actor's Studio" (ABC)

1949

RADIO

Public service by a regional station, Station WWJ (NBC), Detroit, Mich. for "Meet Your Congress," "The Best Weapon," "Protect Your

Child," and "The World Forum"

Public service by a local station, Station KXLJ (NBC), Helena, Mont. for "Legislative Highlights"

Reporting and interpretation of the news, Eric Sevareid (CBS), Washington, D.C.

Entertainment (drama), Jack Benny (CBS)

Entertainment (music), Station WQXR, New York City

Educational program, "Author Meets the Critics" (ABC)

Contribution to international understanding, "United Nations Project" (NBC)

TELEVISION

Entertainment, "The Ed Wynn Show" (CBS)

Education, "Crusade In Europe" (ABC)

Reporting and interpretation of the news, "United Nations in Action" (CBS)

Outstanding children's program, "Kukla, Fran, and Ollie" (NBC)

SPECIAL CITATIONS

To the cartoonist, H. T. Webster, for his weekly cartoon, "Unseen Audience"

To the U.N. and American Broadcasting generally, especially as represented by the National Association of Broadcasters, for broadcast contributions to better international understanding. To Harold W. Ross and *The New Yorker* for their successful Grand Central campaign in behalf of the rights of the so-called captive audience

1950

RADIO

Public service by a regional station, WBBM (CBS), Chicago, Ill. for "The Quiet Answer"

Reporting and interpretation of the news, Elmer Davis (ABC)

Entertainment (drama), "Halls of Ivy" (NBC)

Entertainment (music), Metropolitan Opera (ABC)

Educational "The Quick and the Dead" (NBC)

Winners of the Peabody Award for the outstanding children's program in 1949 were Kukla and Ollie, pictured here sans Fran. (Memory Shop)

Contribution to international understanding, "Radio Free Europe"

TELEVISION
Entertainment, Jimmy Durante (NBC)
Children's program, "Zoo Parade" (NBC); "Saturday At The Zoo" (ABC)

SPECIAL AWARDS
To ABC, its president, Robert E. Kintner, and his associates, Robert Saudek and Joseph McDonald, for their courageous stand in resisting organized pressures and their reaffirmation of basic American principles
To *Providence Journal,* its editor and publisher, Sevellon Brown, and Ben Bagdikian, reporter, for the series of articles analyzing the broadcasts of top commentators, etc.
1951
Radio educational programs, "The Nation's Nightmare" (CBS)
Radio youth programs, "*New York Times* Youth Forums" (WQXR), New York City
Radio entertainment (nonmusical), "Bob and Ray" (NBC)
Radio's contribution to international understanding, Alistair Cooke's "Letter From America," (British Broadcasting Corp.)
Television educational programs, "What in the World," WCAU (CBS), Philadelphia, Pa.
Television entertainment (music), Gian Carlo Menotti and "Amahl and the Night Visitors" (NBC)
Television entertainment (nonmusical), "Celanese Theatre" (ABC)
Television news and interpretation, Ed Murrow and "See it Now" (CBS)
Meritorious local public service by Radio, KPOJ (Mutual), Portland, Ore. for "Careers Unlimited" and "Civic Theatre on the Air"
Meritorious regional public service by radio and television, WSB (NBC), Atlanta, Georgia for "The Pastor's Study" and "Our World Today"
1952
Radio news, Martin Agronsky (ABC)

Radio music, "The New York
Philharmonic Symphony Orchestra"
(CBS); "The Standard Symphony"
(NBC)
Television education, "The Johns
Hopkins Science Review," WAAM,
Baltimore-DuMont, Md.
Television news, "Meet the Press"
(NBC)
Television entertainment, "Mister
Peepers" (NBC); "Your Hit Parade"
(NBC)
Television youth and children's
programs, "Ding Dong School"
(NBC)
Television special award, "Victory At
Sea" (NBC)
Regional public service, including
promotion of international
understanding, Radio Station WIS
(NBC), Columbia, S.C.
Local public service, Television
Station WEWS (ABC, CBS),
Cleveland, Ohio
1953
Radio news, Chet Huntley, KABC
(ABC), Los Angeles, Calif.
Television news, Gerald W. Johnson,
WAAM, Baltimore, Md.
Television music, "NBC Television
Opera Theatre"
Television entertainment, "Television
Playhouse" (NBC); Imogene Coca
(NBC)
Television education, "Cavalcade of
Books," KNXT (CBS), Los Angeles,
Calif., "Camera Three," (WCBS-TV)
New York
Television youth and children's
programs, "Mr. Wizard" (NBC)
Promotion of international
understanding through television,
"Coverage of the Coronation,"
(British Broadcasting Corp.)
Public service by a regional radio-
television station, WSB-AM-FM-TV
(NBC), Atlanta, Ga. especially for
"Removing the Rust from Radio"
and other public services, including
"You and Your Health"
Public service by a local station,
WBAW, Barnwell, S.C., especially
for "Church of Your Choice"
Special award, Edward R. Murrow
(CBS)

1954
Radio-television news, John Daly
(ABC)
Television entertainment, George
Gobel (NBC)
Television education, "Adventure"
(CBS)
Television special awards, "Omnibus"
(CBS); "The Search" (CBS)
Television—youth and children's
programs, "Disneyland" (ABC)
Television national public service,
"Industry on Parade," National
Association of Manufacturers
Television regional public service,
WJAR-TV, Providence, R.I., for
"Hurricane Carol"
Radio entertainment, "Conversation"
(NBC)
Radio education, "Man's Right to
Knowledge" (CBS)
Radio contribution to international
understanding, "Pauline Frederick
at the UN" (NBC)
Radio local public service, KGAK,
Gallup, N.M., for "The Navajo
Hour"
1955
Television news, Douglas Edwards
(CBS)
Television entertainment, Perry Como
(NBC); Jackie Gleason (CBS)
Television dramatic entertainment,
"Producers' Showcase" (NBC)
Television youth and children's
programs, "Lassie" (CBS)
Television education, Dr. Frank
Baxter, KNXT (CBS)
Radio-television music, "Voice of
Firestone" (ABC)
Radio-television public service,
Sylvester L. Weaver, Jr., NBC, for
pioneering program concepts,
especially "Monitor," "Weekday,"
"Wide Wide World," and the
"Spectaculars"
Radio-television promotion of
international understanding, Quincy
Howe (ABC)
Radio education, "Biographies in
Sound" (NBC)
Radio local public service, KIRO
(CBS), Seattle, Wash.
1956
Television news, ABC, John Charles

Daly, and their associates for coverage of the national political conventions

Television entertainment, "The Ed Sullivan Show" (CBS)

Television education, "You Are There" (CBS)

Television youth and/or children's programs, "Youth Wants to Know" (NBC)

Television public service, "World in Crisis" (CBS)

Television promotion of international understanding, "The Secret Life of Danny Kaye,"—UNICEF

Television writing, Rod Serling

Radio news, "Edward P. Morgan and the News" (ABC)

Radio entertainment, "Bob and Ray" (Mutual and NBC)

Radio education, "Books in Profile" (WNYC), New York City

Radio youth and/or children's programs, "Little Orchestra Society Concerts" (WNYC), New York City

Radio-television local-regional public service, "Regimented Raindrops," WOW, Omaha, Neb.

Special radio-television awards: Promotion of international understanding: United Nations Radio and Television; for his outstanding contribution to radio and television through his *New York Times* writings: Jack Gould

1957

Radio and television news, CBS, for depth and range, including "Face the Nation," "See It Now," "The Twentieth Century," and "This Is New York"

Television news, ABC, for "Prologue '58" and other significant news coverage by John Charles Daly and associates

Local radio-television news, Louis M. Lyons (WGBH), Boston, Mass.

Television entertainment (musical), "The Dinah Shore Chevy Show," (NBC)

Television entertainment (nonmusical), "Hallmark Hall of Fame," (NBC) with special mention of "The Green Pastures," "There Shall Be No Night," "On Borrowed

Time," "Twelfth Night," "The Lark," "Yeoman of the Guard"

Television education, "The Heritage Series," (WQED), Pittsburgh, Pa.

Local radio education, "You Are the Jury," (WKAR), East Lansing, Mich.

Television youth and children's programs, "Captain Kangaroo," (CBS)

Local television youth and children's programs, "Wunda Wunda," KING-TV (ABC), Seattle, Wash.

Television public service, "The Last Word" (CBS)

Local television public service, "Panorama" KLZ-TV (CBS), Denver, Colo.

Local radio public service, KPFA-FM, Berkeley, Calif.

Television contribution to international understanding, Bob Hope (NBC)

Special radio-television award, NBC, for its outstanding contribution to education through the series of educational programs fed to educational stations across the country, and for the "Know Your Schools" project by NBC-owned and operated stations; Westinghouse Broadcasting Company Inc. for its Boston Conference and high quality of its public service broadcasting

1958

Television news, "NBC News—The Huntley-Brinkley Report"

Television dramatic entertainment, "Playhouse 90" (CBS)

Television musical entertainment, "Lincoln Presents Leonard Bernstein and the New York Philharmonic" (CBS)

Television entertainment with humor, "The Steve Allen Show" (NBC)

Television education, "Continental Classroom" (NBC)

Television programs for youth, "College News Conference" (ABC)

Television programs for children, "The Blue Fairy," WGN-TV, Chicago, Ill.

Television contribution to international understanding, "M.D. International" (NBC)

Television public service, CBS-TV

Television writing, James Costigan for "Little Moon of Alban" on "Hallmark Hall of Fame" (NBC)

Television special awards, "An Evening with Fred Astaire" (NBC); Orson Welles, "Fountain of Youth" on "Colgate Theatre" (NBC)

Radio news, WNEW, New York City

Radio public service, "The Hidden Revolution" (CBS)

Radio education, "Standard School Broadcast," Standard Oil Co. of Calif.

Radio contribution to international understanding, "Easy as ABC," (ABC-UNESCO)

1959

Television news, "Khrushchev Abroad" (ABC)

Television entertainment (nonmusical), "The Play of The Week" (WNTA-TV), Newark, N.J.; David Susskind for "The Moon and Sixpence" (NBC)

Television entertainment (musical), "The Bell Telephone Hour" (NBC); "Great Music from Chicago" (WGN-TV), Chicago, Ill.

Television education, "The Population Explosion" (CBS); 'Decisions," (WGBH-TV and World Affairs Council), Boston, Mass.

Television contribution to international understanding, "The Ed Sullivan Show" (CBS); "Small World" (CBS)

Local television public service, WDSU-TV, New Orleans, La.

Television special awards, Dr. Frank Stanton (CBS); "The Lost Class of '59" (CBS)

Radio news, "The World Tonight" (CBS)

Radio public service, "Family Living '59" (NBC)

Local radio public service, WCCO, Minneapolis, Minn.

1960

Television news, "The Texaco Huntley-Brinkley Report" (NBC)

Television entertainment, "The Fabulous Fifties" (CBS)

Television education, NBC "White Paper" series

Television youth programs, "G-E College Bowl" (CBS)

Television children's programs, "The Shari Lewis Show" (NBC)

Television contribution to international understanding, CBS 1960 Olympic Coverage

Television public service, "CBS Reports"

Radio entertainment, WQXR, New York City, for "Musical Spectaculars" and overall programming of music

Radio children's programs, Ireene Wickler, WNYC, New York City

Radio public service, Texaco-Metropolitan Opera Network

Radio-television education, Broadcasting and Film Commission, National Council of Churches of Christ in the U.S.A., for such programs as "Look Up and Live" (CBS-TV), "Frontiers of Faith" (NBC-TV), "Pilgrimage" (ABC), and "Talk-Back" (local stations)

Locally produced radio-television programs, WOOD and WOOD-TV, Grand Rapids, Mich.; KPFK, Los Angeles, Calif.; WCKT, Miami, Fla.; and WCCO-TV, Minneapolis, Minn.

Special award, Dr. Frank Stanton (CBS)

1961

Television news, "David Brinkley's Journal" (NBC)

Television entertainment, "The Bob Newhart Show" (NBC)

Television education, "An Age of Kings" (BBC); "Vincent Van Gogh: A Self-Portrait" (NBC)

Television youth and children's programs, "Expedition!" (ABC)

Television contribution to international understanding, Walter Lippmann and CBS

Television public service, "Let Freedom Ring," KSL-TV (CBS), Salt Lake City, Utah

Radio entertainment, WFMT, Chicago, Ill., for its "Fine Arts Entertainment"

Radio entertainment, WNYC, New York City, for "The Reader's Almanac" and "Teen Age Book Talk"

Radio contribution to international

understanding, WRUL (Worldwide Broadcasting), New York City, for coverage of UN General Assembly proceedings in English and Spanish

Special award, Fred Friendly (CBS)

Special award, Capital Cities Broadcasting Corporation for "Verdict for Tomorrow: The Eichmann Trial on Television"

Special award, Newton N. Minow, chairman, Federal Communications Commission

1962

Television news, Walter Cronkite (CBS)

Television entertainment, "Du Pont Show of the Week" (NBC); Carol Burnett (CBS)

Television education, "Biography," Official Films, Inc.

Television youth and children's programs, "Exploring" (NBC); "Walt Disney" (NBC)

Television contribution to international understanding, "Adlai Stevenson Reports" (ABC)

Television public service, "A Tour of the White House with Mrs. John F. Kennedy" (CBS)

Locally produced television, "Elliott Norton Reviews," WGBH-TV, Boston, Mass.; "Books for Our Time," WNDT, New York City; and "San Francisco Pageant," KPIX-TV (ABC) San Francisco, Calif.

Radio news, WQXR, New York City

Radio entertainment, "Adventures in Good Music" (WJR), Detroit, Mich.; "The Eternal Light" (NBC)

Radio education, "Science Editor," KNX (CBS), Los Angeles, Calif.

Radio youth and children's programs, "Carnival of Books," WMAQ (NBC), Chicago, Ill.

Special award, William R. McAndrew and NBC News

Special award, TIO, NAB, for study resulting in "For the Young Viewer: Television Programming Children . . . at the Local Level"

1963

Televison news (Commentary), Eric Sevareid (CBS)

Television entertainment, "The Danny Kaye Show" (CBS); "Mr. Novak" (NBC)

Television education, "American Revolution '63" (NBC); "Saga of Western Man" (ABC)

Television youth programs, "The Dorothy Gordon Forum," (WNBC), New York City (and NBC Radio)

Television children's programs, "Treetop House," (WGN), Chicago, Ill.

Television contribution to international understanding, "Town Meeting of the World" (CBS), and Dr. Frank Stanton

Television Public Service, "CBS Reports: Storm Over the Supreme Court" (CBS)

Radio News, "Sunday Night Monitor" (NBC)

Radio Education, WLW, Cincinnati, Ohio

Radio contribution to international understanding, Voice of America and Edward R. Murrow

Radio public service, KSTP, Minneapolis, Minn.

Special award, Broadcasting industry of the U.S.A. for its coverage of President Kennedy and related events

1964

"CBS Reports"

"Profiles in Courage" (NBC)

William (Bill) H. Lawrence (ABC)

Joyce Hall for "Hallmark Hall of Fame" (NBC)

Julia Child—"The French Chef" (WGBH), Boston, Mass. (and NET)

Intertel (International Television Federation: Australian Broadcasting Corporation, Canadian Broadcasting Corporation, Rediffusion Television, Ltd., London, Westinghouse Broadcasting Company, and National Educational Television)

"Off the Cuff," WBKB (ABC), Chicago, Ill.

"Riverside Radio," (WRVR-FM), New York City

"The Louvre" (NBC)

Burr Tillstrom

The networks and the broadcasting industry "for inescapably

---

confronting the American public with the realities of racial discontent"

1965

Television news, Frank McGee (NBC); Morley Safer (CBS); and KTLA, Los Angeles, Calif.

Television entertainment, "The Julie Andrews Show" (NBC); "My Name is Barbra" (CBS); and "Frank Sinatra—A Man and His Music" (NBC)

Television education, National Educational Television (NET)

Television youth and children's programs, "A Charlie Brown Christmas" (CBS)

Television Public Service, "CBS Report: KKK—The Invisible Empire"

Television innovation, "The National Driver's Test" (CBS)

Television's most inventive art documentary, "The Mystery of Stonehenge" (CBS)

Television special award, "A Visit to Washington with Mrs. Lyndon B. Johnson—On Behalf of a More Beautiful America" (ABC)

Television contribution to international understanding, Xerox Corporation

Radio entertainment, "Music 'til Dawn" (CBS)

Radio public service, WCCO Radio, Minneapolis, Minn.

1966

Television news, Harry Reasoner (CBS)

Television entertainment, "A Christmas Memory: ABC Stage 67"

Television education, "National Geographic Specials" (CBS); "American White Paper: Organized Crime in the United States" (NBC)

Television youth and children's programs, "The World of Stuart Little" (NBC)

Television promotion of international understanding, "The Wide World of Sports" (ABC); "Siberia: A Day in Irkutsk" (NBC)

Television special awards, "Bell Telephone Hour" (NBC); Tom John for "Death of a Salesman," "The Strollin' Twenties," and "Color Me

Barbra" (CBS); "CBS Reports: The Poisoned Air;" National Educational Television

Television-radio public service, "The Dorothy Gordon Youth Forum: Youth and Narcotics—Who Has the Answer?" (WNBC-TV and NBC Radio)

Radio news, Edwin Newman (NBC)

Televison local news-entertainment, "Kup's Show" (WBKB-TV), Chicago, Ill.

Television local music, "Artists' Showcase" (WGN-TV), Chicago; "A Polish Millenium Concert" (WTMJ-TV), Milwaukee, Wis.

Television local public service, "Assignment Four" (KRON-TV), San Francisco, Calif.

Radio local public service, Elmo Ellis (WSB), Atlanta, Ga.

Radio local education, "Community Opinion" (WLIB), New York City

1967

Radio News, Elie Abel and "The World and Washington" (NBC)

Radio Education, "The Eternal Light" (NBC)

Radio-television news analysis and commentary, Eric Sevareid (CBS)

Television entertainment, "CBS Playhouse"; "An Evening at Tanglewood" (NBC)

Television youth or children's programs, "The Children's Film Festival" (CBS); "Mr. Knozit" (WIS-TV)

Television promotion of international understanding, "Africa" (ABC)

Television public service, "The Opportunity Line" (WBBM-TV)

Radio-television special awards, "Meet the Press" (NBC); Bob Hope (NBC)

Television special award, "The Ed Sullivan Show" (CBS)

Special broadcasting education award, Dr. James R. Killian, Jr., chairman, Massachusetts Institute of Technology

1968

Radio news, "Second Sunday" (NBC)

Radio education, Dr. Leonard Reiffel and "The World Tomorrow" (WEEI-CBS), Boston, Mass.

Radio entertainment, "Steinway Hall"

(WQXR), New York City

Radio public service, "Kaleidoscope" (WJR-CBS), Detroit, Mich.

Television news, Charles Kuralt and "On the Road" (CBS)

Television education, Robert Cromie and "Book Beat" (WTTW), Chicago; ABC for its creative 1968 documentaries

Television entertainment, "Playhouse" (NET)

Television youth or children's programs, "Misterogers' Neighborhood" (NET)

Television promotion of international understanding, ABC for 1968 Olympic Games

Television public service, Westinghouse Broadcasting Co. for "One National Indivisible"

Television special award, "CBS Reports: Hunger in America"

1969

Radio news, (WRNG), Atlanta, "When Will It End?"

Radio education, "On Trial: The Man in the Middle" (NBC), New York City

Radio promotion of international understanding, Voice of America, Washington, D.C.

Radio public service, "Higher Horizons" (WLIB), New York City

Television news, "Newsroom" (KQED-TV), San Francisco, Calif.; Frank Reynolds (ABC-TV), New York City

Television education, "The Advocates" (WBGH-TV), Boston, Mass. (and KCET), Los Angeles, Calif.; "Who Killed Lake Erie?" (NBC-TV) New York City

Television entertainment, "Experiment in Television" (NBC-TV), New York City; Curt Gowdy for sports coverage

Television youth or children's programs, Children's Television Workshop, New York City, "Sesame Street"

Television promotion of international understanding "The Japanese" (CBS-TV), New York City

Network television public service, Tom Pettit (NBC-TV), New York

City, for investigative reporting

Local television public service, "The Negro in Indianapolis" (WFBM-TV), Indianapolis, Ind.

Television special award for writing, "J.T." (CBS-TV)

Television special award, Chet Huntley, for his contributions to television news

Special individual award, Bing Crosby, for his outstanding service to broadcasting

1970

Radio news, "Jordan Reports" (NBC Radio), New York City, Douglas Kiker

Radio education, "The Danger Within: A Study of Disunity in America" (NBC Radio)

Radio youth or children's programs, "Listening/4" (WFBE-FM), Flint, Mich.

Radio promotion of international understanding, Voice of America, Garry Moore

Radio public service, WAHT, Lebanon, Pa., "Medical Viewpoint" and "Pearl Harbor, Lest We Forget"

Television news, "60 Minutes" (CBS-TV), New York City

Television news, "Politithon '70" (WPBT), Miami, Fla.

Television entertainment, "Flip Wilson Show" (NBC-TV)

Television entertainment, "Evening at Pops" (PBS), Washington, D.C.

Television entertainment, "The Andersonville Trial," (PBS and KCET), Los Angeles, Calif.

Television education, "Eye of the Storm" (ABC-TV)

Television youth or children's program, "Hot Dog" (NBC-TV); The Dr. Seuss Programs (CBS-TV)

Television promotion of international understanding, "Civilisation" (BBC-TV); "This New Frontier" (WWL-TV), New Orleans, La.

Television public service, "Peace . . . On Our Time: KMEX-TV and The Death of Ruben Salazar"(KMEX-TV), Los Angeles, Calif.; "Migrant: An NBC White Paper" (NBC-TV) New York City

Television special award, "The Selling

of the Pentagon" (CBS-TV), New
York City
1971
Broadcast news, John Rich (NBC
Radio and Television), New York
City
Radio education, "Wisconsin on the
Move," (WHA), Madison, Wis.
Radio youth or children's programs,
"Junior Town Meeting of the Air"
(WWVA), Wheeling, W. Va.
Radio promotion of international
understanding, Voice of America,
Washington, D.C.
Radio public service, "Second
Sunday" (NBC-Radio), New York
City
Radio special award, "The Heart of the
Matter" (WCCO-Radio),
Minneapolis, Minn.; Arthur Godfrey
(CBS-Radio), New York City
Television entertainment, NBC-TV,
New York City, for dramatic
programming; "The American
Revolution: 1770–1783, A
Conversation with Lord North"
(CBS-TV), New York City; "Brian's
Song" (ABC-TV), New York City,
and William Blinn
Television youth or children's
programs, "Make A Wish" (ABC-TV
News)
Television education, "The Turned On
Crisis" (WQED), Pittsburgh, Pa.
Special television education,
Mississippi Authority for
Educational Television and
executive director William Smith,
Jackson, Miss.
Television promotion of international
understanding, "United Nations Day
Concert with Pablo Casals," United
Nations Television, New York City
Television public service, "This Child
is Rated X" (NBC-TV), New York
City
Special television award, George
Heinemann (NBC-TV)
Special award, Dr. Frank Stanton
(CBS)
1972
RADIO
NBC Radio Network, NBC Monitor,
for its return to more traditional
forms of radio programming

KOAC, Corvallis, Oreg., for the
program, "Conversations With Will
Shakespeare and Certain of his
Friends"
Washington, D.C., Schools Radio
Project, for "The Noise Show," an
innovative use of radio in education
KGW, Portland, Ore., for "Open
Door," providing youth an
opportunity to express views about
religious values
Broadcasting Foundation of
America, New York City, for
programs promoting international
understanding
Voice of America, for outstanding
coverage of the American political
conventions and national election,
distributed to a worldwide audience
Group W, New York City, for
"Breakdown," a critical examination
of the nation's most crucial problems
NBC and NBC-owned and operated
stations, for "No-Fault Insurance—
Right Road or Wrong?" and "Second
Sunday: Seven-Part Series on Cities"
National Public Radio, Washington,
D.C., for "All Things Considered,"
an innovative use of investigative
reporting

TELEVISION
Bill Monroe, Washington editor of
the "Today" show, NBC-TV, for his
excellence in news reporting
CBS-TV, for "The Waltons," a
sensitive dramatic interpretation of
life during the Depression
NBC-TV, for three special programs
devoted to Twentieth Century
American music: "Jack Lemmon in
'S Wonderful, 'S Marvelous, 'S
Gershwin;" "Singer Presents Liza
With a Z;" and "The Timex All-Star
Swing Festival"
WHRO-TV, Norfolk, Va., for its
overall classroom programming as
evidenced by "Animals and Such,"
"Writing Time," "People Puzzle,"
and "Dollar Date—A Matter of
Choice"
BBC and NBC-TV, for "The Search
for the Nile," an outstanding series

of documentaries depicting the thirty-five-year search for the source of the Nile River

ABC-TV, for "ABC Afterschool Specials," an innovative series for young people

CBS-TV, for "Captain Kangaroo," a long-running show for young children

WNET, New York, and BBC, for "The Restless Earth," and outstanding use of television as a medium for the promotion of international understanding

WWL-TV, New Orleans, for "China '72: A Hole in the Bamboo Curtain," one of the first non-network documentaries about life in China

NBC-TV, for "Pensions: The Broken Promise," an investigative documentary about the private pension system

WABC-TV, New York, for "Willowbrook: The Last Great Disgrace," a documentary about living conditions of the mentally retarded

ABC-TV, for "XX Olympiad," an outstanding example of a network's coverage of a worldwide sports event

Alistair Cooke, British social historian, for a meaningful perspective look at America in a series presented by BBC & NBC

1973
RADIO
News, A personal award to Lowell Thomas for his contributions to broadcast news

Entertainment, "Lyric Opera Live Broadcasts" and "Music in Chicago" Series (WFMT) Chicago, Ill.; "Project 1 Experiment" for "The Carpenters—Live in Concert" and "Helen Reddy—Live in Concert" (NBC-Radio), New York City

Education, "Second Sunday" for "Communism in the 70's" and "A Right to Death" (NBC-Radio), New York City; "The American Past: Introduction" (KANU-FM), Lawrence, Kans.

Promotion of International

Understanding, "From 18th Street: Destination Peking" (WIND), Chicago, Ill.

Public Service, "Marijuana and the Law" (KNOW), Austin, Tex.

TELEVISION
News, "Close-Up" (ABC News) Special News Award, Peter Lisagor of the *Chicago Daily News* for his contribution to broadcast news

Entertainment, "Myshkin" WTIU, Bloomington, Ind.; a joint award to NBC-TV, ABC-TV, and CBS-TV for their outstanding contributions to television drama as evidenced by "Red Pony" (NBC-TV); "Pueblo" and "The Glass Menagerie" (ABC-TV for ABC-TV Theatre); "CBS Playhouse 90": "*The Catholics*" (CBS-TV)

Education, ABC-TV for its contribution to education as evidenced by "The First and Essential Freedom," "Learning Can be Fun" and "Dusty's Treehouse" (KNXT), Los Angeles, Calif.

Youth and Children, "The Borrowers" ("Hallmark Hall of Fame"), and "Street of the Flower Boxes" "NBC Children's Theatre" (NBC-TV)

Promotion of international understanding, WCAU-TV, "Overture to Friendship: The Philadelphia Orchestra in China" (WCAU-TV)

Public Service, "Home Rule Campaign" (WRC-NBC-TV); a personal award to Pamela Ilott of CBS News for "Lamp Unto My Feet" and "Look Up and Live"

TV Special Award, "The Energy Crisis ... An American White Paper" (NBC-TV)

Special Sports Award, Joe Garagiola, "The Baseball World of Joe Garagiola" (NBC-TV)

1974
KTW-Radio, Seattle, Wash., for "The Hit and Run Players," a satirical series of vignettes that "gives distinguished testimony to the creative vigor characterizing American radio today"

CBS-Radio Network, New York City, for "The CBS Radio Mystery Theatre," which was recognized for "its outstanding effort in the field of contemporary radio drama"

NBC-Radio Network, New York City for the "Second Sunday" series, which was characterized as "a truly noteworthy use of the documentary form in radio"

KFAC-Radio, Los Angeles, Calif., for "Through the Looking Glass," a program designed to introduce young people to classical music, "a subject that has been sadly neglected in broadcasting"

"Conversations from Wingspread," produced by the Johnson Foundation, Racine, Wis., for distribution to radio stations which "distinguished itself in promoting international understanding"

WSB-Radio, Atlanta, Ga., for its "exceptional use of radio in approaching community problems as evidenced by "Suffer the Little Children," "Atlanta: A Portrait in Black and White," and "Henry Aaron: A Man with a Mission"

WMAL-Radio, Washington, D.C., for "Battles Just Begun," "an extraordinary utilization of the entire range of its public affairs capabilities to deal with the problems of the Vietnam veteran"

WNBC-Radio, New York City for "Pledge a Job," which attacked the problem of unemployment in its listening area, "an innovative and effective effort"

WCKT-TV, Miami, Fla., for "a superb series of investigative reports which brought considerable response and change"

NBC Television Network, New York City, for "the distinguished variety and quality of its dramatic programs, as evidenced by "The Execution of Private Slovik," "The Law," and "IBM Presents Clarence Darrow"

CBS Television Network, New York City, for "the exceptionally well done four-part series of dramatic specials based on the life of Benjamin Franklin"

WNET and the Public Broadcasting Service, Washington, D.C., for "bringing 'The Theatre in America' to national television, giving the viewer the finest in regional American theatre"

WGBH-TV, Boston, Mass., "for the exceptional 'NOVA' series, recognizing particularly those programs which were produced in the United States"

ABC Television Network, New York City, for "Free to Be . . . You and Me," a program for young people which the board said "meets the highest standards for excellence both in its production quality and in its concept"

NBC Television Network, New York City, for "Go!," an action-oriented program for children which the board found to be "consistently of the best to be found in today's television world for children"

KING-TV, Seattle, Wash., for "How Come?," a "well-paced, fully literate program which neither talks down to nor over the level of the young audience for which it is intended"

WCCO-TV, Minneapolis, Minn., for "From Belfast with Love," "a superb effort to promote understanding of the situation in Northern Ireland"

ABC Television Network, New York City, for "Sadat: Action Biography," the story of the personal and public life of this pivotal mid-East leader, which the board found to be "exceptionally well done, particularly by interviewer Peter Jennings"

NBC Television Network, New York City, for "Tornado! 4:40 P.M., Xenia, Ohio," "not only for its dramatic impact but for its searching analysis of how the community reacted in the months following"

NPACT—The National Public Affairs Center for Television, Washington, D.C., for "its outstanding overall effort to bring

meaningful public affairs programming to the nation"

KPRC-TV, Houston, Tex., for "The Right Man," the story of the dedication of one man, Dr. Robert Hayes (president of Wiley College) both to a school and to his fellow man, which the board found to be a rewarding, innovative, and exceptionally well done television documentary"

Carl Stern of NBC News, New York City for his "exceptional journalistic enterprise during a time of national crisis"

Fred Graham of CBS News, New York City, for his "thoroughly professional and consistently penetrating reporting during a time of national crisis"

Marilyn Baker, San Francisco, Calif., for her work as an "investigative reporter of the highest order" during the time she was a staff member of KQED-TV

Julian Goodman, Chairman of the Board of the National Broadcasting Company for "his outstanding work in the area of first amendment rights and privileges for broadcasting"

1975

RADIO

Jim Laurie, NBC News, for "his series of outstanding reports covering the fall of Vietnam by remaining in Saigon after the evacuation was completed"

KMOX Radio, St. Louis, for "Sleeping Watchdogs," "an outstanding series of innovative investigative reports into government boards established to protect the consumer"

WGMS, Bethesda, Md. and WGMS-FM, Washington, D.C., for "their combined overall efforts to provide outstanding radio entertainment, as exemplified by 'The Collector's Shelf' and '200 Years of Music in America'"

The Standard School Broadcast, San Francisco, Calif., for "forty-seven years of continuous educational radio service to the citizens of the Far West, making this broadcast the nation's oldest, continuous educational radio program"

WFMT, Chicago, Ill., for "Music in Chicago: Stravinsky '75," "a superlative program which gave listeners a musical treat of the highest order"

WSOU (FM), South Orange, N.J., the student station of Seton Hall University, for "Land of Poetry," a particularly innovative Halloween radio treat which brought young listeners a worthwhile listening experience

VOICE OF AMERICA, Washington, D.C., for "The Battle of Lexington," as part of the excellent series "200 Years Ago Tonight" produced to give listeners overseas insight into what has made America great

WCBS Radio, New York City, for "A Life to Share" which, together with free seminars to aid parents in the study of child development made this one of the great radio public service efforts of the year

KDKB, Mesa, Ariz., for "outstanding contributions to the community it serves through its superior overall public service programming"

WMAL Radio, Washington, D.C., for "overall excellence in the radio documentary as exemplified by "Suffer the Little Children" and "The Legend of the Bermuda Triangle"

TELEVISION

WTOP-TV, Washington, D.C., for "their overall public service effort with particular reference to "Harambee: For My People" and "Everywoman: The Hidden World"

WCKT-TV, Miami, Fla., for "compiling an envious record of outstanding investigative reporting during 1975"

Charles Kuralt, CBS News, New York City, for "On the Road to '76" a first-rate effort to acquaint Americans

with what each state is really like in a prebicentennial year

KABC-TV, Los Angeles, Calif., for "The Dale Car: A Dream or A Nightmare" as a fine example of how an enterprising television news operation can successfully serve the community interests and needs by exposing a notorious con game

CBS-TV, New York City, for "M°A°S°H," a creative entertainment effort that has delighted millions of Americans with first-rate humor

ABC-TV, New York City, for "ABC Theatre: Love Among the Ruins" as television entertainment programming of the highest order

NBC-TV, New York City, for "Weekend," a new and refreshing approach to television programming, providing the viewer with a quality experience

WCVB-TV, Boston, Mass., for "a viewer-oriented programming package which exhibits a quality of service too rarely seen in today's television"

GROUP W, New York, for "Call It Macroni," "a first-rate series of children's programs which permits children to expand their minds through the discovery of new life styles and adventures"

ABC-TV, New York City, for "The ABC Afterschool Specials" that, as a series, has opened new frontiers of children's television programming

Kaiser Broadcasting, San Francisco, Calif., for "Snipets" as an excellent way in which children can learn from television with brief and to-the-point educational and instructional vignettes

Alphaventure, New York City, for "Big Blue Marble," a program which makes children very much aware of the world that lies beyond the borders of the United States

CBS News, New York City, for "Mr. Rooney Goes To Washington," a program that rendered an outstanding and meritorious service

to the citizens of this nation

WWL-TV, New Orleans, for "A Sunday Journal," a locally produced magazine-concept program that reflects the finest in local television

CBS News, New York City, for "The American Assassins," as a shining example of what quality broadcasting service to the American public can be

WAPA-TV, San Juan, Puerto Rico, for "Las Rosas Blancas," reflecting local television drama at its finest

Dr. James Killian, Boston, Mass., for "his outstanding contributions to educational television in the United States"

1977

"Sybil," NBC

"Eleanor and Franklin," ABC

South Carolina Educational Radio Network for "American Popular Song with Alex Wilder and Friends" series

Associated Press Radio for "Garden Plot; Food as a Weapon"

WGIR AM-FM, Manchester, N.H., for "Flashbacks 1976"

WNET-13, New York, for "The Adams Chronicles"

WLBT, Jackson, Miss., for "Power Politics in Mississippi"

Franklin McMahon, WBBM, Chicago, Ill., for "Primary Colors"

Charles Bathold, WHO, Des Moines, Iowa

Hughes Rudd and Bruce Morton, "CBS Morning News"

Sy Pearlman, NBC, New York, for "Weekends' 'Sawyer Brothers' "

KCET-28, Los Angeles, for "Visions"

ABC Sports for "1976 Summer Olympic Games"

Tomorrow Entertainment, Inc., New York, for "Judge Horton and The Scottsboro Boys"

CBS News for "Sixty Minutes"

WETA, Washington, D.C., for "A Conversation with Jimmy Carter"

Perry Como for his Christmas show in Austria

KERA, Dallas, Tex., for "A Thirst in The Garden"

Jim Karayan and the League of Women

Voters, Washington, D.C., for "76 Presidential Debates"

TELEVISION-RADIO   AWARDS—
Writers Guild of America, West, Inc.
To honor superlative scripts on television and radio.
1966
Best written anthology, "The Game," S. Lee Pogostin, "Chrysler Theatre"
Best written comedy, "You Ought to be in Pictures," "Dick Van Dyke," Jack Winter
Best written comedy variety, "The Road to Lebanon," "Danny Thomas Special," Garry Marshall, Jerry Belson
Best written dramatic-episodic, "No Justice for the Judge," "Trials of O'Brien," David Ellis
Best written adaptation, "Lamp at Midnight," "Hallmark Hall of Fame," Robert Hartung
Best written documentary, "The Great Love Affair," CBS News Special, Andrew A. Rooney, Richard Ellison
Best written radio, "The Legend of Le Manh," Voice of America, Sol Panitz
1967
Best written anthology (including adaptations), "Crazier Than Cotton," "Chrysler Theatre," S. Lee Pogostin
Best written comedy-episodic, "Movies Are Better Than Ever," "Honeymooners—Jackie Gleason Show," Marvin Marx, Walter Stone, and Gordon Rod Parker
Best written comedy-nonepisodic, "The Sid Caesar, Imogene Coca, Carl Reiner, Howard Morris Special," CBS Special, Mel Brooks, Sam Denoff, Bill Persky, Carl Reiner, and Mel Tolkin
Best written dramatic-episodic, "The City on the Edge of Forever," "Star Trek," Harlan Ellison
Best written current events documentary, "The Battle for Asia, Part 1, Thailand: The New Front," "NBC News," Robert Rogers
Best written feature documentary, "The Legend of Marilyn Monroe," Theodore Strauss and Terry Sanders
Best written radio, "A Deadly Mistake," "WCBS News Special,"

Peter Woititz
Special award, "The Long, Long Curfew," "Jewish-Federation Council Commitment" series KNXT, Shimon Wincelberg
1968
Best written anthology including adaptations, "Heidi," "NBC Special," Earl Hamner
Best written comedy-episodic, "Viva Smart," "Get Smart," Bill Idelson and Sam Bobrick
Best written comedy-nonepisodic, "Alan King's Wonderful World of Aggravation," "Kraft Music Hall," Sam Bobrick, Ron Clark, Danny Simon, Marty Farrell, and Martin Ragaway
Best written dramatic-episodic, "To Kill a Madman," "Judd for the Defense," Robert Lewin
Best written current events documentary, "Hunger in America," "CBS Reports," Peter Davis and Martin Carr
Best written feature documentary, "Africa," James Fleming, Blaine Littell, and Richard E. Siemanowski (ABC); "Black History—Lost, Strayed or Stolen," CBS, Perry Wolff and Andrew Rooney
Best written radio, "The Problem Children," Susan A. Meyer (WINS)
1969
Best anthology (including adaptations), "Sadbird," "CBS Playhouse," George Bellak
Best comedy episodic, "Funny Boy," "Room 222," Allan Burns
Best dramatic episodic, "An Elephant in a Cigar Box," "Judd for the Defense," Robert Lewin
Best variety, "Norman Rockwell's America," NBC Special, Herbert Baker and Treva Silverman
Best current events documentary, "Fathers and Sons," Harry E. Morgan (CBS)
Best feature documentary, "Max Brod: Portrait of an Artist in his Own Right," "Directions," Shimon Wincelberg (ABC); "The Ship that Wouldn't Die: The USS Franklin," Special Projects, David Davidson (NBC)

Best radio, "No Matter Where You Are," Salvation Army, Robert Juhren

1970

Best anthology (including adaptations), "Tribes," "ABC Movie of the Week," Tracy Keenan Wynn and Marvin Schwartz

Best comedy episodic, "The Valediction," "Room 222," Richard Deroy

Best dramatic episodic, "A Continual Roar of Musketry," NBC, "The Bold Ones," David Rintels

Best variety, "Annie, the Women in the Life of a Man," "Monsanto Nights," Gary Belkin, Peter Bellwood, Thomas Meehan, Herb Sargent, and Judith Viorst

Best current events documentary, "Survival on the Prairie," NBC News, Craig B. Fisher

Best feature documentary, "Gertrude Stein: A Biography," Marianna Morris (NET)

Best radio, "Guerrilla Warfare in Cairo, Illinois: There Are Three Sides to Every Story," (WBBM-FM) Michael Hirsch

1971

Best original anthology, "The Neon Ceiling," "NBC World Premiere," story by Carol Sobieski, screenplay by Carol Sobieski and Howard Rodman

Best adapted anthology, "Brian's Song," William Blinn, "ABC Movie of the Week," based on the book by Gale Sayers

Best comedy episodic, "Thoroughly Unmilitant Mary," "Mary Tyler Moore Show," Martin Cohan (CBS)

Best dramatic episodic, "Par for the Course," Thomas Y. Drake, Herb Bermann, Jerrold Freedman, and Bo May, "The Psychiatrist," story by Thomas Y. Drake (NBC)

Best variety, "The Carol Burnett Show (with Rita Hayworth and James Bailey)," Don Hinkley, Jack Mendelsohn, Stan Hart, Larry Siegel, Woody Kling, Roger Beatty, Arnie Rosen, Kenny Solms, and Gail Parent with writing supervised by Arthur Julian (CBS)

Best current events documentary, "The Selling of the Pentagon," "CBS Reports," Peter F. Davis

Best feature documentary, "An Essay on War," "The Great American Dream Machine," Andrew A. Rooney (NET)

Best radio, "A Walk with Two Shadows," "Voice of America," Sol Panitz; "America the Violent," "2nd Sunday," Edward Hanna (NBC)

1972

Best original anthology, "That Certain Summer," "ABC Movie of the Week," Richard Levinson and William Link

Best adapted anthology, "The Night Stalker," "ABC Movie of the Week," Richard Matheson, novel by Jeff Rice

Best comedy episodic, "Chief Surgeon Who," "M*A*S*H," Larry Gelbart (CBS)

Best dramatic episodic, "King of the Mountain," "Kung Fu," Herman Miller (ABC)

Best variety, "The Trouble with People," "Bell System Family," special, Neil Simon (NBC)

Best current events documentary, "Suffer the Little Children," "NBC News Special," Robert Northshield (NBC)

Best feature documentary, "Guilty by Reason of Race," Robert Northshield (NBC)

Best TV news, "CBS Evening News with Walter Cronkite," Charles West, Rabun Matthews, Gary Gates, and John Merriman (CBS); "Land Fury; The Six O'Clock Report," WCBS-TV News, Richard Cannon (CBS)

Best daytime serial, "Love of Life," Loring Mandel, Nancy Ford, Louis Ringwald, and Max Mc Clellan (CBS)

Best radio, "The Firebrand," USIA, Sol Panitz

Best radio news, "Flashback, 1972," Paul Flynn (WABC Radio); "The Reasoner Report: A Maddened Minority," Joe Cook (ABC Radio)

1973

Best original anthology, "The Marcus-Nelson Murders," "CBS Movie of the Week," Abby Mann (CBS)

Best adapted anthology, "Sunshine," "CBS Movie of the Week," from *Journal of Jacquelyn M. Helton,* Carol Sobieski (CBS)

Best comedy episodic, "Walter's Problem, Part II," "Maude," Bob Weiskopf and Bob Schiller

Best dramatic episodic, "Phoenix Without Ashes," "The Starlost," Harlan Ellison (NBC)

Best variety, "The Burns and Schreiber Comedy Hour,"Norman Barasch, Jack Burns, Avery Schreiber, Bob Ellison, Bob Garland, Carroll Moore, and George Yanok (ABC)

1974

Best original anthology, "The Law," Joel Oliansky, story by William Sackheim and Joel Oliansky, "NBC World Premiere" (NBC)

Best adapted anthology, "The Autobiography of Miss Jane Pittman," Tracy Keenan Wynn, novel by Ernest J. Gaines, "CBS Movie of the Week" (CBS)

Best comedy episodic, "O.R.," "M*A*S*H," Larry Gelbart, Laurence Marks (CBS)

Best dramatic episodic, "Thirty a Month and Found," "Gunsmoke," M. Byrnes (CBS)

Best variety, "The Carol Burnett Show (with Ken Berry and Carl Reiner)," Gary Belkin, Roger Beatty, Arnie Kogen, Bill Richmond, Gene Perret, Rudy Luca, Barry Levinson, Dick Clair, Barry Harman, and Jenna McMahon (CBS)

Best variety special, "Alan King's Energy Crisis, Rising Prices and Assorted Vices Comedy Hour," Norman Steinberg, Alan Uger, Howard Albreeht, Sol Weinstein, John Boni, Thad Mumford, Chevy Chase, Herb Sargent, and Alan King (ABC)

Best current events documentary, "The Palestinians," Edward Stringer (CBS)

Best feature documentary, "The Right to Die," Marlene Sanders (ABC)

Best TV news, "Two Presidents— Transition in the White House," Charles West (CBS)

Best daytime serial, "Search for Tomorrow," Ann Marcus, Joyce Perry, Jerry Adelman, and Ray Goldstone (CBS)

Best radio, "Summer on a Mountain of Spices," EARPLAY/PBS, Harvey Jacobs

Best radio news, "Voices in the Headlines," ABC

1975

Best original anthology, "Queen of the Stardust Ballroom," Jerome Kass, "CBS Special" (CBS)

Best adapted anthology, "Fear on Trial," David W. Rintels, based on book by John Henry Faulk, "CBS Movie of the Week" (CBS); "Hustling," Fay Kanin, based on the book by Gail Sheehy, "ABC Movie of the Week" (ABC)

Best comedy episodic, "Welcome to Korea," "M*A*S*H," Everett Greenbaum, Jim Fritzell, Larry Gelbart (CBS)

Best dramatic episodic, "Prior Consent," "The Law," Arthur Ross, story by Stephen Kandel (NBC)

Best variety, "Lily," Sybil Adelman, Barbara Gallagher, Gloria Banta, Pat Nardo, Stuart Birnbaum, Matt Newman, Lorne Michaels, Marilyn Miller, Earl Pomerantz, Rosie Ruthchild, Lily Tomlin, Jane Wagner (ABC)

Best children's show, "The Superlative Horse," Anna Brandt (CBS)

Best current event documentary, "Mr. Rooney Goes to Washington," Andrew Rooney (CBS)

Best feature documentary, "The Guns of Autumn," V. Drasnin (CBS)

Best TV News, "CBS Evening News," Apr. 29, 1975, Sandor Polster, William H. Moran, Carol Ross (CBS)

Best daytime serial, "Ryan's Hope," Claire Labine, Paul Mayer, Mary Munisteri, Allan Leicht (ABC)

Best radio, "The American Inheritance," Norman Morris, Dale Minor (CBS)

1976

Best original anthology, "The Quality of Mercy," Robert Collins (NBC)

Best adapted anthology, "Sybil,"

Stewart Stern (NBC)
Best comedy episode, "Dear Sigmund," "M*A*S*H," Alan Alda (CBS)
Best dramatic episode, "Crossing the River," Loring Mandel

See Women, Headliners, Women in Communications, Inc.

BUSINESS, ECONOMICS, INDUSTRY

JOHN BATES CLARK AWARD—
American Economic Association
  Presented every two years, this award is for an association member, under 40, who has contributed to the pool of economic knowledge.
  Established 1947.

1947	Paul A. Samuelson
1949	Kenneth E. Boulding
1951	Milton Friedman
1953	no award
1955	James Tobin
1957	Kenneth J. Arrow
1959	Lawrence R. Klein
1961	Robert M. Solow
1963	Hendrik S. Houthakker
1965	Zvi Griliches
1967	Gary S. Becker
1969	Marc Leon Nerlove
1971	Dale W. Jorgenson
1973	Franklin M. Fisher
1975	Daniel McFadden

CORPORATE SOCIAL RESPONSIBILITY ADVERTISING AWARDS—
Esquire magazine (with the University of Michigan's Department of Journalism)
  Esquire describes its award best: ". . . . we salute the vanguard of far-sighted companies who have demonstrated a high degree of social consciousness in addressing themselves to the pressing problems that confront society: ecology, the environment, pollution, credibility gaps, consumerism, etc."
  Established 1972 (temporarily discontinued).

1973	Metropolitan Life Insurance Co.
	Chemical Bank
	IBM
	Xerox Corp.
	Abraham & Straus
	American Motors Corp.
	AT&T
	Atlantic Richfield Co.
	Dow Chemical Co.
	Eastman Kodak Co.
	Ford Motor Co.
	General Motors Corp.
	Halsted & Co.
	Hawaiian Electric Co.
	Mobil Oil Corp.
	National Shawmut Bank of Boston
	Northern States Power Co.
	Owens-Corning Fiberglas Corp.
	Seagram Distillers Co.
	Westinghouse Broadcasting Co.
1974	City of Baltimore

Houston Public Library
Atlantic Richfield Co.
   IBM
Timme Furs
Abbott Laboratories
Bacardi Imports
Chase Manhattan Bank
Crane Co.
Fisher-Price Toys
Knight Newspapers
Pharmaceutical
   Manufacturers Association
The Travelers Insurance
   Companies
Globetrotter
   Communications, Inc.
Liberty National Life
   Insurance Co.
Polaroid Corp.
U.S. Brewers Association
Group W
New York Telephone Co.
State Farm Insurance
   Companies
Worcester County National
   Bank
1975   Exxon Corp.
IBM
St. Regis Paper
Texaco Inc.
Kellogg Co.
American Can Co.
Atlantic Richfield Co.
Blue Cross of Western
   Pennsylvania
Swissair
Eastman Kodak Co.
Continental Oil Co.
WLS-TV
Central Telephone & Utilities
   Co.
Commuter Computer
Metropolitan Life Insurance
   Co.
First National City Bank
The Babcock & Wilcox Co.
Phillips Petroleum Co.
The Standard Oil Company
   of Ohio
Caterpillar Tractor Co.

See Education, Dow Jones Award,
American Assembly of Collegiate
Schools of Business

See Education, Western Electric Fund
Award, American Assembly of Collegiate Schools of Business

EXECUTIVE OF THE YEAR—The
National Management Association
   First you have to be an American industrialist. Then you have to have contributed toward "the preservation and
advancement of the free enterprise system." And then you must have con-
ducted your "personal and business
affairs in keeping with NMA's Code of
Ethics." Meet the qualifications and
you have a shot at being "Executive of
the Year."
   Established 1935.
1935
   C. L. Proctor, Toledo Edison Co.
1936
   Frank H. Adams, Surface
   Combustion Co.
1937
   A. M. Degner, Surface Combustion
   Co.
1938
   C. C. Kendrick, Met 'L' Wood Corp.
1939
   Harry H. Woodhead, Consolidated
   Vultee Aircraft Corp.
1940
   George Spatta, Clark Equipment Co.
1941
   S. C. Allyn, National Cash Register
   Co.
1942
   C. E. Wilson, General Motors Corp.
1943
   J. A. Robertshaw, Robertshaw-
   Fulton Controls
1944
   C. R. Hook, Armco Steel Corp.
1945
   J. H. Kindelberger, North American
   Aviation, Inc.
1946
   Robert E. Gross, Lockheed Aircraft
   Corp.
1947
   Fred Maytag, II, The Maytag Co.
1948
   W. D. Robinson, Briggs
   Manufacturing Co.

1949
George R. Fink, Great Lakes Steel Corp.
1950
Frank H. Irelan, Delco Products Div., GMC
1951
Robert F. Loetscher, Farley & Loetscher Mfg. Co.
1952
Mason M. Roberts, General Motors Corp.
1953
Ralph S. Damon, Trans World Airlines
1954
John T. Beatty, United Specialties Co.
1955
Alva W. Phelps, The Oliver Corp.
1956
Gen. J. T. Mc Narney, Convair
1957
Gen. H. F. Safford, The Ohio Rubber Co.
1958
Thomas E. Millsop, National Steel Corp.
1959
George Romney, American Motors Corp.
1960
Thomas W. Martin, Alabama Power Co.
1961
John Mihalic, Avco Corp.
1962
Frank J. Schaeffer, National Tube Div., U.S. Steel Corp.
1963
Albrecht M. Lederer, A.M. Lederer & Co., Inc.
1964
Floyd D. Gottwald, Ethyl Corp.
1965
Charles C. Gates, Jr., Gates Rubber Co.
1966
Daniel J. Haughton, Lockheed Aircraft Corp.
1967
Russell De Young, The Goodyear Tire & Rubber Co.

1968
Lynn A. Townsend, Chrysler Corp.
1969
D. C. Burnham, Westinghouse Electric Corp.
1970
Robert G. Dunlop, Sun Oil Corp.
1971
George H. Weyerhaeuser, Weyerhaeuser Co.
1972
Frederick G. Jaicks, Inland Steel Co.
1973
Melvin C. Holm, Carrier Corp.
1974
W. Michael Blumenthal, The Bendix Corp.
1975
Willard F. Rockwell, Rockwell International Corp.
1976
William Plummer Drake, Pennwalt Corp.

RAILROAD MAN OF THE YEAR—
Modern Railroads magazine
This prize evolved from being a readers' poll. That ran into problems, since the top executive of the company with the most *MR* magazine readers got the most votes. Now it is based on a staff selection of the individual who was the "key mover" in the most important event in railroading during the previous year.
Established 1964.
1964
D. W. Brosnan, Southern Railway System
1965
Stuart T. Saunders, Pennsylvania Railroad Co.
1966
Stuart T. Saunders, Pennsylvania Railroad Co.
1967
Louis W. Menk, Northern Pacific Railway
1968
William B. Johnson, Illinois Central Railroad
1969
John W. Barriger, Missouri-Kansas-Texas Railroad

1970
John S. Reed, Atchison, Topeka &
Santa Fe Railway Co.
1971
Jervis Langdon, Jr., Penn Central
Transportation Co.
1972
Charles Luna, United
Transportation Union
1973
James W. Germany, Southern Pacific
Transportation Co.
1974
L. Stanley Crane, Southern Railway
System
1975
Frank E. Barnett, Union Pacific
Railroad

1976
Dr. William J. Harris, Jr., Association
of American Railroads

FRANCIS A. WALKER MEDAL—
American Economic Association
The association hands out this award
every five years for a member's career
contribution to economics.
Established 1947.

1947	Wesley C. Mitchell
1952	John Maurice Clark
1957	Frank H. Knight
1962	Jacob Viner
1967	Alvin H. Hansen
1972	Theodore W. Schultz

COWBOYS and INDIANS

THE CHEROKEE HALL OF FAME
—The Cherokee National Historical
Society, Inc.
This honor goes to a deceased indi-
vidual of Cherokee descent who influ-
enced and made significant contribu-
tions to the United States.
Established 1971.

| 1971 | Robert Latham Owen |
| 1972 | James Joseph Clark |

WESTERN HERITAGE AWARDS—
The National Cowboy Hall of Fame
and Western Heritage Center
For creations—in factual television,
fictional television, documentary, movies, music, art books, novels, juvenile
books, nonfiction books, magazine articles, short stories, or poetry—that "best
portray the high principles, spirit, and
individual achievements of the developing west."
Established 1960.

THEATRICAL MOTION PICTURES
1961
The Alamo, Batjac-United Artist

1962
The Comancheros, 20th Century-Fox
1963
The Man Who Shot Liberty Valance,
Paramount Pictures
1964
How the West Was Won, Cinerama-
MGM
1965
Cheyenne Autumn, Warner Brothers
1966
Sons of Katie Elder, Paramount-Hal
Wallis
1967
Appaloosa, Universal Pictures
1968
The War Wagon, Universal Pictures
1969
Will Penny, Paramount Pictures
1970
True Grit, Hal Wallis and Paramount
Pictures
1971
A Man Called Horse, Cinema Center
Films-National General Pictures
1972
The Cowboys, Warner Brothers

Shown with a cowboy's best friend is Robert Redford, disguised as Jeremiah Johnson. (Memory Shop)

1973
   Jeremiah Johnson, Warner Brothers
1974
   The New Land, Warner Brothers
1975   no award
1976
   Bite the Bullet

FACTUAL TELEVISION
   PROGRAMS
1961
   "The Great Lounsberry Scoop,"
   "Death Valley Days"
1962
   "The Real West," "Project 20"
1963
   "The Hat That Wore The West,"
   "Death Valley Days"
1964
   "American Cowboy," "Discovery
   '63"
1965
   "The Hanging Judge," WKY-TV
   "They Went That-a-Way," Wolper
   Productions
1966
   "Custer to the Little Big Horn," ABC

"The Journals of Lewis and Clark,"
NBC
1967
   "An Iron Horse in Silver Pastures,"
   "Discovery"
1968
   "The End of the Trail," "Project
   Twenty"
1969
   "The Bonanza Years," KRON-TV
1970
   "The West of Charles Russell,"
   "Project Twenty"
1971
   "The Last of the Westerners," ABC
   News
1972   no award
1973
   "Gone West," "The America Series"
1974
   "Conrad Schwiering—Mountain
   Painter," KTWO-TV
1975
   "The American Parade: The 34th
   Star," CBS
1976
   "I Will Fight No More Forever,"
   ABC

FICTION TELEVISION PROGRAMS

1961
"Incident at Dragoon Crossing," "Rawhide"
1962
"The Sendoff," "Rawhide"
1963
"The Contender," "Stoney Burke"
1964
"Incident of Iron Bull," "Rawhide"
1965
"Corporal Dasovik," "Rawhide"
1966
"The Horse Fighter," "The Virginian"
1967
"The Intruders," "The Monroes"
"Deathwatch," "Gunsmoke"
1968
"Bitter Autumn," "The Virginian"
1969
"The Buffalo Soldiers," "The High Chaparral"
1970
"The Wish," "Bonanza"
1971
"Run, Simon, Run," ABC Movie of the Week
1972
"Pike" "Gunsmoke"
1973
"Hec," "Hec Ramsey"
1974
"Pioneer Woman," ABC Movie of the Week
1975
"The Little House on the Prairie," NBC
1976
"The Macahans," MGM-TV

WESTERN DOCUMENTARY FILMS

1961
Four Seasons West, Max Howe Film Productions for South Dakota Stockgrowers Assn.
1962
101, WKY-TV
1963
Appaloosa, Fred Rice Productions for Appaloosa Horse Club of America

1964
Pioneer Painter, WKY-TV
1965
Age of the Buffalo, National Film Board of Canada
1966
The Beautiful Tree, Chishkale, University of California Extension Media Center
1967
The Five Civilized Tribes, KTUL-TV
1968
Colorado: Prehistoric Man, Barbre Productions Inc. for State Historical Society of Colorado
Time of the West, Guggenheim Productions, Inc.
1969
Born to Buck, Casey Tibbs Productions
1970
The Golden Spike, Barbre Production, Inc.
1971
Rodeo, Concepts Unlimited, Inc. and Contemporary Films/McGraw Hill
1972
The Last of the Wild Mustangs, Leo Leo Burnett Co. for Marlboro Cigarettes
1973
Bighorn, Marty Stouffer
1974
The Great American Cowboy, Kieth Merrill
1975
Goin' Down the Road, Kieth Merrill
1976
Red Sunday: The Battle of the Little Big Horn, Pyramid Films

NONFICTION BOOKS

1961   no award
1962
The American Heritage Book of Indians, Alvin M. Josephy, Jr. (editor)
1963
Where the West Stayed Young, John Rolph Burroughs
1964
Furs by Astor, John Upton Terrell

1965
  Standing Up Country, C. Gregory Crampton
1966
  The American Heritage History of the Great West, Alvin M. Josephy, Jr., (editor)
1967
  Gold Fever, George W. Groh
1968
  America's Western Frontiers, John A. Hawgood
1969
  The Cattle Towns, Robert Dykstra
  The Enduring Navajo, Laura Gilpin
1970
  The Great Platte River Road, Merrill J. Mattes
1971
  The Great Range Wars, Harry Sinclair Drago
1972
  North America Divided: The Mexican War, Odie B. Faulk and Seymour V. Connor
1973
  The Time of the Buffalo, Tom McHugh
  Carson Valley, Grace Dangberg
  Crimsoned Prairie, S. L. A. Marshall
1974
  Bell Ranch As I Knew It, George Ellis
  Will Rogers: The Man and His Times, Richard Ketchum
  Owyhee Trails, Mike Hanley and Ellis Lucia
  Colorado Summer/Fall/Winter/ Spring, Dave Muench and N. Scott Momaday
1975
  The Warren Wagontrain Raid, Benjamin Capps
  Idaho—A Pictorial Overview, Robert O. Beatty
  Born Grown, Roy P. Stewart
  Colonel Greene and the Copper Skyrocket, C. S. Sonnichsen
  The American, Margaret Sanborn
1976
  Fifty Great Westner Illustrators, Jeff C. Dykes
  Charles F. Lummis: The Man and His West, Keith Lummis
  Butte's Memory Book, Don James

NOVELS
1961   no award
1962
  The Shadow Catcher, James D. Horan
1963
  Fire on the Mountain, Edward Abbey
1964
  Honor Thy Father, Robert Roripaugh
1965
  Little Big Man, Thomas Berger
1966
  Mountain Man, Vardis Fisher
1967
  They Came to a Valley, Bill Gulick
1968
  North to Yesterday, Robert Flynn
1969
  The Buffalo Runners, Fred Grove
1970
  The White Man's Road, Benjamin Capps
1971
  Arfive, A. B. Guthrie
1972
  Pike's Peak: A Family Saga, Frank Waters
1973
  Chiricahua, Will Henry
1974
  The Time It Never Rained, Elmer Kelton
1975
  Centennial, James Michener
1976   no award

JUVENILE BOOKS
1961   no award
1962
  King of the Mountain, Gene Caesar
1963
  The Book of the West, Charles Clifton
1964
  Killer-Of-Death, Betty Baker
1965
  The Greatest Cattle Drive, Paul Wellman
1966
  The Land Rush, Carl G. Hodges
1967
  Mustang: Wild Spirit of the West, Marguerite Henry

1968
Down the Rivers, Westward Ho!,
Eric Scott
1969
Edge of Two Worlds, Weyman Jones
1970
An Awful Name to Live Up To,
Jessie Hosford
1971
And One Was A Wooden Indian,
Betty Baker
1972
The Black Mustanger, Richard
Wormser
1973
Famous American Explorers, Bern
Keating
1974   no award
1975
Susy's Scoundrel, Harold Keith
1976
Owl in the Cedar Tree, Natachee
Scott Momaday

ART BOOKS
1961   no award
1962   no award
1963   no award
1964   no award
1965   no award
1966   no award
1967   no award
1968
*George Caleb Bingham: The
Evolution of an Artist,* E. Maurice
Bloch
1969
The Cowboy in Art, Ed Ainsworth
1970
Olaf Wieghorst, William Reed
1971
*The Story of Harvey Dunn, Artist:
Where Your Heart Is,* Robert
Karolevitz
1972
The Art of the Old West, Paul Rossi
and David Hunt
1973
*Harold Von Schmidt Draws and
Paints the Old West,* Walt Reed
1974
The Lure of the Great West, Frank
Getlein
1975
Edward Borein Cowboy Artist,

Harold Davidson
1976
*Hans Kleiber: Artist of the Bighorn
Mountains,* Emmie D. Mygatt and
Roberta Cheney

MAGAZINE ARTICLES, SHORT
   STORIES, OR POETRY
1961
"The Old Chisholm Trail," *Kiwanis*
"All Legal and Proper," *Ellery
Queen*
1962
"Comanche Son," *Boy's Life* "The
Look of the Last Frontier," *American
Heritage*
1963
"The Prairie Schooner Got Them
There," *American Heritage*
1964
"Nine Years Among the Indians,"
Frontier Times
1965
"Titans of Western Art," *The
American Scene*
1966
"How Lost Was Zebulon Pike,"
American Heritage
1967
"The Red Man's Last Struggle,"
Empire
1968
"The Snows of Rimrock Ridge," *The
Farm Quarterly*
1969
"W. R. Leigh: The Artist's Studio
Collection," *The American Scene*
1970
"Bennett Howell's Cow Country,"
Frontier Times
1971
"Cattle, Guns, and Cowboys,"
Arizona Highways
1972
"Echoes of the Little Bighorn,"
American Heritage
1973
"Horses of the West," *Arizona
Highways*
1974
"40 Years Gatherins'," *The Dude
Ranch*
1975
"George Humphreys, Half Century
with 6666," *Quarter House Journal*

1976
"The Pioneer Woman—Image in
Bronze," *American Art Review*

MUSIC
1961
"The Alamo," Dimitri Tiomkin
1962
"Charles Russell Contata," William
J. May
1963   no award
1964
"How the West Was Won," Alfred
Newman and Ken Darby
1965
"Damon's Road," Herschel Burke
Gilbert
1966
"Hallelujah Trail," Elmer Bernstein
1967   no award
1968
"The End of the Trail," Robert
Russel Bennett
1969   no award
1970
"True Grit," Elmer Bernstein and
Don Black
1971
"Snow Train," John Parker
1972
"The Cowboys," John Williams
1973
"The Train Robbers," Dominic
Frontiere
1974
"Cahill U.S. Marshall," Elmer
Bernstein
1975
"Little House on the Prairie," David
Rose
1976
"Bite the Bullet," Alex North

SPECIAL AWARDS
1970
Arizona Highways magazine
"Death Valley Days"
Swiss National Television Network's
documentary "Far West: the
Indians"
1971
*The Autobiography of Charles
Francis Colcord, 1859–1934*
Yakima Canutt
The Marlboro Man

The Sons of the Pioneers
"Survival on the Prairie,"
NBC News Documentary
1972
John Ford
Dorothy Harmsen, *Harmsen's
Western Americana*
Wyoming Stock Growers Association
Winchester-Western
1973
William Clothier
Ben K. Green, *Some More Horse
Tradin'*
Agnes Wright Spring
Dale Robertson
1974
Alfred Y Allee
Howard Hawks
Luke Short
Dimitri Tiomkin
Korczak Ziolkowski
National Park Service documentary
"The Excavation of Mound Seven"
1975
"Bob Wills and His Texas Playboys:
For the Last Time" (record album)
Delmer Daves
James Whitmore
Watt R. Matthews
Robert Adams, author of *The
Architecture and Art of Early
Hispanic Colorado
Oklahoma Today* magazine
1976
*Spike Van Cleve: An American
Portrait* Spike Van Cleve, principal,
David Hoffman, Director-
Documentary film
Gordon Bowman
Harry Wiland
Margaret Harper
W. C. Lawrence
Joel McCrea
John Champion
George O'Brien
George Shirk

Dancer, choreographer, and writer Agnes de Mille.

DANCE

THE CAPEZIO AWARD—Capezio Foundation

Capezio has chosen to honor the "forces at work within the art itself" rather than individual performances or productions. It has also chosen to give cash—$1,000—"instead of a loving cup or statuette. Such a trophy, however handsome and deeply appreciated can do little more ultimately than stand upon a shelf and gather dust."

Established 1951.

1952	Zachary Solov
1953	Lincoln Kirstein
1954	Doris Humphrey
1955	Louis Horst
1956	Genevieve Oswald
1957	Ted Shawn

1958	Alexandra Danilova
1959	S. Hurok
1960	Martha Graham
1961	Ruth St. Denis
1962	Barbara Karinska
1963	Donald McKayle
1964	Jose Limon
1965	Maria Tallchief
1966	Agnes de Mille
1967	Paul Taylor
1968	Lucia Chase
1969	John Martin
1970	William Kolodney
1971	Arthur Mitchell
1972	La Meri, The Laubins
1973	Isadora Bennett
1974	Robert Joffrey
1975	Robert Irving
1976	Jerome Robbins

DANCE MAGAZINE AWARD—*Dance* magazine

To an exceptional "dance person," be he or she a performer, choreographer, or teacher. This may also be pre-

Ballerina Natalia Makarova.
(Kenn Duncan)

sented to an organization that has contributed to the art.
    Established 1954.
1954   Max Liebman, "Omnibus,"
        Tony Charmoli, Adventure
1955   Moira Shearer, Jack Cole,
        Gene Nelson
1956   Martha Graham, Agnes de
        Mille
1957   Alicia Markova, Lucia Chase,
        Jerome Robbins, Jose Limon
1958   Doris Humphrey, Gene Kelly,
        Igor Youskevitch, Alicia
        Alonso
1959   Dorothy Alexander, Fred
        Astaire, George Balanchine
1960   Merce Cunningham, Igor
        Moiseyev, Maria Tallchief
1961   Melissa Hayden, Gwen
        Verdon, Anna Sokolow
1962   Margot Fonteyn, Bob Fosse,
        Isadora Bennett
1963   Gower Champion, Robert
        Joffrey, Pauline Koner
1964   Edward Villella, John Butler,
        Peter Gennaro
1965   Margaret H'Doubler, Edwin

        Denby, Maya Plisetskaya
1966   Sol Hurok, Carmen De
        Lavallade, Wesleyan
        University Press
1967   Alwin Nikolais, Violette
        Verdy, Eugene Loring
1968   Carla Fracci, Erik Bruhn,
        Katherine Dunham
1969   Sir Frederick Ashton, Carolyn
        Brown, Ted Shawn
1972   Judith Jamison, Anthony
        Dowell
1973   The Christensen Brothers
        (Lew, Harold, and William),
        Rudolf Nureyev
1974   Gerald Arpino, Maurice
        Bejart, Antony Tudor
1975   Cynthia Gregory, Arthur
        Mitchell, Alvin Ailey
1976   E. Virginia Williams,
        Suzanne Farrell, Michael
        Bennett
1977   Murray Louis, Natalia
        Makarova, Peter Martins

See Service, Award of Merit, The Decalogue Society of Lawyers

EDUCATION

See Architecture, Distinguished Service Award, American Institute of Planners

See Broadcasting, The George Foster Peabody Broadcasting Awards, University of Georgia

DOW JONES AWARD—American Assembly of Collegiate Schools of Business

The Dow Jones Co. established this award for individuals who contribute to business and administrative education on the college level.

Established 1973.

1974
Walter Hoving, Tiffany & Company
1975
G. L. Bach, Stanford University
1976
Paul Garner, University of Alabama

WESTERN ELECTRIC FUND AWARD—American Assembly of Collegiate Schools of Business

This goes for innovative learning approaches and technologies in collegiate business administration education. Established 1969.

1970
Dr. John R. Wish, University of Oregon
1971
Dr. William G. Panschar, Indiana University
1972
Dr. John F. Rockart, Massachusetts Institute of Technology
1973
Drs. Mark Hammer and C. Obert Henderson, Washington State University
1974
Dr. Bruce M. Hass, University of Hawaii
1975
Dr. David J. Werner, Southern Illinois University, Edwardsville
1976
Dr. Gerald L. Thompson, Carnegie Mellon University

ELECTIONS

GOVERNORS OF THE STATES

ALABAMA *(Four-Year Term)*
Dec. 1, 1900–Dec. 26, 1900
William D. Jelks (D)
Dec. 26, 1900–June 11, 1901
William J. Samford (D)

June 11, 1901–Apr. 25, 1904
William D. Jelks (D)
Apr. 25, 1904–Mar. 5, 1905
Russell M. Cunningham (D)
Mar. 5, 1905–Jan. 14, 1907
William D. Jelks (D)
Jan. 14, 1907–Jan. 17, 1911
Braxton B. Comer (D)
Jan. 17, 1911–Jan. 18, 1915
Emmet O'Neal (D)
Jan. 18, 1915–Jan. 20, 1919
Charles Henderson (D)

Jan. 20, 1919–Jan. 15, 1923
  Thomas E. Kilby (D)
Jan. 15, 1923–Jan. 17, 1927
  William W. Brandon (D)
Jan. 17, 1927–Jan. 19, 1931
  Bibb Graves (D)
Jan. 19, 1931–Jan. 14, 1935
  Benjamin M. Miller (D)
Jan. 14, 1935–Jan. 17, 1939
  Bibb Graves (D)
Jan. 17, 1939–Jan. 19, 1943
  Frank M. Dixon (D)
Jan. 19, 1943–Jan. 20, 1947
  Chauncey M. Sparks (D)
Jan. 20, 1947–Jan. 15, 1951
  James E. Folsom (D)
Jan. 15, 1951–Jan. 17, 1955
  Gordon Persons (D)
Jan. 17, 1955–Jan. 19, 1959
  James E. Folsom (D)
Jan. 19, 1959–Jan. 14, 1963
  John M. Patterson (D)
Jan. 14, 1963–Jan. 16, 1967
  George C. Wallace (D)
Jan. 16, 1967–May 7, 1968
  Lurleen B. Wallace (D)
May 7, 1968–Jan. 18, 1971
  Albert P. Brewer (D)
Jan. 18, 1971
  George C. Wallace (D)

ALASKA *(Four-Year Term)*
Jan. 3, 1959–Dec. 5, 1966
  William A. Egan (D)
Dec. 5, 1966–Jan. 29, 1969
  Walter J. Hickel (R)
Jan. 29, 1969–Dec. 5, 1970
  Keith H. Miller (R)
Dec. 5, 1970–Dec. 2, 1974
  William A. Egan (D)
Dec. 2, 1974
  Jay S. Hammond (R)

ARIZONA *(Four-Year Term)*
Feb. 14, 1912–Jan. 1, 1917
  George W. P. Hunt (D)
Jan. 1, 1917–Dec. 25, 1917
  Thomas E. Campbell (R)
Dec. 25, 1917–Jan. 6, 1919
  George W. P. Hunt (D)
Jan. 6, 1919–Jan. 1, 1923
  Thomas E. Campbell (R)
Jan. 1, 1923–Jan. 7, 1929
  George W. P. Hunt (D)
Jan. 7, 1929–Jan. 5, 1931

John C. Phillips (R)
Jan. 5, 1931–Jan. 2, 1933
  George W. P. Hunt (D)
Jan. 2, 1933–Jan. 4, 1937
  Benjamin B. Moeur (D)
Jan. 4, 1937–Jan. 2, 1939
  Rawghlie C. Stanford (D)
Jan. 2, 1939–Jan. 6, 1941
  Robert T. Jones (D)
Jan. 6, 1941–May 25, 1948
  Sidney P. Osborn (D)
May 25, 1948–Jan. 1, 1951
  Dan E. Garvey (D)
Jan. 1, 1951—Jan. 3, 1955
  J. Howard Pyle (R)
Jan. 3, 1955–Jan. 5, 1959
  Ernest W. McFarland (D)
Jan. 5, 1959–Jan. 4, 1965
  Paul J. Fannin (R)
Jan. 4, 1965–Jan. 2, 1967
  Sam Goddard (D)
Jan. 2, 1967–Jan. 6, 1975
  Jack Williams (R)
Jan. 6, 1975
  Raul Castro (D)

ARKANSAS *(Two-Year Term)*
Jan. 8, 1901–Jan. 8, 1907
  Jeff Davis (D)
Jan. 8, 1907–Feb. 11, 1907
  John S. Little (D)
Feb. 11, 1907–May 11, 1907
  John I. Moore (D)
May 14, 1907–Jan. 11, 1909
  Xenophon O. Pindall (D)
Jan. 11, 1909–Jan. 15, 1913
  George W. Donaghey (D)
Jan. 15, 1913–Mar. 10, 1913
  Joseph T. Robinson (D)
Mar. 10, 1913–Mar. 13, 1913
  William K. Oldham (D)
Mar. 13, 1913–July 23, 1913
  Junius M. Futrell (D)
July 23, 1913–Jan. 9, 1917
  George W. Hays (D)
Jan. 9, 1917–Jan. 11, 1921
  Charles H. Brough (D)
Jan. 11, 1921–Jan. 13, 1925
  Thomas C. McRae (D)
Jan. 13, 1925–Jan. 11, 1927
  Thomas J. Terrall (D)
Jan. 11, 1927–Mar. 4, 1928
  John E. Martineau (D)
Mar. 4, 1928–Jan. 10, 1933
  Harvey Parnell (D)

Jan. 10, 1933–Jan. 12, 1937
    Junius M. Futrell (D)
Jan. 12, 1937–Jan. 14, 1941
    Carl E. Bailey (D)
Jan. 14, 1941–Jan. 9, 1945
    Homer M. Adkins (D)
Jan. 9, 1945–Jan. 11, 1949
    Benjamin T. Laney (D)
Jan. 11, 1949–Jan. 13, 1953
    Sidney S. McMath (D)
Jan. 13, 1953–Jan. 11, 1955
    Frances A. Cherry (D)
Jan. 11, 1955–Jan. 10, 1967
    Orval E. Faubus (D)
Jan. 10, 1967–Jan. 12, 1971
    Winthrop Rockefeller (R)
Jan. 12, 1971–Jan. 3, 1975
    Dale Bumpers (D)
Jan. 3, 1975–Jan. 14, 1975
    Bob Riley (D)
Jan. 14, 1975
    David Pryor (D)

CALIFORNIA *(Four-Year Term)*
Jan. 10, 1899–Jan. 8, 1901
    Charles S. Thomas (FUS)
Jan. 3, 1899–Jan. 6, 1903
    Henry T. Gage (R & UL)
Jan. 6, 1903–Jan. 8, 1907
    George C. Pardee (R)
Jan. 8, 1907–Jan. 3, 1911
    James N. Gillett (R)
Jan. 3, 1911–Mar. 15, 1917
    Hiram W. Johnson (R, PROG)
Mar. 15, 1917–Jan. 9, 1923
    William D. Stephens (RP PROG)
Jan. 9, 1923–Jan. 4, 1927
    Friend William Richardson (R)
Jan. 4, 1927–Jan. 6, 1931
    Clement C. Young (R)
Jan. 6, 1931–June 2, 1934
    James Rolph, Jr. (R)
June 2, 1934–Jan. 2, 1939
    Frank F. Merriam (R)
Jan. 2, 1939–Jan. 4, 1943
    Culbert L. Olson (D)
Jan. 4, 1943–Oct. 5, 1953
    Earl Warren (R)
Oct. 5, 1953–Jan. 5, 1959
    Goodwin J. Knight (R)
Jan. 5, 1959–Jan. 2, 1967
    Edmund G. Brown (D)
Jan. 2, 1967–Jan. 6, 1975
    Ronald Regan (R)
Jan. 6, 1975

    Edmund G. Brown, Jr. (D)

COLORADO *(Four-Year Term)*
Jan. 10, 1899–Jan. 8, 1901
    Charles S. Thomas (FUS)
Jan. 8, 1901–Jan. 13, 1903
    James B. Orman (FUS)
Jan. 13, 1903–Jan. 10, 1905
    James H. Peabody (R)
Jan. 10, 1905–Mar. 16, 1905
    Alva Adams (D)
Mar. 16, 1905–Mar. 17, 1905
    James H. Peabody (R)
Mar. 17, 1905–Jan. 8, 1907
    Jesse F. McDonald (R)
Jan. 8, 1907–Jan. 12, 1909
    Henry A. Buchtel (R)
Jan. 12, 1909–Jan. 14, 1913
    John F. Shafroth (D)
Jan. 14, 1913–Jan. 12, 1915
    Elias M. Ammons (D)
Jan. 12, 1915–Jan. 9, 1917
    George A. Carlson (R)
Jan. 9, 1917–Jan. 14, 1919
    Julius C. Gunter (D)
Jan. 14, 1919–Jan. 9, 1923
    Oliver H. Shoup (R)
Jan. 9, 1923–Jan. 13, 1925
    William E. Sweet (D)
Jan. 13, 1925–Jan. 11, 1927
    Clarence J. Morley (R)
Jan. 11, 1927–Jan. 10, 1933
    William H. Adams (R)
Jan. 10, 1933–Jan. 3, 1937
    Edwin C. Johnson (R)
Jan. 3, 1937–Jan. 12, 1937
Jan. 12, 1939–Jan. 10, 1943
Jan. 12, 1937–Jan. 10,1939
    Teller Ammons (D)
Jan. 10, 1939–Jan. 12, 1943
    Ralph L. Carr (R)
Jan. 12, 1943–Jan. 14, 1947
    John C. Vivian (R)
Jan. 14, 1947–Apr. 15, 1950
    William L. Knous (D)
Apr. 15, 1950–Jan. 9, 1951
    Walter W. Johnson (D)
Jan. 9, 1951–Jan. 11, 1955
    Dan Thornton (R)
Jan. 11, 1955–Jan. 8, 1957
    Edwin C. Johnson (D)
Jan. 8, 1957–Jan. 8, 1963
    Stephen L. R. McNichols (D)
Jan. 8, 1963–July 16, 1973
    John A. Love (R)

July 16, 1973–Jan. 14, 1975
  John D. Vanderhood (R)
Jan. 14, 1975
  Richard D. Lamm (D)

CONNECTICUT *(Four-Year Term)*
Jan. 4, 1899–Jan. 9, 1901
  George E. Lounsberg (R)
Jan. 9, 1901–Jan. 7, 1903
  George P. McLean (R)
Jan. 7, 1903–Jan. 4, 1905
  Abiram Chamberlain (R)
Jan. 4, 1905–Jan. 9, 1907
  Henry Roberts (R)
Jan. 9, 1907–Jan. 6, 1909
  Rollin S. Woodruff (R)
Jan. 6, 1909–Apr. 21, 1909
  George L. Lilley (R)
Apr. 21, 1909–Jan. 4, 1911
  Frank B. Weeks (R)
Jan. 4, 1911–Jan. 6, 1915
  Simeon E. Baldwin (D)
Jan. 6, 1915–Jan. 5, 1921
  Marcus H. Holcomb (R)
Jan. 5, 1921–Jan. 3, 1923
  Everett J. Lake (R)
Jan. 3, 1923–Jan. 7, 1925
  Charles A. Templeton (R)
Jan. 7, 1925–Jan. 8, 1925
  Hiram Bingham (R)
Jan. 8, 1925–Jan. 7, 1931
  John H. Trumbull (R)
Jan. 7, 1931–Jan. 4, 1939
  Wilbur L. Cross (D)
Jan. 4, 1939–Jan. 8, 1941
  Raymond E. Baldwin (R)
Jan. 8, 1941–Jan. 6, 1943
  Robert A. Hurley (D)
Jan. 6, 1943–Dec. 27, 1946
  Raymond E. Baldwin (R)
Dec. 27, 1946–Jan. 8, 1947
  Wilbert Snow (D)
Jan. 8, 1947–Mar. 7, 1948
  James L. McConaughy (R)
Mar. 7, 1948–Jan. 5, 1949
  James C. Shannon (R)
Jan. 5, 1949–Jan. 3, 1951
  Chester Bowles (D)
Jan. 3, 1951–Jan. 5, 1955
  John D. Lodge (R)
Jan. 5, 1955–Jan. 21, 1961
  Abraham Ribicoff (D)
Jan. 21, 1961–Jan. 6, 1971
  John Dempsey (D)
Jan. 6, 1971–Jan. 8, 1975

Thomas J. Meskill (R)
Jan. 8, 1975
  Ella T. Grasso (D)

DELAWARE *(Four-Year Term)*
Jan. 15, 1901–Jan. 17, 1905
  John Hunn (R)
Jan. 17, 1905–Jan. 19, 1909
  Preston Lea (R)
Jan. 19, 1909–Jan. 21, 1913
  Simeon S. Pennewill (R)
Jan. 21, 1913–Jan. 17, 1917
  Charles R. Miller (R)
Jan. 17, 1917–Jan. 18, 1921
  John G. Townsend, Jr. (R)
Jan. 18, 1921–Jan. 20, 1925
  William D. Denney (R)
Jan. 20, 1925–Jan. 15, 1929
  Robert P. Robinson (R)
Jan. 15, 1929–Jan. 19, 1937
  C. Douglass Buck (R)
Jan. 19, 1937–Jan. 21, 1941
  Richard C. McMullen (D)
Jan. 21, 1941–Jan. 18, 1949
  Walter W. Bacon (R)
Jan. 18, 1949–Jan. 20, 1953
  Elbert N. Carvel (D)
Jan. 20, 1953–Dec. 30, 1960
  J. Caleb Boggs (R)
Dec. 30, 1960–Jan. 17, 1961
  David P. Buckson (R)
Jan. 17, 1961–Jan. 19, 1965
  Elbert N. Carvel (D)
Jan. 19, 1965–Jan. 21, 1969
  Charles L. Terry, Jr. (D)
Jan. 21, 1969–Jan. 16, 1973
  Russell W. Peterson (R)
Jan. 16, 1973–Jan. 18, 1977
  Sherman W. Tribbitt (D)
Jan. 18, 1977
  Pierre S. du Pont (R)

FLORIDA *(Four-Year Term)*
Jan. 8, 1901–Jan. 3, 1905
  William S. Jennings (D)
Jan. 3, 1905–Jan. 5, 1909
  Napoleon B. Broward (D)
Jan. 5, 1909–Jan. 7, 1913
  Albert W. Gilchrist (D)
Jan. 7, 1913–Jan. 2, 1917
  Park Trammell (D)
Jan. 2, 1917–Jan. 4, 1921
  Sidney J. Catts (IP)
Jan. 4, 1921–Jan. 6, 1925
  Cary A. Hardee (D)

Jan. 6, 1925–Jan. 8, 1929
  John W. Martin (D)
Jan. 8, 1929–Jan. 3, 1933
  Doyle E. Carlton (D)
Jan. 3, 1933–Jan. 5, 1937
  David Sholtz (D)
Jan. 5, 1937–Jan. 7, 1941
  Frederick P. Cone (D)
Jan. 7, 1941–Jan. 2, 1945
  Spessard L. Holland (D)
Jan. 2, 1945–Jan. 4, 1949
  Millard F. Caldwell (D)
Jan. 4, 1949–Jan. 6, 1953
  Fuller Warren (D)
Jan. 6, 1953–Sept. 28, 1953
  Daniel T. McCarty (D)
Sept. 28, 1953–Jan. 4, 1955
  Charley E. Johns (D)
Jan. 4, 1955–Jan. 3, 1961
  LeRoy Collins (D)
Jan. 3, 1961–Jan. 5, 1965
  Farris Bryant (D)
Jan. 5, 1965–Jan. 3, 1967
  Haydon Burns (D)
Jan. 3, 1967–Jan. 5, 1971
  Claude R. Kirk, Jr. (R)
Jan. 5, 1971
  Reubin Askew (D)

GEORGIA *(Four-Year Term)*
Oct. 29, 1898–Oct. 25, 1902
  Allen D. Candler (D)
Oct. 25, 1902–June 29, 1907
  Joseph M. Terrell (D)
June 29, 1907–June 26, 1909
  Hoke Smith (D)
June 26, 1909–July 1, 1911
  Joseph M. Brown (D)
July 1, 1911–Nov. 16, 1911
  Hoke Smith (D)
Nov. 16, 1911–Jan. 25, 1912
  John M. Slaton (D)
Jan. 25, 1912–June 28, 1913
  Joseph M. Brown (D)
June 28, 1913–June 26, 1915
  John M. Slaton (D)
June 26, 1915–June 30, 1917
  Nathaniel E. Harris (D)
June 30, 1917–June 25, 1921
  Hugh M. Dorsey (D)
June 25, 1921–June 30, 1923
  Thomas W. Hardwick (D)
June 30, 1923–June 25, 1927
  Clifford M. Walker (D)
June 25, 1927–June 27, 1931

Lamartine G. Hardman (D)
June 27, 1931–Jan. 10, 1933
  Richard B. Russell (D)
Jan. 10, 1933–Jan. 12, 1937
  Eugene Talmadge (D)
Jan. 12, 1937–Jan. 14, 1941
  Eurith D. Rivers (D)
Jan. 14, 1941–Jan. 12, 1943
  Eugene Talmadge (D)
Jan. 12, 1943–Jan. 14, 1947
  Ellis G. Arnall (D)
Jan. 14, 1947–Mar. 18, 1947
  Herman E. Talmadge (D)
Mar. 18, 1947–Nov. 17, 1948
  Melvin E. Thompson (D)
Nov. 17, 1948–Jan. 11, 1955
  Herman E. Talmadge (D)
Jan. 11, 1955–Jan. 13, 1959
  S. Marvin Griffin (D)
Jan. 13, 1959–Jan. 15, 1963
  S. Ernest Vandiver, Jr. (D)
Jan. 15, 1963–Jan. 10, 1967
  Carl Edward Sanders (D)
Jan. 10, 1967–Jan. 12, 1971
  Lester G. Maddox (D)
Jan. 12, 1971–Jan. 14, 1975
  Jimmy Carter (D)
Jan. 14, 1975
  George Busbee (D)

HAWAII *(Four-Year Term)*
Aug. 21, 1959–Dec. 3, 1962
  William F. Quinn (R)
Dec. 3, 1962–Dec. 2, 1974
  John A. Burns (D)
Dec. 2, 1974
  George R. Ariyoshi (D)

IDAHO *(Four-Year Term)*
Jan. 7, 1901–Jan. 5, 1903
  Frank W. Hunt (D-FUS)
Jan. 5, 1903–Jan. 2, 1905
  John T. Morrison (R)
Jan. 2, 1905–Jan. 4, 1909
  Frank R. Gooding (R)
Jan. 4, 1909–Jan. 2, 1911
  James H. Brady (R)
Jan. 2, 1911–Jan. 6, 1913
  James H. Hawley (D)
Jan. 6, 1913–Jan. 4, 1915
  John M. Haines (R)
Jan. 4, 1915–Jan. 6, 1919
  Moses Alexander (D)
Jan. 6, 1919–Jan. 1, 1923
  David W. Davis (R)

Jan. 1, 1923–Jan. 3, 1927
  Charles C. Moore (R)
Jan. 3, 1927–Jan. 5, 1931
  H. Clarence Baldridge (R)
Jan. 5, 1931–Jan. 4, 1937
  C. Ben Ross (D)
Jan. 4, 1937–Jan. 2, 1939
  Barzilla W. Clark (D)
Jan. 2, 1939–Jan. 6, 1941
  Clarence A. Bottolfsen (R)
Jan. 6, 1941–Jan. 4, 1943
  Chase A. Clark (D)
Jan. 4, 1943–Jan. 1, 1945
  Clarence A. Bottolfsen (R)
Jan. 1, 1945–Nov. 17, 1945
  Charles C. Gossett (D)
Nov. 17, 1945–Jan. 6, 1947
  Arnold Williams (D)
Jan. 6, 1947–Jan. 1, 1951
  Charles A. Robins (R)
Jan. 1, 1951–Jan. 3, 1955
  Len B. Jordan (R)
Jan. 3, 1955–Jan. 2, 1967
  Robert E. Smylie (R)
Jan. 2, 1967–Jan. 4, 1971
  Don Samuelson (R)
Jan. 4, 1971–Jan. 24, 1977
  Cecil D. Andrus (D)
Jan. 24, 1977
  John V. Evans (D)

ILLINOIS *(Four-Year Term)*
Jan. 14, 1901–Jan. 9, 1905
  Richard Yates (R)
Jan. 9, 1905–Feb. 3, 1913
  Charles S. Deneen (R)
Feb. 3, 1913–Jan. 8, 1917
  Edward F. Dunne (D)
Jan. 8, 1917–Jan. 10, 1921
  Frank O. Lowden (R)
Jan. 10, 1921–Jan. 14, 1929
  Len Small (R)
Jan. 14, 1929–Jan. 9, 1933
  Louis L. Emmerson (R)
Jan. 9, 1933–Oct. 6, 1940
  Henry Horner (D)
Oct. 6, 1940–Jan. 13, 1941
  John H. Stelle (D)
Jan. 13, 1941–Jan. 10, 1949
  Dwight H. Green (R)
Jan. 10, 1949–Jan. 12, 1953
  Adlai E. Stevenson (D)
Jan. 12, 1953–Jan. 9, 1961
  William G. Stratton (R)
Jan. 9, 1961–May 22, 1968

Otto Kerner (D)
May 22, 1968–Jan. 13, 1969
  Samuel H. Shapiro (D)
Jan. 13, 1969–Jan. 8, 1973
  Richard B. Ogilvie (R)
Jan. 8, 1973–Jan. 10, 1977
  Daniel Walker (D)
Jan. 10, 1977
  James R. Thompson (R)

INDIANA *(Four-Year Term)*
Jan. 14, 1901–Jan. 9, 1905
  Winfield T. Durbin (R)
Jan. 9, 1905–Jan. 11, 1909
  J. Frank Hanly (R)
Jan. 11, 1909–Jan. 13, 1913
  Thomas R. Marshall (D)
Jan. 13, 1913–Jan. 8, 1917
  Samuel M. Ralston (D)
Jan. 8, 1917–Jan. 10, 1921
  James Putnam Goodrich (R)
Jan. 10, 1921–Apr. 30, 1924
  Warren T. McCray (R)
Apr. 30, 1924–Jan. 12, 1925
  Emmett F. Branch (R)
Jan. 12, 1925–Jan. 14, 1929
  Edward Jackson (R)
Jan. 14, 1929–Jan. 9, 1933
  Harry .G. Leslie (R)
Jan. 9, 1933–Jan. 11, 1937
  Paul V. McNutt (D)
Jan. 11, 1937–Jan. 13, 1941
  M. Clifford Townsend (D)
Jan. 13, 1941–Jan. 8, 1945
  Henry F. Schricker (D)
Jan. 8, 1945–Jan. 10, 1949
  Ralph F. Gates (R)
Jan. 10, 1949–Jan. 12, 1953
  Henry F. Schricker (D)
Jan. 12, 1953–Jan. 14, 1957
  George N. Craig (R)
Jan. 14, 1957–Jan. 9, 1961
  Harold W. Handley (R)
Jan. 9, 1961–Jan. 11, 1965
  Matthew E. Welsh (D)
Jan. 11, 1965–Jan. 13, 1969
  Roger D. Branigin (D)
Jan. 13, 1969–Jan. 8, 1973
  Edgar D. Whitcomb (R)
Jan. 8, 1973
  Otis R. Bowen (R)

IOWA *(Four-Year Term)*
Jan. 13, 1898–Jan. 16, 1902
  Leslie M. Shaw (R)

Jan. 16, 1902–Nov. 24, 1908
  Albert B. Cummins (R)
Nov. 24, 1908–Jan. 14, 1909
  Warren Garst (R)
Jan. 14, 1909–Jan. 16, 1913
  Beryl F. Carroll (R)
Jan. 16, 1913–Jan. 11, 1917
  George W. Clarke (R)
Jan. 11, 1917–Jan. 13, 1921
  William L. Harding (R)
Jan. 13, 1921–Jan. 15, 1925
  Nathan E. Kendall (R)
Jan. 15, 1925–Jan. 15, 1931
  John Hammill (R)
Jan. 15, 1931–Jan. 12, 1933
  Daniel W. Turner (R)
Jan. 12, 1933–Jan. 14, 1937
  Clyde L. Herring (D)
Jan. 14, 1937–Jan. 12, 1939
  Nelson G. Kraschel (D)
Jan. 12, 1939–Jan. 14, 1943
  George A. Wilson (R)
Jan. 14, 1943–Jan. 11, 1945
  Bourke B. Hickenlooper (R)
Jan. 11, 1945–Jan. 13, 1949
  Robert D. Blue (R)
Jan. 13, 1949–Nov. 21, 1954
  William S. Beardsley (R)
Nov. 22, 1954–Jan. 13, 1955
  Leo Elthon (R)
Jan. 13, 1955–Jan. 17, 1957
  Leo Arthur Hoegh (R)
Jan. 17, 1957–Jan. 12, 1961
  Herschel C. Loveless (D)
Jan. 12, 1961–Jan. 17, 1963
  Norman A. Erbe (R)
Jan. 17, 1963–Jan. 1, 1969
  Harold E. Hughes (D)
Jan. 1, 1969–Jan. 16, 1969
  Robert D. Fulton (D)
Jan. 16, 1969
  Robert D. Ray (R)

KANSAS *(Four-Year Term)*
Jan. 9, 1899–Jan. 12, 1903
  William E. Stanley (R)
Jan. 12, 1903–Jan. 9, 1905
  Willis J. Bailey (R)
Jan. 9, 1905–Jan. 11, 1909
  Edward W. Hoch (R)
Jan. 11, 1909–Jan. 13, 1913
  Walter R. Stubbs (R)
Jan. 13, 1913–Jan. 11, 1915
  George H. Hodges (D)
Jan. 11, 1915–Jan. 13, 1919

  Arthur Capper (R)
Jan. 13, 1919–Jan. 8, 1923
  Henry J. Allen (R)
Jan. 8, 1923–Jan. 12, 1925
  Jonathan McM. Davis (D)
Jan. 12, 1925–Jan. 14, 1929
  Ben S. Paulen (R)
Jan. 14, 1929–Jan. 12, 1931
  Clyde M. Reed (R)
Jan. 12, 1931–Jan. 9, 1933
  Harry H. Woodring (D)
Jan. 9, 1933–Jan. 11, 1937
  Alfred M. Landon (R)
Jan. 11, 1937–Jan. 9, 1939
  Walter A. Huxman (D)
Jan. 9, 1939–Jan. 11, 1943
  Payne H. Ratner (R)
Jan. 11, 1943–Jan. 13, 1947
  Andrew F. Schoeppel (R)
Jan. 13, 1947–Nov. 28, 1950
  Frank Carlson (R)
Nov. 28, 1950–Jan. 8, 1951
  Frank L. Hagaman (R)
Jan. 8, 1951–Jan. 10, 1955
  Edward F. Arn (R)
Jan. 10, 1955–Jan. 3, 1957
  Frederick L. Hall (R)
Jan. 3, 1957–Jan. 14, 1957
  John McCuish (R)
Jan. 14, 1957–Jan. 9, 1961
  George Docking (D)
Jan. 9, 1961–Jan. 11, 1965
  John Anderson, Jr. (R)
Jan. 11, 1965–Jan. 9, 1967
  William H. Avery (R)
Jan. 9, 1967–Jan. 13, 1975
  Robert B. Docking (D)
Jan. 13, 1975
  Robert F. Bennett (R)

KENTUCKY *(Four-Year Term)*
Jan. 31, 1900–Feb. 3, 1900
  William Goebel (D)
Feb. 3, 1900–Dec. 10, 1907
  John C. W. Beckham (D)
Dec. 10, 1907–Dec. 12, 1911
  August E. Willson (R)
Dec. 12, 1911–Dec. 7, 1915
  James B. McCreary (D)
Dec. 7, 1915–May 19, 1919
  Augustus O. Stanley (D)
May 19, 1919–Dec. 9, 1919
  James D. Black (D)
Dec. 9, 1919–Dec. 11, 1923
  Edwin P. Morrow (R)

Dec. 11, 1923–Dec. 13, 1927
  William J. Fields (D)
Dec. 13, 1927–Dec. 8, 1931
  Flem D. Sampson (R)
Dec. 8, 1931–Dec. 10, 1935
  Ruby Lafoon (D)
Dec. 10, 1935–Oct. 9, 1939
  Albert B. (Happy) Chandler (D)
Oct. 9, 1939–Dec. 7, 1943
  Keen Johnson (D)
Dec. 7, 1943–Dec. 9, 1947
  Simeon S. Willis (R)
Dec. 9, 1947–Nov. 27, 1950
  Earle C. Clements (D)   .
Nov. 27, 1950–Dec. 13, 1955
  Lawrence W. Wetherby (D)
Dec. 13, 1955–Dec. 9, 1959
  Albert B. (Happy) Chandler (D)
Dec. 9, 1959–Dec. 10, 1963
  Bert T. Combs (D)
Dec. 10, 1963–Dec. 12, 1967
  Edward T. Breathitt (D)
Dec. 12, 1967–Dec. 7, 1971
  Louie B. Nunn (R)
Dec. 7, 1971–Dec. 28, 1974
  Wendell H. Ford (D)
Dec. 28, 1974
  Julian Carroll (D)

LOUISIANA *(Four-Year Term)*
May 8, 1900–May 10, 1904
  William W. Heard (D)
May 10, 1904–May 12, 1908
  Newton C. Blanchard (D)
May 12, 1908–May 14, 1912
  Jared 'Y. Sanders (D)
May 14, 1912–May 9, 1916
  Luther E. Hall (D)
May 9, 1916–May 11, 1920
  Ruffin G. Pleasant (D)
May 11, 1920–May 13, 1924
  John M. Parker (D)
May 13, 1924–Oct. 11, 1926
  Henry L. Fuqua (D)
Oct. 11, 1926–May 21, 1928
  Oramel H. Simpson (D)
May 21, 1928–Jan. 25, 1932
  Huey P. Long, Jr. (D)
Jan. 25, 1932–May 10, 1932
  Alvin O. King (D)
May 10, 1932–Jan. 28, 1936
  Oscar K. Allen (D)
Jan. 28, 1936–May 12, 1936
  James A. Noe (D)
May 12, 1936–June 26, 1939

Richard W. Leche (D)
June 26, 1939–May 14, 1940
  Earl K. Long (D)
May 14, 1940–May 9, 1944
  Sam H. Jones (D)
May 9, 1944–May 11, 1948
  James H. Davis (D)
May 11, 1948–May 13, 1952
  Earl K. Long (D)
May 13, 1952–May 8, 1956
  Robert F. Kennon (D)
May 8, 1956–May 10, 1960
  Earl K. Long (D)
May 10, 1960–May 12, 1964
  James H. Davis (D)
May 12, 1964–May 9, 1972
  John J. McKeithen (D)
May 9, 1972
  Edwin W. Edwards (D)

MAINE *(Four-Year Term)*
Jan. 6, 1897–Jan. 2, 1901
  Llewellyn Powers (R)
Jan. 2, 1901–Jan. 4, 1905
  John F. Hill (R)
Jan. 4, 1905–Jan. 6, 1909
  William T. Cobb (R)
Jan. 6, 1909–Jan. 4, 1911
  Bert M. Fernald (R)
Jan. 4, 1911–Jan. 1, 1913
  Frederick W. Plaisted (D)
Jan. 1, 1913–Jan. 6, 1915
  William T. Haines (R)
Jan. 6, 1915–Jan. 3, 1917
  Oakley C. Curtis (D)
Jan. 3, 1917–Jan. 5, 1921
  Carl E. Milliken (R)
Jan. 5, 1921–Jan. 31, 1921
  Frederic H. Parkhurst (R)
Jan. 31, 1921–Jan. 8, 1925
  Percival P. Baxter (R)
Jan. 8, 1925–Jan. 2, 1929
  Ralph O. Brewster (R)
Jan. 2, 1929–Jan. 4, 1933
  William T. Gardiner (R)
Jan. 4, 1933–Jan. 6, 1937
  Louis J. Brann (D)
Jan. 6, 1937–Jan. 1, 1941
  Lewis O. Barrows (R)
Jan. 1, 1941–Jan. 3, 1945
  Sumner Sewall (R)
Jan. 3, 1945–Jan. 5, 1949
  Horace A. Hildreth (R)
Jan. 5, 1949–Dec. 25, 1952
  Frederick G. Payne (R)

Dec. 26, 1952–Jan. 5, 1955
 Burton M. Cross (R)
Jan. 5, 1955–Jan. 3, 1959
 Edmund S. Muskie (D)
Jan. 3, 1959–Jan. 8, 1959
 Robert N. Haskell (R)
Jan. 8, 1959–Dec. 30, 1959
 Clinton A. Clauson (D)
Dec. 30, 1959–Jan. 5, 1967
 John H. Reed (R)
Jan. 5, 1967–Jan. 1, 1975
 Kenneth M. Curtis (D)
Jan. 2, 1975
 James B. Longley (I)

MARYLAND *(Four-Year Term)*
Jan. 10, 1900–Jan. 13, 1904
 John W. Smith (D)
Jan. 13, 1904–Jan. 8, 1908
 Edwin Warfield (D)
Jan. 8, 1908–Jan. 10, 1912
 Austin L. Crothers (D)
Jan. 10, 1912–Jan. 12, 1916
 Phillips L. Goldsborough (R)
Jan. 12, 1916–Jan. 14, 1920
 Emerson C. Harrington (D)
Jan. 14, 1920–Jan. 9, 1935
 Albert C. Ritchie (D)
Jan. 9, 1935–Jan. 11, 1939
 Harry W. Nice (R)
Jan. 11, 1939–Jan. 3, 1947
 Herbert R. O'Conor (D)
Jan. 3, 1947–Jan. 10, 1951
 William P. Lane, Jr. (D)
Jan. 10, 1951–Jan. 14, 1959
 Theodore R. McKeldin (R)
Jan. 14, 1959–Jan. 25, 1967
 J. Millard Tawes (D)
Jan. 25, 1967–Jan. 7, 1969
 Spiro T. Agnew (R)
Jan. 7, 1969
 Marvin Mandel (D)

MASSACHUSETTS *(Four-Year Term)*
Jan. 4, 1900–Jan. 8, 1903
 Winthrop M. Crane (R)
Jan. 8, 1903–Jan. 5, 1905
 John L. Bates (R)
Jan. 5, 1905–Jan. 4, 1906
 William L. Douglas (D)
Jan. 4, 1906–Jan. 7, 1909
 Curtis Guild, Jr. (R)
Jan. 7, 1909–Jan. 5, 1911
 Eben Sumner Draper (D)

Jan. 5, 1911–Jan. 8, 1914
 Eugene N. Foss (D)
Jan. 8, 1914–Jan. 6, 1916
 David I. Walsh (D)
Jan. 6, 1916–Jan. 2, 1919
 Samuel W. McCall (R)
Jan. 2, 1919–Jan. 6, 1921
 Calvin Coolidge (R)
Jan. 6, 1921–Jan. 8, 1925
 Channing H. Cox (R)
Jan. 8, 1925–Jan. 3, 1929
 A. T. Fuller (R)
Jan. 3, 1929–Jan. 8, 1931
 Frank G. Allen (R)
Jan. 8, 1931–Jan. 3, 1935
 Joseph B. Ely (D)
Jan. 3, 1935–Jan. 7, 1937
 James M. Curley (D)
Jan. 7, 1937–Jan. 5, 1939
 Charles F. Hurley (D)
Jan. 5, 1939–Jan. 3, 1945
 Leverett Saltonstall (R)
Jan. 3, 1945–Jan. 2, 1947
 Maurice J. Tobin (D)
Jan. 2, 1947–Jan. 6, 1949
 Robert F. Bradford (R)
Jan. 6, 1949–Jan. 8, 1953
 Paul A. Dever (D)
Jan. 8, 1953–Jan. 3, 1957
 Christian A. Herter (R)
Jan. 3, 1957–Jan. 5, 1961
 Foster J. Furcolo (D)
Jan. 5, 1961–Jan. 3, 1963
 John A. Volpe (R)
Jan. 3, 1963–Jan. 7, 1965
 Endicott Peabody (D)
Jan. 7, 1965–Jan. 22, 1969
 John A. Volpe (R)
Jan. 22, 1969–Jan. 2, 1975
 Francis W. Sargent (R)
Jan. 2, 1975
 Michael S. Dukakis (D)

MICHIGAN *(Four-Year Term)*
Jan. 1, 1901–Jan. 1, 1905
 Aaron T. Bliss (R)
Jan. 1, 1905–Jan. 1, 1911
 Fred M. Warner (R)
Jan. 1, 1911–Jan. 1, 1913
 Chase S. Osborn (R)
Jan. 1, 1913–Jan. 1, 1917
 Woodbridge N. Ferris (D)
Jan. 1, 1917–Jan. 1, 1921
 Albert E. Sleeper (R)

Jan. 1, 1921–Jan. 1, 1927
  Alexander J. Groesbeck (R)
Jan. 1, 1927–Jan. 1, 1931
  Fred W. Green (R)
Jan. 1, 1931–Jan. 1, 1933
  Wilber M. Brucker (R)
Jan. 1, 1933–Jan. 1, 1935
  William A. Comstock (D)
Jan. 1, 1935–Jan. 1, 1937
  Frank D. Fitzgerald (D)
Jan. 1, 1937–Jan. 1, 1939
  Frank Murphy (D)
Jan. 1, 1939–Mar. 16, 1939
  Frank D. Fitzgerald (R)
Mar. 16, 1939–Jan. 1, 1941
  Luren D. Dickinson (R)
Jan. 1, 1941–Jan. 1, 1943
  Murray D. Van Wagoner (D)
Jan. 1, 1943–Jan. 1, 1947
  Harry F. Kelly (R)
Jan. 1, 1947–Jan. 1, 1949
  Kim Sigler (R)
Jan. 1, 1949–Jan. 1, 1961
  G. Mennen Williams (D)
Jan. 1, 1961–Jan. 1, 1963
  John B. Swainson (D)
Jan. 1, 1963–Jan. 22, 1969
  George W. Romney (R)
Jan. 22, 1969
  William G. Milliken (R)

MINNESOTA *(Four-Year Term)*
Jan. 2, 1899–Jan. 7, 1901
  John Lind (D and POP)
Jan. 7, 1901–Jan. 4, 1905
  Samuel R. Van Sant (R)
Jan. 4, 1905–Sept. 21, 1909
  John A. Johnson (D)
Sept. 21, 1909–Jan. 5, 1915
  Adolph O. Eberhart (R)
Jan. 5, 1915–Dec. 30, 1915
  Winfield S. Hammond (D)
Dec. 30, 1915–Jan. 5, 1921
  Joseph A. A. Burnquist (R)
Jan. 5, 1921–Jan. 6, 1925
  Jacob A. O. Preus (R)
Jan. 6, 1925–Jan. 6, 1931
  Theodore Christianson (R)
Jan. 6, 1931–Aug. 22, 1936
  Floyd B. Olson (F-LAB)
Aug. 22, 1936–Jan. 4, 1937
  Hjalmar Petersen (F-LAB)
Jan. 4, 1937–Jan. 2, 1939
  Elmer A. Benson (F-LAB)

Jan. 2, 1939–Apr. 27, 1943
  Harold E. Stassen (R)
Apr. 27, 1943–Jan. 8, 1947
  Edward J. Thye (R)
Jan. 8, 1947–Sept. 27, 1951
  Luther W. Youngdahl (R)
Sept. 27, 1951–Jan. 5, 1955
  C. Elmer Anderson (R)
Jan. 5, 1955–Jan. 2, 1961
  Orville L. Freeman (DFL)
Jan. 2, 1961–Mar. 25, 1963
  Elmer L. Andersen (R)
Mar. 25, 1963–Jan. 2, 1967
  Karl F. Rolvaag (DFL)
Jan. 2, 1967–Jan. 4, 1971
  Harold LeVander (R)
Jan. 4, 1971–Dec. 29, 1976
  Wendell R. Anderson (DFL)
Dec. 29, 1976
  Rudy Perpich (D)

MISSISSIPPI *(Four-Year Term)*
Jan. 16, 1900–Jan. 19, 1904
  Andrew H. Longino (D)
Jan. 19, 1904–Jan. 21, 1908
  James Kimble Vardaman (D)
Jan. 21, 1908–Jan. 16, 1912
  Edmond Favor Noel (D)
Jan. 16, 1912–Jan. 18, 1916
  Earl LeRoy Brewer (D)
Jan. 18, 1916–Jan. 20, 1920
  Theodore Gilmore Bilbo (D)
Jan. 20, 1920–Jan. 22, 1924
  Lee Maurice Russell (D)
Jan. 22, 1924–Mar. 18, 1927
  Henry Lewis Whitfield (D)
Mar. 18, 1927–Jan. 17, 1928
  Dennis Murphree (D)
Jan. 17, 1928–Jan. 19, 1932
  Theodore Gilmore Bilbo (D)
Jan. 19, 1932–Jan. 21, 1936
  Martin Sennett Conner (D)
Jan. 21, 1936–Jan. 16, 1940
  Hugh L. White (D)
Jan. 16, 1940–Dec. 26, 1943
  Paul B. Johnson (D)
Dec. 26, 1943–Jan. 18, 1944
  Dennis Murphree (D)
Jan. 18, 1944–Nov. 2, 1946
  Thomas L. Bailey (D)
Nov. 2, 1946–Jan. 22, 1952
  Fielding L. Wright (D)
Jan. 22, 1952–Jan. 17, 1956
  Hugh L. White (D)

Jan. 17, 1956–Jan. 19, 1960
  J. P. Coleman (D)
Jan. 19, 1960–Jan. 21, 1964
  Ross R. Barnett (D)
Jan. 21, 1964–Jan. 16, 1968
  Paul B. Johnson, Jr. (D)
Jan. 16, 1968–Jan. 18, 1972
  John Bell Williams (D)
Jan. 18, 1972–Jan. 20, 1976
  William Lowe Waller (D)
Jan. 20, 1976
  Charles C. Finch (D)

MISSOURI *(Four-Year Term)*
Jan. 14, 1901–Jan. 9, 1905
  Alexander M. Dockery (D)
Jan. 9, 1905–Jan. 11, 1909
  Joseph W. Folk (D)
Jan. 11, 1909–Jan. 13, 1913
  Herbert S. Hadley (R)
Jan. 13, 1913–Jan. 8, 1917
  Elliot W. Major (D)
Jan. 8, 1917–Jan. 10, 1921
  Frederick D. Gardner (D)
Jan. 10, 1921–Jan. 12, 1925
  Arthur M. Hyde (R)
Jan. 12, 1925–Jan. 14, 1929
  Samuel A. Baker (R)
Jan. 14, 1929–Jan. 9, 1933
  Henry S. Caulfield (R)
Jan. 9, 1933–Jan. 11, 1937
  Guy B. Park (D)
Jan. 11, 1937–Jan. 13, 1941
  Lloyd C. Stark (D)
Jan. 13, 1941–Jan. 8, 1945
  Forrest C. Donnell (R)
Jan. 8, 1945–Jan. 10, 1949
  Phil M. Donnelly (D)
Jan. 10, 1949–Jan. 12, 1953
  Forrest Smith (D)
Jan. 12, 1953–Jan. 14, 1957
  Phil M. Donnelly (D)
Jan. 14, 1957–Jan. 9, 1961
  James T. Blair, Jr. (D)
Jan. 9, 1961–Jan. 11, 1965
  John M. Dalton (D)
Jan. 11, 1965–Jan. 8, 1973
  Warren E. Hearnes (D)
Jan. 8, 1973–Jan. 10, 1977
  Christopher S. Bond (R)
Jan. 10, 1977
  Joseph P. Teasdale (D)

MONTANA *(Four-Year Term)*
Jan. 7, 1901–Apr. 1, 1908
  Joseph K. Toole (D)
Apr. 1, 1908–Jan. 5, 1913
  Edwin L. Norris (D)
Jan. 6, 1913–Jan. 2, 1921
  Samuel V. Stewart (D)
Jan. 3, 1921–Jan. 4, 1925
  Joseph M. Dixon (R)
Jan. 4, 1925–Mar. 13, 1933
  John E. Erickson (D)
Mar. 13, 1933–Dec. 15, 1935
  Frank H. Cooney (D)
Dec. 16, 1935–Jan. 4, 1937
  William E. Holt (D)
Jan. 4, 1937–Jan. 6, 1941
  Roy E. Ayers (D)
Jan. 6, 1941–Jan. 3, 1949
  Samuel C. Ford (R)
Jan. 3, 1949–Jan. 4, 1953
  John W. Bonner (D)
Jan. 4, 1953–Jan. 4, 1961
  J. Hugo Aronson (R)
Jan. 4, 1961–Jan. 25, 1962
  Donald G. Nutter (R)
Jan. 26, 1962–Jan. 6, 1969
  Tim M. Babcock (R)
Jan. 6, 1969–Jan. 1, 1973
  Forrest H. Anderson (D)
Jan. 1, 1973
  Thomas L. Judge (D)

NEBRASKA *(Four-Year Term)*
Jan. 5, 1899–Jan. 3, 1901
  William A. Poynter (FUS)
Jan. 3, 1901–May 1, 1901
  Charles H. Dietrich (R)
May 1, 1901–Jan. 8, 1903
  Ezra P. Savage (R)
Jan. 8, 1903–Jan. 3, 1907
  John H. Mickey (R)
Jan. 3, 1907–Jan. 7, 1909
  George L. Sheldon (R)
Jan. 7, 1909–Jan. 5, 1911
  Ashton C. Shallenberger (D)
Jan. 5, 1911–Jan. 9, 1913
  Chester H. Aldrich (R)
Jan. 9, 1913–Jan. 4, 1917
  John H. Morehead (D)
Jan. 4, 1917–Jan. 9, 1919
  Keith Neville (D)
Jan. 9, 1919–Jan. 3, 1923
  Samuel R. McKelvie (R)
Jan. 4, 1923–Jan. 8, 1925
  Charles W. Bryan (D)

Jan. 8, 1925–Jan. 3, 1929
 Adam McMullen (R)
Jan. 3, 1929–Jan. 8, 1931
 Arthur J. Weaver (R)
Jan. 8, 1931–Jan. 3, 1935
 Charles W. Bryan (D)
Jan. 3, 1935–Jan. 9, 1941
 Robert L. Cochran (D)
Jan. 9, 1941–Jan. 9, 1947
 Dwight P. Griswold (R)
Jan. 9, 1947–Jan. 8, 1953
 Val Peterson (R)
Jan. 8, 1953–Jan. 6, 1955
 Robert Berkey Crosby (R)
Jan. 6, 1955–Jan. 8, 1959
 Victor E. Anderson (R)
Jan. 8, 1959–Sept. 9, 1960
 Ralph G. Brooks (D)
Sept. 9, 1960–Jan. 5, 1961
 Dwight W. Burney (R)
Jan. 5, 1961–Jan. 5, 1967
 Frank B. Morrison (D)
Jan. 5, 1967–Jan. 7, 1971
 Norbert T. Tiemann (R)
Jan. 7, 1971
 J. James Exon (D)

NEVADA *(Four-Year Term)*
Apr. 10, 1896–Jan. 1, 1903
 Reinhold Sadler (SIL R)
Jan. 1, 1903–May 22, 1908
 John Sparks (D & SILVER)
May 22, 1908–Jan. 2, 1911
 Denver S. Dickerson (D)
Jan. 2, 1911–Jan. 4, 1915
 Tasker L. Oddie (R)
Jan. 4, 1915–Jan. 1, 1923
 Emmet D. Boyle (D)
Jan. 1, 1923–Jan. 3, 1927
 James G. Scrugham (D)
Jan. 3, 1927–Mar. 21, 1934
 Frederick B. Balzar (R)
Mar. 21, 1934–Jan. 7, 1935
 Morley I. Griswold (R)
Jan. 7, 1935–Jan. 2, 1939
 Richard Kirman, Sr. (D)
Jan. 2, 1939–July 24, 1945
 Edward P. Carville (D)
July 24, 1945–Jan. 1, 1951
 Vail M. Pittman (D)
Jan. 1, 1951–Jan. 5, 1959
 Charles H. Russell (R)
Jan. 5, 1959–Jan. 2, 1967
 Grant Sawyer (D)

Jan. 2, 1967–Jan. 4, 1971
 Paul D. Laxalt (R)
Jan. 4, 1971
 Mike O'Callaghan (D)

NEW HAMPSHIRE *(Two-Year Term)*
Jan. 3, 1901–Jan. 1, 1903
 Chester B. Jordan (R)
Jan. 1, 1903–Jan. 5, 1905
 Nahum J. Batchelder (R)
Jan. 5, 1905–Jan. 3, 1907
 John McLane (R)
Jan. 3, 1907–Jan. 7, 1909
 Charles M. Floyd (R)
Jan. 7, 1909–Jan. 5, 1911
 Henry B. Quinby (R)
Jan. 5, 1911–Jan. 2, 1913
 Robert P. Bass (R)
Jan. 2, 1913–Jan. 7, 1915
 Samuel D. Felker (D)
Jan. 7, 1915–Jan. 3, 1917
 Rolland H. Spaulding (R)
Jan. 3, 1917–Jan. 2, 1919
 Henry Wilder Keyes (R)
Jan. 2, 1919–Jan. 6, 1921
 John H. Bartlett (R)
Jan. 6, 1921–Jan. 4, 1923
 Albert O. Brown (R)
Jan. 4, 1923–Jan. 1, 1925
 Fred H. Brown (D)
Jan. 1, 1925–Jan. 6, 1927
 John G. Winant (R)
Jan. 6, 1927–Jan. 3, 1929
 Huntley N. Spaulding (R)
Jan. 3, 1929–Jan. 1, 1931
 Charles W. Tobey (R)
Jan. 1, 1931–Jan. 3, 1935
 John G. Winant (R)
Jan. 3, 1935–Jan. 7, 1937
 H. Styles Bridges (R)
Jan. 7, 1937–Jan. 2, 1941
 Francis P. Murphy (R)
Jan. 2, 1941–Jan. 4, 1945
 Robert O. Blood (R)
Jan. 4, 1945–Jan. 6, 1949
 Charles M. Dale (R)
Jan. 6, 1949–Jan. 1, 1953
 Sherman Adams (R)
Jan. 1, 1953–Jan. 6, 1955
 Hugh Gregg (R)
Jan. 6, 1955–Jan. 1, 1959
 Lane Dwinell (R)
Jan. 1, 1959–Jan. 3, 1963
 Wesley Powell (R)

Jan. 3, 1963–Jan. 2, 1969
  John W. King (D)
Jan. 2, 1969–Jan. 4, 1973
  Walter Peterson (R)
Jan. 4, 1973
  Meldrim Thomson, Jr. (R)

NEW JERSEY (*Four-Year Term*)
Jan. 17, 1899–Jan. 21, 1902
  Foster M. Voorhees (R)
Jan. 21, 1902–Jan. 17, 1905
  Franklin Murphy (R)
Jan. 17, 1905–Jan. 21, 1908
  Edward C. Stokes (R)
Jan. 21, 1908–Jan. 17, 1911
  John F. Fort (R)
Jan. 17, 1911–Mar. 1, 1913
  Woodrow Wilson (D)
Mar. 1, 1913–Oct. 28, 1913
  James F. Fielder (D)
Oct. 28, 1913–Jan. 20, 1914
  Leon R. Taylor (D)
Jan. 20, 1914–Jan. 15, 1917
  James F. Fielder (D)
Jan. 15, 1917–May 16, 1919
  Walter E. Edge (R)
May 16, 1919–Jan. 13, 1920
  William N. Runyon (R)
Jan. 13, 1920–Jan. 20, 1920
  Clarence E. Case (R)
Jan. 20, 1920–Jan. 15, 1923
  Edward I. Edwards (D)
Jan. 15, 1923–Jan. 19, 1926
  George S. Silzer (D)
Jan. 19, 1926–Jan. 15, 1929
  Arthur Harry Moore (D)
Jan. 15, 1929–Jan. 19, 1932
  Morgan F. Larson (R)
Jan. 19, 1932–Jan. 3, 1935
  Arthur Harry Moore (D)
Jan. 3, 1935–Jan. 8, 1935
  Clifford R. Powell (R)
Jan. 8, 1935–Jan. 15, 1935
  Horace G. Prall (R)
Jan. 15, 1935–Jan. 18, 1938
  Harold G. Hoffman (R)
Jan. 18, 1938–Jan. 21, 1941
  Arthur Harry Moore (D)
Jan. 21, 1941–Jan. 18, 1944
  Charles Edison (D)
Jan. 18, 1944–Jan. 21, 1947
  Walter E. Edge (R)
Jan. 21, 1947–Jan. 19, 1954
  Alfred E. Driscoll (R)

Jan. 19, 1954–Jan. 16, 1962
  Robert B. Meyner (D)
Jan. 16, 1962–Jan. 20, 1970
  Richard J. Hughes (D)
Jan. 20, 1970–Jan. 15, 1974
  William T. Cahill (R)
Jan. 15, 1974
  Brendan T. Byrne (D)

NEW MEXICO (*Four-Year Term*)
Jan. 6, 1912–Jan. 1, 1917
  William C. McDonald (D)
Jan. 1, 1917–Feb. 18, 1917
  Ezequiel C. de Baca (D)
Feb. 19, 1917–Jan. 1, 1919
  Washington E. Lindsey (R)
Jan. 1, 1919–Jan. 1, 1921
  Octaviano A. Larrazolo (R)
Jan. 1, 1921–Jan. 1, 1923
  Merritt C. Mechem (R)
Jan. 1, 1923–Jan. 1, 1925
  James F. Hinkle (D)
Jan. 1, 1925–Jan. 1, 1927
  Arthur T. Hannett (D)
Jan. 1, 1927–Jan. 1, 1931
  Richard C. Dillon (R)
Jan. 1, 1931–Sept. 25, 1933
  Arthur Seligman (D)
Sept. 25, 1933–Jan. 1, 1935
  Andrew W. Hockenhull (D)
Jan. 1, 1935–Jan. 1, 1939
  Clyde Tingley (D)
Jan. 1, 1939–Jan. 1, 1943
  John E. Miles (D)
Jan. 1, 1943–Jan. 1, 1947
  John J. Dempsey (D)
Jan. 1, 1947–Jan. 1, 1951
  Thomas J. Mabry (D)
Jan. 1, 1951–Jan. 1, 1955
  Edwin L. Mechem (R)
Jan. 1, 1955–Jan. 1, 1957
  John F. Simms (D)
Jan. 1, 1957–Jan. 1, 1959
  Edwin L. Mechem (R)
Jan. 1, 1959–Jan. 1, 1961
  John Burroughs (D)
Jan. 1, 1961–Nov. 30, 1962
  Edwin L. Mechem (R)
Nov. 30, 1962–Jan. 1, 1963
  Tom Bolack (R)
Jan. 1, 1963–Jan. 1, 1967
  Jack M. Campbell (D)
Jan. 1, 1967–Jan. 1, 1971
  David F. Cargo (R)

Jan. 1, 1971–Jan. 1, 1975
  Bruce King (D)
Jan. 1, 1975
  Jerry Apodaca (D)

NEW YORK *(Four-Year Term)*
Jan. 1, 1899–Jan. 1, 1901
  Theodore Roosevelt (R)
Jan. 1, 1901–Jan. 1, 1905
  Benjamin B. Odell, Jr. (R)
Jan. 1, 1905–Jan. 1, 1907
  Frank W. Higgins (R)
Jan. 1, 1907–Oct. 6, 1910
  Charles Evans Hughes (R)
Oct. 6, 1910–Jan. 1, 1911
  Horace White (R)
Jan. 1, 1911–Jan. 1, 1913
  John A. Dix (D)
Jan. 1, 1913–Oct. 17, 1913
  William Sulzer (D)
Oct. 17, 1913–Jan. 1, 1915
  Martin H. Glynn (D)
Jan. 1, 1915–Jan. 1, 1919
  Charles S. Whitman (R)
Jan. 1, 1919–Jan. 1, 1921
  Alfred E. Smith (D)
Jan. 1, 1921–Jan. 1, 1923
  Nathan L. Miller (R)
Jan. 1, 1923–Jan. 1, 1929
  Alfred E. Smith (D)
Jan. 1, 1929–Jan. 1, 1933
  Franklin D. Roosevelt (D)
Jan. 1, 1933–Dec. 3, 1942
  Herbert H. Lehman (D)
Dec. 3, 1942–Jan. 1, 1943
  Charles Poletti (D)
Jan. 1, 1943–Jan. 1, 1955
  Thomas E. Dewey (R)
Jan. 1, 1955–Jan. 1, 1959
  W. Averell Harriman (D)
Jan. 1, 1959–Dec. 18, 1973
  Nelson A. Rockefeller (R)
Dec. 18, 1973–Jan. 1, 1975
  Malcolm Wilson (R)
Jan. 1, 1975
  Hugh Carey (D)

NORTH CAROLINA *(Four-Year Term)*
Jan. 15, 1901–Jan. 11, 1905
  Charles B. Aycock (D)
Jan. 11, 1905–Jan. 12, 1909
  R. B. Glenn (D)
Jan. 12, 1909–Jan. 15, 1913
  W. W. Kitchin (D)

Jan. 15, 1913–Jan. 11, 1917
  Locke Craig (D)
Jan. 11, 1917–Jan. 12, 1921
  Thomas W. Bickett (D)
Jan. 12, 1921–Jan. 14, 1925
  Cameron Morrison (D)
Jan. 14, 1925–Jan. 11, 1929
  Angus Wilton McLean (D)
Jan. 11, 1929–Jan. 5, 1933
  O. Max Gardner (D)
Jan. 5, 1933–Jan. 7, 1937
  John C. B. Ehringhaus (D)
Jan. 7, 1937–Jan. 9, 1941
  Clyde R. Hoey (D)
Jan. 9, 1941–Jan. 4, 1945
  J. Melville Broughton (D)
Jan. 4, 1945–Jan. 6, 1949
  R. Gregg Cherry (D)
Jan. 6, 1949–Jan. 8, 1953
  W. Kerr Scott (D)
Jan. 8, 1953–Nov. 7, 1954
  William B. Umstead (D)
Nov. 7, 1954–Jan. 5, 1961
  Luther H. Hodges (D)
Jan. 5, 1961–Jan. 8, 1965
  Terry Sanford (D)
Jan. 8, 1965–Jan. 3, 1969
  Dan K. Moore (D)
Jan. 3, 1969–Jan. 5, 1973
  Robert W. Scott (D)
Jan. 5, 1973–Jan. 8, 1977
  James E. Holshouser, Jr. (R)
Jan. 8, 1977
  James B. Hunt, Jr. (D)

NORTH DAKOTA *(Four-Year Term)*
Jan. 3, 1899–Jan. 10, 1901
  Frederick B. Fancher (R)
Jan. 10, 1901–Jan. 4, 1905
  Frank White (R)
Jan. 5, 1905–Jan. 9, 1907
  Elmore Y. Sarles (R)
Jan. 9, 1907–Jan. 8, 1913
  John Burke (D)
Jan. 8, 1913–Jan. 3, 1917
  Louis B. Hanna (R)
Jan. 3, 1917–Nov. 23, 1921
  Lynn J. Frazier (R)
Nov. 23, 1921–Jan. 5, 1925
  Ragnvald A. Nestos (R)
Jan. 7, 1925–Aug. 28, 1928
  Arthur G. Sorlie (R)
Aug. 28, 1928–Jan. 9, 1929
  Walter J. Maddock (R)

Jan. 9, 1929–Dec. 31, 1932
  George F. Shafer (R)
Dec. 31, 1932–July 17, 1934
  William Langer (R)
July 17, 1934–Jan. 7, 1935
  Ole H. Olson (R)
Jan. 7, 1935–Feb. 2, 1935
  Thomas H. Moodie (D)
Feb. 2, 1935–Jan. 6, 1937
  Walter Welford (R)
Jan. 6, 1937–Jan. 5, 1939
  William Langer (I)
Jan. 5, 1939–Jan. 4, 1945
  John Moses (D)
Jan. 4, 1945–Jan. 3, 1951
  Fred G. Aandahl (R)
Jan. 3, 1951–Jan. 9, 1957
  C. Norman Brunsdale (R)
Jan. 9, 1957–Jan. 4, 1961
  John E. Davis (R)
Jan. 4, 1961–Jan. 2, 1973
  William L. Guy (D)
Jan. 2, 1973
  Arthur A. Link (D)

OHIO *(Four-Year Term)*
Jan. 8, 1900–Jan. 11, 1904
  George K. Nash (R)
Jan. 11, 1904–Jan. 8, 1906
  Myron T. Herrick (R)
Jan. 8, 1906–June 18, 1906
  John M. Pattison (D)
June 18, 1906–Jan. 11, 1909
  Andrew L. Harris (R)
Jan. 11, 1909–Jan. 13, 1913
  Judson Harmon (D)
Jan. 13, 1913–Jan. 11, 1915
  James M. Cox (D)
Jan. 11, 1915–Jan. 8, 1917
  Frank B. Willis (R)
Jan. 8, 1917–Jan. 10, 1921
  James M. Cox (D)
Jan. 10, 1921–Jan. 8, 1923
  Harry L. Davis (R)
Jan. 8, 1923–Jan. 14, 1929
  Alvin Victor Donahey (D)
Jan. 14, 1929–Jan. 12, 1931
  Myers Y. Cooper (R)
Jan. 12, 1931–Jan. 14, 1935
  George White (D)
Jan. 14, 1935–Jan. 9, 1939
  Martin L. Davey (D)
Jan. 9, 1939–Jan. 8, 1945
  John W. Bricker (R)

Jan. 8, 1945–Jan. 13, 1947
  Frank J. Lausche (D)
Jan. 13, 1947–Jan. 10, 1949
  Thomas J. Herbert (R)
Jan. 10, 1949–Jan. 3, 1957
  Frank J. Lausche (D)
Jan. 3, 1957–Jan. 14, 1957
  John W. Brown (R)
Jan. 14, 1957–Jan. 12, 1959
  C. William O'Neill (R)
Jan. 12, 1959–Jan. 14, 1963
  Michael V. DiSalle (D)
Jan. 14, 1963–Jan. 11, 1971
  James A. Rhodes (R)
Jan. 11, 1971–Jan. 13, 1975
  John J. Gilligan (D)
Jan. 13, 1975
  James A. Rhodes (D)

OKLAHOMA *(Four-Year Term)*
Nov. 16, 1907–Jan. 9, 1911
  Charles N. Haskell (D)
Jan. 9, 1911–Jan. 11, 1915
  Lee Cruce (D)
Jan. 11, 1915–Jan. 13, 1919
  Robert L. Williams (D)
Jan. 13, 1919–Jan. 8, 1923
  James B. A. Robertson (D)
Jan. 8, 1923–Nov. 19, 1923
  John C. Walton (D)
Nov. 19, 1923–Jan. 10, 1927
  Martin E. Trapp (D)
Jan. 10, 1927–Mar. 20, 1929
  Henry S. Johnston (D)
Mar. 20, 1929–Jan. 12, 1931
  William J. Holloway (D)
Jan. 12, 1931–Jan. 14, 1935
  William H. Murray (D)
Jan. 14, 1935–Jan. 9, 1939
  Ernest W. Marland (D)
Jan. 9, 1939–Jan. 11, 1943
  Leon C. Phillips (D)
Jan. 11, 1943–Jan. 13, 1947
  Robert S. Kerr (D)
Jan. 13, 1947–Jan. 8, 1951
  Roy J. Turner (D)
Jan. 8, 1951–Jan. 10, 1955
  Johnston Murray (D)
Jan. 10, 1955–Jan. 12, 1959
  Raymond D. Gary (D)
Jan. 12, 1959–Jan. 6, 1963
  J. Howard Edmondson (D)
Jan. 6, 1963–Jan. 14, 1963
  George P. Nigh (D)

Jan. 14, 1963–Jan. 9, 1967
  Henry L. Bellmon (R)
Jan. 9, 1967–Jan. 11, 1971
  Dewey F. Bartlett (R)
Jan. 11, 1971–Jan. 13, 1975
  David Hall (D)
Jan. 13, 1975
  David L. Boren (D)

OREGON *(Four-Year Term)*
Jan. 9, 1899–Jan. 14, 1903
  Theodore T. Geer (R)
Jan. 14, 1903–Mar. 1, 1909
  George E. Chamberlain (D)
Mar. 1, 1909–June 17, 1910
  Frank W. Benson (R)
June 17, 1910–Jan. 10, 1911
  Jay Bowerman (R)
Jan. 10, 1911–Jan. 12, 1915
  Oswald West (D)
Jan. 12, 1915–Mar. 3, 1919
  James Withycombe (R)
Mar. 3, 1919–Jan. 8, 1923
  Ben W. Olcott (R)
Jan. 8, 1923–Jan. 10, 1927
  Walter M. Pierce (D)
Jan. 10, 1927–Dec. 21, 1929
  Isaac L. Patterson (R)
Dec. 22, 1929–Jan. 12, 1931
  A. W. Norblad (R)
Jan. 12, 1931–Jan. 14, 1935
  Julius L. Meier (I)
Jan. 14, 1935–Jan. 9, 1939
  Charles H. Martin (D)
Jan. 9, 1939–Jan. 11, 1943
  Charles A. Sprague (R)
Jan. 11, 1943–Oct. 28, 1947
  Earl Snell (R)
Oct. 30, 1947–Jan. 10, 1949
  John H. Hall (R)
Jan. 10, 1949–Dec. 27, 1952
  Douglas McKay (R)
Dec. 27, 1952–Jan. 31, 1956
  Paul L. Patterson (R)
Feb. 1, 1956–Jan. 14, 1957
  Elmo Smith (R)
Jan. 14, 1957–Jan. 12, 1959
  Robert D. Holmes (D)
Jan. 12, 1959–Jan. 9, 1967
  Mark O. Hatfield (R)
Jan. 9, 1967–Jan. 13, 1975
  Tom McCall (R)
Jan. 13, 1975
  Robert W. Straub (D)

PENNSYLVANIA *(Four-Year Term)*
Jan. 17, 1899–Jan. 20, 1903
  William A. Stone (R)
Jan. 20, 1903–Jan. 15, 1907
  Samuel W. Pennypacker (R)
Jan. 15, 1907–Jan. 17, 1911
  Edwin S. Stuart (R)
Jan. 17, 1911–Jan. 19, 1915
  John K. Tener (R)
Jan. 19, 1915–Jan. 21, 1919
  Martin G. Brumbaugh (R)
Jan. 21, 1919–Jan. 16, 1923
  William C. Sproul (R)
Jan. 16, 1923–Jan. 18, 1927
  Gifford Pinchot (R)
Jan. 18, 1927–Jan. 20, 1931
  John S. Fisher (R)
Jan. 20, 1931–Jan. 15, 1935
  Gifford Pinchot (R, PROG)
Jan. 15,1935–Jan. 17, 1939
  George H. Earle (D)
Jan. 17, 1939–Jan. 19, 1943
  Arthur H. James (R)
Jan. 19, 1943–Jan. 2, 1947
  Edward Martin (R)
Jan. 2, 1947–Jan. 21, 1947
  John C. Bell, Jr. (R)
Jan. 21, 1947–Jan. 16, 1951
  James H. Duff (R)
Jan. 16, 1951–Jan. 18, 1955
  John S. Fine (R)
Jan. 18, 1955–Jan. 20, 1959
  George M. Leader (D)
Jan. 20, 1959–Jan. 15, 1963
  David L. Lawrence (D)
Jan. 15, 1963–Jan. 17, 1967
  William W. Scranton (R)
Jan. 17, 1967–Jan. 19, 1971
  Raymond P. Shafer (R)
Jan. 19, 1971
  Milton J. Shapp (D)

RHODE ISLAND *(Two-Year Term)*
May 29, 1900–Dec. 16, 1901
  William Gregory (R)
Dec. 16, 1901–Jan. 6, 1903
  Charles D. Kimball (R)
Jan. 6, 1903–Jan. 3, 1905
  Lucius F. C. Garvin (D)
Jan. 3, 1905–Jan. 1, 1907
  George H. Utter (R)
Jan. 1, 1907–Jan. 5, 1909
  James H. Higgins (D)
Jan. 5, 1909–Jan. 5, 1915
  Aram J. Pothier (R)

Jan. 5, 1915–Jan. 4, 1921
   R. Livingston Beeckman (R)
Jan. 4, 1921–Jan. 2, 1923
   Emery J. San Souci (R)
Jan. 2, 1923–Jan. 6, 1925
   William S. Flynn (D)
Jan. 6, 1925–Feb. 4, 1928
   Aram J. Pothier (R)
Feb. 4, 1928–Jan. 3, 1933
   Norman S. Case (R)
Jan. 3, 1933–Jan. 5, 1937
   Theodore F. Green (D)
Jan. 5, 1937–Jan. 3, 1939
   Robert E. Quinn (D)
Jan. 3, 1939–Jan. 7, 1941
   William H. Vanderbilt (R)
Jan. 7, 1941–Oct. 6, 1945
   J. Howard McGrath (D)
Oct. 6, 1945–Dec. 19, 1950
   John O. Pastore (D)
Dec. 19, 1950–Jan. 2, 1951
   John S. McKiernan (D)
Jan. 2, 1951–Jan. 6, 1959
   Dennis J. Roberts (D)
Jan. 6, 1959–Jan. 3, 1961
   Christopher Del Sesto (R)
Jan. 3, 1961–Jan. 1, 1963
   John A. Notte, Jr. (D)
Jan. 1, 1963–Jan. 7, 1969
   John H. Chafee (R)
Jan. 7, 1969–Jan. 2, 1973
   Frank Licht (D)
Jan. 2, 1973–Jan. 4, 1977
   Philip W. Noel (D)
Jan. 4, 1977
   J. Joseph Garrahy (D)

SOUTH CAROLINA *(Four-Year Term)*
June 2, 1899–Jan. 20, 1903
   Miles B. McSweeney (D)
Jan. 20, 1903–Jan. 15, 1907
   Duncan C. Heyward (D)
Jan. 15, 1907–Jan. 17, 1911
   Martin F. Ansel (D)
Jan. 17, 1911–Jan. 14, 1915
   Coleman L. Blease (D)
Jan. 14, 1915–Jan. 19, 1915
   Charles A. Smith (D)
Jan. 19, 1915–Jan. 21, 1919
   Richard I. Manning (D)
Jan. 21, 1919–May 20, 1922
   Robert A. Cooper (D)
May 20, 1922–Jan. 16, 1923
   Wilson G. Harvey (D)

Jan. 16, 1923–Jan. 18, 1927
   Thomas G. McLeod (D)
Jan. 18, 1927–Jan. 20, 1931
   John G. Richards (D)
Jan. 20, 1931–Jan. 15, 1935
   Ibra C. Blackwood (D)
Jan. 15, 1935–Jan. 17, 1939
   Olin D. Johnston (D)
Jan. 17, 1939–Nov. 4, 1941
   Burnet R. Maybank (D)
Nov. 4, 1941–Feb. 27, 1942
   Joseph E. Harley (D)
Mar. 2, 1942–Jan. 19, 1943
   Richard M. Jeffries (D)
Jan. 19, 1943–Jan. 2, 1945
   Olin D. Johnson (D)
Jan. 2, 1945–Jan. 21, 1947
   Ransome J. Williams (D)
Jan. 21, 1947–Jan. 16, 1951
   J. Strom Thurmond (D)
Jan. 16, 1951–Jan. 18, 1955
   James F. Byrnes (D)
Jan. 18, 1955–Jan. 20, 1959
   George Bell Timmerman, Jr. (D)
Jan. 20, 1959–Jan. 15, 1963
   Ernest F. Hollings (D)
Jan. 15, 1963–Apr. 22, 1965
   Donald S. Russell (D)
Apr. 22, 1965–Jan. 19, 1971
   Robert E. McNair (D)
Jan. 19, 1971–Jan. 21, 1975
   John C. West (D)
Jan. 21, 1975
   James Edwards (R)

SOUTH DAKOTA *(Four-Year Term)*
Jan. 8, 1901–Jan. 3, 1905
   Charles N. Herreld (R)
Jan. 3, 1905–Jan. 8, 1907
   Samuel H. Elrod (R)
Jan. 8, 1907–Jan. 5, 1909
   Coe I. Crawford (R)
Jan. 5, 1909–Jan. 7, 1913
   Robert S. Vessey (R)
Jan. 7, 1913–Jan. 2, 1917
   Frank M. Byrne (R)
Jan. 2, 1917–Jan. 4, 1921
   Peter Norbeck (R)
Jan. 4, 1921–Jan. 6, 1925
   William H. McMaster (R)
Jan. 6, 1925–Jan. 4, 1927
   Carl Gunderson (R)
Jan. 4, 1927–Jan. 6, 1931
   William J. Bulow (D)

Jan. 6, 1931–Jan. 3, 1933
  Warren E. Green (R)
Jan 3, 1933–Jan. 5, 1937
  Tom Berry (D)
Jan. 5, 1937–Jan. 3, 1939
  Leslie Jensen (R)
Jan. 3, 1939–Jan. 5, 1943
  Harlan J. Bushfield (R)
Jan. 5, 1943–Jan. 7, 1947
  Merrell Q. Sharpe (R)
Jan. 7, 1947–Jan. 2, 1951
  George T. Mickelson (R)
Jan. 2, 1951–Jan. 4, 1955
  Sigurd Anderson (R)
Jan. 4. 1955–Jan. 6, 1959
  Joe Foss (R)
Jan. 6, 1959–Jan. 3, 1961
  Ralph E. Herseth (D)
Jan. 3, 1961–Jan. 5, 1965
  Archie M. Gubbrud (R)
Jan. 5, 1965–Jan. 7, 1969
  Nils A. Boe (R)
Jan. 7, 1969–Jan. 5, 1971
  Frank L. Farrar (R)
Jan. 5, 1971
  Richard F. Kneip (D)

TENNESSEE *(Four-Year Term)*
Jan. 16, 1899–Jan. 19, 1903
  Benton McMillin (D)
Jan. 19, 1903–Mar. 21, 1905
  James B. Frazier (D)
Mar. 21, 1905–Jan. 17, 1907
  John I. Cox (D)
Jan. 17, 1907–Jan. 26, 1911
  Malcolm R. Patterson (D)
Jan. 26, 1911–Jan. 17, 1915
  Ben W. Hooper (R)
Jan. 17, 1915–Jan. 15, 1919
  Thomas C. Rye (D)
Jan. 15, 1919–Jan. 15, 1921
  Albert H. Roberts (D)
Jan. 15, 1921–Jan. 16, 1923
  Alfred A. Taylor (R)
Jan. 16, 1923–Oct. 2, 1927
  Austin Peay (D)
Oct. 3, 1927–Jan. 17, 1933
  Henry H. Horton (D)
Jan. 17, 1933–Jan. 15, 1937
  Hill McAlister (D)
Jan. 15, 1937–Jan. 16, 1939
  Gordon Browning (D)
Jan. 16, 1939–Jan. 16, 1945
  Prentice Cooper (D)

Jan. 16, 1945–Jan. 17, 1949
  James N. McCord (D)
Jan. 17, 1949–Jan. 15, 1953
  Gordon Browning (D)
Jan. 15, 1953–Jan. 19, 1959
  Frank G. Clement (D)
Jan. 19, 1959–Jan. 15, 1963
  Buford Ellington (D)
Jan. 15, 1963–Jan. 16, 1967
  Frank G. Clement (D)
Jan. 16, 1967–Jan. 16, 1971
  Buford Ellington (D)
Jan. 16, 1971–Jan. 18, 1975
  Winfield Dunn (R)
Jan. 18, 1975
  Ray Blanton (D)

TEXAS *(Four-Year Term)*
Jan. 17, 1899–Jan. 20, 1903
  Joseph D. Sayers (D)
Jan. 20, 1903–Jan. 15, 1907
  Samuel W. T. Lanham (D)
Jan. 15, 1907–Jan. 17, 1911
  Thomas M. Campbell (D)
Jan. 17, 1911–Jan. 19, 1915
  Oscar B. Colquitt (D)
Jan. 19, 1915–Aug. 25, 1917
  James E. Ferguson (D)
Aug. 25, 1917–Jan. 18, 1921
  William P. Hobby (D)
Jan. 18, 1921–Jan. 20, 1925
  Pat M. Neff (D)
Jan. 20, 1925–Jan. 18, 1927
  Miriam A. Ferguson (D)
Jan. 18, 1927–Jan. 20, 1931
  Dan Moody (D)
Jan. 20, 1931–Jan. 17, 1933
  Ross S. Sterling (D)
Jan. 17, 1933–Jan. 15, 1935
  Miriam A. Ferguson (D)
Jan. 15, 1935–Jan. 17, 1939
  James V. Allred (D)
Jan. 17, 1939–Aug. 4, 1941
  W. Lee O'Daniel (D)
Aug. 4, 1941–Jan. 21, 1947
  Coke R. Stevenson (D)
Jan. 21, 1947–July 11, 1949
  Beauford H. Jester (D)
July 11, 1949–Jan. 15, 1957
  Allan Shivers (D)
Jan. 15, 1957–Jan. 15, 1963
  Price Daniel (D)
Jan. 15, 1963–Jan. 21, 1969
  John B. Connally (D)

Jan. 21, 1969–Jan. 16, 1973
  Preston Smith (D)
Jan. 16, 1973
  Dolph Briscoe (D)

UTAH *(Four-Year Term)*
Jan. 6, 1896–Jan. 2, 1905
  Heber Manning Wells (R)
Jan. 2, 1905–Jan. 4, 1909
  John C. Cutler (R)
Jan. 4, 1909–Jan. 1, 1917
  William Spry (R)
Jan. 1, 1917–Jan. 3, 1921
  Simon Bamberger (D)
Jan. 3, 1921–Jan. 5, 1925
  Charles R. Mabey (R)
Jan. 5, 1925–Jan. 2, 1933
  George H. Dern (D)
Jan. 2, 1933–Jan. 6, 1941
  Henry H. Blood (D)
Jan. 6, 1941–Jan. 3, 1949
  Herbert B. Maw (D)
Jan. 3, 1949–Jan. 7, 1957
  J. Bracken Lee (R)
Jan. 7, 1957–Jan. 4, 1965
  George Dewey Clyde (R)
Jan. 4, 1965–Jan. 3, 1977
  Calvin L. Rampton (D)
Jan. 3, 1977
  Scott M. Matheson (D)

VERMONT *(Two-Year Term)*
Oct. 4, 1900–Oct. 3, 1902
  William W. Stickney (R)
Oct. 3, 1902–Oct. 6, 1904
  John G. McCullough (R)
Oct. 6, 1904–Oct. 4, 1906
  Charles J. Bell (R)
Oct. 4, 1906–Oct. 8, 1908
  Fletcher D. Proctor (D)
Oct. 8, 1908–Oct. 5, 1910
  George H. Prouty (R)
Oct. 5, 1910–Oct. 3, 1912
  John A. Mead (R)
Oct. 3, 1912–Jan. 7, 1915
  Allen M. Fletcher (R)
Jan. 7, 1915–Jan. 4, 1917
  Charles W. Gates (R)
Jan. 4, 1917–Jan. 9, 1919
  Horace F. Graham (R)
Jan. 9, 1919–Jan. 6, 1921
  Percival W. Clement (R)
Jan. 6, 1921–Jan. 4, 1923
  James Hartness (R)

Jan. 4, 1923–Jan. 8, 1925
  Redfield Proctor (R)
Jan. 8, 1925–Jan. 6, 1927
  Franklin S. Billings (R)
Jan. 6, 1927–Jan. 8, 1931
  John E. Weeks (R)
Jan. 8, 1931–Jan. 10, 1935
  Stanley C. Wilson (R)
Jan. 10, 1935–Jan. 7, 1937
  Charles M. Smith (R)
Jan. 7, 1937–Jan. 9, 1941
  George D. Aiken (R)
Jan. 9, 1941–Jan. 4, 1945
  William H. Wills (R)
Jan. 4, 1945–Jan. 9, 1947
  Mortimer R. Proctor (R)
Jan. 9, 1947–Jan. 16, 1950
  Ernest W. Gibson (R)
Jan. 16, 1950–Jan. 4, 1951
  Harold J. Arthur (R)
Jan. 4, 1951–Jan. 6, 1955
  Lee E. Emerson (R)
Jan. 6, 1955–Jan. 8, 1959
  Joseph B. Johnson (R)
Jan. 8, 1959–Jan. 5, 1961
  Robert T. Stafford (R)
Jan. 5, 1961–Jan. 10, 1963
  Frank Ray Keyser, Jr. (R)
Jan. 10, 1963–Jan. 9, 1969
  Philip H. Hoff (D)
Jan. 9, 1969–Jan. 4, 1973
  Deane C. Davis (R)
Jan. 4, 1973–Jan. 6, 1977
  Thomas P. Salmon (D)
Jan. 6, 1977
  Richard A. Snelling (R)

VIRGINIA *(Four-Year Term)*
Jan. 1, 1898–Jan. 1, 1902
  James Hoge Tyler (D)
Jan. 1, 1902–Feb. 1, 1906
  Andrew J. Montague (D)
Feb. 1, 1906–Feb. 1, 1910
  Claude A. Swanson (D)
Feb. 1, 1910–Feb. 1, 1914
  William H. Mann (D)
Feb. 1, 1914–Feb. 1, 1918
  Henry C. Stuart (D)
Feb. 1, 1918–Feb. 1, 1922
  Westmoreland Davis (D)
Feb. 1, 1922–Feb. 1, 1926
  E. Lee Trinkle (D)
Feb. 1, 1926–Jan. 15, 1930
  Harry F. Byrd (D)

Jan. 15, 1930–Jan. 17, 1934
  John G. Pollard (D)
Jan. 17, 1934–Jan. 19, 1938
  George C. Peery (D)
Jan. 19, 1938–Jan. 21, 1942
  James H. Price (D)
Jan. 21, 1942–Jan. 16, 1946
  Colgate W. Darden, Jr. (D)
Jan. 16, 1946–Jan. 18, 1950
  William M. Tuck (D)
Jan. 18, 1950–Jan. 20, 1954
  John S. Battle (D)
Jan. 20, 1954–Jan. 11, 1958
  Thomas B. Stanley (D)
Jan. 11, 1958–Jan. 13, 1962
  James Lindsay Almond, Jr. (D)
Jan. 13, 1962–Jan. 15, 1966
  Albertis S. Harrison, Jr. (D)
Jan. 16, 1966–Jan. 17, 1970
  Mills E. Godwin, Jr. (D)
Jan. 17, 1970–Jan. 12, 1974
  Linwood Holton (R)
Jan. 12, 1974
  Mills E. Godwin, Jr. (R)

WASHINGTON *(Four-Year Term)*
Jan. 11, 1897–Dec. 26, 1901
  John R. Rogers (PP, D)
Dec. 26, 1901–Jan. 9, 1905
  Henry McBride (R)
Jan. 9, 1905–Jan. 27, 1909
  Albert E. Mead (R)
Jan. 27, 1909–Mar. 28, 1909
  Samuel G. Cosgrove (R)
Mar. 29, 1909–Jan. 11, 1913
  Marion E. Hay (R)
Jan. 11, 1913–June 14, 1919
  Ernest Lister (D)
June 14, 1919–Jan. 12, 1925
  Louis F. Hart (R)
Jan. 12, 1925–Jan. 9, 1933
  Roland H. Hartley (R)
Jan. 9, 1933–Jan. 13, 1941
  Clarence D. Martin (D)
Jan. 13, 1941–Jan. 8, 1945
  Arthur B. Langlie (R)
Jan. 8, 1945–Jan. 10, 1949
  Monrad C. Wallgren (D)
Jan. 10, 1949–Jan. 14, 1957
  Arthur B. Langlie (R)

Jan. 14, 1957–Jan. 11, 1965
  Albert D. Rosellini (D)
Jan. 11, 1965–Jan. 12, 1977
  Daniel J. Evans (R)
Jan. 12, 1977
  Dixy Lee Ray (D)

WEST VIRGINIA *(Four-Year Term)*
Mar. 4, 1901–Mar. 4, 1905
  Albert B. White (R)
Mar. 4, 1905–Mar. 4, 1909
  William M. O. Dawson (R)
Mar. 4, 1909–Marc. 4, 1913
  William E. Glasscock (R)
Mar. 4, 1913–Mar. 4, 1917
  Henry D. Hatfield (R)
Mar. 4, 1917–Mar. 4, 1921
  John J. Cornwell (D)
Mar. 4, 1921–Mar. 4, 1925
  Ephraim F. Morgan (R)
Mar. 4, 1925–Mar. 4, 1929
  Howard M. Gore (R)
Mar. 4, 1929–Mar. 4, 1933
  William G. Conley (R)
Mar. 4, 1933–Jan. 18, 1937
  Herman G. Kump (D)
Jan. 18, 1937–Jan. 13, 1941
  Homer A. Holt (D)
Jan. 13, 1941–Jan. 15, 1945
  Matthew M. Neely (D)
Jan. 15, 1945–Jan. 17, 1949
  Clarence W. Meadows (D)
Jan. 17, 1949–Jan. 19, 1953
  Okey L. Patteson (D)
Jan. 19, 1953–Jan. 14, 1957
  William C. Marland (D)
Jan. 14, 1957–Jan. 16, 1961
  Cecil H. Underwood (R)
Jan. 16, 1961–Jan. 18, 1965
  William W. Barron (D)
Jan. 18, 1965–Jan. 13, 1969
  Hulett C. Smith (D)
Jan. 13, 1969–Jan. 17, 1977
  Arch A. Moore, Jr. (R)
Jan. 17, 1977
  John D. Rockefeller 4th (D)

WISCONSIN *(Four-Year Term)*
Jan. 7, 1901–Jan. 1, 1906
  Robert M. LaFollette (R)
Jan. 1, 1906–Jan. 2, 1911
  James O. Davidson (R)
Jan. 2, 1911–Jan. 4, 1915
  Francis E. McGovern (R)

Jan. 4, 1915–Jan. 3, 1921
  Emanuel L. Philipp (R)
Jan. 3, 1921–Jan. 3, 1927
  John J. Blaine (R)
Jan. 3, 1927–Jan. 7, 1929
  Fred R. Zimmerman (R)
Jan. 7, 1929–Jan. 5, 1931
  Walter J. Kohler, Sr. (R)
Jan. 5, 1931–Jan. 2, 1933
  Philip F. LaFollette (R)
Jan. 2, 1933–Jan. 7, 1935
  Albert G. Schmedeman (D)
Jan. 7, 1935–Jan. 2, 1939
  Philip F. LaFollette (PROG)
Jan. 2, 1939–Jan. 4, 1943
  Julius P. Heil (R)
  Orland S. Loomis (PROG)°
Jan. 4, 1943–Mar. 12, 1947
  Walter S. Goodland (R)
Mar. 12, 1947–Jan. 1, 1951
  Oscar Rennebohm (R)
Jan. 1, 1951–Jan. 7, 1957
  Walter J. Kohler, Jr. (R)
Jan. 7, 1957–Jan. 5, 1959
  Vernon W. Thomson (R)
Jan. 5, 1959–Jan. 7, 1963
  Gaylord A. Nelson (D)
Jan. 7, 1963–Jan. 4, 1965
  John W. Reynolds (D)
Jan. 4, 1965–Jan. 4, 1971
  Warren P. Knowles (R)
Jan. 4, 1971
  Patrick J. Lucey (D)

WYOMING *(Four-Year Term)*
Jan. 2, 1899–Apr. 28, 1903
  DeForest Richards (R)
Apr. 28, 1903–Jan. 2, 1905
  Fenimore C. Chatterton (R)
Jan. 2, 1905–Jan. 2, 1911
  Bryant B. Brooks (R)
Jan. 2, 1911–Jan. 4, 1915
  Joseph M. Carey (D)
Jan. 4, 1915–Feb. 26, 1917
  John B. Kendrick (D)
Feb. 26, 1917–Jan. 6, 1919
  Frank L. Houx (D)
Jan. 6, 1919–Jan. 1, 1923
  Robert D. Carey (R)
Jan. 1, 1923–Oct. 2, 1924
  William B. Ross (D)
Oct. 2, 1924–Jan. 5, 1925
  Frank E. Lucas (R)

°Elected, but died before taking office.

Jan. 5, 1925–Jan. 3, 1927
  Nellie T. Ross (D)
Jan. 3, 1927–Feb. 18, 1931
  Frank C. Emerson (R)
Feb. 18, 1931–Jan. 2, 1933
  Alonzo M. Clark (R)
Jan. 2, 1933–Jan. 2, 1939
  Leslie A. Miller (D)
Jan. 2, 1939–Jan. 4, 1943
  Nels H. Smith (R)
Jan. 4, 1943–Jan. 3, 1949
  Lester C. Hunt (D)
Jan. 3, 1949–Jan. 1, 1951
  Arthur G. Crane (R)
Jan. 1, 1951–Jan. 3, 1953
  Frank A. Barrett (R)
Jan. 3, 1953–Jan. 3, 1955
  Clifford Joy Rogers (R)
Jan. 3, 1955–Jan. 5, 1959
  Milward L. Simpson (R)
Jan. 5, 1959–Jan. 2, 1961
  John J. Hickey (D)
Jan. 2, 1961–Jan. 6, 1963
  Jack R. Gage (D)
Jan. 7, 1963–Jan. 2, 1967
  Clifford P. Hansen (R)
Jan. 2, 1967–Jan. 6, 1975
  Stanley K. Hathaway (R)
Jan. 6, 1975
  Ed Herschler (D)

UNITED STATES PRESIDENTS

Mar. 4, 1897–Mar. 3, 1901
  William McKinley
Mar. 4, 1901–Sept 14, 1901
  William McKinley
Sept. 14, 1901–Mar. 3, 1905
  Theodore Roosevelt
Mar. 4, 1905–Mar. 3, 1909
  Theodore Roosevelt
Mar. 4, 1909–Mar. 3, 1913
  William H. Taft
Mar. 4, 1913–Mar. 3, 1921
  Woodrow Wilson
Mar. 4, 1921–Aug. 2, 1923
  Warren G. Harding

Aug. 3, 1923–Mar. 3, 1925
Calvin Coolidge
Mar. 4, 1925–Mar. 4, 1929
Calvin Coolidge
Mar. 4, 1929–Mar. 3, 1933
Herbert C. Hoover
Mar. 4, 1933–Jan. 20, 1937
Franklin D. Roosevelt
Jan. 20, 1937–Jan. 20, 1941
Franklin D. Roosevelt
Jan. 20, 1941–Jan. 20, 1945
Franklin D. Roosevelt
Jan. 20, 1945–Apr. 12, 1945
Franklin D. Roosevelt
Apr. 12, 1945–Jan. 20, 1949
Harry S. Truman
Jan. 20, 1949–Jan. 20, 1953
Harry S. Truman
Jan. 20, 1953–Jan. 20, 1957
Dwight D. Eisenhower
Jan. 20, 1957–Jan. 20, 1961
Dwight D. Eisenhower
Jan. 20, 1961–Nov. 22, 1963
John F. Kennedy
Nov. 22, 1963–Jan. 20, 1965
Lyndon B. Johnson
Jan. 20, 1965–Jan. 20, 1969
Lyndon B. Johnson
Jan. 20, 1969–Jan. 20, 1973
Richard M. Nixon
Jan. 20, 1973–Aug. 9, 1974
Richard M. Nixon
Aug. 9, 1974–Jan. 20, 1977
Gerald R. Ford
Jan. 20, 1977–
Jimmy E. Carter

UNITED STATES SENATORS

ALABAMA

Class 2 *
Mar. 4, 1877–June 11, 1907
John T. Morgan (D)

*This designation has nothing to do with how well a Senator is doing his job. Rather, the Senate is divided so that every two years, one third of its seats expires.

June 18, 1907–Mar. 1, 1920
John H. Bankhead (D)
Mar. 5, 1920–Nov. 2, 1920
Braxton B. Comer (D)
Nov. 2, 1920–Mar. 3, 1931
J. Thomas Heflin (D)
Mar. 4, 1931–June 12, 1946
John H. Bankhead II (D)
June 15, 1946–Nov. 5, 1946
George R. Swift (D)
Nov. 6, 1946
John Sparkman (D)

Class 3
Mar. 4, 1897–July 27, 1907
Edmund W. Pettus (D)
Aug. 6, 1907–Aug. 8, 1913
Joseph F. Johnston (D)
May 11, 1914–Mar. 3, 1915
Francis S. White (D)
Mar. 4, 1915–Mar. 3, 1927
Oscar W. Underwood (D)
Mar. 4, 1927–Aug. 19, 1937
Hugo Black (D)
Aug. 20, 1937–Jan. 10, 1938
Dixie Bibb Graves (D)
Jan. 11, 1938–Jan. 2, 1969
Lister Hill (D)
Jan. 3, 1969
James B. Allen (D)

ALASKA

Class 2
Jan. 3, 1959–Dec. 11, 1968
E. L. Bartlett (D)
Dec. 24, 1968
Ted Stevens (R)

Class 3
Jan. 3, 1959–Jan. 2, 1969
Ernest Gruening (D)
Jan. 3, 1969
Mike Gravel (D)

ARIZONA

Class 1
Mar. 27, 1912–Jan. 2, 1941
Henry Fountain Ashurst (D)
Jan. 3, 1941–Jan. 2, 1953
Ernest W. McFarland (D)
Jan. 3, 1953–Jan. 2, 1965
Barry Goldwater (R)

Jan. 3, 1965–Jan. 2, 1977
    Paul J. Fannin (R)
Jan. 2, 1977
    Dennis DeConcini (D)

Class 3
Mar. 27, 1912–Mar. 3, 1921
    Marcus A. Smith (D)
Mar. 4, 1921–Mar. 3, 1927
    Ralph H. Cameron (R)
Mar. 4, 1927–Jan. 2, 1969
    Carl Hayden (D)
Jan. 3, 1969
    Barry Goldwater (R)

ARKANSAS

Class 2
Mar. 20, 1885–Mar. 3, 1907
    James H. Berry (D)
Mar. 4, 1907–Jan. 3, 1913
    Jeff Davis (D)
Jan. 6, 1913–Jan. 29, 1913
    John N. Heiskell (D)
Jan. 29, 1913–Mar. 3, 1913
    William M. Kavanaugh (D)
Mar. 10, 1913–July 14, 1937
    Joseph T. Robinson (D)
Nov. 15, 1937–Mar. 31, 1941
    John E. Miller (D)
Apr. 1, 1941–Jan. 2, 1943
    Lloyd Spencer (D)
Jan. 3 1943
    John L. McClellan (D)

Class 3
Mar. 4, 1885–Mar. 3, 1903
    James K. Jones (D)
Mar. 4, 1903–Oct. 1, 1916
    James P. Clarke (D)
Nov. 8, 1916–Mar. 2, 1921
    William F. Kirby (D)
Mar. 4, 1921–Nov. 6, 1931
    Thaddeus H. Caraway (D)
Nov. 13, 1931–Jan. 2, 1945
    Hattie W. Caraway (D)
Jan. 3, 1945–Dec. 31, 1974
    J. William Fulbright (D)
Jan. 3, 1975
    Dale Bumpers (D)

CALIFORNIA

Class 1
Feb. 7, 1900–Mar. 3, 1905
    Thomas R. Bard (R)
Mar. 4, 1905–Mar. 3, 1911
    Frank P. Flint (R)
Mar. 4, 1911–Mar. 3, 1917
    John D. Works (R)
Apr. 2, 1917–Aug. 6, 1945
    Hiram W. Johnson (R)
Aug. 26, 1945–Jan. 2, 1959
    William F. Knowland (R)
Jan. 3, 1959–July 30, 1964
    Clair Engle (D)
Aug. 4, 1964–Dec. 31, 1964
    Pierre Salinger (D)
Jan. 1, 1965–Jan. 2, 1971
    George Murphy (R)
Jan. 2, 1971–Jan. 2, 1977
    John V. Tunney (D)
Jan. 3, 1977
    S. I. Hayakawa (R)

Class 3
July 26, 1893–Mar. 3, 1915
    George C. Perkins (R)
Mar. 4, 1915–Mar. 3, 1921
    James D. Phelan (D)
Mar. 4, 1921–Mar. 3, 1933
    Samuel M. Shortridge (R)
Mar. 4, 1933–Nov. 8, 1938
    William Gibbs McAdoo (D)
Nov. 9, 1938–Jan. 2, 1939
    Thomas M. Storke (D)
Jan. 3, 1939–Nov. 30, 1950
    Sheridan Downey (D)
Dec. 4, 1950–Jan. 1, 1953
    Richard M. Nixon (R)
Jan. 2, 1953–Jan. 2, 1969
    Thomas H. Kuchel (R)
Jan. 3, 1969
    Alan Cranston (D)

COLORADO

Class 2
Mar. 4, 1889–Mar. 3, 1901
    Edward O. Wolcott (R)
Mar. 4, 1901–Mar. 3, 1907
    Thomas M. Patterson (D)
Mar. 4, 1907–Mar. 3, 1913
    Simon Guggenheim (R)
Mar. 4, 1913–Mar. 3, 1919
    John F. Shafroth (D)

Mar. 4, 1919–Mar. 3, 1931
    Lawrence C. Phipps (R)
Mar. 4, 1931–Jan. 2, 1937
    Edward P. Costigan (D)
Jan. 3, 1937–Jan. 2, 1955
    Edwin C. Johnson (D)
Jan. 3, 1955–Jan. 2, 1973
    Gordon Allott (R)
Jan. 3, 1973
    Floyd K. Haskell (D)

Class 3
Mar. 4, 1885–Mar. 3, 1909
    Henry M. Teller (R, I SIL R, D)
Mar. 4, 1909–Jan. 11, 1911
    Charles J. Hughes, Jr. (D)
Jan. 15, 1913–Mar. 3, 1921
    Charles S. Thomas (D)
Mar. 4, 1921–Mar. 24, 1923
    Samuel D. Nicholson (R)
May 17, 1923–Nov. 30, 1924
    Alva B. Adams (D)
Dec. 1, 1924–Mar. 3, 1927
    Rice W. Means (R)
Mar. 4, 1927–Aug. 27, 1932
    Charles W. Waterman (R)
Sept. 26, 1932–Dec. 6, 1932
    Walter Walker (D)
Dec. 7, 1932–Mar. 3, 1933
    Karl C. Schuyler (R)
Mar. 4, 1933–Dec. 1, 1941
    Alva B. Adams (D)
Dec. 20, 1941–Jan. 2, 1957
    Eugene D. Millikin (R)
Jan. 3, 1957–Jan. 2, 1963
    John A. Carroll (D)
Jan. 3, 1963–Jan. 2, 1975
    Peter H. Dominick (R)
Jan. 3, 1975
    Gary Hart (D)

CONNECTICUT

Class 1
Mar. 4, 1881–Mar. 3, 1905
    Joseph R. Hawley (R)
Mar. 4, 1905–Mar. 3, 1911
    Morgan G. Bulkeley (R)
Mar. 4, 1911–Mar. 3, 1929
    George P. McLean
Mar. 4, 1929–Jan. 2, 1935
    Frederic C. Walcott (R)
Jan. 3, 1935–Jan. 16, 1945
    Francis Maloney (D)

Feb. 15, 1945–Nov. 5, 1946
    Thomas C. Hart (R)
Dec. 27, 1946–Dec. 17, 1949
    Raymond E. Baldwin (R)
Dec. 17, 1949–Jan. 2, 1953
    William Benton (D)
Jan. 3, 1953–Jan. 2, 1959
    William A. Purtell (R)
Jan. 3, 1959–Jan. 2, 1971
    Thomas J. Dodd (D)
Jan. 3, 1971
    Lowell P. Weicker, Jr. (R)

Class 3
Mar. 4, 1879–Apr. 21, 1905
    Orville H. Platt (R)
May 10, 1905–Oct. 14, 1924
    Frank B. Brandegee (R)
Dec. 17, 1924–Mar. 3, 1933
    Hiram Bingham (R)
Mar. 4, 1933–Jan. 2, 1939
    Augustine Lonergan (D)
Jan. 3, 1939–Jan. 2, 1945
    John A. Danaher (R)
Jan. 3, 1945–July 28, 1952
    Brien McMahon (D)
Aug. 29, 1952–Nov. 4, 1952
    William A. Purtell (R)
Nov. 5, 1952–Jan. 2, 1963
    Prescott Bush (R)
Jan. 3, 1963
    Abraham Ribicoff (D)

DELAWARE

Class 1
Mar. 2, 1903–Mar. 3, 1905
    L. Heisler Ball (R)
June 13, 1906–Mar. 3, 1917
    Henry A. du Pont (R)
Mar. 4, 1917–July 2, 1921
    Josiah O. Wolcott (D)
July 7, 1921–Nov. 6, 1922
    T. Coleman du Pont (R)
Nov. 7, 1922–Mar. 3, 1929
    Thomas F. Bayard, Jr. (R)
Mar. 4, 1929–Jan. 2, 1941
    John G. Townsend, Jr. (R)
Jan. 3, 1941–Jan. 2, 1947
    James M. Tunnell (D)
Jan. 3, 1947–Dec. 31, 1970
    John J. Williams (R)
Jan. 1, 1971
    William V. Roth, Jr. (R)

200 ELECTIONS

Class 2

Jan. 19, 1897–Mar. 3, 1901
  Richard R. Kenney (R)
Mar. 2, 1903–Mar. 3, 1907
  James F. Allee (R)
Mar. 4, 1907–Mar. 3, 1913
  Harry A. Richardson (R)
Mar. 4, 1913–Mar. 3, 1919
  Willard Saulsbury, Jr. (D)
Mar. 4, 1919–Mar. 3, 1925
  L. Heisler Ball (R)
Mar. 4, 1925–Dec. 9, 1928
  T. Coleman du Pont (R)
Dec. 10, 1928–Jan. 2, 1937
  Daniel O. Hastings (R)
Jan. 3, 1937–Jan. 2, 1943
  James H. Hughes (D)
Jan. 3, 1943–Jan. 2, 1949
  C. Douglass Buck (R)
Jan. 3, 1949–Jan. 2, 1961
  J. Allen Frear, Jr. (D)
Jan. 3, 1961–Jan. 2, 1973
  J. Caleb Boggs (R)
Jan. 3, 1973
  Joseph R. Biden, Jr. (D)

FLORIDA

Class 1

Apr. 19, 1899–Mar. 3, 1911
  James P. Taliaferro (D)
Mar. 4, 1911–Mar. 3, 1917
  Nathan P. Bryan (D)
Mar. 4, 1917–May 8, 1936
  Park Trammell (D)
May. 26, 1936–Nov. 3, 1936
  Scott M. Loftin (D)
Nov. 4, 1936–Sept. 18, 1946
  Charles O. Andrews (D)
Sept. 25, 1946–Jan. 2, 1971
  Spessard L. Holland (D)
Jan. 3, 1971
  Lawton Chiles (D)

Class 3

May 24, 1897–Dec. 23, 1907
  Stephen R. Mallory (D)
Dec. 25, 1907–Mar. 22, 1908
  William J. Bryan (D)
Mar. 27, 1908–Mar. 3, 1909
  William H. Milton
Mar. 4, 1909–June 17, 1936
  Duncan U. Fletcher (D)
July 1, 1936–Nov. 3, 1936
  William L. Hill (D)

Nov. 4, 1936–Jan. 2, 1951
  Claude Pepper (D)
Jan. 3, 1951–Jan. 2, 1969
  George A. Smathers (D)
Jan. 3, 1969–Dec. 31, 1974
  Edward J. Gurney (R)
Jan. 2, 1975
  Richard Stone (D)

GEORGIA

Class 2

Mar. 4, 1895–Feb. 14, 1914
  Augustus O. Bacon (D)
Mar. 2, 1914–Nov. 3, 1914
  William S. West (D)
Nov. 4, 1914–Mar. 3, 1919
  Thomas W. Hardwick (D)
Mar. 4, 1919–Apr. 18, 1932
  William J. Harris (D)
Apr. 25, 1932–Jan. 11, 1933
  John S. Cohen (D)
Jan. 12, 1933–Jan. 21, 1971
  Richard B. Russell (D)
Feb. 1, 1971,–Nov. 7, 1972
  David H. Gambrell (D)
Nov. 8, 1972
  Sam Nunn (D)

Class 3

Mar. 4, 1897–Nov. 13, 1910
  Alexander S. Clay (D)
Nov. 17, 1910–July 14, 1911
  Joseph M. Terrell (D)
Dec. 4, 1911–Mar. 3, 1921
  Hoke Smith (D)
Mar. 4, 1921–Sept. 26, 1922
  Thomas E. Watson (D)
Oct. 3, 1922–Nov. 21, 1922
  Rebecca L. Felton (D)
Nov. 22, 1922–Jan. 2, 1957
  Walter F. George (D)
Jan. 3, 1957
  Herman E. Talmadge (D)

HAWAII

Class 1
Aug. 21, 1959
  Hiram L. Fong (R)
  Spark M. Matsundga (D)

Class 3
Aug. 21, 1959–Jan. 2, 1963
  Oren E. Long (D)

Jan. 3, 1963
    Daniel K. Inouye (D)

IDAHO

Class 2
Dec. 18, 1890–Mar. 3, 1901
    George L. Shoup (R)
Mar. 4, 1901–Mar. 3, 1907
    Fred T. Dubois (D)
Mar. 4, 1907–Jan. 19, 1940
    William E. Borah (R)
Jan. 27, 1940–Nov. 10, 1945
    John Thomas (R)
Nov. 17, 1945–Nov. 5, 1946
    Charles C. Gossett (D)
Nov. 6, 1946–Jan. 2, 1949
    Henry C. Dworshak (R)
Jan. 3, 1949–Oct. 8, 1949
    Bert H. Miller (D)
Oct. 14, 1949–July 23, 1962
    Henry C. Dworshak (R)
Aug. 6, 1962–Jan. 2, 1973
    Len B. Jordan (R)
Jan. 3, 1973
    James A. McClure (R)

Class 3
Mar. 4, 1897–Mar. 3, 1903
    Henry Heitfeld (POP)
Mar. 4, 1903–Oct. 17, 1912
    Weldon B. Heyburn (R)
Nov. 18, 1912–Feb. 5, 1913
    Kirtland I. Perky (D)
Feb. 6, 1913–Jan. 13, 1918
    James H. Brady (R)
Jan. 22, 1918–Jan. 14, 1921
    John F. Nugent (D)
Jan. 15, 1921–June 24, 1928
    Frank R. Gooding (R)
June 30, 1928–Mar. 3, 1933
    John Thomas (R)
Mar. 4, 1933–Jan. 2, 1939
    James P. Pope (D)
Jan. 3, 1939–Jan. 2, 1945
    D. Worth Clark (D)
Jan. 3, 1945–Jan. 2, 1951
    Glen H. Taylor (D)
Jan. 3, 1951–Jan. 2, 1957
    Herman Welker (R)
Jan. 3, 1957
    Frank Church (D)

ILLINOIS

Class 2
Mar. 4, 1883–Mar. 3, 1913
    Shelby M. Cullom (R)
Mar. 26, 1913–Mar. 3, 1919
    James Hamilton Lewis (D)
Mar. 4, 1919–Feb. 25, 1925
    Medill McCormick (R)
Feb. 26, 1925–Mar. 3, 1931
    Charles S. Deneen (R)
Mar. 4, 1931–Apr. 9, 1939
    James Hamilton Lewis (D)
Apr. 14, 1939–Nov. 21, 1940
    James M. Slattery (D)
Nov. 22, 1940–Jan. 2, 1949
    C. Wayland Brooks (R)
Jan. 3, 1949–Jan. 2, 1967
    Paul H. Douglas (D)
Jan. 3, 1967
    Charles H. Percy (R)

Class 3
Mar. 4, 1897–Mar. 3, 1903
    William E. Mason (R)
Mar. 4, 1903–Mar. 3, 1909
    Albert J. Hopkins (R)
June 18, 1909–July 13, 1912
    William Lorimer (R)
Mar. 26, 1913–Mar. 3, 1921
    Lawrence Y. Sherman (R)
Mar. 4, 1921–Dec. 7, 1926
    William B. McKinley (R)
    Frank L. Smith (R)*
Dec. 3, 1928–Mar. 3, 1933
    Otis F. Glenn (R)
Mar. 4, 1933–Jan. 2, 1939
    William H. Dietrich (D)
Jan. 3, 1939–Jan. 2, 1951
    Scott W. Lucas (D)
Jan. 3, 1951–Sept. 7, 1969
    Everett McKinley Dirksen (R)
Sept. 17, 1969–Nov. 16, 1970
    Ralph Tyler Smith (R)
Nov. 17, 1970
    Adlai E. Stevenson III (D)

INDIANA

Class 1
Mar. 4, 1899–Mar. 3, 1911
    Albert J. Beveridge (R)

*Hanky-panky investigations of foul campaign practices kept Smith from taking his seat.

Mar. 4, 1911–Mar. 3, 1917
   John W. Kern (D)
Mar. 4, 1917–Mar. 3, 1923
   Harry S. New (R)
Mar. 4, 1923–Oct. 14, 1925
   Samuel M. Ralston (D)
Oct. 20, 1925–Jan. 2, 1935
   Arthur R. Robinson (R)
Jan. 3, 1935–Jan. 2, 1941
   Sherman Minton (D)
Jan. 3, 1941–Jan. 2, 1947
   Raymond E. Willis (R)
Jan. 3, 1947–Jan. 2, 1959
   William E. Jenner (R)
Jan. 3, 1959–Jan. 2, 1977
   Vance Hartke (D)
Jan. 3, 1977
   Richard G. Lugar (R)

Class 3
Mar. 4, 1897–Mar. 3, 1905
   Charles W. Fairbanks (R)
Mar. 4, 1905–Mar. 3, 1909
   James A. Hemenway (R)
Mar. 4, 1909–Mar. 14, 1916
   Benjamin F. Shively (D)
Mar. 20, 1916–Nov. 7, 1916
   Thomas Taggart (D)
Nov. 8, 1916–Mar. 3, 1933
   James E. Watson (R)
Mar. 4, 1933–Jan. 25, 1944
   Frederick Van Nuys (D)
Jan. 28, 1944–Nov. 13, 1944
   Samuel D. Jackson (D)
Nov. 14, 1944–Jan. 2, 1945
   William E. Jenner (R)
Jan. 3, 1945–Jan. 2, 1963
   Homer E. Capehart (R)
Jan. 3, 1963
   Birch Bayh (D)

IOWA

Class 2
Aug. 22, 1900–Oct. 15, 1910
   Jonathan P. Dolliver (R)
Nov. 12, 1910–Apr. 11, 1911
   Lafayette Young (R)
Apr. 12, 1911–Feb. 24, 1922
   William S. Kenyon (R)
Feb. 24, 1922–Dec. 1, 1922
   Charles A. Rawson (R)
Dec. 2, 1922–Apr. 12, 1926
   Smith W. Brookhart (R)

Apr. 12, 1926–Mar. 3, 1931
   Daniel F. Steck (D)
Mar. 4, 1931–Jan. 2, 1937
   L. J. Dickinson (R)
Jan. 19, 1937–Jan. 2, 1943
   Clyde L. Herring (D)
Jan. 14, 1943–Jan. 2, 1949
   George A. Wilson (R)
Jan. 3, 1949–Jan. 2, 1955
   Guy M. Gillette (D)
Jan. 3, 1955–Jan. 2, 1961
   Thomas E. Martin (R)
Jan. 3, 1961–Jan. 2, 1973
   Jack Miller (R)
Jan. 3, 1973
   Dick Clark (D)

Class 3
Mar. 4, 1873–Aug. 4, 1908
   William B. Allison (R)
Nov. 24, 1908–July 30, 1926
   Albert B. Cummins (R)
Aug. 7, 1926–Mar. 3, 1927
   David W. Stewart (R)
Mar. 4, 1927–Mar. 3, 1933
   Smith W. Brookhart (R)
Mar. 4, 1933–July 16, 1936
   Richard Louis Murphy (D)
Nov. 4, 1936–Jan. 2, 1945
   Guy M. Gillette (D)
Jan. 3, 1945–Jan. 2, 1969
   Bourke B. Hickenlooper (R)
Jan. 3, 1969–Jan. 2, 1975
   Harold E. Hughes (D)
Jan. 3, 1975
   John C. Culver (D)

KANSAS

Class 2
Mar. 4, 1895–Mar. 3, 1901
   Lucien Baker (R)
Mar. 4, 1901–June 4, 1906
   Joseph R. Burton (R)
June 11, 1906–Jan. 23, 1907
   Alfred W. Benson (R)
Jan. 23, 1907–Mar. 3, 1913
   Charles Curtis (R)
Mar. 4, 1913–Mar. 3, 1919
   William H. Thompson (D)
Mar. 4, 1919–Jan. 2, 1949
   Arthur Capper (R)
Jan. 3, 1949–Jan. 21, 1962
   Andrew F. Schoeppel (R)

Jan. 31, 1962
James B. Pearson (R)

Class 3
Mar. 4, 1897–Mar. 3, 1903
William A. Harris (D)
Mar. 4, 1903–Mar.3, 1909
Chester I. Long (R)
Mar. 4, 1909–Mar. 3, 1915
Joseph L. Bristow (R)
Mar. 4, 1915–Mar. 3, 1929
Charles Curtis (R)
Apr. 1, 1929–Nov. 30, 1930
Henry J. Allen (R)
Dec. 1, 1930–Jan. 2, 1939
George McGill (D)
Jan. 3, 1939–Nov. 8, 1949
Clyde M. Reed (R)
Dec. 2, 1949–Nov. 28, 1950
Harry Darby (R)
Nov. 29, 1950–Jan. 2, 1969
Frank Carlson (R)
Jan. 3, 1969
Robert Dole (R)

KENTUCKY

Class 2
Feb. 15, 1893–Mar. 3, 1901
William Lindsay (D)
Mar. 4, 1901–Mar. 3, 1907
Joseph C. S. Blackburn (D)
Mar. 4, 1907–Mar. 3, 1913
Thomas H. Paynter (D)
Mar. 4, 1913–Aug. 28, 1918
Ollie M. James (D)
Sept. 7, 1918–Mar. 3, 1919
George B. Martin (D)
Mar. 4, 1919–Mar. 3, 1925
A. Owsley Stanley (D)
Mar. 4, 1925–Jan. 9, 1930
Fred M. Sackett (R)
Jan. 9, 1930–Nov. 30, 1930
John M. Robsion (R)
Dec. 1, 1930–Mar. 3, 1931
Ben M. Williamson (D)
Mar. 4, 1931–Oct. 3, 1939
Marvel M. Logan (D)
Oct. 10, 1939–Nov. 1, 1945
Albert B. Chandler (D)
Nov. 19, 1945–Nov. 5, 1946
William A. Stanfill (R)
Nov. 6, 1946–Jan. 2, 1949
John Sherman Cooper (R)

Jan. 3, 1949–Mar. 8, 1951
Virgil Chapman (D)
Mar. 19, 1951–Nov. 4, 1952
Thomas R. Underwood (D)
Nov. 5, 1952–Jan. 2, 1955
John Sherman Cooper (R)
Jan. 3, 1955–Apr. 30, 1956
Alben W. Barkley (D)
June 21, 1956–Nov. 6, 1956
Robert Humphreys (D)
Nov. 7, 1956–Jan. 2, 1973
John Sherman Cooper (R)
Jan. 3, 1973
Walter (Dee) Huddleston (D)

Class 3
Mar. 4, 1897–Mar. 3, 1903
William J. Deboe (R)
Mar. 4, 1903–Mar. 3, 1909
James B. McCreary (D)
Mar. 4, 1909–May 23, 1914
William O. Bradley (R)
June 16, 1914–Mar. 3, 1915
Johnson N. Camden Jr. (D)
Mar. 4, 1915–Mar. 3, 1921
John C. W. Beckham (D)
Mar. 4, 1921–Mar. 3, 1927
Richard P. Ernst (R)
Mar. 4, 1927–Jan. 19, 1949
Alben W. Barkley (D)
Jan. 20, 1949–Nov. 26, 1950
Garrett L. Withers (D)
Nov. 27, 1950–Jan. 2, 1957
Earle C. Clements (D)
Jan. 3, 1957–Dec. 16, 1968
Thruston B. Morton (R)
Dec. 17, 1968–Dec. 27, 1974
Marlow W. Cook (R)
Dec. 28, 1974
Wendell H. Ford (D)

LOUISIANA

Class 2
Dec. 31, 1892–Mar. 3, 1901
Donelson Caffery (D)
Mar. 4, 1901–Mar. 3, 1913
Murphy J. Foster (D)
Mar. 4, 1913–Mar. 3, 1931
Joseph E. Ransdell (D)
Jan. 25, 1932–Sept. 10, 1935
Huey P. Long (D)
Jan. 31, 1936–Jan. 2, 1937
Rose McConnell Long (D)

Jan. 3, 1937–July 27, 1972
    Allen J. Ellender (D)
Aug. 1, 1972–Nov. 13, 1972
    Elaine S. Edwards (D)
Nov. 14, 1972
    J. Bennett Johnston, Jr. (D)

Class 3
Mar. 4, 1897–June 28, 1910
    Samuel D. McEnery (D)
Dec. 7, 1910–Mar. 3, 1915
    John R. Thornton (D)
Mar. 4, 1915–Apr. 12, 1918
    Robert F. Broussard (D)
Apr. 22, 1918–Nov. 5, 1918
    Walter Guion (D)
Nov. 6, 1918–Mar. 3, 1921
    Edward J. Gay (D)
Mar. 4, 1921–Mar. 3, 1933
    Edwin S. Broussard (D)
Mar. 4, 1933–May 14, 1948
    John H. Overton (D)
May 18, 1948–Dec. 30, 1948
    William C. Feazel (D)
Dec. 31, 1948
    Russell B. Long (D)

MAINE

Class 1
Mar. 4, 1881–Mar. 3, 1911
    Eugene Hale (R)
Mar. 4, 1911–Mar. 3, 1917
    Charles F. Johnson (D)
Mar. 4, 1917–Jan. 2, 1941
    Frederick Hale (R)
Jan. 3, 1941–Jan. 2, 1953
    Ralph O. Brewster (R)
Jan. 3, 1953–Jan. 2, 1959
    Frederick G. Payne(R)
Jan. 3, 1959
    Edmund S. Muskie (D)

Class 2
Mar. 18, 1881–Aug. 8, 1911
    William P. Frye (R)
Sept. 23, 1911–Mar. 3, 1913
    Obadiah Gardner (D)
Mar. 4, 1913–June 16, 1916
    Edwin C. Burleigh (R)
Sept. 12, 1916–Aug. 23, 1926
    Bert M. Fernald (R)
Nov. 30, 1926–Mar. 3, 1931
    Arthur R. Gould (R)

Mar. 4, 1931–Jan. 2, 1949
    Wallace H. White, Jr. (R)
Jan. 3, 1949–Jan. 2, 1973
    Margaret Chase Smith (R)
Jan. 3, 1973
    William D. Hathaway (D)

MARYLAND

Class 1
Mar. 4, 1899–Mar. 3, 1905
    Louis E. McComas (R)
Mar. 4, 1905–Nov. 25, 1912
    Isidor Rayner (D)
Nov. 29, 1912–Jan. 28, 1914
    William P. Jackson (R)
Jan. 29, 1914–Mar. 3, 1917
    Blair Lee (D)
Mar. 4, 1917–Mar. 3, 1923
    Joseph I. France (R)
Mar. 4, 1923–Mar. 3, 1929
    William Cabell Bruce (D)
Mar. 4, 1929–Jan. 2, 1935
    Phillips Lee Goldsborough (R)
Jan. 3, 1935–Jan. 2, 1947
    George W. Radcliffe (D)
Jan. 3, 1947–Jan. 2, 1953
    Herbert R. O'Conor (D)
Jan. 3, 1953–Jan. 2, 1965
    J. Glenn Beall (R)
Jan. 3, 1965–Jan. 2, 1971
    Joseph D. Tydings (D)
Jan. 3, 1971–Jan. 2, 1977
    J. Glenn Beall, Jr. (R)
Jan. 3, 1977
    Paul S. Sarbanes (D)

Class 3
Mar. 4, 1897–Mar. 3, 1903
    George L. Wellington (R)
Mar. 4, 1903–June 4, 1906
    Arthur P. Gorman (D)
June 8, 1906–Mar. 17, 1908
    William Pinkney Whyte (D)
Mar. 25, 1908–Mar. 3, 1921
    John Walter Smith (D)
Mar. 4, 1921–Mar. 3, 1927
    Ovington E. Weller (R)
Mar. 4, 1927–Jan. 2, 1951
    Millard E. Tydings (D)
Jan. 3, 1951–Jan. 2, 1963
    John Marshall Butler (R)
Jan. 3, 1963–Jan. 2, 1969
    Daniel B. Brewster (D)

Jan. 3, 1969
    Charles McC. Mathias, Jr. (R)

MASSACHUSETTS

Class 1
Mar. 4, 1893–Nov. 9, 1924
    Henry Cabot Lodge (R)
Nov. 13, 1924–Dec. 5, 1926
    William M. Butler (R)
Dec. 6, 1926–Jan. 2, 1947
    David I. Walsh (D)
Jan. 3, 1947–Jan. 2, 1953
    Henry Cabot Lodge, Jr. (R)
Jan. 3, 1953–Dec. 22, 1960
    John F. Kennedy (D)
Dec. 27, 1960–Nov. 6, 1962
    Benjamin A. Smith II (D)
Nov. 7, 1962
    Edward M. Kennedy (D)

Class 2
Mar. 4, 1877–Sept. 30, 1904
    George F. Hoar (R)
Oct. 12, 1904–Mar. 3, 1913
    Winthrop Murray Crane (R)
Mar. 4, 1913–Mar. 3, 1919
    John W. Weeks (R)
Mar. 4, 1919–Mar. 3, 1925
    David I. Walsh (D)
Mar. 4, 1925–Mar. 3, 1931
    Frederick H. Gillett (R)
Mar. 4, 1931–Mar. 3, 1937
    Marcus A. Coolidge (D)
Jan. 3, 1937–Feb. 3, 1944
    Henry Cabot Lodge, Jr. (R)
Feb. 8, 1944–Dec. 19, 1944
    Sinclair Weeks (R)
Jan. 10, 1945–Jan. 2, 1967
    Leverett Saltonstall (R)
Jan. 3, 1967
    Edward W. Brooke (R)

MICHIGAN

Class 1
Jan. 23, 1895–Mar. 3, 1911
    Julius C. Burrows (R)
Mar. 4, 1911–Mar. 3, 1923
    Charles E. Townsend (R)
Mar. 4, 1923–Mar. 23, 1928
    Woodbridge N. Ferris (D)
Mar. 31, 1928–Apr. 18, 1951
    Arthur H. Vandenberg (R)

Apr. 22, 1951–Nov. 4, 1952
    Blair Moody (D)
Nov. 5, 1952–Jan. 2, 1959
    Charles E. Potter (R)
Jan. 3, 1959–Jan. 2, 1977
    Philip A. Hart (D)
Jan. 3, 1977
    Donald W. Riegle, Jr. (D)

Class 2
Mar. 4, 1889–Aug. 10, 1902
    James McMillan (R)
Sept. 27, 1902–Jan. 24, 1907
    Russell A. Alger (R)
Feb. 6, 1907–Mar. 3, 1919
    William Alden Smith (R)
Mar. 4, 1919–Nov. 18, 1922
    Truman H. Newberry (R)
Nov. 29, 1922–Oct. 22, 1936
    James Couzens (R)
Nov. 19, 1936–Jan. 2, 1943
    Prentiss M. Brown (D)
Jan. 3, 1943–Jan. 2, 1955
    Homer Ferguson (R)
Jan. 3, 1955–Apr. 30, 1966
    Patrick V. McNamara (D)
May 11, 1966
    Robert P. Griffin (R)

MINNESOTA

Class 1
Dec. 5, 1900–Jan. 23, 1901
    Charles A. Towne (D)
Jan. 23, 1901–Mar. 3, 1917
    Moses E. Clapp (R)
Mar. 4, 1917–Mar. 3, 1923
    Frank B. Kellogg (R)
Mar. 4, 1923–Jan. 2, 1947
    Henrik Shipstead (F-LAB, R)
Jan. 3, 1947–Jan. 2, 1959
    Edward J. Thye (R)
Jan. 3, 1959–Jan. 2, 1971
    Eugene J. McCarthy (DFL)
Jan. 3, 1971
    Hubert H. Humphrey (DFL)

Class 2
Mar. 4, 1895–Apr. 28, 1923
    Knute Nelson (R)
July 16, 1923–Mar. 3, 1925
    Magnus Johnson (F-LAB)
Mar. 4, 1925–Dec. 22, 1935
    Thomas D. Schall (R)

Dec. 27, 1935–Nov. 3, 1936
Elmer A. Benson (F-LAB)
Nov. 4, 1936–Jan. 2, 1937
Guy V. Howard (R)
Jan. 3, 1937–Aug. 31, 1940
Ernest Lundeen (F-LAB)
Oct. 14, 1940–Nov. 17, 1942
Joseph H. Ball (R)
Nov. 18, 1942–Jan. 2, 1943
Arthur E. Nelson (R)
Jan. 3, 1943–Jan. 2, 1949
Joseph H. Ball (R)
Jan. 3, 1949–Dec. 29, 1964
Hubert H. Humphrey (DFL)
Dec. 30, 1964–Dec. 30, 1976
Walter F. Mondale (DFL)
Dec. 30, 1976
Wendell Anderson (D)

MISSISSIPPI

Class 1
Oct. 8, 1897–Mar. 3, 1911
Hernando D. Money (D)
Mar. 4, 1911–Mar. 3, 1923
John Sharp Williams (D)
Mar. 4, 1923–Jan. 2, 1935
Hubert D. Stephens (D)
Jan. 3, 1935–Jan. 2, 1947
Theodore G. Bilbo (D)
Nov. 5, 1947
John C. Stennis (D)

Class 2
May 31, 1898–Mar. 3, 1901
William V. Sullivan (D)
Mar. 4, 1901–Dec. 22, 1909
Anselm J. McLaurin (D)
Dec. 27, 1909–Feb. 22, 1910
James Gordon (D)
Feb. 23, 1910–Mar. 3, 1913
Le Roy Percy (D)
Mar. 4, 1913–Mar. 3, 1919
James K. Vardaman (D)
Mar. 4, 1919–June 22, 1941
Pat Harrison (D)
June 30, 1941–Sept. 28, 1941
James O. Eastland (D)
Sept. 29, 1941–Jan. 2, 1943
Wall Doxey (D)
Jan. 3, 1943
James O. Eastland (D)

MISSOURI

Class 1
Mar. 4, 1875–Mar. 3, 1905
Francis M. Cockrell (D)
Mar. 18, 1905–Mar. 3, 1911
William Warner (R)
Mar. 4, 1911–Mar. 3, 1929
James A. Reed (D)
Mar. 4, 1929–Jan. 2, 1935
Roscoe C. Patterson (R)
Jan. 3, 1935–Jan. 18, 1945
Harry S. Truman (D)
Jan. 18, 1945–Jan. 2, 1947
Frank P. Briggs (D)
Jan. 3, 1947–Jan. 2, 1953
James P. Kem (R)
Jan. 3, 1953–Jan. 2, 1977
Stuart Symington (D)
Jan. 3, 1977
John C. Danforth (R)

Class 3
Mar. 4, 1879–Mar. 3, 1903
George G. Vest (D)
Mar. 4, 1903–Apr. 14, 1918
William J. Stone (D)
Apr. 30, 1918–Nov. 5, 1918
Xenophon P. Wilfley (D)
Nov. 6, 1918–May 16, 1925
Selden P. Spencer (R)
May 25, 1925–Dec. 5, 1926
George H. Williams (R)
Dec. 6, 1926–Feb. 3, 1933
Harry B. Hawes (D)
Feb. 3, 1933–Jan. 2, 1945
Bennett Champ Clark (D)
Jan. 3, 1945–Jan. 2, 1951
Forrest C. Donnell (R)
Jan. 3, 1951–Sept. 13, 1960
Thomas C. Hennings, Jr. (D)
Sept. 23, 1960–Dec. 27, 1968
Edward V. Long (D)
Dec. 28, 1968
Thomas F. Eagleton (D)

MONTANA

Class 1
Mar. 7, 1901–Mar. 3, 1905
Paris Gibson (D)
Mar. 4, 1905–Mar. 3, 1911
Thomas H. Carter (R)
Mar. 4, 1911–Mar. 3, 1923
Henry L. Myers (D)

Mar. 4, 1923–Jan. 2, 1947
 Burton K. Wheeler (D)
Jan. 3, 1947–Jan. 2, 1953
 Zales N. Ecton (R)
Jan. 3, 1953–Jan. 2, 1977
 Mike Mansfield (D)
Jan. 3, 1977
 John Melcher (D)

Class 2
Mar. 4, 1895–Mar. 3, 1901
 Thomas H. Carter (R)
Mar. 4, 1901–Mar. 3, 1907
 William A. Clark (D)
Mar. 4, 1907–Mar. 3, 1913
 Joseph M. Dixon (R)
Mar. 4, 1913–Mar. 2, 1933
 Thomas J. Walsh (D)
Mar. 13, 1933–Nov. 6, 1934
 John E. Erickson (D)
Nov. 7, 1934–Jan. 2, 1961
 James E. Murray (D)
Jan. 3, 1961
 Lee Metcalf (D)

NEBRASKA

Class 1
Dec. 13, 1899–Mar. 28, 1901
 William V. Allen (POP)
Mar. 28, 1901–Mar. 3, 1905
 Charles H. Dietrich (R)
Mar. 4, 1905–Mar. 3, 1911
 Elmer J. Burkett (R)
Mar. 4, 1911–Mar. 3, 1923
 Gilbert M. Hitchcock (D)
Mar. 4, 1923–Mar. 11, 1933
 Robert B. Howell (R)
May 24, 1933–Nov. 6, 1934
 William H. Thompson (D)
Nov. 7, 1934–Jan. 2, 1935
 Richard C. Hunter (D)
Jan. 3, 1935–Jan. 2, 1941
 Edward R. Burke (D)
Jan. 3, 1941–July 1, 1954
 Hugh Butler (R)
July 3, 1954–Nov. 7, 1954
 Sam W. Reynolds (R)
Nov. 8, 1954–Dec. 31, 1976
 Roman L. Hruska (R)
Jan. 1, 1977
 Edward Zorinsky (D)

Class 2
Mar. 4, 1895–Mar. 3, 1901
 John M. Thurston (R)
Mar. 28, 1901–Mar. 3, 1907
 Joseph H. Millard (R)
Mar. 4, 1907–Mar. 3, 1913
 Norris Brown (R)
Mar. 4, 1913–Jan. 2, 1943
 George W. Norris (R, I)
Jan. 3, 1943–Nov. 29, 1951
 Kenneth S. Wherry (R)
Dec. 10, 1951–Nov. 4, 1952
 Fred A. Seaton (R)
Nov. 5, 1952–Apr. 12, 1954
 Dwight Griswold (R)
Apr. 16, 1954–Nov. 7, 1954
 Eva Bowring (R)
Nov. 8, 1954–Dec. 31, 1954
 Hazel H. Abel (R)
Jan. 1, 1955
 Carl T. Curtis (R)

NEVADA

Class 1
Mar. 4, 1887–Mar. 3, 1905
 William M. Stewart (R)
Mar. 4, 1905–June 5, 1912
 George S. Nixon (R)
July 1, 1912–Jan. 29, 1913
 William A. Massey (R)
Jan. 29, 1913–Nov. 10, 1940
 Key Pittman (D)
Nov. 27, 1940–Dec. 6, 1942
 Berkeley L. Bunker (D)
Dec. 7, 1942–June 23, 1945
 James G. Scrugham (D)
July 25, 1945–Jan. 2, 1947
 E. P. Carville (D)
Jan. 3, 1947–Jan. 2, 1959
 George W. Malone (R)
Jan. 3, 1959
 Howard W. Cannon (D)

Class 3
Mar. 4, 1873–Mar. 3, 1903
 John P. Jones (R)
Mar. 4, 1903–Dec. 24, 1917
 Francis G. Newlands (D)
Jan. 12, 1918–Mar. 3, 1921
 Charles B. Henderson (D)
Mar. 4, 1921–Mar. 3, 1933
 Tasker L. Oddie (R)
Mar. 4, 1933–Sept. 28, 1954
 Patrick A. McCarran (D)

Oct. 1, 1954–Dec. 1, 1954
    Ernest S. Brown (R)
Dec. 2, 1954–Dec. 17, 1974
    Alan Bible (D)
Dec. 18, 1974
    Paul Laxalt (R)

NEW HAMPSHIRE

Class 2
June 19, 1889–Mar. 3, 1901
    William E. Chandler (R)
Mar. 4, 1901–Mar. 3, 1913
    Henry E. Burnham (R)
Mar. 13, 1913–Mar. 3, 1919
    Henry F. Hollis (D)
Mar. 4, 1919–Jan. 2, 1937
    Henry W. Keyes (R)
Jan. 3, 1937–Nov. 26, 1961
    Styles Bridges (R)
Dec. 7, 1961–Nov. 6, 1962
    Maurice J. Murphy, Jr. (R)
Nov. 7, 1962
    Thomas J. McIntyre (D)

Class 3
Mar. 4, 1891–Aug. 17, 1918
    Jacob H. Gallinger (R)
Sept. 2, 1918–Nov. 5, 1918
    Irving W. Drew (R)
Nov. 6, 1918–Mar. 3, 1933
    George H. Moses (R)
Mar. 4, 1933–Jan. 2, 1939
    Fred H. Brown (D)
Jan. 3, 1939–July 24, 1953
    Charles W. Tobey (R)
Aug. 14, 1953–Nov. 7, 1954
    Robert W. Upton (R)
Nov. 8, 1954–Dec. 31, 1974
    Norris Cotton (R)
Jan. 1, 1975–Jan. 2, 1975
    Louis C. Wyman (R)
Aug. 8, 1975–Sept. 18, 1975
    Norris Cotton (R)
Sept. 18, 1975
    John A. Durkin (D)

NEW JERSEY

Class 1
Mar. 4, 1899–Mar. 3, 1911
    John Kean (R)
Mar. 4, 1911–Mar. 3, 1917
    James E. Martine (D)

Mar. 4, 1917–Mar. 3, 1923
    Joseph S. Frelinghuysen (R)
Mar. 4, 1923–Mar. 3, 1929
    Edward I. Edwards (D)
Mar. 4, 1929–Jan. 3, 1935
    Hamilton F. Kean (R)
Jan. 3, 1935–Jan. 18, 1938
    A. Harry Moore (D)
Jan. 18, 1938–Nov. 8, 1938
    John Milton (D)
Nov. 9, 1938–Nov. 22, 1943
    W. Warren Barbour (R)
Nov. 26, 1943–Dec. 6, 1944
    Arthur Walsh (D)
Dec. 7, 1944–Jan. 2, 1959
    H. Alexander Smith (R)
Jan. 3, 1959
    Harrison A. Williams, Jr. (D)

Class 2
Mar. 4, 1895–Dec. 27, 1901
    William J. Sewell (R)
Jan. 29, 1902–Mar. 3, 1907
    John F. Dryden (R)
Mar. 4, 1907–Mar. 3, 1913
    Frank O. Briggs (R)
Mar. 4, 1913–Jan. 30, 1918
    William Hughes (D)
Feb. 23, 1918–Mar. 3, 1919
    David Baird (R)
Mar. 4, 1919–Nov. 21, 1929
    Walter E. Edge (R)
Nov. 30, 1929–Dec. 2, 1930
    David Baird, Jr. (R)
Dec. 3, 1930–Oct. 5, 1931
    Dwight W. Morrow (R)
Dec. 1, 1931–Jan. 2, 1937
    W. Warren Barbour (R)
Apr. 15, 1937–Jan. 2, 1943
    William H. Smathers (D)
Jan. 3, 1943–Jan. 2, 1949
    Albert W. Hawkes (R)
Jan. 3, 1949–Jan. 2, 1955
    Robert C. Hendrickson (R)
Jan. 3, 1955
    Clifford P. Case (R)

NEW MEXICO

Class 1
Mar. 27, 1912–Mar. 3, 1917
    Thomas B. Catron (R)
Mar. 4, 1917–Dec. 20, 1927
    Andrieus A. Jones (D)

Dec. 29, 1927–Dec. 6, 1928
  Bronson Cutting (R)
Dec. 7, 1928–Mar. 3, 1929
  Octaviano A. Larrazolo (R)
Mar. 4, 1929–May 6, 1935
  Bronson Cutting (R)
May 11, 1935–Nov. 18, 1962
  Dennis Chavez (D)
Nov. 30, 1962–Nov. 3, 1964
  Edwin L. Mechem (R)
Nov. 4, 1964–Nov. 3, 1976
  Joseph M. Montoya (D)
Nov. 4, 1976
  Harrison "Jack" Schmitt (R)

Class 2
Mar. 27, 1912–Mar. 4, 1921
  Albert B. Fall (R)
Mar. 11, 1921–Mar. 3, 1925
  Holm O. Bursum (R)
Mar. 4, 1925–June 24, 1933
  Sam G. Bratton (D)
Oct. 10, 1933–Jan. 2, 1949
  Carl A. Hatch (D)
Jan. 3, 1949–Jan. 2, 1973
  Clinton P. Anderson (D)
Jan. 3, 1973
  Pete V. Domenici (R)

NEW YORK

Class 1
Mar. 4, 1899–Mar. 3, 1911
  Chauncey M. Depew (R)
Mar. 31, 1911–Mar. 3, 1917
  James A. O'Gorman (D)
Mar. 4, 1917–Mar. 3, 1923
  William M. Calder (R)
Mar. 4, 1923–June 17, 1938
  Royal S. Copeland (D)
Dec. 3, 1938–Jan. 2, 1947
  James M. Mead (D)
Jan. 3, 1947–Jan. 2, 1959
  Irving M. Ives (R)
Jan. 3, 1959–Jan. 2, 1965
  Kenneth B. Keating (R)
Jan. 3, 1965–June 6, 1968
  Robert F. Kennedy (D)
Sept. 10, 1968–Jan. 2, 1971
  Charles E. Goodell (R)
Jan. 3, 1971–Jan. 2, 1977
  James L. Buckley (C-R)
Jan. 3, 1977
  Daniel Patrick Moynihan (D)

Class 3
Mar. 4, 1897–Mar. 3, 1909
  Thomas C. Platt (R)
Mar. 4, 1909–Mar. 3, 1915
  Elihu Root (R)
Mar. 4, 1915–Mar. 3, 1927
  James W. Wadsworth, Jr. (R)
Mar. 4, 1927–June 28, 1949
  Robert F. Wagner (D)
July 7, 1949–Nov. 8, 1949
  John Foster Dulles (R)
Nov. 9, 1949–Jan. 2, 1957
  Herbert H. Lehman (D)
Jan. 9, 1957
  Jacob K. Javits (R)

NORTH CAROLINA

Class 2
Mar. 4, 1895–Mar. 3, 1901
  Marion Butler (POP)
Mar. 4, 1901–Mar. 3, 1931
  Furnifold M. Simmons (D)
Mar. 4, 1931–Dec. 15, 1946
  Josiah W. Bailey (D)
Dec. 18, 1946–Dec. 30, 1948
  William B. Umstead (D)
Dec. 31, 1948–Mar. 6, 1949
  J. Melville Broughton (D)
Mar. 29, 1949–Nov. 26, 1950
  Frank P. Graham (D)
Nov. 27, 1950–June 23, 1953
  Willis Smith (D)
July 10, 1953–Nov. 28, 1954
  Alton A. Lennon (D)
Nov. 29, 1954–Apr. 16, 1958
  W. Kerr Scott (D)
Apr. 19, 1958–Jan. 2, 1973
  B. Everett Jordan (D)
Jan. 3, 1973
  Jesse Helms (R)

Class 3
Jan. 23, 1895–Mar. 3, 1903
  Jeter C. Pritchard (R)
Mar. 4, 1903–Dec. 12, 1930
  Lee S. Overman (D)
Dec. 13, 1930–Dec. 4, 1932
  Cameron Morrison (D)
Dec. 5, 1932–Jan. 2, 1945
  Robert R. Reynolds (D)
Jan. 3, 1945–May 12, 1954
  Clyde R. Hoey (D)
June 5, 1954–Dec. 31, 1974
  Sam J. Ervin, Jr. (D)

Jan. 3, 1975
    Robert Morgan (D)

NORTH DAKOTA

Class 1
Mar. 4, 1899–Mar. 3, 1923
    Porter J. McCumber (R)
Mar. 4, 1923–Jan. 2, 1941
    Lynn J. Frazier (R)
Jan. 3, 1941–Nov. 8, 1959
    William Langer (R)
Nov. 19, 1959–Aug. 7, 1960
    C. Norman Brunsdale (R)
Aug. 8, 1960
    Quentin N. Burdick (D)

Class 3
Mar. 4, 1891–Mar. 3, 1909
    Henry C. Hansbrough (R)
Mar. 4, 1909–Oct. 21, 1909
    Martin N. Johnson (R)
Nov. 10, 1909–Jan. 31, 1910
    Fountain L. Thompson (R)
Feb. 1, 1910–Feb. 1, 1911
    William E. Purcell (D)
Feb. 2, 1911–Mar. 3, 1921
    Asle J. Gronna (R)
Mar. 4, 1921–June 22, 1925
    Edwin F. Ladd (R)
Nov. 14, 1925–Jan. 2, 1945
    Gerald P. Nye (R)
Jan. 3, 1945–Mar. 3, 1945
    John Moses (D)
Mar. 12, 1945
    Milton R. Young (R)

OHIO

Class 1
Mar. 5, 1897–Feb. 15, 1904
    Marcus A. Hanna (R)
Mar. 2, 1904–Mar. 3, 1911
    Charles W. F. Dick (R)
Mar. 4, 1911–Mar. 3, 1923
    Atlee Pomerene (D)
Mar. 4, 1923–Jan. 2, 1935
    Simeon D. Fess (R)
Jan. 3, 1935–Jan. 2, 1941
    Vic Donahey (D)
Jan. 3, 1941–Sept. 30, 1945
    Harold H. Burton (R)
Oct. 8, 1945–Nov. 5, 1946
    James W. Huffman (D)

Nov. 6, 1946–Jan. 2, 1947
    Kingsley A. Taft (R)
Jan. 3, 1947–Jan. 2, 1959
    John W. Bricker (R)
Jan. 3, 1959–Jan. 2, 1971
    Stephen M. Young (D)
Jan. 3, 1971–Jan. 2, 1977
    Robert Taft, Jr. (R)
Jan. 3, 1977
    Howard M. Metzenbaum (D)

Class 3
Mar. 4, 1897–Mar. 3, 1909
    Joseph B. Foraker (R)
Mar. 4, 1909–Mar. 3, 1915
    Theodore E. Burton (R)
Mar. 4, 1915–Jan. 13, 1921
    Warren G. Harding (R)
Jan. 14, 1921–Mar. 30, 1928
    Frank B. Willis (R)
Apr. 4, 1928–Dec. 14, 1928
    Cyrus Locher (D)
Dec. 15, 1928–Oct. 28, 1929
    Theodore E. Burton (R)
Nov. 5, 1929–Nov. 30, 1930
    Roscoe C. McCulloch (R)
Dec. 1, 1930–Jan. 2, 1939
    Robert J. Bulkley (D)
Jan. 3, 1939–July 31, 1953
    Robert A. Taft (R)
Nov. 10, 1953–Dec. 2, 1954
    Thomas A. Burke (D)
Dec. 16, 1954–Jan. 2, 1957
    George H. Bender (R)
Jan. 3, 1957–Jan. 2, 1969
    Frank J. Lausche (D)
Jan. 3, 1969–Jan. 4, 1974
    William B. Saxbe (R)
Jan. 4, 1974–Dec. 23, 1974
    Howard M. Metzenbaum (D)
Dec. 23, 1974
    John Glenn (D)

OKLAHOMA

Class 2
Dec. 11, 1907–Mar. 3, 1925
    Robert L. Owen (D)
Mar. 4, 1925–Mar. 3, 1931
    William B. Pine (R)
Mar. 4, 1931–Jan. 2, 1937
    Thomas P. Gore (D)
Jan. 3, 1937–Jan. 2, 1943
    Josh Lee (D)

Jan. 3, 1943–Jan. 2, 1949
  Edward H. Moore (R)
Jan. 3, 1949–Jan. 1, 1963
  Robert S. Kerr (D)
Jan. 7, 1963–Nov. 3, 1964
  J. Howard Edmondson (D)
Nov. 4, 1964–Jan. 2, 1973
  Fred R. Harris (D)
Jan. 3, 1973
  Dewey F. Bartlett (R)

Class 3
Dec. 11, 1907–Mar. 3, 1921
  Thomas P. Gore (D)
Mar. 4, 1921–Mar. 3, 1927
  John W. Harreld (R)
Mar. 4, 1927–Jan. 2, 1951
  Elmer Thomas (D)
Jan. 3, 1951–Jan. 2, 1969
  A. S. Mike Monroney (D)
Jan. 3, 1969
  Henry Bellmon (R)

OREGON

Class 2
Mar. 4, 1895–Mar. 3, 1901
  George W. McBride (R)
Mar. 4, 1901–Dec. 8, 1905
  John H. Mitchell (R)
Dec. 13, 1905–Jan. 23, 1907
  John M. Gearin (D)
Jan. 23, 1907–Mar. 3, 1907
  Frederick W. Mulkey (R)
Mar. 4, 1907–Mar. 3, 1913
  Jonathan Bourne, Jr. (R)
Mar. 4, 1913–May 23, 1917
  Harry Lane (D)
May 29, 1917–Nov. 5, 1918
  Charles L. McNary (R)
Nov. 6, 1918–Dec. 17, 1918
  Frederick W. Mulkey (R)
Dec. 18, 1918–Feb. 25, 1944
  Charles L. McNary (R)
Mar. 4, 1944–Jan. 2, 1955
  Guy Cordon (R)
Jan. 3, 1955–Mar. 9, 1960
  Richard L. Neuberger (D)
Mar. 16, 1960–Nov. 8, 1960
  Hall S. Lusk (D)
Nov. 9, 1960–Jan. 2, 1967
  Maurine B. Neuberger (D)
Jan. 10, 1967
  Mark O. Hatfield (R)

Class 3
Oct. 8, 1898–Mar. 3, 1903
  Joseph Simon (R)
Mar. 4, 1903–Mar. 3, 1909
  Charles W. Fulton (R)
Mar. 4, 1909–Mar. 3, 1921
  George E. Chamberlain (D)
Mar. 4, 1921–Mar. 3, 1927
  Robert N. Stanfield (R)
Mar. 4, 1927–Jan. 31, 1938
  Frederick Steiwer (R)
Feb. 1, 1938–Nov. 8, 1938
  Alfred Evan Reames (D)
Nov. 9, 1938–Jan. 2, 1939
  Alexander G. Barry (R)
Jan. 3, 1939–Jan. 2, 1945
  Rufus C. Holman (R)
Jan. 3, 1945–Jan. 2, 1969
  Wayne L. Morse (R, I, D)
Jan. 3, 1969
  Robert W. Packwood (R)

PENNSYLVANIA

Class 1
Jan. 17, 1901–May 28, 1904
  Matthew S. Quay (R)
June 10, 1904–Mar. 4, 1909
  Philander C. Knox (R)
Mar. 17, 1909–Mar. 3, 1917
  George T. Oliver (R)
Mar. 4, 1917–Oct. 12, 1921
  Philander C. Knox (R)
Oct. 24, 1921–Aug. 2, 1922
  William E. Crow (R)
Aug. 8, 1922–Jan. 2, 1935
  David A. Reed (R)
Jan. 3, 1935–Jan. 2, 1947
  Joseph F. Guffey (D)
Jan. 3, 1947–Jan. 2, 1959
  Edward Martin (R)
Jan. 3, 1959–Jan. 2, 1977
  Hugh Scott (R)
Jan. 3, 1977
  H. John Heinz (R)

Class 3
Mar. 4, 1897–Dec. 31, 1921
  Boies Penrose (R)
Jan. 9, 1922–Mar. 3, 1927
  George Wharton Pepper (R)
  William S. Vare (R)
Dec. 11, 1929–Dec. 1, 1930
  Joseph R. Grundy (R)

Dec. 2, 1930–Jan. 2, 1945
  James J. Davis (R)
Jan. 3, 1945–Jan. 2, 1951
  Francis J. Myers (D)
Jan. 16, 1951–Jan. 2, 1957
  James H. Duff (R)
Jan. 3, 1957–Jan. 2, 1969
  Joseph S. Clark (D)
Jan. 3, 1969
  Richard S. Schweiker (R)

RHODE ISLAND

Class 1
Oct. 5, 1881–Mar. 3, 1911
  Nelson W. Aldrich (R)
Mar. 4, 1911–Mar. 3, 1917
  Henry F. Lippitt (R)
Mar. 4, 1917–Mar. 3, 1929
  Peter G. Gerry (D)
Mar. 4, 1929–Jan. 2, 1935
  Felix Hebert (R)
Jan. 3, 1935–Jan. 2, 1947
  Peter G. Gerry (D)
Jan. 3, 1947–Aug. 23, 1949
  J. Howard McGrath (D)
Aug. 24, 1949–Dec. 18, 1950
  Edward L. Leahy (D)
Dec. 19, 1950–Jan. 2, 1977
  John O. Pastore (D)
Jan. 3, 1977
  John H. Chafee (R)

Class 2
Mar. 4, 1895–Mar. 3, 1907
  George Peabody Wetmore (R)
Jan. 22, 1908–Mar. 3, 1913
  George Peabody Wetmore (R)
Mar. 4, 1913–Aug. 18, 1924
  LeBaron B. Colt (R)
Nov. 5, 1924–Jan. 2, 1937
  Jesse H. Metcalf (R)
Jan. 3, 1937–Jan. 2, 1961
  Theodore F. Green (D)
Jan. 3, 1961
  Claiborne Pell (D)

SOUTH CAROLINA

Class 2
Mar. 4, 1895–July 3, 1918
  Benjamin R. Tillman (D)
July 6, 1918–Nov. 5, 1918
  Christie Benet (D)

Nov. 6, 1918–Mar. 3, 1919
  William P. Pollock (D)
Mar. 4, 1919–Mar. 3, 1925
  Nathaniel B. Dial (D)
Mar. 4, 1925–Mar. 3, 1931
  Coleman L. Blease (D)
Mar. 4, 1931–July 8, 1941
  James F. Byrnes (D)
July 17, 1941–Aug. 1, 1941
  Alva M. Lumpkin (D)
Aug. 5, 1941–Nov. 4, 1941
  Roger C. Peace (D)
Nov. 5, 1941–Sept. 1, 1954
  Burnet R. Maybank (D)
Sept. 6, 1954–Dec. 23, 1954
  Charles E. Daniel (D)
Dec. 24, 1954–Apr. 4, 1956
  Strom Thurmond (D)
Apr. 5, 1956–Nov. 6, 1956
  Thomas A. Wofford (D)
Nov. 7, 1956
  Strom Thurmond (D, R)

Class 3
May 27, 1897–Mar. 3, 1903
  John L. McLaurin (D)
Mar. 4, 1903–Feb. 20, 1908
  Asbury C. Latimer (D)
Mar. 6, 1908–Mar. 3, 1909
  Frank B. Gary (D)
Mar. 4, 1909–Nov. 17, 1944
  Ellison D. Smith (D)
Nov. 20, 1944–Jan. 2, 1945
  Wilton E. Hall (D)
Jan. 3, 1945–Apr. 18, 1965
  Olin D. Johnston (D)
Apr. 22, 1965–Nov. 8, 1966
  Donald Russell (D)
Nov. 9, 1966
  Ernest F. Hollings (D)

SOUTH DAKOTA

Class 2
Nov. 2, 1889–Mar. 3, 1901
  Richard F. Pettigrew (R)
Mar. 4, 1901–Mar. 3, 1913
  Robert J. Gamble (R)
Mar. 4, 1913–Mar. 3, 1925
  Thomas Sterling (R)
Mar. 4, 1925–Mar. 3, 1931
  William H. McMaster (R)
Mar. 4, 1931–Jan. 2, 1943
  William J. Bulow (D)

Jan. 3, 1943–Sept. 27, 1948
　　Harlan J. Bushfield (R)
Oct. 6, 1948–Dec. 26, 1948
　　Vera C. Bushfield (R)
Dec. 31, 1948–Jan. 2, 1973
　　Karl E. Mundt (R)
Jan. 3, 1973
　　James Abourezk (D)

Class 3
Mar. 4, 1891–July 1, 1901
　　James H. Kyle (I)
July 11, 1901–Mar. 3, 1909
　　Alfred B. Kittredge (R)
Mar. 4, 1909–Mar. 3, 1915
　　Coe I. Crawford (R)
Mar. 4, 1915–Mar. 3, 1921
　　Edwin S. Johnson (D)
Mar. 4, 1921–Dec. 20, 1936
　　Peter Norbeck (R)
Dec. 29, 1936–Nov. 8, 1938
　　Herbert E. Hitchcock (D)
Nov. 9, 1938–Jan. 2, 1939
　　Gladys Pyle (R)
Jan. 3, 1939–Jan. 2, 1951
　　J. Chandler Gurney (R)
Jan. 3, 1951–June 22, 1962
　　Francis Case (R)
July 9, 1962–Jan. 2, 1963
　　Joe H. Bottum (R)
Jan. 3, 1963
　　George McGovern (D)

TENNESSEE

Class 1
Mar. 4, 1887–Mar. 9, 1905
　　William B. Bate (D)
Mar. 21, 1905–Mar. 3, 1911
　　James B. Frazier (D)
Mar. 4, 1911–Mar. 3, 1917
　　Luke Lea (D)
Mar. 4, 1917–Jan. 2, 1953
　　Kenneth D. McKellar (D)
Jan. 3, 1953–Jan. 2, 1971
　　Albert Gore (D)
Jan. 3, 1971–Jan. 2, 1977
　　Bill Brock (R)
Jan. 3, 1977
　　James R. Sasser (D)

Class 2
July 20, 1897–Mar. 3, 1901
　　Thomas B. Turley (D)

Mar. 4, 1901–Mar. 3, 1907
　　Edward W. Carmack (D)
Mar. 4, 1907–Mar. 31, 1912
　　Robert L. Taylor (D)
Apr. 8, 1912–Jan. 24, 1913
　　Newell Sanders (R)
Jan. 24, 1913–Mar. 3, 1913
　　William R. Webb (D)
Mar. 4, 1913–Mar. 3, 1925
　　John K. Shields (D)
Mar. 4, 1925–Aug. 24, 1929
　　Lawrence D. Tyson (D)
Sept. 2, 1929–Mar. 3, 1931
　　William E. Brock (D)
Mar. 4, 1931–Mar. 3, 1933
　　Cordell Hull (D)
Mar. 4, 1933–Apr. 23, 1937
　　Nathan L. Bachman (D)
May 6, 1937–Nov. 8, 1938
　　George L. Berry (D)
Jan. 16, 1939–Jan. 2, 1949
　　Tom Stewart (D)
Jan. 3, 1949–Aug. 10, 1963
　　Estes Kefauver (D)
Aug. 20, 1963–Nov. 3, 1964
　　Herbert S. Walters (D)
Nov. 4, 1964–Jan. 2, 1967
　　Ross Bass (D)
Jan. 3, 1967
　　Howard H. Baker, Jr. (R)

TEXAS

Class 1
Mar. 4, 1899–Mar. 3, 1923
　　Charles A. Culberson (D)
Mar. 4, 1923–Mar. 3, 1929
　　Earle B. Mayfield (D)
Mar. 4, 1929–Jan. 2, 1953
　　Tom Connally (D)
Jan. 3, 1953–Jan. 14, 1957
　　Price Daniel (D)
Jan. 15, 1957–Apr. 28, 1957
　　William A. Blakley (D)
Apr. 29, 1957–Jan. 2, 1971
　　Ralph Yarborough (D)
Jan. 3, 1971
　　Lloyd M. Bentsen, Jr.

Class 2
Mar. 4, 1895–Mar. 3, 1901
　　Horace Chilton (D)
Mar. 4, 1901–Jan. 3, 1913
　　Joseph W. Bailey (D)

Jan. 4, 1913–Jan. 29, 1913
  Rienzi M. Johnston (D)
Jan. 29, 1913–Apr. 9, 1941
  Morris Sheppard (D)
Apr. 21, 1941–June 26, 1941
  Andrew Jackson Houston (D)
Aug. 4, 1941–Jan. 2, 1949
  W. Lee O'Daniel (D)
Jan. 3, 1949–Jan. 3, 1961
  Lyndon B. Johnson (D)
Jan. 3, 1961–June 14, 1961
  William A. Blakley (D)
June 15, 1961
  John G. Tower (D)

UTAH
Class 1
Jan. 23, 1901–Mar. 3, 1905
  Thomas Kearns (R)
Mar. 4, 1905–Mar. 3, 1917
  George Sutherland (R)
Mar. 4, 1917–Jan. 2, 1941
  William H. King (D)
Jan. 3, 1941–Jan. 2, 1947
  Abe Murdock (D)
Jan. 3, 1947–Jan. 2, 1959
  Arthur V. Watkins (R)
Jan. 3, 1959–Jan. 2, 1977
  Frank E. Moss (D)
Jan. 3, 1977
  Orrin G. Hatch (R)

Class 3
Mar. 4, 1897–Mar. 3, 1903
  Joseph L. Rawlins (D)
Mar. 4, 1903–Mar. 3, 1933
  Reed Smoot (R)
Mar. 4, 1933–Jan. 2, 1951
  Elbert D. Thomas (D)
Jan. 3, 1951–Dec. 20, 1974
  Wallace F. Bennett (R)
Dec. 21, 1974
  Jake Garn (R)

VERMONT

Class 1
Nov. 2, 1891–Mar. 4, 1908
  Redfield Proctor (R)
Mar. 24, 1908–Oct. 20, 1908
  John W. Stewart (R)
Oct. 21, 1908–Mar. 3, 1923
  Carroll S. Page (R)
Mar. 4, 1923–Dec. 17, 1930
  Frank L. Greene (R)

Dec. 23, 1930–Mar. 31, 1931
  Frank C. Partridge (R)
Apr. 1, 1931–Aug. 2, 1946
  Warren R. Austin (R)
Nov. 1, 1946–Jan. 2, 1959
  Ralph E. Flanders (R)
Jan. 3, 1959–Sept. 10, 1971
  Winston L. Prouty (R)
Sept. 16, 1971
  Robert T. Stafford (R)

Class 3
Oct. 18, 1900–July 12, 1923
  William P. Dillingham (R)
Nov. 6, 1923–Oct. 6, 1933
  Porter H. Dale (R)
Nov. 21, 1933–June 20, 1940
  Ernest W. Gibson (R)
June 24, 1940–Jan. 2, 1941
  Ernest W. Gibson, Jr. (R)
Jan. 10, 1941–Jan. 2, 1975
  George D. Aiken (R)
Jan. 3, 1975
  Patrick J. Leahy (D)

VIRGINIA

Class 1
Mar. 4, 1887–June 29, 1910
  John W. Daniel (D)
Aug. 1, 1910–Mar. 3, 1933
  Claude A. Swanson (D)
Mar. 4, 1933–Nov. 10, 1965
  Harry Flood Byrd (D)
Nov. 12, 1965
  Harry F. Byrd, Jr. (D, I)

Class 2
Mar. 4, 1895–Nov. 12, 1919
  Thomas S. Martin (D)
Feb. 2, 1920–May 28, 1946
  Carter Glass (D)
May 31, 1946–Nov. 5, 1946
  Thomas G. Burch (D)
Nov. 6, 1946–Dec. 30, 1966
  A. Willis Robertson (D)
Dec. 31, 1966–Jan. 2, 1973
  William B. Spong, Jr. (D)
Jan. 3, 1973
  William Lloyd Scott (R)

WASHINGTON

Class 1
Mar. 4, 1899–Mar. 3, 1905
  Addison G. Foster (R)
Mar. 4, 1905–Mar. 3, 1911
  Samuel H. Piles (R)
Mar. 4, 1911–Mar. 3, 1923
  Miles Poindexter (R)
Mar. 4, 1923–Jan. 2, 1935
  Clarence C. Dill (D)
Jan. 3, 1935–Dec. 16, 1940
  L. B. Schwellenbach (D)
Dec. 19, 1940–Jan. 10, 1945
  Mon C. Wallgren (D)
Jan. 10, 1945–Dec. 25, 1946
  Hugh B. Mitchell (D)
Dec. 26, 1946–Jan. 2, 1953
  Harry P. Cain (R)
Jan. 3, 1953
  Henry M. Jackson (D)

Class 3
Mar. 4, 1897–Mar. 3, 1903
  George Turner (D)
Mar. 4, 1903–Mar. 3, 1909
  Levi Ankeny (R)
Mar. 4, 1909–Nov. 19, 1932
  Wesley L. Jones (R)
Nov. 22, 1932–Mar. 3, 1933
  Elijah S. Grammer (R)
Mar. 4, 1933–Nov. 13, 1944
  Homer T. Bone (D)
Dec. 14, 1944
  Warren G. Magnuson (D)

WEST VIRGINIA

Class 1
Mar. 4, 1899–Mar. 3, 1911
  Nathan B. Scott (R)
Mar. 4, 1911–Mar. 3, 1917
  William E. Chilton (D)
Mar. 4, 1917–Mar. 3, 1923
  Howard Sutherland (R)
Mar. 4, 1923–Mar. 3, 1929
  Matthew M. Neely (D)
Mar. 4, 1929–Jan. 2, 1935
  Henry D. Hatfield (R)
June 21, 1935–Jan. 2, 1941
  Rush D. Holt (D)
Jan. 3, 1941–Feb. 28, 1956
  Harley M. Kilgore (D)
Mar. 13, 1956–Nov. 6, 1956
  William R. Laird III (D)

Nov. 7, 1956–Jan. 2, 1959
  Chapman Revercomb (R)
Jan. 3, 1959
  Robert C. Byrd (D)

Class 2
Mar. 4, 1895–Jan. 4, 1911
  Stephen B. Elkins (R)
Jan. 9, 1911–Jan. 31, 1911
  Davis Elkins (R)
Feb. 1, 1911–Mar. 3, 1913
  Clarence W. Watson (D)
Mar. 4, 1913–Mar. 3, 1919
  Nathan Goff (R)
Mar. 4, 1919–Mar. 3, 1925
  Davis Elkins (R)
Mar. 4, 1925–Mar. 3, 1931
  Guy D. Goff (R)
Mar. 4, 1931–Jan. 12, 1941
  Matthew M. Neely (D)
Jan. 13, 1941–Nov. 17, 1942
  Joseph Rosier (D)
Nov. 18, 1942–Jan. 2, 1943
  Hugh Ike Shott (R)
Jan. 3, 1943–Jan. 2, 1949
  Chapman Revercomb (R)
Jan. 3, 1949–Jan. 18, 1958
  Matthew M. Neely (D)
Jan. 25, 1958–Nov. 4, 1958
  John D. Hoblitzell, Jr. (R)
Nov. 5, 1958
  Jennings Randolph (D)

WISCONSIN

Class 1
Mar. 4, 1899–Mar. 3, 1905
  Joseph V. Quarles (R)
Jan. 4, 1906–June 18, 1925
  Robert M. LaFollette (R)
Sept. 30, 1925–Jan. 2, 1947
  R. M. LaFollette, Jr. (R, PROG)
Jan. 3, 1947–May 2, 1957
  Joseph R. McCarthy (R)
Aug. 28, 1957
  William Proxmire (D)

Class 3
Mar. 4, 1897–May 1, 1907
  John Coit Spooner (R)
May 17, 1907–Mar. 3, 1915
  Isaac Stephenson (R)
Mar. 4, 1915–Oct. 21, 1917
  Paul O. Husting (D)

Apr. 18, 1918–Mar. 3, 1927
  Irvine L. Lenroot (R)
Mar. 4, 1927–Mar. 3, 1933
  John J. Blaine (R)
Mar. 4, 1933–Jan. 2, 1939
  F. Ryan Duffy (D)
Jan. 3, 1939–Jan. 2, 1963
  Alexander Wiley (R)
Jan. 8, 1963
  Gaylord Nelson (D)

WYOMING

Class 1
Jan. 23, 1895–Mar. 3, 1917
  Clarence D. Clark (R)
Mar. 4, 1917–Nov. 3, 1933
  John B. Kendrick (D)
Jan. 1, 1934–Jan. 2, 1953
  Joseph C. O'Mahoney (D)
Jan. 3, 1953–Jan. 2, 1959
  Frank A. Barrett (R)
Jan. 3, 1959–Jan. 2, 1977
  Gale W. McGee (D)

Jan. 3, 1977
  Malcolm Wallop (R)

Class 2
Mar. 4, 1895–Nov. 24, 1929
  Francis E. Warren (R)
Dec. 5, 1929–Nov. 30, 1930
  Patrick J. Sullivan (R)
Dec. 1, 1930–Jan. 2, 1937
  Robert D. Carey (R)
Jan. 3, 1937–Jan. 2, 1943
  Harry H. Schwartz (D)
Jan. 3, 1943–Jan. 2, 1949
  E. V. Robertson (R)
Jan. 3, 1949–June 19, 1954
  Lester C. Hunt (D)
June 24, 1954–Nov. 28, 1954
  Edward D. Crippa (R)
Nov. 29, 1954–Jan. 2, 1961
  Joseph C. O'Mahoney (D)
Jan. 3, 1961–Nov. 6, 1962
  John Joseph Hickey (D)
Nov. 7, 1962–Jan. 2, 1967
  Milward L. Simpson (R)
Jan. 3, 1967
  Clifford P. Hansen (R)

FASHION

COTY AMERICAN FASHION CRITICS' AWARD (The Winnie)—Coty, Inc.

The American fashion press chooses the American fashion designer that has a significant effect on how the country dressed the year before. In 1968, the fashion writers decided to give a nod to men's wear, also.

Established 1942.

1943
  Winnie, Norman Norell
  Special award, Lilly Dache
  Special award, John Frederics
1944
  Winnie, Claire McCardell
  Special award, Sally Victor
  Special award, Phelps Associates

1945
  Winnie, Gilbert Adrian
  Winnie, Tina Leser
  Winnie, Emily Wilkens
1946
  Winnie, Clare Potter
  Winnie, Omar Kiam of Ben Reig
  Winnie, Vincent Monte-Sano
1947
  Winnie, Nettie Rosenstein
  Winnie, Mark Mooring
  Winnie, Jack Horwitz
  Winnie, Adele Simpson
1948
  Winnie, Hattie Carnegie
  Special award, Esther Dorothy
  (Furrier)

Special award, Joseph DeLeo
(Furrier)
Special award, Maximilian
1949
Winnie, Pauline Trigere
Special award, Toni Owen
Special award, David Evins
1950
Winnie, Bonnie Cashin
Winnie, Charles James
Special award, Mabel and Charles
Julianelli
Special award, Nancy Melcher
1951
Winnie, Jane Derby
Return award, Norman Norell
Return award, Pauline Trigere
Special award, Vera Maxwell
Special award, Anne Fogarty
Special award, Sylvia Pedlar
1952
Winnie, Ben Zuckerman
Winnie, Ben Sommers of Capezio
Special award, Harvey Berin and his
designer, Karen Stark
Special award, Sydney Wragge of B.
H. Wragge
1953
Winnie, Tholmas F. Brigance
Special award, Mattie Talmack and
her designer John Moore
Special award, Helen Lee
1954
Winnie, James Galanos
Special award, Charles James
1955
Winnie, Jeanne Campbell
Winnie, Anne Klein
Winnie, Herbert Kasper
Special award, Adolfo
1956
Winnie, Luis Estevez
Winnie, Sally Victor
Return award, James Galanos
Special award, Gertrude and Robert
Goldworm
Hall of Fame award, Norman Norell
1957
Winnie, Leslie Morris
Winnie, Sydney Wragge
Special award, Emeric Partos
1958
Hall of Fame award (Posthumous),
Claire McCardell
Winnie, Arnold Scaasi

Return award, Ben Zuckerman
Special award, Donald Brooks
Special award, Jean Schlumberger
1959
Hall of Fame award, Pauline Trigere
Hall of Fame award, James Galanos
1960
Winnie, Ferdinando Sarmi
Winnie, Jacques Tiffeau
Special award, Rudi Gernreich
Special award, Sol Klein of Nettie
Rosenstein Jewelry
Special award, Roxane of Samuel
Winston
1961
Hall of Fame award, Ben Zuckerman
Winnie, Bill Blass
Winnie, Gustave Tassell
Special award, Bonnie Cashin
Special award, Mr. Kenneth
1962
Winnie, Donald Brooks
Special award, Halston
1963
Winnie, Rudi Gernreich
Return award, Bill Blass
Special award, Arthur and Theodora
Edelman
Special award, Betty Yokova of A.
Neustadter
1964
Winnie, Geoffrey Beene
Return award, Jacques Tiffeau of
Tiffeau & Busch
Return special award, Sylvia Pedlar
of Iris Lingerie
Special award, David Webb
1965
Special award, Anna Potok of
Maximilian
Special award, Tzaims Luksus
Special award, Gertrude Seperack
Special award, Pablo
Joint special award, Sylvia de Gay,
Bill Smith, Victor Joris, Leo
Narducci, Don Simonelli, Gayle
Kirkpatrick, Stanley Herman, Edie
Gladstone, Deanna Littell
1966
Winnie, Dominic
Return award, Rudi Gernreich
Return award, Geoffrey Beene
Special award, Kenneth Jay Lane
1967
Hall of Fame award, Rudi Gernreich

Return award, Donald Brooks
Winnie, Oscar de la Renta
Special award, Beth and Herbert
Levine
1968
Return award, Bonnie Cashin
Return award, Oscar de la Renta
Winnie, George Halley
Winnie, Luba
Special award, Count Giorgio di
Sant'Angelo
First Coty award for men's fashion
design, Bill Blass
1969
Winnie, Stan Herman
Winnie, Victor Joris
Return award, Anne Klein
Special award, Adolfo
Special award, Halston
Special award, Julian Tomchin
1970
Hall of Fame award, Bill Blass
Winnie, Giorgio di Sant'Angelo
Winnie, Chester Weinberg
Return award, Herbert Kasper
Coty award for men's fashion design,
Ralph Lauren
Joint special awards for costume
jewelry design, Alexis Kirk, Cliff
Nicholson, Marty Ruza, Bill Smith,
Daniel Stoenescu and Steven Brody
of Cadoro
Special award, Will and Eileen
Richardson
1971
Hall of Fame citation, Bill Blass
Hall of Fame award, Anne Klein
Winnie, Halston
Winnie, Betsey Johnson of Alley Cat
Coty award for men's fashion design,
Larry Kane of Raffles Wear
Special award, John Kloss of Cira
Special award, Nancy Knox of
Renegades
Special award, Elsa Peretti
Special award, Levi Strauss
1972
Hall of Fame, Bonnie Cashin
Return award, Halston
Winnie, John Anthony
Special award, Dorothy Weatherford
for Mountain Artisans
Special men's fashion awards,
Alexander Shields, Pinky Wolman
and Dianne Beaudry of Flo Toronto,

Alan Rosanes of Gordonn Gregory
Ltd., Robert Margolis of A. Smile,
Inc.
1973
Hall of Fame award, Oscar de la
Renta
Coty menswear return award, Ralph
Lauren
Winnie, Stephen Burrows
Winnie, Calvin Klein
Coty menswear award, Piero Dimitri
Special award, Clovis Ruffin
Special accessory awards, Michael
Moraux of Dubaux, Joe Famolare,
Don Kline, Herbert and Beth Levine,
Judith Leiber, Celia Sebiri
1974
Hall of Fame award, Geoffrey Beene
Hall of Fame award, Halston
Coty menswear return award, Piero
Dimitri
Return award, Calvin Klein
Winnie, Ralph Lauren
Coty menswear award, Bill
Kaiserman for Rafael
Special menswear award for jewelry,
Aldo Cipullo
Special lingerie awards, Fernando
Sanchez, Stan Herman, John Kloss,
Bill Tice, Stephen Burrows
Special menswear awards, Sal
Cesarani, John Weitz
1975
Hall of Fame citation, Geoffrey
Beene
Hall of Fame award, Calvin Klein
Hall of Fame award, for menswear,
Piero Dimitri
Coty menswear return award, Bill
Kaiserman for Rafael
Winnie, Carol Horn
Coty menswear award, Chuck
Howard and Peter Wrigley for the
"Mark of the Lion" collection (Anne
Klein Studio)
Special award for swimsuits, Monika
Tilley for Elon
Special menswear award for leather
design, Nancy Knox of Intercuerros
Special awards for fur design, Bill
Blass for Revillon America,
Fernando Sanchez for Revillon
America, Calvin Klein for Alixandre,
Viola Sylbert for Alixandre

1976
Winnie, Mary McFadden
Return award, Ralph Lauren
Return award, John Anthony
Hall of Fame award, Kasper
Special award, Barbara Dulien for
Workwear Corp.
Menswear trophy, Sal Cesarani

Hall of Fame award for menswear,
Bill Kaiserman of Rafael
Special award menswear, Ronald
Kolodzie for Eye-ful,
Lowell Judson for Roytex,
Robert Schafer for Burma-Bibas,
Vicky Davis

GRAPHICS

See Achievement, The Gold Medal
Awards, The American Academy of
Arts and Letters

MEDALLIST AWARD—The American Institute of Graphic Arts
  Posters, album covers, books, packaging, magazine covers—all are graphic arts. To win this medal, one must have made a "distinguished contribution" to the field.
Established 1920.

1920	Norman T. A. Munder
1922	Daniel Berkeley Updike
1924	John C. Agar, Stephen H. Horgan
1925	Bruce Rogers
1926	Burton Emmett
1927	Timothy Cole, Frederic W. Goudy
1929	William A. Dwiggins
1930	Henry Watson Kent
1931	Dard Hunter
1932	Porter Garnett
1934	Henry Lewis Bullen
1935	J. Thompson Willing
1936	Rudolph Ruzicka
1939	William A. Kittredge
1940	Thomas M. Cleland
1941	Carl Purington Rollins
1942	Edwin and Robert Grabhorn
1944	Edward Epstean
1945	Frederic G. Melcher
1946	Stanley Morison
1947	Elmer Adler
1948	Lawrence C. Wroth
1950	Earnest Elmo Calkins, Alfred A. Knopf
1951	Harry L. Gage
1952	Joseph Blumenthal
1953	George Macy
1954	Will Bradley, Jan Tschichold
1955	P. J. Conkwright
1956	Ray Nash
1957	Dr. M. F. Agha
1958	Ben Shahn
1959	May Massee
1960	Walter Paepcke
1961	Paul A. Bennett
1962	Willem Sandberg
1963	Saul Steinberg
1964	Josef Albers
1965	Leonard Baskin
1966	Paul Rand
1967	Romana Javitz
1968	Dr. Giovanni Mardersteig
1969	Dr. Robert L. Leslie
1970	Herbert Bayer
1971	Will Burtin
1972	Milton Glaser
1973	Richard Avedon, Allen Hurlburt, Philip Johnson
1974	Robert Rauschenberg
1975	Bradbury Thompson
1976	Jerome Snyder, Henry Wolf

FLAG-WAVING

**AMERICA'S DEMOCRATIC LEG-
ACY AWARD**—Anti - Defamation
League of B'nai B'rith
"For distinguished contributions to
the enrichment of America's Demo-
cratic Legacy."
Established 1948.
1948
Mrs. Eleanor Roosevelt
Darryl Zanuck, Producer
Dore Schary, Writer-producer
Barney Balaban, President
Paramount Pictures
Charles E. Wilson, Chairman,
President's Committee on Civil
Rights
1949
Harry S. Truman
1950
J. Howard McGrath, U. S. Attorney
General
1951
Henry Ford II
1952
Herbert H. Lehman, U. S. Senator
1953
Dwight D. Eisenhower
1954-1955
Carnegie Corporation
Ford Foundation
Rockefeller Foundation
1956
Herbert H. Lehman, U. S. Senator
James P. Mitchell, U. S. Secretary of
Labor
Charles P. Taft, Mayor of Cincinnati
1957
The 85th Congress of the United
States
1958
Columbia Broadcasting System
Look magazine
The *New York Times*
1959
Actors' Equity Association
Dramatists Guild
League of New York Theatres
Society of Stage Directors and

Choreographers
1960
Harvard University
University of Notre Dame
Brandeis University
1961
Adlai E. Stevenson, U. S.
Ambassador to the U. N.
1962
John F. Kennedy
1963
Eugene Carson Blake, United
Presbyterian Church
A. Philip Randolph, Brotherhood of
Sleeping Car Porters
Walter Reuther, United Auto
Workers
Roy Wilkins, NAACP
1964
Lyndon B. Johnson
1965
Arthur J. Goldberg, U. S.
Ambassador to the U. N.
1966
Nicholas deB. Katzenbach, Under
Secretary of State
1967
John W. Gardner, National Urban
Coalition
1968   no award
1969
Earl Warren, Former Chief Justice,
U. S. Supreme Court
1970   no award
1971
Abraham Joshua Heschel, Jewish
Theological Seminary of America
1972   no award
1973
Jacob K. Javits, U. S. Senator
Abraham A. Ribicoff, U. S. Senator
1974   no award
1975   no award
1976
Saul Bellow, Author

**DISTINGUISHED SERVICE MED-
AL**—The American Legion

Novelist Saul Bellow (left) receiving his Nobel prize from Sweden's King Carl Gustaf. (Wide World Photos)

Qualifications? "Outstanding service to the nation and to the program of the American Legion."

Established 1929. (The award before 1929 was made prior to the Legion's "adoption of definite regulations.")

1921	Marshall Foch (France)
	Adm. Beatty (Great Britain)
	Gen. Baron Jacques (Belgium)
	Gen. Diaz (Italy)
	Charles Bertrand (France)
1922	Gen. John J. Pershing
1923	Adm. R. E. Coontz
	Gen. Josef Haller (Poland)
1926	Ignace Jan Paderewski (Poland)
1927	Comte Francois Marie Robert DeJean (France)
1928	Lord Allenby (Great Britain)
1929	Judge Kenesaw M. Landis
1930	Adm. William S. Sims
1942	Gen. Douglas MacArthur
1943	Adm. Ernest J. King
	Gen. George C. Marshall
1944	Henry Ford
	Frank Knox
	Gen. H. H. Arnold

1945	Franklin D. Roosevelt
	Henry L. Stimson
	Ernest Taylor (Ernie) Pyle
	Adm. Chester Nimitz
	Brig. Gen. Theodore Roosevelt
	Gen. Dwight D. Eisenhower
1946	William Randolph Hearst
	Bob Hope
	Maj. Gen. Lewis B. Hershey
	J. Edgar Hoover
	Cordell Hull
1947	Fred M. Vinson
	Edward Martin
	Wm. S. Knudsen
1949	President Harry S. Truman
	George Herman (Babe) Ruth
	Gen. Frank Parker
1950	Rep. Edith Nourse Rogers
	Maj. Gen. Milton A. Reckord
	Charles F. Johnson, Jr.
1951	Maj. Gen. Charles P. Summerall
1953	Royal C. Johnson
1954	Maj. Gen. George A. White
1955	Dr. Jonas E. Salk
	Maj. Gen. Ellard A. Walsh
1956	Vice Adm. Joel T. Boone

Actor Pat O'Brien, pictured here in costume for Marine Raiders, *won the American Legion's Distinguished Service Medal. (Memory Shop)*

	Charles Stewart Mott
1957	Bishop Fulton J. Sheen
	Gen. Mark W. Clark
1958	Bernard M. Baruch
1959	Sen. Robert S. Kerr
1961	John F. Kennedy
1962	Gen. Lucius D. Clay
	Dr. Thomas A. Dooley
1963	Francis Cardinal Spellman, Archbishop of New York
1964	Dr. Charles W. Mayo
1965	James F. Byrnes
	Herbert Clark Hoover
1966	Capt. Roger H. C. Donlon
1967	Tom C. Clark
1968	Lyndon B. Johnson
	Gen. William C. Westmoreland
1969	Richard M. Nixon
1970	Rep. Olin E. Teague
1971	Hon. Richard Brevard Russell
	Hon. L. Mendel Rivers
1972	DeWitt Wallace
	Sen. John C. Stennis
1974	Henry F. Kissinger
	Rep. F. Edward Hebert
1975	Harry W. Colmery
1976	Pat O'Brien

SPLENDID AMERICAN AWARD—
The Thomas A. Dooley Foundation

Dr. Thomas A. Dooley was a naval officer who stayed behind in Asia after the Korean conflict was stalemated. He established some 17 health programs and clinics in 14 countries. After Dr. Dooley's death in 1961, the foundation was set up to continue his work. Authors of the best-selling novel, *The Ugly American,* sponsored the Splendid American Award to "honor those Americans whose personal accomplishments have well reflected the meaning and purpose of the United States to the world community." Established 1964.

1964	Henry Cabot Lodge
1965	Dean Rusk
	Bob Hope
1966	Edwin O. Reischauer
	Danny Kaye
1967	Daniel K. Inouye
	Kirk Douglas
1968	John H Glenn, Jr.
	Eugene R. Black
1969	Samuel F. Pryor
	Duke Ellington

Pauline V. Delli-Carpini accepts the American Society of Interior Designers award from the society's president, Richard Jones, for Belgian Linens. (Courtesy of ASID)

1970	no award	1972	no award
1971	Perle M. Mesta	1973	Spiro T. Agnew
	Lowell Thomas		Frank Sinatra
	Reader's Digest		

INTERIOR DESIGN

INTERNATIONAL DESIGN
AWARD—American Society of Interior Designers

Here is an award for professionals and nonprofessionals who "have made substantial contributions toward improving design standards of our manmade environment." Some awards are presented to a project and those involved in its planning and execution.

Established 1975 (previously given by the American Institute of Interior Designers).

1975
 Ontario Place, Toronto, Canada
 Reyner Banham, University College, London, England
 Thomas Lawson McCall, Former Governor of Oregon
 John Entenza, University of Illinois
 Pedestrian Mall, Munich, Germany
1976
 Porters of Racine, Racine, Wis.
 Belgian Linens Association, New York, N.Y.
 Contract Interiors for Business, Inc.

JOURNALISM

See Broadcasting, The George Foster Peabody Broadcasting Awards, University of Georgia

HEYWOOD BROUN AWARD—The Newspaper Guild
This is the investigative reporter's award. It goes for righting wrongs, exposes, revelations, and stories leading to indictments and, in one case, a presidential resignation.
Established 1941.
1941
Tom O'Connor, *PM*, for revealing hazardous mine conditions
1942
Dillard Stokes, *Washington Post*, for uncovering a Nazi propaganda network in the U. S.
1943
Milton J. Lapine, I. L. Kenen, William M. Davy, E. George Green, *Cleveland Union Leader*, for series of wartime ads
1944
Nathan Robertson, *PM*, for distinguished Washington coverage
1945
Larry Guerin, *New Orleans Item*, for his local and state coverage
1946
James McGuire, Jack McPhaul, Karin Walsh, *Chicago Times*, for helping free a prisoner unjustly convicted of murder
1947
Bert Andrews, *New York Herald Tribune*, for exposing disregard for civil rights in State Department security dismissals
1948
Elias A. McQuaid, *New Hampshire News* (Manchester), for uncovering fraud in state contract awards
1949
Herbert L. Block, *Washington Post*, for editorial cartoons
Ted Poston, *N. Y. Post*, for

courageous coverage of Florida rape trial
1950
Leonard Jackson, *Bay City* (Mich.) *Times*, for exposing exploitation of migrant farm workers
1951
Jack Steele, *New York Herald Tribune*, for exposing corruption in federal government bureaus
1952
Wallace Turner, *Portland Oregonian*, for exposing fraud in sale of Indian timberlands
1953
Ralph S. O'Leary, *Houston Post*, for his exposé of The Minute Women in Texas
1954
Anthony Lewis, *Washington Daily News*, for helping reinstate federal employee wrongly fired as security risk
1955
Clark R. Mollenhoff, Cowles Newspapers, stories leading to reinstatement of security "risk" and new security rules
1956
Wallace Turner, William Lambert, *Portland Oregonian*, stories leading to racket indictments of union, police, and city officials
1957
Aaron Epstein, *Daytona Beach Journal & News*, stories leading to redevelopment of Negro slums
Arthur W. Geiselman, Jr., *York Gazette & Daily*, stories leading to community reforms
1958
George N. Allen, *N. Y. World-Telegram & Sun*, on-the-scene investigation of delinquencies in New York City schools
1959
William Haddad, Joseph Kahn, *New York Post*, exposing graft and

mismanagement in New York City slum clearance
1960
Harry Allen, Frank Drea, *Toronto Telegram,* exposing exploitation of Italian immigrant workers
1961
Michael Mok, *N. Y. World-Telegram & Sun,* for exposing conditions in New York City mental hospital
Dale Wright, *N. Y. World-Telegram & Sun,* for disclosing exploitation of migrant workers
1962
Morton Mintz, *Washington Post,* report on thalidomide leading to protective legislation
1963
Arthur W. Geiselman, Jr., *York Gazette & Daily,* stories leading to prosecution of housing code violations
Samuel Stafford, *Washington Daily News,* expose of abuses in distribution of surplus food
1964
Gene Goltz, *Houston Post,* stories leading to indictment of local officials charged with theft and conspiracy involving public funds
1965
John Frasca, *Tampa Tribune,* stories leading to release of innocent man convicted and imprisoned for robbery
1966
Gene Miller, *Miami Herald,* stories leading to release of two persons unjustly convicted of murder
1967
Robert Wyrick, *Today,* Cocoa, Fla., stories exposing county government corruption, leading to indictments and convictions
1968
Mike Royko, *Chicago Daily News,* columns pleading the cause of the underdog, leading to redress for the abused
1969
William Lambert, *Life,* article resulting in Justice Fortas' resignation and reexamination of ethics in public life

1970
Donald Singleton, *New York Daily News,* series spotlighting problems of crime in nation's largest city
1971
Aaron Latham, *Washington Post,* series examining failures of Junior Village, the Capital's home for homeless children
1972
Carl Bernstein, Bob Woodward, *Washington Post,* series exposing political ramifications of the Watergate Affair
1973
Donald L. Barlett, James B. Steele, *Philadelphia Inquirer,* series exposing uneven sentencing and discrimination by judges and prosecutors
1974
Selwyn Raab, *New York Times,* article revealing new evidence calling into question convictions of two men for triple murder
1975
Kent Pollock, *Philadelphia Inquirer,* series documenting the spread of police brutality in the City of Brotherly Love

FOURTH ESTATE AWARD—The American Legion
This is subtitled "public relations recognition award," and goes for "an outstanding service to the community, state or nation, which service shall have been in accordance with or the furtherance of established American Legion policies or programs." John Wayne was a shoo-in.
Established 1958.
1958
Jim Lucas
1959
Advertising Council, Inc., *Chicago Tribune, U.S. News and World Report*
1960
Hearst Newspapers
1961
Scripps–Howard Newspapers, Jack L. Warner (Warner Brothers Pictures)

1962
  Fulton Lewis, Jr.
1963
  The Copley Press, Inc., *This Week*
  magazine
1964
  Chicago Tribune,
  Mississippi Publishers Corp.
1965
  Clark Mollenhoff (Cowles
  Publications), Paul Harvey
  (American Broadcasting Co.),
  Golden West Broadcasters
1966
  Mutual Broadcasting System,
  The Booth Newspapers,
  Columbus Dispatch
1967
  St. Louis Globe-Democrat
1968
  William S. White (United Feature
  Syndicate)
1969
  George W. Healy, Jr. (*New Orleans
  Times-Picayune and State*)
  Raymond J. McHugh (Copley News
  Service)
1970
  James Geddes Stahlman (*The
  Banner,* Nashville, Tenn.), Jenkin
  Lloyd Jones (*The Tribune,* Tulsa,
  Okla.)
1971
  Anheuser Busch, Inc., John Wayne
1972
  Agustin Edwards (*El Mercurio,*
  Santiago, Chile)
1973
  Clare Booth Luce
1974
  James J. Kilpatrick, Jr.
1975
  Jim Bishop
1976
  Thomas P. Chisman (Bicentennial
  Radio Network)
  Vic Cantone (cartoonist)

GAVEL AWARD—American Bar Association
  For movies, television shows, newspapers, and magazines that present a good case for the legal profession.
  Established 1958.

1958
Movies
  United Artists Corp., *Twelve Angry
  Men*
Television
  Columbia Broadcasting System,
  "The Greeg Case" and "The Verdict
  Is Yours"
  National Broadcasting Co., "An Act
  of Law," and "American Trial by
  Jury"
Newspapers
  Cleveland Plain Dealer, editorials on
  court administration
  Richmond (Va.) *News Leader,*
  weekly legal column
  St. Petersburg (Fla.) *Times,*
  editorials and articles on law and the
  courts
Magazines
  Life, Crime in the U.S. series
1959
Movies   no award
Television
  American Broadcasting Co., "Day in
  Court"
  Columbia University Press, "The
  Constitution: Whose
  Interpretation?"
Newspapers
  St. Louis Post-Dispatch, series on the
  U.S. Supreme Court
  Moline (Ill.) *Daily Dispatch,*
  editorials and articles on
  modernizing the Illinois court
  system
Magazines
  Southern Telephone News (Atlanta,
  Ga.), series on law in American life
  Time, Inc., *Time* magazine coverage
  of Law Day U.S.A.
1960
Movies   no award
Television
  KPIX-TV, San Francisco
  (Westinghouse), "A Life in Balance"
  WRC-TV, Washington, D.C. (NBC),
  series on the role of the juvenile
  court
  Piasano Productions, *Perry Mason*
  series for dramatizing basic legal
  safeguards afforded the accused
  Tulane University (New Orleans,
  La.), "With Justice for All" from
  Close-Up series

Radio
WRCV (NBC) (Philadelphia, Pa.), "Law in Action"
WHAS (Louisville, Ky.), "It's the Law"
Newspapers
Washington Post, editorials on the constitutional role of the Supreme Court
Pittsburgh Post-Gazette, editorials and articles explaining the roles of judges and lawyers
The Oregonian (Portland, Oreg.), a special Law Day U.S.A. section
Lindsay-Schaub Newspapers (Decatur, Ill.), series on first National Conference of Judicial Selection and Court Administration
Magazines   no award
1961
Movies   no award
Television
Armstrong Circle Theatre, dramatization on the work of Legal Aid Societies
University of Michigan Television Center (Ann Arbor, Mich.), *Blessings of Liberty* series dramatizing constitutional rights of Americans
CBS Reports, documentary production, "A Real Case of Murder"
Radio
KMOX (St. Louis, Mo.), "A Case in Point," dramatizing the role of a lawyer
Newspapers
Hartford Times, series on newly reorganized system of state courts
Christian Science Monitor, series documenting an alien's murder trial
Chicago Tribune, Robert Wiedrich (author), series analyzing the congestion in Chicago courts
Magazines   no award
1962
Movies
Stanley Kramer Corp., *Judgment at Nuremburg*
Television
CBS Television Network, "Iron Man" segment of *The Defenders* series
Radio
WRFB (Tallahassee, Fla.), "So

Highly We Value," dramatizing significant men and events in American legal history
Newspapers
Christian Science Monitor, Emilie Tavel (author), for journalistic enterprise in support of steps to strengthen the probate court system in Massachusetts
Washington Post, James E. Clayton (author), for articles interpreting decisions of the Supreme Court on major constitutional issues
Magazines
Fortune, for a definitive article on the court congestion problem, "The Crisis in the Courts"
Boy's Life, for a series of illustrated, educational articles on the historical origins of our legal system

1963
Newspapers
Washington Post, for distinguished interpretative reporting of the Supreme Court decisions on constitutional issues of great national significance
Chicago Tribune, for a series of editorials backing adoption of the judicial amendment of the Illinois constitution to modernize the courts there
Chicago Daily News, for articles and editorials supporting the organized bar campaign to modernize the Illinois courts
Chicago Sun-Times, for reportorial and editorial support of the judicial amendment
Television
National Broadcasting Co., "The Judge"
Columbia Broadcasting System, CBS Reports, a two-part documentary, "Storm Over the Supreme Court"
Radio
WMAQ (Chicago, Ill.), "A Look at the Law" series
KYW (Cleveland, Ohio),"A Look at the Law" series
Movies
Universal-International Pictures, *To Kill a Mockingbird*

Publications
 The Research Institute of America,
 for a series of educational booklets
 explaining preventative law
1964
Newspapers
 Washington Star, for analytical
 reporting, under deadline, of
 important Supreme Court decisions
 Oklahoma City Times, Robert
 McMillin (author), for a series on a
 court ruling for reapportionment of
 the Oklahoma legislature's western
 district
Television
 CBS News Division, for "CBS
 Reports" documentary, "The Crisis
 of Presidential Succession"
 University of Michigan Television
 Center (Ann Arbor, Mich.), for a
 20-part series, "A Quest for
 Certainty"
 Plautus Productions, for "Blacklist,"
 a segment of "The Defenders" series
Radio
 KMPC, (Los Angeles, Calif.),
 "Heritage" series
Movies
 Brandon Films, *The Great Rights,* an
 animated film
Books
 American Heritage Publishing Co.,
 for a series of articles analyzing
 historic decisions of the Supreme
 Court which helped to shape
 American democracy
 J. B. Lippincott Co., Herbert
 Mitgang (author), *The Man Who
 Rode the Tiger*
Magazines
 Look, for a series on legal issues
1965
Newspapers
 Kansas City Kansan, for an eleven-
 part series analyzing the 1964 Code
 of Civil Procedures in the Kansas
 Courts
 Louisville Times, for a twenty-four-
 part series on the Kentucky Court of
 Appeals
 Toledo Blade, for comprehensive
 reporting, editorial interpretation of
 court decisions, legislative
 enactments, and organized bar
 efforts to improve the courts

Worcester (Mass.) *Daily Telegram,*
 for a series on judicial trends
Television
 CBS News Division, "Gideon's
 Trumpet: The Poor Man and the
 Law," a "CBS Reports"
 documentary
 National Broadcasting Co., "The
 Magnificent Yankee"
 Robert Saudek Associates, Inc., for
 the "Profiles of Courage" segment on
 Charles Evans Hughes
Radio
 WIBG (Philadelphia, Pa.),
 "Government of Man by Law" series
Wire Services
 Gannett News Service, *Crime and
 the U.S. Supreme Court* series
Magazines
 Life, "Storm Center of Justice"
Books
 McGraw Hill, A. L. Todd (author),
 Justice on Trial
1966
Newspapers
 Christian Science Monitor for a ten-
 part series on the nature and impact
 of significant changes in the
 administration of criminal justice
 St. Petersburg (Fla.) *Times* for
 editorials urging modernization of
 the Florida judicial system and the
 nonpartisan selection of judges
Television
 CBS News Division, "Abortion and
 the Law"
 WCAU-TV Philadelphia, Pa.,
 "Girard College: The Will and the
 Wall"
Radio
 KMPC (Los Angeles, Calif.) for its
 editorial on the Watts riots, "The
 Second Civil War"
 WMAL (Washington, D. C.), "The
 Abused Witness"
Magazines
 Time for its law sections and the
 essay, "The Revolution in Criminal
 Justice"
 Look, for its story on reform in the
 Chicago police department
1967
Newspapers
 Washington Post, Leonard Downie,
 Jr. (author), for a seven-part series

leading to reforms in Washington's Court of General Sessions

Washington Post, John P. MacKenzie (author), for articles interpreting significant Supreme Court decisions

Daily Oklahoman and Times, for editorials leading to a petition calling for a statewide referendum on court reforms

Toledo Blade, for pioneering leadership in formulating a voluntary code of fair practices in crime news coverage

Television

NBC News, for its "Meet the Press" documentary on the President's Commission on Law Enforcement

NBC News, "The Statesman

WTVN-TV, (Columbus, Ohio), "View from the High Bench"

WNBC-TV, (New York City), "Due Process for the Accused" series, three segments

Radio

Group W, "Crime and Punishment in the 60s" series, four segments

Magazines

Time, "Moving the Constitution into the Police Station"

Look, Fletcher Knebel (author), for an article on the jury system in the U.S.

Look, Julius Horowitz (author), "The Lady Fights Back"

1968

Newspapers

Christian Science Monitor, Howard James (author), *Crisis in the Courts* series

Los Angeles Times, Ronald J. Ostrow (author), for a series of interpretative articles on Supreme Court decisions

St. Louis Post-Dispatch, James C. Millstone (author), for articles on the decision-making process of the Supreme Court

Louisville Courier-Journal, for its adoption of a code to protect fair trial

Philadelphia Inquirer, G. Warren Nutter (author), for a ten-part series contrasting legal, social, and political institutions in the U.S. and the Soviet Union

Television

National Broadcasting Co., "Justice for All?"

American Broadcasting Co., "A Case of Libel"

Twentieth-Century Fox, Television, Inc., "Commitment" segment of "Judd for the Defense" series

Magazines

Newsweek, Peter Janssen (author), "The 'New' Law vs. Tradition"

Saturday Evening Post, Stewart Alsop (author), "The Supreme Court Asks a Question: Is It Fair?"

Radio

WMAL, (Washington, D.C.), "Perspective—D. C. Crime Report" series

WEEI, (Boston, Mass.), "Benzaquin's Notepad" series

News Service

Newhouse National News Service, Jack C. Landau (author), a series examining the American military justice

1969

Newspapers

New York Times magazine, Herbert Mitgang (author), for an article detailing the work of community lawyers for the poor and disadvantaged

Minneapolis Star, Austin Wehrwein (author), for editorials and commentaries on developments in law and the administration of justice

Anchorage Daily News, C. Robert Zelnick (author), for a survey of the state's administration of justice

Riverside Press-Enterprise, for a series on crime and the courts

Washington Post, for the book, *Ten Blocks from the White House*

Radio

NBC Radio News, "The Cop and the Court"

WJR (Detroit, Mich.), "The Rule of Law" series

KLAC (Los Angeles, Calif.), "Law for the Laymen" series

Television

CBS News Division, "Justice Black and the Bill of Rights"

WMAQ-TV, (Chicago, Ill.), "The Quality of Justice"

1970

Newspapers

Kankakee (Ill.) *Daily Journal,* for an in-depth probe into conditions affecting the administration of justice

Niagara Falls (N.Y.) *Gazette,* for a series on the quality of justice in the lower courts

Evansville (Ind.) *Courier,* for the publication of the complete study on local crime and law enforcement problems

Washington Evening Star, for a series detailing the problems in the D.C. courts

Christian Science Monitor, for a series on the brutal conditions in juvenile detention homes

Louisville Courier-Journal, for a series describing the archaic court conditions

New York Times, for a series examining the problems of free press-fair trial

Chicago Sun-Times, for series on legal subjects of public imports, including the need for more Black lawyers

Parade, "They Learn the Law— Before It's Too Late"

Television

NBC News Division, "Voices on the Inside" and "Between Two Rivers"

Universal City Studios, Inc., "The DA: Murder One"

American Broadcasting Co., "The Young Lawyers"

National Educational Television, "The Warren Years"

WNED-TV (Buffalo, N.Y.), "Are Campus Disorders Out of Hand?"

Radio

KFWB (Los Angeles, Calif.) "Ignorance and the Law" series

Magazines

Psychology Today, for the contribution to original research concerning attitudes toward the law, court, crime and punishment, and the penal system rights

1971

Newspapers

The Record-Chronicle, (Denton, Tex.), for a series explaining the legal steps that occur from the time of arrest to the trial

Spartanburg (S. Car.) *Journal,* series on how each court in the judicial system operates

St. Petersburg (Fla.) *Times,* series on the quality of Florida prisons

Valley News, (Van Nuys, Calif.), series on court decisions expanding individual rights

Milwaukee Journal, for editorials favoring efforts to update Wisconsin's judicial system

Milwaukee Journal, Law Day U.S.A. supplement

Minneapolis Star, for weekly columns, *Judging the Law*

Christian Science Monitor, for a series examining the state of American prisons

Kansas City Star, for a series of editorials on the problems of criminal justice and penal reform

The National Observer, for a series interpreting major Supreme Court decisions

Television

CBS News, for the "CBS Reports" documentary, "Justice in America, Part I, Some Are More Equal than Others"

NBC News, "This Child is Rated X: An NBC White Paper on Juvenile Justice"

Midwestern Educational Television, Inc. (St. Paul, Minn.), "The Baseball Glove" series

WGBH-TV (Boston, Mass.) and KCET-TV (Los Angeles, Calif.) (joint award), "The Advocates" segment, "Jail with No Bail"

Radio

WNBC (New York City), for a series of educational documentaries on the operation of the New York City court system.

KXYZ (Houston, Tex.), for a six-part series on the courts and the law, with special recognition for the segment, "Old Fashioned Citizenship"

KEEL (Shreveport, La.), "Angola: The Crime of Louisiana Punishment"

Movies

Groverton Production and Universal

Television, for the movie that was
made for television that launched the
ABC's series "Owen Marshall,
Counselor at Law"
Magazines
Newsweek, for its special report,
"Justice on Trial"
Books
The University of Michigan Press
(Ann Arbor, Mich.) *Assault of
Privacy: Computers Data Banks, and
Dossiers*
1973
Newspapers
Illinois State Register, for an
eighteen-part series on the many
facets of the American criminal
justice system
Tucson Daily Citizen, for an
investigative series on the lax
administrative practices of the Pima
County probate system
St. Louis Post-Dispatch, for a series
on the new forces and ideas taking
place in the legal profession
St. Louis Globe-Democrat, for an
investigative series uncovering
corruption in the city's Municipal
Court
Detroit Free Press, for a series
exploring conditions that are
weakening the ability of the legal
system to function properly
Parade, for an article outlining the
problems of the deaf in obtaining
proper legal representation
Television
NBC, Time-Life Films, "Inventing a
Nation"
NBC News, "Guilty by Reason of
Race"
KNXT-TV, (Los Angeles, Calif.),
"Rape"
WKBF-TV, (Cleveland, Ohio), "The
Crime of Our Courts" series
KING-TV (Seattle, Wash.), "Are
Prisons for People?"
WMAR-TV (Baltimore, Md.), "Bars
to Progress"
New Hampshire Network/WENH-
TV(Durham, N.H.), "Society's Child"
Radio
KTOK, Oklahoma City, "Poverty in
the Courtroom" and "Behind the
Walls of Big Mac"

WCCO (Minneapolis/St. Paul,
Minn.), "You and the Jury: Law Day
1972
Movies
Dick Berg—Metromedia Production,
Heat of Anger, a made-for-television
movie
Magazines
Apartment Ideas (Des Moines,
Iowa), for articles on legal problems
common to apartment renters
Harper's, "Your Phone is a Party
Line"
Readers Digest, for its series examining
the juvenile court system in America
Time, "Up from Coverture"
1974
Newspapers
Poughkeepsie (N.Y.) *Journal,* Ed
Baron and Joe Tinkleman (authors),
for a special study of New York
State's new drug law
Kansas City Star, Harry Jones, Jr.,
and J. J. Maloney (authors), series
examining the prisons of Missouri
and Kansas and the federal
institutions in those states
Philadelphia Inquirer, Donald L.
Bartlett and James B. Steele
(authors), for series revealing
patterns of discrimination and bias,
extreme disparity in sentencing, and
jailing of innocent persons by some
judges
Birmingham News Dimension
supplement, Peggy Roberson
(author), for article on plea
bargaining in Birmingham
Orlando (Fla.) *Sentinel Star,* James
Bacchus (author), series disclosing
practices and procedures needing
reform in Florida's penal
system
Television
ABC News, "The First and Essential
Freedom"
CBS News, for its series of reports on
the "CBS Evening News" dealing
with Supreme Court decisions
NBC News, "Watergate: The
President Speaks" and "How
Watergate Changed Government"
WRC-TV, NBC (Washington, D.C.),
"News 4 Washington Probe: By
Reason of Insanity"

KPIX-TV (San Francisco, Calif.), "A Case of Arson"

WMAR-TV (Baltimore, Md.), "There Ought To Be a Law"

WTIC-TV (Hartford, Conn.), "The Nine-Year-Old Norfolk Prison"

KYTV (Springfield, Mo.), "START Inmates: Experimental Man"

WNET-TV PBS, (New York City), "Bill Moyers' Journal: An Essay on Watergate"

Radio

KNX Newsradio, CBS (Los Angeles, Calif.), "Is Our Flag Still There?"

WMAL (Washington, D.C.), "The Legend of Lenient Justice"

National Public Radio, "All Things Considered" and "Every Tenth American"

Movies   no award

Magazines

Philadelphia, John Guinther (author), "The Last Whole Justice Catalog"

The New Yorker, Richard Harris (author), "Annals of Law: Boston Criminal Courts"

Wire Services and Syndicates

Public Insights Syndicate, (North Hollywood, Calif.) Harry Humphreys (author), *Ideas, Issues and Insights*

Books

David McKay Company, Inc., James F. Simon (author), *In His Own Image: The Supreme Court in Richard Nixon's America*

1975

Newspapers

Sharon Herald (Grove City, Pa.), Teresa Spatara (author), for its eighteen-part series on crime and criminal justice

Albuquerque Journal, Scott Beaven (author), series on the way New Mexico treats its mentally ill and retarded

Minneapolis Tribune, Frank Premack, Peter Vanderpoel, and Doug Stone (authors), for its series on the Hennepin County juvenile system

Chicago Sun-Times, Roger Simon and Patrick Oster (authors), for its in-depth investigation of the Cook

County criminal justice system

Television

American television industry and ABC News, NBC News, CBS News and PBS for pool coverage and broadcast of the House Judiciary Committee impeachment proceedings

KATU (Portland, Oreg.), "Is It Justice?"

WCCO-TV (Minneapolis, Minn.), "The Time Machine"

WTTW (Chicago, Ill.), "Criminal Court"

Indiana University Radio and Television Service, "The Role of the Lawyer"

Complete Channel TV, Inc. (Madison, Wis.), "Halfway to Somewhere"

CBS News, "What's It All About" series

NBC, "A Case of Rape"

WNBC-TV (New York City), "Legal Ethics: What's Happening?" segment of the "Critical Issues: Critical Minds" series

Radio

CBS News Radio, "A Hearing for American Justice" series

NBC News Radio, "Capital Punishment: Dead or Alive"

WCBS/Newsradio (New York City), "Rape: The Law and You" series

WHLO (Akron, Ohio), "Inside the Grand Jury" series

American Forces Network, "High Crimes and Misdemeanors"

WWVA (Wheeling, W. Va.), for coverage by Jerry Kelanic of the investigation, indictment and trial of Tony Boyle

Magazines

Philadephia magazine, James N. Riggio (author), "The Paint Job"

The New Yorker, Richard Harris (author), "A Scrap of Black Cloth"

Newsweek, David M. Alpern (author), "All About Impeachment"

Books

Charles Scribner's Sons, John P. MacKenzie (author), *The Appearance of Justice*

News Syndicates

McGraw-Hill World News, Daniel

B. Moskowitz (author), *Your World Tomorrow* series
Theatre
Dome Productions (Los Angeles, Calif.), for the one-man play, *Clarence Darrow*
1976
Movies   no award
Theatre   no award
Books
Yale University Press, Alexander M. Bickel (author), *The Morality of Consent*
Television
CBS News, "The Case Against Milligan"
WMAQ-TV, NBC (Chicago, Ill.), "When Is Justice Coming?"
WCVB-TV (Boston, Mass.), "Crime: The War We're Losing"

ROBERT F. KENNEDY JOURNAL-ISM AWARDS—Robert F. Kennedy Journalism Awards Committee
For articles or broadcasts dealing with the problems of disadvantaged Americans.
Established 1968.
1968
CBS, "Black History: Lost, Stolen or Strayed," Andrew A. Rooney, Producer
WMCA-Radio, New York City, for continuing special coverage of the problems of poverty and discrimination in New York City and New York State
Nick Kotz, *Des Moines Register* and *Tribune*, for his continuing coverage of poverty in America
David Nevin, *Life*, "These Murdered Old Mountains"
1969
ABC, "Black Fiddler: Prejudice and the Negro," Howard Enders, Producer
NBC, "Between Two Rivers" from the "First Tuesday" series, Tom Pettit, Reporter
WRC-TV (Washington, D. C.), "Perspective: New Set of Eyes," Bill Leonard, Producer
WJR Radio (Detroit, Mich), "I Am Not Alone," Phil Jones, reporter

Linda Rockey, *Chicago Sun-Times*, series on the problems of hunger
Dallas Kinney and Kent Pollock, *Palm Beach Post-Times*, "Migration to Misery" series
Fred C. Shapiro, *The New Yorker*, "The Whitmore Confessions"
1970
Westinghouse Broadcasting Co., "When You Reach December"
NBC, "Migrant: An NBC White Paper," Martin Carr, Producer
Ralph Looney, *Albuquerque Tribune*, series on the Navajos
Jerome Watson and Sam Washington, *Chicago Sun-Times*, series on Illinois State Schools for the Mentally Retarded
Ruben Salazar, *Los Angeles Times*, columns on the culture and alienation of Chicanos
The New Thing (arts workshop in the inner city of Washington, D. C.), "This is the Home of Mrs. Levant Graham," Topper Carew, Producer
1971
Jon Nordheimer, *New York Times*, "From Dakto to Detroit: Death of a Troubled Hero"
Patrick Zier and Joanne Wragg, *Lakeland* (Fla.) *Ledger*, "The Battle for Dignity"
Beekman Winthrop, *New South*, "Worms Turn People Off"
Newsweek, "Justice on Trial," by Edward Kosner, Peter Goldman and Don Holt
Group W, "The Suburban Wall," Paul Altmeyer, Producer
Doug Fox, KTOK-Radio, series on "The Business of Being Black"
1972
Jean Heller, The Associated Press, "The Tuskegee Syphilis Study"
WABC-TV (New York City), "Willowbrook: The Last Great Disgrace," written and reported by Geraldo Rivera
1973
John Guinther, *Philadelphia Magazine*, "The Only Good Indian"
Bob Dotson, WKY-TV (Oklahoma

City, Okla.), "Through the Looking Glass Darkly"

Dolores Katz and Jo Thomas, *Detroit Free Press,* "Psychosurgery—On Trial"

1974

Mike Masterson, *Hot Springs* (Ark.) *Sentinel-Record,* feature stories, editorials, and columns on poverty and discrimination

Loretta Schwartz, *Philadelphia Magazine,* "Nothing to Eat"

Martin Berman, Peter Lance, and Geraldo Rivera, WABC-TV (New York City), "The Willowbrook Case: The People vs. the State of New York"

Terence Gurley, WWVA-Radio (Wheeling, W. Va.), "Back to Bloody Harlan"

1975

Gene Miller and the *Miami Herald,* coverage of the Pitts-Lee case

Michael O'Brien, the *Miami News,* (photojournalism), "John Madden: His Last Days"

Tom Pettit, NBC News, "Feeding the Poor"

Bob Cain and Cathleen Gurley, WWVA Radio, Wheeling, W. Va., "Care and Feeding of America"

The Cavalier Daily, University of Virginia, "Benign Neglect"

MURRAY KRAMER AWARD—Boston University

This goes to a sports journalist—in broadcasting, print, or even a cartoonist—who covers intercollegiate athletics. Note that it took Kramer, a sports columnist for the *Boston Record-American,* three years to win his own award.

Established 1965.

1965

Arthur Sampson, *Boston Herald-Traveler*

1966

Don Gillis, WHDH-TV Boston

1967

Murray Kramer, *Boston Record-American*

1968

Cliff Sundberg, *Boston Herald-Traveler*

1969

Roy Mumpton, *Worcester Telegram & Gazette*

1970

Jerry Nason, *Boston Globe*

1971

Dick Dew, *United Press International*

1972

Walter "Red" Smith, Nationally syndicated columnist

1973

Joe Concannon, *Boston Globe*

1974

Bob Monahan, *Boston Globe*

1975

Joe Giuliotti, *Boston Herald-American*

1976

Phil Bissell, *Boston Herald-American*

NATIONAL CITATION AWARD— William Allen White Foundation

When you win this award your medallion reads: "American journalist who exemplifies William Allen White ideals in service to his profession and his community." William Allen White was a small-town editor-publisher whose influence extended far beyond the circulation boundaries of his *Emporia* (Kans.) *Gazette.*

Established 1950.

1950	James B. Reston
1951	Ernest K. Lindley
1952	Erwin D. Canham
1953	Palmer Hoyt
1954	Grove Patterson
1955	Norman E. Isaacs
1956	Roy A. Roberts
1957	Irving Dilliard
1958	Jenkin Lloyd Jones
1959	Ben Hibbs
1960	Jules Dubios
1961	Hodding Carter
1962	Bernard Kilgore
1963	Paul Miller
1964	Clark R. Mollenhoff
1965	Earl J. Johnson
1966	Gardner Cowles
1967	Wes Gallagher
1968	Mark Ethridge
1969	Walter Cronkite
1970	Eugene Pulliam

1971	Vermont Royster
1972	John S. Knight
1973	Barry Bingham, Sr.
1974	Arthur O. Sulzberger
1975	Otis Chandler
1976	Peter Lisagor

See Pulitzer Prize

SCIENCE WRITING AWARD IN PHYSICS AND ASTRONOMY—The American Institute of Physics and the United States Steel Foundation

This goes to a writer or broadcaster who manages to clarify the complexities and scientific mumbo-jumbo of physics so that the average person with intelligence above 100 and education beyond second grade can understand it. Or as the institute phrases it: "For noteworthy writing, broadcasting, or televising about physics and astronomy in the media of mass communications."

1968
William J. Perkinson, *Baltimore Evening Sun*
1969   No award
1970
Clarence P. Gilmore, Metromedia Television
1971
Kenneth F. Weaver, *National Geographic*
1972
Jerry E. Bishop, *Wall Street Journal*
1973
Edward Edelson, *New York Daily News*
1974
Patrick Young, *The National Observer*
1975
Tom Alexander, *Fortune*
1976
Frederic Golden, *Time*

SCIENCE WRITING AWARD IN PHYSICS AND ASTRONOMY—The American Institute of Physics and the United States Steel Foundation

Unlike the preceding award, this is presented to a scientist who has written for the mass media.

1969
Dr. Kip S. Thorne, California Institute of Technology
1970   No award
1971
Robert H. March, University of Wisconsin
1972
Dr. Dietrich Schroeer, University of North Carolina (UNC) at Chapel Hill
1973
Dr. Banesh Hoffmann, Queens College of The City University of New York
1974
Dr. Robert D. Chapman, The Laboratory for Solar Physics at NASA/Goddard Space Flight Center
1975
Robert H. March, University of Wisconsin
1976
Jeremy Bernstein, Stevens Institute of Technology

SIGMA DELTA CHI AWARDS FOR DISTINGUISHED SERVICE IN JOURNALISM—The Society of Professional Journalists, Sigma Delta Chi

Sigma Delta Chi is the largest and oldest journalism society, with humble beginnings back in 1909 in Greencastle, Indiana. Today it has more than 145 campus chapters and 125 professional chapters. It also has quite a few award categories.
Established 1932.

GENERAL REPORTING

1939	Meigs O. Frost
1940	Basil Brewer
1941	no award
1942	Jack Vincent
1943	Julius M. Klein
	Ralph S. O'Leary
1944	Edward J. Doherty
1945	James P. McGuire
	John J. McPhaul
1946	John M. McCullough
1947	George Goodwin
1948	Richard C. Looman
1949	Bob Considine
1950	Edward B. Simmons
1951	Victor Cohn

1952	Chalmers M. Roberts
1953	Carl T. Rowan
1954	Richard Hyer
	William P. Walsh
1955	Victor Cohn
1956	Alfred Kuettner
1957	Pierre J. Huss
1958	Victor Cohn
1959	Saul Pett
1960	Robert Colby Nelson
1961	Joseph Newman
1962	Oscar Griffin
1963	Jimmy Breslin
1964	J. Harold Brislin
1965	Alton Blakeslee
1966	Stanley W. Penn
	Monroe W. Karmin
1967	Charles Nicodemus
1968	Haynes Johnson
1969	Seymour M. Hersh
1970	*Washington Post* Staff Writers
1971	James B. Steele
	Donald L. Barlett
1972	William F. Reed, Jr.
	James M. Bolus
1973	James R. Polk
1974	Frank Sutherland
1975	*Detroit Free Press* Reporters:
	William Mitchell
	Billy Bowles
	Kirk Cheyfitz
	Julie Morris
	Tom Hennessey
	James Harper
	Jim Neubacher

EDITORIAL WRITING

1939	W. W. Waymack
1940	Allen Drury
1941	no award
1942	Alexander Kendrick
1943	Milton Lehman
1944	Felix R. McKnight
1945	Francis P. Locke
1946	John W. Hillman
1947	Alan Barth
1948	Virginius Dabney
1949	John Crider
1950	Bradley L. Morison
1951	Robert M. White II
1952	Virginius Dabney
1953	John N. Reddin
1954	Robert Estabrook
1955	James Jackson Kilpatrick

1956	Sylvan Meyer
1957	Vermont Royster
1958	J. D. Maurice
1959	Cecil Prince
1960	Hodding Carter III
1961	James A. Clendinen
1962	Karl E. Meyer
1963	H. G. Davis, Jr.
1964	J. O. Emmerich
1965	Alfred G. Dickson
1966	Duane Croft
1967	Robert E. Fisher
1968	Robert M. White II
1969	Albert Cawood
1970	John R. Harrison
1972	Joanna Wragg
1972	John R. Harrison
1973	Frank W. Corrigan
1974	Michael Pakenham
1975	William Duncliffe

WASHINGTON CORRESPONDENCE

1942	Drew Pearson
	Robert S. Allen
1943	Sam O'Neal
1944	Marquis W. Childs
1945	Peter Edson
1946	Wallace R. Deuel
1947	Bert Andrews
1948	W. McNeil Lowry
1949	Jack Steele
1950	William K. Hutchinson
1951	John Hightower
1952	Clark R. Mollenhoff
1953	Richard L. Wilson
1954	Clark R. Mollenhoff
1955	Joseph and Stewart Alsop
1956	Bem Price
1957	Robert T. Hartmann
1958	James Reston
1959	Vance Trimble
1960	James Clayton
	Julius Duscha
	Murrey Marder
	Bernard Nossiter
1961	James Marlow
1962	Jules Witcover
1963	Jerry Landauer
1964	Louis M. Kohlmeier
1965	Nick Kotz
1966	Richard Harwood
1967	Jack C. Landau
1968	Joe Western

1969	Ronald J. Ostrow
	Robert Jackson
1970	Jared D. Stout
1971	Neil Sheehan
	The *New York Times*
1972	Carl Bernstein
	Robert Woodward
1973	James M. Naughton
	John M. Crewdson
	Ben A. Franklin
	Christopher Lydon
	Agis Salpukas
1974	Seth Kantor
1975	James Risser

FOREIGN CORRESPONDENCE

1939	Kenneth T. Downs
1940	Leland Stowe
1941	no award
1942	Keith Wheeler
1943	Frederick Kuh
1944	Frederick Kuh
1945	Arnaldo Cortesi
1946	Charles Gratke
1947	Daniel DeLuce
1948	Nat Barrows
1949	Kingsbury Smith
1950	Keyes Beech
	Dan Whitehead
1951	Ferdinand Kuhn
1952	Ernest S. Pisko
1953	Alexander Campbell
1954	Carl T. Rowan
1955	Carl T. Rowan
1956	Russell Jones
1957	Harrison E. Salisbury
1958	John Strohm
1959	William H. Stringer
1960	Smith Hempstone, Jr.
1961	Gaston Coblentz
1962	William J. Woestendiek
1963	Malcolm W. Browne
1964	Henry Shapiro
1965	James Nelson Goodsell
1966	Robert S. Elegant
1967	Peter Arnett
1968	Clyde H. Fernsworth
	Henry Kamm
	Tad Szulc
1969	Anatole Shub
1970	Hugh Mulligan
1971	Peter Arnett
	Bernard Gavzer
1972	Charlotte Saikowski

1973	Jacques Leslie
1974	Donald L. Barlett
	James B. Steele
1975	Sydney H. Schanberg

NEWS PHOTOGRAPHY

1946	Frank Q. Brown
1947	Paul Calvert
1948	Frank Jurkoski
1949	*Chicago Daily News*
1950	David Douglas Duncan
1951	Edward DeLuga
	Roger Wrenn
1952	Robert I. Wendlinger
1953	Bill Wilson
1954	Leslie Dodds
1955	Richard B. Yager
1956	Dan Tompkins
1957	Eldred C. Reaney
1958	Andrew St. George
1959	Andrew Lopez
1960	J. Parke Randall
1961	Peter Leibing
1962	Cliff DeBear
1963	Bob Jackson
1964	Dom Ligato
1965	Henry Herr Gill
1966	Ray Mews
1967	Catherine Leroy
1968	Edward T. Adams
1969	Horst Faas
1970	John P. Filo
1971	Dong Jun Kim
1972	Huynh Cong (Nick) Ut
1973	Anthony K. Roberts
1974	Werner Baum
1975	Stanley J. Forman

EDITORIAL CARTOONING

1942	Jacob Burck
1943	Charles Werner
1944	Henry Barrow
1945	Reuben L. Goldberg
1946	Dorman H. Smith
1947	Bruce Russell
1948	Herbert Block
1949	Herbert Block
1950	Bruce Russell
1952	Herbert Block
	Bruce Russell
1952	Cecil Jensen
1953	John Fischetti
1954	Calvin Alley

Cartoonist Tony Auth.

1955	John Fischetti
1956	Herbert Block
1957	Scott Long
1958	Clifford H. Baldowski
1959	Charles Gordon Brooks
1960	Dan Dowling
1961	Frank Interlandi
1962	Paul F. Conrad
1963	William H. "Bill" Mauldin
1964	Charles O. Bissell
1965	Roy Justus
1966	Patrick B. Oliphant
1967	Eugene C. Payne
1968	Paul F. Conrad
1969	Bill Mauldin
1970	Paul Conrad
1971	Hugh Haynie
1972	Bill Mauldin
1973	Paul Szep
1974	Mike Peters
1975	Tony Auth

PUBLIC SERVICE IN NEWSPAPER
  JOURNALISM

1949	*Star-Gazette*, Moose Lake, Minn.
1950	*Atlanta* (Ga.) *Journal*

1951	*Chicago Sun-Times*
1952	*Wall Street Journal*
1953	*Chicago Daily News*
	Houston Post
1954	*Cleveland Plain Dealer*
1955	*The Register-Pajaronian*, Watsonville, Calif.
1956	*The Oregonian*, Portland, Oreg.
1957	*Des Moines Register* and *Tribune*
	Minneapolis (Minn.) *Star* and *Tribune*
1958	*Tampa* (Fla.) *Tribune*
1959	*Atlanta* (Ga.) *Constitution*
1960	*The Daily Commercial*, Leesburg, Fla.
1961	*San Gabriel Valley Daily Tribune*, West Covina, Calif.
1962	*Pascagoula* (Miss.) *Chronicle*
1963	*Chicago Daily News*
1964	*McComb* (Miss.) *Enterprise-Journal*
1965	*Miami Herald*
1966	*Los Angeles Times*
	Long Island Press
1967	*Newsday*, Garden City, N. Y.
1968	*St. Louis Globe-Democrat*

Magazine writer Mike Mallowe.

1969	*Chicago Daily News*
1970	*Newsday,* Garden City, N. Y.
1971	*Boston Globe*
1972	Sun Newspapers, Omaha, Neb.
1973	*Newsday,* Garden City, N. Y.
1974	*Indianapolis Star*
1975	*Louisville Courier-Journal*

MAGAZINE REPORTING

1949	Lester Velie
1950	Gordon Schendel
1951	Bill Davidson
1952	Bill Davidson
1953	James P. O'Donnell
1954	Marshall MacDuffie
1955	Fletcher Knebel
1956	John Bartlow Martin
1957	Harold H. Martin
1958	John L. Cobbs
1959	John Robert Coughlan
1960	Hobart Rowen
1961	Joseph Morschauser
1962	Peter Goldman
1963	Theodore H. White
1964	Sam Castan
1965	Ben H. Bagdikian

1966	John G. Hubbell
1967	William Lambert
1968	Kristin Hunter
1969	William Lambert
1970	David L. Chandler
1971	Arthur Hadley
1972	Thomas Thompson
1973	Floyd Miller
1974	John Guinther
1975	Mike Mallowe

PUBLIC SERVICE IN MAGAZINE
   JOURNALISM

1949	*Collier's*
1950	*Collier's*
1951	*McCall's*
1952	*Look*
1953	*Look*
1954	*Saturday Evening Post*
1955	*Look*
1956	*Life*
1957	*The Reporter*
1958	*Life*
1959	*Saturday Evening Post*
1960	*Saturday Review*
1961	*Look*
1962	*Look*

1963	*Look*
1964	*Look*
1965	*Reader's Digest*
1966	*Life*
1967	*Philadelphia Magazine*
1968	*Life*
1969	*Philadelphia Magazine*
1970	*The Washingtonian Magazine*
1971	*New Orleans Magazine*
1972	*Philadelphia Magazine*
1973	*Philadelphia Magazine*
1974	*Philadelphia Magazine*
1975	*Philadelphia Magazine*

RADIO REPORTING

1946	Allen Stout
1947	James C. McNamara
1948	George J. O'Connor
1949	Sid Pletzsch
1950	Jack E. Krueger
1951	Jim Monroe
1952	Charles and Eugene Jones
1953	Gordon Gammack
1954	Richard Chapman
1955	John Chancellor
1956	Edward J. Green
1957	Dave Muhlstein
1958	Winston Burdett
1959	Donald H. Weston
1960	Frederick A. Goerner
1961	KDKA Radio News Staff (Pittsburgh, Pa.) Wip Robinson and Frank O'Roark, WSVA (Harrisonburg, Va.)
1962	WINS News Staff, (New York City)
1963	WINS News Staff (New York City)
1964	WNEW Radio News (New York City)
1965	WNEW Radio News (New York City)
1966	KTBC Radio News (Austin, Tex.)
1967	WJR News (Detroit, Mich.)
1968	KFWB News Radio (Los Angeles, Calif.)
1969	Ed Joyce, WCBS (New York City)
1970	Bob White, KRLD (Dallas, Tex.)
1971	John Rich, NBC

1972	Val Hymes, WTOP Radio (Washington, D. C.)
1973	Eric Engberg, Group W, Westinghouse
1974	Jim Mitchell, Gary Franklin, Herb Humphries, and Hank Allison, KFWB Radio (Los Angeles, Calif.)
1975	WHBF AM-FM Radio News Team (Rock Island, Ill.)

PUBLIC SERVICE IN RADIO JOURNALISM

1949	Station WTTS (Bloomington, Ind.)
1950	Station WAVZ (New Haven, Conn.)
1951	Station WMAQ (Chicago, Ill.)
1952	Station WMT (Cedar Rapids, Ia.)
1953	CBS Radio Network
1954	CBS Radio Network
1955	Station WMAQ (Chicago, Ill.)
1956	CBS Radio Network
1957	Station KNX (Los Angeles, Calif.)
1958	CBS Radio Network
1959	WIP Radio (Philadelphia, Pa.)
1960	WBT Radio (Charlotte, N. C.)
1961	Station KNUZ (Houston, Tex.)
1962	WBZ (Boston, Mass.)
1963	Station WSB (Atlanta, Ga.)
1964	KSEN (Shelby, Mont.)
1965	WCCO Radio (Minneapolis-St. Paul, Minn.)
1966	WIBW Radio (Topeka, Kans.)
1967	Westinghouse Broadcasting Co., Inc.
1968	WBZ Radio (Boston, Mass.)
1969	Station WHN (New York City)
1970	WWDC (Washington, D. C.)
1971	WBZ Radio (Boston, Mass.)
1972	WGAR Radio (Cleveland, Ohio)
1973	WMAL Radio (Washington, D. C.)
1974	WIND (Chicago, Ill.)
1975	WRVA Radio (Richmond, Va.)

EDITORIALIZING ON RADIO

1963	Station WRTA (Altoona, Pa.)
1964	WXYZ (Detroit Mich.)
1965	KDKA Radio (Pittsburgh, Pa.)
1966	Station W-A-I-T (Chicago, Ill.)
1967	WSBA Radio (York-Lancaster-Harrisburg, Pa.)
1968	Theodore Jones, WCRB (Waltham, Mass.)
1969	WWDC Radio (Washington, D. C.)
1970	WLPR Radio (Mobile, Ala.)
1971	WSOC-AM (Charlotte, N. C.)
1972	Frank Reynolds, ABC News (New York City)
1973	WGRG Radio (Pittsfield, Mass.)
1974	Jim Branch, WRFM (New York City)
1975	Charles B. Cleveland, WIND (Chicago, Ill.)

TELEVISION REPORTING

1952	Charles and Eugene Jones
1953	no award
1954	Spencer Allen
1955	Paul Alexander
	Gael Boden
1956	Ernest Leiser
	Jerry Schwartzkopff
	Julian B. Hoshal
	Dick Hance
1957	Jim Bennett
1958	WBBM-TV News Department (Chicago, Ill.)
1959	WGN-TV News Department (Chicago, Ill.)
1960	WTVJ-TV News Department (Miami, Fla.)
1961	WKY-TV (Oklahoma City, Okla.)
1962	KWTV News (Oklahoma City, Okla.)
1963	WBAP-TV (Fort Worth, Tex.)
1964	WFGA-TV (Jacksonville, Fla.)
1965	Morley Safer, CBS News
1966	WSB-TV News (Atlanta, Ga.)
1967	John Laurence, CBS News
1968	Station KNXT (Los Angeles, Calif.)

1969	WCCO Television News (Minneapolis, Minn.)
1970	KBTV (Denver, Colo.)
1971	Robert Schakne, CBS News
1972	Laurens Pierce, CBS News
1973	Steve Young and Roger Sims, CBS News
1974	Lee Louis, KGTV10 (San Diego, Calif.)
1975	WHAS-TV News (Louisville, Ky.)

PUBLIC SERVICE IN TV JOURNALISM

1952	Station WBNS-TV (Columbus, Ohio)
1953	Station WHAS-TV (Louisville, Ky.)
1954	Dumont Television Network American Broadcasting Company
1955	Station KAKE-TV (Wichita, Kans.)
1956	Station KPIX (San Francisco, Calif.)
1957	Station WBZ-TV (Boston, Mass.)
1958	Station KNXT (Hollywood, Calif.)
1959	Station WBZ-TV (Boston, Mass.)
1960	NBC Television Network
1961	Station KHOU-TV (Houston, Tex.)
1962	KGW-TV (Portland, Oreg.)
1963	KDKA-TV (Pittsburgh, Pa.) National Broadcasting Co.
1964	Columbia Broadcasting System
1965	WABC-TV (New York City)
1966	KLZ-TV (Denver, Colo.)
1967	National Broadcasting Co.
1968	WIBW-TV (Topeka, Kans.)
1969	WDSU-TV (New Orleans, La.)
1970	KING-TV (Seattle, Wash.)
1971	Columbia Broadcasting System
1972	WABC-TV (New York City)
1973	WSOC-TV News (Charlotte, N. C.)
1974	ABC News
1975	WCKT-TV (Miami, Fla.)

EDITORIALIZING ON TELEVISION

1963   Tom Martin, KFDA-TV (Amarillo, Tex.)
1964   KDKA-TV (Pittsburgh, Pa.)
1965   WTOP-TV (Washington, D.C.)
1966   WFBM-TV (Indianapolis, Ind.)
1967   KWTV (Oklahoma City, Okla.)
1968   WOOD-TV (Grand Rapids, Mich.)
1969   KCPX Television (Salt Lake City, Utah)
1970   WCCO-TV (Minneapolis, Minn.)
1971   Robert Schulman, WHAS-TV (Louisville, Ky.)
1972   WCKT-TV (Miami, Fla.)
1973   KRON-TV (San Francisco, Calif.)
1974   Jay Lewis, WSFA-TV (Montgomery, Ala.)
1975   Don McGaffin and Charles Royer, KING-TV (Seattle, Wash.)

RESEARCH ABOUT JOURNALISM

1935   Oscar W. Riegel
1936   Ralph O. Nafziger
1937   Alfred McClung Lee
1938   Frank Luther Mott
1939   Norval Neil Luxon
1940   Paul F. Lazarsfeld
1941   no award
1942   no award
1943   no award
1944   Earl English
1945   Frank Thayer
1946   Ralph D. Casey
       Bruce Lannes Smith
       Harold D. Lasswell
1947   James E. Pollard
1948   J. Edward Gerald
1949   Edwin Emery
1950   Robert S. Harper
1951   no award
1952   Curtis D. MacDougall
1953   Harold L. Cross
1954   Edwin Emery
       Henry Ladd Smith
1956   Theodore B. Peterson

1957   Frank Luther Mott
1958   L. John Martin
1959   Warren C. Price
1960   Leonard W. Levy
1961   Burton Paulu
1962   Theodore E. Kruglak
1963   David P. Forsyth
1964   John Hohenberg
1965   William L. Rivers
1966   Kenneth E. Olson
1967   John Hohenberg
1968   William A. Hachten
1969   Ronald T. Farrar
1970   William Small
1971   John C. Merrill
       Ralph L. Lowenstein
1972   William Small
1973   Philip Meyer
1974   Loren Ghiglione
1975   Marvin Barrett

COURAGE IN JOURNALISM
(discontinued)

1939   *New Orleans* (La.) *States*
1942   *Guthrie County Vedette* (Panora, Ia.)
1943   *Lowell* (Mass.) *Sunday Telegram*
1944   *Milwaukee Journal*
1945   *New Orleans* (La.) *States*
1946   *Kansas City* (Mo.) *Star*
1947   *Memphis Press-Scimitar*

NEWSPAPER CARTOONING
(discontinued)

1948   *Philadelphia Inquirer*
       Ed Dodd
1950   Milton Caniff

RADIO OR TV COMMENTARY
(discontinued)

1961   KDKA-TV (Pittsburgh, Pa.)
1962   Harold Keen, WFMB-TV (San Diego, Calif.)

RADIO OR TV NEWSWRITING
(discontinued)

1939   Albert Warner
1940   Cecil Brown
1942   Fulton Lewis, Jr.

1946	Harry M. Cochran
1947	Alex Dreier
1948	Merrill Mueller
1949	Elmer Davis
1950	Leo O'Brien
	Howard Maschmeier
1951	William E. Griffith, Jr.
1952	Clifton Utley
1953	Charles J. Chatfield
1954	Reuven Frank
1955	Charles Shaw
1956	Howard K. Smith
1957	Jerry Rosholt
1958	Harold R. Meier
1959	Gene Marine
1960	David Brinkley

SPECIAL AWARDS
(discontinued)
1943   Raymond Clapper
(posthumous) "William Allen White Memorial Award"

WAR CORRESPONDENCE
(discontinued)
1943   Ernie Pyle (Raymond Clapper Memorial Award)
1944   Ernie Pyle (human interest) Henry T. Gorrell (spot news)
1945   John Graham Dowling

GOLD KEY AWARDS OF 1932–34
(discontinued)
Paul Scott Mowrer
Philip Hale
Franklin P. Adams
Alexander Dana Noyes
Jay N. (Ding) Darling
Casper S. Yost

THE CARR VAN ANDA AWARD—
Ohio University
For "enduring contributions to journalism."
Established 1968.
1968
Turner Catledge, *New York Times*
Edward W. Barrett, Columbia University School of Journalism
Walter Cronkite, CBS News
1969
Wes Gallagher, Associated Press
Margaret Bourke-White, photojournalist
Osborne Elliott, *Newsweek*

1970
John S. Knight, Knight Newspapers
Gordon Parks, *Life*
Howard K. Smith, ABC News
1971
James Reston, *New York Times*
Norman Cousins, *Saturday Review*
1972
Pauline Frederick, NBC News
Richard Leonard, *Milwaukee Journal*
1973
William Attwood, *Newsday*
Harry Reasoner, ABC News
1974
Otis Chandler, *Los Angeles Times*
Shana Alexander, *Newsweek*
1975
Katharine Graham, *Washington Post*
Philip Meyer, Knight Newspapers
Eric Sevareid, CBS News
1976
A. M. Rosenthal, *New York Times*
Pat Carbine, *Ms.*

See Women, Headliners, Women in Communications, Inc.

JOHN PETER ZENGER AWARD—
University of Arizona
For distinguished service in behalf of freedom of the press and the people's right to know.
Established 1954.
1954
Palmer Hoyt, *Denver Post*
1955
Basil L. Walters, *Chicago Daily News*
1956
James S. Pope, *Louisville Courier Journal*
1957
James R. Wiggins, *Washington Post* and *Times Herald*
1958
John E. Moss, chairman, House Government Information Subcommittee
1959
Herbert Brucker, *Hartford Courant*
1960
Virgil M. Newton, Jr., *Tampa Tribune*

Washington Postmistress Katharine Graham receives the John Peter Zenger Award from George Ridge.

1961
Clark R. Mollenhoff, Cowles Publications
1962
John H. Colburn, *Richmond Times-Dispatch* (now with Landmark Communications, Inc.)
1963
James B. Reston, *New York Times*
1964
John N. Heiskell, *Arkansas Gazette*
1965
Eugene C. Pulliam, *Arizona Republic* and *Phoenix Gazette*
1966
Arthur Krock, *New York Times*
1967
John S. Knight, Knight Newspapers, Inc.
1968
Wes Gallagher, The Associated Press

1969
J. Edward Murray, *Arizona Republic* (now with the *Detroit Free Press*)
1970
Erwin D. Canham, *Christian Science Monitor*
1971
New York Times
1972
Dan Hicks, Jr., *Monroe County Observer*
1973
Katharine M. Graham, *Washington Post*
1974
Thomas E. Gish, *The Mountain Eagle*
1975
Seymour M. Hersh, *New York Times*
1976
Donald F. Bolles, *Arizona Republic*

MILITARY

H. H. ARNOLD AWARD—Air Force Association
Aerospace's "Man of the Year."
Established 1948.
1948
W. Stuart Symington, secretary of the Air Force
1949
Maj. Gen. William H. Tunner and the men of the Berlin Airlift
1950
Airmen of the United Nations in the Far East
1951
Lt. Gen. Curtis E. LeMay and the personnel of Strategic Air Command
1952
Lyndon B. Johnson, U.S. senator
Joseph C. O'Mahoney, U.S senator
1953
Gen. Hoyt S. Vandenberg, former chief of staff, United States Air Force
1954
John Foster Dulles, secretary of state
1955
Gen. Nathan F. Twining, chief of staff, United State Air Force
1956
W. Stuart Symington, U.S. senator
1957
Edward P. Curtis, special assistant to the president
1958
Maj. Gen. Bernard A. Schriever, commander, Ballistic Missile Division, ARDC
1959
Gen. Thomas S. Power, commander in chief, Strategic Air Command
1960
Gen. Thomas D. White, chief of staff, United States Air Force
1961
Lyle S. Garlock, assistant secretary of the Air Force
1962
Dr. A. C. Dickieson, Bell Telephone Laboratories
John R. Pierce, Bell Telephone

Laboratories
1963
363d Tactical Reconnaissance Wing, TAC, 4080th Strategic Wing, Strategic Air Command
1964
Gen. Curtis E. LeMay, chief of staff, United States Air Force
1965
Second Air Division, PACAF, United States Air Force
1966
8th, 12th, 355th, 366th, and 388th Tactical Fighter Wings; 432d and 460th Tactical Reconnaissance Wings
1967
Gen. William W. Momyer, commander, 7th Air Force, PACAF
1968
Col. Frank Borman, Capt. James Lovell, Lt. Col. William Anders, Apollo 8 Crew
1969
no award
1970
J. L. Atwood, Lt. Gen. Samuel C. Phillips, Neil Armstrong, Col. Edwin E. Aldrin, Jr., Col. Michael Collins, Apollo 11 Team
1971
Dr. John S. Foster, Jr., director of defense research and engineering
1972
Air Units of the Allied Forces in SEA (Air Force, Navy, Army, Marine Corps, and the Vietnamese Air Force)
1973
Gen. John D. Ryan, United States Air Force
1974
Gen. George S. Brown, chairman, Joint Chiefs of Staff
1975
James R. Schlesinger, secretary of defense
1976
Barry M. Goldwater, U.S. senator

Clara Bow and Charles "Buddy" Rogers in Wings. *(Memory Shop)*

MOTION PICTURES and STAGE

ACADEMY AWARDS (OSCARS)
—The American Academy of Motion Picture Arts and Sciences.
"The envelope, please."
Established 1927.
1927–1928
Best Picture, *Wings*
Best actor, Emil Jannings, *The Last Command, The Way of All Flesh*
Best supporting actor, no award
Best actress, Janet Gaynor, *Seventh Heaven, Street Angel, Sunrise*
Best supporting actress, no award
Best director, Frank Borzage, *Seventh Heaven;* Lewis Milestone, *Two Arabian Knights*
1928–1929
Best picture, *Broadway Melody*

Best actor, Warner Baxter, *In Old Arizona*
Best supporting actor, no award
Best actress, Mary Pickford, *Coquette*
Best supporting actress, no award
Best director, Frank Lloyd, *The Divine Lady*
1929–1930
Best picture, *All Quiet on the Western Front*
Best actor, George Arliss, *Disraeli*
Best supporting actor, no award
Best actress, Norma Shearer, *The Divorcee*
Best supporting actress, no award
Best director, Lewis Milestone, *All Quiet on the Western Front*

Katharine Hepburn, who won an Oscar for Morning Glory, *perches on co-star Adolphe Menjou's chair. (Memory Shop)*

1930–1931
Best picture, *Cimarron*
Best actor, Lionel Barrymore, *A Free Soul*
Best supporting actor, no award
Best actress, Marie Dressler, *Min and Bill*
Best supporting actress, no award
Best director, Norman Taurog, *Skippy*

1931–1932
Best picture, *Grand Hotel*
Best actor, Wallace Beery, *The Champ;* Fredric March, *Dr. Jekyll and Mr. Hyde*
Best supporting actor, no award
Best actress, Helen Hayes, *The Sin of Madelon Claudet*
Best supporting actress, no award
Best director, Frank Borzage, *Bad Girl*

1932–1933
Best picture, *Cavalcade*
Best actor, Charles Laughton, *The Private Life of Henry VIII*
Best supporting actor, no award
Best actress, Katharine Hepburn, *Morning Glory*

Best supporting actress, no award
Best director, Frank Lloyd, *Cavalcade*

1934
Best picture, *It Happened One Night*
Best actor, Clark Gable, *It Happened One Night*
Best supporting actor, no award
Best actress, Claudette Colbert, *It Happened One Night*
Best supporting actress, no award
Best director, Frank Capra, *It Happened One Night*

1935
Best picture, *Mutiny on the Bounty*
Best actor, Victor McLaglen, *The Informer*
Best supporting actor, no award
Best actress, Bette Davis, *Dangerous*
Best supporting actress, no award
Best director, John Ford, *The Informer*

1936
Best picture, *The Great Ziegfeld*
Best actor, Paul Muni, *The Story of Louis Pasteur*
Best supporting actor, Walter Brennan, *Come and Get It*

Best actress, Luise Rainer, *The Great Ziegfeld*
Best supporting actress, Gale Sondergaard, *Anthony Adverse*
Best director, Frank Capra, *Mr. Deeds Goes to Town*

1937
Best picture, *The Life of Emile Zola*
Best actor, Spencer Tracy, *Captains Courageous*
Best supporting actor, Joseph Schildkraut, *The Life of Emile Zola*
Best actress, Luise Rainer, *The Good Earth*
Best supporting actress, Alice Brady, *In Old Chicago*
Best director, Leo McCarey, *The Awful Truth*

1938
Best picture, *You Can't Take It with You*
Best actor, Spencer Tracy, *Boys Town*
Best supporting actor, Walter Brennan, *Kentucky*
Best actress, Bette Davis, *Jezebel*
Best supporting actress, Fay Bainter, *Jezebel*
Best director, Frank Capra, *You Can't Take It with You*

1939
Best picture, *Gone With the Wind*
Best actor, Robert Donat, *Goodbye, Mr. Chips*
Best supporting actor, Thomas Mitchell, *Stagecoach*
Best actress, Vivien Leigh, *Gone With the Wind*
Best supporting actress, Hattie McDaniel, *Gone With the Wind*
Best director, Victor Fleming, *Gone With the Wind*

1940
Best picture, *Rebecca*
Best actor, James Stewart, *The Philadelphia Story*
Best supporting actor, Walter Brennan, *The Westerner*
Best actress, Ginger Rogers, *Kitty Foyle*
Best supporting actress, Jane Darwell, *The Grapes of Wrath*
Best director, John Ford, *The Grapes of Wrath*

1941
Best picture, *How Green Was My Valley*
Best actor, Gary Cooper, *Sergeant York*
Best supporting actor, Donald Crisp, *How Green Was My Valley*
Best actress, Joan Fontaine, *Suspicion*
Best supporting actress, Mary Astor, *The Great Lie*
Best director, John Ford, *How Green Was My Valley*

1942
Best picture, *Mrs. Miniver*
Best Actor, James Cagney, *Yankee Doodle Dandy*
Best supporting actor, Van Heflin, *Johnny Eager*
Best actress, Greer Garson, *Mrs. Miniver*
Best supporting actress, Teresa Wright, *Mrs. Miniver*
Best director, William Wyler, *Mrs. Miniver*

1943
Best picture, *Casablanca*
Best actor, Paul Lukas, *Watch on the Rhine*
Best supporting actor, Charles Coburn, *The More the Merrier*
Best actress, Jennifer Jones, *The Song of Bernadette*
Best supporting actress, Katina Paxinou, *For Whom the Bell Tolls*
Best director, Michael Curtiz, *Casablanca*

1944
Best picture, *Going My Way*
Best actor, Bing Crosby, *Going My Way*
Best supporting actor, Barry Fitzgerald, *Going My Way*
Best actress, Ingrid Bergman, *Gaslight*
Best supporting actress, Ethel Barrymore, *None But the Lonely Heart*
Best director, Leo McCarey, *Going My Way*

1945
Best picture, *The Lost Weekend*
Best actor, Ray Milland, *The Lost Weekend*
Best supporting actor, James Dunn,

Laurence Olivier as Hamlet.
(Memory Shop)

A Tree Grows in Brooklyn
Best actress, Joan Crawford, *Mildred Pierce*
Best supporting actress, Anne Revere, *National Velvet*
Best director, Billy Wilder, *The Lost Weekend*
1946
Best picture, *The Best Years of Our Lives*
Best actor, Fredric March, *The Best Years of Our Lives*
Best supporting actor, Harold Russell, *The Best Years of Our Lives*
Best actress, Olivia de Havilland, *To Each His Own*
Best supporting actress, Anne Baxter, *The Razor's Edge*
Best director, William Wyler, *The Best Years of Our Lives*
1947
Best picture, *Gentleman's Agreement*
Best actor, Ronald Colman, *A Double Life*
Best supporting actor, Edmund Gwenn, *Miracle on 34th Street*
Best actress, Loretta Young, *The Farmer's Daughter*

Best supporting actress, Celeste Holm, *Gentleman's Agreement*
Best director, Elia Kazan, *Gentleman's Agreement*
1948
Best picture, *Hamlet*
Best actor, Laurence Olivier, *Hamlet*
Best supporting actor, Walter Huston, *The Treasure of the Sierra Madre*
Best actress, Jane Wyman, *Johnny Belinda*
Best supporting actress, Claire Trevor, *Key Largo*
Best director, John Huston, *The Treasure of the Sierra Madre*
1949
Best picture, *All the King's Men*
Best actor, Broderick Crawford, *All the King's Men*
Best supporting actor, Dean Jagger, *Twelve O'Clock High*
Best actress, Olivia de Havilland, *The Heiress*
Best supporting actress, Mercedes McCambridge, *All the King's Men*
Best director, Joseph L. Mankiewicz, *A Letter to Three Wives*

1950
Best picture, *All About Eve*
Best actor, Jose Ferrer, *Cyrano de Bergerac*
Best supporting actor, George Sanders, *All About Eve*
Best actress, Judy Holliday, *Born Yesterday*
Best supporting actress, Josephine Hull, *Harvey*
Best director, Joseph L. Mankiewicz, *All About Eve*

1951
Best picture, *An American in Paris*
Best actor, Humphrey Bogart, *The African Queen*
Best supporting actor, Karl Malden, *A Streetcar Named Desire*
Best actress, Vivien Leigh, *A Streetcar Named Desire*
Best supporting actress, Kim Hunter, *A Streetcar Named Desire*
Best director, George Stevens, *A Place in the Sun*

1952
Best picture, *The Greatest Show on Earth*
Best actor, Gary Cooper, *High Noon*
Best supporting actor, Anthony Quinn, *Viva Zapata!*
Best actress, Shirley Booth, *Come Back, Little Sheba*
Best supporting actress, Gloria Grahame, *The Bad and the Beautiful*
Best director, John Ford, *The Quiet Man*

1953
Best picture, *From Here to Eternity*
Best actor, William Holden, *Stalag 17*
Best supporting actor, Frank Sinatra, *From Here to Eternity*
Best actress, Audrey Hepburn, *Roman Holiday*
Best supporting actress, Donna Reed, *From Here to Eternity*
Best director, Fred Zinnemann, *From Here to Eternity*

1954
Best picture, *On The Waterfront*
Best actor, Marlon Brando, *On The Waterfront*
Best supporting actor, Edmond O'Brien, *The Barefoot Contessa*
Best actress, Grace Kelly, *The Country Girl*
Best supporting actress, Eva Marie Saint, *On The Waterfront*
Best director, Elia Kazan, *On The Waterfront*

1955
Best picture, *Marty*
Best actor, Ernest Borgnine, *Marty*
Best supporting actor, Jack Lemmon, *Mister Roberts*
Best actress, Anna Magnani, *The Rose Tattoo*
Best supporting actress, Jo Van Fleet, *East of Eden*
Best director, Delbert Mann, *Marty*

1956
Best picture, *Around the World in 80 Days*
Best actor, Yul Brynner, *The King and I*
Best supporting actor, Anthony Quinn, *Lust for Life*
Best actress, Ingrid Bergman, *Anastasia*
Best supporting actress, Dorothy Malone, *Written on the Wind*
Best director, George Stevens, *Giant*

1957
Best picture, *The Bridge on the River Kwai*
Best actor, Alec Guinness, *The Bridge on the River Kwai*
Best supporting actor, Red Buttons, *Sayonara*
Best actress, Joanne Woodward, *The Three Faces of Eve*
Best supporting actress, Miyoshi Umeki, *Sayonara*
Best director, David Lean, *The Bridge on the River Kwai*

1958
Best picture, *Gigi*
Best actor, David Niven, *Separate Tables*
Best supporting actor, Burl Ives, *The Big Country*
Best actress, Susan Hayward, *I Want to Live*
Best supporting actress, Wendy Hiller, *Separate Tables*
Best director, Vincente Minnelli, *Gigi*

1959
Best picture, *Ben-Hur*
Best actor, Charlton Heston, *Ben-Hur*

Leslie Caron was Gigi, the little girl who grew up in the most delightful way. (Memory Shop)

Best supporting actor, Hugh Griffith, *Ben-Hur*
Best actress, Simone Signoret, *Room at the Top*
Best supporting actress, Shelley Winters, *The Diary of Anne Frank*
Best director, William Wyler, *Ben-Hur*

1960
Best Picture, *The Apartment*
Best actor, Burt Lancaster, *Elmer Gantry*
Best supporting actor, Peter Ustinov, *Spartacus*
Best Actress, Elizabeth Taylor, *Butterfield 8*
Best supporting actress, Shirley Jones, *Elmer Gantry*
Best director, Billy Wilder, *The Apartment*

1961
Best picture, *West Side Story*
Best actor, Maximilian Schell, *Judgment at Nuremberg*
Best supporting actor, George Chakiris, *West Side Story*
Best actress, Sophia Loren, *Two Women*

Best supporting actress, Rita Moreno, *West Side Story*
Best director, Jerome Robbins and Robert Wise, *West Side Story*

1962
Best picture, *Lawrence of Arabia*
Best actor, Gregory Peck, *To Kill a Mockingbird*
Best supporting actor, Ed Begley, *Sweet Bird of Youth*
Best actress, Anne Bancroft, *The Miracle Worker*
Best supporting actress, Patty Duke, *The Miracle Worker*
Best director, David Lean, *Lawrence of Arabia*

1963
Best picture, *Tom Jones*
Best actor, Sidney Poitier, *Lilies of the Field*
Best supporting actor, Melvyn Douglas, *Hud*
Best actress, Patricia Neal, *Hud*
Best supporting actress, Margaret Rutherford, *The V.I.Ps*
Best director, Tony Richardson, *Tom Jones*

1964
Best picture, *My Fair Lady*
Best actor, Rex Harrison, *My Fair Lady*
Best supporting actor, Peter Ustinov, *Topkapi*
Best actress, Julie Andrews, *Mary Poppins*
Best supporting actress, Lila Kedrova, *Zorba the Greek*
Best director, George Cukor, *My Fair Lady*

1965
Best picture, *The Sound of Music*
Best actor, Lee Marvin, *Cat Ballou*
Best supporting actor, Martin Balsam, *A Thousand Clowns*
Best actress, Julie Christie, *Darling*
Best supporting actress, Shelley Winters, *A Patch of Blue*
Best director, Robert Wise, *The Sound of Music*

1966
Best picture, *A Man for All Seasons*
Best actor, Paul Scofield, *A Man for All Seasons*
Best supporting actor, Walter Matthau, *The Fortune Cookie*
Best actress, Elizabeth Taylor, *Who's Afraid of Virginia Woolf?*
Best supporting actress, Sandy Dennis, *Who's Afraid of Virginia Woolf?*
Best director, Fred Zinnemann, *A Man For All Seasons*

1967
Best picture, *In the Heat of the Night*
Best actor, Rod Steiger, *In the Heat of the Night*
Best supporting actor, George Kennedy, *Cool Hand Luke*
Best actress, Katharine Hepburn, *Guess Who's Coming to Dinner?*
Best supporting actress, Estelle Parsons, *Bonnie and Clyde*
Best director, Mike Nichols, *The Graduate*

1968
Best picture, *Oliver!*
Best actor, Cliff Robertson, *Charly*
Best supporting actor, Jack Albertson, *The Subject Was Roses*
Best actress, Katharine Hepburn, Barbra Streisand, *The Lion in Winter; Funny Girl*
Best supporting actress, Ruth Gordon, *Rosemary's Baby*
Best director, Sir Carol Reed, *Oliver!*

1969
Best picture, *Midnight Cowboy*
Best actor, John Wayne, *True Grit*
Best supporting actor, Gig Young, *They Shoot Horses, Don't They?*
Best actress, Maggie Smith, *The Prime of Miss Jean Brodie*
Best supporting actress, Goldie Hawn, *Cactus Flower*
Best director, John Schlesinger, *Midnight Cowboy*

1970
Best picture, *Patton*
Best actor, George C. Scott, *Patton*
Best supporting actor, John Mills, *Ryan's Daughter*
Best actress, Glenda Jackson, *Women in Love*
Best supporting actress, Helen Hayes, *Airport*
Best director, Franklin Schaffner, *Patton*

1971
Best picture, *The French Connection*
Best actor, Gene Hackman, *The French Connection*
Best supporting actor, Ben Johnson, *The Last Picture Show*
Best actress, Jane Fonda, *Klute*
Best supporting actress, Cloris Leachman, *The Last Picture Show*
Best director, William Friedkin, *The French Connection*

1972
Best picture, *The Godfather*
Best actor, Marlon Brando, *The Godfather*
Best supporting actor, Joel Grey, *Cabaret*
Best actress, Liza Minnelli, *Cabaret*
Best supporting actress, Eileen Heckart, *Butterflies Are Free*
Best director, Bob Fosse, *Cabaret*

1973
Best picture, *The Sting*
Best actor, Jack Lemmon, *Save the Tiger*
Best supporting actor, John Houseman, *The Paper Chase*
Best actress, Glenda Jackson, *A Touch of Class*
Best supporting actress, Tatum

Gene Hackman, as the The French Connection*'s Popeye Doyle. (Memory Shop)*

O'Neal, *Paper Moon*
Best director, George Roy Hill, *The Sting*
1974
Best picture, *The Godfather, Part II*
Best actor, Art Carney, *Harry and Tonto*
Best supporting actor, Robert DeNiro, *The Godfather, Part II*
Best actress, Ellen Burstyn, *Alice Doesn't Live Here Anymore*
Best supporting actress, Ingrid Bergman, *Murder on the Orient Express*
Best director, Francis Ford Coppola, *The Godfather, Part II*
1975
Best picture, *One Flew Over the Cuckoo's Nest*
Best actor, Jack Nicholson, *One Flew Over the Cuckoo's Nest*
Best supporting actor, George Burns, *The Sunshine Boys*
Best actress, Louise Fletcher, *One Flew Over the Cuckoo's Nest*
Best supporting actress, Lee Grant, *Shampoo*
Best director, Milos Forman, *One*

Flew Over the Cuckoo's Nest
1976
Best picture, *Rocky*
Best actor, Peter Finch, *Network*
Best supporting actor, Jason Robards, Jr. *All the President's Men*
Best actress, Faye Dunaway, *Network*
Best supporting actress, Beatrice Straight, *Network*
Best director, John Avildsen, *Rocky*

See Achievement, The Gold Medal Awards, The American Academy of Arts and Letters

AWARDS—National Board of Review of Motion Pictures
The board bills itself as the "oldest group in the business of selecting the ten best films of the year."
Established 1930.
1930   *All Quiet on the Western Front*
        Holiday
        Laughter
        The Man from Blankley's
        Men Without Women

Morocco
Outward Bound
Romance
The Street of Chance
Tol'able David

1931   Cimarron
City Lights
City Streets
Dishonored
The Front Page
The Guardsman
Quick Millions
Rango
Surrender
Tabu

1932   I Am a Fugitive from a Chain
    Gang
As You Desire Me
A Bill of Divorcement
A Farewell to Arms
Madame Racketeer
Payment Deferred
Scarface
Tarzan
Trouble in Paradise
Two Seconds

1933   Topaze
Berkeley Square
Cavalcade
Little Women
Mama Loves Papa
The Pied Piper
She Done Him Wrong
State Fair
Three Cornered Moon
Zoo in Budapest

1934   It Happened One Night
The Count of Monte Cristo
Crime Without Passion
Eskimo
The First World War
The Lost Patrol
Lot in Sodom
No Greater Glory
The Thin Man
Viva Villa

1935   The Informer
Alice Adams
Anna Karenina
David Copperfield
The Gilded Lily
Les Miserables
The Lives of the Bengal
    Lancers
Mutiny on the Bounty

Ruggles of Red Gap
Who Killed Cock Robin

1936   Mr. Deeds Goes to Town
The Story of Louis Pasteur
Modern Times
Fury
Winterset
The Devil Is a Sissy
Ceiling Zero
Romeo and Juliet
The Prisoner of Shark Island
The Green Pastures

1937   Night Must Fall
The Life of Emile Zola
Black Legion
Camille
Make Way for Tomorrow
The Good Earth
They Won't Forget
Captains Courageous
A Star Is Born
Stage Door

1938   The Citadel
Snow White and the Seven
    Dwarfs
The Beachcomber
To the Victor
Sing You Sinners
The Edge of the World
Of Human Hearts
Jezebel
South Riding
Three Comrades

1939   Confessions of a Nazi Spy
Wuthering Heights
Stagecoach
Ninotchka
Young Mr. Lincoln
Crisis
Goodbye, Mr. Chips
Mr. Smith Goes to
    Washington
The Roaring Twenties
U-Boat 29

1940   The Grapes of Wrath
The Great Dictator
Of Mice and Men
Our Town
Fantasia
The Long Voyage Home
Foreign Correspondent
The Biscuit Eater
Gone With the Wind
Rebecca

1941   Citizen Kane

How Green Was My Valley
The Little Foxes
The Stars Look Down
Dumbo
High Sierra
Here Comes Mr. Jordan
Tom, Dick and Harry
The Road to Zanzibar
The Lady Eve

1942 In Which We Serve
One of Our Aircraft Is
  Missing
Mrs. Miniver
Journey for Margaret
Wake Island
The Male Animal
The Major and the Minor
Sullivan's Travels
The Moon and Sixpence
The Pied Piper

1943 The Ox-Bow Incident
Watch on the Rhine
Air Force
Holy Matrimony
The Hard Way
Casablanca
Lassie Come Home
Bataan
The Moon Is Down
The Next of Kin

1944 None But the Lonely Heart
Going My Way
The Miracle of Morgan's
  Creek
Hail the Conquering Hero
The Song of Bernadette
Wilson
Meet Me in St. Louis
Thirty Seconds Over Tokyo
Thunder Rock
Lifeboat

1945 The True Glory
The Lost Weekend
The Southerner
The Story of G. I. Joe
The Last Chance
Colonel Blimp
A Tree Grows in Brooklyn
The Fighting Lady
The Way Ahead
The Clock

1946 Henry V
Open City
The Best Years of Our Lives
Brief Encounter

A Walk in the Sun
It Happened at the Inn
My Darling Clementine
The Diary of a Chambermaid
The Killers
Anna and the King of Siam

1947 Monsieur Verdoux
Great Expectations
Shoe-shine
Crossfire
Boomerang!
Odd Man Out
Gentleman's Agreement
To Live in Peace
It's a Wonderful Life
The Overlanders

1948 Paisan
Day of Wrath
The Search
The Treasure of the Sierra
Madre
Louisiana Story
Hamlet
The Snake Pit
Johnny Belinda
Joan of Arc
The Red Shoes

1949 The Bicycle Thief
The Quiet One
Intruder in the Dust
The Heiress
Devil in the Flesh
Quartet
Germany, Year Zero
Home of the Brave
A Letter to Three Wives
The Fallen Idol

1950 Sunset Boulevard
All About Eve
The Asphalt Jungle
The Men
Edge of Doom
Twelve O'Clock High
Panic in the Streets
Cyrano de Bergerac
No Way Out
Stage Fright

1951 A Place in the Sun
The Red Badge of Courage
An American in Paris
Death of a Salesman
Detective Story
A Streetcar Named Desire
Decision Before Dawn
Strangers on a Train

Quo Vadis
Fourteen Hours

1952
The Quiet Man
High Noon
Limelight
Five Fingers
The Snows of Kilimanjaro
The Thief
The Bad and the Beautiful
Singin' in the Rain
Above and Beyond
My Son John

1953
Julius Caesar
Shane
From Here to Eternity
Martin Luther
Lili
Roman Holiday
Stalag 17
Little Fugitive
Mogambo
The Robe

1954
On the Waterfront
Seven Brides for Seven
  Brothers
The Country Girl
A Star Is Born
Executive Suite
The Vanishing Prairie
Sabrina
20,000 Leagues Under the Sea
The Unconquered
Beat the Devil

1955
Marty
East of Eden
Mister Roberts
Bad Day at Black Rock
Summertime
The Rose Tattoo
A Man Called Peter
Not as a Stranger
Picnic
The African Lion

1956
Around the World in Eighty
  Days
Moby Dick
The King and I
Lust for Life
Friendly Persuasion
Somebody Up There Likes
  Me
The Catered Affair
Anastasia
The Man Who Never Was
Bus Stop

1957
The Bridge on the River Kwai
Twelve Angry Men
The Spirit of St. Louis
The Rising of the Moon
Albert Schweitzer
Funny Face
The Bachelor Party
The Enemy Below
A Hatful of Rain
A Farewell to Arms

1958
The Old Man and the Sea
Separate Tables
The Last Hurrah
The Long Hot Summer
Windjammer
Cat on a Hot Tin Roof
The Goddess
The Brothers Karamazov
Me and the Colonel
Gigi

1959
The Nun's Story
Ben-Hur
Anatomy of a Murder
The Diary of Anne Frank
Middle of the Night
The Man Who Understood
  Women
Some Like It Hot
Suddenly, Last Summer
On the Beach
North by Northwest

1960
The Alamo
Sons and Lovers
The Sundowners
Inherit the Wind
Sunrise at Campobello
Elmer Gantry
Home from the Hill
The Apartment
Wild River
The Dark at the Top of the
  Stairs

1961
Question 7
The Hustler
West Side Story
The Innocents
The Hoodlum Priest
Summer and Smoke
The Young Doctors
Judgment at Nuremberg
One, Two, Three
Fanny

1962
The Longest Day
Billy Budd
The Miracle Worker

Lawrence of Arabia
Long Day's Journey Into
  Night
Whistle Down the Wind
Requiem for a Heavyweight
A Taste of Honey
Birdman of Alcatraz
War Hunt
1963 Tom Jones
Lilies of the Field
All the Way Home
Hud
This Sporting Life
Lord of the Flies
The L-Shaped Room
The Great Escape
How the West Was Won
The Cardinal
1964 Becket
My Fair Lady
Girl with Green Eyes
The World of Henry Orient
Zorba the Greek
Topkapi
The Chalk Garden
The Finest Hours
Four Days in November
Seance on a Wet Afternoon
1965 The Eleanor Roosevelt Story
The Agony and the Ecstasy
Doctor Zhivago
Ship of Fools
The Spy Who Came in from
  the Cold
Darling
The Greatest Story Ever Told
A Thousand Clowns
The Train
The Sound of Music
1966 A Man for All Seasons
Born Free
Alfie
Who's Afraid of Virginia
  Woolf?
The Bible
Georgy Girl
Years of Lightning, Day of
  Drums
It Happened Here
The Russians Are Coming,
  The Russians Are Coming
Shakespeare Wallah
1967 Far From the Madding
  Crowd
The Whisperers

Ulysses
In Cold Blood
The Family Way
The Taming of the Shrew
Doctor Dolittle
The Graduate
The Comedians
Accident
1968 The Shoes of the Fisherman
Romeo and Juliet
The Yellow Submarine
Charly
Rachel, Rachel
The Subject Was Roses
The Lion in Winter
Planet of the Apes
Oliver!
2001: A Space Odyssey
1969 They Shoot Horses, Don't
  They?
Ring of Bright Water
Topaz
Goodbye, Mr. Chips
Battle of Britain
The Loves of Isadora
The Prime of Miss Jean
  Brodie
Support Your Local Sheriff
True Grit
Midnight Cowboy
1970 Patton
Kes
Women in Love
Five Easy Pieces
Ryan's Daughter
I Never Sang for My Father
Diary of a Mad Housewife
Love Story
The Virgin and the Gypsy
Tora, Tora, Tora
1971 Macbeth
The Boy Friend
One Day in the Life of Ivan
  Denisovitch
The French Connection
The Last Picture Show
Nicholas and Alexandra
The Go-Between
King Lear
Peter Rabbit and Tales of
  Beatrix Potter
Death in Venice
1972 Cabaret
Man of La Mancha
The Godfather

Sounder
1776
*The Effect of Gamma Rays on
Man-in-the-Moon Marigolds*
Deliverance
The Ruling Class
The Candidate
Frenzy
1973　*The Sting*
Paper Moon
The Homecoming
Bang the Drum Slowly
Serpico
O Lucky Man
The Last American Hero
The Hireling
The Day of the Dolphin
The Way We Were
1974　*The Conversation*
Murder on the Orient Express
Chinatown
The Last Detail
Harry and Tonto
A Woman Under the Influence
Thieves Like Us
Lenny
Daisy Miller
The Three Musketeers
1975　*Barry Lyndon* and *Nashville*
(tie)
Conduct Unbecoming
*One Flew Over the Cuckoo's
Nest*
Lies My Father Told Me
Dog Day Afternoon
The Day of the Locust
The Passenger
Hearts of the West
Farewell My Lovely
*Alice Doesn't Live Here
Anymore*
1976　*All the President's Men*
Network
Rocky
The Last Tycoon
The Seven Per Cent Solution
The Front
The Shootist
Family Plot
Silent Movie
Obsession

See Books, Award of Merit Medal, The
American Academy of Arts and Letters

and The National Institute of Arts and
Letters

See Cowboys and Indians, Western
Heritage Awards, The National Cowboy Hall of Fame and Western Heritage Center

RICHARD C. CRAVEN AWARD—
The American Humane Association
The Patsy Award goes to animals in
starring roles. The Craven Award goes
to animals in supporting spots. Don't
think it's easy being a "falling horse."
Established 1951.
1951
Tamba Tamba, chimpanzee
1952
Smoky, fighting stallion
1953
Brackett, jumping horse
1954
Cocaine, falling horse
1955
Flash, falling and lay-down horse
1956
Flame, German Shepherd dog
1957
King Cotton, white stallion
1958
Roy Rogers and Trigger, 25th
anniversary in show business
1959
Baldy, rearing horse
1960
Sharkey, Dempsey, Choctaw, Joker,
four-up horse team
1961　no award
1962　no award
1963
Mickey O'Boyle, fighting horse
1964　no award
1965
Little Buck, falling and lay-down
horse
1966
Smoky, trick horse
1967　no award
1968　no award
1969　no award
1970　no award
1971
Kilroy, falling horse

1972
Cocaine, falling horse (30 years old,
also won award 1954)
1973   no award
1974   no award
1975   no award
1976   no award

THE VALENTINE DAVIES AWARD
—Writers Guild of America, West, Inc.
For someone "whose contribution to the motion picture community has brought dignity and honor to writers everywhere."
Established 1962.
1962   Mary McCall, Jr.
1963   Allen Rivkin
1964   Morgan Cox
1965   James R. Webb
1966   Leonard Spigelgass
1967   Edmund H. North
1968   George Seaton
1969   Dore Schary
1970   Richard Murphy
1971   Daniel Taradash
1972   Michael Blankfort, Norman Corwin
1973   William Ludwig
1974   Ray Bradbury, Philip Dunne
1975   Fay Kanin
1976   Winston Miller
1977   Carl Foreman

THE DELIA AUSTRAIN AWARD—
The Drama League of New York, Inc.
For the "most distinguished performance" of the New York theatre season.
Established 1935.
1935
Katharine Cornell, *Romeo and Juliet*
1936
Helen Hayes, *Victoria Regina*
1937
Maurice Evans, *Richard III*
1938
Cedric Hardwicke, *Shadow and Substance*
1939
Raymond Massey, *Abe Lincoln in Illinois*
1940
Paul Muni, *Key Largo*
1941
Paul Lukas, *Watch on the Rhine*

1942
Judith Evelyn, *Angel Street*
1943
Alfred Lunt, Lynn Fontanne, *The Pirate*
1944
Elisabeth Bergner, *The Two Mrs. Carrolls*
1945
Mady Christians, *I Remember Mama*
1946
Louis Calhern, *The Magnificent Yankee*
1947
Ingrid Bergman, *Joan of Lorraine*
1948
Judith Anderson, *Medea*
1949
Robert Morley, *Edward My Son*
1950
Grace George, *The Velvet Glove*
1951
Claude Rains, *Darkness at Noon*
1952
Julie Harris, *I Am A Camera*
1953
Shirley Booth, *Time of the Cuckoo*
1954
Josephine Hull, *The Solid Gold Cadillac*
1955
Viveca Lindfors, *Anastasia*
1956
David Wayne, *The Ponder Heart*
1957
Eli Wallach, *Major Barbara*
1958
Ralph Bellamy, *Sunrise at Campobello*
1959
Cyril Ritchard, *The Pleasure of His Company*
1960
Jessica Tandy, *Five Finger Exercise*
1961
Hume Cronyn, *Big Fish, Little Fish*
1962
Paul Scofield, *A Man For All Seasons*
1963
Charles Boyer, *Lord Pengo*
1964
Alec Guinness, *Dylan*
1965
John Gielgud, *Tiny Alice*

1966
Richard Kiley, *Man of La Mancha*
1967
Rosemary Harris, *The Wild Duck*
1968
Zoe Caldwell, *The Prime of Miss Jean Brodie*
1969
Alec McCowen, *Hadrian The Seventh*
1970
James Stewart, *Harvey*
1971
Anthony Quayle, *Sleuth*
1972
Eileen Atkins, Claire Bloom, *Vivat! Vivat! Regina*
1973
Alan Bates, *Butley*
1974
Christopher Plummer, *The Good Doctor*
1975
John Wood, *Sherlock Holmes*
1976
Eva Le Gallienne, *The Royal Family*

THE GOLDEN SCROLL AWARD—
The Academy of Science Fiction, Fantasy, and Horror Films
The best films of the year—but limited to the best fantasy, horror, and science fiction.
Established 1973 (winners before 1976 are unavailable)
1976
Best actress, Blythe Danner, *Futureworld*
Best actor, David Bowie, *The Man Who Fell to Earth;* Gregory Peck, *The Omen*
Best actress, supporting, Bette Davis, *Burnt Offerings*
Best actor, supporting, Jay Robinson, *Train Ride to Hollywood*
Best director, Dan Curtis, *Burnt Offerings*
Best writer, Jimmy Sangster
Best cinematography, Ernest Laszlo, *Logan's Run*
Best executive achievement, Gene Roddenberry
Best music, David Raksin
Best costume, Bill Thomas, *Logan's Run*

Best publicist, Dan Morgan, *Logan's Run*
Best film criticism, Arthur Knight
Best art direction, Dale Hennesy, *Logan's Run*
Best set direction, Robert De Vestel, *Logan's Run*
Best special effects, L. B. Abbott
Best animation, Charles M. Jones
Best make-up, William Tuttle, *Logan's Run*
Best Science Fiction, *Logan's Run*
Best fantasy, *The Holes*
Best horror, *Burnt Offerings*
Special award, *King Kong*

See Journalism, Gavel Award, American Bar Association

LAUREL AWARD FOR SCREEN WRITING ACHIEVEMENT—Writers Guild of America, West, Inc.
To a guild member who "has advanced the literature of the motion picture through the years. . . ."
Established 1953.

1953	Sonya Levien
1954	Dudley Nichols
1955	Robert Riskin
1956	Julius and Philip Epstein
	Albert Hackett
	Frances Goodrich
1957	Charles Brackett
	Billy Wilder
1958	John Lee Mahin
1959	Nunnally Johnson
1960	Norman Krasna
1961	George Seaton
1962	Philip Dunne
1963	Joseph L. Mankiewicz
1964	John Huston
1965	Sidney Buchman
1966	Isobel Lennart
1967	Richard Brooks
1968	Casey Robinson
1969	Carl Foreman
1970	Dalton Trumbo
1971	James Poe
1972	Ernest Lehman
1973	William Rose
1974	Paddy Chayefsky
1975	Preston Sturges
1976	Michael Wilson
1977	Samson Raphaelson

Screenwriter Paddy Chayefsky in his pre-beard days. (Memory Shop)

LIFE ACHIEVEMENT AWARD—
The American Film Institute

For "an individual whose talent has in a fundamental way contributed to the filmmaking art; whose accomplishments have been acknowledged by scholars, critics, professional peers, and the general public; and whose work has stood the test of time." The *New York Times* has called this "one of Hollywood's most prestigious awards."

Established 1973.

1973	John Ford, director
1974	James Cagney, actor
1975	Orson Welles, director, actor, writer
1976	William Wyler, director
1977	Bette Davis, actress

MAN OF THE YEAR AWARD—
Hasty Pudding Theatricals, Harvard University

Not to be confused with the Harvard Lampoon Worst awards, this is for a man who "has made the most outstanding contribution to the acting profession during the past year."

Established 1967.

1967	Bob Hope
1968	Paul Newman
1969	Bill Cosby
1970	Robert Redford
1971	James Stewart
1972	Dustin Hoffman
1973	Jack Lemmon
1974	Peter Falk
1975	Warren Beatty
1976	Robert Blake

GEORGE JEAN NATHAN AWARD FOR DRAMATIC CRITICISM—
George Jean Nathan Trust and Manufacturers Hanover Trust

The heads of the English Departments at Cornell, Princeton, and Yale Universities decide which American in the past theatrical year (July 1 to June 30) has written the best criticism of drama. Articles, essays, treatises, and books are all eligible.

1958–1959
Harold Clurman, drama critic, *The Nation, Lies Like Truth*
1959–1960
Professor C. L. Barber, professor of

English, Amherst College, for
Shakespeare's Festive Comedy
1960–1961
Jerry Tallmer, drama critic, *The
Village Voice*
1961–1962
Robert Brustein, theater critic, *The
New Republic*
1962–1963
Walter Kerr, drama critic, the *New
York Herald Tribune, The Theater in
Spite of Itself*
1963–1964
Elliot Norton, drama critic, *Boston
Record American and Sunday
Advertiser*
1964–1965
Gerald Weales, associate professor of
English, University of Pennsylvania
1965–1966
Eric Russell Bentley, professor of
dramatic literature, Columbia
University
1966–1967
Elizabeth Hardwick, advisory editor,
New York Review of Books
1967–1968
Martin Gottfried, drama critic,
Women's Wear Daily, for *A Theater
Divided: The Postwar American
Stage*
1968–1969
John Lahr, drama critic, *Evergreen
Review* and *The Village Voice*
1969–1970
John Simon, drama critic, *Hudson
Review* and *New York* magazine
1970–1971
Richard Gilman, professor of
playwriting and criticism, Yale
Drama School, for *Common and
Uncommon Masks: Writings on
Theatre 1961–1970*
1971–1972
Jay Carr, theater and music critic,
Detroit News
1972–1973
StanleyKauffmann, film and theater
critic *New Republic*
1973–1974
Albert Bermel, theater critic, *The
New Leader*
1975–1976
Michael Goldman, professor of
English, Princeton University, *The*

*Actor's Freedom: Toward a Theory
of Drama*

**NEW YORK DRAMA CRITICS CIR-
CLE AWARDS**—New York Drama
Critics Circle
For the best plays opening on Broad-
way during the previous year chosen
by those who see them all.
Established 1935.
1935–1936
Best American play, *Winterset*
1936–1937
Best American play, *High Tor*
1937–1938
Best American play, *Of Mice and
Men*
Best foreign play, *Shadow and
Substance*
1938–1939
Best American play, no award
Best foreign play, *The White Steed*
1939–1940
Best American play, *The Time of
Your Life*
1940–1941
Best American play, *Watch on the
Rhine*
Best foreign play, *The Corn is Green*
1941–1942
Best American play, no award
Best foreign play, *Blithe Spirit*
1942–1943
Best American Play, *The Patriots*
1943–1944
Best American play, no award
Best foreign play, *Jacobowsky and
the Colonel*
1944–1945
Best American play, *The Glass
Menagerie*
1945–1946
Best musical, *Carousel*
1946–1947
Best American play, *All My Sons*
Best foreign play, *No Exit*
Best musical, *Brigadoon*
1947–1948
Best American play, *A Streetcar
Named Desire*
Best foreign play, *The Winslow Boy*
1948–1949
Best American play, *Death of a
Salesman*
Best foreign play, *The Madwoman of
Chaillot*

Princeton professor Michael Goldman won the George Jean Nathan Award for Dramatic Criticism and $10,000 in 1975-1976. (Matar Studio, Inc.)

Best musical, *South Pacific*

1949–1950

Best American play, *The Member of the Wedding*

Best foreign play, *The Cocktail Party*

Best musical, *The Consul*

1950–1951

Best American play, *Darkness at Noon*

Best foreign play, *The Lady's Not for Burning*

Best musical, *Guys and Dolls*

1951–1952

Best American play, *I Am a Camera*

Best foreign play, *Venus Observed*

Best musical, *Pal Joey*

Special citation, *Don Juan in Hell*

1952–1953

Best American play, *Picnic*

Best foreign play, *The Love of Four Colonels*

Best musical, *Wonderful Town*

1953–1954

Best American play, *Teahouse of the August Moon*

Best foreign play, *Ondine*

Best musical, *The Golden Apple*

1954–1955

Best American play, *Cat on a Hot Tin Roof*

Best foreign play, *Witness for the Prosecution*

Best musical, *The Saint of Bleecker Street*

1955–1956

Best American play, *The Diary of Anne Frank*

Best foreign play, *Tiger at the Gates*

Best musical, *My Fair Lady*

1956–1957

Best American play, *Long Day's Journey into Night*

Best foreign play, *The Waltz of the Toreadors*

Best musical, *The Most Happy Fella*

1957–1958

Best American play, *Look Homeward, Angel*

Best foreign play, *Look Back in Anger*

Best musical, *The Music Man*

1958–1959

Best American play, *A Raisin in the Sun*

Best musical, *Company*

Best foreign play, *The Visit*
Best musical, *La Plume de Ma Tante*
1959–1960
  Best American play, *Toys in the Attic*
  Best foreign play, *Five Finger Exercise*
  Best musical, *Fiorello!*
1960–1961
  Best American play, *All the Way Home*
  Best foreign play, *A Taste of Honey*
  Best musical, *Carnival*
1961–1962
  Best American play, *The Night of the Iguana*
  Best foreign play, *A Man for All Seasons*
  Best musical, *How to Succeed in Business Without Really Trying*
1962–1963
  Best of year, *Who's Afraid of Virginia Woolf?*
  Special citation, *Beyond the Fringe*
1963–1964
  Best of year, *Luther*
  Best musical, *Hello, Dolly!*
  Special citation, *The Trojan Women*
1964–1965
  Best of year, *The Subject Was Roses*
  Best musical, *Fiddler on the Roof*
1965–1966
  Best of year, *The Persecution and Assassination of Marat as Performed by the Inmates of the Asylum of Charenton Under the Direction of the Marquis de Sade*
  Best musical, *Man of La Mancha*
1966–1967
  Best of year, *The Homecoming*
  Best musical, *Cabaret*
1967–1968
  Best of year, *Rosencrantz and Guildenstern Are Dead*
  Best musical, *Your Own Thing*
1968–1969
  Best of year, *The Great White Hope*
  Best musical, *1776*
1969–1970
  Best of year, *Borstal Boy*
  Best American play, *The Effect of Gamma Rays on Man-in-the-Moon Marigolds*
1970–1971
  Best of year, *Home*
  Best American play, *The House of Blue Leaves*

Best musical, *Follies*
1971–1972
  Best of year, *That Championship Season*
  Best foreign play, *The Screens*
  Best musical, *Two Gentlemen of Verona*
  Special citation, *Sticks and Bones*
  Special citation, *Old Times*
1972–1973
  Best of year, *The Changing Room*
  Best American play, *The Hot l Baltimore*
  Best musical, *A Little Night Music*
1973–1974
  Best of year, *The Contractor*
  Best American play, *Short Eyes*
  Best musical, *Candide*
1974–1975
  Best of year, *Equus*
  Best American play, *The Taking of Miss Janie*
  Best musical, *A Chorus Line*
1975–1976
  Best of year, *Travesties*
  Best American play, *Streamers*
  Best musical, *Pacific Overtures*
1976–1977
  Best of year, *Otherwise Engaged*
  Best American play, *American Buffalo*
  Best musical, *Annie*

THE NEW YORK FILM CRITICS CIRCLE AWARDS—New York Film Critics Circle

The New York movie critics, in the "circle," decide what they liked best. Established 1935.

1935
  Best picture, *The Informer* (director, John Ford)
  Best actor, Charles Laughton (*Mutiny on the Bounty* and *Ruggles of Red Gap*)
  Best actress, Greta Garbo (*Anna Karenina*)
  Best direction, John Ford (*The Informer*)
1936
  Best picture, *Mr. Deeds Goes to Town* (director, Frank Capra)
  Best actor, Walter Huston (*Dodsworth*)

Best actress, Luise Rainer *(The Great Ziegfeld)*
Best direction, Rouben Mamoulian *(The Gay Desperado)*
Best foreign film, *La Kermesse Heroique* (director, Jacques Feyder; French)

1937
Best picture, *The Life of Emile Zola* (director, William Dieterle)
Best actor, Paul Muni *(The Life of Emile Zola)*
Best actress, Greta Garbo *(Camille)*
Best direction, Gregory La Cava *(Stage Door)*
Best foreign film, *Mayerling* (director, Anatole Litvak; French)

1938
Best picture, *The Citadel* (director, King Vidor)
Best actor, James Cagney *(Angels With Dirty Faces)*
Best actress, Margaret Sullavan *(Three Comrades)*
Best direction, Alfred Hitchcock *(The Lady Vanishes)*
Best foreign film, *Grande Illusion* (director, Jean Renoir; French)

1939
Best picture, *Wuthering Heights* (director, William Wyler)
Best actor, James Stewart *(Mr. Smith Goes to Washington)*
Best actress, Vivien Leigh *(Gone With the Wind)*
Best direction, John Ford *(Stagecoach)*

1940
Best picture, *The Grapes of Wrath* (director, John Ford)
Best actor, Charles Chaplin *(The Great Dictator)*
Best actress, Katharine Hepburn *(The Philadelphia Story)*
Best direction, John Ford *(The Grapes of Wrath* and *The Long Voyage Home)*

1941
Best picture, *Citizen Kane* (director, Orson Welles)
Best actor, Gary Cooper *(Sergeant York)*
Best actress, Joan Fontaine *(Suspicion)*

Best direction, John Ford *(How Green Was My Valley)*

1942
Best picture, *In Which We Serve* (directors, Noel Coward, David Lean)
Best actor, James Cagney *(Yankee Doodle Dandy)*
Best actress, Agnes Moorehead *(The Magnificent Ambersons)*
Best direction, John Farrow *(Wake Island)*

1943
Best picture, *Watch on the Rhine* (director, Herman Shumlin)
Best actor, Paul Lukas *(Watch on the Rhine)*
Best actress, Ida Lupino *(The Hard Way)*
Best direction, George Stevens *(The More the Merrier)*

1944
Best picture, *Going My Way* (director, Leo McCarey)
Best actor, Barry Fitzgerald *(Going My Way)*
Best actress, Tallulah Bankhead *(Lifeboat)*
Best direction, Leo McCarey *(Going My Way)*

1945
Best picture, *The Lost Weekend* (director, Billy Wilder)
Best actor, Ray Milland *(The Lost Weekend)*
Best actress, Ingrid Bergman *(Spellbound* and *The Bells of St. Mary's)*
Best direction, Billy Wilder *(The Lost Weekend)*

1946
Best picture, *The Best Years of Our Lives* (director, William Wyler)
Best actor, Laurence Olivier *(Henry V)*
Best actress, Celia Johnson *(Brief Encounter)*
Best direction, William Wyler *(The Best Years of Our Lives)*

1947
Best picture, *Gentleman's Agreement* (director, Elia Kazan)
Best actor, William Powell *(Life With Father* and *The Senator Was Indiscreet)*

Best actress, Deborah Kerr (*Black Narcissus* and *The Adventuress*)
Best direction, Elia Kazan (*Gentleman's Agreement* and *Boomerang*)
Best foreign film, *To Live in Peace* (director, Luigi Zampa; Italian)
1948
Best picture, *The Treasure of the Sierra Madre* (director, John Huston)
Best actor, Laurence Olivier (*Hamlet*)
Best actress, Olivia de Havilland (*The Snake Pit*)
Best direction, John Huston (*The Treasure of the Sierra Madre*)
Best foreign film, *Paisan* (director, Roberto Rossellini; Italian)
1949
Best picture, *All the King's Men* (director, Robert Rossen)
Best actor, Broderick Crawford (*All the King's Men*)
Best actress, Olivia de Havilland (*The Heiress*)
Best direction, Carol Reed (*The Fallen Idol*)
Best foreign film, *The Bicycle Thief* (Vittorio De Sica; Italian)
1950
Best picture, *All About Eve* (director, Joseph L. Mankiewicz)
Best actor, Gregory Peck (*Twelve O'Clock High*)
Best actress, Bette Davis (*All About Eve*)
Best direction, Joseph L. Mankiewicz (*All About Eve*)
Best foreign film, *Ways of Love* (directors, Rossellini, Pagnol, Renoir; Italian/French)
1951
Best picture, *A Streetcar Named Desire* (director, Elia Kazan)
Best actor, Arthur Kennedy (*Bright Victory*)
Best direction, Elia Kazan (*A Streetcar Named Desire*)
Best foreign film, *Miracle in Milan* (director, Vittorio De Sica; Italian)
1952
Best picture, *High Noon* (director, Fred Zinnemann)
Best actor, Ralph Richardson (*Breaking the Sound Barrier*)

Best actress, Shirley Booth (*Come Back, Little Sheba*)
Best direction, Fred Zinnemann (*High Noon*)
Best foreign film, *Forbidden Games* (director, René Clement; French)
1953
Best picture, *From Here To Eternity* (director, Fred Zinnemann)
Best actor, Burt Lancaster (*From Here To Eternity*)
Best actress, Audrey Hepburn (*Roman Holiday*)
Best direction, Fred Zinnemann (*From Here To Eternity*)
Best foreign film, *Justice Is Done* (director, Andre Cayatte; French)
1954
Best picture, *On The Waterfront* (director, Elia Kazan)
Best actor, Marlon Brando (*On The Waterfront*)
Best actress, Grace Kelly (*The Country Girl*)
Best direction, Elia Kazan (*On The Waterfront*)
Best foreign film, *Gate of Hell* (director, Teinosuke Kinugasa; Japanese)
1955
Best picture, *Marty* (director, Delbert Mann)
Best actor, Ernest Borgnine (*Marty*)
Best actress, Anna Magnani (*The Rose Tattoo*)
Best direction, David Lean (*Summertime*)
Best foreign film, *Umberto D* (director, Vittorio De Sica; Italian) and *Diabolique* (director, Henri-Georges Clouzot; French)
1956
Best picture, *Around the World in 80 Days* (director, Michael Anderson)
Best actor, Kirk Douglas (*Lust for Life*)
Best actress, Ingrid Bergman (*Anastasia*)
Best direction, John Huston (*Moby Dick*)
Best foreign film, *La Strada* (director, Frederico Fellini; Italian)
1957
Best picture, *The Bridge on the River Kwai* (director, David Lean)

Best actor, Alec Guinness *(The Bridge on the River Kwai)*
Best actress, Deborah Kerr *(Heaven Knows, Mr. Allison)*
Best direction, David Lean *(The Bridge on the River Kwai)*
Best foreign film, *Gervaise* (director, René Clement; French)

1958
Best picture, *The Defiant Ones* (director, Stanley Kramer)
Best actor, David Niven *(Separate Tables)*
Best actress, Susan Hayward *(I Want To Live)*
Best direction, Stanley Kramer *(The Defiant Ones)*
Best foreign film, *My Uncle, Mr. Hulot* (director, Jacques Tati; French)

1959
Best picture, *Ben-Hur* (director, William Wyler)
Best actor, James Stewart *(Anatomy of a Murder)*
Best actress, Audrey Hepburn *(The Nun's Story)*
Best direction, Fred Zinnemann *(The Nun's Story)*
Best foreign film, *The 400 Blows* (director, Francois Truffaut; French)

1960
Best picture, *The Apartment* (director, Billy Wilder) and *Sons and Lovers* (director, Jack Cardiff)
Best actor, Burt Lancaster *(Elmer Gantry)*
Best actress, Deborah Kerr *(The Sundowners)*
Best directors, Billy Wilder *(The Apartment)* and Jack Cardiff *(Sons and Lovers)*
Best foreign film, *Hiroshima, Mon Amour* (Director, Alain Resnais; French-Japanese)

1961
Best picture, *West Side Story* (directors, Robert Wise and Jerome Robbins)
Best actor, Maximilian Schell *(Judgement at Nuremberg)*
Best actress, Sophia Loren *(Two Women)*
Best direction, Robert Rossen *(The Hustler)*

Best foreign film, *La Dolce Vita* (director, Frederico Fellini; Italian)

1962   no award
1963
Best picture, *Tom Jones* (director, Tony Richardson)
Best actor, Albert Finney *(Tom Jones)*
Best actress, Patricia Neal *(Hud)*
Best direction, Tony Richardson *(Tom Jones)*
Best foreign film, *8 1/2* (director, Frederico Fellini; Italian)

1964
Best picture, *My Fair Lady* (director, George Cukor)
Best actor, Rex Harrison *(My Fair Lady)*
Best actress, Kim Stanley *(Seance on a Wet Afternoon)*
Best direction, Stanley Kubrick *(Dr. Strangelove, Or How I Learned to Stop Worrying and Love the Bomb)*
Best foreign film, *That Man From Rio* (director, Philippe De Broca; French)

1965
Best picture, *Darling* (director John Schlesinger)
Best actor, Oskar Werner *(Ship of Fools)*
Best actress, Julie Christie *(Darling)*
Best direction, John Schlesinger *(Darling)*
Best foreign film, *Juliet of the Spirits* (director, Frederico Fellini; Italian)

1966
Best picture, *A Man for All Seasons* (director, Fred Zinnemann)
Best actor, Paul Scofield *(A Man for All Seasons)*
Best actress, Elizabeth Taylor *(Who's Afraid of Virginia Woolf?)* and Lynn Redgrave *(Georgy Girl)*
Best direction, Fred Zinnemann *(A Man for All Seasons)*
Best foreign film, *The Shop on Main Street* (directors, Jan Kadar and Elmer Klos; Czechoslovakian)

1967
Best picture, *In the Heat of the Night* (director, Norman Jewison)
Best actor, Rod Steiger *(In the Heat of the Night)*

Best actress, Edith Evans *(The Whisperers)*
Best direction, Mike Nichols *(The Graduate)*
Best foreign film, *La Guerre Est Finie* (director, Alain Resnais; French)

1968
Best picture, *The Lion in Winter* (director, Anthony Harvey)
Best actor, Alan Arkin *(The Heart Is A Lonely Hunter)*
Best actress, Joanne Woodward *(Rachel, Rachel)*
Best direction, Paul Newman *(Rachel, Rachel)*
Best foreign film, *War and Peace* (director, Serge Bondarchuk; Russian)

1969
Best picture, *"Z"* (director, Costa-Gavras)
Best actor, Jon Voight *(Midnight Cowboy)*
Best actress, Jane Fonda *(They Shoot Horses, Don't They?)*
Best direction, Costa-Gavras *("Z")*

1970
Best picture, *Five Easy Pieces* (director, Bob Rafelson)
Best actor, George C. Scott *(Patton)*
Best actress, Glenda Jackson *(Women in Love)*
Best direction, Bob Rafelson *(Five Easy Pieces)*

1971
Best picture, *A Clockwork Orange* (director, Stanley Kubrick)
Best actor, Gene Hackman *(French Connection)*
Best actress, Jane Fonda *(Klute)*
Best direction, Stanley Kubrick *(A Clockwork Orange)*

1972
Best picture, *Cries and Whispers* (director, Ingmar Bergman)
Best actor, Laurence Olivier *(Sleuth)*
Best actress, Liv Ullman *(Cries and Whispers)*
Best direction, Ingmar Bergman *(Cries and Whispers)*
Best foreign film, *The Sorrow and The Pity*

1973
Best picture, *Day For Night*

(director, Francois Truffaut)
Best actor, Marlon Brando *(The Godfather)*
Best actress, Joanne Woodward *(The Effect of Gamma Rays on Man-in-the-Moon Marigolds)*
Best direction, Francois Truffaut *(Day For Night)*

1974
Best picture, *Amarcord* (director, Frederico Fellini)
Best actor, Jack Nicholson *(Chinatown)*
Best actress, Liv Ullmann *(Scenes From A Marriage)*
Best direction, Ingmar Bergman *(Scenes From A Marriage)*

1975
Best picture, *Nashville* (director, Robert Altman)
Best actor, Jack Nicholson *(One Flew Over the Cuckoo's Nest)*
Best actress, Isabelle Adjani *(The Story of Adele H)*
Best direction, Robert Altman *(Nashville)*

1976

PATSY AWARDS—The American Humane Association
Humans have their Oscars and Emmys, animals have their Patsys.
Established 1951.

1951
Francis—talking mule, *Francis*
California—Palomino horse, *The Palomino*
Pierre—chimpanzee, *My Friend Irma Goes West*

1952
Rhubarb—cat, *Rhubarb*
Francis—talking mule, *Francis Goes to the Races*
Cheta—chimpanzee, *Tarzan's Peril*

1953
Jackie—African lion, *Fearless Fagin*
Bonzo—chimpanzee, *Bonzo Goes to College*
Trigger—Roy Roger's horse, *Son of Paleface*

1954
Laddie—Collie dog, *Hondo*
Francis—talking mule, *Francis Covers the Big Town*
Jackie—African lion, *Androcles and the Lion*

1955
   Gypsy—black stallion, *Gypsy Colt*
   Francis—talking mule, *Francis Joins
   the WACS*
   Esmeralda—seal, *20,000 Leagues
   Under the Sea*
1956
   Wildfire—bull terrier, dog, *It's a
   Dog's Life*
   Francis—talking mule, *Francis Joins
   the Navy*
   Faro—dog, *The Kentuckian*
1957
   Samantha—goose, *Friendly
   Persuasion*
   War Winds—black stallion, *Giant*
   Francis—talking mule, *Francis in the
   Haunted House*
1958
Movie
   Spike—dog, *Old Yeller*
   Beauty—horse, *Wild is the Wind*
   Kelly—dog, *Kelly and Me*
T.V.
   Lassie—collie, "Lassie"
   Cleo—bassett hound, "The People's
   Choice"
   Rin Tin Tin— German shepherd,
   "Rin Tin Tin"
1959
Movie
   Pyewacket—cat, *Bell, Book and
   Candle*
   Tonka—horse, *Tonka*
   Harry—hare, *Geisha Boy*
T.V.
   Lassie—collie, "Lassie"
   Asta—dog, "The Thin Man"
   Rin Tin Tin—German shepherd,
   "Rin Tin Tin"
1960
Movie
   Shaggy—Old English sheepdog, *The
   Shaggy Dog*
   Herman—pigeon, *The Gazebo*
   North Wind—horse, *The Sad Horse*
T.V.
   Asta—dog, "The Thin Man"
   Lassie—collie, "Lassie"
   Fury, "Bachelor Father"
   Jasper, "Bachelor Father"
1961
Movie
   Cotton—white horse, *Pepe*
   Spike—dog, *A Dog of Flanders*

   Mr. Stubbs—chimpanzee, *Visit to a
   Small Planet*
   Skip, *Visit to a Small Planet*
T.V.
   Tramp—old English sheepdog, "My
   Three Sons"
   Lassie—collie, "Lassie"
   Fury—horse, "Bachelor Father"
1962
Movie
   Cat—cat, *Breakfast at Tiffany's*
   Pete—dog, *The Silent Call*
   Flame—horse, *The Clown and the
   Kid*
T.V.
   Mister Ed—horse, "Mister Ed"
   Lassie—collie, "Lassie"
   Tramp—old English sheepdog, "My
   Three Sons"
1963
Movie
   Big Red—dog, *Big Red*
   Sydney—elephant, *Jumbo*
   Zamba—African lion, *The Lion*
T.V.
   Mister Ed—horse, "Mister Ed"
   Lassie—collie, "Lassie"
   Tramp—Old English sheepdog, "My
   Three Sons"
1964
Movie
   Tom Dooley—hound dog, *Savage
   Sam*
   Pluto—dog, *My Six Loves*
   Raunchy—jaguar, *Rampage*
T.V.
   Lassie—collie, "Lassie"
   Mister Ed—horse, "Mister Ed"
1964
T.V.
   Tramp—dog, "My Three Sons"
1965
Movie
   Patrina—tiger, *A Tiger Walks*
   Storm—dog, *Goodbye Charlie*
   Junior—dog, *Island of the Blue
   Dolphins*
T.V.
   Flipper—porpoise, "Flipper"
   Lassie—collie, "Lassie"
   Mister Ed—horse, "Mister Ed"
1966
Movie
   Syn—Siamese cat, *That Darn Cat*

Clarence—African lion, *Clarence, the Cross-Eyed Lion*
Judy—chimpanzee, *The Monkey's Uncle*
T.V.
Flipper—porpoise, "Flipper"
Lord Nelson—dog, "Please Don't Eat the Daisies"
Higgins—dog, "Petticoat Junction"
1967
Movie
Elsa—African lionness, *Born Free*
Duke—dog, *The Ugly Dachshund*
Vindicator—bull, *The Rare Breed*
T.V
Judy—chimpanzee, "Daktari"
Flipper—porpoise, "Flipper"
Arnold—pig, "Green Acres"
1968
Movie
Gentle Ben—bear, *Gentle Giant*
Sir Tom—mountain lion, *The Cat*
Sophie—sea lion, *Dr. Doolittle*
T.V.
Arnold—pig, "Green Acres"
Gentle Ben—bear, "Gentle Ben"
Judy—chimpanzee, "Daktari"
T.V. Commercial
Samba, Jr.—African lion, Dreyfus Fund
1969
Movie
Albarado—horse, *Horse in the Gray Flannel Suit*
T.V.
Arnold—pig (continuing series), "Green Acres"
Timmy—chimpanzee (single episode), "Beverly Hillbillies"
T.V. Commercial
Chauncey—cougar, Ford Motor Company
1970
Movie
Rascal—raccoon, *Rascal*
T.V.
Scruffy—dog (continuing series), "The Ghost and Mrs. Muir"
Algae—seal (single episode), "The Ghost and Mrs. Muir"
1971
Movie
Sancho—wolf, *The Wild Country*
T.V.
Arnold—pig (continuing series),

"Green Acres"
Lassie's three puppies (single episode), "Lassie"
Margie—elephant (single episode) "Wonderful World of Disney"
1972
Movie
Ben—rat, *Willard*
T.V.
Pax—dog (continuing series), "Longstreet"
Ott—horse (single episode), "Lassie"
1973
Movie
Ben—rat, *Ben*
T.V.
Farouk—German shepherd (single episode), "Ironside"
T.V. commercial
Morris—yellow tiger cat, Nine Lives Cat Food
1974
Movie
Alpha—dolphin, *The Day of the Dolphin*
T.V.
Midnight—cat (continuing series), "Mannix" and "Barnaby Jones"
Caesar—Doberman Pinscher (single episode), "Trapped"
T.V. commercial
Scruffy—dog, Chuckwagon Dog Food
1975
Movie
Tonto—yellow cat, *Harry and Tonto*
T.V.
Elsa—lion (continuing series), "Born Free"
Ginger & cubs—coyote family (single episode), "The Indestructible Outcasts"
T.V. commercial
Lawrence—red deer, Hartford Insurance

See Pulitzer Prize

MRS. ANN RADCLIFFE AWARDS—
The Count Dracula Society
The society doesn't vant to suck your blood, it just wants to give awards for the best horror in the movies, literature, and on television.

*The symbol of the Count
Dracula Society, naturally.*

Established 1962.
(no dates available until 1976)
Vincent Price
Robert Quarry
Peter Lorre
Lon Chaney, Jr.
John Carradine
Alfred Hitchcock
Rod Serling
Ray Bradbury
Karl Freund
Francis Lederer
Rouben Mamoulian
George Pal
Fritz Lang
Boris Karloff
Roger Corman
Robert Block
Dr. Russell Kirk
Jonathan Frid
Bud Abbott
Roddy McDowall
Barbara Steele
Peter Cushing
Christopher Lee
1976
Jay Robinson, cinema
Leonard Wolf, literature

Gene Roddenberry, television
Jim Rumph, special award
Radu Florescu, special award
Don Johnson, special award

ST. CLAIR BAYFIELD AWARD—Actor's Equity Association and Mrs. Kathleen St. Clair Bayfield
This is a very specialized award, going to an unfeatured actor or actress appearing in a Shakespearean production. The production must be presented within 50 miles of New York City. The award is named after a character actor who was a charter member of Actor's Equity.
Established 1973.
1973   Barnard Hughes
1974   Randall Duc Kim
1975   John Glover
1976   Caroline McWilliams

SCREEN AWARDS—Writers Guild of America, West, Inc.
A motion picture is a fusion of many talents—director, actors, cinematographers, costume designers, etc. But whom better for the Writers Guild to

Director Billy Wilder took home the best screenwriter award in 1950, 1954, 1957, 1959, and 1960. (Memory Shop)

honor when choosing its best pictures, than the screenwriter? The various categories—comedy, drama, adaptations —varied somewhat over the years. But the honor has always been for American movies exclusively.
Established 1948.

1948
Best comedy, *Sitting Pretty,* screenplay by F. Hugh Herbert, from the novel by Gwen Davenport
Best drama, *The Snake Pit,* screenplay by Frank Partos and Millen Brand, based on the novel by Mary Jane Ward
Best western, *The Treasure of the Sierra Madre,* screenplay by John Huston
Best musical, *Easter Parade,* screenplay by Sidney Sheldon, Frances Goodrich, and Albert Hackett, story by Frances Goodrich and Albert Hackett
Screenplay dealing most ably with problems of the American scene (the Robert Meltzer Award), *The Snake Pit,* screenplay by Frank Partos and

Millen Brand, based on the novel by Mary Jane Ward
1949
Best comedy, *A Letter to Three Wives,* screenplay by Joseph L. Mankiewicz, from Vera Caspary's adaptation of John Klempner's novel
Best drama, *All the King's Men,* screenplay by Robert Rossen from the novel by William Penn Warren
Best western, *Yellow Sky,* screenplay by Lamar Trotti, story by W. R. Burnett
Best musical, *On the Town,* story and screenplay by Betty Comden and Adolph Green, from their musical play, based on an idea by Jerome Robbins
Screenplay dealing most ably with problems of the American scene (the Robert Meltzer Award), *All the King's Men,* screenplay by Robert Rossen from the novel by William Penn Warren
1950
Best comedy, *All About Eve,* screenplay by Joseph L. Mankiewicz, based on "The Wisdom

of Eve," a short story and radio play by Mary Orr

Best drama, *Sunset Boulevard,* original story and screenplay by Charles Brackett, Billy Wilder, and D. M. Marshman, Jr.

Best western, *Broken Arrow,* screenplay by Michael Blankfort, based on *Blood Brother,* a novel by Elliott Arnold

Best musical, *Annie Get Your Gun,* screenplay by Sidney Sheldon, based on the musical play by Herbert and Dorothy Fields, with music and lyrics by Irving Berlin

Screenplay dealing most ably with problems of the American scene (the Robert Meltzer Award), *The Men,* story and screenplay by Carl Foreman

1951

Best comedy, *Father's Little Dividend,* screenplay by Frances Goodrich and Albert Hackett, based on characters created by Edward Street in his book *Father of the Bride*

Best drama, *A Place in the Sun,* screenplay by Michael Wilson and Harry Brown, based on *An American Tragedy,* the novel by Theodore Dreiser, and the play, as adapted by Patrick Kearney

Best low-budget film, *The Steel Helmet,* story and screenplay by Samuel Fuller

Best musical, *An American In Paris,* story and screenplay by Alan Jay Lerner

Screenplay dealing most ably with problems of the American scene (the Robert Meltzer Award), *Bright Victory,* screenplay by Robert Buckner, from *Lights Out,* a novel by Baynard Kendrick

1952

Best comedy, *The Quiet Man,* screenplay by Frank S. Nugent, from "Green Rushes", a short story by Maurice Walsh

Best drama, *High Noon,* screenplay by Carl Foreman, based on "The Tin Star," a magazine story by John W. Cunningham

Best musical, *Singin' in the Rain,* screenplay by Betty Comden and Adolph Green, suggested by the song of the same title

1953

Best comedy, *Roman Holiday,* screenplay by Ian McLellan Hunter and John Dighton. Story by Ian McLellan Hunter

Best drama, *From Here to Eternity,* screenplay by Daniel Taradash, from the novel by James Jones

Best musical, *Lili,* screenplay by Helen Deutsch, story by Paul Gallico

1954

Best comedy, *Sabrina,* screenplay by Billy Wilder, Samuel Taylor, and Ernest Lehman, based on *Sabrina Fair,* the play by Samuel Taylor

Best drama, *On the Waterfront,* screen story and screenplay by Budd Schulberg, based on articles by Malcolm Johnson, entitled: "Crime on the Waterfront"

Best musical, *Seven Brides for Seven Brothers,* screenplay by Albert Hackett, Frances Goodrich, and Dorothy Kingsley, from "The Sobbin Women," a story by Stephen Vincent Benet

1955

Best comedy, *Mr. Roberts,* screenplay by Frank Nugent and Joshua Logan, from the play by Thomas Heggen and Joshua Logan, based on Thomas Heggen's novel

Best drama, *Marty,* original screenplay by Paddy Chayefsky

Best musical, *Love Me or Leave Me,* screenplay Daniel Fuchs and Isobel Lennart, story by Daniel Fuchs

1956

Best comedy, *Around the World in 80 Days,* screenplay by James Poe, John Farrow, and S. J. Perelman, based on the novel by Jules Verne

Best drama, *Friendly Persuasion,* screenplay by Michael Wilson, from the book by Jessamyn West

Best musical, *The King and I,* screenplay by Ernest Lehman, from the Rodgers and Hammerstein musical, as based on *Anna and the King of Siam,* a book by Margaret Landon

1957

Best comedy, *Love in the Afternoon,*

screenplay by Billy Wilder and I. A. L. Diamond adapted from *Ariane,* a novel by Claude Anet

Best drama, *12 Angry Men,* story and screenplay by Reginald Rose, from his own television play

Best musical, *Les Girls,* screenplay by John Patrick, story by Vera Caspary

1958

Best comedy, *Me and the Colonel,* screenplay by S. N. Behrman and George Froeschel, based on *Jacobowsky and the Colonel,* a play by Franz Werfel

Best drama, *The Defiant Ones,* story and screenplay by Harold Jacob Smith and Nathan E. Douglas

Best musical, *Gigi,* screenplay by Alan Jay Lerner, based on the Colette novel

1959

Best comedy, *Some Like It Hot,* screenplay by Billy Wilder and I. A. L. Diamond, suggested by a story by Robert Thoeren and M. Logan

Best drama, *The Diary of Anne Frank,* screenplay by Frances Goodrich and Albert Hackett, adapted from the book, *Anne Frank, the Diary of a Young Girl,* and the play by Goodrich and Hackett

Best musical, *The Five Pennies,* screenplay by Melville Shavelson and Jack Rose. Story by Robert Smith, based on the life of Loring "Red" Nichols

1960

Best comedy, *The Apartment,* story and screenplay by Billy Wilder and I. A. L. Diamond

Best drama, *Elmer Gantry,* screenplay by Richard Brooks, based on the Sinclair Lewis novel

Best musical, *Bells Are Ringing,* story and screenplay by Betty Comden and Adolph Green, from their own musical play

1961

Best comedy, *Breakfast at Tiffany's,* screenplay by George Axelrod, based on the Truman Capote novel

Best drama, *The Hustler,* screenplay by Sidney Carroll and Robert Rossen, from the novel by Walter Tevis

Best musical, *West Side Story,* screenplay by Ernest Lehman, from the musical play by Arthur Laurents

1962

Best comedy, *That Touch of Mink,* original screenplay by Stanley Shapiro and Nate Monaster

Best drama, *To Kill a Mockingbird,* screenplay by Horton Foote, based on the Harper Lee novel

Best musical, *The Music Man,* screenplay by Marion Hargrove, based on the musical play by Meredith Willson, from a story by Meredith Willson and Franklin Lacey

1963

Best comedy, *Lilies of the Field,* screenplay by James Poe, from the novel by William E. Barrett

Best drama, *Hud,* screenplay by Harriet Frank, Jr. and Irving Ravetch, from *Horseman, Pass By,* novel by Larry McMurtry

Best musical, no award

1964

Best comedy, *Dr. Strangelove: Or How I Learned to Stop Worrying and Love the Bomb,* screenplay by Stanley Kubrick, Peter George, and Terry Southern, story by Peter George, from his novel, *Red Alert*

Best drama, *Becket,* screenplay by Edward Anhalt, based on the play by Jean Anouilh

Best musical, *Mary Poppins* screenplay by Bill Walsh and Don Da Gradi, based on books by P. L. Travers

1965

Best comedy, *A Thousand Clowns,* screenplay by Herb Gardner, from his own play

Best drama, *The Pawnbroker,* screenplay by Morton Fine and David Friedkin, from the novel by Edward Lewis Wallant

Best musical, *The Sound of Music,* screenplay by Ernest Lehman, from the Rodgers and Hammerstein musical; book by Howard Lindsay and Russel Crouse, based on *The Trapp Family Singers* by Maria Augusta Trapp

1966

Best comedy, *The Russians are Coming, The Russians Are Coming,* screenplay by William Rose, from *The Off-Islanders,* a novel by Nathaniel Benchley
Best drama, *Who's Afraid of Virginia Woolf?* screenplay by Ernest Lehman, from the play by Edward Albee
Best musical, no award

1967

Best comedy, *The Graduate,* screenplay by Calder Willingham and Buck Henry, from the novel by Charles Webb
Best drama, *Bonnie and Clyde,* story and screenplay by David Newman and Robert Benton
Best musical, *Thoroughly Modern Millie,* story and screenplay by Richard Morris
Best original screenplay, *Bonnie and Clyde,* story and screenplay by David Newman and Robert Benton

1968

Best comedy, *The Odd Couple,* screenplay by Neil Simon, from his own play
Best drama, *The Lion in Winter,* screenplay by James Goldman, from his own play
Best musical, *Funny Girl,* screenplay by Isobel Lennart, from her own musical play and original story
Best original screenplay, *The Producers,* story and screenplay by Mel Brooks

1969

Best comedy, *Bob & Carol & Ted & Alice,* story and screenplay by Paul Mazursky and Larry Tucker
Best comedy adapted from another medium, *Goodbye, Columbus,* screenplay by Arnold Schulman, based on the book by Philip Roth
Best drama written directly for the screen, *Butch Cassidy and the Sundance Kid,* story and screenplay by William Goldman
Best drama adapted from another medium, *Midnight Cowboy,* screenplay by Waldo Salt, based on the novel by James Leo Herlihy

1970

Best comedy written directly for the screen, *The Out-of-Towners,* Neil Simon
Best comedy adapted from another medium, *M*A*S*H,* screenplay by Ring Lardner, Jr., from the novel by Richard Hooker
Best drama written directly for the screen, *Patton,* screen story and screenplay by Francis Ford Coppola and Edmund H. North
Best drama adapted from another medium, *I Never Sang For My Father,* screenplay by Robert Anderson, based on his play

1971

Best comedy written directly for the screen, *The Hospital,* Paddy Chayefsky
Best comedy adapted from another medium, *Kotch,* screenplay by John Paxton, novel by Katherine Topkins
Best drama written directly for the screen *Sunday Bloody Sunday,* Penelope Gilliatt
Best drama adapted from another medium, *The French Connection,* screenplay by Ernest Tidyman, book by Robin Moore

1972

Best comedy written directly for the screen, *What's Up, Doc?,* Buck Henry, David Newman and Robert Benton, story by Peter Bogdanovich
Best comedy adapted from another medium, *Cabaret,* Jay Presson Allen, screenplay; play by John Van Druten; and stories by Christopher Isherwood, based on musical play's book by Joe Masteroff
Best drama written directly for the screen, *The Candidate,* Jeremy Larner
Best drama adapted from another medium, *The Godfather,* screenplay by Mario Puzo and Francis Ford Coppola; novel by Puzo

1973

Best comedy written directly for the screen, *A Touch of Class,* Melvin Frank and Jack Rose
Best comedy adapted from another medium, *Paper Moon,* screenplay by

Alvin Sargent, novel by Joe David Brown
Best drama written directly for the screen, *Save the Tiger*, Steve Shagan
Best drama adapted from another medium, *Serpico*, screenplay by Waldo Salt and Norman Wexler, book by Peter Maas

1974
Best comedy written directly for the screen, *Blazing Saddles*, screenplay by Mel Brooks, Norman Steinberg, Andrew Bergman, Richard Pryor, and Alan Uger, story by Andrew Bergman
Best comedy adapted from another medium, *The Apprenticeship of Duddy Kravitz*, screenplay by Mordecai Richler, adaptation by Lionel Chetwynd, novel by Richler
Best drama written directly for the screen, *Chinatown*, Robert Towne
Best drama adapted from another medium, *The Godfather—Part II*, screenplay by Francis Ford Coppola and Mario Puzo; novel by Puzo

1975
Best comedy written directly for the screen, *Shampoo* Robert Towne and Warren Beatty
Best comedy adapted from another medium, *Sunshine Boys*, screenplay by Neil Simon, from his play
Best drama written directly for the screen, *Dog Day Afternoon*, Frank Pierson
Best drama adapted from another medium, *One Flew Over the Cuckoo's Nest*, screenplay by Lawrence Hauben and Bo Goldman, novel by Ken Kesey

1976
Best comedy written directly for the screen, *The Bad News Bears*, Bill Lancaster
Best comedy adapted from another medium, *The Pink Panther Strikes Again*, Frank Waldman and Blake Edwards
Best drama written directly for the screen, *Network*, Paddy Chayefsky
Best drama adpted from another medium, *All the President's Men*, William Goldman

THE TIMES "10 BEST"—The New York Times
The movie critics of the Gray Old Lady decide which films they liked best.
Established 1924
1924
The Dramatic Life of Abraham Lincoln, The Thief of Bagdad, Beau Brummel, Merton of the Movies, The Sea Hawk, He Who Gets Slapped, The Marriage Circle, In Hollywood with Potash and Perlmutter, Peter Pan, Isn't Life Wonderful?
1925
The Big Parade, The Last Laugh, The Unholy Three, The Gold Rush, The Merry Widow, The Dark Angel, Don Q, Son of Zorro, Ben-Hur, Stella Dallas, A Kiss for Cinderella
1926
Variety, Beau Geste, What Price Glory, Potemkin, The Grand Duchess and the Waiter, The Black Pirate, Old Ironsides, Moana, La Boheme, So This Is Paris
1927
The King of Kings, Chang, The Way of All Flesh, Wings, Seventh Heaven, Sunrise, Service for Ladies, Quality Street, Underworld, Stark Love
1928
The Circus, Street Angel, Czar Ivan the Terrible, The Last Command, White Shadows of the South Seas, The Patriot, The End of St. Petersburg, Show People, Homecoming, Four Devils
1929
The Love Parade, Disraeli, Hallelujah, The Passion of Jeanne d'Arc, The Taming of the Shrew, Bulldog Drummond, They Had to See Paris, The Sky Hawk, The Virginian, Sally
1930
With Byrd at the South Pole, All Quiet on the Western Front, Journey's End, Lightnin', The Devil to Pay, Outward Bound, Tom Sawyer, Holiday, Abraham Lincoln, Anna Christie
1931
The Guardsman, City Lights, The Smiling Lieutenant, Arrowsmith,

Tabu, Bad Girl, Frankenstein,
Skippy, Private Lives, A Connecticut
Yankee
1932
Maedchen in Uniform, Trouble in
Paradise, Der Raub der Mona Lisa,
Grand Hotel, Dr. Jekyll and Mr.
Hyde, The Mouthpiece, One Hour
with You, A Bill of Divorcement, The
Doomed Battalion, Reserved for
Ladies
1933
Cavalcade, Reunion in Vienna,
Morgenrot, State Fair, Dinner at
Eight, Berkeley Square, The Private
Life of Henry VIII, Little Women,
The Invisible Man, His Double Life
1934
It Happened One Night, The House
of Rothschild, The Battle, The Thin
Man, Catherine the Great, The First
World War, One Night of Love, The
Lost Patrol, Man of Aran, Our Daily
Bread
1935
The Informer, Ruggles of Red Gap,
David Copperfield, Lives of a
Bengal Lancer, Les Miserables, The
Scoundrel, Chapayev, The Man Who
Knew Too Much, Sequoia, Love Me
Forever
1936
La Kermesse Heroique (or, Carnival
in Flanders), Fury, Dodsworth, Mr.
Deeds Goes to Town, Winterset,
Romeo and Juliet, The Green
Pastures, The Ghost Goes West, The
Story of Louis Pasteur, These Three,
The Great Ziegfeld
1937
The Life of Emile Zola, The Good
Earth, Stage Door, Captains
Courageous, They Won't Forget,
Make Way for Tomorrow, I Met Him
in Paris, A Star Is Born, Camille,
Lost Horizon
1938
Snow White and the Seven Dwarfs,
The Citadel, To the Victor,
Pygmalion, A Slight Case of Murder,
Three Comrades, The Lady
Vanishes, The Adventures of Robin
Hood, A Man to Remember, Four
Daughters

1939
Made For Each Other, Stagecoach,
Wuthering Heights, Dark Victory,
Juarez, Goodbye, Mr. Chips, The
Women, Mr. Smith Goes to
Washington, Ninotchka, Gone With
the Wind
1940
The Grapes of Wrath, The Baker's
Wife, Rebecca, Our Town, The
Mortal Storm, Pride and Prejudice,
The Great McGinty, The Long
Voyage Home, The Great Dictator,
Fantasia
1941
The Lady Eve, Citizen Kane, Major
Barbara, Sergeant York, The Stars
Look Down, Here Comes Mr. Jordan,
Target for Tonight, Dumbo, How
Green Was My Valley, One Foot in
Heaven
1942
In Which We Serve, Journey for
Margaret, Casablanca, One of Our
Aircraft Is Missing, Wake Island,
Mrs. Miniver, Yankee Doodle
Dandy, The Gold Rush, Woman of
the Year, Sullivan's Travels
1943
Air Force, Desert Victory, The Ox-
Bow Incident, The More the Merrier,
For Whom the Bell Tolls, Report
From the Aleutians, Watch on the
Rhine, Corvette K-225, Sahara,
Madame Curie
1944
Destination Tokyo, The Miracle of
Morgan's Creek, The Purple Heart,
Going My Way, Wilson, Hail the
Conquering Hero, Thirty Seconds
Over Tokyo, None But the Lonely
Heart, Meet Me In St. Louis,
National Velvet
1945
A Tree Grows in Brooklyn, The Way
Ahead, Anchors Aweigh, Pride of the
Marines, The House on Ninety-
Second Street, Story of G.I. Joe,
Spellbound, The Last Chance, The
Lost Weekend, They Were
Expendable
1946
Open City, Road to Utopia, The
Green Years, Henry V, Notorious,
Brief Encounter, The Well-Digger's

Daughter, The Best Years of Our Lives, My Darling Clementine, Stairway to Heaven
1947
The Yearling, Great Expectations, Miracle on 34th Street, Crossfire, Life With Father, Shoe Shine, Gentleman's Agreement, To Live In Peace, The Bishop's Wife, The Fugitive
1948
Treasure of Sierra Madre, The Pearl, The Search, A Foreign Affair, Louisiana Story, Hamlet, Johnny Belinda, Apartment for Peggy, The Red Shoes, The Snake Pit
1949
Command Decision, A Letter to Three Wives, The Quiet One, Lost Boundaries, Pinky, The Heiress, All the King's Men, Battleground, The Fallen Idol, Intruder in the Dust
1950
The Titan—Story of Michelangelo, Twelve O'Clock High, Father of the Bride, The Asphalt Jungle, Destination Moon, The Men, Sunset Boulevard, Trio, All About Eve, Born Yesterday
1951
Fourteen Hours, The Brave Bulls, Oliver Twist, A Place in the Sun, People Will Talk, A Streetcar Named Desire, An American In Paris, Detective Story, Death of a Salesman, Decision Before Dawn
Best Foreign Film
Rashomon
1952
The Greatest Show on Earth, Cry, the Beloved Country, Viva Zapata!, Five Fingers, High Noon, Ivanhoe, The Quiet Man, Limelight, Breaking Through the Sound Barrier, Come Back, Little Sheba
1953
Moulin Rouge, Lili, Shane, Julius Caesar, Man on a Tightrope, Stalag 17, From Here to Eternity, Roman Holiday, Martin Luther, The Conquest of Everest
1954
The Glenn Miller Story, Genevieve, Knock on Wood, Mr. Hulot's Holiday, Seven Brides for Seven

Brothers, On the Waterfront, The Little Kidnappers, Sabrina, The Country Girl, Romeo and Juliet
1955
The Bridges at Toko-Ri, Bad Day at Black Rock, A Man Called Peter, Marty, The Great Adventure, Mister Roberts, The Phenix City Story, It's Always Fair Weather, Oklahoma!, The Prisoner
1956
Richard III, The King and I, Moby Dick, Bus Stop, Lust for Life, The Silent World, Giant, Around the World in 80 Days, Friendly Persuasion, Anastasia
Best Foreign Films
The Proud and the Beautiful (French), *Rififi* (French), *La Strada* (Italian), *The Grand Maneuver* (French), *The Magnificent Seven* (Japanese)
1957
The Great Man, Funny Face, 12 Angry Men, The Green Man, A Hatful of Rain, Silk Stockings, Love in the Afternoon, Les Girls, Sayonara, The Bridge on the River Kwai
Best Foreign Films
We Are All Murderers (French), *Gold of Naples* (Italian), *The Red Balloon* (French), *Torero!* (Mexican), *Passionate Summer* (French), *The Last Bridge* (German), *Cabiria* (Italian), *Gervaise* (French), *Odet* (Danish), *Smiles of a Summer Night* (Swedish)
1958
Teacher's Pet, Gigi, The Goddess, God's Little Acre, Cat on a Hot Tin Roof, The Defiant Ones, Damn Yankees, The Horse's Mouth, I Want to Live!, A Night to Remember
Best Foreign Films
Gates of Paris (French), *Rouge et Noir* (French), *Case of Dr. Laurent* (French), *The Captain from Koepenick* (German), *Panther Panchali* (Indian), *Inspector Maigret* (French), *The Seventh Seal* (Swedish), *My Uncle* (French), *Witches of Salem* (French), *He Who Must Die* (French)

1959
The Diary of Anne Frank, Room at the Top, The Nun's Story, Porgy and Bess, Anatomy of a Murder, A Hole in the Head, North by Northwest, Pillow Talk, Ben-Hur, On The Beach
Best Foreign Films
The Devil Strikes at Night (German), *Forbidden Fruit* (French), *Aparajito* (Indian), *The Roof* (Italian), *Wild Strawberries* (Swedish), *The Magician* (Swedish), *The Lovers* (French), *The 400 Blows* (French), *The Cousins* (French), *Black Orpheus* (French-Brazilian)

1960
I'm All Right, Jack, The Apartment, Pyscho, Elmer Gantry, Sunrise at Campobello, The Entertainer, Inherit the Wind, The Angry Silence, Exodus, Tunes of Glory
Best Foreign Films
Rosemary (German), *Ikiru* (Japanese), *The Cranes Are Flying* (Russian), *Hiroshima Mon Amour* (French), *The World of Apu* (Indian), *Never on Sunday* (Greek), *The Virgin Spring* (Swedish), *General della Rovere* (Italian), *The Big Deal on Madonna Street* (Italian), *The Ballad of a Soldier* (Russian)

1961
The Facts of Life, A Raisin in the Sun, Saturday Night and Sunday Morning, Fanny, The Hustler, Splendor in the Grass, West Side Story, El Cid, Judgment at Nuremberg, One, Two, Three
Best Foreign Films
Don Quixote (Russian), *Breathless* (French), *La Dolce Vita* (Italian), *The Bridge* (German), *Two Women* (Italian), *Ashes and Diamonds* (Polish), *Rocco and His Brothers* (Italian), *Purple Noon* (French), *Girl with a Suitcase* (Italian), *A Summer to Remember* (Russian)

1962
Lover Come Back, Last Year at Marienbad, Whistle Down the Wind, A Taste of Honey, Divorce—Italian Style, The Longest Day, Long Day's Journey Into Night, Sundays and Cybele, Freud, Electra

1963
Heavens Above!, The L-Shaped Room, Hud, Cleopatra, 8 1/2, Tom Jones, Any Number Can Win, The Sound of Trumpets, It's a Mad, Mad, Mad, Mad World, America, America

1964
Dr. Strangelove, or How I Learned to Stop Worrying and Love the Bomb, The Servant, That Man From Rio, One Potato, Two Potato, A Hard Day's Night, Woman in the Dunes, Mary Poppins, My Fair Lady, The Americanization of Emily, Marriage Italian Style

1965
The Pawnbroker, Ship of Fools, Darling, Repulsion, Juliet of the Spirits, The Eleanor Roosevelt Story, Red Desert, Kwaidan, To Die in Madrid, Thunderball

1966
The Shop on Main Street, The Gospel According to St. Matthew, Dear John, Morgan!, The Russians Are Coming, The Russians Are Coming, Who's Afraid of Virginia Woolf?, Georgy Girl, Loves of a Blonde, A Man for All Seasons, Blow-Up

1967
La Guerre Est Finie, Ulysses, The Hunt, In the Heat of the Night, Father, Elvira Madigan, Closely Watched Trains, Cool Hand Luke, In Cold Blood, The Graduate

1968
Charlie Bubbles, The Two of Us, Belle de Jour, Faces, Les Carabiniers, The Bride Wore Black, The Fifth Horseman Is Fear, Petulia, Rosemary's Baby, A Report on the Party and the Guests

1969
Alice's Restaurant, The Damned, If..., La Femme Infidele, Midnight Cowboy, Stolen Kisses, Topaz, True Grit, The Wild Bunch, "Z"

1970
The Ballad of Cable Hogue, Catch-22, Fellini Satyricon, Little Big Man, Loving, M*A*S*H*, Ma Nuit Chez Maud (My Night at Maud's), The Passion of Anna, Tristana, The Wild Child

1971

Bed and Board, Carnal Knowledge, Claire's Knee, A Clockwork Orange, The Conformist, Derby, The French Connection, The Last Picture Show, Le Boucher, Sunday Bloody Sunday

1972

Chloe in the Afternoon, Cries and Whispers, The Discreet Charm of the Bourgeosie, Fat City, Frenzy, The Godfather, The Heartbreak Kid, Tokyo Story, Traffic, Two English Girls

1973

American Graffiti, Day For Night, Heavy Traffic, Last Tango in Paris, The Long Goodbye, Love, Mean Streets, Memories of Underdevelopment, Playtime, Sleeper

1974

Amarcord, Badlands, California Split, Claudine, Daisy Miller, Harry and Tonto, Lacombe Lucien, Man is Not a Bird, Le Petit Theatre de Jean Renoir, The Phantom of Liberty, Scenes From a Marriage

1975

Alice Doesn't Live Here Anymore, Barry Lyndon, Distant Thunder, Hearts and Minds, Love and Death, The Magic Flute, Nashville, Shampoo, The Story of Adele H, Swept Away By an Unusual Destiny in the Blue Sea of August

1976

King Kong, Seven Beauties, All the President's Men, Face to Face, La Chienne, Network, The Seven Per Cent Solution, The Memory of Justice, Works of Rainer Werner Fassbinder, Taxi Driver

ANTOINETTE PERRY ("TONY") AWARDS—League of New York Theaters and Producers

It's got to be a biggie; it has its own television presentation show.

1947

Best actress, play, Ingrid Bergman, *Joan of Lorraine;* Helen Hayes, *Happy Birthday*

Best actor, play, José Ferrer, *Cyrano de Bergerac;* Fredric March, *Years Ago*

Best supporting actress, play, Patricia Neal, *Another Part of the Forest*

Best supporting actor, musical, David Wayne, *Finian's Rainbow*

Best director, Elia Kazan, *All My Sons*

1948

Best play, Thomas Heggen, Joshua Logan, *Mister Roberts*

Best actress, musical, Grace Hartman, *Angel in the Wings*

Best actor, musical, Paul Hartman, *Angel in the Wings*

Best actress, play, Judith Anderson, *Medea;* Katharine Cornell, *Antony and Cleopatra;* Jessica Tandy, *A Streetcar Named Desire*

Best actor, play, Henry Fonda, *Mister Roberts;* Paul Kelly, *Command Decision;* Basil Rathbone, *The Heiress*

1949

Best play, Arthur Miller, *Death of a Salesman*

Best book, musical, Bella and Samuel Spewack, *Kiss Me Kate*

Best composer and lyricist, musical, Cole Porter, *Kiss Me Kate*

Best actress, musical, Nanette Fabray, *Love Life*

Best actor, musical, Ray Bolger, *Where's Charley?*

Best actress, play, Martita Hunt, *The Madwoman of Chaillot*

Best actor, play, Rex Harrison, *Anne of the Thousand Days*

Best supporting actress, play, Shirley Booth, *Goodbye, My Fancy*

Best supporting actor, play, Arthur Kennedy, *Death of a Salesman*

Best director, Elia Kazan, *Death of a Salesman*

1950

Best play, T. S. Eliot, *The Cocktail Party*

Best musical, Oscar Hammerstein II, and Joshua Logan, *South Pacific*

Best composer, Richard Rodgers, *South Pacific*

Best actress, musical, Mary Martin, *South Pacific*

Best actor, musical, Ezio Pinza, *South Pacific*

Best actress, play, Shirley Booth, *Come Back, Little Sheba*
Best actor, play, Sidney Blackmer, *Come Back, Little Sheba*
Best supporting actress, musical, Juanita Hall, *South Pacific*
Best supporting actor, musical, Myron McCormick, *South Pacific*
Best director, Joshua Logan, *South Pacific*

1951
Best play, Tennessee Williams, *The Rose Tattoo*
Best musical, Jo Swerling and Abe Burrows, *Guys and Dolls*
Best composer and lyricist, Frank Loesser, *Guys and Dolls*
Best actress, musical, Ethel Merman, *Call Me Madam*
Best actor, musical, Robert Alda, *Guys and Dolls*
Best actress, play, Uta Hagen, *The Country Girl*
Best actor, play, Claude Rains, *Darkness at Noon*
Best supporting actress, musical, Isabel Bigley, *Guys and Dolls*
Best supporting actor, musical, Russell Nype, *Call Me Madam*
Best supporting actress, play, Maureen Stapleton, *The Rose Tattoo*
Best supporting actor, play, Eli Wallach, *The Rose Tattoo*
Best director, George S. Kaufman, *Guys and Dolls*

1952
Best play, Jan de Hartog, *The Fourposter*
Best musical, Oscar Hammerstein II, *The King and I*
Best actress, musical, Gertrude Lawrence, *The King and I*
Best actor, musical, Phil Silvers, *Top Banana*
Best actress, play, Julie Harris, *I Am a Camera*
Best actor, play, José Ferrer, *The Shrike*
Best supporting actress, musical, Helen Gallagher, *Pal Joey*
Best supporting actor, musical, Yul Brynner, *The King and I*
Best supporting actress, play, Marian Winters, *I Am a Camera*

Best supporting actor, play, John Cromwell, *Point of No Return*
Best director, José Ferrer, *The Shrike, The Fourposter, Stalag 17*

1953
Best play, Arthur Miller, *The Crucible*
Best musical, Joseph Fields, Jerome Chodorov, *Wonderful Town*
Best composer, Leonard Bernstein, *Wonderful Town*
Best actress, musical, Rosalind Russell, *Wonderful Town*
Best actor, musical, Thomas Mitchell, *Hazel Flagg*
Best actress, play, Shirley Booth, *Time of the Cuckoo*
Best actor, play, Tom Ewell, *The Seven Year Itch*
Best supporting actress, musical, Sheila Bond, *Wish You Were Here*
Best supporting actor, musical, Hiram Sherman, *Two's Company*
Best supporting actress, play, Beatrice Straight, *The Crucible*
Best supporting actor, play, John Williams, *Dial M for Murder*
Best director, Joshua Logan, *Picnic*

1954
Best play, John Patrick, *The Teahouse of the August Moon*
Best musical, Charles Lederer & Luther Davis, *Kismet*
Best composer, Alexander Borodin, *Kismet*
Best actress, musical, Dolores Gray, *Carnival in Flanders*
Best actor, musical, Alfred Drake, *Kismet*
Best actress, play, Audrey Hepburn, *Ondine*
Best actor, play, David Wayne, *The Teahouse of the August Moon*
Best supporting actress, musical, Gwen Verdon, *Can-Can*
Best supporting actor, musical, Harry Belafonte, *John Murray Anderson's Almanac*
Best supporting actress, play, Jo Van Fleet, *The Trip to Bountiful*
Best supporting actor, play, John Kerr, *Tea and Sympathy*
Best director, Alfred Lunt, *Ondine*

1955

Best play, Joseph Hayes, *The Desperate Hours*

Best musical, George Abbott & Richard Bissell, *The Pajama Game*

Best composer and lyricist, Richard Adler & Jerry Ross, *The Pajama Game*

Best actress, musical, Mary Martin, *Peter Pan*

Best actor, musical, Walter Slezak, *Fanny*

Best actress, play, Nancy Kelly, *The Bad Seed*

Best actor, play, Alfred Lunt, *Quadrille*

Best supporting actress, musical, Carol Haney, *The Pajama Game*

Best supporting actor, musical, Cyril Ritchard, *Peter Pan*

Best supporting actress, play, Patricia Jessell, *Witness for the Prosecution*

Best supporting actor, play, Francis L. Sullivan, *Witness for the Prosecution*

Best director, Robert Montgomery, *The Desperate Hours*

1956

Best play, Frances Goodrich & Albert Hackett, *The Diary of Anne Frank*

Best musical, George Abbott & Douglass Wallop, *Damn Yankees*

Best composer and lyricist, Richard Adler & Jerry Ross, *Damn Yankees*

Best actress, musical, Gwen Verdon, *Damn Yankees*

Best actor, musical, Ray Walston, *Damn Yankees*

Best actress, play, Julie Harris, *The Lark*

Best actor,play, Paul Muni, *Inherit the Wind*

Best supporting actress, musical, Lotte Lenya, *The Threepenny Opera*

Best supporting actor, musical, Russ Brown, *Damn Yankees*

Best supporting actress, play, Una Merkel, *The Ponder Heart*

Best supporting actor, play, Ed Begley, *Inherit the Wind*

Best director, Tyrone Guthrie, *The Matchmaker*

1957

Best play, Eugene O'Neill, *Long Day's Journey Into Night*

Best musical, Alan Jay Lerner, *My Fair Lady*

Best composer, Frederick Loewe, *My Fair Lady*

Best actress, musical, Judy Holliday, *Bells Are Ringing*

Best actor, musical, Rex Harrison, *My Fair Lady*

Best actress, play, Margaret Leighton, *Separate Tables*

Best actor, play, Fredric March, *Long Day's Journey Into Night*

Best supporting actress, musical, Edith Adams, *Li'l Abner*

Best supporting actor, musical, Sydney Chaplin, *Bells Are Ringing*

Best supporting actress, play, Peggy Cass, *Auntie Mame*

Best supporting actor, play, Frank Conroy, *The Potting Shed*

Best director, Moss Hart, *My Fair Lady*

1958

Best play, Dore Schary, *Sunrise at Campobello*

Best musical, Meredith Willson & Franklin Lacey, *The Music Man*

Best composer and lyricist, Meredith Willson, *The Music Man*

Best actress, musical, Thelma Ritter, *New Girl in Town;* Gwen Verdon, *New Girl in Town*

Best actor, musical, Robert Preston, *The Music Man*

Best actress, play, Helen Hayes, *Time Remembered*

Best actor, play, Ralph Bellamy, *Sunrise at Campobello*

Best supporting actress, musical, Barbara Cook, *The Music Man*

Best supporting actor, musical, David Burns, *The Music Man*

Best supporting actress, play, Anne Bancroft, *Two for the Seesaw*

Best supporting actor, play, Henry Jones, *Sunrise at Campobello*

Best director, play, Vincent J. Donehue, *Sunrise at Campobello*

1959

Best play, Archibald MacLeish, *J.B.*

Best musical, Herbert & Dorothy Fields, Sidney Sheldon & David Shaw, *Redhead*

Best composer, Albert Hague, *Redhead*

Best actress, musical, Gwen Verdon, *Redhead*

Best actor, musical, Richard Kiley, *Redhead*

Best actress, play, Gertrude Berg, *A Majority of One*

Best actor, play, Jason Robards, Jr., *The Disenchanted*

Best supporting actress, musical, Pat Stanley, *Goldilocks*; Cast, *La Plume de Ma Tante*

Best supporting actor, musical, Russell Nype, *Goldilocks*; Cast, *La Plume de Ma Tante*

Best supporting actress, play, Julie Newmar, *The Marriage-Go-Round*

Best supporting actor, play, Charlie Ruggles, *The Pleasure of His Company*

Best director, Elia Kazan, *J.B.*

1960

Best play, William Gibson, *The Miracle Worker*

Best musical, Jerome Weidman, & George Abbott, *Fiorello!*

Best composers, Jerry Bock, *Fiorello!*; Richard Rodgers, *The Sound of Music*

Best actress, musical, Mary Martin, *The Sound of Music*

Best actor, musical, Jackie Gleason, *Take Me Along*

Best actress, play, Anne Bancroft, *The Miracle Worker*

Best actor, play, Melvyn Douglas, *The Best Man*

Best supporting actress, musical, Patricia Neway, *The Sound of Music*

Best supporting actor, musical, Tom Bosley, *Fiorello!*

Best supporting actress, play, Anne Revere, *Toys in the Attic*

Best supporting actor, play, Roddy McDowall, *The Fighting Cock*

Best director, play, Arthur Penn, *The Miracle Worker*

Best director, musical, George Abbott, *Fiorello!*

1961

Best play, Jean Anouilh, *Becket*

Best musical, Michael Stewart, *Bye, Bye Birdie*

Best actress, musical, Elizabeth Seal, *Irma la Douce*

Best actor, musical, Richard Burton, *Camelot*

Best actress, play, Joan Plowright, *A Taste of Honey*

Best actor, play, Zero Mostel, *Rhinoceros*

Best supporting actress, musical, Tammy Grimes, *The Unsinkable Molly Brown*

Best supporting actor, musical, Dick Van Dyke, *Bye, Bye Birdie*

Best supporting actress, play, Colleen Dewhurst, *All the Way Home*

Best supporting actor, play, Martin Gabel, *Big Fish, Little Fish*

Best director, play, Sir John Gielgud, *Big Fish, Little Fish*

Best director, musical, Gower Champion, *Bye, Bye Birdie*

1962

Best play, Robert Bolt, *A Man for All Seasons*

Best musical, Abe Burrows, Jack Weinstock, Willie Gilbert, *How to Succeed in Business Without Really Trying*

Best composer, Richard Rodgers, *No Strings*

Best actress, musical, Anna Maria Alberghetti, *Carnival*; Diahann Carroll, *No Strings*

Best actor, musical, Robert Morse, *How to Succeed in Business Without Really Trying*

Best actress, play, Margaret Leighton, *Night of the Iguana*

Best actor, play, Paul Scofield, *A Man for All Seasons*

Best supporting actress, musical, Phyllis Newman, *Subways Are for Sleeping*

Best supporting actor, musical, Charles Nelson Reilly, *How to Succeed in Business Without Really Trying*

Best supporting actress, play, Elizabeth Ashley, *Take Her, She's Mine*

Best supporting actor, play, Walter Matthau, *A Shot in the Dark*

Best director, play, Noel William, *A Man for All Seasons*

Best director, musical, Abe Burrows, *How to Succeed in Business Without Really Trying*

1963
Best play, Edward Albee, *Who's Afraid of Virginia Woolf?*
Best musical, Burt Shevelove, Larry Gelbart, *A Funny Thing Happened on the Way to the Forum*
Best composer and lyricist, Lionel Bart, *Oliver!*
Best actress, musical, Vivien Leigh, *Tovarich*
Best actor, musical, Zero Mostel, *A Funny Thing Happened on the Way to the Forum*
Best actress, play, Uta Hagen, *Who's Afraid of Virginia Woolf?*
Best actor, play, Arthur Hill, *Who's Afraid of Virginia Woolf?*
Best supporting actress, musical, Anna Quayle, *Stop the World—I Want to Get Off*
Best supporting actor, musical, David Burns, *A Funny Thing Happened on the Way to the Forum*
Best supporting actress, play, Sandy Dennis, *A Thousand Clowns*
Best supporting actor, play, Alan Arkin, *Enter Laughing*
Best director, play, Alan Schneider, *Who's Afraid of Virginia Woolf?*
Best director, musical, George Abbott, *A Funny Thing Happened on the Way to the Forum*

1964
Best play, John Osborne, *Luther*
Best musical, Michael Stewart, *Hello, Dolly!*
Best composer and lyricist, Jerry Herman, *Hello, Dolly!*
Best actress, musical, Carol Channing, *Hello, Dolly!*
Best actor, musical, Bert Lahr, *Foxy*
Best actress, play, Sandy Dennis, *Any Wednesday*
Best actor, play, Alec Guinness, *Dylan*
Best supporting actress, musical, Tessie O'Shea, *The Girl Who Came to Supper*
Best supporting actor, musical, Jack Cassidy, *She Loves Me*

Best supporting actress, play, Barbara Loden, *After the Fall*
Best supporting actor, play, Hume Cronyn, *Hamlet*
Best director, play, Mike Nichols, *Barefoot in the Park*
Best director, musical, Gower Champion, *Hello, Dolly!*

1965
Best play, Frank Gilroy, *The Subject Was Roses*
Best musical, Joseph Stein, *Fiddler on the Roof*
Best composer and lyricist, Jerry Bock, and Sheldon Harnick, *Fiddler on the Roof*
Best actress, musical, Liza Minnelli, *Flora, the Red Menace*
Best actor, musical, Zero Mostel, *Fiddler on the Roof*
Best actress, play, Irene Worth, *Tiny Alice*
Best actor, play, Walter Matthau, *The Odd Couple*
Best supporting actress, musical, Maria Karnilova, *Fiddler on the Roof*
Best supporting actor, musical, Victor Spinetti, *Oh, What a Lovely War*
Best supporting actress, play, Alice Ghostley, *The Sign in Sidney Brustein's Window*
Best supporting actor, play, Jack Albertson, *The Subject Was Roses*
Best director, play, Mike Nichols, *Luv* and *The Odd Couple*
Best director, musical, Jerome Robbins, *Fiddler on the Roof*

1966
Best play, Peter Weiss, *Marat/Sade*
Best musical, Dale Wasserman, *Man of La Mancha*
Best composer and lyricist, Mitch Leigh, Joe Darion, *Man of La Mancha*
Best actress, musical, Angela Lansbury, *Mame*
Best actor, musical, Richard Kiley, *Man of La Mancha*
Best actress, play, Rosemary Harris, *The Lion in Winter*
Best actor, play, Hal Holbrook, *Mark Twain Tonight!*
Best supporting actress, musical, Beatrice Arthur, *Mame*

Best supporting actor, musical, Frankie Michaels, *Mame*

Best supporting actress, play, Zoe Caldwell, *Slapstick Tragedy*

Best supporting actor, play, Patrick Magee, *Marat/Sade*

Best director, play, Peter Brook, *Marat/Sade*

Best director, musical, Albert Marre, *Man of La Mancha*

1967

Best play, Harold Pinter, *The Homecoming*

Best musical, Joe Masteroff, *Cabaret*

Best composer and lyricist, John Kander, Fred Ebb, *Cabaret*

Best actress, musical, Barbara Harris, *The Apple Tree*

Best actor, musical, Robert Preston, *I Do! I Do!*

Best actress, play, Beryl Reid, *The Killing of Sister George*

Best actor, play, Paul Rogers, *The Homecoming*

Best supporting actress, musical, Peg Murray, *Cabaret*

Best supporting actor, musical, Joel Grey, *Cabaret*

Best supporting actress, play, Marian Seldes, *A Delicate Balance*

Best supporting actor, play, Ian Holm, *The Homecoming*

Best director, musical, Harold Prince, *Cabaret*

Best director, play, Peter Hall, *The Homecoming*

1968

Best play, Tom Stoppard, *Rosencrantz and Guildenstern Are Dead*

Best musical, Arthur Laurents, *Hallelujah, Baby!*

Best composer and lyricist, Jule Styne, Betty Comden & Adolph Green, *Hallelujah, Baby!*

Best actress, musical, Patricia Routledge, *Darling of the Day;* Leslie Uggams, *Hallelujah, Baby!*

Best actor, musical, Robert Goulet, *The Happy Time*

Best actress, play, Zoe Caldwell, *The Prime of Miss Jean Brodie*

Best actor, play, Martin Balsam, *You Know I Can't Hear You When the Water's Running*

Best supporting actress, musical, Lillian Hayman, *Hallelujah, Baby!*

Best supporting actor, musical, Hiram Sherman, *How Now, Dow Jones*

Best supporting actress, play, Zena Walker, *Joe Egg*

Best supporting actor play, James Patterson, *The Birthday Party*

Best director, musical, Gower Champion, *The Happy Time*

Best director, play, Mike Nichols, *Plaza Suite*

1969

Best play, Howard Sackler, *The Great White Hope*

Best musical, Peter Stone, *1776*

Best actress, musical, Angela Lansbury, *Dear World*

Best actor, musical, Jerry Orbach, *Promises, Promises*

Best actress, play, Julie Harris, *Forty Carats*

Best actor, play, James Earl Jones, *The Great White Hope*

Best supporting actress, musical, Marian Mercer, *Promises, Promises*

Best supporting actor, musical, Ronald Holgate, *1776*

Best supporting actress, play, Jane Alexander, *The Great White Hope*

Best supporting actor, play, Al Pacino, *Does a Tiger Wear A Necktie?*

Best director, musical, Peter Hunt, *1776*

Best director, play, Peter Dews, *Hadrian VII*

1970

Best play, Frank McMahon, *Borstal Boy*

Best musical, Betty Comden, Adolph Green, *Applause*

Best actress, musical, Lauren Bacall, *Applause*

Best actor, musical, Cleavon Little, *Purlie*

Best actress, play, Tammy Grimes, *Private Lives*

Best actor, play, Fritz Weaver, *Child's Play*

Best supporting actress, musical, Melba Moore, *Purlie*

Best supporting actor, musical, René Auberjonois, *Coco*

Best supporting actress, play, Blythe Danner, *Butterflies Are Free*
Best supporting actor, play, Ken Howard, *Child's Play*
Best director, musical, Ron Field, *Applause*
Best director, play, Joseph Hardy, *Child's Play*

1971

Best play, Anthony Shaffer, *Sleuth*
Best musical, George Furth, *Company*
Best lyrics, musical, Stephen Sondheim, *Company*
Best actress, musical Helen Gallagher, *No, No, Nanette*
Best actor, musical, Hal Linden, *The Rothschilds*
Best actress, play, Maureen Stapleton, *Gingerbread Lady*
Best actor, play, Brian Bedford, *The School for Wives*
Best supporting actress, musical, Patsy Kelly, *No, No, Nanette*
Best supporting actor, musical, Keene Curtis, *The Rothschilds*
Best supporting actress, play, Rae Allen, *And Miss Reardon Drinks a Little*
Best supporting actor, play, Paul Sand, *Story Theatre*
Best director, musical, Harold Prince, *Company*
Best director, play, Peter Brook, *A Midsummer Night's Dream*

1972

Best play, David Rabe, *Sticks and Bones*
Best musical, John Guare & Mel Shapiro, *Two Gentlemen of Verona*
Best book, musical, John Guare & Mel Shapiro, *Two Gentlemen of Verona*
Best score, musical, Stephen Sondheim, *Follies*
Best actress, musical, Alexis Smith, *Follies*
Best actor, musical, Phil Silvers, *A Funny Thing Happened on the Way to the Forum*
Best actress, play, Sada Thompson, *Twigs*
Best actor, play, Cliff Gorman, *Lenny*
Best supporting actress, musical, Linda Hopkins, *Inner City*
Best supporting actor, musical, Larry Blyden, *A Funny Thing Happened on the Way to the Forum*
Best supporting actress, play, Elizabeth Wilson, *Sticks and Bones*
Best supporting actor, play, Vincent Gardenia, *The Prisoner of Second Avenue*
Best director, musical, Harold Prince & Michael Bennett, *Follies*
Best director, play, Mike Nichols, *The Prisoner of Second Avenue*

1973

Best play, Jason Miller, *That Championship Season*
Best musical & book, Hugh Wheeler, *A Little Night Music*
Best score, musical, Stephen Sondheim, *A Little Night Music*
Best actress, musical, Glynis Johns, *A Little Night Music*
Best actor, musical, Ben Vereen, *Pippin*
Best actress, play, Julie Harris, *The Last of Mrs. Lincoln*
Best actor, play, Alan Bates, *Butley*
Best supporting actress, musical, Patricia Elliot, *A Little Night Music*
Best supporting actor, musical, George S. Irving, *Irene*
Best supporting actress, play, Leora Dana, *The Last of Mrs. Lincoln*
Best supporting actor, play, John Lithgow, *The Changing Room*
Best director, musical, Bob Fosse, *Pippin*
Best director, play, A. J. Antoon, *That Championship Season*

1974

Best play, Joseph A. Walker, *The River Niger*
Best musical, Robert Nemiroff, & Charlotte Zaltzberg, *Raisin*
Best book, musical, Hugh Wheeler, *Candide*
Best score, musical, Frederick Loewe, music, Alan Jay Lerner, lyrics, *Gigi*
Best actress, musical, Virginia Capers, *Raisin*
Best actor, musical, Christopher Plummer, *Cyrano*
Best actress, play, Colleen Dewhurst, *A Moon for the Misbegotten*
Best actor, play, Michael Moriarty, *Find Your Way Home*

Best supporting actress, musical, Janie
Sell, *Over Here!*
Best supporting actor, musical, Tommy
Tune, *Seesaw*
Best supporting actress, play, Frances
Sternhagen, *The Good Doctor*
Best supporting actor, play, Ed
Flanders, *A Moon for the
Misbegotten*
Best director, musical, Harold Prince,
Candide
Best director, play, José Quintero, *A
Moon for the Misbegotten*

1975
Best play, Peter Shaffer, *Equus*
Best musical, William F. Brown, *The
Wiz*
Best book, musical, James Lee Barrett,
Peter Udell & Philip Rose,
Shenandoah
Best score, musical, Charlie Smalls,
The Wiz
Best actress, musical, Angela
Lansbury, *Gypsy*
Best actor, musical, John Cullum,
Shenandoah
Best actress, play, Ellen Burstyn, *Same
Time, Next Year*
Best actor, play, John Kani, Winston
Ntshona, *Sizwe Banzi Is Dead* and
The Island
Best supporting actress, musical, Dee
Dee Bridgewater, *The Wiz*
Best supporting actor, musical, Ted
Ross, *The Wiz*
Best supporting actress, play, Rita
Moreno, *The Ritz*
Best supporting actor, play, Frank
Langella, *Seascape*
Best director, musical, Geoffrey
Holder, *The Wiz*
Best director, play, John Dexter, *Equus*

1976
Best play, Michael Cristofer, *The
Shadow Box*
Best musical & book, Thomas Meehan,
Annie
Best score, musical, Charles Strouse,
music, Martin Charnin lyrics, *Annie*
Best actress, musical, Dorothy Loudon,
Annie
Best actor, musical, Barry Bostwick,
Robber Bridegroom

Best actress, play, Julie Harris, *The
Belle of Amherst*
Best actor, play, Al Pacino, *The Basic
Training of Pavlo Hummel*
Best featured actress, musical, Delores
Hall, *Your Arms Too Short to Box
With God*
Best featured actor, musical, Lenny
Baker, *I Love My Wife*
Best featured actress, play, Tarzana
Beverly, *For Colored Girls Who
Have Considered Suicide/When the
Rainbow is Enuf*
Best featured actor, play, Jonathan
Pryce, *Comedians*
Best director, musical, Gene Saks, *I
Love My Wife*
Best director, play, Gordon Davidson,
The Shadow Box

WOMAN OF THE YEAR AWARD—
Hasty Pudding Theatricals, Harvard
University
To quote Hasty P.: "The Hasty Pudding Theatricals has long held womanhood and the performing arts in high esteem and it is honored to present this award in recognition of great artistic skill and feminine qualities." Forgive them. After all, Harvard was an all-male bastion. (How did Mamie Eisenhower sneak in there?)
Established 1951.

1951	Gertrude Lawrence
1952	Barbara Bel Geddes
1953	Mamie Eisenhower
1954	Shirley Booth
1955	Debbie Reynolds
1956	Peggy Ann Garner
1957	Carroll Baker
1958	Katharine Hepburn
1959	Joanne Woodward
1960	Carol Lawrence
1961	Jane Fonda
1962	Piper Laurie
1963	Shirley Maclaine
1964	Rosalind Russell
1965	Lee Remick
1966	Ethel Merman
1967	Lauren Bacall
1968	Angela Lansbury
1969	Carol Burnett
1970	Dionne Warwick

1971	Carol Channing	1974	Faye Dunaway
1972	Ruby Keeler	1975	Valerie Harper
1973	Liza Minnelli	1976	Bette Midler

MUSIC

See Achievement, Marjorie Peabody Waite Award

AMATEUR MUSIC FAMILY OF THE YEAR—American Music Conference

The criteria for this award are 1) the family must be amateur musicians, 2) a majority of the family must play an instrument, 3) the family must play at least four instruments, and 4) the family "must be active in the community through its music."
Established 1971.

1971
The William Boyer Family, Kirkwood, Mo.

1972
The Paul W. Rigsbee Family, Marion, Ohio

1973
The James Cunningham Family, Pittsburgh, Pa.
The Robert Knaff Family, Bethesda, Md.

1974
The Earl Sterns Family, Lock Haven, Pa.

1975
The Tom Wagner Family, Edison, Ohio

1976
The Norman Burdick Family, Williamstown, Mass.

ARTS AND LETTERS AWARD—The National Institute of Arts and Letters

To help composers who are not members of the institute continue their creative work; a prize of $3,000.
Established 1941.

1941   Frederick Woltmann

1942	Bernard Hermann
	Edward Margetson
	Robert McBride
1943	Paul Creston
	William Schuman
1944	Nicolai Berezowsky
	David Diamond
	Burrill Phillips
1945	William Bergsma
	Jerzy Fitelberg
	Gian Carlo Menotti
1946	Marc Blitzstein
	Norman Dello Joio
	Otto Luening
	Peter Mennin
	Robert Palmer
	Robert Ward
1947	Alexei Haieff
	Ulysses Kay
	Norman Lockwood
1948	Henry Cowell
	Lou Harrison
	Vincent Persichetti
1949	John Cage
	Louis Mennini
	Stefan Wolpe
1950	Elliott C. Carter
	Andrew Imbrie
	Ben Weber
1951	Alan Hovhaness
	Leon Kirchner
	Frank Wigglesworth
1952	Robert Kurka
	John Lessard
	Howard Swanson
1953	Peggy Glanville-Hicks
	Roger Goeb
	Nikolai Lopatnikoff
1954	Ingolf Dahl
	Colin McPhee
	Hugo Weisgall
1955	Henry Brant

The Amateur Music Family of 1976 was the Norman Burdick brood, (back row) Tracey, Todd, Scott, Shawn, and Norman; (front row) Ross, Betsey, and Liza.

	Irving Fine		Mel Powell
	Adolph Weiss		Russell Smith
1956	Ross Lee Finney		Vladimir Ussachevsky
	Robert Moevs	1964	Leslie Bassett
	Jacques Louis Monod		Gordon Binkerd
1957	Lukas Foss		Hall Overton
	Lee Hoiby		Julia Perry
	Seymour Shifrin	1965	Mario Davidovsky
1958	Arnold Franchetti		Gerald Humel
	Hunter Johnson		Earl Kim
	Billy Jim Layton		Harvey Sollberger
1959	Milton Babbitt	1966	Walter Aschaffenburg
	John Bavicchi		Richard Hoffman
	Mark Bucci		John MacIvor Perkins
	Noel Lee		Ralph Shapey
1960	Arthur Berger	1967	George H. Crumb
	Easley Blackwood		Donald Martino
	Salvatore Martirano		Julian Orbon
	Gunther Schuller		Charles Wuorinen
1961	Ramiro Cortes	1968	David Del Tredici
	Halsey Stevens		William Flanagan
	Lester Trimble		Ned Rorem
	Yehudi Wyner		Francis Thorne
1962	Ernst Bacon	1969	Michael Brozen
	John LaMontaine		Jacob R. Druckman
	George Rochberg		Nicolas Roussakis
	William Sydeman		Claudio Spies
1963	Chou Wen-chung	1970	William Albright

Arnold Elston
Morton Feldman
George Bach Wilson
1971 Sydney Hodkinson
Fred Lerdahl
Roger Reynolds
Loren Rush
1972 Earle Brown
John Eaton
John Harbison
William Overton Smith
1973 John C. Heiss
Betsy Jolas
Barbara Kolb
Curry Tison Street
1974 Richard Felciano
Raoul Pleskow
Phillip Rhodes
Olly W. Wilson
1975 Marc-Antonio Consoli
Charles Dodge
Daniel Perlongo
Christian Wolff
1976 Dominick Argento
Robert Helps
Robert Hall Lewis
Richard Wernick

AWAPA AWARD—The Academy of Wind and Percussion Arts and the National Band Association

The "Oscar" of the band world, this honor is given to someone who has contributed "to the furthering of the excellence of bands and of band music."

1961 William D. Revelli
1962 Karl L. King
1965 Harold D. Bachman
Glenn Cliffe Bainum
1968 Merle Evans
1969 Harry Guggenheim
Al G. Wright
Paul V. Yoder
1970 Toshio Akiyama
1971 Richard Franko Goldman
1972 Richard M. Nixon
John Paynter
1973 Sir Vivian Dunn
Traugott Rohner
1974 Jan Molenaar
1975 Frederick Fennell

COUNTRY MUSIC ASSOCIATION AWARDS—Country Music Association

The association gives awards in ten categories. "Entertainer of the Year" goes for "the act displaying greatest competence in all aspects of the entertainment field . . . not only for recorded performance, but also for the in-person performance, staging, public acceptance, attitude, leadership, and overall contribution to the Country Music image."

The "Single of the Year" cannot be a track selected off an album, but must be a song that was actually released as a single. Voting on "Album of the Year" takes in account the artist's performance, musical background, engineering, packaging, design, and liner notes. "Song of the Year" is awarded to the songwriter. "Female Vocalist of the Year" and "Male Vocalist of the Year" is based on recorded and in-person performances. To win the "Vocal Group of the Year," the group must have two or more people who do not usually perform as singles. On the other hand, "Vocal Duo of the Year" are two performers who generally perform alone. The remaining categories are for an instrumental group and an instrumentalist.

Established 1967 (Vocal Duo was added in 1970.)

EXTERTAINER OF THE YEAR

1967 Eddy Arnold
1968 Glen Campbell
1969 Johnny Cash
1970 Merle Haggard
1971 Charley Pride
1972 Loretta Lynn
1973 Roy Clark
1974 Charlie Rich
1975 John Denver
1976 Mel Tillis

SINGLE OF THE YEAR

1967 "There Goes My Everything," Jack Greene (Decca)

The Country Music Association award winners for 1976. The blonde in the middle is none other than Dolly Parton.

1968	"Harper Valley P.T.A.," Jeannie C. Riley (Plantation)		*Prison,* Johnny Cash (Columbia)
1969	"A Boy Named Sue," Johnny Cash (Columbia)	1969	*Johnny Cash at San Quentin Prison,* Johnny Cash (Columbia)
1970	"Okie From Muskogee," Merle Haggard (Capitol)	1970	*Okie From Muskogee,* Merle Haggard (Capitol)
1971	"Help Me Make It Through the Night," Sammi Smith (Mega)	1971	*I Won't Mention It Again,* Ray Price (Columbia)
1972	"Happiest Girl in the Whole U.S.A.," Donna Fargo (Dot)	1972	*Let Me Tell You About a Song,* Merle Haggard (Capitol)
1973	"Behind Closed Doors," Charlie Rich (Epic)	1973	*Behind Closed Doors,* Charlie Rich (Epic)
1974	"Country Bumpkin," Cal Smith (MCA)	1974	*A Very Special Love Song,* Charlie Rich (Epic)
1975	"Before the Next Teardrop Falls," Freddy Fender (ABC/Dot)	1975	*A Legend In My Time,* Ronnie Milsap (RCA)
1976	"Good Hearted Woman," Willie Nelson and Waylon Jennings	1976	*Wanted—The Outlaws,* Willie Nelson, Jessi Colter, and Thompall

ALBUM OF THE YEAR

SONG OF THE YEAR

1967	*There Goes My Everything,* Jack Greene, (Decca)	1967	"There Goes My Everything," Dallas Frazier
1968	*Johnny Cash at Folsom*	1968	"Honey," Bobby Russell

1969	"Carroll County Accident," Bob Ferguson
1970	"Sunday Morning Coming Down," Kris Kristofferson
1971	"Easy Loving," Freddie Hart
1972	"Easy Loving," Freddie Hart
1973	"Behind Closed Doors," Kenny O'Dell
1974	"Country Bumpkin," Don Wayne
1975	"Back Home Again," John Denver
1976	"Rhinestone Cowboy," Larry Weiss

FEMALE VOCALIST OF THE YEAR

1967	Loretta Lynn
1968	Tammy Wynette
1969	Tammy Wynette
1970	Tammy Wynette
1971	Lynn Anderson
1972	Loretta Lynn
1973	Loretta Lynn
1974	Olivia Newton-John
1975	Dolly Parton
1976	Dolly Parton

MALE VOCALIST OF THE YEAR

1967	Jack Greene
1968	Glen Campbell
1969	Johnny Cash
1970	Merle Haggard
1971	Charley Pride
1972	Charley Pride
1973	Charlie Rich
1974	Ronnie Milsap
1975	Waylon Jennings
1976	Ronnie Milsap

VOCAL GROUP OF THE YEAR

1967	The Stoneman Family
1968	Porter Wagoner and Dolly Parton
1969	Johnny Cash and June Carter
1970	The Glaser Brothers
1971	The Osborne Brothers
1972	The Statler Brothers
1973	The Statler Brothers
1974	The Statler Brothers
1975	The Statler Brothers
1976	The Statler Brothers

VOCAL DUO OF THE YEAR

1970	Porter Wagoner and Dolly Parton
1971	Porter Wagoner and Dolly Parton
1972	Conway Twitty and Loretta Lynn
1973	Conway Twitty and Loretta Lynn
1974	Conway Twitty and Loretta Lynn
1975	Conway Twitty and Loretta Lynn
1976	Waylon Jennings and Willie Nelson

INSTRUMENTAL GROUP OR BAND OF THE YEAR

1967	The Buckaroos
1968	The Buckaroos
1969	Danny Davis and the Nashville Brass
1970	Danny Davis and the Nashville Brass
1971	Danny Davis and the Nashville Brass
1972	Danny Davis and the Nashville Brass
1973	Danny Davis and the Nashville Brass
1974	Danny Davis and the Nashville Brass
1975	Roy Clark and Buck Trent
1976	Roy Clark and Buck Trent

INSTRUMENTALIST OF THE YEAR

1967	Chet Atkins
1968	Chet Atkins
1969	Chet Atkins
1970	Jerry Reed
1971	Jerry Reed
1972	Charlie McCoy
1973	Charlie McCoy
1974	Don Rich
1975	Johnny Gimble
1976	Hargus "Pig" Robbins

See Cowboys and Indians, Western Heritage Awards, The National Cowboy Hall of Fame and Western Heritage Center

GOLD BATON AWARD—The American Symphony Orchestra League
For service to music and the arts.
Established 1948.

1948   Ernest La Prade, NBC Orchestras of the Nations" radio program
1952   John B. Ford, president of the Detroit Sympathy Orchestra
1956   Mrs. Marjorie Merriweather Post, vice president of the Washington National Symphony
1958   The Study Committee on Orchestra Legal Documents: Samuel Rosenbaum, Henry B. Cabot, Dudley T. Easby, Jr., Charles Garside, and Henry Allen Moe
1959   Leonard Bernstein, conductor, New York Philharmonic
1960   Association of Junior Leagues of America, Charles Farnsley, Former mayor of Louisville
1961   Arthur Judson, Former manager, New York Philharmonic
1962   The Women's Associations of Symphony Orchestras
1963   John D. Rockefeller, 3rd Officers and directors of Lincoln Center for the Performing Arts
1964   Dr. Richard Lert, music director, Pasadena Symphony Paul Mellon, A. W. Mellon Educational and Charitable Trusts, Richard King Mellon Charitable Trusts, Howard Heinz Endowment
1965   American Federation of Musicians
1966   The Ford Foundation
1967   American Telephone and Telegraph Co.
1968   Leopold Stokowski Mrs. Jouett Shouse
1969   The New York State Council on the Arts
1970   Mrs. Helen M. Thompson
1971   Martha Baird Rockefeller
1972   Amyas Ames
1973   Danny Kaye
1974   Nancy Hanks and the

National Council on the Arts
1975   John S. Edwards, manager of the Chicago Symphony
1976   Arthur Fiedler
1977   Avery Fisher Alcoa Foundation

GOLD RECORD AWARDS—Recording Industry Association of America
Easy award to win—just sell one million or more copies of a single record or a half a million albums and it's all yours. An (s) denotes a single.
Established 1958.

1958   "Catch A Falling Star" (s), Perry Como
       Oklahoma, Gordon MacRae
       "He's Got the Whole World In His Hands" (s), Laurie London
       "Hard Headed Woman" (s), Elvis Presley
       "Patricia" (s), Perez Prado
1959   "Tom Dooley" (s), Kingston Trio
       Hymns, Ernie Ford
       Johnny's Greatest Hits, Johnny Mathis
       Music Man, Original Cast
       Sing Along with Mitch, Mitch Miller
       South Pacific, Rodgers and Hammerstein
       Peter Gunn, Henry Mancini
1960   *Student Prince*, Mario Lanza
       60 Years of Music, Honoring 30 Great Artists
       Elvis, Elvis Presley
       Pat's Great Hits, Pat Boone
       Kingston Trio at Large, Kingston Trio
       Kingston Trio, Kingston Trio
       More Sing Along with Mitch, Mitch Miller
       Heavenly, Johnny Mathis
       Warm, Johnny Mathis
       Love Is the Thing, Nat King Cole
       Here We Go Again, Kingston Trio
       From the Hungry i, Kingston Trio
       Sound of Music, Original Cast

Singing the blues sold a lot of records for Diana Ross, both as a solo and as a Supreme. (Memory Shop)

Merry Christmas, Johnny Mathis
Christmas Sing Along, Mitch Miller
Still More! Sing Along, Mitch Miller

1961   "Calcutta" (s), Lawrence Welk
Calcutta Album, Lawrence Welk
Come Dance With Me, Frank Sinatra
Sold Out, Kingston Trio
Glenn Miller Story, Glenn Miller Orchestra
Christmas Carols, Mantovani
Theatre Land, Mantovani
Film Encores Vol. I, Mantovani
Gems Forever, Mantovani
Strauss Waltzes, Mantovani
Spirituals, Ernie Ford
Elvis' Golden Records, Elvis Presley
Belafonte at Carnegie Hall, Harry Belafonte
Tchaikovsky Concerto, Van Cliburn
Big Bad John (s), Jimmy Dean

Encore—Golden Hits, The Platters
Blue Hawaii, Elvis Presley

1962   "The Lion Sleeps" (s), The Tokens
Holiday Sing Along with Mitch, Mitch Miller
Party Sing Along with Mitch, Mitch Miller
More Johnny's Greatest Hits, Johnny Mathis
West Side Story, Original Cast
Camelot, Original Cast
Flower Drum Song, Original Cast
Theme from a Summer Place, Billy Vaughn
Blue Hawaii, Billy Vaughn
Sail Along Silvery Moon, Billy Vaughn
Bob Newhart Button Down Mind, Bob Newhart
Saturday Night Sing Along With Mitch, Mitch Miller
Memories Sing Along with Mitch, Mitch Miller
Sentimental Sing Along with Mitch, Mitch Miller

Star Carol, Ernie Ford
Nearer the Cross, Ernie Ford
"Can't Help Falling in Love"
(s), Elvis Presley
*Frank Sinatra Sings for Only
the Lonely,* Frank Sinatra
Nice 'N' Easy, Frank Sinatra
Songs for Swingin' Lovers,
Frank Sinatra
String Along, Kingston Trio
*Music, Martinis, and
Memories,* Jackie Gleason
Music for Lovers Only, Jackie
Gleason
Judy at Carnegie Hall, Judy
Garland
Happy Times Sing Along,
Mitch Miller
Memories Are Made of This,
Ray Conniff
Concert in Rhythm, Ray
Conniff
'S Marvelous, Ray Conniff
"I Can't Stop Loving You"
(s), Ray Charles
*Modern Sounds in Country
and Western Music,* Ray
Charles
"Roses Are Red" (s), Bobby
Vinton
"Theme from a Summer
Place" (s), Percy Faith
Breakfast at Tiffany's, Henry
Mancini
This is Sinatra, Frank Sinatra
Bouquet, Percy Faith Strings
So Much In Love, Ray
Conniff
Faithfully, Johnny Mathis
Swing Softly, Johnny Mathis
Open Fire, Two Guitars,
Johnny Mathis
Peter, Paul, and Mary, Peter,
Paul, and Mary
My Son The Folk Singer,
Allan Sherman
The First Family, Vaughn
Meader

1963   *West Side Story,* Original
Soundtrack
Glorious Sound of Christmas,
Eugene Ormandy-
Philadelphia Orchestra
1812 Overture-Tschaikovsky,
Antal Dorati and the
Minneapolis Symphony

"Hey Paula" (s), Paul and
Paula
Exodus, Original Soundtrack
Calypso, Harry Belafonte
G. I. Blues, Elvis Presley
*Season's Greetings from Perry
Como,* Perry Como
VIVA, Percy Faith
The Music Man, Soundtrack
Time Out, Dave Brubeck
Quartet
*I Left My Heart in San
Francisco,* Tony Bennett
Elvis' Christmas Album,
Elvis Presley
Girls, Girls, Girls, Elvis
Presley
*Belafonte Returns to Carnegie
Hall,* Harry Belafonte
Belafonte, Harry Belafonte
Jump-Up-Calypso, Harry
Belafonte
Moving, Peter, Paul, and
Mary
Exodus, Mantovani
Days of Wine and Roses,
Andy Williams
*Moon River and Other Great
Movie Themes,* Andy
Williams
Handel's Messiah, Eugene
Ormandy—Philadelphia
Orchestra
Christmas With Conniff, Ray
Conniff
The Lord's Prayer, Mormon
Tabernacle Choir
Porgy and Bess, Original
Soundtrack
Folk Song Sing Along, Mitch
Miller
In the Wind, Peter, Paul, and
Mary
"Sugar Shack" (s), Jim Gilmer
and the Fireballs
Singing Nun, Soeur Sourire

1964   *My Fair Lady,* Original Cast
*John Fitzgerald Kennedy—A
Memorial Album*
Carousel, Motion Picture
Soundtrack
The King and I, Motion
Picture Soundtrack
Ramblin' Rose, Nat King Cole
Meet The Beatles, The
Beatles

"I Want to Hold Your Hand" (s), The Beatles
"Can't Buy Me Love" (s), The Beatles
Honey In the Horn, Al Hirt
The Beatles' Second Album, The Beatles
The Second Barbra Streisand Album, Barbara Streisand
Hello, Dolly!, Original Cast
Hello, Dolly!, Louis Armstrong
The Wonderful World of Andy Williams, Andy Williams
"Everybody Loves Somebody" (s), Dean Martin
Christmas Hymns and Carols, Robert Shaw
Victory At Sea, Volume I, Robert Russell Bennett
"Rag Doll" (s), The Four Seasons
Something New, The Beatles
"A Hard Day's Night" (s), The Beatles
The Best of the Kingston Trio, Kingston Trio
Unforgettable, Nat King Cole
Funny Gril, Original Cast
Ramblin, New Christy Minstrels
The Barbra Streisand Album, Barbra Streisand
"Oh, Pretty Woman" (s), Roy Orbinson
Johnny Horton's Greatest Hits, Johnny Horton
Cotton Candy, Al Hirt
The Andy Williams Christmas Album, Andy Williams
Call Me Irresponsible, Andy Williams
My Fair Lady, Movie Soundtrack
"I Feel Fine" (s), The Beatles
Beatles '65, The Beatles
The Beatles Story, The Beatles
Mary Poppins, Movie Soundtrack

1965 *Glad All Over*, The Dave Clark Five
Peter, Paul and Mary in Concert, Peter, Paul and Mary

Everybody Loves Somebody, Dean Martin
Wonderful of Golden Hits, Andre Kostelanetz
Barbra Streisand/The Third Album, Barbra Streisand
Ring of Fire, Johnny Cash
Beach Boys in Concert, The Beach Boys
All Summer Long, The Beach Boys
Sugar Lips, Al Hirt
"Downtown" (s), Petula Clark
People, Barbra Streisand
The Sound of Music, Movie Soundtrack
Trini Lopez at PJ's, Trini Lopez
"King of the Road" (s), Roger Miller
Getz/Gilberto, Stan Getz
"Mrs. Brown You've Got a Lovely Daughter" (s), Herman's Hermits
Beatles VI, The Beatles
"(I Can't Get No) Satisfaction" (s), The Rolling Stones
Dear Heart, Andy Williams
"Wooly Bully" (s), Sam the Sham and the Pharaohs
Help!, The Beatles
"I'm Henry VIII, I Am" (s), Herman's Hermits
Introducing Herman's Hermits, Herman's Hermits
Herman's Hermits on Tour, Herman's Hermits
More Encore of Golden Hits, The Platters
Return of Roger Miller, Roger Miller
"Help!" (s), The Beatles
"Eight Days a Week" (s), The Beatles
"I Got You Babe" (s), Sonny and Cher
Great Songs From My Fair Lady, Andy Williams
Gunfire Ballads & Trail Songs, Marty Robbins
Look at Us, Sonny and Cher
The Beach Boys Today, The Beach Boys
The Pink Panther, Henry Mancini

Out of Our Heads, The Rolling Stones
"Yesterday" (s), The Beatles
Fiddler on the Roof, Original Cast
Surfer Girl, The Beach Boys
Surfin' USA, The Beach Boys
Sinatra's Sinatra, Frank Sinatra
Welcome to the LBJ Ranch
My Name is Barbra, Barbra Streisand
The Door Is Still Open to My Heart, Dean Martin
"A Lover's Concerto" (s), The Toys
Going Places, Herb Alpert and the Tijuana Brass
Whipped Cream & Other Delights, Herb Alpert and the Tijuana Brass
Rubber Soul, The Beatles

1966   *My Name Is Barbra, Two,* Barbra Streisand
"We Can Work It Out" (s), The Beatles
The Best of Herman's Hermits, Herman's Hermits
December's Children, Rolling Stones
Joan Baez, Vol. 2, Joan Baez
Joan Baez, Joan Baez
September of My Years, Frank Sinatra
Joan Baez in Concert, Joan Baez
A Man and His Music, Frank Sinatra
Summer Days, Beach Boys
Golden Hits, Roger Miller
"Ballad of the Green Berets" (s), SSGT. Barry Sadler
Ballads of the Green Berets, SSGT. Barry Sadler
"Sounds of Silence" (s), Simon & Garfunkel
"These Boots Are Made for Walkin'!", (s), Nancy Sinatra
"Lightnin' Strikes" (s), Lou Christie
Roy Orbison's Greatest Hits, Roy Orbison
"No Where Man" (s), The Beatles
Living Language Spanish

Living Language French
Color Me Barbra, Barbra Streisand
I'm The One Who Loves You, Dean Martin
Big Hits (High Tide and Green Grass), Rolling Stones
Oliver, Original Cast
"Soul and Inspiration" (s), Righteous Brothers
South of the Border, Herb Alpert's Tijuana Brass
The Lonely Bull, Herb Alpert and the Tijuana Brass
What Now My Love, Herb Alpert and the Tijuana Brass
Herb Alpert's Tijuana Brass Volume 2, Herb Alpert's Tijuana Brass
My World, Eddy Arnold
South Pacific, Original Cast
"California Dreamin' " (s), The Mamas and the Papas
"Monday, Monday" (s), The Mamas and the Papas
If You Can Believe Your Eyes and Ears, The Mamas and the Papas
Yesterday and Today, The Beatles
"Paperback Writer" (s), The Beatles
"When a Man Loves a Woman" (s), Percy Sledge
The Best of Jim Reeves, Jim Reeves
The Best of the Animals, The Animals
Dang Me, Roger Miller
Gold Vault of Hits, Four Seasons
Aftermath, Rolling Stones
"Lil' Red Riding Hood" (s), Sam the Sham and The Pharaohs
Dr. Zhivago, Soundtrack
Think Ethnic, Smothers Brothers
Strangers in the Night, Frank Sinatra
Revolver, The Beatles
"Hanky Panky" (s), Tommy James and the Shondells
The Dave Clark Five's Greatest Hits, Dave Clark
"Yellow Submarine" (s), The Beatles

"Summer in the City" (s), The Lovin' Spoonful

Somewhere My Love, Ray Conniff

The Shadow of Your Smile, Andy Williams

"Sunny" (s), Bobby Hebb

The Best of Al Hirt, Al Hirt

I Started Out as a Child, Bill Cosby

Wonderfulness, Bill Cosby

Why Is There Air?, Bill Cosby

Bill Cosby Is a Very Funny Fellow, Right?, Bill Cosby

"Cherish" (s), Association

Jeanette MacDonald and Nelson Eddy Favorites, Jeanette MacDonald and Nelson Eddy

Perry Como Sings Merry Christmas Music, Perry Como

"Last Train to Clarksville" (s), The Monkees

The Monkees, The Monkees

Elvis Presley, Elvis Presley

Elvis' Gold Records, Vol. 2, Elvis Presley

Elvis' Gold Records, Vol. 3, Elvis Presley

Dean Martin Sings Again, Dean Martin

Boots, Nancy Sinatra

"96 Tears" (s), ? (Question Mark) and the Mysterians

"Soul and Inspiration, Righteous Brothers

"I'm a Believer" (s), The Monkees

"Winchester Cathedral" (s), New Vaudeville Band

The Mamas and The Papas, The Mamas and the Papas

Bobby Vinton's Greatest Hits, Bobby Vinton

"Battle of New Orleans" (s), Johnny Horton

"Good Vibrations" (s), Beach Boys

Little Deuce Coupe, Beach Boys

Shut Down—Vol. 2, Beach Boys

Winchester Cathedral, New Vaudeville Band

1967

Spanish Eyes, Al Martino

Just Like Us, Paul Revere and the Raiders

More of the Monkees, The Monkees

"Snoopy vs. The Red Baron" (s), The Guardsmen

"Mellow Yellow" (s), Donovan

S. R. O., Herb Alpert and the Tijuana Brass

Got Love If You Want It, The Rolling Stones

Till, Roger Williams

Songs of the Fabulous Fifties Part 1, Roger Williams

Songs of the Fabulous Fifties Part 2, Roger Williams

Roger Williams' Greatest Hits, Roger WIlliams

Yakety Sax, Boots Randolph

That's Life, Frank Sinatra

Lou Rawls Live!, Lou Rawls

The Two Sides of the Smothers Brothers, Smothers Brothers

Between the Buttons, The Rolling Stones

"A Little Bit Me, a Little Bit You" (s), The Monkees

Midnight Ride, Paul Revere and the Raiders

"Penny Lane" (s), The Beatles

"Sugartown" (s), Nancy Sinatra

Thoroughly Modern Millie, Original Soundtrack

The Best of Mancini, Henry Mancini

An Evening with Belafonte, Harry Belafonte

Best of the Beach Boys, Beach Boys

"There's a Kind of Hush (All Over the Land)" (s), Herman's Hermits

Winchester Cathedral, Lawrence Welk

Spirit of '67, Paul Revere and the Raiders

"Somethin' Stupid" (s), Frank and Nancy Sinatra

The Mamas & the Papas Deliver, The Mamas and the Papas

Born Free, Roger Williams
"This Diamond Ring" (s), Gary Lewis
"Ruby Tuesday" (s), The Rolling Stones
"Happy Together" (s), The Turtles
Mame, Original Cast
Headquarters, The Monkees
My Cup Runneth Over, Ed Ames
"Respect" (s), Aretha Franklin
"Green Onions" (s), Booker T. and the MG's
"Stranger on the Shore" (s), Mr. Acker Bilk
Stranger on the Shore, Mr. Acker Bilk
I Never Loved a Man the Way I Love You, Aretha Franklin
"I Never Loved a Man the Way I Love You" (s), Aretha Franklin
"Groovin" (s), The Young Rascals
Sergeant Pepper's Lonely Hearts Club Band, The Beatles
"Sweet Soul Music (s), Arthur Conley
Man of La Mancha, Original Cast
Revenge, Bill Cosby
Parsley, Sage, Rosemary & Thyme, Simon and Garfunkel
Born Free, Andy Williams
The Best of the Lovin' Spoonful, The Lovin' Spoonful
Themes for Young Lovers, Percy Faith and His Orchestra
I Walk the Line, Johnny Cash
"Pleasant Valley Sunday" (s), The Monkees
"Windy" (s), The Association
Surrealistic Pillow, Jefferson Airplane
"Little Bit O'Soul" (s), Music Explosion
"Georgy Girl" (s), The Seekers
Flowers, The Rolling Stones
A Man and a Woman, Soundtrack
Ebb Tide, Earl Grant
Blue Midnight, Bert Kaempfert
Sounds Like, Herb Alpert and the Tijuana Brass
Sergio Mendes and Brasil '66, Sergio Mendes and Brasil '66
Sounds of Silence, Simon and Garfunkel
Paul Revere & The Raiders Greatest Hits, Paul Revere and the Raiders
Blonde on Blonde, Bob Dylan
Highway 61, Bob Dylan
Bringing It All Back Home, Bob Dylan
"Baby I Love You" (s), Aretha Franklin
"Ode to Billie Joe" (s), Bobbie Gentry
"All You Need Is Love" (s), The Beatles
The Doors, The Doors
"Light My Fire" (s), The Doors
"Can't Take My Eyes Off You" (s), Frankie Valli
2nd Vault of Golden Hits, The Four Seasons
"The Letter" (s), The Box Tops
Ode to Billie Joe, Bobbie Gentry
"Come Back When You Grow Up" (s), Bobby Vee and The Strangers
Tony Bennett's Greatest Hits Volume III, Tony Bennett
"To Sir with Love" (s), Lulu
Pisces, Aquarius, Capricorn and Jones Ltd., The Monkees
"Daydream Believer" (s), The Monkees
"Soul Man" (s), Sam and Dave
Sinatra at the Sands, Frank Sinatra
Along Comes the Association, The Association
"Never My Love" (s), The Association
Their Satanic Majesty's Request, Rolling Stones
Release Me, Engelbert Humperdinck
Herb Alpert's Ninth, Herb

Alpert and the Tijuana Brass
Magical Mystery Tour, The
Beatles
"Hello Goodbye" (s), The
Beatles
Merry Christmas to All, Ray
Conniff
"Incense and Peppermints"
(s), Strawberry Alarm Clock
*The Rain, the Park and Other
Things,* The Cowsills
*The Button-Down Mind
Strikes Back,* Bob Newhart
Insight Out, The Association

1968 *Jim Nabors Sings,* Jim Nabors
Bob Dylan's Greatest Hits,
Bob Dylan
"Chain of Fools" (s), Aretha
Franklin
Strange Days, The Doors
"Skinny Legs and All" (s), Joe
Tex
"Judy in Disguise with
Glasses" (s), John Fred and
the Playboys
"Bend Me, Shape Me" (s),
The American Breed
Dream With Dean, Dean
Martin
Guantanamera, The
Sandpipers
"Woman, Woman" (s), The
Union Gap
*Farewell to the First Golden
Era,* The Mamas and the
Papas
"Green Tambourine" (s), The
Lemon Pipers
I Say a Little Prayer, Dionne
Warwick
How Great Thou Art, Elvis
Presley
"Valleri" (s), The Monkees
Distant Drums, Jim Reeves
"Love Is Blue" (s), Paul
Mauriat
Blooming Hits, Paul Mauriat
and Orchestra
"Simon Says" (s), 1910
Fruitgum Company
Best of Buck Owens, Buck
Owens
"(Sittin' On) The Dock of the
Bay" (s), Otis Redding
Doctor Dolittle, Original
Soundtrack

The Byrds' Greatest Hits, The
Byrds
Welcome to My World, Dean
Martin
Houston, Dean Martin
Are You Experienced, Jimi
Hendrix
John Wesley Harding, Bob
Dylan
The Graduate, Soundtrack
The Best of Eddy Arnold,
Eddy Arnold
The Great Caruso, Mario
Lanza
"Since You've Been Gone"
(s), Aretha Franklin
"Honey" (s), Bobby
Goldsboro
"Young Girl" (s), Union Gap
*Modern Sounds in Country
and Western Music, Vol. 2,*
Ray Charles
Greatest Hits, Ray Charles
"Lady Madonna" (s), The
Beatles
Loving You, Elvis Presley
Turtles' Greatest Hits, The
Turtles
*The Birds, the Bees and the
Monkees,* The Monkees
Gigi, Soundtrack
Bookends, Simon and
Garfunkel
*Somewhere There's a
Someone,* Dean Martin
"Cry Like a Baby" (s), Box
Tops
Persuasive Percussion, Enoch
Light
*Songs I Sing on the Jackie
Gleason Show,* Frank
Fontaine
Love, Andy, Andy Williams
"Cowboys to Girls" (s), The
Intruders
Doris Day's Greatest Hits,
Doris Day
Disraeli Gears, Cream
"Tighten Up" (s), Archie Bell
and the Drells
Merry Christmas, Andy
Williams
"Mrs. Robinson" (s), Simon
and Garfunkel
"Yummy, Yummy, Yummy"
(s), Ohio Express

"Beautiful Morning" (s), The Rascals
Glenn Miller and His Orchestra, Glenn Miller
To Russell, My Brother, Whom I Slept With, Bill Cosby
"Grazing in the Grass" (s), Hugh Masekela
"Lady Willpower" (s), Gary Puckett and the Union Gap
The Beat of the Brass, Herb Alpert and the Tijuana Brass
"This Guy's in Love with You" (s), Herb Alpert
"Think" (s), Aretha Franklin
Wheels of Fire, Cream
Groovin', The Rascals
Vanilla Fudge, Vanilla Fudge
"The Horse" (s), Cliff Nobles and Company
Collections, The Rascals
Somewhere My Love, Roger Williams
Waiting for the Sun, The Doors
The Good, the Bad, and the Ugly, Original Soundtrack
A Man and His Soul, Ray Charles
Lady Soul, Aretha Franklin
"People Got to Be Free" (s), The Rascals
"Harper Valley PTA" (s), Jeannie C. Riley
"Hello, I Love You" (s), The Doors
Look Around, Sergio Mendes and Brasil '66
The Young Rascals, The Rascals
Time Peace—The Rascals Greatest Hits, The Rascals
"Slip Away" (s), Clarence Carter
"Hey Jude" (s), The Beatles
Camelot, Original Soundtrack
"Stoned Soul Picnic" (s), The 5th Dimension
"Born to Be Wild" (s), Steppenwolf
"1, 2, 3, Red Light" (s), 1910 Fruitgum Company
"Turn Around, Look at Me" (s), The Vogues

"Sunshine of Your Love" (s), Cream
Feliciano, Jose Feliciano
Axis: Bold as Love, Jimi Hendrix
"I Say a Little Prayer" (s), Aretha Franklin
Cheap Thrills, Janis Joplin with Big Brother and the Holding Company
By the Time I Get to Phoenix, Glen Campbell
Gentle on My Mind, Glen Campbell
My Love Forgive Me, Robert Goulet
Johnny Cash at Folsom Prison, Johnny Cash
Honey, Andy Williams
"Little Green Apples" (s), O. C. Smith
Purple Onion, Smothers Brothers
"Who's Making Love" (s), Johnnie Taylor
Wichita Lineman, Glen Campbell
Electric Ladyland, Jimi Hendrix
"Those Were the Days" (s), Mary Hopkin
The Kinks Greatest Hits, The Kinks
Honey, Bobby Goldsboro
Dean Martin Christmas Album, Dean Martin
Steppenwolf, Steppenwolf
"Girl Watcher" (s), The O'Kaysions
"Midnight Confession" (s), Grassroots
"Fire" (s), Crazy World of Arthur Brown
Aretha Now, Aretha Franklin
In-A-Gadda-Da-Vida, Iron Butterfly
Fresh Cream, Cream
The Time Has Come, Chambers Brothers
Walt Disney Presents The Jungle Book, Original Soundtrack
The Beatles, The Beatles
The Christmas Album, Herb Alpert and the Tijuana Brass
"I Love How You Love Me"

(s), Bobby Vinton
"Over You" (s), The Union Gap
Harper Valley PTA, Jeannie C. Riley
Funny Girl, Soundtrack
Beggars Banquet, The Rolling Stones
The Sea, The San Sebastian Strings

1969   *Walt Disney Presents The Story of Mary Poppins*, Storyteller LP
"Chewy, Chewy" (s), The Ohio Express
Hey Little One, Glen Campbell
"Abraham, Martin & John" (s), Dion
"See Saw" (s), Aretha Franklin
The Christmas Song, Nat King Cole
The Lettermen!!!. . and "Live", The Lettermen
"Soulful Strut" (s), Young Holt Limited
Wildflowers, Judy Collins
"Wichita Lineman" (s), Glen Campbell
Album 1700, Peter, Paul, and Mary
Gentry/Campbell, Bobbie Gentry and Glen Campbell
Dean Martin's Greatest Hits, Volume 1, Dean Martin
Yellow Submarine, The Beatles
Steppenwolf The Second, Steppenwolf
"Touch Me" (s), The Doors
"Everday People" (s), Sly and the Family Stone
Who Will Answer?", Ed Ames
Boots With Strings, Boots Randolph
"The Worst That Can Happen" (s), The Brooklyn Bridge
Dionne Warwick's Greatest Hits, Dionne Warwick
"Can I Change My Mind" (s), Tyrone Davis
"Hooked on a Feeling" (s), B. J. Thomas
"Too Weak to Fight" (s),

Clarence Carter
"Stormy" (s), The Classics IV
A Man Without Love, Engelbert Humperdinck
The Last Waltz, Engelbert Humperdinck
The Association's Greatest Hits, The Association
Build Me Up Buttercup" (s), The Foundations
Wednesday Morning 3 A.M., Simon & Garfunkel
Wonderland By Night, Bert Kaempfert
Bert Kaempfert's Greeatest Hits, Bert Kaempfert
"Dizzy" (s), Tommy Roe
Drummer Boy, Harry Simeone
200 MPH, Bill Cosby
Hair, Original Cast
It Must Be Him, Ray Conniff
Young Girl, Union Gap
"Magic Carpet Ride" (s), Steppenwolf
"Sheila" (s), Tommy Roe
"Sweet Pea" (s), Tommy Roe
"Indian Giver" (s), 1910 Fruitgum Company
His Hand in Mine, Elvis Presley
"It's Your Thing" (s) Isley Brothers
Blood, Sweat and Tears, Blood, Sweat and Tears
"Time of the Season" (s), The Zombies
Galveston, Glen Campbell
Freedom Suite, The Rascals
Goodbye, Cream
Donovan's Greatest Hits, Donovan
"Hair" (s), The Cowsills
2001: A Space Odyssey, Soundtrack
Soulin,' Lou Rawls
"Only The Strong Survive" (s), Jerry Butler
"Aquarius/Let The Sunshine In" (s), 5th Dimension
Best of the Lettermen, The Lettermen
Nashville Skyline, Bob Dylan
Fever Zone, Tom Jones
Help Yourself, Tom Jones
"This Magic Moment" (s), Jay and the Americans

"Get Back" (s), The Beatles with Billy Preston
Equinox, Sergio Mendes and Brasil '66
A Day in the Life, Wes Montgomery
Fool on the Hill, Sergio Mendes and Brasil '66
The Righteous Brothers Greatest Hits, The Righteous Brothers
"Oh Happy Day" (s), Edwin Hawkins' Singers
This Is Tom Jones, Tom Jones
H. Williams's Greatest Hits, H. Williams
The Very Best of Connie Francis, Connie Francis
How the West Was Won, Soundtrack
Your Cheatin' Heart, Hank Williams
"You Make Me So Very Happy" (s), Blood, Sweat, and Tears
The Best of Herman's Hermits Vol. II, Herman's Hermits
The Stripper and Other Fun Songs for the Family, David Rose and Orchestra
There's a Kind of Hush All Over the World, Herman's Hermits
"Chokin' Kind" (s), Joe Simon
"Gitarzan" (s), Roy Stevens
"Grazin' in the Grass" (s), Friends of Distinction
"In The Ghetto" (s), Elvis Presley
"Love Theme from Romeo and Juliet" (s), Mancini
"These Eyes" (s), The Guess Who
Romeo and Juliet, Soundtrack
Tom Jones Live! Tom Jones
"In the Year 2525" (s), Zager and Evans
The Age of Aquarius, 5th Dimension
"Love Can Make You Happy" (s), Mercy
"Ballad of John and Yoko" (s), The Beatles

Elvis TV Special, Elvis Presley
Ball, Iron Butterfly
Led Zeppelin, Led Zeppelin
"Spinning Wheel" (s), Blood, Sweat, and Tears
"One" (s), Three Dog Night
Johnny Cash's Greatest Hits, Johnny Cash
"Color Him Father" (s), The Winstons
Oliver, Soundtrack
The Soft Parade, The Doors
Johnny Cash at San Quentin, Johnny Cash
"A Boy Named Sue" (s), Johnny Cash
Switched on Bach, Walter Carlos
Three Dog Night, Three Dog Night
"Sweet Caroline" (s), Neil Diamond
Tommy, The Who
Blind Faith, Blind Faith
Happy Heart, Andy Williams
"Honky Tonk Women" (s), The Rolling Stones
Gentle on My Mind, Dean Martin
"Sugar, Sugar" (s), The Archies
Through the Past, Darkly, The Rolling Stones
The Good, the Bad, and the Ugly, Hugo Montenegro
A Warm Shade of Ivory, Henry Mancini
Glen Campbell—'Live', Glen Campbell
Alice's Restaurant, Arlo Guthrie
Realization, Johnny Rivers
"Put a Little Love In Your Heart" (s), Jackie DeShannon DeShannon
Golden Greats, Gary Lewis
Crosby, Stills, and Nash, Crosby, Stills, and Nash
"I'll Never Fall In Love Again" (s), Tom Jones
"Little Woman" (s), Bobby Sherman
"Get Together" (s), Youngbloods
Who Knows Where the Time

Goes, Judy Collins
"Jean" (s), Oliver
Golden Instrumentals, Billy
Vaughn and Orchestra
"Galveston" (s), Glen
Campbell
"Baby, I Love You" (s), Andy
Kim
Jimi Hendrix Smash Hits,
Jimi Hendrix
Abbey Road, The Beatles
"Something" (s), The Beatles
"Tom Jones—Live at Las
Vegas, Tom Jones
"Laughing" (s), The Guess
Who
"Suspicious Minds" (s), Elvis
Presley
*Rudolph, the Red Nosed
Reindeer,* Gene Autry
Best of Cream, Cream
Best of the Bee Gees, The Bee
Gees
Led Zeppelin II, Led
Zeppelin
Green Green Grass, Tom
Jones
Let It Bleed, Rolling Stones
The Band, The Band
Santana, Santana
*The Child Is Father to the
Man,* Blood, Sweet, and Tears
Kozmic Blues, Janis Joplin
Stand! Sly and the Family Stone
"Wedding Bell Blues" (s),
The 5th Dimension
"Na Na Hey Hey Kiss Him
Goodbye" (s), Steam
"Take a Letter Maria" (s),
R. B. Greaves
Cycles, Frank Sinatra
Suitable for Framing, Three
Dog Night
Hot Buttered Soul, Isaac
Hayes
"Going in Circles" (s),
Friends of Distinction
From Vegas to Memphis,
Elvis Presley
"Smile a Little Smile for Me"
(s), Flying Machine
Chicago Transit Authority,
Chicago Transit Authority
"Raindrops Keep Falling on
My Head" (s), B. J. Thomas
"Back Field in Motion" (s),

1970

Mel and Tim
Buddy Holly Story, Buddy
Holly and The Crickets
Honey, Ray Conniff
"Jet Plane" (s), Peter, Paul,
and Mary
"That'll Be the Day" (s),
Buddy Holly and The
Crickets
"Holly Holy" (s), Neil
Diamond
Engelbert, Engelbert
Humperdinck
Engelbert Humperdinck,
Engelbert Humperdinck
"And When I Die" (s), Blood,
Sweat, and Tears
Captured Live At the Forum,
Three Dog Night
Easy Rider, Soundtrack
"Jam Up and Jelly Tight" (s),
Tommy Roe
The Best of Charley Pride,
Charley Pride
"La La La (If I Had You)" (s),
Bobby Sherman
"Don't Cry Daddy" (s), Elvis
Presley
Volunteers, Jefferson Airplane
Crown of Creation, Jefferson
Airplane
"Venus" (s), The Shocking
Blue
From Elvis in Memphis,
Elvis Presley
Hello, I'm Johnny Cash,
Johnny Cash
See What Tomorrow Brings,
Peter, Paul, and Mary
"Jingle Jangle" (s), The
Archies
Alive Alive-o! Feliciano
Bridge Over Troubled Water,
Simon and Garfunkel
"Thank You (Falettinme Be
Mice Elf Agin)" (s), Sly &
The Family Stone
Bobby Sherman, Bobby
Sherman
"Without Love" (s), Tom
Jones
Mantovani's Golden Hits,
Mantovani
Try A Little Kindness, Glen
Campbell
Get Together, Andy Williams

Morrison Hotel, The Doors
"Bridge Over Troubled
Water" (s), Simon &
Garfunkel
Goin' Out of My Head, The
Lettermen
Hey Jude, The Beatles
My Way, Frank Sinatra
*The Plastic Ono Band—Live
Peace in Toronto,* The Plastic
Ono Band
"Hey There Lonely Girl" (s),
Eddie Holman
"Let It Be" (s), The Beatles
"Didn't I (Blow Your Mind
This Time)" (s), The
Delfonics
Monster, Steppenwolf
"Rainy Night in Georgia" (s),
Brook Benton
Feliciano/10 to 23, Feliciano
Deja Vu, Crosby, Stills, Nash,
and Young
Up-Up and Away, 5th
Dimension
Warm, Herb Alpbert and the
Tijuana Brass
"The Rapper" (s), The
Jaggerz
"Easy Come, Easy Go" (s),
Bobby Sherman
*A Gift from a Flower to a
Garden,* Donovan
*Don't Come Home a Drinkin'
(With Lovin' On Your Mind),*
Loretta Lynn
"Whole Lotta Love" (s), Led
Zeppelin
Chicago, Chicago
"Arizona" (s), Mark Lindsay
Tammy's Greatest Hits,
Tammy Wynette
Claudine, Claudine Longet
Joe Cocker, Joe Cocker
"Love Grows (Where My
Rosemary Goes)" (s), Edison
Lighthouse
"Spirit in the Sky" (s),
Norman Greenbaum
Tom, Tom Jones
A Song Will Rise, Peter, Paul
and Mary
McCartney, Paul McCartney
"House of the Rising Son" (s),
Frijid Pink
Midnight Cowboy,
Soundtrack

"Turn Back the Hands of
Time" (s), Tyrone Davis
"Give Me Just A Little More
Time" (s), Chairmen of the
Board
*The 5th Dimension—Greatest
Hits,* 5th Dimension
*Butch Cassidy and the
Sundance Kid,* Burt
Bacharach
*The Ventures Play Telstar,
The Lonely Bull and Others,*
The Ventures
Golden Greats, The Ventures
American Woman, The Guess
Who
"American Woman" (s), The
Guess Who
Let It Be, The Beatles
Woodstock
Band of Gypsys, Jimi
Hendrix
"Love on a Two-Way Street"
(s), The Moments
Hurt So Bad, The Lettermen
"Cecilia" (s), Simon and
Garfunkel
Self Portrait, Bob Dyland
"Which Way You Goin'
Billy" (s), Poppy Family
"Everything is Beautiful" (s),
Ray Stevens
Grand Funk, Grand Funk
Railroad
Here Comes Bobby, Bobby
Sherman
Blood, Sweat and Tears 3,
Blood, Sweat, and Tears
"Hitchin' a Ride" (s), Vanity
Fair
"Mama Told Me (Not To
Come)" (s), Three Dog Night
Live Steppenwolf,
Steppenwolf
Golden Grass, Grass Roots
It Ain't Easy, Three Dog
Night
*Raindrops Keep Fallin' On
My Head,* B. J. Thomas
*To Our Children's Children's,
Children,* Moody Blue
"Band of Gold" (s), Freda
Payne
*The Devil Made Me Buy This
Dress,* Flip Wilson

Absolutely Live, The Doors
"Ride Captain Ride" (s),
Blues Image
Live at Leeds, The Who
Here Where There Is Love,
Dionne Warwick
Valley of the Dolls, Dionne
Warwick
"Make It With You" (s), Bread
"O-O-H Child" (s), The
Stairsteps
"(They Long To Be) Close To
You" (s), The Carpenters
Closer to Home, Grand Funk
Railroad
"The Wonder of You" (s),
Elvis Presley
Mountain Climbing,
Climbing
"In the Summertime" (s),
Mungo Jerry
Mad Dogs & Englishmen, Joe
Cocker
"Julie, Do Ya Love Me" (s),
Bobby Sherman
"Patches" (s), Clarence Carter
"Spill the Wine" (s), Eric
Burdon and War
"Candida" (s), Dawn
Days of Future Passed,
Moody Blues
*On The Threshold of a
Dream,* Moody Blues
Okie From Muskogee, Merle
Haggard and The Strangers
Led Zeppelin III, Led
Zeppelin
Edizione D'Oro, Four
Seasons
On Time, Grand Funk
Railroad
*Everybody Knows This Is
Nowhere,* Neil Young With
Crazy Horse
*Best of Peter, Paul and Mary
(Ten Years Together),* Peter,
Paul and Mary
Sweet Baby James, James
Taylor
Stage Fright, The Band
Paint Your Wagon,
Soundtrack
Abraxas, Santana
"Don't Play That Song" (s),
Aretha Franklin
Sesame Street, Original Cast

"Cracklin' Rosie" (s), Neil
Diamond
With Love, Bobby, Bobby
Sherman
Get Yer Ya-Ya's Out!, Rolling
Stones
A Question of Balance, The
Moody Blues
*Jimi Hendrix/Otis Redding at
Monterey,* Monterey Pop
Soundtrack
"I Think I love You" (s), The
Partridge Family
After The Gold Rush, Neil
Young
"Groovy Situation" (s), Gene
Chandler
Make It Easy On Yourself,
Burt Bacharach
Close to You, The Carpenters
"We've Only Just Begun" (s),
The Carpenters
Reach Out, Burt Bacharach
*With a Little Help from My
Friends,* Joe Cocker
Gold, Neil Diamond
Benefit, Jethro Tull
Merry Christmas, Bing
Crosby
Share the Land, The Guess
Who
"Snowbird" (s), Anne Murray
*Sly and the Family Stone's
Greatest Hits,* Sly and the
Family Stone
Nancy and Lee, Nancy
Sinatra and Lee Hazlewood
Frank Sinatra's Greatest Hits,
Frank Sinatra
Live Album, Grand Funk
Railroad
"Somebody Has Been
Sleeping In My Bed" (s), 100
Proof
Stephen Stills, Stephen Stills
*Jim Nabors' Christmas
Album,* Jim Nabors
Super Session, Bloomfield/
Kooper/Stills
Touching You, Touching Me,
Neil Diamond
In Search of the Lost Chord,
The Moody Blues
"One Less Bell To Answer"
(s), 5th Dimension
New Morning, Bob Dylan

"Instant Karma" (s), John Ono Lennon
"My Sweet Lord" (s), George Harrison
"Down on the Corner" (s), Creedence Clearwater Revival
"Travelin' Band" (s), Creedence Clearwater Revival
"Bad Moon Rising" (s), Creedance Clearwater Revival
"Up Around the Bend" (s) Creedence Clearwater Revival
Cosmo's Factory, Creedence Clearwater Revival
Willy and The Poor Boys, Creedence Clearwater Revival
Green River, Creedence Clearwater Revival
Bayou Country, Creedence Clearwater Revival
Creedence Clearwater Revival, Creedence Clearwater Revival
"Lookin' Out My Back Door" (s), Creedence Clearwater Revival
All Things Must Pass, George Harrison
"Knock Three Times" (s), Dawn
The Partrdige Family Album, The Partridge Family
Pendulum, Creedence Clearwater Revival
The Freewheelin' Bob Dylan, Bob Dylan
John Barleycorn Must Die, Traffic
We Made It Happen, Engelbert Humperdinck
Jesus Christ Superstar, Various Artists
Ladies of the Canyon, Joni Mitchell
Dean Martin's Greatest Hits Vol. II, Dean Martin
Portrait, 5th Dimension
In My Life, Judy Collins
1971 "Groove Me" (s), King Floyd
"Gypsy Woman" (s), Brian Hyland
I Who Have Nothing, Tom Jones

Taproot Manuscript, Neil Diamond
Plastic Ono Band, John Lennon
Love Story, Soundtrack
"Rose Garden" (s), Lynn Anderson
"One Bad Apple" (s), The Osmonds
Chicago III, Chicago
The Worst of Jefferson Airplane, Jefferson Airplane
Elton John, Elton John
On Stage February 1970, Elvis Presley
Charley Pride's 10th Album, Charley Pride
Just Plain Charley, Charley Pride
Charley Pride in Person, Charley Pride
Pearl, Janis Joplin
For The Good Times, Ray Price
"Precious, Precious" (s), Jackie Moore
"Doesn't Somebody Want to be Wanted" (s), The Partridge Family
The Fightin' Side of Me, Merle Haggard and the Strangers
"Have You Ever Seen the Rain" (s), Creedence Clearwater Revival
Gary Puckett and the Union Gap's Greatest Hits, Gary Puckett and the Union Gap
"Don't Let the Green Grass Fool You" (s), Wilson Pickett
Tumbleweed Connection, Elton John
Love Story, Andy Williams
Rose Garden, Lynn Anderson
Up to Date, Partridge Family
"She's a Lady" (s), Tom Jones
"Amos Moses" (s), Jerry Reed
"Lonely Days" (s), Bee Gees
The Cry of Love, Jimi Hendrix
Woodstock II, Woodstock
Friends, Elton John
Whales and Nightingales, Judy Collins
If I Could Only Remember

My Name, David Crosby
"Joy to the World" (s), Three Dog Night
Naturally, Three Dog Night
Steppenwolf 7, Steppenwolf
Golden Bisquits, Three Dog Night
Steppenwolf Gold, Steppenwolf
Greatest Hits, Herb Alpert and the Tijuana Brass
"For All We Know" (s), The Carpenters
Four Way Street, Crosby, Stills, Nash and Young
"The Battle Hymn of Lt. Calley" (s), Terry Nelson
"Help Me Make It Through The Night" (s), Sammi Smith
Stoney End, Barbra Streisand
Survival, Grand Funk Railroad
Mud Slide Slim and the Blue Horizon, James Taylor
"Put Your Hand in the Hand" (s) Ocean
Greatest Hits, Barbra Streisand
"Proud Mary" (s), Ike & Tina Turner
Paranoid, Black Sabbath
Sticky Fingers, Rolling Stones
Tea For the Tillerman, Cat Stevens
"Bridge Over Troubled Water" (s) Aretha Franklin
Sweetheart, Englebert Humperdinck
"Want Ads" (s), Honey Cone
Nantucket Sleigh Ride, Mountain
Love's Lines Angles and Rhymes, 5th Dimension
"Stay Awhile" (s), The Bells
Carpenters, The Carpenters
Tapestry, Carole King
Ram, Paul and Linda McCartney
Black Sabbath, Black Sabbath
If You Could Read My Mind, Gordon Lightfoot
The Best of the Guess Who, The Guess Who
Hawaii 5-0, The Ventures
"Don't Knock My Love" (s),
Wilson Pickett
"Indian Reservation" (s), The Raiders
Aqualung, Jethro Tull
Aretha Franklin at the Fillmore West, Aretha Franklin
Burt Bacharach, Burt Bacharach
"Rainy Days and Mondays" (s), The Carpenters
"It's Too Late" (s), Carole King
L. A. Woman, The Doors
Every Picture Tells a Story, Rod Stewart
"Treat Her Like a Lady" (s), Cornelius Brothers & Sister Rose
"It Don't Come Easy" (s), Ringo Starr
Emerson, Lake, and Palmer, Emerson, Lake and Palmer
B.S. & T. 4, Blood, Sweat & Tears
"Don't Pull Your Love" (s), Hamilton, Joe Frank and Reynolds
"Take Me Home, Country Roads" (s), John Denver
Layla, Derek and The Dominos
Chapter Two, Roberta Flack
Stephen Stills 2, Stephen Stills
Songs for Beginners, Graham Nash
Tarkus, Emerson, Lake, and Palmer
"How Can You Mend A Broken Heart" (s), Bee Gees
"Spanish Harlem" (s), Aretha Franklin
"Bring The Boys Home" (s), Freda Payne
"Sweet and Innocent" (s), Donny Osmond
"Signs" (s), Five Man Electrical Band
Bark, Jefferson Airplane
Every Good Boy Deserves Favour, Moody Blues
"You've Got a Friend" (s), James Taylor
"She's Not Just Another Woman" (s), The 8th Day

Osmonds, The Osmond Brothers

Andy Williams' Greatest Hits, Andy Williams

Poems, Prayers and Promises, John Denver

Who's Next, The Who

"Uncle Albert/Admiral Halsey" (s), Paul and Linda McCartney

"Ain't No Sunshine" (s), Bill Withers

"Stick-Up" (s), Honey Cone

Master of Reality, Black Sabbath

Sound Magazine, Partridge Family

Imagine, John Lennon

"Maggie May" (s), Rod Stewart

Santana, Santana

Harmony, Three Dog Night

"Go Away Little Girl" (s), Donny Osmond

"Superstar" (s), The Carpenters

Fiddler on the Roof, Soundtrack

Teaser and The Firecat, Cat Stevens

"The Night They Drove Old Dixie Down" (s), Joan Baez

Allman Brothers Band at Fillmore East, The Allman Brothers

James Gang Rides Again, James Gang

"Tired of Being Alone" (s), Al Green

"Thin Line Between Love and Hate" (s), The Persuaders

A Partridge Family Christmas Card, Partridge Family

There's a Riot Goin' On, Sly and the Family Stone

Live At Carnegie Hall, Chicago

Blue, Joni Mitchell

Grateful Dead, Grateful Dead

Led Zeppelin, Led Zeppelin

"Yo-Yo" (s), The Osmonds

"Gypsys, Tramps, and Thieves" (s), Cher

E Pluribus Funk, Grand Funk Railroad

"Easy Loving" (s), Freddie Hart

"Family Affair" (s), Sly and the Family Stone

"Trapped by a Thing Called Love" (s), Denise LaSalle

Barbra Joan Streisand, Barbra Streisand

Rainbow Bridge, Jimi Hendrix

"Scorpio" (s), Dennis Coffey and the Detroit Guitar Band

A Space in Time, Ten Years After

Carole King Music, Carole King

Candles in the Rain, Melanie

All in the Family, Original Cast

"Rock Steady" (s), Aretha Franklin

The Donny Osmond Album, Donny Osmond

"Cherish" (s), David Cassidy

"Brand New Key" (s), Melanie

Live, 5th Dimension

The World of Johnny Cash, Johnny Cash

Dionne Warwicke Story—Decade of Gold, Dionne Warwicke

"An Old Fashioned Love Song" (s), Three Dog Night

"Clean Up Woman" (s), Betty Wright

1972 "You Are Everything" (s), The Stylistics

"American Pie" (s), Don McLean

American Pie, Don McLean

Bob Dylan's Greatest Hits, Vol. II, Bob Dylan

The Concert of Bangla Desh, George Harrison and Friends

Aerie, John Denver

"Drowning in the Sea of Love" (s), Joe Simon

"Let's Stay Together" (s), Al Green

"Baby I'm A Want You" (s), Bread

She's a Lady, Tom Jones

Wildlife, Wings

Meaty, Beaty, Big and Bouncy, The Who

"Sunshine" (s), Jonathan Edwards
Stones, Neil Diamond
Loretta Lynn's Greatest Hits, Loretta Lynn
Homemade, The Osmonds
Hot Rocks, Rolling Stones
To You with Love, Donny Osmond
"I'd Like to Teach the World to Sing" (s), The New Seekers
Killer, Alice Cooper
Blessed Are, Joan Baez
Any Day Now, Joan Baez
Leon Russell and The Shelter People, Leon Russell
A Nod is as Good as a Wink . . . to a Blind Horse, Faces
Low Spark of High Heeled Boys, Traffic
Charley Pride Sings Heart Songs, Charley Pride
Harvest, Neil Young
Madman Across the Water, Elton John
"Precious and Few" (s), Climax
Rockin' the Fillmore, Humble Pie
"Hurting Each Other" (s), The Carpenters
Paul Simon, Paul Simon
Nilsson Schmilsson, Nilsson
"Without You" (s), Nilsson
"Day After Day" (s), Badfinger
"Kiss an Angel Good Mornin'!" (s), Charley Pride
Baby I'm A Want You, Bread
America, America
Fragile, Yes
"The Lion Sleeps Tonight" (s), Robert John
"I Gotcha" (s), Joe Tex
"Jungle Fever" (s), The Chakachas
"Puppy Love" (s), Donny Osmond
"A Horse with No Name" (s), America
"Down by the Lazy River" (s), The Osmonds
Tom Jones Live At Caesars Palace, Tom Jones
Another Time, Another Place, Engelbert Humperdinck

"Ain't Understanding Mellow" (s), Jerry Butler and Brenda Lee Eager
Eat a Peach, The Allman Brothers Band
Cher, Cher Bono
"Betcha by Golly, Wow" (s), The Stylistics
Pictures at an Exhibition, Emerson, Lake, and Palmer
"The First Time Ever I Saw Your Face" (s), Roberta Flack
"Day Dreaming" (s), Aretha Franklin
First Take, Roberta Flack
Quiet Fire, Roberta Flack
Young, Gifted and Black, Aretha Franklin
"Heart of Gold" (s), Neil Young
Let's Stay Together, Al Green
"Look What You've Done For Me" (s), Al Green
All I Ever Need Is You, Sonny and Cher
Blood, Sweat and Tears
Greatest Hits, Blood, Sweat and Tears
Glen Campbell's Greatest Hits, Glen Campbell
Hello Darlin', Conway Twitty
Partridge Family Shopping Bag, Partridge Family
Thick as a Brick, Jethro Tull
Hendrix in the West, Jimi Hendrix
Phase III, The Osmonds
Exile on Main Street, Rolling Stones
Graham Nash and David Crosby, Graham Nash and David Crosby
Manassas, Stephen Stills
Mark, Don, and Mel, Grand Funk Railroad
Mardi Gras, Creedence Clearwater Revival
Gather Me, Melanie
"Lean on Me" (s), Bill Withers
13, The Doors
"Nice to Be with You" (s), Gallery
Joplin in Concert, Janis Joplin
"Outa-Space" (s), Billy Preston

All Day Music, War
"Slippin' Into Darkness" (s), War
Live in Concert, James Gang
"Troglodyte" (s), The Jimmy Castor Bunch
Cherish, David Cassidy
Simon and Garfunkel's Greatest Hits, Simon and Garfunkel
School's Out, Alice Cooper
A Song for You, The Carpenters
Thirds, James Gang
"Last Night I Didn't Get to Sleep At All" (s), 5th Dimension
History of Eric Clapton, Eric Clapton
Amazing Grace, Aretha Franklin
Roberta Flack and Donny Hathaway, Roberta Flack and Donny Hathaway
"Daddy Don't You Walk So Fast" (s), Wayne Newton
"Walking in the Rain with the One I Love" (s), Love Unlimited
Honky Chateau, Elton John
Sonny and Cher Live, Sonny and Cher
"Song Sung Blue" (s), Neil Diamond
Seven Separate Fools, Three Dog Night
Never a Dull Moment, Rod Stewart
Cheech and Chong, Cheech and Chong
"Hey Girl" (s), Donny Osmond
Chicago V, Chicago
"Sylvia's Mother" (s), Dr. Hook and the Medicine Show
"How Do You Do" (s), Mouth and MacNeal
"Too Late to Turn Back Now" (s), Cornelius Brothers and Sister Rose
Elvis as Recorded at Madison Square Garden, Elvis Presley
Carlos Santana and Buddy Miles 'Live', Carlos Santana and Buddy Miles
"Brandy" (s), Looking Glass

"Alone Again (Naturally)" (s), Gilbert O'Sullivan
Their Sixteen Greatest Hits, The Grassroots
Donny Hathaway Live, Donny Hathaway
Bib Bambu, Cheech and Chong
"Candy Man" (s), Sammy Davis, Jr.
"The Happiest Girl in the Whole U.S.A." (s), Donna Fargo
Procol Harum 'Live' in Concert with the Edmonton Symphony Orchestra, Procol Harum
"Power of Love" (s), Joe Simon
"I'm Still in Love with You" (s), Al Green
Love Theme from The Godfather, Andy Williams
Moods, Neil Diamond
"Back Stabbers" (s), The O'Jays
"Where Is the Love" (s), Roberta Flack and Donny Hathaway
Trilogy, Emerson, Lake and Palmer
Still Bill, Bill Withers
Super Fly (Original Motion Picture Soundtrack), Curtis Mayfield
Smokin', Humble Pie
What You Hear Is What You Get, Ike and Tina Turner
"Long Cool Woman (In A Black Dress)" (s), The Hollies
"Ding-A-Ling" (s), Chuck Berry
Carney, Leon Russell
"Get On the Good Foot" (s), James Brown
"Everybody Plays the Fool" (s), The Main Ingredient
"Baby Don't Get Hooked on Me" (s), Mac Davis
FM & AM, George Carlin
"Black and White" (s), Three Dog Night
Phoenix, Grand Funk Railroad
Catch Bull at Four, Cat Stevens

"Use Me" (s), Bill Withers
The Best of Charley Pride, Charley Pride
Easy Loving, Freddie Hart
The London Chuck Berry Session, Chuck Berry
"Burning Love" (s), Elvis Presley
Demons and Wizards, Uriah Heep
"I'll Be Around" (s), The Spinners
Close to the Edge, Yes
"Freddie's Dead (Theme from 'Super Fly')" (s), Curtis Mayfield
Rhymes and Reasons, Carole King
The Best of Merle Haggard, Merle Haggard
Rock of Ages, The Band
Machine Head, Deep Purple
"Go All the Way" (s), Raspberries
Black Sabbath—Vol. IV, Black Sabbath
Love It to Death, Alice Cooper
Stand Up, Jethro Tull
Living in the Past, Jethro Tull
Caravanserai, Santana
"Saturday in the Park" (s), Chicago
"I Can See Clearly Now" (s), Johnny Nash
Guitar Man, Bread
"If You Don't Know Me by Now" (s), Harold Melvin and The Blue Notes
Seventh Sojourn, Moody Blues
"Garden Party" (s), Rick Nelson
It's a Beautiful Day, It's A Beautiful Day
"I'd Love You To Want Me" (s), Lobo
I'm Still in Love With You, Al Green
"Mr. and Mrs. Jones" (s), Billy Paul
Chilling, Thrilling Sounds of The Haunted House, Soundtrack
No Secrets, Carly Simon

Greatest Hits on Earth, 5th Dimension
Godspell, Original cast
"I'm Stone in Love With You" (s), The Stylistics
The Partridge Family at Home with Their Greatest Hits, Partridge Family
Tommy, London Symphony Orchestra and Chamber Choir with Guest Soloists
The World Is a Ghetto, War
Summer Breeze, Seals & Crofts
Europe '72, Grateful Dead
"You Ought to Be with Me" (s), Al Green
One Man Dog, James Taylor
Homecoming, America
"Nights in White Satin" (s), Moody Blues
"I Am Woman" (s), Helen Reddy
Summer of '42, Peter Nero
An Anthology, Duane Allman
Manna, Bread
On the Waters, Bread
For the Roses, Joni Mitchell
Hot August Night, Neil Diamond
Portrait of Donny, Donny Osmond
The Osmonds 'Live', The Osmonds
Son of Schmilsson, Nilsson
Rocky Mountain High, John Denver

1973 *Long John Silver,* Jefferson Airplane
"Funny Face" (s), Donna Fargo
"You're So Vain" (s), Carly Simon
"It Never Rains in Southern California" (s), Albert Hammond
More Hot Rocks (Big Hits and Fazed Cookies), Rolling Stones
"Super Fly" (s), Curtis Mayfield
The Magician's Birthday, Uriah Heep
Crazy Horses, The Osmonds
Too Young, Donny Osmond
Creedence Gold, Creedence

Clearwater Revival
"Rockin' Pneumonia and the Boogie Flu" (s), Johnny Rivers
The Happiest Girl in the Whole U. S. A., Donna Fargo
Loggins & Messina, Loggins and Messina
"Crocodile Rock" (s), Elton John
"Love Jones" (s), Brighter Side of Darkness
"Love Train" (s), The O'Jays
360 Degrees of Billy Paul, Billy Paul
Don't Shoot Me I'm Only the Piano Player, Elton John
World Wide 50 Gold Award Hits, Vol. 1, Elvis Presley
Elvis—Aloha from Hawaii via Satellite, Elvis Presley
Live Concert at the Forum, Barbra Streisand
"Could It Be I'm Falling in Love" (s), The Spinners
"Harry Hippie" (s), Bobby Womack & Peace
The Stylistics, The Stylistics
"Killing Me Softly with His Song" (s), Roberta Flack
"The World Is a Ghetto" (s), War
"Cisco Kid" (s), War
Around the World with Three Dog Night, Three Dog Night
I Am Woman, Helen Reddy
Shoot Out at the Fantasy Factory, Traffic
"Your Mama Don't Dance" (s), Loggins & Messina
"Dueling Banjos" (s), Eric Weissberg
Bueling Banjos, Soundtrack from *Deliverance* as performed by Eric Weissberg & Steve Mandel
Baby Don't Get Hooked on Me, Mac Davis
Wattstax—The Living Word, Various Artists
"Last Song" (s), Edward Bear
"Clair" (s), Gilbert O'Sullivan
In Concert, Derek and the Dominos
Billion Dollar Babies, Alice Cooper

Kenny Rogers and the First Edition Greatest Hits, Kenny Rogers and the First Edition
"Ain't No Woman" (s), Four Tops
"The Night the Lights Went Out in Georgia" (s), Vicki Lawrence
"Tie A Yellow Ribbon Round the Old Oak Tree" (s), Dawn
"The Cover of Rolling Stone" (s), Dr. Hook and The Medicine Show
"Break Up to Make Up" (s), The Stylistics
Houses of the Holy, Led Zeppelin
The Best of Bread, Bread
Who Do We Think We Are!, Deep Purple
The Beatles 1962–1966, The Beatles
The Beatles 1966–1970, The Beatles
The Dark Side of the Moon, Pink Floyd
"Call Me (Come Back Home)" (s), Al Green
The Divine Miss M, Bette Midler
"Little Willy" (s), The Sweet
They Only Come Out At Night, Edgar Winter Group
Back Stabbers, The O'Jays
Sittin's In, Loggins & Messina
"Funky Worm" (s), Ohio Players
Yessongs, Yes
The Yes Album, Yes
"Sing" (s), The Carpenters
"Pillow Talk" (s), Sylvia
"Leaving Me" (s), Independents
Red Rose Speedway, Paul McCartney and Wings
William E. McEuen Presents Will the Circle Be Unbroken, The Nitty Gritty Dirt Band
Can't Buy a Thrill, Steely Dan
Made in Japan, Deep Purple
Living in the Material World, George Harrison
Curtis, Curtis Mayfield
Back to the World, Curtis Mayfield

"I'm Gonna Love You Just a
Little More Baby" (s), Barry
White
Now and Then, The
Carpenters
Class Clown, George Carlin
*The Sensational Charley
Pride,* Charley Pride
From Me to You, Charley
Pride
The Country Way, Charley
Pride
Round 2, The Stylistics
There Goes Rhymin' Simon,
Paul Simon
"Frankenstein" (s), Edgar
Winter Group
Moving Waves, Focus
Diamond Girl, Seals & Crofts
Fantasy, Carole King
"Will It Go Round in Circles"
(s), Billy Preston
Leon Live, Leon Russell
Elvis—That's the Way It Is,
Elvis Presley
Live at the Sahara Tahoe,
Isaac Hayes
"Playground in My Mind"
(s), Clint Holmes
The Captain and Me, Doobie
Brothers
"Drift Away" (s), Dobie Gray
"My Love" (s), Paul
McCartney and Wings
Call Me, Al Green
"One of a Kind (Love Affair)"
(s), Spinners
Spinners, Spinners
Chicago VI, Chicago
"Natural High" (s),
Bloodstone
*Dick Clark: 20 Years of Rock
'n' Roll,* Original Artists
"Doin' It to Death" (s), Fred
Wesley and the JB's
"Shambala" (s), Three Dog
Night
"Bad Bad Leroy Brown" (s),
Jim Croce
A Passion Play, Jethro Tull
"Give Your Baby a Standing
Ovation" (s), The Dells
Foreigner, Cat Stevens
"Yesterday Once More" (s),
The Carpenters

"The Morning After" (s),
Maureen McGovern
Cabaret, Original Soundtrack
Fresh, Sly & the Family Stone
We're an American Band,
Grand Funk Railroad
Brothers and Sisters, Allman
Brothers Band
Toulouse Street, Doobie
Brothers
"Brother Louis" (s), Stories
Killing Me Softly, Roberta
Flack
Farewell Andromeda, John
Denver
"Monster Mash" (s), Bobby
Pickett
"Here I Am (Come and Take
Me)" (s), Al Green
"Smoke on the Water" (s),
Deep Purple
"Delta Dawn" (s), Helen
Reddy
"Live and Let Die" (s), Paul
McCartney and Wings
"Behind Closed Doors" (s),
Charlie Rich
Jesus Christ Superstar,
Original Movie Soundtrack
Anticipation, Carly Somon
Deliver the Word, War
"If You Want Me To Stay" (s),
Sly and the Family Stone
Bloodshot, J. Geils Band
"Twelfth of Never" (s),
Donny Osmond
My Best of You, Donny
Osmond
Love Devotion Surrender,
Carlos Santana and
Mahavishnu John
McLaughlin
"Get Down" (s), Gilbert
O'Sullivan
Long Hard Climb, Helen
Reddy
Beginnings, Allman Brothers
Band
Goats Head Soup, Rolling
Stones
Focus 3, Focus
"That Lady" (s), Isley
Brothers
Los Cochinos, Cheech and
Chong
"We're an American Band"

(s), Grand Funk Railroad
"Loves Me Like a Rock" (s),
Paul Simon
"Say, Has Anybody Seen My
Sweet Gypsy Rose" (s), Dawn
"Half-Breed" (s), Cher
Goodbye Yellow Brick Road,
Elton John
Cyan, Three Dog Night
Sing It Again Rod, Rod
Stewart
Uriah Heep Live, Uriah Heep
"Midnight Train to Georgia"
(s), Gladys Knight and the
Pips
"I Believe in You (You
Believe in Me)" (s), Johnny
Taylor
Angel Clare, Arthur
Garfunkel
Quadrophenia, The Who
Meddle, Pink Floyd
Jonathan Livingston Seagull,
Neil Diamond/Original
Movie Soundtrack
*The Golden Age of Rock 'n'
Roll,* Sha Na Na
Life and Times, Jim Croce
*The Smoker You Drink, The
Player You Get,* Joe Walsh
Imagination, Gladys Knight
and the Pips
I've Got So Much to Give,
Barry White
"Heart Beat—It's A
Lovebeat" (s), The DeFranco
Family featuring Tony
DeFranco
Head to the Sky, Earth, Wind
& Fire
"Why Me" (s), Kris
Kristofferson
Ringo, Ringo Starr
*The Silver Tongued Devil and
I,* Kris Kristofferson
3 + 3, Isley Brothers
"Angie" (s), Rolling Stones
*You Don't Mess Around with
Jim,* Jim Croce
Behind Closed Doors, Charlie
Rich
Joy, Isaac Hayes
Welcome, Santana
Jesus Was a Capricorn, Kris
Kristofferson
Mind Games, John Lennon

1974

I Got a Name, Jim Croce
The Joker, Steve Miller Band
"Paper Roses" (s), Marie
Osmond
Muscle of Love, Alice Cooper
Full Sail, Loggins & Messina
Time Fades Away, Neil
Young
Band on the Run, Paul
McCartney and Wings
"The Most Beautiful Girl" (s),
Charlie Rich
John Denver's Greatest Hits,
John Denver
The Singles 1969–1973, The
Carpenters
"Top of the World" (s), The
Carpenters
Brain Salad Surgery,
Emerson, Lake, and Palmer
Bette Midler, Bette Midler
"Show and Tell" (s), Al
Wilson
"Space Race" (s), Billy
Preston
"If You're Ready" (s), Staple
Singers
Snowbird, Anne Murray
Dylan, Dylan
American Graffiti, Movie
Soundtrack
"The Love I Lost" (s), Harold
Melvin and the Blue Notes
"Photograph" (s), Ringo Starr
"Just You and Me" (s),
Chicago
"Time in a Bottle" (s), Jim
Croce
"Goodbye Yellow Brick Road
(s), Elton John
"Americans" (s), Byron
MacGregor
"Leave Me Alone (Ruby Red
Dress)" (s), Helen Reddy
The Early Beatles, The
Beatles
"The Joker" (s), Steve Miller
Band
"Smokin' in the Boys Room"
(s), Brownsville Station
The Lord's Prayer, Jim
Nabors
Ship Ahoy, The O'Jays
Livin' for You, Al Green
Eagles, Eagles
Colors of the Day, Judy
Collins

Hot Cakes, Carly Simon
Planet Waves, Bob Dylan
Johnny Winter Live, Johnny Winter
"I Have Got To Use My Imagination" (s), Gladys Knight and the Pips
"You're Sixteen" (s), Ringo Starr
"The Way We Were" (s) Barbra Streisand
The Pointer Sisters, The Pointer Sisters
Alone Together, Dave Mason
"Never, Never, Gonna Give Ya Up" (s), Barry White
"Love's Theme" (s), Love Unlimited Orchestra
Under the Influence of Love Unlimited, Love Unlimited
Stone Gon', Barry White
Live—Full House, J. Geils Band
Tales from Topographic Oceans, Yes
"Let Me Be There" (s), Olivia Newton-John
"Seasons in the Sun" (s), Terry Jacks
"Until You Come Back to Me" (s), Aretha Franklin
"Jungle Boogie" (s), Kool and The Gang
The Way We Were, Barbra Streisand
Court and Spark, Joni Mitchell
Ummagumma, Pink Floyd
Half Breed, Cher
Sweet Freedom, Uriah Heep
Laid Back, Greg Allman
"Spiders and Snakes" (s), Jim Stafford
Unborn Child, Seals and Crofts
War Live, War
The Payback, James Brown
Chicago VII, Chicago
Burn, Deep Purple
Sabbath, Bloody Sabbath, Black Sabbath
"Dark Lady" (s), Cher
"Rock On" (s), David Essex
Tubular Bells, Mike Oldfield
"Hooked on a Feeling" (s),
Blue Swede
"Sunshine on my Shoulder" (s), John Denver
Shinin' On, Grand Funk Railroad
"TSOP" (s), MFSB
What Were Once Vices Are Now Habits, The Doobie Brothers
"The Lord's Prayer" (s), Sister Janet Mead
"Lookin' for a Love" (s), Bobby Womack
Buddha and the Chocolate Box, Cat Stevens
"Bennie and the Jets" (s) Elton John
"The Best Thing That Ever Happened to Me" (s), Gladys Knights and the Pips
Love Is the Message, MFSB
Hard Labor, Three Dog Night
"The Payback" (s), James Brown
The Sting, Original Motion Picture Soundtrack
Very Special Love Songs, Charlie Rich
"Come and Get Your Love" (s), Redbone
Head Hunters, Herbie Hancock
"The Streak" (s), Ray Stevens
"The Loco-Motion" (s), Grand Funk Railroad
Rhapsody in White, Love Unlimited Orchestra
The Best of the Best of Merle Haggard, Merle Haggard
Bachman-Turner Overdrive II, Bachman-Turner Overdrive
"Just Don't Want to Be Lonely" (s), The Main Ingredient
Wild and Peaceful, Kool and the Gang
Maria Muldaur, Maria Muldaur
"Mockingbird" (s), Carly Simon and James Taylor
Open Our Eyes, Earth, Wind and Fire
Pretzel Logic, Steely Dan
"The Show Must Go On" (s), Three Dog Night

The Way We Were, Original
Soundtrack Recording
Mighty Love, The Spinners
"You Make Me Feel Brand
New" (s), The Stylistics
Tres Hombres, Z. Z. Top
"Be Thankful for What You
Got" (s), William DeVaughn
It's Been a Long Time, The
New Birth
Sundown, Gordon Lightfoot
"Band on the Run" (s), Paul
McCartney and Wings
On the Border, Eagles
"Billy Don't Be a Hero" (s),
Bo Donaldson and the
Heywoods
Love Song for Jeffrey, Helen
Reddy
*Claudine—Motion Picture
Soundtrack,* Gladys Knight
and the Pips
"The Entertainer" (s),
Original Motion Picture
Soundtrack from *The Sting*
Live Rhymin', Paul Simon
Ziggy Stardust, David Bowie
"For the Love of Money" (s),
The O'Jays
On Stage, Loggins and
Messina
"Sundown" (s), Gordon
Lightfoot
"Hollywood Swinging" (s),
Kool and the Gang
Back Home Again, John
Denver
"Rock the Boat" (s), The Hues
Corporation
Skin Tight, Ohio Players
Caribou, Elton John
The Great Gatsby, Original
Soundtrack Recording from
the Paramount Picture
Before the Flood, Bob Dylan
and the Band
Workingman's Dead, The
Grateful Dead
American Beauty, The
Grateful Dead
"On and On" (s), Gladys
Knight and the Pips
Shock Treatment, The Edgar
Winter Group
That's a Plenty, The Pointer
Sisters

"Annie's Song" (s), John
Denver
Diamond Dogs, Bowie
"If You Love Me (Let Me
Know)" (s), Olivia Newton-
John
"Feel Like Makin' Love" (s),
Roberta Flack
461 Ocean Boulevard, Eric
Clapton
"Tell Me Something Good"
(s), Rufus
"The Night Chicago Died"
(s), Paper Lace
Let's Put It All Together, The
Stylistics
"(You're) Having My Baby"
(s), Paul Anka
Endless Summer, The Beach
Boys
"Sideshow" (s), Blue Magic
"The Air That I Breathe" (s),
The Hollies
Not Fragile, Bachman-Turner
Overdrive
"Journey to the Center of the
Earth," Rich Wakeman
Rags to Rufus, Rufus
"Don't Let the Sun Go Down
on Me" (s), Elton John
*If You Love Me, Let Me
Know,* Olivia Newton-John
His 12 Greatest Hits, Neil
Diamond
Bridge of Sighs, Robin
Trower
"Can't Get Enough of Your
Love, Babe" (s), Barry White
So Far, Crosby, Stills, Nash,
and Young
Can't Get Enough, Barry
White
"I Shot the Sheriff" (s), Eric
Clapton
*Welcome Back, My Friends,
to the Show That Never Ends
—Ladies and Gentlemen,*
Emerson, Lake & Palmer
Bad Company, Bad Company
"I'm Leaving It (All) Up to
You" (s), Donny and Marie
Osmond
Moontan, Golden Earring
Second Helping, Lynyrd
Skynyrd
Desperado, Eagles

*The Souther-Hillman-Furay
Band,* The Souther-Hillman-
Furay Band
Stop and Smell the Roses,
Mac Davis
On the Beach, Neil Young
Santana's Greatest Hits,
Santana
"Rock Me Gently" (s), Andy
Kim
The Beach Boys in Concert,
The Beach Boys
"Then Came You" (s), Dionne
Warwicke and the Spinners
Black Oak Arkansas, Black
Oak Arkansas
"I Honestly Love You" (s),
Olivia Newton-John
Body Heat, Quincy Jones
*Cheech and Chong's Wedding
Album,* Cheech & Chong
Bachman-Turner Overdrive,
Bachman-Turner Overdrive
Let Me Be There, Olivia
Newton-John
Alice Cooper's Greatest Hits,
Alice Cooper
"Nothing from Nothing, (s),
Billy Preston
Wrap Around Joy, Carole
King
*Photographs and Memories,
His Greatest Hits,* Jim Croce
Wall and Bridges, John
Lennon
There Won't Be Anymore,
Charlie Rich
"Skin Tight" (s), Ohio Players
Serenade, Neil Diamond
Holiday, America
It's Only Rock 'N' Roll, The
Rolling Stones
Live It Up, The Isley Brothers
When the Eagle Flies, Traffic
David Live, David Bowie
Small Talk, Sly & the Family
Stone
War Child, Jethro Tull
Greatest Hits, Elton John
I Feel a Song, Gladys Knight
and the Pips
Anka, Paul Anka
"Do It ('Til You're Satisfied),
(s), B. T. Express
Mother Lode, Loggins &
Messina

1975

Miles of Aisles, Joni Mitchell
*I Don't Know How to Love
Him,* Helen Reddy
"Kung Fu Fighting" (s), Carl
Douglas
"I Can Help" (s), Billy Swan
This Is the Moody Blues,
Moody Blues
*Here's Johnny . . . Magic
Moments from the Tonight
Show,* Various Artists
Melodies of Love, Bobby
Vinton
"My Melody of Love" (s),
Bobby Vinton
Odds and Sods, The Who
Goodnight Vienna, Ringo
Starr
"When Will I See You Again"
(s), The Three Degrees
"You Ain't Seen Nothing Yet"
(s), Bachman-Turner
Overdrive
Fire, Ohio Players
Dark Horse, George Harrison
Verities and Balderdash,
Harry Chapin
Me and Bobby McGee, Kris
Kristofferson
Roadwork, Edgar Winter
New and Improved, The
Spinners
Relayer, Yes
"You're the First, the Last,
My Everything" (s), Barry
White
Free and Easy, Helen Reddy
*All the Girls in the World
Beware!!!,* Grand Funk
Railroad
*Pronounced Leh-nerd Skin-
nerd,* Lynyd Skynyrd
Late for the Sky, Jackson
Browne
The Best of Bread: Vol. II,
Bread
Rufusized, Rufus
"Cat's in the Cradle" (s),
Harry Chapin
"Back Home Again" (s), John
Denver
Butterfly, Barbra Streisand
*Elvis—A Legendary
Performer, Vol. I,"* Elvis
Presley
Did You Think to Pray,

*The pelvis known as Elvis
(Presley, that is) had
more than his share of Gold
Records. (Memory Shop)*

Charley Pride
(Country) Charley Pride,
Charley Pride
Stormbringer, Deep Purple
"Angie Baby" (s), Helen
Reddy
*Al Green Explores Your
Mind,* Al Green
Average White Band, Average
White Band
*Joy to the World—Their
Greatest Hits,* Three Dog
Night
So What, Joe Walsh
Caught Up, Millie Jackson
"Sha-La-La (Make Me
Happy)" (s), Al Green
"Fire" (s), Ohio Players
"Lucy in the Sky With
Diamonds" (s), Elton John
"Mandy" (s), Barry Manilow
Heart Like a Wheel, Linda
Ronstadt
Dawn's New Ragtime Follies,
Dawn
"Please Mr. Postman" (s),
Carpenters
Blood on the Tracks, Bob
Dylan

An Evening with John Denver,
John Denver
Dragon Fly, Jefferson
Starship
I'm Leaving It All Up to You,
Marie and Donny Osmond
*Have You Never Been
Mellow,* Olivia Newton-John
Something/Anything?, Todd
Rundgren
Energized, Foghat
Together for the First Time,
Bobby Bland/B. B. King
"Have You Never Been
Mellow" (s), Olivia Newton-
John
"Pick Up the Pieces" (s),
Average White Band
Physical Graffiti, Led
Zeppelin
Do It ('Til You're Satisfied),
B. T. Express
A Touch of Gold Volume II,
Johnny Rivers
Johnny Rivers' Golden Hits,
Johnny Rivers
Tommy, Original Soundtrack
Recording
Perfect Angel, Minnie
Riperton

"Lady Marmalade" (s), LaBelle

Chicago VIII, Chicago

Tuneweaving, Tony Orlando & Dawn

"My Eyes Adored You" (s), Frankie Valli

"Lovin' You" (s), Minnie Riperton

White Gold, Love Unlimited Orchestra

Just Another Way to Say I Love You, Barry White

That's the Way of the World, Earth, Wind, and Fire

Phoebe Snow, Phoebe Snow

"Black Water" (s), The Doobie Brothers

Get Your Wings, Aerosmith

"Philadelphia Freedom" (s), The Elton John Band

Spirit of America, The Beach Boys

Styx II, Styx

"Chevy Van" (s), Sammy Johns

Eldorado, The Electric Light Orchestra

Nightbirds, LaBelle

Straight Shooter, Bad Company

Katy Lied, Steely Dan

Sun Goddess, Ramsey Lewis

Captain Fantastic and the Brown Dirt Cowboy, Elton John

"Before the Next Teardrop Falls" (s), Freddy Fender

"(Hey Won't You Play) Another Somebody Done Somebody Wrong Song" (s), B. J. Thomas

Four Wheel Drive, Bachman-Turner Overdrive

Stampede, The Doobie Brothers

Welcome to My Nightmare, Alice Cooper

Venus & Mars, Wings

"He Don't Love You (Like I Love You)" (s), Tony Orlando & Dawn

Survival, The O'Jays

Janis Joplin's Greatest Hits, Janis Joplin

Hearts, America

Horizon, Carpenters

"Shining Star" (s), Earth, Wind, and Fire

Live in London, The O'Jays

"Love Won't Let Me Wait" (s), Major Harris

"Thank God I'm a Country Boy" (s), John Denver

"The Hustle" (s), Van McCoy and the Soul City Symphony

Fandango, Z. Z. Top

Nuthin' Fancy, Lynyrd Skynyrd

One of These Nights, Eagles

The Heat Is On, The Isley Brothers, featuring Fight the Power

To Be True, Harold Melvin and the Blue Notes featuring Theodore Pendergrass

"Love Will Keep Us Together" (s), Captain and Tennille

Young Americans, David Bowie

Chocolate Chip, Isaac Hayes

Barry Manilow II, Barry Manilow

"Wildfire" (s), Michael Murphey

Cut the Cake, Average White Band

Why Can't We Be Friends?, War

Fire on the Mountain, The Charlie Daniels Band

Love Will Keep Us Together, Captain and Tennille

"Express" (s), B. T. Express

Made in the Shade, The Rolling Stones

Toys in the Attic, Aerosmith

"Magic" (s), Pilot

The Marshall Tucker Band, The Marshall Tucker Band

Cat Stevens Greatest Hits, Cat Stevens

Honey, Ohio Players

Light of Worlds, Kool and the Gang

"Why Can't We Be Friends?" (s), War

"Jive Talkin'!" (s), Bee Gees

Red Octopus, Jefferson Starship

Don't Cry Now, Linda
Ronstadt
*Before the Next Teardrop
Falls,* Freddy Fender
"Listen to What the Man
Said" (s), Paul McCartney
and Wings
"Rhinestone Cowboy" (s),
Glen Campbell
Funny Lady (Original
Soundtrack Recording),
Barbra Streisand and James
Caan
"Someone Saved My Life
Tonight" (s), Elton John
Aerosmith, Aerosmith
"Fight the Power Part I" (s),
The Isley Brothers
Between the Lines, Janis Ian
Gorilla, James Taylor
"Fallin' In Love" (s),
Hamilton, Joe Frank, and
Reynolds
"Please Mister Please" (s),
Olivia Newton-John
Wish You Were Here, Pink
Floyd
"Wasted Days and Wasted
Nights" (s), Freddy Fender
Pick of the Litter, Spinners
Windsong, John Denver
"Mr. Jaws" (s), Dickie
Goodman
*Tony Orlando and Dawn's
Greatest Hits,* Tony Orlando
and Dawn
Clearly Love, Olivia Newton-
John
I'll Play for You, Seals and
Crofts
Is It Something I Said?,
Richard Pryor
Win, Lose Or Draw, The
Allman Brothers Band
Prisoner in Disguise, Linda
Ronstadt
For Everyman, Jackson
Browne
Blow by Blow, Jeff Beck
Born to Run, Bruce
Springsteen
Ain't No 'Bout-A-Doubt It,
Graham Central Station
"Fame" (s), David Bowie

Kris and Rita: Full Moon,
Kris Kristofferson and Rita
Coolidge
The Six Wives of Henry VIII,
Rick Wakeman
Rock of the Westies, Elton
John
Rocky Mountain Christmas,
John Denver
Raunch 'n' Roll, Black Oak
Arkansas
Where We All Belong, The
Marshall Tucker Band
Wind on the Water, David
Crosby and Graham Nash
Foghat, Foghat
Extra Texture, George
Harrison
Sedaka's Back, Neil Sedaka
Diamonds and Rust, Joan
Baez
Piano Man, Billy Joel
"Feelings" (s), Morris Albert
Minstrel in the Gallery, Jethro
Tull
"They Just Can't Stop It
(Games People Play)" (s),
Spinners
*Still Crazy After All These
Years,* Paul Simon
"Do It Anyway You Wanna"
(s), Peoples Choice
Blue Sky-Night Thunder,
Michael Murphey
*Chicago IX—Chicago's
Greatest Hits,* Chicago
"I'm Sorry" (s), John Denver
Sheer Heart Attack, Queen
Judith, Judy Collins
"Let's Do It Again" (s), The
Staple Singers
"Bad Blood" (s), Neil Sedaka
*History—America's Greatest
Hits,* America
"Fly, Robin, Fly" (s), Silver
Convention
Helen Reddy's Greatest Hits,
Helen Reddy
Alive!, Kiss
"Island Girl" (s), Elton John
*The Hissing of Summer
Lawns,* Joni Mitchell
*Seals and Crofts Greatest
Hits,* Seals and Crosts
Fleetwood Mac, Fleetwood
Mac

Breakaway, Art Garfunkel
Gratitude, Earth, Wind, and Fire
Family Reunion, O'Jays
Save Me, Silver Convention
The Who By Numbers, The Who
"Saturday Night" (s), Bay City Rollers
"The Way I Want to Touch You" (s), Captain and Tennille
The Best of Carly Simon, Carly Simon
The Hungry Years, Neil Sedaka
Atlantic Crossing, Rod Stewart
"Convoy" (s), C. W. McCall
Head On, Bachman-Turner Overdrive
Main Course, Bee Gees
Trying to Get the Feeling, Barry Manilow
Rhinestone Cowboy, Glen Campbell
Bay City Rollers, Bay City Rollers

1976   "Love Rollercoaster" (s), Ohio Players
High on the Hog, Black Oak Arkansas
"I Write the Songs" (s), Barry Manilow
"I Love Music" (s), The O'Jays
Wake Up Everybody, Harold Melvin and the Blue Notes
"You Sexy Thing" (s), Hot Chocolate
Rufus—Featuring Chaka Khan, Rufus—Featuring Chaka Khan
Desire, Bob Dylan
Numbers, Cat Stevens
Mona Bone Jakon, Cat Stevens
Love to Love You Baby, Donna Summer
No Way to Treat a Lady, Helen Reddy
A Christmas Album, Barbra Streisand
Face the Music, The Electric Light Orchestra

"Proud Mary" (s), Creedence Clearwater Revival
Black Bear Road, C. W. McCall
Searchin' for a Rainbow, Marshall Tucker Band
Bare Trees, Fleetwood Mac
Run with the Pack, Bad Company
Inseparable, Natalie Cole
"Theme from S.W.A.T." (s), Rhythm Heritage
"Love to Love You Baby" (s), Donna Summer
"Fox on the Run" (s), Sweet
Eagles, Their Greatest Hits 1971–75, Eagles
The Best of Jethro Tull, Jethro Tull
Station to Station, David Bowie
"Singasong" (s), Earth, Wind, and Fire
Frampton Comes Alive, Peter Frampton
Sweet Thing, Rufus— Featuring Chaka Khan
The Dream Weaver, Gary Wright
Barry White's Greatest Hits, Barry White
Will O' the Wisp, Leon Russell
A Night at the Opera, Queen
Song of Joy, Captain and Tennille
Red Headed Stranger, Willie Nelson
"Disco Lady" (s), Johnny Taylor
"50 Ways to Leave Your Lover" (s), Paul Simon
Fool for the City, Foghat
Bustin' Out, Pure Prairie League
Thoroughbred, Carole King
Wings at the Speed of Sound, Paul McCartney and Wings
"December, 1963" (s), The Four Seasons
The Outlaws, The Outlaws, Waylon Jennings, Willie Nelson, Thompall Glasser
Brass Construction, Brass Construction

Presence, Led Zeppelin
Eargasm, Johnnie Taylor
Apostrophe, Frank Zappa
"Lonely Night" (s), Captain
and Tennille
"Love Hurts" (s), Nazareth
Hair of the Dog, Nazareth
City Life, Blackbyrds
2nd Anniversary, Gladys
Knight and the Pips
Lazy Afternoon, Barbra
Streisand
"Boogie Fever" (s), The
Sylvers
"Dream Weaver" (s), Gary
Wright
Destroyer, Kiss
Black and Blue, The Rolling
Stones
Membership Connection,
Parliament
Come on Over, Olivia
Newton-John
"Right Back Where We
Started From" (s), Maxine
Nightingale
*You've Never Been This Far
Before—Baby's Gone,*
Conway Twitty
Here and There, Elton John
Takin' It to the Streets, The
Doobie Brothers
Look Out for No. 1, The
Brothers Johnson
Bitches Brew, Miles Davis
"Only Sixteen" (s), Dr. Hook
Hideaway, America
"Welcome Back Kotter" (s),
John Sebastian
"I.O.U." (s), Jimmy Dean
Rocks, Aerosmith
Souvenirs, Dan Fogelberg
All the Love in the World,
Mac Davis
Desolation Boulevard, Sweet
Harvest for the World, Isley
Brothers
Bohemian Rhapsody, Queen
Breezin', George Benson
"Get Up and Boogie" (s),
Silver Convention
Contradiction, Ohio Players
"Silly Love Songs" (s), Wings
Amigos, Santana

Rock 'n' Roll Music, The
Beatles
"Kiss and Say Goodbye" (s),
The Manhattans
*Twelve Dreams of Dr.
Sardonicus,* Spirit
Ole' ELO, Electric Light
Orchestra
"Shannon" (s), Henry Gross
Chicago X, Chicago
Beautiful Noise, Neil
Diamond
*Fooled Around and Fell in
Love,* Elvin Bishop
Love Trilogy, Donna Summer
"Sara Smile" (s), Daryl Hall
and John Oates
Spitfire, Jefferson Starship
Natalie, Natalie Cole
Sparkle, Aretha Franklin
Second Childhood, Phoebe
Snow
All-Time Greatest Hits,
Johnny Mathis
A Kind of Hush, The
Carpenters
"Afternoon Delight" (s),
Starland Vocal Band
Silk Degrees, Boz Scaggs

GRAMMY WINNERS—National Academy of Recording Arts and Sciences.
Sciences.
The record industry's biggie.
1958
Record of the year, *Nel Blu Dipinto Di Blu (Volare),* Domenico Modugno
Album of the year, *The Music From Peter Gunn,* Henry Mancini
Song of the year, *Nel Blu Dipinto Di Blu (Volare),* Domenico Modugno
Best female vocal, *Ella Fitzgerald Sings the Irving Berlin Song Book,* Ella Fitzgerald
Best male vocal, *Catch A Falling Star,* Perry Como
Best orchestra performance, *Billy May's Big Fat Brass*
Best dance band performance, *Basie*
Best vocal group or chorus performance, *That Old Black Magic,* Louis Prima and Keely Smith
Best individual jazz performance, *Ella Fitzgerald Sings the Duke Ellington Song Book*

Best group jazz performance, *Basie*
Best comedy performance, *The Chipmunk Song*, David Seville
Best country and western performance, *Tom Dooley*, The Kingston Trio
Best rhythm and blues performance, *Tequila*, The Champs
Best arrangement, *The Music From Peter Gunn*, Henry Mancini; arrangement, Henry Mancini
Best engineered classical, *Duets with a Spanish Guitar*, Laurindo Almeida and Salli Terri; engineer, Sherwood Hall, III
Best engineered nonclassical, *The Chipmunk Song*, David Seville; engineer, Ted Keep
Best musical composition first recorded and released in 1958 (over 5 minutes), *Cross Country Suite*, composer Nelson Riddle
Best original cast, Broadway or TV, *The Music Man*, Meredith Willson
Best sound track album, *Gigi*, Andre Previn
Best spoken word performance, *The Best of the Stan Freberg Shows*
Best children's album, *The Chipmunk Song*, David Seville
Best classical orchestral performance, *Gaiete Parisienne*, Felix Slatkin conductor, Hollywood Bowl Symphony Orchestra
Best classical instrumental performance (with concerto scale accompaniment), *Tchaikovsky: Concerto No. 1, in B-Flat Minor, Op. 23*, Van Cliburn, pianist
Best classical instrumentalist (other than concerto scale), *Segovia Golden Jubilee*
Best classical chamber music performance, *Beethoven Quartet 130*, Hollywood String Quartet
Best classical vocal soloist performance, *Operatic Recital*, Renata Tebaldi
Best classical operatic choral performance, *Virtuoso*, Roger Wagner Chorale
1959
Record of the year, *Mack The Knife*, Bobby Darin
Album of the year, *Come Dance With Me*, Frank Sinatra
Song of the year, *The Battle of New Orleans*, composer Jimmy Driftwood
Best vocal female performance, *But Not For Me*, Ella Fitzgerald
Best vocal male performance, *Come Dance With Me*, Frank Sinatra
Best dance band performance, *Anatomy of a Murder*, Duke Ellington
Best orchestra, *Like Young*, David Rose Orchestra with Andre Previn
Best choral performance, *Battle Hymn of the Republic*, Mormon Tabernacle Choir; Richard Condie, conductor
Best jazz soloist, *Ella Swings Lightly*, Ella Fitzgerald
Best jazz group, *Dig Chicks*, Jonah Jones
Best classical orchestra, *Debussy: Images for Orchestra*, Boston Symphony; Charles Munch, conductor
Best classical concerto or instrumental soloist (full orchestra), *Rachmaninoff Piano Concerto No. 3*, Van Cliburn; Kiril Kondrashin conductor, symphony of the air
Best classical opera cast or choral, *Mozart: The Marriage of Figaro*, Erich Leinsdorf, conductor, Vienna Philharmonic Orchestra
Best classical vocal soloist, *Bjoerling In Opera*, Jussi Bjoerling
Best classical chamber music, *Beethoven: Sonata No. 21, In C, Op. 53 (Waldstein): Sonata No. 18, In E-Flat, Op. 31, No. 3*; Artur Rubinstein, Pianist
Best classical instrumental soloist, *Beethoven: Sonata No. 21, In C, Op. 53 (Waldstein); Sonata No. 18, In E-Flat, Op. 31, No. 3*, Artur Rubinstein, Pianist
Best musical composition first recorded and released in 1959 (5 minutes), *Anatomy Of A Murder*, Duke Ellington, Composer
Best sound track album, *Anatomy Of A Murder (Motion Picture)*, Duke Ellington
Best sound track album, original cast, *Porgy and Bess*, Motion Picture Cast

Best Broadway show album, *Gypsy,* Ethel Merman; *Redhead,* Gwen Verdon
Best comedy—spoken word, *Inside Shelley Berman*
Best comedy—musical, *The Battle of Kookamonga,* Homer and Jethro
Best spoken word, *A Lincoln Portrait,* Carl Sandburg
Best country and western, *The Battle of New Orleans,* Johnny Horton
Best rhythm and blues, *What A Difference A Day Makes,* Dinah Washington
Best folk, *The Kingston Trio At Large*
Best children's album, *Peter And The Wolf,* Peter Ustinov, Narrator; von Karajan, conductor, Philharmonia Orchestra
Best arrangement, *Come Dance With Me,* Frank Sinatra; arrangement, Billy May
Best engineering—classical, *Victory At Sea, Vol. 1,* Robert Russell Bennett; engineer, Lewis W. Layton
Best engineering—Novelty, *Alvin's Harmonica,* David Seville; engineer, Ted Keep
Best engineering—other, *Belafonte at Carnegie Hall,* engineer, Robert Simpson

1960
Record of the year, *Theme From A Summer Place,* Percy Faith
Album of the year, *Button Down Mind,* Bob Newhart
Song of the year, *Theme From Exodus,* composer, Ernest Gold
Best female vocal single, *Mack The Knife,* Ella Fitzgerald
Best female vocal album, *Mack The Knife—Ella In Berlin,* Ella Fitzgerald
Best male vocal single, *Georgia On My Mind,* Ray Charles
Best male vocal—album, *Genius Of Ray Charles,* Ray Charles
Best band for dancing, *Dance With Basie*
Best arrangement, *Mr. Lucky,* Henry Mancini
Best orchestra, *Mr. Lucky,* Henry Mancini

Best vocal group, *We Got Us,* Eydie Gorme/Steve Lawrence
Best chorus, *Songs Of The Cowboy,* Norman Luboff Choir
Best jazz—solo or small group, *West Side Story,* Andre Previn
Best jazz—large group, *Blues And The Beat,* Henry Mancini
Best classical orchestra, *Bartok: Music for Strings, Percussion and Celeste,* Fritz Reiner, conductor, Chicago Symphony
Best classical chamber music, *Conversations With The Guitar,* Laurindo Almeida
Best classical concerto or instrumental soloist, *Brahms: Piano Concerto No. 2 in B-Flat,* Sviatoslav Richter; Erich Leinsdorf, conductor, Chicago Symphony
Best classical instrumental soloist or duo, *The Spanish Guitars of Laurindo Almeida,* Laurindo Almeida
Best classical vocal soloist, *A Program of Song,* Leontyne Price
Best classical opera production, *Puccini: Turandot,* Erich Leinsdorf, conductor, Rome Opera House, Chorus and Orchestra
Best contemporary classical composition, *Orchestral Suite From Tender Land Suite,* Aaron Copland, composer
Best classical choral (including oratorio), *Handel: The Messiah,* Sir Thomas Beecham, conductor, Royal Philharmonic Orchestra and Chorus
Best sound track music score, *Exodus,* Ernest Gold, composer
Best sound track original cast, *Can Can,* Frank Sinatra, original cast, Cole Porter, composer
Best show album (original cast), *The Sound Of Music,* Mary Martin, Richard Rodgers, Oscar Hammerstein, composers
Best comedy (spoken word), *Button Down Mind Strikes Back,* Bob Newhart
Best comedy (musical), *Jonathan and Darlene Edwards in Paris,* Jonathan and Darlene Edwards (Jo Stafford and Paul Weston)
Best performance (spoken word),

F.D.R. Speaks, (Franklin D. Roosevelt); Robert Blalek

Best pop single artist, *Georgia On My Mind,* Ray Charles

Best country and western, *El Paso,* Marty Robbins

Best rhythm and blues, *Let The Good Times Roll,* Ray Charles

Best folk, *Swing Dat Hammer,* Harry Belafonte

Best children's album, *Let's All Sing With The Chipmunks,* David Seville

Best engineering, classical, *Spanish Guitars of Laurindo Almeida,* engineer, Hugh Davies

Best engineering, pop, *Ella Fitzgerald Sings the George and Ira Gershwin Song Book,* engineer, Luis P. Valentin

Best engineering, novelty, *The Old Payola Roll Blues,* Stan Freberg; engineer, John Kraus

Best jazz composition of more than five minutes duration, *Sketches of Spain,* Miles Davis and Gil Evans

1961

Record of the year, *Moon River,* Henry Mancini

Album of the year, *Judy At Carnegie Hall,* Judy Garland

Classical album of the year, *Stravinsky Conducts, 1960: Le Sacre Du Printemps; Petrouchka;* Igor Stravinsky, conductor, Columbia Symphony

Song of the year, *Moon River;* Composers, Henry Mancini and Johnny Mercer

Best instrumental theme version, *African Waltz;* Composer, Galt MacDermott

Best female solo vocal, *Judy At Carnegie Hall;* Judy Garland

Best male solo vocal, *Lollipops And Roses,* Jack Jones

Best Jazz—soloist or small group (instrumental), *Andre Previn Plays Harold Arlen;* Andre Previn

Best Jazz—large group, *West Side Story,* Stan Kenton

Best original jazz composition, *African Waltz;* Composer, Galt MacDermott

Best orchestra—for dancing, *Up A Lazy River;* Si Zentner

Best orchestra—non dancing, *Breakfast at Tiffany's,* Henry Mancini

Best arrangment, *Moon River,* Henry Mancini, arrangement

Best vocal group, *High Flying,* Lambert, Hendricks and Ross

Best chorus, *Great Band With Great Voices,* Johnny Mann Singers, Si Zentner Orchestra

Best sound track of score, *Breakfast At Tiffany's,* Henry Mancini

Best sound track of original cast, *West Side Story,* Johnny Green, Saul Chaplin, Sid Ramin and Irwin Kostal

Best original cast show album, *How To Succeed In Business Without Really Trying;* composer, Frank Loesser

Best comedy, *An Evening With Mike Nichols And Elaine May*

Best spoken word, *Humor In Music;* Leonard Bernstein, conductor, New York Philharmonic symphony

Best Engineering—pop, *Judy At Carnegie Hall,* Judy Garland; engineer, Robert Arnold

Best Engineering—novelty, *Stan Freberg Presents The United States Of America;* engineer, John Kraus

Best children's album, *Prokofiev: Peter And The Wolf;* Leonard Bernstein, conductor, New York Philharmonic Orchestra

Best rock and roll, *Let's Twist Again,* Chubby Checker

Best country & western, *Big Bad John,* Jimmy Dean

Best rhythm and blues, *Hit the Road Jack,* Ray Charles

Best folk, *Belafonte Folk Singers At Home and Abroad;* Belafonte Folk Singers

Best gospel or other religious, *Everytime I Feel the Spirit;* Mahalia Jackson

Best classical—orchestra, *Ravel: Daphnis Et Chloe;* Charles Munch, conductor, Boston Symphony Orchestra

Best classical—chamber music, *Beethoven: Serenade, Op. 8 Kodaly Duo For Violin & Cello, Op. 7,*

Jascha Heifetz, Gregory Piatigorsky, William Primrose
Best classical—instrumental soloist (with orchestra), *Bartok: Concerto No. 1 for Violin and Orchestra;* Isaac Stern; Eugene Ormandy, conductor, Philharmonic Orchestra
Best classical—instrumental soloist or duo without orchestra, *Reverie for Spanish Guitars,* Laurindo Almeida
Best opera, *Puccini: Madame Butterfly;* Gabriele Santini, conductor, Rome Opera Chorus and Orchestra
Best classical—choral, *Bach: B Minor Mass;* Robert Shaw Chorale; Robert Shaw, conductor
Best classical—vocal soloist, *The Art of the Prima Donna,* Joan Sutherland; Molinari-Pradelli, conductor, Royal Opera House Orchestra
Best contemporary classical composition, *Discantus,* composer, Laurindo Almeida, *Movements For Piano and Orchestra,* composer, Igor Stravinsky
Best engineering—classical, *Ravel: Daphnis Et Chloe,* Munch, conductor, Boston Symphony; engineer, Lewis W. Layton
1962
Record of the year, *I Left My Heart In San Francisco,* Tony Bennett
Album of the year, *The First Family,* Vaughn Meader
Classical album of the year, *Columbia Records Presents Vladimir Horowitz*
Song of the year, *What Kind of Fool Am I,* composers, Leslie Bricusse and Anthony Newley
Best instrumental theme, *A Taste of Honey,* composers, Bobby Scott and Ric Marlow
Best female solo vocal, *Ella Swings Brightly With Nelson Riddle,* Ella Fitzgerald
Best male solo vocal, *I Left My Heart In San Francisco,* Tony Bennett
Best Jazz—soloist or small group (instrumental), *Desafinado,* Stan Getz
Best jazz—Large group instrumental, *Adventures In Jazz,* Stan Kenton

Best original jazz composition, *Cast Your Fate To The Winds;* composer, Vince Guaraldi
Best orchestra—for dancing, *Fly Me to The Moon Bossa Nova;* Joe Harnell
Best orchestra or instrumentalist with orchestra—not for jazz or dancing, *The Colorful Peter Nero*
Best instrumental arrangement, *Baby Elephant Walk,* Mancini and Orchestra; arrangement, Henry Mancini
Best background arrangement, *I Left My Heart In San Francisco,* Tony Bennett; arrangement, Marty Manning
Best vocal group, *If I Had A Hammer;* Peter, Paul and Mary
Best chorus, *Presenting The New Christy Minstrels;* The New Christy Minstrels
Best original cast show album, *No Strings,* Original Broadway Cast; composer, Richard Rodgers
Best classical orchestra, *Stravinsky: The Firebird Ballet;* Igor Stravinsky, conductor, Columbia Symphony
Best classical—chamber music, *The Heifetz— Piatigorsky Concerts With Primrose, Pennario and Guests*
Best classical—instrumental soloist(s) (with orchestra), *Stravinsky: Concerto In D For Violin;* Isaac Stern, Stravinsky, conductor, Columbia Symphony
Best classical—instrumental soloist or duo (without orchestra), Columbia Records Presents Vladimir Horowitz
Best opera, *Verdi: Aida;* George Solti, conductor, Rome Opera House Orchestra and Chorus
Best classical—choral, *Bach: St. Matthew Passion,* Philharmonia Choir
Best classical—vocal soloist, *Wagner: Gotterdamerung—* Brunhilde's Immolations Scene/ *Wesendonck Songs,* Eileen Farrell; Bernstein, conductor, New York Philharmonic
Best classical composition by contemporary composer, *The Flood,* composer, Igor Stravinsky
Best engineering—classical, *Strauss:*

Also Sprach Zarathustra Op. 30; Reiner, conductor, Chicago Symphony, engineer; Lewis W. Layton

Best comedy, *The First Family,* Vaughn Meader

Best spoken word, *The Story-Teller: A Session With Charles Laughton*

Best engineering—other than novelty or classical, *Hatari!,* Henry Mancini; engineer, Al Schmitt

Best engineering—Novelty, *The Civil War, Vol. I,* Fennell; engineer, Robert Fine

Best children's, *Saint-Saens: Carnival of the Animals/Britten: Young Person's Guide To The Orchestra,* Leonard Bernstein

Best rock and roll, *Alley Cat,* Bent Fabric

Best country and western, *Funny Way of Laughin',* Burl Ives

Best rhythm and blues, *I Can't Stop Loving You,* Ray Charles

Best Folk, *If I Had A Hammer;* Peter, Paul and Mary

Best Gospel or other religious, *Great Songs of Love And Faith,* Mahalia Jackson

1963

Record of the year, *The Days of Wine And Roses,* Henry Mancini

Album of the year, *The Barbra Streisand Album,* Barbra Streisand

Classical album of the year, *Britten: War Requiem;* Benjamin Britten, conductor, London Symphony Orchestra and Chorus (London)

Song of the year, *The Days of Wine and Roses;* composers, Henry Mancini and Johnny Mercer

Best instrumental theme, *More (Theme From "Mondo Cane");* composers, Norman Newell, Nino Oliviero, and Riz Ortolani

Best female vocal, *The Barbra Streisand Album,* Barbra Streisand

Best male vocal, *Wives And Lovers,* Jack Jones

Best instrumental jazz—soloist or small group, *Conversations With Myself,* Bill Evans

Best instrumental jazz—large group, *Encore: Woody Herman, 1963*

Best original jazz composition, *Gravy Waltz,* composers, Steve Allen, Ray Brown

Best Performance orchestra—for dancing, *This Time By Basie! Hits of The 50's And 60's,* Count Basie

Best performance orchestra or instrumentalist with orchestra—not jazz/dancing, *Java,* Al Hirt

Best instrumental arrangement, *I Can't Stop Loving You,* Count Basie; arrangement, Quincy Jones

Best background arrangement, *The Days of Wine and Roses,* Mancini; arrangement, Henry Mancini

Best vocal group, *Blowin' In The Wind;* Peter, Paul and Mary

Best chorus, *Bach's Greatest Hits,* The Swingle Singers

Best original score, *Tom Jones,* John Addison, conductor; composer, John Addison

Best score original cast show album, *She Loves Me,* Original Cast; composers, Jerry Bock, Sheldon Harnick

Best classical orchestra, *Bartok: Concerto for Orchestra;* Erich Leinsdorf, Boston Symphony Orchestra

Best classical—chamber music, *Evening of Elizabethan Music;* Julian Bream Consort

Best classical—instrumental soloist(s) (with orchestra), *Tchaikovsky: Concerto No. 1 in B-Flat Minor For Piano and Orchestra,* Artur Rubinstien, Leinsdorf, conductor, Boston Symphony Orchestra

Best classical—instrumental soloist or duo (without orchestra), *The Sound of Horowitz;* Vladimir Horowitz

Best opera, *Puccini: Madama Butterfly;* Erich Leinsdorf, conductor, RCA Italiana Opera Orchestra and Chorus

Best classical choral, *Britten: War Requiem;* David Willcocks, director, Bach Choir; Edward Chapman, director, Highgate School Choir; Benjamin Britten, conductor, London Symphony Orchestra and Chorus

Best classical—vocal soloist (with/ without orchestra), *Great Scenes From Gershwin's Porgy And Bess,* Leontyne Price

Best classical composition by contemporary composer, *War Requiem;* composer Benjamin Britten

Best engineered classical, *Puccini; Madama Butterfly;* Leinsdorf, conductor; engineer Lewis Layton

Best comedy, *Hello Mudduh, Hello Faddah;* Allan Sherman

Best spoken word, *Who's Afraid of Virginia Woolf?;* Edward Albee

Best engineered—nonclassical, Charade, Mancini Orchestra and Chorus; engineer, James Malloy

Best engineered—special or novel effects, *Civil War Vol. II;* Frederick Fennell; engineer, Robert Fine

Best children's, *Bernstein Conducts for Young People;* Leonard Bernstein, conductor New York Philharmonic

Best rock and roll, *Deep Purple,* Nino Tempo and April Stevens

Best country and western, *Detroit City,* Bobby Bare

Best rhythm and blues, *Busted,* Ray Charles

Best folk, *Blowin' In The Wind;* Peter, Paul and Mary

Best gospel or other religious, *Dominique,* Soeur Sourire (The Singing Nun)

1964

Record of the Year, *The Girl From Ipanema,* Stan Getz, Astrud Gilberto

Album of the year, *Getz/Gilberto,* Stan Getz, Joao Gilberto

Classical album of the year, *Bernstein: Symphony No. 3 ("Kaddish");* Leonard Bernstein, conductor, New York Philharmonic

Song of the year, *Hello, Dolly!;* composer, Jerry Herman

Best instrumental composition (nonjazz), *The Pink Panther Theme;* Composer Henry Mancini

Best female vocal, *"People,"* Barbra Streisand

Best male vocal, *Hello, Dolly!;* Louis Armstrong

Best instrumental jazz—small group, *Getz/Gilberto;* Stan Getz

Best instrumental jazz performance —large group, *Guitar From Ipanema,* Laurindo Almeida

Best original jazz composition, *The Cat;* composer, Lalo Schifrin

Best instrumental performance— (nonjazz), *Pink Panther;* Henry Mancini

Best instrumental arrangement, *Pink Panther,* Henry Mancini; arrangement, Henry Mancini

Best accompaniment arrangement, *People,* Barbra Streisand; arrangement Peter Matz

Best vocal group, *A Hard Day's Night,* The Beatles

Best chorus, *The Swingle Singers Going Baroque,* The Swingle Singers

Best original score, *Mary Poppins,* Julie Andrews, Dick Van Dyke; composers, Richard M. Sherman and Robert B. Sherman

Best score from an original cast show album, *Funny Girl,* Barbra Streisand, original cast; composer, Jule Styne and Bob Merrill

Best comedy, *I Started Out as a Child,* Bill Cosby

Best spoken word, *BBC Tribute to John F. Kennedy;* That Was The Week That Was, Cast

Best engineered recording, *Getz/ Gilberto,* Stan Getz, Joao Gilberto; engineer, Phil Ramone

Best engineered—special or novel effects, *The Chipmunks Sing the Beatles;* engineer, Dave Hassinger

Best children's, *Mary Poppins,* Julie Andrews, Dick Van Dyke

Best rock and roll, *Downtown;* Petula Clark

Best rhythm and blues, *How Glad I Am;* Nancy Wilson

Best folk, *We'll Sing in the Sunshine;* Gale Garnett

Best gospel or other religious, *Great Gospel Songs;* Tennessee Ernie Ford

Best country and western single, *Dang Me;* Roger Miller

Best country and western album, *Dang Me/Chug-A-Lug;* Roger Miller

Best country and western female vocal, *Here Comes My Baby,* Dottie West

Grammy winner Louis Armstrong pictured here with Billie Holiday, who was no slouch when it came to music either. (Memory Shop)

Best country and western male vocal, *Dang Me,* Roger Miller

Best country and western song, *Dang Me,* composer Roger Miller

Best orchestra, *Mahler: Symphony No. 5 in C Sharp Minor, Berg: "Wozzeck" Excerpts;* Erich Leinsdorf, conductor, Boston Symphony

Best chamber performance, *Beethoven: Trio No. 1 in E Flat Op. 1, No. 1,* (Jacob Lateiner, piano; Jascha Heifetz, Gregor Piatigorsky

Best vocal chamber music, *It Was a Lover and His Lass, (Morley, Byrd and others)*; New York Pro Musica, Noah Greenberg, conductor

Best performance—instrumental soloist(s) (with orchestra), *Prokofieff: Concerto No. 1 in D Major for Violin,* Isaac Stern; Ormandy conductor, Philadelphia Orchestra

Best performance—Instrumental soloist (without orchestra), *Vladimir Horowitz Plays Beethoven, Debussy, Chopin (Beethoven: Sonata No. 8, "Pathetique"; Debussy: Preludes;*

Chopin: Etudes and Scherzos 1–4

Best opera, *Bizet: Carmen*; von Karaja, conductor, Vienna Philharmonica Orchestra and Chorus

Best choral, *Britten: A Ceremony of Carols*, Robert Shaw, Robert Shaw Chorale

Best vocal soloist, *Berlioz: Nuits D'Ete (Song Cycle)/Falla: El Amor Brujo;* Reiner, conductor, Chicago Symphony, Leontyne Price

Best composition by a contemporary composer, *Piano Concerto;* composer Samuel Barber

1965

Record of the year, *A Taste of Honey;* Herb Alpert and the Tijuana Brass

Album of the year, *September of My Years,* Frank Sinatra

Album of the year—classical, *Horowitz at Carnegie Hall (An Historic Return)*; Vladimir Horowitz

Song of the year, *The Shadow of Your Smile (Love Theme from the Sandpiper)*; composers, Paul Francis

The Beatles in more innocent days. (Memory Shop)

Webster and Johnny Mandel
Best female vocal, *My Name is Barbra*, Barbra Streisand
Best male vocal, *It Was a Very Good Year*, Frank Sinatra
Best instrumental nonjazz, *A Taste of Honey*, Herb Alpert and the Tijuana Brass
Best vocal group, *We Dig Mancini*; Anita Kerr Singers
Best chorus, *Anyone for Mozart?*; The Swingle Singers
Best original score, *The Sandpiper*, Robert Armbruster Orchestra; composer, Johnny Mandel
Best score from an original show album, *On A Clear Day*; composers, Alan Lerner, Burton Lane
Best comedy, *Why Is There Air?*, Bill Cosby
Best spoken word, *John F. Kennedy —As We Remember Him*; Goddard Lieberson, producer
Best children's, *Dr. Seuss Presents "Fox In Sox"—Green Eggs and Ham*; Marvin Miller
Best instrumental jazz—small group,

The "In" Crowd, Ramsey Lewis Trio
Best instrumental jazz—large group, *Ellington '66*; Duke Ellington Orchestra
Best original jazz composition, *Jazz Suite on the Mass Texts*; composer, Lalo Schifrin
Best instrumental arrangements, *A Taste of Honey*; Herb Alpert and the Tijuana Brass; Arrangement, Herb Alpert
Best accompaniment arrangement, *It Was a Very Good Year*, Frank Sinatra; arrangement, Gordon Jenkins
Best contemporary (Rock and Roll) single, *King of the Road*; Roger Miller
Best contemporary (Rock and Roll) female vocal, *I Know A Place*, Petula Clark
Best contemporary (Rock and Roll) male vocal, *King of the Road*, Roger Miller
Best contemporary (Rock and Roll) group, *Flowers on the Wall*, The Statler Brothers

Best rhythm and blues, *Papa's Got a Brand New Bag,* James Brown

Best folk, *An Evening with Belafonte/Makeba,* Harry Belafonte, Miriam Makeba

Best gospel or other religious, *Southland Favorites,* George Beverly Shea and the Anita Kerr Singers

Best country and western single, *King of the Road,* Roger Miller

Best country and western album, *The Return of Roger Miller,* Roger Miller

Best country and western female vocal, *Queen of the House,* Jody Miller

Best country and western male vocal, *King of the Road,* Roger Miller

Best country and western song, *King of the Road;* songwriter, Roger Miller

Best engineered recording, *A Taste of Honey,* Herb Alpert and the Tijuana Brass; engineer, Larry Levine

Best engineered recording—classical, *Horowitz at Carnegie Hall —An Historic Return,* Vladimir Horowitz; engineer, Fred Plaut

Best classical orchestra, *Ives: Symphony No. 4,* Leopold Stokowski; conductor, American Symphony Orchestra

Best classical chamber music, *Bartok: The Six String Quartets,* Juilliard String Quartet

Best classical—instrumental soloist(s), *Beethoven: Concerto No. 4 in G Major for Piano and Orchestra,* Artur Rubinstein; Erich Leinsdorf, conductor, Boston Symphony

Best classical—instrumental soloist (without orchestra), *Horowitz at Carnegie Hall—An Historic Return,* Vladimir Horowitz

Best Opera, *Berg: Wozzeck;* Karl Bohm, conductor Orchestra of the German Opera, Berlin

Best choral, *Stravinsky: Symphony of Psalms/Poulenc: Gloria;* Robert Shaw Chorale, RCA Victor Symphony Orchestra

Best vocal—with/without orchestra, *Strauss: Salome (Dance of the Seven Veils, Interlude, Finale Scene) The Egyptian Helen (Awakening Scene),* Leontyne Price

Best composition by a contemporary classical composer, *Symphony No. 4;* composer, Charles Ives

1966

Record of the year, *Strangers in the Night,* Frank Sinatra

Album of the year, *Sinatra A Man and His Music,* Frank Sinatra

Song of the year, *Michelle;* songwriters, John Lennon and Paul McCartney

Best instrumental theme, *Batman Theme;* composer, Neal Hefti

Best female vocal, *If He Walked Into My Life,* Eydie Gorme

Best male vocal, *Strangers in the Night,* Frank Sinatra

Best instrumental (nonjazz), *What Now My Love,* Herb Alpert and the Tijuana Brass

Best vocal group, *A Man and A Woman,* Anita Kerr Singers

Best chorus performance, *Somewhere, My Love (Lara's Theme from "Dr. Zhivago"),* Ray Conniff and Singers

Best original score, *Dr. Zhivago,* composer, Maurice Jarre

Best score from an original cast show album, *Mame,* composer, Jerry Herman

Best comedy, *Wonderfulness,* Bill Cosby

Best spoken word, *Edward R. Murrow—A Reporter Remembers, Vol. 1 The War Years,* Edward R. Murrow

Best children's, *Dr. Seuss Presents: "If I Ran the Zoo" and "Sleep Book,"* Marvin Miller

Best instrumental jazz group, *Goin' Out of My Head,* Wes Montgomery

Best original jazz composition, *In The Beginning God;* composer, Duke Ellington

Best contemporary Rock and Roll, *Winchester Cathedral,* New Vaudeville Band

Best contemporary (Rock and Roll) solo vocal, *Eleanor Rigby,* Paul McCartney

Best contemporary (Rock and Roll) group, *Monday, Monday,* The Mamas and The Papas

Best rhythm and blues, *Crying Time,* Ray Charles

Best rhythm and blues solo vocal, *Crying Time,* Ray Charles

Best rhythm and blues group, *Hold It Right There,* Ramsey Lewis

Best folk, *Blues in the Street,* Cortella Clark

Best sacred, *Grand Old Gospel,* Porter Wagoner and the Blackwood Bros.

Best country and western, *Almost Persuaded,* David Houston

Best country and western female vocal, *Don't Touch Me,* Jeannie Seely

Best country and western male vocal, *Almost Persuaded,* David Houston

Best country and western song, *Almost Persuaded,* songwriters, Billy Sherrill and Glenn Sutton

Best instrumental arrangement, *What Now My Love,* Herb Alpert and the Tijuana Brass; arrangement, Herb Alpert

Best accompaniment arrangement, *Strangers in the Night,* Frank Sinatra; arrangement, Ernie Freeman

Classical album of the year, *Ives: Symphony No. 1 in D Minor;* Morton Gould, conductor, Chicago Symphony; arrangement, Howard Scott

Best classical orchestra, *Mahler: Symphony No. 6 in A Minor;* Erich Leinsdorf, conductor, Boston Symphony

Best chamber music, *Boston Symphony Chamber Players*

Best performance—instrumental soloist(s), *Baroque Guitar,* Julian Bream

Best opera, *Wagner: Die Walkure;* Georg Solti, conductor, Vienna Philharmonic

Best classical choral, *Handel: Messiah;* Robert Shaw, conductor, Robert Shaw Chorale and Orchestra

Ives: Music for Chorus (Gen. Wm. Booth Enters Into Heaven, Serenity, The Circus Band, etc.); Gregg Smith, conductor, Columbia Chamber Orchestra; Gregg Smith Singers, Ithaca College Concert Choir/ George Bragg, conductor, Texas Boys Choir

Best classical vocal soloist, *Prima Donna,* Leontyne Price; Molinari-Pradelli, conductor, RCA Italiana Opera Orchestra

1967

Record of the year, *Up, Up And Away,* 5th Dimension

Album of the year, *Sgt. Pepper's Lonely Hearts Club Band,* The Beatles

Song of the year, *Up, Up and Away;* songwriter, Jim Webb

Best instrumental theme, *Mission: Impossible;* composer, Lalo Schifrin

Best female vocal, *Ode to Billy Joe,* Bobbie Gentry

Best male vocal, *By The Time I Get to Phoenix,* Glen Campbell

Best instrumental, *Chet Atkins Picks The Best,* Chet Atkins

Best vocal group, *Up, Up and Away,* 5th Dimension

Best performance chorus, *Up, Up and Away,* Johnny Mann Singers

Best original score, *Mission: Impossible;* composer, Lalo Schifrin

Best score from an original cast show album, *Cabaret;* composers, Fred Ebb and John Kander

Best comedy, *Revenge,* Bill Cosby

Best instrumental jazz—small group, *Mercy, Mercy, Mercy,* Cannonball Adderley Quintet

Best instrumental jazz—large group, *Far East Suite,* Duke Ellington

Best contemporary single, *Up, Up and Away,* 5th Dimension

Best contemporary album, *Sgt. Pepper's Lonely Hearts Club Band,* The Beatles

Best contemporary female solo vocal, *Ode to Billie Joe,* Bobby Gentry

Best contemporary male solo vocal, *By the Time I Get to Phoenix,* Glen Campbell

Best contemporary group, *Up, Up and Away,* 5th Dimension

Best rhythm and blues, *Respect,* Aretha Franklin

Best rhythm and blues female solo vocal, *Respect,* Aretha Franklin

Best rhythm and blues male solo vocal, *Dead End Street,* Lou Rawls

Best rhythm and blues group (2 or

Composer-conductor Leonard Bernstein (left) getting his National Music Award from Robert Campbell, a director of the American Music Conference.

more), *Soul Man*, Sam and Dave
Best sacred, *How Great Thou Art*, Elvis Presley
Best gospel, *More Grand Old Gospel*, Porter Wagoner and the Blackwood Bros.
Best folk, *Gentle on My Mind*, John Hartford
Best country and western, *Gentle on My Mind*, Glen Campbell
Best country and western female solo vocal, *I Don't Wanna Play House*, Tammy Wynette
Best country and western male solo vocal, *Gentle on My Mind*, Glen Campbell
Best country and western—duet, trio or group, *Jackson*, Johnny Cash, June Carter
Best country and western song, *Gentle on My Mind*; songwriter, John Hartford
Best spoken word, *Gallant Men*, Sen. Everett M. Dirksen
Best children's, *Dr. Seuss: How The Grinch Stole Christmas*, Boris Karloff
Best instrumental arrangement, *Alfie*, Burt Bacharach Orchestra;

arrangement, Burt Bacharach
Best accompaniment arrangement, *Ode to Billie Joe*, Bobbie Gentry; arrangement, Jimmie Haskell
Best engineered recording, *Sgt. Pepper's Lonely Hearts Club Band*, The Beatles; engineer, G. E. Emerick
Best engineered recording— classical, *The Glorious Sound of Brass*, Philadelphia Brass Ensemble; engineer, Edward T. Graham
Album of the year—classical, *Berg: Wozzeck*; Pierre Boulez, Paris National Opera
Mahler: Symphony No. 8 in E Flat Major ("Symphony of a Thousand"); Leonard Bernstein, conductor, London Symphony Orchestra
Best classical orchestra, *Stravinsky: Firebird and Petrouchka Suites*; Igor Stravinsky, conductor, Columbia Symphony
Best chamber music, *West Meets East*, Ravi Shankar and Yehudi Menuhin
Best classical—instrumental, soloist(s), *Horowitz In Concert*
Best opera, *Berg: Wozzeck*, Pierre

Boulez and Paris National Opera
Best classical choral, *Mahler:
Symphony No. 8 in E Flat Major,*
Leonard Bernstein, conductor,
London Symphony Orchestra
Orff: Catulli Carmina, Robert Page,
conductor, Temple University
Chorus; Eugene Ormandy,
conductor, Philadelphia Orchestra
Best classical vocal soloist, *Prima
Donna, Volume 2,* Leontyne Price;
Molinari-Pradelli, conductor, RCA
Italiana Opera Orchestra

1968

Record of the year, *Mrs. Robinson,*
Simon and Garfunkel
Album of the year, *By the Time I Get
to Phoenix,* Glen Campbell
Song of the year, *Little Green
Apples;* songwriter, Bobby Russell
Best instrumental arrangement,
Classical Gas, Mason Williams;
arrangement, Mike Post
Best accompaniment arrangement,
MacArthur Park, Richard Harris;
arrangement, Jim Webb
Best contemporary—pop female
vocal, *Do You Know the Way to San
Jose,* Dionne Warwicke
Best contemporary—pop male vocal,
Light My Fire, Jose Feliciano
Best contemporary—pop vocal, duo
or group, *Mrs. Robinson,* Simon and
Garfunkel
Best contemporary—pop chorus,
*Mission Impossible/Norwegian
Wood,* Alan Copeland Singers
Best contemporary—pop
instrumental, *Classical Gas,* Mason
Williams
Best rhythm and blues female vocal,
Chain Of Fools, Aretha Franklin
Best rhythm and blues male vocal,
(Sittin' On) The Dock of the Bay, Otis
Redding
Best rhythm and blues—duo or
group, *Cloud Nine,* The Temptations
Best rhythm and blues song, *(Sittin'
On) the Dock of the Bay;*
songwriters, Otis Redding and Steve
Cropper
Best country female vocal, *Harper
Valley P.T.A.,* Jeannie C. Riley
Best country male vocal, *Folsom
Prison Blues,* Johnny Cash

Best country—duo or group, *Foggy
Mountain Breakdown,* Flatt and
Scruggs
Best country song, *Little Green
Apples;* songwriter, Bobby Russell
Best sacred, *Beautiful Isle of
Somewhere,* Jack Hess
Best gospel, *The Happy Gospel of
the Happy Goodmans,* Happy
Goodman Faily
Best soul gospel, *The Soul of Me,*
Dottie Rambo
Best folk, *Both Sides Now,* Judy
Collins
Best instrumental theme, *Classical
Gas,* composer, Mason Williams
Best original score, *The Graduate;*
songwriter, Paul Simon; additional
music, Dave Grusin
Best score from an original cast show
album, *Hair;* composer, Gerome
Ragni, James Rado, and Galt
MacDermott
Best comedy, *To Russell, My
Brother, Whom I Slept With,* Bill
Cosby
Best spoken word, *Lonesome Cities,*
Rod McKuen
Best instrumental jazz—small group,
*Bill Evans at the Montreux Jazz
Festival,* Bill Evans Trio
Best instrumental jazz—large group,
And His Mother Called Him Bill,
Duke Ellington
Best classical orchestra, Boulez
Conducts Debussy; Pierre Boulez,
conductor, New Philharmonia
Orchestra
Best chamber music, *Gabrieli:
Canzoni for Brass, Winds, Strings
and Organ,* E. Power Biggs with
Edward Tarr Ensemble and Gabrieli
Consort; Vittorio Negri, conductor
Best opera recording, *Mozart: Cosi
Fan Tutte;* Erich Leinsdorf,
conductor, New Philharmonia
Orchestra and Ambrosian Opera
Chorus
Best performance—instrumental
soloist(s), *Horowitz on Television*
Best choral, *The Glory of Gabrieli,*
Vittorio Negri, conductor; Gregg
Smith Singers, Texas Boys Choir,
George Bragg, director; Edward Tarr
Ensemble with E. Power Biggs

Best classical vocal soloist, *Rossini Rarities*, Montserrat Caballe; Cillario, conductor, RCA Italiana Opera Orchestra and Chorus
Best engineered—classical, *Mahler: Symphony No. 9 in D Major;* Solti, conductor, London Symphony Orchestra; engineer, Gordon Parry

1969

Record of the year, *Aquarius/Let the Sunshine In,* 5th Dimension
Album of the year, *Blood, Sweat and Tears,* Blood, Sweat and Tears
Song of the year, *Games People Play*; songwriter, Joe South
Best instrumental arrangement, *Love Theme from Romeo and Juliet,* Henry Mancini; arrangement, Henry Mancini
Best accompaniment arrangement, *Spinning Wheel,* Blood, Sweat and Tears; arrangement, Fred Lipsius
Best engineered recording, *Abbey Road,* The Beatles; engineers, Geoff Emerick and Phillip McDonald
Best contemporary female vocal, *Is That All There Is,* Peggy Lee
Best contemporary male vocal, *Everybody's Talkin',* Harry Nilsson
Best contemporary group vocal, *Aquarius/Let the Sunshine In,* 5th Dimension
Best contemporary chorus, *Love Theme from Romeo and Juliet,* Percy Faith Orchestra and Chorus
Best contemporary instrumental, *Variations on a Theme by Eric Satie,* Blood, Sweat and Tears
Best contemporary song, *Games People Play*; songwriter, Joe South
Best rhythm and blues—female vocal, *Share Your Love With Me,* Aretha Franklin
Best rhythm and blues—male vocal, *The Chokin' Kind,* Joe Simon
Best rhythm and blues—vocal group or duo, *It's Your Thing,* The Isley Brothers
Best rhythm and blues instrumental, *Games People Play,* King Curtis
Best rhythm and blues song, *Color Him Father,* songwriter, Richard Spencer
Best soul gospel, *Oh Happy Day,* Edwin Hawkins Singers
Best country female vocal, *Stand By Your Man,* Tammy Wynette
Best country male vocal, *A Boy Named Sue,* Johnny Cash
Best country duo or group, *MacArthur Park,* Waylon Jennings and The Kimberleys
Best country instrumental, *The Nashville Brass Featuring Danny Davis Play More Nashville Sounds*
Best country song, *A Boy Named Sue;* songwriter, Shel Silverstein
Best sacred, *Ain't That Beautiful Singing,* Jake Hess
Best gospel, *In Gospel Country,* Porter Wagoner and The Blackwood Brothers
Best folk, *Clouds,* Joni Mitchell
Best instrumental theme, *Midnight Cowboy;* composer, John Barry
Best original score, *Butch Cassidy and the Sundance Kid;* composer, Burt Bacharach
Best score from an original cast show album, *Promises, Promises;* composer, Burt Bacharach and Hal David
Best children's, *Peter, Paul & Mommy,* Peter, Paul and Mary
Best comedy, *Bill Cosby*
Best spoken word, *We Love You, Call Collect,* Art Linkletter and Diane
Best instrumental jazz—small group, *Willow Weep For Me,* Wes Montgomery
Best instrumental jazz—large group, *Walking in Space,* Quincy Jones
Album of the year, classical, *Switched-On Bach,* Walter Carlos
Best classical orchestra, *Boulez Conducts Debussy, Vol. 2 "Images Pour Orchestre;* Pierre Boulez, conductor, Cleveland Orchestra
Best chamber music, *Gabrieli: Antiphonal Music of Gabrieli (Canzoni for Brass Choirs);* The Philadelphia, Cleveland, and Chicago Brass Ensembles
Best instrumental soloist(s), *Switched-On Bach,* Walter Carlos
Best opera, *Wagner: Siegfried;* Herbert von Karajan, conductor, Berlin Philharmonic
Best choral, *Berio: Sinfonia,* Swingle Singers; New York Philharmonic, Luciano Berlo, conductor

Best classical vocal soloist, *Barber: Two Scenes From "Antony and Cleopatra"/Knoxville: Summer of 1915,* Leontyne Price; Schippers, conductor, New Philharmonia

Best engineered classical, *Switched-On Bach,* Walter Carlos; engineer, Walter Carlos

1970

Record of the year, *Bridge Over Troubled Water,* Simon and Garfunkel

Album of the year, *Bridge Over Troubled Water,* Simon and Garfunkel

Song of the year, *Bridge Over Troubled Water;* Songwriter, Paul Simon

Best instrumental arrangement, *Theme From "Z,"* Henry Mancini; arrangement, Henry Mancini

Best accompaniment arrangement, *Bridge Over Troubled Water,* Simon and Garfunkel; arrangement, Paul Simon, Arthur Garfunkel, Jimmie Haskell, Ernie Freeman, Larry Knechtel

Best engineered, *Bridge Over Troubled Water,* Simon and Garfunkel; engineer, Roy Halee

Best contemporary female vocal, *I'll Never Fall In Love Again,* Dionne Warwicke

Best contemporary male vocal, *Everything Is Beautiful,* Ray Stevens

Best contemporary group vocal, *Close To You,* Carpenters

Best contemporary instrumental, *Theme from "Z" and Other Film Music,* Henry Mancini

Best contemporary song, *Bridge Over Troubled Water,* songwriter, Paul Simon

Best rhythm and blues—female vocal, *Don't Play That Song,* Aretha Franklin

Best rhythm and blues—male vocal, *The Thrill Is Gone,* B. B. King

Best rhythm and blues—vocal, duo or group, *Didn't I (Blow Your Mind This Time),* The Delfonics

Best rhythm and blues song, *Patches;* songwriters, Ronald Dunbar and General Johnson

Best soul gospel, *Every Man Wants to Be Free,* Edwin Hawkins Singers

Best country female vocal, *Rose Garden,* Lynn Anderson

Best country male vocal, *For The Good Times,* Ray Price

Best country—duo or group, *If I Were a Carpenter,* Johnny Cash and June Carter

Best country instrumental, *Me & Jerry,* Chet Atkins and Jerry Reed

Best country song, *My Woman, My Woman, My Wife;* songwriter, Marty Robbins

Best sacred, *Everything Is Beautiful,* Jake Hess

Best gospel, *Talk About the Good Times,* Oak Ridge Boys

Best ethnic, *Good Feelin',* T-Bone Walker

Best instrumental composition, *Airport Love Theme,* composer, Alfred Newman

Best original score, *Let It Be;* composers, John Lennon, Paul McCartney, George Harrison, Ringo Starr

Best score from original cast show album, *Company;* composer, Stephen Sondheim

Best children's, *Sesame Street,* Joan Cooney, producer

Best comedy, *The Devil Made Me Buy This Dress,* Flip Wilson

Best spoken word, *Why I Oppose the War in Vietnam,* Dr. Martin Luther King, Jr.

Best jazz—small group, *Alone,* Bill Evans

Best jazz—large group, *Bitches Brew,* Miles Davis

Classical album of the year, *Berlioz: Les Troyens,* Colin Davis, Royal Opera House Orchestra

Best Classical orchestra, *Stravinsky: Le Sacre Du Printemps;* Pierre Boulez, conductor, Cleveland Orchestra

Best classical instrumental soloist(s), *Brahms: Double Concerto (Concerto in A Minor for Violin and Cello),* David Oistrakh and Mstislav Rostropovich

Best chamber music, *Beethoven: The Complete Piano Trios,* Eugene Istomin, Isaac Stern, Leonard Rose

Best opera, *Berlioz: Les Troyens;* Colin Davis, conductor, Royal Opera

House Orchestra and Chorus
Best vocal soloist—classical,
Schubert: Lieder, Dietrich Fischer-
Dieskau
Best choral, *Ives: New Music of
Charles Ives;* Gregg Smith,
conductor, Gregg Smith Singers and
Columbia Chamber Ensemble
Best engineered classical,
Stravinsky: Le Sacre Du Printemps;
Boulez, conductor, Cleveland
Orchestra; engineers, Fred Plaut,
Ray Moore, Arthur Kendy
1971
Record of the year, *It's Too Late,*
Carole King;
Album of the year, *Tapestry,* Carole
King
Song of the year, *You've Got a
Friend,* songwriter, Carole King
Best instrumental arrangement,
Theme from Shaft, arrangement,
Isaac Hayes and Johnny Allen
Best accompaniment arrangement,
Uncle Albert/Admiral Halsey, Paul
and Linda McCartney; arrangement,
Paul McCartney
Best engineered, *Theme from Shaft,*
Isaac Hayes; engineers, David
Purple, Ron, Capone, Henry Bush
Best pop female vocal, *Tapestry,*
Carole King
Best pop male vocal, *You've Got a
Friend,* James Taylor
Best pop vocal group, *Carpenters,*
Carpenters
Best pop instrumental, *Smackwater
Jack,* Quincy Jones
Best rhythm and blues—female
vocal, *Bridge Over Troubled Water,*
Aretha Franklin
Best rhythm and blues—male vocal,
A Natural Man, Lou Rawls
Best rhythm and blues vocal group,
Proud Mary, Ike and Tina Turner
Best rhythm and blues song, *Ain't No
Sunshine;* songwriter, Bill Withers
Best soul gospel, *Put Your Hand in
the Hand of the Man from Galilee,*
Shirley Caesar
Best country female vocal, *Help Me
Make It Through the Night,* Sammi
Smith
Best country male vocal, *When
You're Hot, You're Hot,* Jerry Reed

Best country vocal—group, *After the
Fire Is Gone,* Conway Twitty and
Loretta Lynn
Best country instrumental,
Snowbird, Chet Atkins
Best country song, *Help Me Make It
Through the Night;* songwriter, Kris
Kristofferson
Best sacred, *Did You Think to Pray,*
Charley Pride
Best gospel, *Let Me Live,* Charley
Pride
Best ethnic, *They Call Me Muddy
Waters,* Muddy Waters
Best instrumental composition,
Theme from Summer of '42;
composer Michel Legrand
Best original score written for
motion picture, *Shaft,* composer,
Isaac Hayes
Best score from an original cast show
album, *Godspell;* composer, Stephen
Schwartz
Best children's, *Bill Cosby Talks to
Kids about Drugs*
Best comedy, *This Is a Recording,*
Lily Tomlin
Best spoken word, *Desiderata,* Les
Crane
Best jazz—soloist, *The Bill Evans
Album*
Best jazz—group, *The Bill Evans
Album,* Bill Evans Trio
Best jazz—big band, *New Orleans
Suite,* Duke Ellington
Classical album of the year,
Horowitz Plays Rachmaninoff,
Vladimir Horowitz; producers,
Richard Killough, Thomas Frost
Best classical—orchestra, *Mahler:
Symphony No 1 in D Major;* Carlo
Maria Giulini, conductor, Chicago
Symphony Orchestra
Best classical—instrumental soloist
or soloists (with Orchestra), *Villa-
Lobos: Concerto for Guitar,* Julian
Bream; (Andre Previn, conductor,
London Symphony)
Best classical—instrumental soloist
or soloists (without Orchestra),
Horowitz Plays Rachmaninoff,
Vladimir Horowitz
Best chamber music, *Debussy:
Quartet in G Minor/Ravel: Quartet in
F Major,* Juilliard Quartet

Best opera, *Verdi: Aida;* Erich
Leinsdorf, conductor, London
Symphony Orchestra, (Price,
Domingo, Milnes, Bumbry,
Raimondi); producer Richard Mohr
Best classical vocal soloist, *Leontyne
Price Sings Robert Schumann*
Best choral classical (other than
opera), *Berlioz: Requiem,* Colin
Davis, conductor, London
Symphony Orchestra; Russell
Burgess, conductor, Wandsworth
School Boys Choir; Arthur Oldham,
conductor, London Symphony
Chorus
Best engineered classical, *Berlioz:
Requiem,* Colin Davis, conductor,
London Symphony Orchestra;
Russell Burgess, conductor,
Wandsworth School Boys Choir;
Oldham, conductor, London
Symphony Chorus; engineer,
Vittorio Negri
1972
Record of the year, *The First Time
Ever I Saw Your Face,* Roberta Flack
Album of the year, *The Concert for
Bangla Desh,* George Harrison, Ravi
Shankar, Bob Dylan, Leon Russell,
Ringo Starr, Billy Preston, Eric
Clapton, Klaus Voormann
Song of the year, *The First Time
Ever I Saw Your Face*; songwriter,
Ewan MacColl
Best instrumental arrangement,
Theme from the French Connection,
Don Ellis; arrangement, Don Ellis
Best accompaniment arrangement,
*What Are You Doing the Rest of Your
Life,* Sarah Vaughn; arrangement,
Michel Legrand
Best engineered, *Moods,* Neil
Diamond; engineer, Armin Steiner
Best jazz—soloist, *Alone at Last,*
Gary Burton
Best jazz—group, *First Light,*
Freddie Hubbard
Best jazz—big band, *Toga Brava
Suite,* Duke Ellington
Best pop female vocal, *I Am Woman,*
Helen Reddy
Best pop male vocal, *Without You,*
Nilsson
Best pop vocal—duo, group or
chorus, *Where Is the Love,* Roberta

Flack, Donny Hathaway
Best pop instrumental performer,
Outa-Space, Billy Preston
Best pop instrumental arranger,
composer, orchestra and/or choral
leader, *Black Moses,* Isaac Hayes
Best rhythm and blues female vocal,
Young, Gifted & Black, Aretha
Franklin
Best rhythm and blues male vocal,
Me & Mrs. Jones, Billy Paul
Best rhythm and blues vocal—duo,
group or chorus, *Papa Was a Rolling
Stone,* The Temptations
Best rhythm and blues instrumental,
Papa Was a Rolling Stone, The
Temptations; conductor, Paul Riser
Best rhythm and blues song, *Papa
Was a Rolling Stone;* songwriters,
Barrett Strong and Norman Whitfield
Best soul gospel, *Amazing Grace,*
Aretha Franklin
Best country female vocal, *Happiest
Girl in the Whole USA,* Donna Fargo
Best country male vocal, *Charley
Pride Sings Heart Songs*
Best country vocal—duo or group,
Class of '57, The Statler Bros.
Best country instrumental, *Charlie
McCoy/The Real McCoy,* Charlie
McCoy
Best country song, *Kiss An Angel
Good Mornin';* songwriter, Ben
Peters
Best inspirational, *He Touched Me,*
Elvis Presley
Best gospel *Love,* Blackwood Bros.
Best ethnic, *The London Muddy
Waters Session,* Muddy Waters
Best children's, *The Electric
Company;* Project Director,
Christopher Cerf, Lee Chamberlin,
Bill Cosby, Rita Moreno; Prod. &
Music Dir: Joe Raposo
Best comedy, *FM & AM,* George
Carlin
Best spoken word, *Lenny;* producer,
Bruce Botnick
Best instrumental composition,
Brian's Song, Michel Legrand
Best original score written for
motion picture or television special,
The Godfather; composer, Nino Rota
Best score from an original cast show
album, *Don't Bother Me, I Can't*

Cope; composer, Micki Grant; producer, Jerry Ragavoy

Album of the year—classical, *Mahler: Symphony No. 8;* Georg Solti, conductor, Chicago Symphony Orchestra, Vienna Boys Choir, Vienna State Opera Chorus, Vienna Singverein Chorus and Soloists; producer, David Harvey

Best classical orchestra, *Mahler: Symphony No. 7;* Georg Solti, conductor, Chicago Symphony Orchestra

Best opera, *Berlioz: Benvenuto Cellini;* Colin Davis, conductor, BBC Symphony, Chorus of Covent Garden; producer, Erik Smith

Best choral, *Mahler: Symphony No. 8;* Georg Solti, conductor

Best chamber music, *Julian & John,* Julian Bream, John Williams

Best instrumental soloist—with orchestra, *Brahms: Concerto No. 2,* Artur Rubinstein

Best instrumental soloist—without orchestra, *Horowitz Plays Chopin,* Vladimir Horowitz

Best vocal soloist, *Brahms: Die Schone Magelone,* Dietrich Fischer-Dieskau

Best engineered, *Mahler: Symphony No. 8,* engineers, Gordon Parry, Kenneth Wilkinson

1973

Record of the year, *Killing Me Softly With His Song,* Roberta Flack;

Album of the year, *Innervisions,* Stevie Wonder

Song of the year, *Killing Me Softly With His Song;* songwriter, Norman Gimbel, Charles Fox

Best instrumental arrangement, *Summer in the City,* Quincy Jones; arrangement, Quincy Jones

Best accompaniment arrangement, *Live and Let Die,* Paul McCartney and Wings; arrangement, George Martin

Best engineered (non-classical), *Innervisions,* Stevie Wonder; engineers, Robert Margouleff and Malcolm Cecil

Best jazz—soloist, *God Is in the House,* Art Tatum

Best jazz—group, *Supersax Plays Bird,* Supersax

Best jazz—big band, *Giant Steps,* Woody Herman

Best pop female vocal, *Killing Me Softly With His Song,* Roberta Flack

Best pop male vocal, *You Are the Sunshine of my Life,* Stevie Wonder

Best pop vocal—duo, group, or chorus, *Neither One of Us (Wants to Be the First to Say Goodbye),* Gladys Knight and The Pips

Best pop instrumental, *Also Sprach Zarathustra (2001),* Eumir Deodato

Best rhythm and blues female vocal, *Master of Eyes,* Aretha Franklin

Best rhythm and blues male vocal, *Superstition,* Stevie Wonder

Best rhythm and blues vocal—duo, group, or chorus, *Midnight Train to Georgia,* Gladys Knight and The Pips

Best rhythm and blues instrumental, *Hang on Sloopy,* Ramsey Lewis

Best rhythm and blues song, *Superstition,* songwriter, Stevie Wonder

Best soul gospel, *Loves Me Like a Rock,* Dixie Hummingbirds

Best country female vocal, *Let Me Be There,* Olivia Newton-John

Best country male vocal, *Behind Closed Doors,* Charlie Rich

Best country vocal—duo or group, *From the Bottle to the Bottom,* Kris Kristofferson, Rita Coolidge

Best country instrumental, *Dueling Banjos,* Eric Weissberg, Steve Mandell

Best country song, *Behind Closed Doors,* songwriter, Kenny O'Dell

Best inspirational, *Let's Just Praise the Lord,* Bill Gaither Trio

Best gospel, *Release Me (From My Sin),* Blackwood Brothers

Best ethnic or traditional, *Then and Now,* Doc Watson

Best children's, *Sesame Street Live,* Sesame Street Cast; Joe Raposo, producer

Best comedy, *Los Cochinos,* Cheech and Chong

Best spoken word, *Jonathan Livingston Seagull,* Richard Harris

Best instrumental composition, *Last Tango in Paris;* composer, Gato Barbieri
Album of best original score, written for a motion picture, *Jonathan Livingston Seagull;* composer, Neil Diamond
Best score from the original cast show album, *A Little Night Music;* composer, Stephen Sondheim; producer, Goddard Lieberson
Classical album of the year, *Bartok: "Concerto For Orchestra;* Pierre Boulez, conductor, New York Philharmonic Orchestra; producer, Thomas Z. Shepard
Best classical orchestra, *Bartok: Concerto for Orchestra;* Pierre Boulez, conductor, New York Philharmonic Orchestra
Best opera, *Bizet: Carmen;* Leonard Bernstein, conductor, Metropolitan Opera Orchestra, Manhattan Opera Chorus (Horne, McCracken, Maliponte, Kraus); producer, Thomas W. Mowrey
Best choral classical, *Walton: Belshazzar's Feast;* Andre Previn, conductor, London Symphony Orchestra, Arthur Oldham, conductor, London Symphony Orchestra Chorus
Best chamber music, *Joplin: The Red Back Book;* Gunther Schuller and New England Conservatory Ragtime Ensemble
Best classical instrumental soloist (with orchestra), *Beethoven: "Concerti (5) for Piano and Orchestra,* Vladimir Ashkenazy; Solti, conductor, Chicago Symphony)
Best classical instrumental soloist (without orchestra), *(Scriabin) Horowitz Plays Scriabin,* Vladimir Horowitz
Best classical vocal soloist, *Puccini: Heroines (La Boheme, La Rondine, Tosca, Manon Lescaut),* Leontyne Price, Downes, conductor, New Philharmonia
Best engineered (classical), *Bartok: Concerto for Orchestra;* Pierre Boulez conductor, New York Philharmonic; engineers, Edward T.

Graham, Raymond Moore

1974

Record of the year, *I Honestly Love You,* Olivia Newton-John;
Album of the year, *Fulfillingness' First Finale,* Stevie Wonder
Song of the year, *The Way We Were;* songwriters, Marilyn and Alan Bergman, Marvin Hamlisch
Best instrumental arrangement, *Threshold,* Pat Williams; arrangement, Pat Williams
Best accompaniment arrangement, *Down to You,* Joni Mitchell; arrangement, Joni Mitchell and Tom Scott
Best engineered (non-classical), *Band on the Run,* Paul McCartney & Wings; engineer, Geoff Emerick
Best jazz—soloist, *First Recordings,* Charlie Parker
Best jazz—group, *The Trio,* Oscar Peterson, Joe Pass, Niels Pedersen
Best jazz—big band, *Thundering Herd,* Woody Herman
Best pop female vocal, *I Honestly Love You,* Olivia Newton-John
Best pop male vocal, *Fulfillingness' First Finale,* Stevie Wonder
Best pop vocal—duo, group, or chorus, *Band on the Run,* Paul McCartney & Wings
Best pop instrumental, *The Entertainer,* Marvin Hamlisch
Best rhythm and blues—female vocal, *Ain't Nothing Like the Real Thing,* Aretha Franklin
Best rhythm and blues—male vocal, *Boogie on Reggae Woman,* Stevie Wonder
Best rhythm and blues vocal—duo, group, or chorus, *Tell Me Something Good,* Rufus
Best rhythm and blues instrumental, *TSOP (The Sound of Philadelphia),* MFSB
Best rhythm and blues song, *Living for the City;* songwriter, Stevie Wonder
Best soul gospel, *In the Ghetto,* James Cleveland & the Southern California Community Choir
Best country female vocal, *Love Song,* Anne Murray

Best country male vocal, *Please Don't Tell Me How the Story Ends,* Ronnie Milsap

Best country vocal—duo or group, *Fairytale,* The Pointer Sisters

Best country instrumental, *The Atkins-Travis Traveling Show,* Chet Atkins and Merle Travis

Best country song, *A Very Special Love Song;* songwriters, Norris Wilson and Billy Sherrill

Best inspirational, *How Great Thou Art,* Elvis Presley

Best gospel, *The Baptism of Jesse Taylor,* Oak Ridge Boys

Best ethnic or traditional, *Two Days in November,* Doc and Merle Watson

Best children's album, *Winnie the Pooh & Tigger Too,* Sebastian Cabot, Sterling Holloway, Paul Winchell

Best comedy, *That Nigger's Crazy,* Richard Pryor

Best spoken word, *Good Evening,* Peter Cook and Dudley Moore

Best instrumental composition, *Tubular Bells (Theme From "The Exorcist");* composer, Mike Oldfield

Album of best original score written for a motion picture or a television special, *The Way We Were;* composer, Marvin Hamlisch, Alan and Marilyn Bergman

Best score from the original cast show album, *Raisin;* composers, Judd Woldin and Robert Brittan; producer, Thomas Z. Shepard

Classical album of the year, *Berlioz: Symphonie Fantastique;* Georg Solti, conductor, Chicago Symphony; producer, David Harvey

Best classical orchestra, *Berlioz: Symphonie Fantastique;* Georg Solti, conductor, Chicago Symphony

Best opera, *Puccini: La Boheme;* Georg Solti, conductor; producer, Richard Mohr

Best choral classical (other than opera), *Berlioz: The Damnation of Faust;* conductor, Colin Davis

Best chamber music, *Brahms & Schumann Trios,* Artur Rubinstein, Henryk Szeryng and Pierre Fournier

Best classical instrumental soloist or soloists (with orchestra), *Shostakovich: Violin Concerto No. 1,* David Oistrakh

Best classical instrumental soloist or soloists (without orchestra), *Albeniz: Iberia,* Alicia de Larrocha

Best classical vocal soloist, *Leontyne Price Sings Richard Strauss*

Best engineered classical, *Berlioz: Symphonie Fantastique;* engineer, Kenneth Wilkinson

1975

Record of the year, *Love Will Keep Us Together,* Captain and Tennille

Album of the year, *Still Crazy After All These Years,* Paul Simon;

Song of the year, *Send in the Clowns;* songwriter, Stephen Sondheim

Best instrumental arrangement, *The Rockford Files,* Mike Post; arrangement, Mike Post, Pete Carpenter

Best accompaniment arrangement, *Misty,* Ray Stevens; arrangement, Ray Stevens

Best engineered, *Between the Lines,* Janis Ian; engineer, Brooks Arthur, Larry Alexander and Russ Payne

Best jazz soloist, *Oscar Peterson and Dizzy Gillespie,* Dizzy Gillespie

Best jazz—group, *No Mystery,* Chick Corea and Return To Forever

Best jazz—big band, *Images,* Phil Woods with Michel Legrand and His Orchestra

Best pop female vocal, *At Seventeen,* Janis Ian

Best pop male vocal, *Still Crazy After All These Years,* Paul Simon

Best pop vocal by a duo, group or chorus, *Lyin' Eyes,* Eagles

Best pop instrumental, *The Hustle,* Van McCoy and the Soul City Symphony

Best rhythm and blues female vocal *This Will Be,* Natalie Cole

Best rhythm and blues male vocal, *Living for the City,* Ray Charles

Best rhythm and blues vocal by a duo, group, or chorus, *Shining Star,* Earth, Wind & Fire

Best rhythm and blues instrumental, *Fly, Robin, Fly,* Silver Convention

Best rhythm and blues song, *Where Is the Love;* songwriters, Harry

Wayne Casey, Richard Finch, Willie Clarke, Betty Wright
Best soul gospel, *Take Me Back,* Andrae Crouch and the Disciples
Best country female vocal, *I Can't Help It (If I'm Still In Love With You),* Linda Ronstadt
Best country male vocal, *Blues Eyes Crying In the Rain,* Willie Nelson
Best country vocal by a duo or group, *Lover Please,* Kris Kristofferson and Rita Coolidge
Best country instrumental, *The Entertainer,* Chet Atkins
Best country song, *(Hey Won't You Play) Another Somebody Done Somebody Wrong Song;* songwriters, Chips Moman and Larry Butler
Best inspirational, *Jesus, We Just Want To Thank You,* The Bill Gaither Trio
Best gospel, *No Shortage,* Imperials
Best ethnic or traditional, *The Muddy Waters Woodstock Album,* Muddy Waters
Best latin, *Sun Of Latin Music,* Eddie Palmieri
Best children's album, *The Little Prince,* Richard Burton, narrator
Best comedy, *Is It Something I Said,* Richard Pryor
Best spoken word, *Give 'Em Hell Harry,* James Whitmore
Best instrumental composition, *Images*; composer, Michel Legrand
Album of best original score written for motion picture or television special, Jaws; composer, John Williams
Album of the year—classical, *Beethoven: Symphonies (9) Complete;* Georg Solti conductor, the Chicago Symphony Orchestra; producer, Ray Minshull
Best classical orchestra, *Ravel: Daphnis Et Chloe (Complete Ballet);* Pierre Boulez, conductor, New York Philharmonic
Best opera, *Mozart: Cosi Fan Tutte;* Colin Davis, conductor, Royal Opera House, Covent Garden; Principal Solos, Caballe, Baker, Gedda, Ganzarolli, Van Allan, Cotrubas; producer, Erik Smith
Best choral classical, *Orff: Carmina*

Burana; Robert Page director, Cleveland Orchestra Chorus and Boys Choir; Michael Tilson Thomas, conductor, Cleveland Orchestra; soloists, Blegen, Binder, Riegel
Best chamber music, *Schubert: "Trios Nos. 1 in B flat Maj. Op. 99 & 2 in E Flat Major, Op. 100 (The Piano Trios),* Artur Rubinstein, Henryk Szeryng, Pierre Fournier
Best classical instrumental soloist (with orchestra), *Ravel: "Concerto for Left Hand & Concerto for piano in G Maj./Faure: Fantasie For Piano & Orchestra,* Alicia de Larrocha; De Burgos & Foster, conductors, London Philharmonic
Best classical instrumental soloist (without orchestra), *Bach: Sonatas & Partitas for Violin Unaccompanied,* Nathan Milstein
Best classical vocal soloist, *Mahler: Kindertotenlieder,* Janet Baker; Bernstein, conductor, Israel Philharmonic
1976
Record of the year, *This Masquerade,* George Benson
Album of the year, *Songs In the Key of Life,* Stevie Wonder;
Song of the year, *I Write the Songs;* songwriter, Bruce Johnston
Best instrumental arrangement, Leprechaun's Dream, Chick Corea; arrangement, Chick Corea
Best accompaniment arrangement, *If You Leave Me Now,* Chicago; arrangements, Jimmie Haskell and James William Guercio
Best arrangement for voices— duo, group or chorus; *Afternoon Delight,* Starland Vocal Band; arrangements, Starland Vocal Band
Best engineered (nonclassical), *Breezin,* George Benson; engineer, Al Schmitt
Best producer of the year, Stevie Wonder *Songs in the Key of Life*
Best jazz vocal, *Fitzgerald & Pass . . . Again,* Ella Fitzgerald
Best jazz group, Count Basie *Basie & Zoot*
Best jazz soloist, Chick Corea, *The Leprechaun*
Best jazz big band, *The Ellington*

Suites, Duke Ellington
Best pop female vocal, *Hasten Down the Wind,* Linda Ronstadt
Best pop male vocal, *Songs in the Key of Life,* Stevie Wonder
Best pop vocal—duo group, or chorus, *If You Leave Me Now,* Chicago
Best pop instrumental, *Breezin',* George Benson
Rhythm and blues vocal—female, *Sophisticated Lady (She's a Different Lady),* Natalie Cole
Best rhythm and blues vocal—male, *I Wish,* Stevie Wonder
Best rhythm and blues vocal—duo group, *You Don't Have to Be a Star (to Be in My Show),* Marilyn McCoo, Billy Davis Jr.
Best rhythm and blues instrumental, *Theme from Good King Bad,* George Benson
Best rhythm and blues song, *Lowdown,* Boz Scaggs; songwriters, Boz Scaggs, David Paich
Best soul gospel, *How I Got Over,* Mahalia Jackson
Best country female vocal, *Elite Hotel,* Emmylou Harris
Best country male vocal, *(I'm a) Stand By My Woman Man,* Ronnie Milsap
Best country vocal—duo or group, *The End Is Not In Sight (The Cowboy Tune),* Amazing Rhythm Aces
Best Country Instrumental, *Chester & Lester,* Chet Atkins, Les Paul
Best country song, *Broken Lady;* Larry Gatlin, songwriter
Best inspirational, *The Astonishing, Outrageous, Amazing, Incredible, Unbelievable, Different World of Gary S. Paxton,* Gary S. Paxton
Best gospel (other than soul gospel), *Where the Soul Never Dies,* Oak Ridge Boys
Best ethnic or traditional, *Mark Twang,* John Hartford
Best latin, *Unfinished Masterpiece,* Eddie Palmieri
Best children's album, *Prokofiev: Peter And The Wolf/Saint Saens: Carnival Of The Animals,* Hermione Gingold, Karl Bohm

Best comedy, *Bicentennial Nigger,* Richard Pryor
Best spoken word, *Great American Documents,* Orson Welles, Henry Fonda, Helen Hayes, James Earl Jones
Best instrumental composition, *Bellavia,* Chuck Mangione; composer, Chuck Mangione
Album of best original score written for a motion picture or television special, *Car Wash;* Norman Whitefield, composer
Best cast show album, *Bubbling Brown Sugar;* Hugh and Luigi, producers
Album of the year (classical), *Beethoven: The Five Piano Concertos;* Artur Rubinstein and Daniel Barenboim conductors, the London Philharmonic; producer, Max Wilcox
Best classical orchestral, *Strauss: Also Sprach Zarathustra;* Georg Solti, conductor, the Chicago Symphony; producer, Ray Minshull
Best opera, *Gershwin: Porgy & Bess;* Lorin Maazel, conductor the Cleveland Orchestra and Chorus; producer, Michael Woolcook
Best choral classical (other than opera), *Rachmaninoff: The Bells;* Arthur Oldham, chorus master of London Symphony Chorus; Andre Previn, conductor London Symphony Orchestra
Best chamber music, *The Art of Courtly Love;* David Munrow conductor, Early Music Consort of London
Best classical instrumental soloist or soloists (with orchestra), *Beethoven: The Five Piano Concertos,* Artur Rubinstein, piano; Daniel Barenboim conductor, London Philharmonic
Best classical instrumental soloist or soloists (without orchestra), *Horowitz Concerts 1975/76,* Vladimir Horowitz, piano
Best classical vocal soloist, *Herbert: Music Of Victor Herbert,* Beverly Sills

CHARLES E. IVES AWARDS—The National Institute of Arts and Letters

This prize is divided each year between furthering the publication and performance of the music of Charles Ives and a scholarship to enable a young composer to continue studying.

Established 1970.

SCHOLARSHIP
1970	Joseph C. Schwantner
1971	Louis Smith Weingarden
1972	Thomas Janson
	Robert J. Krupnick
	Michael Seyfrit
1973	Philip Caldwell Carlsen
	Robert Gerster
	Peter Lieberson
1974	Paul Alan Levi
	Allen Shearer
	Ira Taxin
1975	Chester Biscardi
	Stephen Chatman
	David Koblitz
1976	

IVES GRANT
1970	John Kirkpatrick
1971	Vivian Perlis
1972	Harold Farberman
1973	The Charles E. Ives Society
1974	The Charles E. Ives Society
1975	The Charles E. Ives Society
1976	The Charles E. Ives Society

LAUREL LEAF AWARD—American Composers Alliance

For giving American music encouragement.

Established 1950.
1951	Radio Station WGBH, Boston, Mass.
1952	Maro and Anahid Ajemian
1953	Dr. Herman Neuman
1954	Green Bay (Wisc.) Symphonette
1955	George Szell
1956	Robert Whitney
1957	Howard Hanson
	Juilliard String Quartet
1958	Thor Johnson
1959	Martha Graham
	Jack Benny

1960	Howard Mitchell
	Oliver Daniel
1961	Mrs. Helen Thompson
	William Strickland
1962	Bethany Beardslee
	Hugh Ross
	Samuel Rosenbaum
1963	Claire Reis
	Carl Haverlin
1964	Walter Hinrichsen
	Margaret L. Crofts
	Max Pollikoff
1965	Henry Cowell
	Avery Claflin
	Elizabeth Ames
1966	Henry A. Moe
	Lawrence Morton
1967	Radio Station WBAI
	Fromm Foundation
	Composers Forum
1968	Aaron Copland
1969	Group for Contemporary Music
1970	Otto Luening
	Harris Danziger
1971	The Alice M. Ditson Fund
1972	Leopold Stokowski
1973	The MacDowell Colony
1974	Theresa Sterne
1975	Nelson Rockefeller
1976	Gunther Schuller

NATIONAL MUSIC AWARDS—American Music Conference

To honor musicians, lyricists, and composers who have contributed to American music from the drum rolls of the Revolution through the present.

Established 1976.

Harold Arlen
Louis (Satchmo) Armstrong
Milton Babbitt
Samuel Barber
William (Count) Basie
Mrs. H. H. A. Beach
Leon Bismarck (Bix) Beiderbecke
Irving Berlin
Leonard Bernstein
Charles Edward Anderson (Chuck) Berry
William Billings
Jimmy Blanton
Clifford Brown
John Cage

Hoagland Howard (Hoagy) Carmichael
Benjamin Carr
Bennett Lester (Benny) Carter
Elliott Carter
George Whitefield Chadwick
Ray Charles (Ray Charles Robinson)
Charles (Charlie) Christian
George M. Cohan
Nat (King) Cole (Nathaniel Adams Coles)
Aaron Copland
Henry Cowell
Miles Davis, Jr.
Norman Dello Joio
B. G. (George Gard) (Buddy) DeSylva
Robert Nathaniel Dett
Warren (Baby) Dodds
Walter Donaldson
Thomas A. Dorsey
Paul Dresser
Edward Kennedy (Duke) Ellington
Daniel Decatur Emmett
Gil (Ian Ernest Gilmore Green) Evans
Arthur Farwell
Ella Fitzgerald
Stephen Collins Foster
William Henry Fry
George Gershwin
Ira Gershwin
Stanley (Stan) Getz
Henry Franklin Belknap Gilbert
John Birks (Dizzy) Gillespie
Benjamin David (Benny) Goodman
Louis Moreau Gottschalk
Charles Tomlinson Griffes
Woody Guthrie
Oscar Hammerstein II
W. C. (William Christopher) Handy
Howard Harold Hanson
Roy Harris
Lorenz Hart
Coleman Hawkins
Anthony Philip Heinrich
Fletcher Henderson
Victor Herbert
Woodrow Charles (Woody) Herman
James Hewitt
John Hill Hewitt
Earl (Fatha) Hines
Billie Holiday
Francis Hopkinson
Charles Ives
Mahalia Jackson

Milton (Milt) Jackson
J. J. (James) Johnson
James Price Johnson
Robert Johnson
Scott Joplin
Stanley Newcomb (Stan) Kenton
Jerome Kern
Leon Kirchner
Gene Krupa
Eddie Lang
James Melvin (Jimmie) Lunceford
James Lyon
Edward MacDowell
Daniel Gregory Mason
Lowell Mason
Gian-Carlo Menotti
John H. (Johnny) Mercer
Thelonius Monk
Douglas Stuart Moore
John Knowles Paine
Charles Christopher (Charlie or Bird or Yardbird) Parker
Horatio Parker
Cole Porter
Earl (Bud) Powell
Chano Pozo (Luciano Pozo Gonzales)
Donald Matthew (Don) Redman
Alexander Reinagle
Wallingford Riegger
Maxwell (Max) Roach
James Charles (Jimmie) Rodgers
Richard Rodgers
George Frederick Root
George Russell
Henry Russell
William Howard Schuman
Roger Sessions
Bessie Smith
John Philip Sousa
Arthur (Art) Tatum
Deems Taylor
Weldon John (Jack) Teagarden
Virgil Thomson
Leonard Joseph (Lennie) Tristano
Edgard Varese
Sarah Vaughan
Joe (Giuseppe) Venuti
Harry Von Tilzer
Thomas (Fats) Waller
Harry Warren
Richard A. Whiting
Hank Williams
Bob Wills
Henry Clay Work

Vincent Youmans
Lester (Pres) Young

See Pulitzer Prize

See Service, Award of Merit, The Decalogue Society of Lawyers

PHOTOGRAPHY

See Architecture, Fine Arts Medal, The American Institute of Architects

See Architecture, Architectural Photography Medal, The American Institute of Architects

ASMP AWARDS—American Society of Magazine Photographers
The society gives various awards to photojournalists for outstanding work or to individuals who have contributed in some way to the profession.
1953
Henri Cartier-Bresson
Dr. Roland S. Potter, the inventor of Varigam
Roy Stryker
1954
Ernst Haas
Alexey Brodovitch
1955
Robert Capa
Werner Bischof
Dr. John A. Leermakers, assistant director, Kodak Research Laboratories and to Eastman Kodak and its technical staff for significant advance in photographic emulsion-making technology
Wayne Miller
Edward Steichen
1956
Ylla
Dr. Roman Vishniac
1957
Richard Avedon
Will Connell
Allen F. Gifford, for the development of Anscochrome

1958
Marty Forscher, for improving the tools of our profession
Emil Schulthess
Wilson Hicks
1960
Gordon Parks
Dr. Edwin H. Land, for his development of the 4 x 5 Polaroid back
Richard Simon, for his outstanding record in the photographic book-publishing field
David Douglas Duncan
1961
Irving Penn
The Japanese Camera Industry, for its high professional standards
The John Simon Guggenheim Foundation
1962
Brian Brake
George Silk
Bill Brandt
1963
Gjon Mili
1964
Art Kane
The Polaroid Corporation, for the production of the electronic shutter
Berenice Abbott
Charles Moore
1965
David Linton
Ralph Baum
Morris Gordon
Imogen Cunningham

Lennart Nilsson
Harold E. Edgerton

FOUNDERS AWARDS
Allan Gould
Michael Elliot
Ewing Krainin
Ike Vern
Bradley Smith
John Adam Knight
1966
  Andreas Feininger
  Victor Hasselblad, for his designs of
  a truly modern camera system
1967
  Photographer of the Year award to all
  the Vietnam war photographers,
  living and dead. The award was
  symbolically presented to Bernard
  Kolenberg, the first U.S.
  photographer to perish in Vietnam,
  in the name of his colleagues
  Dr. Charles Wycoff, for his
  contribution to the development of
  extended range films
  Dr. Dennis Gabor, Dr. Emmett
  Leith, Juris Upatnieks, for their
  exploration and development of the
  Hologram
1968
  David Douglas Duncan, for his
  outstanding coverage of the Vietnam
  War and for his book, *I Protest*
  Cornell Capa
  Lisette Model
  Dr. Homer E. Newell, for his leading
  role in the development of U.S.
  spacecraft whose extraordinary
  photographs of the moon constituted
  a new era in photography
  Leopold Godowski and Leopold
  Manners, for the first practical
  multilayer photographic color film
  based on color coupling reaction
  Dr. Alexander Smakula, for his
  contribution in perfecting the
  technique of antireflection coatings
  which enhanced images and made
  possible advanced designs in lenses
  Beaumont Newhall
  Grace Mayer, for her unflagging
  devotion to photography
1969
  Hiro
  Fritz Gruger

Ben Rose
Yoichi R. Okamoto
Romana Javits, for making the New
York Public Library picture file a
vital source of pictorial information
Edwin L. Wisherd, on the occasion
of his fiftieth year on the
photographic staff of *National
Geographic* magazine and for his
pioneering to make miniature camera
photography an accepted standard
for modern photojournalism
James Van Derzee
Dr. Ott. Schade, for effecting a
marriage of electronics and optics
which made sophisticated designs of
lenses possible
Oscar Barnack, for developing the
concept of the Leica camera
1970
  Bruce Davidson
  Diane Arbus
  Jerry Uelsmann
  Jacob Deschin, for bringing his
  special skill of criticism and
  journalism to bear upon our
  profession
  Dr. Walter Clark, for the
  development of the Ektachrome
  Infrared Aero Film
  Dr. Peter C. Goldmark, for his
  development of the Electronic Video
  Recording (EVR) system of visual
  recording for CBS-TV
1972
  David B. Eisendrath
  Lee D. Witkin, for his leadership in
  the photographic gallery movement
1975
  Philippe Halsman
  Arnold Newman
  Donald McCullin
  Alexander Liberman, for his editorial
  design excellence
  Dr. Edwin H. Land, for developing
  the revolutionary photographic
  technology of Polaroid's SX 70
  camera

HONOR ROLL
1961
  Man Ray
1962
  Roy Stryker
  Alexey Brodovitch

Edward Steichen
Will Connell
1963
   Dorothea Lange
   Walker Evans
   Cecil Beaton
   Paul Strand
   George Hoyningen-Huene
1964
   Margaret Bourke-White
1965
   Andre Kertesz
1966
   Ansel Adams
   Brassai
1967
   Dr. Roman Vishniac

Bill Brandt
1968
   Beaumont Newhall
1969
   Fritz Gruber
1970
   W. Eugene Smith
1971
   Ernst Haas
1972
   Henri Cartier-Bresson
1975
   Cornell Capa

See Pulitzer Prize

POETRY

See Achievement, Gold Medal Awards, The American Academy of Arts and Letters

LITERATURE

BOLLINGEN PRIZE IN POETRY—
Yale University Library
   This prize goes for either a poet's life work or a particular poem published in the year preceding the presentation of the award.
   Established 1949.
1949   Wallace Stevens
1950   John Crowe Ransom
1951   Marianne Moore
1952   William Carlos Williams
       Archibald MacLeish
1953   W. H. Auden
1954   Leonie Adams
       Louise Bogan
1955   Conrad Aiken

1956   Allen Tate
1957   e. e. cummings
1958   Theodore Roethke
1959   Delmore Schwartz
1960   Ivor Winters
1961   John Hall Wheelock
       Richard Eberhart
1962   Robert Frost
1965   Horace Gregory
1967   Robert Penn Warren
1969   John Berryman
       Karl (Jay) Shapiro
1971   Richard P. Wilbur
       Mona Van Duyn
1973   Archie R. Ammons

See Books, Award of Merit Medal, The American Academy of Arts and Letters and The National Institute of Arts and Letters

COPERNICUS AWARD—The Academy of American Poets and the Copernicus Society of America
   Ten thousand dollars worth of recog-

nition for lifetime achievement of a poet older than forty-five.
Established 1974.

1974	Robert Lowell
1975	Kenneth Rexroth
1976	Robert Penn Warren

See Cowboys and Indians, Western Heritage Awards, The National Cowboy Hall of Fame and Western Heritage Center

THE FELLOWSHIP OF THE ACADEMY OF AMERICAN POETS
—The Academy of American Poets
For distinguished poetic achievement. In 1969 the amount of the award went from $5,000 to $10,000.
Established 1937.

1946	Edgar Lee Masters
1947	Ridgely Torrence
1948	Percy MacKaye
1950	e. e. cummings
1952	Padraic Colum
1953	Robert Frost
1954	Louise Townsend Nicholl
	Dr. Oliver St. John Gogarty
1955	Rolfe Humphries
1956	Dr. William Carlos Williams
1957	Conrad Aiken
1958	Robinson Jeffers
1959	Louise Bogan
	Leonie Adams
1960	Jesse Stuart
1961	Horace Gregory
1962	John Crowe Ransom
1963	Ezra Pound
	Allen Tate
1964	Elizabeth Bishop
1965	Marianne Moore
1966	Archibald MacLeish
	John Berryman
1967	Mark Van Doren
1968	Stanley Kunitz
1969	Richard Eberhart
	Anthony Hecht
1970	Howard Nemerov
1971	James Wright
1972	W. D. Snodgrass
1973	W. S. Merwin
1974	Leonie Adams
1975	Robert Hayden
1976	J. V. Cunningham

GOLD MEDAL—The Poetry Society of America
For "excellence in poetry"

1930	Jessie Rittenhouse
	Clinton Scollard
	George Edward Woodberry
	Bliss Carman
1941	Robert Frost
1942	Edgar Lee Masters
1943	Edna St. Vincent Millay
1947	Gustav Davidson
1951	Wallace Stevens
1952	Carl Sandburg
1955	Leonora Speyer
1967	Marianne Moore
1974	John Hall Wheelock
1976	A. M. Sullivan

THE LAMONT POETRY SELECTION—The Academy of American Poets
A prize for a first book of poems. Since 1975, winning the prize insures there will be a second book.
Established 1954.

1954
Constance Carrier, *The Middle Voice*
1955
Donald Hall, *Exiles and Marriages*
1956
Philip Booth, *Letter from a Distant Land*
1957
Daniel Berrigan, S. J., *Time Without Number*
1958
Ned O'Gorman, *The Night of the Hammer*
1959
Donald Justice, *The Summer Anniversaries*
1960
Robert Mezey, *The Lovemaker*
1961
X. J. Kennedy, *Nude Descending a Staircase*
1962
Edward Field, *Stand Up, Friend, With Me*
1963
no award
1964
Adrien Stoutenberg, *Heroes, Advise Us*

1965
Henri Coulette, *The War of the Secret Agents*
1966
Kenneth O. Hanson, *The Distance Anywhere*
1967
James Scully, *The Marches*
1968
Jane Cooper, *The Weather of Six Mornings*
1969
Marvin Bell, *A Probable Volume of Dreams*
1970
William Harmon, *Treasury Holiday*
1971
Stephen Dobyns, *Concurring Beasts*
1972
Peter Everwine, *Collecting the Animals*
1973
Marilyn Hacker, *Presentation Piece*
1974
John Balaban, *After Our War*
1975
Lisel Mueller, *The Private Life*
1976
Larry Levis, *The Afterlife*

THE HAROLD MORTON LANDON AWARD—The Academy of American Poets

For a published translation of poetry from any foreign language into English.

Established 1976.
1976
Robert Fitzgerald, for the *Iliad* of Homer

THE EDGAR ALLAN POE AWARD
—The Academy of American Poets and the Copernicus Society of America

To win, you must be a poet, forty-five years old or younger who has recently published a book of poems. What you win is $5,000.

Established 1974.

1974   Mark Strand
1975   Charles Simic
1976   Charles Wright

See Pulitzer Prize

THE WALT WHITMAN AWARD—
The Academy of American Poets and the Copernicus Society of America

This is for any American citizen who has not had a book of poems published. The winner gets his book published, $1,000, and a guaranteed one thousand copies go to Academy members and friends.

Established 1974.
1975
Reg Saner, *Climbing into the Roots*
1976
Laura Gilpin, *The House-Pocus of the Universe*

SCIENCE

See Achievement, Frank A. Chambers Award, Air Pollution Control Association

See Achievement, Gold Medal for Distinguished Archaeological Achievement

See Achievement, S. Smith Griswold Award, Air Pollution Control Association

See Achievement, Richard Beatty Mellon Award, Air Pollution Control Association

ROGER ADAMS AWARD IN ORGANIC CHEMISTRY—American Chemical Society, Organic Reactions, Inc., and Organic Syntheses, Inc.

Ten thousand dollars worth of recognition and encouragement for "outstanding contributions to research in organic chemistry defined in the broadest sense."
Established 1959.

1959	D. H. R. Barton
1961	Robert B. Woodward
1963	Paul D. Bartlett
1965	Arthur C. Cope
1967	John D. Roberts
1969	Vladimir Prelog
1971	Herbert C. Brown
1973	George Wittig
1975	Rolf Huisgen
1977	William S. Johnson

AERO-ACOUSTICS AWARD—American Institute of Aeronautics and Astronautics

An award hurrahed by anyone who lives within ten miles of an airport, this is given for contribution to aircraft community noise reduction.
Established 1973.

| 1975 | Michael J. Lighthill |
| 1976 | Herbert Ribner |

AEROSPACE COMMUNICATION AWARD—American Institute of Aeronautics and Astronautics

This goes for contributions in such areas as satellite communication between points on earth, communication to spacecraft in earth orbit or in interplanetary journey, and communications between spacecraft and aircraft. Over and out, Captain Kirk.
Established 1967.

1968	Donald D. Williams
	Harold A. Rosen
1969	Eberhardt Rechtin
1970	Edmund J. Habib
1971	Siegfried H. Reiger
1972	Wilbur Pritchard
1973	no award
1974	Arthur C. Clark
1975	no award
1976	Robert F. Garbarini

AIRCRAFT DESIGN AWARD—American Institute of Aeronautics and Astronautics

For an original concept in aircraft design or design technology.
Established 1968.

1969	Harold W. Adams
1970	Harrison A. Storms
1971	Joseph F. Sutter
1972	Ben R. Rich
1973	Herman D. Barkey
1974	Richard T. Whitcomb
1975	Walter E. Fellers
1976	Kendall Perkins

THE FRANCIS AMORY PRIZE—American Academy of Arts and Sciences

A very specific science award, this prize is given for work dealing with male and female reproductive and genito-urinary systems. Discovering testosterone is one way of winning.
Established 1912.

1940	Ernest Laquer
	Joseph Francis McCarthy
	Carl Richard Moore
	Hugh Hampton Young
1947	Alexander Benjamin Gutman
	Charles Brenton Huggins
	Willem Johan Kolff
	Guy Frederic Marrian
	George Nicholas Papanicolaou
	Selman Abraham Waksman
1954	Frederic E. B. Foley
	Choh Hao Li
	Thaddeus R. R. Mann
	Terence J. Millin
	Warren O. Nelson
	Frederick J. Wallace
	Lawson Wilkins
1961	J. Hartwell Harrison, David M. Hume, and Joseph E. Murray
	John P. Merrill, Benjamin F. Miller, and George W. Thorn
	Harry Goldblatt and Eugene F. Poutasse
	Eugene M. Bricker and Justin J. Cordonnier
1968	Geoffrey Wingfield Harris
	Hans Henriksen Ussing
1975	Karl Sune Detlof Bergström
	Min-Chueh Chang

Howard Guy Williams-
Ashman

JOHNNY APPLESEED AWARD—
Men's Garden Clubs of America
For pioneering some branch of horti-
culture in the spirit of John Chapman,
aka Johnny Appleseed. "This award is
given for outstanding work in horticul-
ture in a spirit of service away from his
vocation." One doesn't need to be a
member of the MGCA to win, but one
must be a man.
Established 1939.

1939	Carleton Morse
	John Marvin Yoste
1940	John McLaren
	August Kock
1941	Adolph Mueller
1942	Henry Hicks
	Jens Jenson
1943	no award
1944	no award
1945	John Bacher
	Adolph Jaenicke
1946	Fred Edmunds
	Lester Morris
1947	no award
1948	Liberty Hyde Bailey
1949	Dr. David Fairchild
1950	Dr. E. J. Kraus
1951	Arie den Boer
1952	no award
1953	George Terziev
1954	George W. Kelly
1955	James Henry, Jr.
1956	Henry J. Benninger
1957	Dr. A. H. Hermann
1958	no award
1959	Herbert Ferris Crisler
1960	Arthur W. Solomon, Sr.
1961	Harvey Foster Stoke
1962	Wister Henry
1963	no award
1964	George Pedlow
1965	David Dowen
1966	Clarence E. Godshalk
1967	Dr. Rupert Streets
1968	Perry Davis
1969	Frank Curto
1970	Leo F. Simon
1971	Barnie Kennedy
1972	George E. Allen
1973	Edgar Friedrich
1974	Robert Vine

1975	no award
1976	no award

**AWARD FOR CREATIVE INVEN-
TION—**American Chemical Society
and Corporation Associates
For inventors who successfully apply "research in chemistry and/or
chemical engineering" to "the material
prosperity and happiness of people."
Established 1966.

1968	William G. Pfann
1969	J. Paul Hogan
1970	Gordon K. Teal
1971	S. Donald Stookey
1972	H. Tracy Hall
1973	Carl Djerassi
1974	Charles C. Price
1975	James D. Idol, Jr.
1976	Manuel M. Baizer
1977	Herman A. Bruson

**AWARD FOR DISTINGUISHED
SERVICE IN THE ADVANCEMENT
OF INORGANIC CHEMISTRY—**
American Chemical Society and Mal-
linckrodt, Inc.
"To recognize distinguished services
to the advancement of inorganic chem-
istry."
Established 1963.

1965	Robert W. Parry
1966	George H. Cady
1967	Henry Taube
1968	William N. Lipscomb, Jr.
1969	Anton B. Burg
1970	Ralph G. Pearson
1971	Joseph Chatt
1972	John C. Bailar, Jr.
1973	Ronald J. Gillespie
1974	F. Albert Cotton
1975	Fred Basolo
1976	Daryle H. Busch
1977	James L. Hoard

**AWARD IN ANALYTICAL CHEMIS-
TRY—**American Chemical Society and
Fisher Scientific Company
For outstanding work in analytical
chemistry, pure or applied, done in ei-
ther the United States or Canada.
Established 1947.

1948	N. Howell Furman
1949	G. E. F. Lundell
1950	Isaac M. Kolthoff

1951	H. H. Willard
1952	Melvin G. Mellon
1953	Donald D. Van Slyke
1954	G. Frederick Smith
1955	Ernest H. Swift
1956	Harvey Diehl
1957	John H. Yoe
1958	James J. Lingane
1959	James I. Hoffman
1960	Philip J. Elving
1961	Herbert A. Laitinen
1962	H. A. Liebhafsky
1963	David N. Hume
1964	John Mitchell, Jr.
1965	Charles N. Reilley
1966	Lyman C. Craig
1967	Lawrence T. Hallett
1968	Lockhart B. Rogers
1969	Roger G. Bates
1970	Charles V. Banks
1971	George H. Morrison
1972	W. Wayne Meinke
1973	James D. Winefordner
1974	Philip W. West
1975	Sidney Siggia
1976	Howard V. Malmstadt
1977	George G. Guilbault

AWARD IN CHEMICAL EDUCATION—American Chemical Society and Union Carbide Corporation.

"To recognize outstanding contributions to chemical education."

Established 1950.

1952	Joel H. Hildebrand
1953	Howard J. Lucas
1954	Raymond E. Kirk
1955	Gerrit Van Zyl
1956	Otto M. Smith
1957	Norris W. Rakestraw
1958	Frank E. Brown
1959	Harry F. Lewis
1960	Arthur F. Scott
1961	John C. Bailar, Jr.
1962	William G. Young
1963	Edward L. Haenisch
1964	Alfred B. Garrett
1965	Theodore A. Ashford
1966	W. Conway Pierce
1967	Louis F. Fieser
1968	William F. Kieffer
1969	L. Carroll King
1970	Hubert N. Alyea
1971	Laurence E. Strong
1972	J. Arthur Campbell

1973	Robert C. Brasted
1974	George S. Hammond
1975	William T. Lippincott
1976	Leallyn B. Clapp
1977	Robert W. Parry

AWARD IN CHROMATOGRAPHY— American Chemical Society and SUPELCO, Inc.

"To recognize outstanding contributions to the fields of chromatography." In case "chromatography" isn't a word that crops up in your usual breakfast conversation, it's the process of separating gases, liquids, or solids by getting the various molecules to stick to the surface of another substance.

Established 1959.

1961	Harold H. Strain
1962	L. Zechmeister
1963	Waldo E. Cohn
1964	Stanford Moore
	William H. Stein
1965	Stephen Dal Nogare
1966	Kurt A. Kraus
1967	J. Calvin Giddings
1968	Lewis G. Longsworth
1969	Morton Beroza
1970	Julian F. Johnson
1971	no award
1972	J. J. Kirkland
1973	Albert Zlatkis
1974	Lockhart B. Rogers
1975	Egon Stahl
1976	James S. Fritz
1977	Raymond P. W. Scott

AWARD IN ORGANIC CHEMISTRY —American Chemical Society and Monsanto Company

For fundamental research in inorganic chemistry.

Established 1960.

1962	F. Albert Cotton
1963	Daryle H. Busch
1964	Fred Basolo
1965	Earl L. Muetterties
1966	Geoffrey Wilkinson
1967	John L. Margrave
1968	Jack Halpern
1969	Russell S. Drago
1970	Neil Bartlett
1971	Jack Lewis
1972	Theodore L. Brown
1973	M. F. Hawthorne

1974	Lawrence F. Dahl
1975	James P. Collman
1976	Richard H. Holm
1977	no award

AWARD IN PETROLEUM CHEMIS-TRY—American Chemical Society and The Lubrizol Corporation

For American and Canadian research achievements in petroleum chemistry. The winner gets $5,000, a certificate, and $350 in traveling expenses to collect the award.

Established 1948.

1949	Bruce H. Sage
1950	Kenneth S. Pitzer
1951	Louis Schmerling
1952	Vladimir Haensel
1953	Robert W. Schiessler
1954	Arthur P. Lien
1955	Frank Ciapetta
1956	Milburn J. O'Neal, Jr.
1957	C. Gardner Swain
1958	Robert P. Eischens
1959	George C. Pimentel
1960	Robert W. Taft, Jr.
1961	George S. Hammond
1962	Harold Hart
1963	John P. McCullough
1964	George A. Olah
1965	Glen A. Russell
1966	James Wei
1967	Andrew Streitwieser, Jr.
1968	Keith U. Ingold
1969	Alan Schriesheim
1970	Lloyd R. Snyder
1971	Gerasimos J. Karabatsos
1972	Paul G. Gassman
1973	Joe W. Hightower
1974	no award
1975	no award
1976	John H. Sinfelt
1977	Sidney W. Benson

HERBERT BLOCH AWARD—The American Society of Criminology

For outstanding service to the society and the profession.

Established 1961.

1966
Charles L. Newman, Pennsylvania State University
1967
Donal MacNamara, John Jay College of Criminal Justice

1968	no award
1969	no award
1970	no award
1971	no award
1972	Freda Adler, Temple University
1973	C. Ray Jeffery, Florida State University, Tallahassee
1974	Albert Morris
1975	no award
1976	no award

BORDEN AWARD IN NUTRITION—Borden Foundation

For research in the nutritional significance of a food or a food component.

Established 1944.

1944	E. V. McCollum
1945	H. H. Mitchell
1946	P. C. Jeans
	Genevieve Stearns
1947	L. A. Maynard
1948	C. A. Cary
1949	H. J. Deuel, Jr.
1950	H. C. Sherman
1951	P. Gyorgy
1952	M. Kleiber
1953	H. H. Williams
1954	A. F. Morgan
	A. H. Smith
1955	A. G. Hogan
1956	F. M. Strong
1957	no award
1958	L. D. Wright
1959	H. Steenbock
1960	R. G. Hansen
1961	K. Schwarz
1962	H. A. Barker
1963	Arthur L. Black
1964	G. K. Davis
1965	A. E. Harper
1966	R. T. Holman
1967	R. H. Barnes
1968	C. L. Comar
1969	H. P. Broquist
1970	L. M. Henderson
1971	H. E. Sauberlich
1972	S. J. Gershoff
1973	A. L. Tappel
1974	David Kritchevsky
1975	W. G. Hoekstra
1976	D. B. Zilversmit

CHANUTE FLIGHT AWARD—
American Institute of Aeronautics and Astronautics

"For outstanding contribution made by a pilot or test personnel to the advancement of the art, science, and technology of aeronautics." Named after a pioneer American aeronautical investigator.

Established 1939.

1939	Edmund T. Allen
1940	Howard Hughes
1941	Melvin N. Gough
1942	A. L. MacClain
1943	William H. McAvoy
1944	Benjamin S. Kelsey
1945	Robert T. Lamson
	Elliott Merrill
1946	Ernest A. Cutrell
1947	Lawrence A. Clousing
1948	Herbert H. Hoover
1949	Frederick M. Trapnell
1950	Donald B. MacDiarmid
1951	Marion E. Carl
1952	John C. Seal
1953	W. T. Bridgeman
1954	George E. Cooper
1955	Albert Boyd
1956	A. M. Johnston
1957	Frank K. Everest
1958	A. Scott Crossfield
1959	John P. Reeder
1960	Joseph J. Tymczyszyn
1961	Joseph A. Walker
1962	Neil Armstrong
1963	E. J. Bechtold
1964	Fred J. Drinkwater, III
	Robert C. Innis
1965	Alvin S. White
1966	Donald F. McKusker
	John L. Swigert, Jr.
1967	Milton O. Thompson
1968	William J. Knight
1969	William C. Park
1970	Jerauld P. Gentry
1971	William M. Magruder
1972	Donald R. Segner
1973	Cecil W. Powell
1974	Charles A. Sewell
1975	Alan L. Bean
	Owen K. Garriott
	Jack R. Lousma
1976	Thomas Stafford

KARL TAYLOR COMPTON GOLD MEDAL—American Institute of Physics

For "High statesmanship in physics."

Established 1957.

1957
George B. Pegram
1960
Karl K. Darrow, Bell Telephone Laboratories
1964
Henry A. Barton, retired director American Institute of Physics
1967
Alan T. Waterman, first director of the National Science Foundation
1970
Frederick Seitz
1971
Ralph A. Sawyer
1974
Samuel A. Goudsmit, former editor-in-chief of the American Physical Society

COMPUTER SCIENCES MAN OF THE YEAR—Data Processing Management Association

For contributions to the field of computer sciences.

Established 1969.

1969
Commander Grace Murray Hopper, director, Navy programming languages group, Office of Information Systems Planning and Development, United States Navy
1970
Frederick Phillips Brooks, Jr., Ph.D., chairman of the department of computer and information science, University of North Carolina
1971   no award
1972
Robert C. Cheek, president, Westinghouse Tele-Computer Systems Corp., Pittsburgh, Pa.
1973
Dr. Carl Hammer, director of computer sciences, UNIVAC Division, Sperry Rand Corporation, Washington, D. C.
1974
Edward L. Glaser, head of the

computing and information sciences at Case Western Reserve University, Cleveland, Ohio
1975
Willis H. Ware, senior computer scientist, The Rand Corporation, Santa Monica, Calif.
Donald L. Bitzer, Ph.D. director, Computer-Based Education Research Laboratory, University of Illinois, Urbana, Ill.
1976
Dr. Gene M. Amdahl, chairman of the board of Amdahl Corporation, Sunnyvale, Calif.

CULLUM GEOGRAPHICAL MEDAL—American Geographical Society

"To those who distinguish themselves by geographical discoveries or in the advancement of geographical science."
Established 1896.

1896	Robert E. Peary
1897	Fridtjof Nansen
1899	Sir John Murray
1901	Thomas C. Mendenhall
1902	A. Donaldson Smith
1903	The Duke of the Abruzzi
1904	Georg von Neumayer
	Sven Hedin
1906	Robert Falcon Scott
	Robert Bell
1908	William Morris Davis
1909	Francisco P. Moreno
	Sir Ernest Shackleton
1910	Hermann Wagner
1911	Jean B. E. A. Charcot
1914	Ellen Churchill Semple
	John Scott Keltie
1917	George W. Goethals
1918	Frederick Haynes Newell
1919	Emmanuel de Margerie
	Henry Fairfield Osborn
1921	Albert I, Prince of Monaco
1922	Edward A. Reeves
1924	Jovan Cvijic
1925	Pedro C. Sanchez
	Lucien Gallois
	Harvey C. Hayes
1929	Hugh Robert Mill
	Jean Brunhes
	Alfred Hettner
	Jules de Schokalsky

1930	Curtis F. Marbut
1931	Mark Jefferson
1932	Bertram Thomas
1935	Douglas Johnson
1938	Louise Arner Boyd
1939	Emmanuel de Martonne
1940	Robert Cushman Murphy
1943	Arthur Robert Hinks
1948	Hugh Hammond Bennett
1950	Hans W. Ahlmann
1952	Roberto Almagia
1954	British Everest Expedition
1956	J. Russell Smith
1958	Charles Warren Thornthwaite
1959	Albert Paddock Crary
1961	William Maurice Ewing
1962	Richard Joel Russell
1963	Rachel Louise Carson
1964	John Leighly
1965	Kirtley Fletcher Mather
1967	Peter Haggett
1968	Luna B. Leopold
1969	Neil A. Armstrong
	Edwin E. Aldrin, Jr.
	Michael Collins
1973	Bruce Heezen
1975	Rene Dubos

THE CHARLES P. DALY MEDAL—American Geographical Society

"For valuable or distinguished geographical services or labors."
Established 1902.

1902	Robert E. Peary
1906	Thorvald Thoroddsen
1908	George Davidson
1909	William W. Rockhill
	Charles Chaille-Long
1910	Grove Karl Gilbert
1912	Roald Amundsen
1913	Alfred H. Brooks
1914	Albrecht Penck
1915	Paul Vidal de la Blache
1917	George G. Chisholm
1918	Vilhjalmur Stefansson
1920	George Otis Smith
1922	Sir Francis Younghusband
	Adolphus W. Greely
	Ernest de K. Leffingwell
1924	Claude H. Birdseye
	Knud Rasmussen
1925	Robert A. Bartlett
	David L. Brainard
1927	Alois Musil
1929	Filippo De Filippi
	Emile Feliz Gautier

358   SCIENCE

1930	Joseph B. Tyrrell
	Nelson H. Darton
	Lauge Koch
1931	Gunnar Isachsen
1935	Roy Chapman Andrews
1938	Alexander Forbes
1939	Herbert John Fleure
1940	Carl Ortwin Sauer
1941	Julio Garzon Nieto
1943	Sir Halford J. Mackinder
1948	Henri Baulig
1950	Laurence Dudley Stamp
1952	J. M. Wordie
1954	John K. Wright
1956	Raoul Blanchard
1959	Richard Hartshorne
1961	Theodore Monod
1962	Osborn Maitland Miller
1963	Henry Clifford Darby
1964	Jean Gottmann
1965	William Skinner Cooper
1966	Torsten Hagerstrand
1967	Marston Bates
1968	O. H. K. Spate
1969	Paul B. Sears
	William O. Field
1971	Gilbert F. White
1973	Walter Sullivan
1974	Walter Wood

THE GEORGE DAVIDSON MEDAL — American Geographical Society

For "exceptional achievement in research or exploration in the Pacific Ocean or the land's bordering thereon."
Established 1946.

1952	George B. Cressey
1972	F. Raymond Fosberg
1974	Joseph Spencer
1975	Shinzo Kiuchi

DE FLOREZ TRAINING AWARD— American Institute of Aeronautics and Astronautics

For improving aerospace training.
Established 1965.

1965	Lloyd L. Kelly
1966	Warren J. North
1967	Edwin H. Link
1968	Joseph La Russa
1969	Gifford Bull
1970	Harold G. Miller
1971	Walter P. Moran

1972	James W. Campbell
1973	Carroll H. Woodling
1974	Hugh Harrison Hurt, Jr.
1975	John C. Dusterberry
1976	John E. Duberg

LOUIS I. DUBLIN AWARD—American Association of Suicidology

"For outstanding service and contribution to the field of suicide prevention."

1971	Karl Menninger
1972	Edwin Shneidman
1973	Norman Farberow
1974	Reverend Chad Varah
1975	Robert Felix
1976	Theodore Curphey

LOUIS H. BAUER FOUNDERS AWARD—Aerospace Medical Association

For contributions to space medicine.
Established 1961.

1961	Lt. Col. Stanley C. White
1962	Don Flickinger
1963	Col. Paul A. Campbell
1964	Col. William K. Douglas
1965	Hubertus Strughold
1966	Charles A. Berry
1967	RADM Frank B. Voris
1968	James N. Waggoner
1969	Maj. Gen. Otis O. Benson, Jr.
1970	Walton L. Jones
1971	Maj. Gen. James W. Humphreys
1972	Capt. Ralph L. Christy
1973	Karl H. Houghton
1974	Willard R. Hawkins
1975	Col. John Pickering
1976	Lawrence F. Dietlein

THE PASSANO AWARD—The Passano Foundation

This goes for medical research, with emphasis on work that has immediate clinical value. Seven past winners have also won the Nobel prize.
Established 1945.

1945
  Edwin Joseph Cohn, Harvard Medical School
1946
  Ernest William Goodpasture, Vanderbilt University

1947
Selman A. Waksman, New Jersey
Agricultural Experiment Station
1948
Alfred Blalock, Johns Hopkins
University School of Medicine
Helen Brooke Taussig, Johns
Hopkins University School of
Medicine
1949
Oswald Theodore Avery, Rockefeller
Institute for Medical Research
1950
Edward Calvin Kendall, Mayo
Clinic
Philip Showalter Hench, Mayo
Clinic
1951
Philip Levine, Ortho Research
Foundation, Raritan, N.J.
Alexander S. Wiener, Jewish
Hospital, Brooklyn, N.Y.
1952
Herbert McLean Evans, University
of California
1953
John Franklin Enders, Harvard
Medical School; Children's
Hospital, Boston, Mass.
1954
Homer William Smith, New York
University College of Medicine
1955
Vincent duVigneaud, Cornell
University Medical College
1956
George Nicholas Papanicolaou,
Cornell University Medical College
1957
William Mansfield Clark, Johns
Hopkins University
1958
George Washington Corner,
American Philosophical Society
1959
Stanhope Bayne-Jones, former
technical director of research, Office
of the Surgeon General
1960
Rene J. Dubos, Rockefeller
University
1961
Owen H. Wangensteen, University
of Minnesota Medical School

1962
Albert H. Coons, Harvard Medical
School
1963
Horace W. Magoun, University of
California School of Medicine, Los
Angeles
1964
Keith R. Porter, Harvard University
George E. Palade, Rockefeller
University
1965
Charles B. Huggins, Ben May
Laboratory for Cancer Research,
Chicago, Ill.
1966
John T. Edsall, Harvard University
1967
Irvine H. Page, Cleveland Clinic
Foundation
1968
John Eager Howard, Johns Hopkins
University School of Medicine
1969
George Herbert Hitchings, vice
president in charge of research,
Burroughs Wellcome & Company
1970
Paul Charles Zamecnik,
Massachusetts General Hospital
1971
Stephen W. Kuffler, Harvard Medical
School
1972
Kimishige Ishizaka, Johns Hopkins
University School of Medicine
Teruko Ishizaka, Johns Hopkins
University School of Medicine
1973
Roger W. Sperry, California Institute
of Technology
1974
Seymour S. Cohen, University of
Colorado School of Medicine,
Denver.
Baruch S. Blumberg, The Institute
for Cancer Research, Fox Chase,
Philadelphia
1975
Henry G. Kunkel, Rockefeller
University
Joan Argetsinger Steitz, Yale
University
1976
Roger Guillemin, Salk Institute

Ralph A. Bradshaw, Washington
University School of Medicine

EMINENT ECOLOGIST CITATION
—Ecological Society of America
For important and significant contributions to ecology. You don't have to be a society member to win, but since 1960, winners have received free lifetime membership.
Established 1954.
1954
H. S. Conrad, botany, Grinnell
1955
A. H. Wright, zoology, Cornell
1956
G. B. Rigg, botany, University of Washington
1957
D. P. Schmidt, herpetology, Chicago
1958
A. W. Sampson, forestry, University of California
1959
H. A. Gleason, botany, New York Botanical Garden
1960
W. P. Cottam, botany, University of Utah
1961
Charles Elton, animal ecology, Oxford University
1962
G. E. Hutchinson, limnology, Yale
1963
W. Cooper, botany, Minnesota
1964
S. R. Dice, zoology, Michigan
1965
Paul B. Sears, botany, retired
1966
A. Redfield, marine biology, retired
1967
A. E. Emerson, zoology, retired
1968
Victor Shelford, zoology, retired
1969
Stanley Cain, botany, University of Michigan
1970
Murray F. Buell, botany, Rutgers
1971
Thomas Park, zoology, University of Chicago

1972
Ruth Patrick, limnology, Academy of Natural Sciences
1973   no award
1974
Eugene P. Odum, ecosystem ecology, University of Georgia
1975
C. H. Muller, ecology-community-allelopathy, University of California, Santa Barbara
1976
Alton Tindsey, Purdue University

FLUID AND PLASMADYNAMICS AWARD—American Institute of Aeronautics and Astronautics
We defer to the Institute's description of the award: ". . . for outstanding contribution to the understanding of the behavior of liquids and gases in motion or of the physical properties and dynamical behavior of matter in the plasma state as related to the needs in aeronautics and astronautics.
Established 1975.
1976   Mark Markovin

GARVAN MEDAL—American Chemical Society
This one goes to distinguished American female chemists.
Established 1936.

1937	Emma P. Carr
1940	Mary E. Pennington
1941	no award
1942	Florence B. Seibert
1943	no award
1944	no award
1945	no award
1946	Icie G. Macy-Hoobler
1947	Mary Laura Sherrill
1948	Gerty T. Cori
1949	Agnes Fay Morgan
1950	Pauline Beery Mack
1951	Katherine B. Blodgett
1952	Gladys A. Emerson
1953	Leonora N. Bilger
1954	Betty Sullivan
1955	Grace Medes
1956	Allene R. Jeans
1957	Lucy W. Pickett
1958	Arda A. Green
1959	Dorothy V. Nightingale
1960	Mary L. Caldwell

1961	Sarah Ratner
1962	Helen M. Dyer
1963	Mildred Cohn
1964	Birgit Vennesland
1965	Gertrude E. Perlmann
1966	Mary L. Peterman
1967	Marjorie J. Vold
1968	Gertrude B. Elion
1969	Sofia Simmonds
1970	Ruth R. Benerito
1971	Mary Fieser
1972	Jean'ne M. Shreeve
1973	Mary L. Good
1974	Joyce J. Kaufman
1975	Marjorie C. Caserio
1976	Isabella L. Karle
1977	Marjorie G. Horning

GODDARD ASTRONAUTICS AWARD—American Institute of Aeronautics and Astronautics

Until 1975 this award was presented for contributions in the engineering science of propulsion and energy conversion. Now it goes for contributions to astronautics in general.
Established 1948.

1948	John Shesta
1949	Calvin M. Bolster
1950	Lovell Lawrence, Jr.
1951	Robert C. Truax
1953	Richard W. Porter
1953	David A. Young
1954	A. M. O. Smith
1955	E. N. Hall
1956	Chandler C. Ross
1957	Thomas F. Dixon
1958	Richard B. Canright
1959	Samuel K. Hoffman
1960	Theodore von Karman
1961	Wernher von Braun
1962	Robert R. Gilruth
1965	Frank Whittle
1966	Hans J. P. von Ohain
	A. W. Blackman
	George D. Lewis
1967	Robert O. Bullock
	Irving A. Johnson
	Seymour Lieblein
1968	Donald C. Berkey
	Ernest C. Simpson
	James E. Worsham
1969	Perry W. Pratt
	Stanley G. Hooker
1970	Gerhard Neumann

1972	Howard E. Schumacher
	Brian Brimelow
	Gary Plourde
1973	Edward S. Taylor
1974	Paul D. Castenholz
	Richard Mulready
	John Sloop
1975	George Rosen
	Gordon Holbrook
1976	Edward Price
1977	James S. Martin

JAMES T. GRADY AWARD FOR INTERPRETING CHEMISTRY FOR THE PUBLIC—American Chemical Society.

For translating the gobbledygook so the public might understand it.
Established 1955.

1957	David H. Killeffer
1958	William L. Laurence
1959	Alton L. Blakeslee
1960	Watson Davis
1961	David Dietz
1962	John F. Baxter
1963	Lawrence Lessing
1964	Nate Haseltine
1965	Isaac Asimov
1966	Frank E. Carey
1967	Irving S. Bengelsdorf
1968	Raymond A. Bruner
1969	Walter Sullivan
1970	Robert C. Cowen
1971	Victor Cohn
1972	Dan Q. Posin
1973	O. A. Battista
1974	Ronald Kotulak
1975	Jon Franklin
1976	Gene Bylinsky
1977	Patrick Young

HALEY SPACE FLIGHT AWARD—American Institute of Aeronautics and Astronautics

Originally called the Astronautics Award, this was renamed in 1966 to honor Andrew G. Haley, a founder of the American Rocket Society. ". . . for outstanding contribution by an astronaut or flight test personnel to the advancement of the art, science, or technology of astronautics."
Established 1954.

1954	Theodore von Karman
1955	Wernher von Braun

1956	Joseph Kaplan
1957	Krafft Ehricke
1958	Ivan C. Kincheloe, Jr.
1959	Walter R. Dornberger
1960	A. Scott Crossfield
1961	Alan Shepard
1962	John H. Glenn, Jr.
1963	Walter M. Schirra, Jr.
	Gordon Cooper
1964	Walter C. Williams
1965	Joseph S. Bleymaier
1966	Neil A. Armstrong
	David R. Scott
1967	Edward H. White, II
1968	Virgil I. Grissom
1969	Donn F. Eisele
	R. Walter Cunningham
	Walter M. Schirra, Jr.
1970	Frank Borman
	James A. Lovell, Jr.
	William Anders
1971	John Swigert
	Fred W. Haise, Jr.
	James A. Lovell, Jr.
1972	David Worden
	David Scott
	James Irwin
1973	John Young
	Thomas Mattingly, II
	Charles Duke, Jr.
1974	Paul J. Weitz
	Charles Conrad, Jr.
	Joseph R. Kerwin
1975	Gerald Carr
	William Pogue
	Edward Gibson
1976	William H. Dana

HODGKINS MEDAL—Smithsonian Institution

"To recognize research and investigation of the interrelationship between the atmosphere and the welfare of man."

Established 1895.

1895	John, Lord Rayleigh and Professor William Ramsay
1899	Professor James Dewar
1902	Professor J. J. Thomson
1965	Sidney Chapman
	Joseph Kaplan
	Marcel Nicolet

JEFFRIES MEDICAL RESEARCH AWARD—American Institute of Aeronautics and Astronautics

John Jeffries was an American doctor "who made the earliest recorded scientific observations from the air." The medal honors contribution to aerospace medical research.

Established 1940.

1940	Louis H. Bauer
1941	Harry G. Armstrong
1942	Edward C. Schneider
1943	Eugene G. Reinartz
1944	Harold E. Wittingham
1945	John C. Adams
1946	Malcolm C. Grow
1947	J. Winifred Tice
1948	W. Randolph Lovelace, II
1949	A. D. Tuttle
1950	Otis O. Bensen, Jr.
1951	John R. Poppen
1952	John Stapp
1953	Charles F. Gell
1954	James P. Henry
1955	Wilbur E. Kellum
1956	Ross A. McFarland
1957	David C. Simons
1958	Hubertus Strughold
1959	Don Flickinger
1960	Joseph W. Kittinger
1961	Ashton Graybiel
1962	James L. Goddard
1963	no award
1964	Eugene Konecci
1965	William K. Douglas
1966	Charles A. Berry
1967	Charles I. Barron
1968	Loren D. Carlson
1969	Frank B. Voris
1970	Walton L. Jones
1971	Richard St. Johnston
1972	Roger G. Ireland
1973	Karl H. Houghton
1974	Malcolm Clayton Lancaster
1975	Lawrence F. Dietlein
1976	Harald Von Beckh

THE LANGLEY MEDAL—Smithsonian Institution

To recognize "specially meritorious investigations in connection with the science of aviation and space flight." Mr. Samuel P. Langley was the third secretary of the Smithsonian as well as

a "pioneer student of human flight." Established 1909.

1909	William and Orville Wright
1913	Glenn H. Curtiss
	Gustave Eiffel
1927	Charles A. Lindbergh
1929	Charles Matthews Manley
	Adm. Richard E. Byrd
1935	Joseph Sweetman Ames
	Jerome C. Hunsaker
1960	Robert H. Goddard
1962	Hugh Latimer Dryden
1964	Alan B. Shephard, Jr.
1967	Wernher von Braun

THE IRVING LANGMUIR AWARD IN CHEMICAL PHYSICS—American Chemical Society and The General Electric Foundation

For interdisciplinary research in chemistry and physics.

The asterisks (*) designate selection and presentation made by the Division of Chemical Physics of the American Physical Society

Established 1964.

1965	John H. Van Vleck*
1966	H. S. Gutowsky
1967	John C. Slater*
1968	Henry Eyring
1969	Charles P. Slichter*
1970	John A. Pople
1971	Michael E. Fisher*
1972	Harden M. McConnell
1973	Peter M. Rentzepis*
1974	Harry G. Drickamer
1975	Robert H. Cole*
1976	John S. Waugh

DAVID LIVINGSTONE CENTENARY MEDAL—American Geographical Society

"Dr. Livingstone, I presume?" Established by the Hispanic Society of America, this honors scientific geographic achievement in the southern hemisphere.

Established 1913.

1916	Sir Douglas Mawson
1917	Theodore Roosevelt
	Manuel Vincente Ballivian
1918	Candido Rondon
1920	William Speirs Bruce
	Alexander Hamilton Rice

1923	Griffith Taylor
1924	Frank Wild
1925	Luis Riso Patron
1926	Erich von Drygalski
1929	Richard E. Byrd
1930	Jose M. Sobral
	Laurence M. Gould
1931	Hjalmar Riiser-Larsen
1935	Lars Christensen
1936	Lincoln Ellsworth
1939	John R. Rymill
1945	Isaiah Bowman
1948	Frank Debenham
1950	Robert L. Pendleton
1952	Carlos Delgado de Carvalho
1956	George McCutchen McBride
1958	Paul Allman Siple
1959	William Edward Rudolph
1965	Bassett McGuire
1966	Preston E. James
1968	William H. Phelps, Jr.
1972	Akin L. Mabogunje

THE SAMUEL FINLEY BREESE MORSE MEDAL—American Geographical Society

The inventor of the telegraph left money in his will to establish this medal "for the encouragement of Geographical Research."

Established 1872.

1928	Sir George Hubert Wilkins
1945	Archer M. Huntington
1952	Gilbert Grosvenor
1966	Charles B. Hitchcock
1968	Wilma B. Fairchild

NATIONAL MEDAL OF SCIENCE
—National Medal of Science Committee

The committee nominates and the president (of the United States, that is) selects scientists who have made contributions to biology, engineering, mathematics, and physics.

1962

Theodore von Karman, professor of aeronautical engineering, California Institute of Technology

1963

Luis Walter Alvarez, professor of physics, University of California

Vannevar Bush, administrator, electrical engineer, former president,

Carnegie Institution of Washington and honorary chairman M. I. T. Corp.

John Robinson Pierce, executive director, Communications Division Systems, Bell Telephone Laboratories

Cornelis B. van Niel, professor of microbiology, Stanford University

Norbert Wiener, professor of mathematics, Massachusetts Institute of Technology

1964

Roger Adams, professor of chemistry, University of Illinois

Othmar H. Ammann, consulting engineer, Ammann and Whitney, Rye, N.Y.

Theodosius Dobzhansky, member, the Rockefeller Institute

Charles Stark Draper, head, department of aeronautics and astronautics, Massachusetts Institute of Technology

Soloman Lefschetz, professor of mathematics, Princeton University

Neal Elgar Miller, professor of psychology, Yale University

Harold Marston Morse, professor of mathematics, Institute for Advanced Studies

Marshall Warren Nirenberg, chief, section of biochemical genetics, National Institutes of Health

Julian Schwinger, professor of physics, Harvard University

Harold Clayton Urey, professor of chemistry, University of California

Robert Burns Woodward, professor of chemistry, Harvard University

1965

John Bardeen, professor of electrical engineering and physics, University of Illinois

Hugh L. Dryden, former deputy administrator, National Aeronautics and Space Administration

Clarence Leonard Johnson, vice president for advanced development projects, Lockheed Aircraft Corporation

Peter J. W. Debye, professor of chemistry, Cornell University

Leon M. Lederman, professor of physics, Columbia University

Warren Kendall Lewis, professor of chemical engineering, Massachusetts Institute of Technology

Francis Peyton Rous, member, The Rockefeller Institute

William Walden Rubey, professor of geology and geophysics, University of California

George Gaylord Simpson, professor of Vertebrate Paleontology, Harvard University

Donald D. Van Slyke, research chemist, Brookhaven National Laboratories

Oscar Zariski, professor of mathematics, Harvard University

1966

Jacob Bjerknes, professor of meteorology, University of California in Los Angeles

Subrahmanyan Chandrasekhar, professor of theoretical astrophysics, University of Chicago

Henry Eyring, dean, Graduate School, University of Utah

E. F. Knipling, Director, entomology research division, U.S. Department of Agriculture

Fritz A. Lipman, professor of biochemistry, Rockefeller University

John W. Milnor, professor of mathematics, Princeton University

William C. Rose, professor of chemistry, University of Illinois

Claude E. Shannon, Donner Professor of Science, Massachusetts Institute of Technology

J. H. Van Vleck, professor of physics, Harvard University

Sewall Wright, professor of genetics, University of Wisconsin

Vladimir Kosma Zworykin, honorary vice president, Radio Corporation of America

1967

J. W. Beams, professor of physics, University of Virginia

A. Francis Birch, professor of geological sciences, Harvard University

Gregory Breit, professor of physics, Yale University

Paul J. Cohen, professor of mathematics, Stanford University

Kenneth S. Cole, senior research biophysicist, National Institutes of Health

Louis Plack Hammett, professor of chemistry, Columbia University

Harry F. Harlow, professor of psychology, University of Wisconsin

Michael Heidelberger, professor of immunochemistry, New York University

G. B. Kistiakowsky, professor of chemistry, Harvard University

Edwin Herbert Land, president, Polaroid Corp.

Igor I. Sikorsky, former engineering manager, Sikorsky Aircraft Division of United Aircraft Corp.

Alfred Henry Sturtevant, professor of biology, California Institute of Technology

1968

Horace Albert Barker, professor of biochemistry, University of California

Paul D. Bartlett, professor of chemistry, Harvard University

Bernard B. Brodie, chief, laboratory of chemical pharmacology, National Institutes of Health

Detlev W. Bronk, president emeritus, Rockefeller University

J. Presper Eckert, vice president, Remington Rand, Univac division, Sperry Rand Corp.

Herbert Friedman, superintendent, atmosphere and astrophysics division, Naval Research Laboratory

Jay L. Lush, professor of animal breeding, Iowa State University

N. M. Newmark, professor of civil engineering, University of Illinois

Jerzy Neyman, professor of mathematics, University of California

Lars Onsager, professor of chemistry, Yale University

B. F. Skinner, professor psychology, Harvard University

Eugene P. Wigner, professor of mathematical physics, Princeton University

1969

Herbert C. Brown, professor of chemistry, Purdue University

William Feller, professor of mathematics, Princeton University

Robert Joseph Huebner, chief, viral carcinogenesis branch, National Cancer Institute, National Institutes of Health

Jack S. C. Kilby, manager, customer requirements department, Texas Instruments, Inc.

Ernst Mayr, director and professor, Museum of Comparative Zoology, Harvard University

W. K. H. Panofsky, director and professor, Stanford Linear Accelerator Center, Stanford University

1970

Richard D. Brauer, professor of mathematics, Harvard University

Robert H. Dicke, Cyrus Fogg Brackett Professor of Physics, Princeton University

Barbara McClintock, distinguished service member, Carnegie Institution of Washington, Cold Spring Harbor, N.Y.

George E. Mueller, senior vice president, General Dynamics Corp.

Albert B. Sabin, president, Weizmann Institute of Science, Rehovoth, Israel

Allan R. Sandage, staff member, Hale Observatories, Carnegie Institution of Washington, California Institute of Technology

John C. Slater, professor of physics and chemistry, University of Florida

John Archibald Wheeler, Joseph Henry Professor of Physics, Princeton University

Saul Winstein, professor of chemistry, University of California in Los Angeles

1971   no award

1972   no award

1973

Daniel I. Arnon, professor and chairman of the department of cell physiology and biochemist in the agricultural experiment station, University of California

Carl Djerassi, professor of chemistry, Stanford University

Harold E. Edgerton, professor

emeritus, Massachusetts Institute of Technology

William Maurice Ewing, distinguished professor of electrical engineering, The Marine Institute, The University of Texas Medical Branch at Galveston

Arie J. Haagen-Smit, professor of biochemistry, California Institute of Technology

Vladimir Haensel, vice president for research and development, Universal Oil Products Company

Frederick Seitz, president, Rockefeller University

Earl W. Sutherland, Jr. professor of biochemistry, University of Miami

John W. Tukey, professor of statistics, Princeton University

Richard Travis Whitcomb, aeronautical engineer, Langley Research Center

Robert R. Wilson, director, Fermi National Accelerator Laboratory, Weston, Ill.

1974

Nicolaas Bloembergen, professor of applied physics, Harvard University

Britton Chance, director, Johnson Research Foundation and chairman, department of biophysics, University of Pennsylvania

Erwin Chargaff, professor of biochemistry, Columbia University

Paul John Flory, Jackson Wood Professor of Chemistry, Stanford University

William A. Fowler, professor of physics, California Institute of Technology

Kurt Godel, professor of mathematics, Institute for Advanced Study

Rudolf Kompfner, professor of applied physics, Stanford University

James V. Neel, Lee R. Dice Professor of Human Genetics, University of Michigan Medical School

Linus Pauling, professor of chemistry, Stanford University

Ralph Brazelton Peck, consultant

foundation engineer and professor emeritus, University of Illinois

K. S. Pitzer, professor of chemistry, University of California

James A. Shannon, special adviser to the president, Rockefeller University

Abel Wolman, professor emeritus sanitary engineering, Johns Hopkins University

1975

John Backus, IBM staff member, San Jose Research Laboratory, San Jose, Calif.

Manson Benedict, institute professor emeritus, Massachusetts Institute of Technology

Hans A. Bethe, Emeritus John Wendell Anderson Professor of Physics, Cornell University

Shiing-shen Chern, professor of mathematics, University of California

George Bernard Dantzig, professor of operations research and computer science, Stanford University

Hallowell Davis, director emeritus of research, and emeritus professor of otolaryngology, Central Institute for the Deaf, Washington University

Paul Gyorgy, professor emeritus of pediatrics and consultant, University of Pennsylvania Medical School Philadelphia General Hospital

Sterling B. Hendricks, formerly chief chemist Beltsville plant industry station, U. S. Department of Agriculture

Joseph Oakland Hirschfelder, Homer Adkins Professor of Theoretical Chemistry, University of Wisconsin, Madison

William H. Pickering, director, Jet Propulsion Laboratory, California Institute of Technology

Lewis Hastings Sarett, president, Merck, Sharp & Dohme Research Laboratories, Rahway, N.J.

Frederick Emmons Terman, provost emeritus, Stanford University

Orville Alvin Vogel, professor emeritus Department of Agronomy

*Scientist and Vitamin C
advocate Linus Pauling.
(Wide World Photos)*

and Soils, Washington State
University

E. Bright Wilson, Theodore
Williams Richards Professor of
Chemistry, Harvard University

Chien-Shiung Wu, Michael I. Pupin
Professor of Chemistry, Columbia
University

See Nobel Prize

**THE JAMES FLACK NORRIS
AWARD IN PHYSICAL ORGANIC
CHEMISTRY**—American   Chemical
Society, Northeastern Section
  For outstanding contributions to
physical organic chemistry.
  Established 1963.

1965	Christopher K. Ingold
1966	Louis P. Hammett
1967	Saul Winstein
1968	George S. Hammond
1969	Paul D. Bartlett
1970	Frank H. Westheimer
1971	Cheves Walling
1972	Stanley J. Cristol
1973	Kenneth B. Wiberg

1974	Gerhard L. Closs
1975	Kurt M. Mislow
1976	Howard E. Zimmerman
1977	Edward M. Arnett

**THE   OSBORNE   AND   MENDEL
AWARD**—The Nutrition Foundation
  For nutrition research.
  Established 1949.

1949	W. C. Rose
1950	C. A. Elvehjem
1951	E. E. Snell
1952	Icie Macy Hoobler
1953	V. du Vigneaud
1954	L. A. Maynard
1955	E. V. McCollum
1956	A. G. Hogan
1957	G. R. Cowgill
1958	P. Gyorgy
1959	Grace A. Goldsmith
1960	N. S. Scrimshaw
1961	Max K. Horwitt
1962	William J. Darby
1963	James B. Allison
1964	L. Emmett Holt, Jr.
1965	D. M. Hegsted
1966	H. H. Mitchell

1967	Samuel Lepkovsky
1968	C. H. Hill
1969	H. N. Munro
1970	R. B. Alfin-Slater
1971	Walter Mertz
1972	E. T. Mertz
1973	H. F. DeLuca
1974	DeWitt S. Goodman
1975	B. Connor Johnson
1976	Myron Winick

CHARLES LATHROP PARSONS AWARD—American Chemical Society

This goes to a society member for public service.

Established 1952.

1952	Charles L. Parsons
1955	James B. Conant
1958	Roger Adams
1961	George B. Kistiakowsky
1964	Glenn T. Seaborg
1967	Donald F. Hornig
1970	W. Albert Noyes, Jr.
1973	Charles C. Price
1974	Russell W. Peterson
1976	William O. Baker

PHYSICIAN'S RECOGNITION AWARD—American Medical Association

Although we would like to list the recipients of this award, the following figures explain why we didn't.

Year	Total presented
1969–1970	14,795
1970–1971	8,822
1971–1972	5,450
1972–1973	11,498
1973–1974	12,448
1974–1975	16,798
1975–1976	29,389

MARY SOPER POPE AWARD—Cranbrook Institute of Science

"For noteworthy and distinguished accomplishment in the field of plant sciences."

Established 1946.

1947	Frans Verdoorn
1948	William Vogt
1949	Charles Deam
1950	Jens C. Clausen
	David D. Keck
	William M. Hiesey

1951	Martin Cardenas
1952	E. Lucy Braun
1954	Irving W. Bailey
1959	Kenneth W. Neatby
1962	Edmund H. Fulling
1964	Edgar T. Wherry
1966	Karl and Hally Jolivette Sax
1970	Stanley Adair Cain

PRIESTLY MEDAL—American Chemistry Society

For "distinguished services to chemistry."

Established 1922.

1923	Ira Remsen
1926	Edgar F. Smith
1929	Francis P. Garvan
1932	Charles L. Parsons
1935	William A. Noyes
1938	Marston T. Bogert
1941	Thomas Midgley, Jr.
1944	James B. Conant
1945	Ian Heilbron
1946	Roger Adams
1947	Warren K. Lewis
1948	Edward R. Weidlein
1949	Arthur B. Lamb
1950	Charles A. Kraus
1951	E. J. Crane
1952	Samuel C. Lind
1953	Robert Robinson
1954	W. Albert Noyes, Jr.
1955	Charles A. Thomas
1956	Carl S. Marvel
1957	Farrington Daniels
1958	Ernest H. Volwiler
1959	H. I. Schlesinger
1960	Wallace R. Brode
1961	Louis P. Hammett
1962	Joel H. Hildebrand
1963	Peter J. W. Debye
1964	John C. Bailar, Jr.
1965	William J. Sparks
1966	William O. Baker
1967	Ralph Connor
1968	William G. Young
1969	Kenneth S. Pitzer
1970	Max Tishler
1971	Frederick D. Rossini
1972	George B. Kistiakowsky
1973	Harold C. Urey
1974	Paul J. Flory
1975	Henry Eyring
1976	George S. Hammond
1977	Henry Gilman

REED AERONAUTICS AWARD—
American Institute of Aeronautics and Astronautics

This is the institute's biggie, going for notable achievement in aeronautical science and engineering. Established 1933.

1934	C. G. Rossby
	H. G. Willett
1935	Frank W. Caldwell
1936	Edward S. Taylor
1937	Eastman N. Jacobs
1938	Alfred Victor de Forest
1939	George J. Mead
1940	Hugh L. Dryden
1941	Theodore von Karman
1942	Igor I. Sikorsky
1943	Sanford A. Moss
1944	Fred E. Weick
1945	Charles S. Draper
1946	Robert T. Jones
1947	Galen B. Schubauer
	Harold K. Skramstad
1948	George W. Brady
1949	George S. Schairer
1950	Robert R. Gilruth
1951	E. H. Heinemann
1952	John Stack
1953	Ernest G. Stout
1954	Clark B. Millikan
1955	H. Julian Allen
1956	Clarence L. Johnson
1957	R. L. Bisplinghoff
1958	Victor E. Carbonera
1959	Karel J. Bossart
1960	John W. Becker
1961	Alfred J. Eggers, Jr.
1962	Walter C. Williams
1964	Abe Silverstein
1965	Arthur E. Raymond
1966	Clarence J. Johnson
1967	Adolph Busemann
1968	William H. Cook
1969	Rene H. Miller
1970	Richard T. Whitcomb
1971	Ira Grant Hedrick
1972	Max Munk
1973	I. E. Garrick
1974	Willis Hawkins
1975	Antonio Ferri
1976	George Spangenberg
1977	William C. Dietz

THE RUMFORD MEDAL—American Academy of Arts and Sciences

Back in 1796, Benjamin Thompson, also known as Count Rumford, decided to use his $5,000 in three per cent U.S. government bonds as the basis for an award. The award would be given for discoveries in heat or light. The interest on the capital would be the prize money. Heat and light were expanded in the twentieth century to all forms of radiant energy. The other twentieth century change? The $5,000 worth of bonds has expanded to $100,000. Established 1796.

1900	Carl Barus
1901	Elihu Thomson
1902	George Ellery Hale
1903	no award
1904	Ernest Fox Nichols
1905	no award
1906	no award
1907	Edward Goodrich Acheson
1908	no award
1909	Robert Williams Wood
1910	Charles Gordon Curtis
1911	James Mason Crafts
1912	Frederic Eugene Ives
1915	Joel Stebbins
1914	William David Coolidge
1915	Charles Greeley Abbot
1916	no award
1917	Percy Williams Bridgman
1918	Theodore Lyman
1919	no award
1920	Irving Langmuir
1921	no award
1922	no award
1923	no award
1924	no award
1925	Henry Norris Russell
1926	Arthur Holly Compton
1927	no award
1928	Edward Leamington Nichols
1929	no award
1930	John Stanley Plaskett
1931	Karl Taylor Compton
1932	no award
1933	Harlow Shapley
1934	no award
1935	no award
1936	no award
1937	William Weber Coblentz
1938	no award
1939	George Russell Harrison
1940	no award
1941	Vladimir Kosma Zworykin

1942	no award
1943	Charles Edward Mees
1944	no award
1945	Edwin Herbert Land
1946	no award
1947	Edmund Newton Harvey
1948	no award
1949	Ira Sprague Bowen
1950	no award
1951	Herbert E. Ives
1952	no award
1953	Lars Onsager
	Enrico Fermi
	Willis E. Lamb, Jr.
1954	no award
1955	James Franck
1956	no award
1957	Subrahmanyan Chandrasekhar
1958	no award
1959	George Wald
1960	no award
1961	Charles Hard Townes
1962	no award
1963	Hans Albrecht Bethe
1964	no award
1965	Samuel Cornette Collins
	William David McElroy
1966	no award
1967	Robert Henry Dicke
	Cornelis B. Van Niel
1968	Maarten Schmidt
1969	no award
1970	no award
1971	M.I.T. Group:

John A. Ball
Alan H. Barrett
Bernard F. Burke
Joseph C. Carter
Patricia P. Crowther
James M. Moran, Jr.
Alan E. E. Rogers
Canadian Group:
Norman W. Broten
R. M. Chisholm
John A. Galt
Herbert P. Gush
Thomas H. Legg
Jack L. Locke
Charles W. McLeish
Roger S. Richards
Jui Lin Yen
NRAO-Cornell Group:
C. C. Baret
Barry G. Clark

Marshall H. Cohen
David L. Jauncey
Kenneth I. Kellermann

| 1972 | no award |
| 1973 | E. Bright Wilson |

EDWIN SUTHERLAND AWARD—
The American Society of Criminology
For contributions to criminology theory.
Established 1960.

1960
Thorsten Sellin, University of Pennsylvania
1961
Orlando Wilson, police superintendent of Chicago; professor emeritus, University of California
1962
Negley Teeters, Temple University
1963
Herbert Wechsler, Columbia University Law School
Walter Reckless, Ohio State University
1964
Hon. J. C. McRuer, chairman of the Royal Commission on Civil Rights, former chief justice of Ontario
1965   no award
1966
George Vold, University of Minnesota
1967
Donald R. Cressey, University of California, Santa Barbara
1968
Denis Szabo, University of Montreal
1969
Lloyd Ohlin, Harvard University Law School
1970
Alfred Lindesmith, University of Indiana
1971
Marshall Clinard, University of Wisconsin
1972
Leslie Wilkins, State University of New York at Albany
1973
Edwin Lemert, University of California

1974
Simon Dinitz, Ohio State University
1975
C. Ray Jeffery, Florida State University
1976
Daniel Glaster, University of Southern California

AUGUST VOLLMER AWARD—The American Society of Criminology
"For an outstanding report of research in the field of criminology."
Established 1959.
1960
Marvin Wolfgang, University of Pennsylvania
Paul Bohannon, Northwestern University
1961
Sheldon and Eleanor Glueck, Harvard University Law School
1962
James Bennett, director, U. S. Bureau of Prisons
1963
Austin MacCormick, executive director, The Osborne Association
1964
Hon. J. Adrien Robert, director, Montreal Police Department; chief, Quebec Provincial Police
1965   no award
1966
Judge George Edwards, former justice of the Supreme Court of Michigan, police commissioner of Detroit, justice of the U. S. Circuit Court of Appeals
1967
Howard Leary, police commissioner of New York
1968
Myrl Alexander, director, U. S. Bureau of Prisons
1969
Hon. Joseph Tydings, U. S. senator, Maryland
1970
Milton Rector, executive director of the National Council on Crime and Delinquency
1971   no award
1972
Jerome Skolnick, University of California, Berkeley

1973
E. Preston Sharpe, general secretary of the American Correctional Association
1974
Patrick Murphy, president of the Police Foundation
Sol Rubin, counsel emeritus, National Council on Crime and Delinquency
1975   no award
1976
Patricia M. Wald, litigation director, Mental Health Law Project, Washington, D.C.

BRADFORD WASHBURN AWARD
—Boston Museum of Science
Dr. Washburn was the director of the museum. To honor him, the museum established this award to be given "to an individual anywhere in the world who has made an outstanding contribution toward public understanding of science, appreciation of its fascination, and the vital role it plays in all our lives."
Established 1964.
1964
Melville Bell Grosvenor, president, The National Geographic Society
1965
Captain Jacques-Yves Cousteau, director, Institut Oceangraphique et Musee, Monaco
1966
Gerard Piel, publisher, *Scientific American*
1967
Donald Baxter MacMillan, Rear Admiral, United States Navy Reserve (retired)
1968
George Wald, professor of biology, Harvard University
1969
Sir George Taylor, director, Royal Botanic Gardens, Kew, England
1970
Walter Cronkite, senior CBS News Correspondent
1972
Walter Sullivan, science editor, the *New York Times*

Nutritionist Jean Mayer.
(Museum of Science, Boston)

1973
  Rene Dubos, professor of biology, Rockefeller University, New York, N.Y.

1974
  Dr. Jane Goodall
  Baron Hugo Van Lawick

1975
  Professor Jean Mayer, Department of Nutrition, Harvard School of Public Health
1976
  Dr. Richard M. Eakin, Department of Zoology, University of California, Berkeley

SERVICE

AMERICAN BAR ASSOCIATION MEDAL—American Bar Association
  For service to the cause of American jurisprudence.
  Established 1929.
  1929   Samuel Williston
  1930   Elihu Root
  1931   Oliver Wendell Holmes

  1932   John Henry Wigmore
  1933   no award
  1934   George Woodward Wickersham
  1935   no award
  1936   no award
  1937   no award
  1938   Herbert Harley

Mickey Mouse's old man,
Walt Disney. (Memory Shop)

1939	Edgar Bronson Tolman
1940	Roscoe Pound
1941	George Wharton Pepper
1942	Charles Evans Hughes
1943	John J. Parker
1944	Hatton W. Sumners
1945	no award
1946	Carl McFarland
1947	William L. Ransom
1948	Arthur T. Vanderbilt
1949	no award
1950	Orie L. Phillips
1951	Reginald Heber Smith
1952	Harrison Tweed
1953	Frank E. Holman
1954	George M. Morris
1955	no award
1956	Robert G. Storey
1957	William Clarke Mason
1958	E. Smythe Gambrell
1959	Greenville Clark
1960	William A. Schnader
1961	Jacob Mark Lashly
1962	Tom C. Clark
1963	Felix Frankfurter
1964	Henry S. Drinker
1965	Edmund M. Morgan
1966	Charles S. Rhyne

1967	Roger J. Traynor
1968	J. Edward Lumbard
1969	Walter V. Schaefer
1970	Frank C. Haymond
1971	Whitney North Seymour
1972	Harold J. Gallagher

See Architecture, Distinguished Service Award, American Institute of Planners

THE AUDUBON MEDAL—National Audubon Society
For distinguished individual service to conservation.
Established 1946.

1947	Dr. Hugh Bennett
1949	Dr. Ira N. Gabrielson
1950	John D. Rockefeller, Jr.
1952	Louis Bromfield
1955	Walt Disney
1956	Dr. Ludlow Griscom
1959	Dr. Olaus J. Murie
1960	Jay N. Darling
1961	Dr. Clarence Cottam
1962	William O. Douglas
1963	Rachel Carson
1964	Laurance S. Rockefeller

1966	Dr. A. Starker Leopold
1967	Stewart L. Udall
1968	Fairfield Osborn
1969	Horace M. Albright
1972	Roger Tory Peterson
1973	Barbara Ward
1974	Tom McCall, governor of Oregon
1975	Maurice Strong
1976	John Oakes, chief editorial writer, New York Times

AWARD FOR DISTINGUISHED SERVICE TO THE ARTS—The

American Academy of Arts and Letters and the National Institute of Arts and Letters

For distinguished service to the arts. Established 1941.

1941	Robert Moses
1944	Samuel S. McClure
1949	Mrs. Edward MacDowell
1952	Mrs. Simon Guggenheim
1954	Senator J. William Fulbright
1955	Henry Allen Moe
1957	Francis Henry Taylor
1958	Lincoln Kirstein
1959	Mrs. Elizabeth Ames
1962	Paul Mellon
1963	Mrs. Hugh Bullock
1965	Miss Frances Steloff
1968	Alfred H. Barr, Jr.
1969	Leopold Stokowski
1970	Martha Graham
1973	Felicia Geffen
1974	Walker Evans
1975	George Balanchine

AWARD FOR OUTSTANDING LAW ENFORCEMENT ACHIEVEMENT

—Society of Professional Investigators

For "meritorious service in the field of investigation" and law enforcement. Established 1956.

1957
Robert F. Kennedy, chief counsel, U. S. Senate Select Committee on Improper Activities in the Labor or Management Field
1958
Edgar D. Croswell, N. Y. State Police sergeant who uncovered the meeting of notorious characters at Apalachin, N. Y.
1959
Detective Division of the New York City Police Department
1960
Arthur H. Christy, chief of the criminal division, U. S. Attorney's Office, Southern District, New York City
1961
Urbanus Edmund Baughman, chief, U. S. Secret Service
1962
Charles "Pat" Ward, agent-in-charge, New York office, Federal Bureau of Narcotics
1963
Joseph Kaitz, New York commissioner, Waterfront Commission of New York Harbor
1964
Michael J. Murphy, police commissioner, New York City
1965
William A. O'Connor, superintendent, Port of New York Authority Police Department
1966
Alfred J. Scotti, Chief assistant, District Attorney's Office, New York County
1967
Sanford D. Garelik, Chief inspector, New York City Police Department
1968
John F. Malone, Assistant director, Federal Bureau of Investigation
1969
Albert E. Whitaker, agent-in-charge, U. S. Secret Service, New York City
1970
John L. Barry, police commissioner, Suffolk County (N. Y.) Police Department
1971
Louis J. Lefkowitz, attorney general, state of New York
1972
Myles J. Ambrose, special assistant attorney general for drug abuse law enforcement
1973
Clarence M. Kelley, director, Federal Bureau of Investigation
1974
Michael J. Codd, police commissioner, New York City

1975
  William C. Connelie,
  superintendent, New York State
  Police
1976
  Mario Merola, district attorney of
  Bronx County, New York City

AWARD OF MERIT—The Decalogue Society of Lawyers
  The society uses a five-point criteria in awarding this honor. The criteria all involve contributions not only to the "Jewish community" but to the nation and in some cases the world as well. The contributions must be in outstanding service, leadership, promotion of Jewish causes, artistic contributions to culture, and the influence of a person's writing, music, art, choreography.
  Established 1941.

1941   Barnet Hodes
1942   Marshall Field
1943   Col. Frank Knox
1944   Wendell L. Willkie
1945   Leo Lerner
1946   Bartley C. Crum
1947   Bishop Bernard J. Sheil
1948   Rabbi Stephen S. Wise
1949   Col. Jacob M. Arvey
1950   Dr. Percy L. Julian
1951   Judge Harry M. Fisher
1952   Governor Adlai E. Stevenson
1953   Professor Albert Einstein
1954   Hon. Harry S. Truman
1955   Senator Herbert Lehman
1956   Dr. Edward J. Sparling
1957   Mrs. Eleanor Roosevelt
1958   Judge Simon E. Sobeloff
1959   Philip M. Klutznick
1960   Judge Julius H. Miner
1961   Hon. Arthur J. Goldberg
1962   Senator Jacob K. Javits
1963   Hon. Michael A. Musmanno
1964   Rabbi Mordecai M. Kaplan
1965   Dr. Albert B. Sabin
1966   Hon. Paul H. Douglas
1967   Hon. Abraham L. Marovitz
1968   Senator Charles H. Percy
1969   Professor Rene Cassin
1970   Ramsey Clark
1971   Sir Georg Solti
1972   Hon. Sidney R. Yates
1973   Justice William O. Douglas

1974   no award
1975   Saul Bellow

See Broadcasting, The George Foster Peabody Broadcasting Awards, University of Georgia

BRONZE MEDAL—Citizens Budget Commission, Inc.
  This goes for outstanding service to New York City.
  Established 1951.

1953   Joseph M. Proskauer
1954   Devereux C. Josephs
1955   Stanley M. Isaacs
1956   David Rockefeller
       Bernard F. Gimbel
1957   Herbert H. Lehman
1958   Harrison Tweed
1959   James Felt
1960   Samuel D. Leidesdorf
1961   John D. Rockefeller, 3rd
       James Felt
1962   David M. Heyman
       Emma Alden Rothblatt
1963   Austin J. Tobin
       Mrs. Charles S. Payson
1964   Percy Uris
1965   Othmar Hermann Ammann
1966   Earl B. Schwulst
1967   Thomas P. F. Hoving
1968   McGeorge Bundy
1969   Robert W. Dowling
1970   Walter Cronkite
1971   Jacob K. Javits
1972   Arthur Levitt
1973   William J. Ronan
       George Champion
1974   Abraham Beame (as comptroller)
1975   J. Peter Grace
1976   Richard R. Shinn

EUGENE V. DEBS AWARD—Eugene V. Debs Foundation
  Given in the fields of labor, public service, and education.
  Established 1965.

1966   John L. Lewis, labor
1967   Norman Thomas, public service
1968   A. Philip Randolph, labor
1969   Walter Reuther, labor
1970   H. E. Gilbert, labor
1971   Patrick E. Gorman, labor

1972   Dorothy Day, public service
1973   Michael Harrington, public
service
1974   Arthur Schlesinger, Jr.,
education
1975   Ruben Levin, labor
1976   Martin H. Miller, labor

DISTINGUISHED PUBLIC SER-VICE AWARDS—Department of Health, Education, and Welfare

For "outstanding contributions to the growth and development of the Department, for exceptional services in or for the Department as an institution committed to combating all the conditions that prevent individual fulfillment or stunt human growth."
Established 1968.
1968
Lister Hall, U. S. senator from Alabama
Carl Elliott, former U. S. congressman
1971
Dr. William Middleton, nongovernment scientist
Dr. Alfred Gilman, nongovernment scientist
Mr. Maurice Warsaw, president of Grand Central, Inc.
1972
WRC-TV, Washington, D.C., an owned and operated television station of the National Broadcasting Company—for the production of 94 half-hour television programs (the "YOU" series) in their studios exclusively for the dissemination of information about the department, at no expense to the department
1974
Dr. Elizabeth M. Boggs, Ph.D. chairwoman, National Advisory on Developmental Disabilities
Lawrence Arnstein, also known as "Mr. Public Health," for his unique contributions to development of public health and welfare programs since 1913. He provided leadership for a lobbying campaign that broke down public resistance, making possible the founding of the School of Public Health at the University of California in Berkeley

DISTINGUISHED SERVICE AWARD—United States Department of the Treasury

The highest treasury award for a nonemployee who has given "outstanding assistance to the Department."
Established 1963.
1964   Robert G. Rouse
J. Vaughan Gary
1965   Frank R. Milliken
1966   William C. Decker
1968   Francis M. Bator
Edward M. Bernstein
Kermit Gordon
Walter W. Heller
Andre Mayer
David Rockefeller
Robert V. Roosa
Frazar B. Wilde
Harold Boeschenstein
Eugene N. Beesley
Roger M. Blough
Bert S. Cross
Paul L. Davies
Frederic G. Donner
G. Keith Funston
Thomas S. Gates, Jr.
Frank R. Milliken
David Packard
Sidney J. Weinberg
Henry S. Wingate
Albert L. Nickerson
Edward R. Fried
William McChesney Martin, Jr.
Robert M. McKinney
Reno Odlin
Charles A. Coombs
1969   Alfred Hayes
J. L. Robertson
1971   James M. Roche
1976   James S. Fish

See Flag-Waving, Distinguished Service Medal, The American Legion

CHARLES EVANS HUGHES AWARD—National Conference of Christians and Jews

"For courageous leadership in governmental, civic, and humanitarian affairs." Named in honor of the former Supreme Court justice.
Established 1965.

1965
  Edmund (Pat) G. Brown, California governor
  Leroy Collins, Florida governor
  Nelson Aldrich Rockefeller, New York governor
  George Romney, Michigan governor
1966
  Dwight D. Eisenhower, General of the Army
1967
  Harry S. Truman
  Edward W. Brooke, U. S. senator
  Hon. Paul H. Douglas
1968
  Lewis L. Strauss, Admiral, retired
  John W. Gardner
1969
  Ivan Allen, Jr.
  Chief Justice Earl Warren
1970
  Hon. Constance Baker Motley
  Rev. Theodore M. Hesburgh
1971
  Gen. Lucius D. Clay
  Associate Justice Tom C. Clark
  Walter E. Washington
1972
  Jerome H. Holland
1973
  Henry A. Kissinger, secretary of state
1974
  David Rockefeller
1975
  Hon. Brooks Hays
  Hon. Linwood Holton
  Robert D. Murphy
1976
  John D. deButts, AT & T

**HELEN KELLER INTERNA-
TIONAL AWARD**—Helen Keller International, Inc.

The group giving this award was called the American Foundation for Overseas Blind, Inc., before changing its name in 1977. The award is presented for work with the blind or for work in blindness prevention.
Established 1960.
1960
  Col. Edwin A. Baker, Canada: founder and managing director, Canadian National Institute for the

Blind; president, World Council for the Welfare of the Blind
1968
  George L. Raverat, France: director, European office AFOB
1970
  Sir John F. Wilson, United Kingdom: director and chief executive officer, Royal Commonwealth Society for the Blind
1971
  Lord Fraser of Lonsdale, United Kingdom: chairman, St. Dunstan's, London
1973
  James S. Adams, United States: industrialist and investment banker; president, Research to Prevent Blindness, Inc.; director, AFOB
1976
  Dr. John Ferree, United States: director, National Society for the Prevention of Blindness; member, AFOB's Advisory Committee on Blindness Prevention

THE MURRAY-GREEN AWARD FOR COMMUNITY SERVICE—American Federation of Labor and Congress of Industrial Organizations
Originally this was called the Philip Murray Award. It became the Murray-Green Award in 1956. It is presented to those who have improved the "health, welfare, and recreation of people everywhere."
Established 1947.

1947	Gen. Omar N. Bradley
1958	Sen. Robert F. Wagner
1951	Sen. James E. Murray
1953	United Automobile Workers
	United Nations Children's Emergency Fund
	Wilbur F. Maxwell
	Robert H. MacRae
	Oscar R. Ewing
1954	The Menninger Foundation
1955	Eleanor Roosevelt
1956	Herbert H. Lehman
1957	Dr. Jonas E. Salk
1958	Bob Hope
1959	President Harry S. Truman
1960	Mrs. Agnes E. Meyer
1962	Gov. Luis Munoz Marin

*James S. Adams,
industrialist, investment
banker, and president of
Research to Prevent
Blindness.*

1963	Gen. Alfred M. Gruenther
1964	Sen. Estes Kefauver
1965	Henry J. Kaiser
1966	Mr. and Mrs. Sargent Shriver
1967	Dr. Albert B. Sabin
1968	Wilbur J. Cohen
1969	Sen. Paul A. Douglas
1970	John W. Gardner
1971	Jerry Lewis
1972	A. Philip Randolph
1973	President Lyndon B. Johnson
1974	Sen. Hubert H. Humphrey

See Music, Gold Baton Award, The American Symphony Orchestra League

NOAA AWARD—The U. S. Department of Commerce, National Oceanic and Atmospheric Administration

For service and contribution to NOAA.

Established 1970.

1971

Harold L. Crutcher, scientific advisor, National Climatic Center, EDS, Asheville, N. C.

Robert S. Dietz, research oceanographer, Atlantic Oceanographic and Meteorological Laboratories, Miami, Fla.

Roy L. Fox, retired director, National Weather Service's Central Region, Kansas City, Mo.

Raymond L. Joiner, digital computer systems analyst, National Climatic Center, EDS, Asheville, N. C.

Robert A. McCormick, Air Resources Laboratories, Raleigh, N. C.

Donald F. Moore, NOAA assistant administrator for policy and plans

1972

Herbert P. Benner, radarmeteorologist, National Weather Service's Western Region Headquarters, Salt Lake City, Utah

Dr. Clayton E. Jensen, leader, NOAA's environmental monitoring activities

Dr. Kikuro Miyakoda, Environmental Research Laboratories' Geophysical Fluid Dynamics Laboratory, Princeton, N. J.

Dr. Joanne Simpson, director, ERL's Florida-based experimental meteorology laboratory

Dr. Charles A. Whitten, National Ocean Survey

1973

Dr. James R. Wait, director of the Environmental Research Laboratories' Theoretical Study Group

Walter D. Komhry, chief of the Geophysical Monitoring Techniques and Standards Group of ERL's Air Resources Laboratories

Dr. Clifford A. Spohn, director of operations for the National Environmental Satellite Service, Suitland, Md.

William R. Long, forecaster of floods, credited with saving thousands of lives in 1968 in northern New Jersey and again in 1972 in the Pittsburgh, Pa., area

Bob E. Finley, for consumer educational materials produced by the National Marketing Services Office

Morris R. Jones, innovator in distribution of the NOS nautical and aeronautical charts and related publications

1974

Dr. Douglas H. Sargeant, director of the U. S. Project Office of GATE— the Atlantic Tropical Experiment of the Global Atmospheric Research Project—for program administration and management

Robert E. Johnson, chief, Systems Integration Division, Systems Development Office, National Weather Service, Silver Spring, Md.

Dr. Donald J. Williams, director of the Boulder, Colo., based Environmental Research Laboratories' space environment laboratory

Joseph Dracup, supervisory geodesist of the National Geodetic Survey, Rockville, Md.

Burton L. Tinker, food technologist at the Northeast Utilization Research Center of the National Marine Fisheries Service, Gloucester, Mass.

1975

Dr. Lester Machta, director of the Environmental Research Laboratories' Air Resources

Laboratory, Silver Spring, Md.

Cdr. R. Lawrence Swanson, project manager for ERL's marine ecosystems analysis (MESA) program New York Bight Project, Stony Brook, N. Y.

Dr. Harry R. Glahn, deputy director of the National Weather Service's techniques development laboratory, Silver Spring, Md.

Ernest S. Ethridge, official-in-charge of the NWS office at Shreveport, La.

Russell T. Norris, retired director of the National Marine Fisheries Service's Northeast Region, Gloucester, Mass.

1976

William L. Peck, retired deputy regional director of the National Marine Fisheries Service Northwest Region, Seattle, Wash.

Dr. Andrew J. Kemmerer, chief of the Technology Division of the National Marine Fisheries Service southeast fisheries center, Bay St. Louis, Miss.

Dr. Syukuro Manabe, research meteorologist at the Environmental Research Laboratories' Geophysical Fluid Dynamics Laboratory, Princeton, N. J.

Herman F. Mondschein, hydrologist-in-charge at the National Weather Service, River Forecast Center, Kansas City, Mo.

Richard L. Rutkowski, physical science technician and diver at ERL's Atlantic Oceanographic and Meteorological Laboratories, Miami, Fla.

PRESIDENTIAL MEDAL OF FREE-DOM

For those "who contribute to the quality of American life," this is the nation's highest civilian award.

Established 1963.

1963

Marian Anderson, singer

Ralph J. Bunche, undersecretary to U.N.

Ellsworth Bunker, diplomat

Pablo Casals, cellist

Genevieve Caulfield, educator

James B. Conant, educator

John F. Enders, bacteriologist

Felix Frankfurter, jurist
Karl Holton, youth authority
John XXIII, Pope
John F. Kennedy, U.S. President
Robert J. Kiphuth, director of
athletics
Edwin H. Land, inventor
Herbert H. Lehman, statesman
Robert A. Lovett, statesman
J. Clifford MacDonald, educator
John J. McCloy, statesman, banker
George Meany, labor leader
Alexander Meiklejohn, philosopher
Ludgwig Mies van der Rohe,
architect
Jean Monnet, statesman
Luis Munoz-Marin, Puerto Rican
governor
Clarence B. Randall, industrialist
Rudolf Serkin, pianist
Edward Steichen, photographer
George W. Taylor, educator
Alan T. Waterman, scientist
Mark S. Watson, journalist
Annie D. Wauneka, worker in public
health
E. B. White, author
Thornton Wilder, author
Edmund Wilson, critic, author
Andrew N. Wyeth, artist
1964
Dean Acheson, statesman
Detlev W. Bronk, neurophysiologist
Aaron Copland, composer
William de Kooning, artist
Walt Disney, movie maker,
cartoonist
J. Frank Dobie, author
Lena F. Edwards, doctor
Thomas Stearns Eliot, poet
Lynn Fontanne, actress
John W. Gardner, educator
Rev. Theodore M. Hesburgh,
educator
Clarence L. Johnson, engineer
Frederick R. Kappel, telephone
executive
Helen A. Keller, educator
John L. Lewis, labor leader
Walter Lippmann, journalist
Alfred Lunt, actor
Ralph Emerson McGill, journalist
Samuel Eliot Morison, historian
Lewis Mumford, urban planner,
author

Edward R. Murrow, broadcast
journalist
Reinhold Niebuhr, theologian
Leontyne Price, singer
A. Philip Randolph, labor leader
Carl Sandburg, poet
John Steinbeck, author
Helen B. Taussig, doctor
Carl Vinson, legislator
Thomas J. Watson, Jr., industrialist
Paul Dudley White, physician
1967
Ellsworth Bunker, diplomat
Eugene M. Locke, diplomat
Robert W. Komer, government
employe
1968
Robert S. McNamara, government
official
James Webb, NASA administrator
1969 (by President Johnson)
Eugene R. Black, banker
McGeorge Bundy, government
official
Clark M. Clifford, statesman
Michael E. DeBakey, surgeon
David Dubinsky, labor leader
Henry Ford II, industrialist
Ralph Ellison, author
W. Averell Harriman, statesman
Bob Hope, comedian
Edgar Kaiser, industrialist
Mary Lasker, philanthropist
John W. Macy, Jr. government
official
Gregory Peck, actor
Laurance S. Rockefeller,
conservationist
Walt. W. Rostow, government official
Dean Rusk, statesman
Merriman Smith, journalist
Cyrus R. Vance, government official
William S. White, journalist
Roy Wilkins, civil rights leader
Whitney M. Young, civil rights
leader
1969 (by President Nixon)
Col. Edwin E. Aldrin, Jr., astronaut
Neil A. Armstrong, astronaut
Lt. Col. Michael Collins, astronaut
Duke Ellington, musician
1970
Apollo 13 Mission Operations Team
Earl Charles Behrens, journalist
Edward T. Folliard, journalist

Fred Wallace Haise, Jr., astronaut
William M. Henry, journalist
Arthur Krock, journalist
David Lawrence, journalist
George Gould Lincoln, journalist
James A. Lovell, Jr., astronaut
Raymond Moley, journalist
Eugene Ormandy, conductor
Adela Rogers St. Johns, journalist
John Leonard Swigert, Jr., astronaut
1971
Sam Goldwyn, film producer
Manlio Brosio, NATO secretary
general
William J. Hopkins, White House
executive clerk
1972
Lila and DeWitt Wallace, founders
of *Readers' Digest*
John Paul Vann, Vietnam adviser
1973
John Ford, movie director
William P. Rogers, diplomat
1974
Melvin R. Laird, government official
Dr. Charles L. Lowman, doctor
Paul G. Hoffman, statesman
1975 no award
1976
David K. E. Bruce, ambassador
Artur Rubinstein, conductor
U.S. Olympic Team (Jesse Owen),
olympics
Martha Graham, dancer
1977
I. W. Able, labor leader
John Bardeen, physicist
Irving Berlin, songwriter
Normal Borlaug, agricultural
scientist
Gen. Omar M. Bradley, officer, U.S.
Army
Adm. Arleigh Burke, officer, U.S.
Navy
Bruce Catton, Civil War historian
Joe DiMaggio, baseball player
Ariel Durant, writer, historian,
philosopher
Will Durant, writer, historian,
philosopher
Judge Henry J. Friendy
Lady Bird Johnson, former first lady
Archibald MacLeish, poet,
playwright
James Michener, author

Nelson A. Rockefeller, former U.S.
vice-president
Norman Rockwell, artist
Katherine Felene Shouse,
performing arts
James D. Watson, educator, scientist
Arthur Fiedler, conductor
Lowell Thomas, newscaster
Alexander Calder, sculptor
Georgia O'Keeffe, artist

PUBLIC SERVICE AWARD—The
Advertising Council
In the words of the Council: "The
social consciousness of American business leaders is one of the distinguish-
ing marks of the American form of cap-
italism. It is a quality too little
honored." The Council hopes to make
up for that with this award.
Established 1954.

1954	Charles E. Wilson
1955	Clarence Francis
1956	Paul G. Hoffman
1957	Sidney J. Weinberg
1958	George M. Humphrey
1959	Roy E. Larsen
1960	Neil McElroy
1961	Henry Ford II
1962	Lucius D. Clay
1963	John J. McCloy
1964	Charles G. Mortimer
1965	David Sarnoff
1966	John A. McCone
1967	John T. Connor
1968	Robert S. McNamara
1969	Frank Stanton
1970	James M. Roche
1971	David Rockefeller
1972	Thomas J. Watson, Jr.
1973	Howard J. Morgens
1974	Katharine Graham
1975	J. Paul Austin
1976	Arthur M. Wood

**ROCKEFELLER PUBLIC SERVICE
AWARD**—Princeton University
Established by John D. III, this is
awarded "to men and women whose
careers in the Federal Service have
been marked by sustained excellence."
Ten thousand dollars goes along with
the honor. The award was originally
designed to give recipients time for
leaves to study, write, or travel. How-

ever, after Congress passed the Government Employees Training Act in 1958, the awards were redesigned to honor employees with distinguished careers.

Established 1952.

ADMINISTRATION
1960

Robert M. Ball, deputy director, bureau of Old-Age and Survivors Insurance, Social Security Administration, Department of Health, Education, and Welfare

1961

Elmer B. Staats, deputy director, Bureau of the Budget, Executive Office of the President

1962

J. Stanley Baughman, president, Federal National Mortgage Association, Housing and Home Finance Agency

1963

Eugene W. Weber, chief, Civil Works Planning Division, Office of the Chief of Engineers, Department of the Army

1964

William D. Carey, executive assistant director, bureau of the budget, Executive Office of the President

1965

Bertrand M. Harding, deputy commissioner, Internal Revenue Service, Department of the Treasury

1966

Millard Cass, deputy under secretary, Department of Labor

1967

Donald A. Williams, administrator, Soil Conservation Service, Department of Agriculture

1968

Artemus E. Weatherbee, assistant secretary for administration, Department of the Treasury

1969

Arthur E. Hess, deputy commissioner, Social Security Administration, Department of Health, Education, and Welfare

1970

Ben Posner, assistant director for administration, U. S. Information Agency

FOREIGN AFFAIRS OR INTERNATIONAL OPERATIONS
1960

Charles E. Bohlen, special assistant to the secretary of state, Department of State

1961

Livingston T. Merchant, ambassador to Canada, Department of State

1962

Liewellyn E. Thompson, ambassador to the U.S.S.R., Department of State

1963

Henry Loomis, director, International Broadcasting Service, United States Information Agency

1964

Charles W. Yost, deputy United States representative to the United Nations, Department of State

1965

U. Alexis Johnson, deputy under secretary for political affairs, Department of State

1966

John M. Leddy, assistant secretary for European affairs, Department of State

1967

Foy D. Kohler, deputy under secretary for political affairs, Department of State

1968

Leonard C. Meeker, legal adviser, Department of State

1969

Philip C. Habib, senior adviser, U. S. Delegation, Paris Negotiations on Vietnam, Department of State
John F. Thomas, director, Intergovernmental Committee for European Migration

1970

Spurgeon M. Keeny, Jr., assistant director, Science and Technology Bureau, U.S. Arms Control and Disarmament Agency

THE GENERAL WELFARE OR
  NATIONAL RESOURCES
1960
  Richard E. McArdle, chief, Forest
  Service, Department of Agriculture
  Conrad L. Wirth, director, National
  Park Service, Department of the
  Interior
1961
  Thomas B. Nolan, director,
  Geological Survey, Department of
  the Interior
1962
  Morris H. Hansen, assistant director
  for research and development,
  Bureau of the Census, Department of
  Commerce
1963
  Gabriel O. Wessenauer, manager of
  power, Tennessee Valley Authority
1964
  Gordon E. Howard, assistant
  commissioner, Urban Renewal
  Administration, Housing and Home
  Finance Agency
1965
  Margaret G. Arnstein, senior nursing
  adviser for international health, U.S.
  Public Health Service, Department
  of Health, Education, and Welfare
  Huntington Cairns, secretary,
  treasurer, and general counsel,
  National Gallery of Art
1966
  David D. Thomas, deputy
  administrator, Federal Aviation
  Agency
1967
  Wilbur J. Cohen, under secretary,
  Department of Health, Education,
  and Welfare
1968
  Edward C. Crafts, director, Bureau
  of Outdoor Recreation, Department
  of the Interior
1969
  William T. Pecora, director,
  Geological Survey, Department of
  the Interior
1970
  Aaron M. Altschul, special assistant
  to the secretary for nutrition
  improvement, Department of
  Agriculture

LAW, LEGISLATION, OR
  REGULATION
1960
  Leonard Niederlehner, deputy
  general counsel, Department of
  Defense
1961
  Colin F. Stam, chief of staff, Joint
  Committee on Internal Revenue
  Taxation, United States Congress
1962
  Reginald G. Conley, assistant
  general counsel, Department of
  Health, Education, and Welfare
1963
  Carl M. Marcy, chief of staff, Senate
  Foreign Relations Committee,
  United States Congress
1964
  Harold F. Reis, first assistant, Office
  of Legal Counsel, Department of
  Justice
1965
  Robert F. Keller, general counsel,
  General Accounting Office
1966
  John R. Blandford, chief counsel,
  House Committee on Armed
  Services, United States Congress
1967
  Philip Elman, commissioner,
  Federal Trade Commission
1968
  David Ferber, solicitor, Securities
  and Exchange Commission
  Irving M. Pollack, director, Division
  of Trading and Markets, Securities
  and Exchange Commission
1969
  Ashley Foard, deputy general
  counsel, Department of Housing and
  Urban Development
1970
  David L. Norman, deputy assistant
  attorney general, Civil Rights
  Division, Department of Justice

SCIENCE, TECHNOLOGY, OR
  ENGINEERING
1960
  Sterling Brown Hendricks, chief
  scientist, Mineral Nutrition
  Laboratory for Pioneering Research,
  Agricultural Research Service,
  Department of Agriculture

1961

Robert H. Felix, director, Institute of Mental Health, National Institutes of Health, Department of Health, Education, and Welfare

1962

Hugh L. Dryden, deputy administrator, National Aeronautics and Space Administration

1963

Allen V. Astin, director, National Bureau of Standards, Department of Commerce

1964

James A. Shannon, director, National Institutes of Health, Department of Health, Education, and Welfare

1965

William B. McLean, technical director, U. S. Naval Ordnance Test Station, China Lake, Department of Navy

1966

Edward F. Knipling, director, Entomology Division, Agricultural Research Service, Department of Agriculture

1967

Herbert Friedman, superintendent, Atmosphere and Astrophysics Division, Hulburt Center for Space Research, Department of the Navy

1968

Abe Silverstein, director, Lewis Research Center, National Aeronautics and Space Administration

1969

John W. Evans, director, Sacramento Peak Observatory, Department of the Air Force

1970

Robert J. Huebner, chief, Viral Carcinogenesis Branch, National Cancer Institute, National Institutes of Health, Department of Health, Education, and Welfare

AT LARGE

1969

A special award honoring man's first landing on the Moon

Robert R. Gilruth, director, Manned Spacecraft Center, National Aeronautics and Space Administration

1971

Samuel M. Cohn, assistant director for budget review, Office of Management and Budget, Executive Office of the President

Mary Lee Mills, nurse-consultant, Community Health Service, Department of Health, Education, and Welfare

Joseph J. Sisco, assistant secretary for Near Eastern and South Asian affairs, Department of State

Luna B. Leopold, senior research hydrologist, U.S. Geological Survey, Department of the Interior

Robert Solomon, adviser to the Board and Director, Division of International Finance, Board of Governors, Federal Reserve System

1972

Vernon D. Acree, commissioner of customs, Bureau of Customs, Department of the Treasury

Samuel C. Adams, Jr., assistant administrator, Bureau for Africa, Agency for International Development

Barbara M. White, special assistant to the director, United States Information Agency

Wallace P. Rowe, chief, Laboratory of Viral Diseases, National Institutes of Health, Department of Health, Education, and Welfare

Laurence N. Woodworth, chief of staff, Joint Committee on Internal Revenue Taxation, United States Congress

1973

Phillip S. Hughes, director, Office of Federal Elections, General Accounting Office

Martin M. Cummings, director, National Library of Medicine, National Institutes of Health, Department of Health, Education, and Welfare

David D. Newsom, assistant secretary for African affairs, Department of State

Vincent E. McKelvey, director, U. S. Geological Survey, Department of the Interior

Ruth M. Davis, director, Institute for Computer Sciences and Technology, National Bureau of Standards, Department of Commerce
1976
Dale Bertsch, executive director of the Miami Valley Regional Planning Commission, Dayton, Ohio
Ira DeMent, Montgomery, Ala., United States attorney for the middle district of Alabama
Herbert Sturz, director of the Vera Institute of Justice in New York City
Ernest G. Green, executive director of the Recruitment and Training Program in New York City
Bernice Sandler, director of the Project on the Status and Education of Women of the Association of American Colleges in Washington, D. C.
Donald S. Brown, mission director, United States Agency for International Development, Egypt
David Shear, director of the Office of Sahel and Francophone West Africa, AID

MARGARET SANGER AWARD—
Planned Parenthood-World Population
Well, you can safely bet that no mother of eighteen children is going to get this award, which goes for leadership in family planning.
Established 1966.

1966	Lyndon B. Johnson
	Rev. Martin Luther King, Jr.
	Dr. Carl G. Hartman
	Gen. William H. Draper
1967	John D. Rockefeller III
1968	Hon. Ernest Gruening
1969	Lord Caradon
1970	Hon. Joseph D. Tydings
1971	Dr. Louis M. Hellman
1972	Dr. Alan F. Guttmacher
1973	Dr. Christopher Tietze
	Sarah Lewit
1974	Harriet F. Pilpel, Esq.
1975	Cass Canfield
1976	Dr. John Rock

See Science, Johnny Appleseed Award, Men's Garden Clubs of America

See Science, Award for Distinguished Service in the Advancement of Inorganic Chemistry, American Chemical Society and Mallinckrodt, Inc.

See Science, Louis I. Dublin Award, American Association of Suicidology

See Science, NOAA Award, the U.S. Department of Commerce, National Oceanic and Atmospheric Administration

See Science, Priestly Medal. American Chemical Society

SECRETARY OF DEFENSE AWARD FOR OUTSTANDING PUBLIC SERVICE—United States Department of Defense
For a private citizen who has contributed to the department.
Dr. Ann P. Ulrey, coauthor of *Analysis: For Managers of People and Things*
Fount L. Robison, for services to the YMCA and USO
Professor Rodney C. Loehr, professor, University of Minnesota and supporter of ROTC
J. Kevin Murphy, chairman, National POW/MIA Scholarship Committee
Robert C. Lewis, vice president, American National Red Cross
Dr. John Dunworth, dean, Teachers College, Ball State University, Muncie, Ind.
Thurston Hassell, contributor to military photography as an employee of Fairchild Camera and Instrument Corporation
Lotte Duker, citizen of the Federal Republic of Germany who contributed to friendly relationships between the German-American community
Raymond Weeks, director of Veterans Day, Birmingham, Ala.

See Sports, Boxing Hall of Fame, Amateur Athletic Union

SPORTS

AUTO RACING

GRAND PRIX FORMULA I WINNERS
1950	Nino Farina, Italy
1951	Juan Fangio, Argentina
1952	Alberto Ascari, Italy
1953	Alberto Ascari, Italy
1954	Juan Fangio, Argentina
1955	Juan Fangio, Argentina
1956	Juan Fangio, Argentina
1957	Juan Fangio, Argentinia
1958	Mike Hawthorne, England
1959	Jack Brabham, Australia
1960	Jack Brabham, Australia
1961	Phil Hill, United States
1962	Graham Hill, England
1963	Jim Clark, Scotland
1964	John Surtees, England
1965	Jim Clark, Scotland
1966	Jack Brabham, Australia
1967	Denis Hulme, New Zealand
1968	Graham Hill, England
1969	Jackie Stewart, Scotland
1970	Jochen Rindt, Austria
1971	Jackie Stewart, Scotland
1972	Emerson Fittipaldi, Brazil
1973	Jackie Stewart, Scotland
1974	Emerson Fittipaldi, Brazil
1975	Niki Lauda, Austria
1976	

INDIANAPOLIS 500
1911	Ray Harrison
1912	Joe Dawson
1913	Jules Goux
1914	Rene Thomas
1915	Ralph DePalma
1916	Dario Resta
1917	Race Cancelled
1918	Race Cancelled
1919	Howdy Wilcox
1920	Gaston Chevrolet
1921	Tommy Milton
1922	Jimmy Murphy
1923	Tommy Milton
1924	L. L. Corum—Joe Boyer
1925	Pete DePaolo
1926	Frank Lockhart
1927	George Souders
1928	Louis Meyer
1929	Ray Keech
1930	Billy Arnold
1931	Louis Schneider
1932	Fred Frame
1933	Louis Meyer
1934	Bill Cummings
1935	Kelly Petillo
1936	Louis Meyer
1937	Wilbur Shaw
1938	Floyd Roberts
1939	Wilbur Shaw
1940	Wilbur Shaw
1941	Floyd David—Mauri Rose
1942	Race cancelled
1943	Race cancelled
1944	Race cancelled
1945	Race cancelled
1946	George Robinson
1947	Mauri Rose
1948	Mauri Rose
1949	Bill Holland
1950	Johnnie Parsons
1951	Lee Wallard
1952	Troy Ruttman
1953	Bill Vukovich
1954	Bill Vukovich
1955	Bob Sweikert
1956	Pat Flaherty
1957	Sam Hanks
1958	Jimmy Bryan
1959	Rodger Ward
1960	Jim Rathmann
1961	A. J. Foyt
1962	Rodger Ward
1963	Parnelli Jones
1964	A. J. Foyt
1965	Jim Clark
1966	Graham Hill
1967	A. J. Foyt
1968	Bobby Unser

1969	Mario Andretti
1970	Al Unser
1971	Al Unser
1972	Mark Donohue
1973	Gordon Johncock
1974	Johnny Rutherford
1975	Bobby Unser
1976	Johnny Rutherford

UNITED STATES AUTO CLUB NATIONAL WINNERS (previously American Automobile Association)

1902	Harry Harkness
1903	Barney Oldfield
1904	George Heath
1905	Victor Hemery
1906	Joe Tracy
1907	Eddie Bald
1908	Louis Strang
1909	Bert Dingley
	George Robertson
1910	Ray Harroun
1911	Ralph Mulford
1912	Ralph DePalma
1913	Earl Cooper
1914	Ralph DePalma
1915	Earl Cooper
1916	Dario Resta
1917	Earl Cooper
1918	Ralph Mulford
1919	Howard Wilcox
1920	Tommy Milton
1921	Tommy Milton
1922	Jimmy Murphy
1923	Eddie Hearne
1924	Jimmy Murphy
1925	Pete DePaolo
1926	Harry Hartz
1927	Pete DePaolo
1928	Louis Meyer
1929	Louis Meyer
1930	Billy Arnold
1931	Louis Schneider
1932	Bob Carey
1933	Louis Meyer
1934	Bill Cummings
1935	Kelly Petillo
1936	Mauri Rose
1937	Wilbur Shaw
1938	Floyd Roberts
1939	Wilbur Shaw
1940	Rex Mays
1941	Rex Mays
1942	No winner
1943	No winner

1944	No winner
1945	No winner
1946	Ted Horn
1947	Ted Horn
1948	Ted Horn
1949	Johnny Parsons
1950	Henry Banks
1951	Tony Bettenhausen
1952	Chuck Stevenson
1953	Sam Hawks
1954	Jimmy Bryan
1955	Bob Sweikert
1956	Jimmy Bryan
1957	Jimmy Bryan
1958	Tony Bettenhausen
1959	Rodger Ward
1960	A. J. Foyt
1961	A. J. Foyt
1962	Rodger Ward
1963	A. J. Foyt
1964	A. J. Foyt
1965	Mario Andretti
1966	Mario Andretti
1967	A. J. Foyt
1968	Bobby Unser
1969	Mario Andretti
1970	Al Unser
1971	Joe Leonard
1972	Joe Leonard
1973	Roger McCluskey
1974	Bobby Unser
1975	A. J. Foyt

UNITED STATES AUTO CLUB NATIONAL STOCK CAR CHAMPIONS (previously named the American Automobile Association)

1950	Jay Frank
1951	Rodger Ward
1952	Marshall Teague
1953	Frank Mundy
1954	Marshall Teague
1955	Frank Lundy
1956	Johnny Mantz
1957	Jerry Unser
1958	Fred Lorenzen
1959	Fred Lorenzen
1960	Norm Nelson
1961	Paul Goldsmith
1962	Paul Goldsmith
1963	Don White
1964	Parnelli Jones
1965	Norm Nelson
1966	Norm Nelson

1967	Don White
1968	A. J. Foyt
1969	Roger McCluskey
1970	Roger McCluskey
1971	Butch Hartman
1972	Butch Hartman
1973	Butch Hartman
1974	Butch Hartman
1975	Ramo Scott
1976	Ray Darnell

NATIONAL ASSOCIATION FOR STOCK CAR AUTO RACING (NASCAR) GRAND NATIONAL DIVISION

1949	Red Byron
1950	Bill Rexford
1951	Herb Thomas
1952	Tim Flock
1953	Herb Thomas
1954	Lee Petty
1955	Tim Flock
1956	Buck Baker
1957	Buck Baker
1958	Lee Petty
1959	Lee Petty
1960	Rex White
1961	Ned Jarrett
1962	Joe Weatherly
1963	Joe Weatherly
1964	Richard Petty
1965	Ned Jarrett
1966	David Pearson
1967	Richard Petty
1968	David Pearson
1969	David Pearson
1970	Bobby Isaac
1971	Richard Petty
1972	Richard Petty
1973	Benny Parsons
1974	Richard Petty
1975	Richard Petty

USAC CALIFORNIA 500

1971	Jeo Leonard
1972	Roger McCluskey
1973	Wally Dallenbach
1974	Bobby Unser
1975	A. J. Foyt
1976	Bobby Unser

DAYTONA 500 WINNERS

1961	Marvin Panch
1972	Fireball Roberts
1963	Tiny Lund

1964	Richard Petty
1965	Fred Lorenzen
1966	Richard Petty
1967	Mario Andretti
1968	Cale Yarborough
1969	Lee Roy Yarborough
1970	Pete Hamilton
1971	Richard Petty
1972	A. J. Foyt
1973	Richard Petty
1974	Richard Petty
1975	Benny Parsons
1976	David Pearson

UNITED STATES GRAND PRIX

1959	Bruce McLaren
1960	Stirling Moss
1961	Ines Ireland
1962	Jim Clark
1963	Graham Hill
1964	Graham Hill
1965	Graham Hill
1966	Jim Clark
1967	Jim Clark
1968	Jackie Stewart
1969	Jochen Rindt
1970	Emerson Fittipaldi
1971	Francis Cevert
1972	Jackie Stewart
1973	Ronnie Peterson
1974	Carlos Reutemann
1975	Niki Lauda

BASEBALL

WORLD SERIES

1903	Boston Red Sox
1904	series not played
1905	New York Giants
1906	Chicago White Sox
1907	Chicago Cubs
1908	Chicago Cubs
1909	Pittsburgh Pirates
1910	Philadelphia Athletics
1911	Philadelphia Athletics
1912	Boston Red Sox
1913	Philadelphia Athletics
1914	Boston Braves
1915	Boston Red Sox
1916	Boston Red Sox
1917	Chicago White Sox
1918	Boston Red Sox

1919	Cincinnati Reds		1974	Oakland A's
1920	Cleveland Indians		1975	Cincinnati Reds
1921	New York Giants		1976	Cincinnati Reds
1922	New York Giants			
1923	New York Yankees			

AMERICAN LEAGUE PENNANT WINNERS (in 1969 became the Eastern and Western Divisions)

1924	Washington Senators		1901	Chicago White Sox
1925	Pittsburgh Pirates		1902	Philadelphia Athletics
1926	St. Louis Cardinals		1903	Boston Red Sox
1927	New York Yankees		1904	Boston Red Sox
1928	New York Yankees		1905	Philadelphia Athletics
1929	Philadelphia Athletics		1906	Chicago White Sox
1930	Philadelphia Athletics		1907	Detroit Tigers
1931	St. Louis Cardinals		1908	Detroit Tigers
1932	New York Yankees		1909	Detroit Tigers
1933	New York Giants		1910	Philadelphia Athletics
1934	St. Louis Cardinals		1911	Philadelphia Athletics
1935	Detroit Tigers		1912	Boston Red Sox
1936	New York Yankees		1913	Philadelphia Athletics
1937	New York Yankees		1914	Philadelphia Athletics
1938	New York Yankees		1915	Boston Red Sox
1939	New York Yankees		1916	Boston Red Sox
1940	Cincinnati Reds		1917	Chicago White Sox
1941	New York Yankees		1918	Boston Red Sox
1942	St. Louis Cardinals		1919	Chicago White Sox
1943	New York Yankees		1920	Cleveland Indians
1944	St. Louis Cardinals		1921	New York Yankees
1945	Detroit Tigers		1922	New York Yankees
1946	St. Louis Cardinals		1923	New York Yankees
1947	New York Yankees		1924	Washington Senators
1948	Cleveland Indians		1925	Washington Senators
1949	New York Yankees		1926	New York Yankees
1950	New York Yankees		1927	New York Yankees
1951	New York Yankees		1928	New York Yankees
1952	New York Yankees		1929	Philadelphia Athletics
1953	New York Yankees		1930	Philadelphia Athletics
1954	New York Giants		1931	Philadelphia Athletics
1955	Brooklyn Dodgers		1932	New York Yankees
1956	New York Yankees		1933	Washington Senators
1957	Milwaukee Braves		1934	Detroit Tigers
1958	New York Yankees		1935	Detroit Tigers
1959	Los Angeles Dodgers		1936	New York Yankees
1960	Pittsburgh Pirates		1937	New York Yankees
1961	New York Yankees		1938	New York Yankees
1962	New York Yankees		1939	New York Yankees
1963	Los Angeles Dodgers		1940	Detroit Tigers
1964	St. Louis Cardinals		1941	New York Yankees
1965	Los Angeles Dodgers		1942	New York Yankees
1966	Baltimore Orioles		1943	New York Yankees
1967	St. Louis Cardinals		1944	St. Louis Cardinals
1968	Detroit Tigers		1945	Detroit Tigers
1969	New York Mets		1946	Boston Red Sox
1970	Baltimore Orioles		1947	New York Yankees
1971	Pittsburgh Pirates		1948	Cleveland Indians
1972	Oakland A's			
1973	Oakland A's			

1949	New York Yankees
1950	New York Yankees
1951	New York Yankees
1952	New York Yankees
1953	New York Yankees
1954	Cleveland Indians
1955	New York Yankees
1956	New York Yankees
1957	New York Yankees
1958	New York Yankees
1959	Chicago White Sox
1960	New York Yankees
1961	New York Yankees
1962	New York Yankees
1963	New York Yankees
1964	New York Yankees
1965	Minnesota Twins
1966	Baltimore Orioles
1967	Boston Red Sox
1968	Detroit Tigers
1969	Baltimore Orioles (Eastern Division)
1970	Baltimore Orioles (Eastern Division)
1971	Baltimore Orioles (Eastern Division)
1972	Oakland A's (Western Division)
1973	Oakland A's (Western Division)
1974	Oakland A's (Western Division)
1975	Boston Red Sox (Eastern Division)
1976	New York Yankees (Eastern Division)

NATIONAL LEAGUE PENNANT WINNERS (in 1969 Eastern and Western divisions played for pennant)

1900	Brooklyn Dodgers
1901	Pittsburgh Pirates
1902	Pittsburgh Pirates
1903	Pittsburgh Pirates
1904	New York Giants
1905	New York Giants
1906	Chicago Cubs
1907	Chicago Cubs
1908	Chicago Cubs
1909	Pittsburgh Pirates
1910	Chicago Cubs
1911	New York Giants
1912	New York Giants
1913	New York Giants
1914	Boston Braves
1915	Philadelphia Phillies
1916	Brooklyn Dodgers
1917	New York Giants
1918	Chicago Cubs
1919	Cincinnati Reds
1920	Brooklyn Dodgers
1921	New York Giants
1922	New York Giants
1923	New York Giants
1924	New York Giants
1925	Pittsburgh Pirates
1926	St. Louis Cardinals
1927	Pittsburgh Pirates
1928	St. Louis Cardinals
1929	Chicago Cubs
1930	St. Louis Cardinals
1931	St. Louis Cardinals
1932	Chicago Cubs
1933	New York Giants
1934	St. Louis Cardinals
1935	Chicago Cubs
1936	New York Giants
1937	New York Giants
1938	Chicago Cubs
1939	Cincinnati Reds
1940	Cincinnati Reds
1941	Brooklyn Dodgers
1942	St. Louis Cardinals
1943	St. Louis Cardinals
1944	St. Louis Cardinals
1945	Chicago Cubs
1946	St. Louis Cardinals
1947	Brooklyn Dodgers
1948	Boston Braves
1949	Brooklyn Dodgers
1950	Philadelphia Phillies
1951	New York Giants
1952	Brooklyn Dodgers
1953	Brooklyn Dodgers
1954	New York Giants
1955	Brooklyn Dodgers
1956	Brooklyn Dodgers
1957	Milwaukee Braves
1958	Milwaukee Braves
1959	Los Angeles Dodgers
1960	Pittsburgh Pirates
1961	Cincinnati Reds
1962	San Francisco Giants
1963	Los Angeles Dodgers
1964	St. Louis Cardinals
1965	Los Angeles Dodgers
1966	Los Angeles Dodgers
1967	St. Louis Cardinals
1968	St. Louis Cardinals

1969 New York Mets (Eastern
Division)
1970 Cincinnati Reds (Western
Division)
1971 Pittsburgh Pirates (Eastern
Division)
1972 Cincinnati Reds (Western
Division)
1973 New York Mets (Eastern
Division)
1974 Los Angeles Dodgers
(Western Division)
1975 Cincinnati Reds (Western
Division)
1976 Cincinnati Reds (Western
Division)

ROOKIE OF THE YEAR WINNERS
1947
Jackie Robinson, first base, Brooklyn
Dodgers
1948
Alvin Dark, shortstop, Boston Braves

AMERICAN LEAGUE
1949
Roy Sievers, outfield, St. Louis
Cardinals
1950
Walt Dropo, first base, Boston Red
Sox
1951
Gil McDougald, third base, New
York Yankees
1952
Harry Byrd, pitcher, Philadelphia
Athletics
1953
Harvey Kuenn, shortstop, Detroit
Tigers
1954
Bob Grim, pitcher, New York
Yankees
1955
Herb Score, pitcher, Cleveland
Indians
1956
Luis Aparicio, shortstop, Chicago
White Sox
1957
Tony Kubek, outfield, New York
Yankees
1958
Albie Pearson, outfield, Washington
Senators

1959
Bob Allison, outfield, Washington
Senators
1960
Ron Hansen, shortstop, Baltimore
Orioles
1961
Don Schwall, pitcher, Boston Red
Sox
1962
Tom Tresh, shortstop, New York
Yankees
1963
Gary Peters, pitcher, Chicago White
Sox
1964
Tony Oliva, outfield, Minnesota
Twins
1965
Curt Blefary, outfield, Baltimore
Orioles
1966
Tommie Agee, outfield, Chicago
White Sox
1967
Rod Carew, second base, Minnesota
Twins
1968
Stan Bahnsen, pitcher, New York
Yankees
1969
Lou Piniella, outfield, Kansas City
Royals
1970
Thurman Munson, catcher, New
York Yankees
1971
Chris Chambliss, first base,
Cleveland Indians
1972
Carlton Fisk, catcher, Boston Red Sox
1973
Al Bumbry, outfield, Baltimore
Orioles
1974
Mike Hargrove, first base, Texas
Rangers
1975
Fred Lynn, outfield, Boston Red Sox
1976

NATIONAL LEAGUE
1949
Don Newcombe, pitcher, Brooklyn
Dodgers

1950
   Sam Jethroe, outfield, Boston Braves
1951
   Willie Mays, outfield, New York
   Giants
1952
   Joe Black, pitcher, Brooklyn Dodgers
1953
   Jim Gilliam, second base, Brooklyn
   Dodgers
1954
   Wally Moon, outfield, St. Louis
   Cardinals
1955
   Bill Virdon, outfield, St. Louis
   Cardinals
1956
   Frank Robinson, outfield, Cincinnati
   Reds
1957
   Jack Sanford, pitcher, Philadelphia
   Phillies
1958
   Orlanda Cepeda, first base, San
   Francisco Giants
1959
   Willie McCovey, first base, San
   Francisco Giants
1960
   Frank Howard, outfield, Los Angeles
   Dodgers
1961
   Billy Williams, outfield, Chicago
   Cubs
1962
   Ken Hubbs, second base, Chicago
   Cubs
1963
   Pete Rose, second base, Cincinnati
   Reds
1964
   Richie Allen, third base,
   Philadelphia Phillies
1965
   Jim Lefebvre, second base, Los
   Angeles Dodgers
1966
   Tommy Helms, third base,
   Cincinnati Reds
1967
   Tom Seaver, pitcher, New York Mets
1968
   Johnny Bench, catcher, Cincinnati
   Reds

1969
   Ted Sizemore, second base, Los
   Angeles Dodgers
1970
   Carl Morton, pitcher, Montreal
   Expos
1971
   Earl Williams, catcher, Atlanta
   Braves
1972
   Jon Matlack, pitcher, New York Mets
1973
   Gary Matthews, outfield, San
   Francisco Giants
1974
   Bake McBride, outfield, St. Louis
   Cardinals
1975
   John Montefusco, pitcher, San
   Francisco Giants
1976

MOST VALUABLE PLAYER—
AMERICAN LEAGUE
1931
   Lefty Grove, pitcher, Philadelphia
   Athletics
1932
   Jimmy Foxx, first base, Philadelphia
   Athletics
1933
   Jimmy Foxx, first base, Philadelphia
   Athletics
1934
   Mickey Cochrane, catcher, Detroit
   Tigers
1935
   Henry Greenberg, first base, Detroit
   Tigers
1936
   Lou Gehrig, first base, New York
   Yankees
1937
   Charley Gehringer, first base, Detroit
   Tigers
1938
   Jimmy Foxx, first base, Boston Red
   Sox
1939
   Joe DiMaggio, outfield, New York
   Yankees
1940
   Hank Greenberg, outfield, Detroit
   Tigers

The American League's most valuable player in 1956, 1957, and 1962, Yankee Mickey Mantle. (Memory Shop)

1941
Joe DiMaggio, outfield, New York Yankees
1942
Joe Gordon, second base, New York Yankees
1943
Spurgeon Chandler, pitcher, New York Yankees
1944
Hal Newhouser, pitcher, Detroit Tigers
1945
Hal Newhouser, pitcher, Detroit Tigers
1946
Ted Williams, outfield, Boston Red Sox
1947
Joe DiMaggio, outfield, New York Yankees
1948
Lou Boudreau, shortstop, Cleveland Indians
1949
Ted Williams, outfield, Boston Red Sox

1950
Phil Rizzuto, shortstop, New York Yankees
1951
Yogi Berra, catcher, New York Yankees
1952
Bobby Shantz, pitcher, Philadelphia Athletics
1953
Al Rosen, third base, Cleveland Indians
1954
Yogi Berra, catcher, New York Yankees
1955
Yogi Berra, catcher, New York Yankees
1956
Mickey Mantle, outfield, New York Yankees
1957
Mickey Mantle, outfield, New York Yankees
1958
Jackie Jensen, outfield, Boston Red Sox

1959
Nellie Fox, second base, Chicago White Sox
1960
Roger Maris, outfield, New York Yankees
1961
Roger Maris, outfield, New York Yankees
1962
Mickey Mantle, outfield, New York Yankees
1963
Elston Howard, catcher, New York Yankees
1964
Brooks Robinson, third base, Baltimore Orioles
1965
Zoilo Versalles, shortstop, Minnesota Twins
1966
Frank Robinson, outfield, Baltimore Orioles
1967
Carl Yastrzemski, outfield, Boston Red Sox
1968
Denny McLain, pitcher, Detroit Tigers
1969
Harmon Killebrew, third base, Minnesota Twins
1970
John (Boog) Powell, first base, Baltimore Orioles
1971
Vida Blue, pitcher, Oakland A's
1972
Richie Allen, Chicago White Sox
1973
Reggie Jackson, outfield, Oakland A's
1974
Jeff Burroughs, shortstop, Texas Rangers
1975
Fred Lynn, outfield, Boston Red Sox
1976
Thurman Munson, catcher, New York Yankees

MOST VALUABLE PLAYER— NATIONAL LEAGUE
1931
Frank Frisch, second base, St. Louis Cardinals

1932
Charles Klein, outfield, Philadelphia Phillies
1933
Carl Hubbell, pitcher, New York Giants
1934
Dizzy Dean, pitcher, St. Louis Cardinals
1935
Gabby Hartnett, catcher, Chicago Cubs
1936
Carl Hubbell, pitcher, New York Giants
1937
Joe Medwick, outfield, St. Louis Cardinals
1938
Ernie Lombardi, catcher, Cincinnati Reds
1939
Bucky Walters, pitcher, Cincinnati Reds
1940
Frank McCormick, first base, Cincinnati Reds
1941
Dolph Camilli, first base, Brooklyn Dodgers
1942
Mort Cooper, pitcher, St. Louis Cardinals
1943
Stan Musial, outfield, St. Louis Cardinals
1944
Martin Marion, shortstop, St. Louis Cardinals
1945
Phil Cavarretta, first base, Chicago Cubs
1946
Stan Musial, first base, St. Louis Cardinals
1947
Bob Elliott, third base, Boston Braves
1948
Stan Musial, outfield, St. Louis Cardinals
1949
Jackie Robinson, second base, Brooklyn Dodgers

1950
Jim Konstanty, pitcher, Philadelphia Phillies
1951
Roy Campanella, catcher, Brooklyn Dodgers
1952
Hank Sauer, outfield, Chicago Cubs
1953
Roy Campanella, catcher, Brooklyn Dodgers
1954
Willie Mays, outfield, New York Giants
1955
Roy Campanella, catcher, Brooklyn Dodgers
1956
Don Newcombe, pitcher, Brooklyn Dodgers
1957
Henry Aaron, outfield, Milwaukee Braves
1958
Ernie Banks, shortstop, Chicago Cubs
1959
Ernie Banks, shortstop, Chicago Cubs
1960
Dick Groat, shortstop, Pittsburgh Pirates
1961
Frank Robinson, outfield, Cincinnati Reds
1962
Maury Wills, shortstop, Los Angeles Dodgers
1963
Sandy Koufax, pitcher, Los Angeles Dodgers
1964
Ken Boyer, third base, St. Louis Cardinals
1965
Willie Mays, outfield, San Francisco Giants
1966
Roberto Clemente, outfield, Pittsburgh Pirates
1967
Orlando Cepeda, first base, St. Louis Cardinals
1968
Bob Gibson, pitcher, St. Louis Cardinals

1969
Willie McCovey, first base, San Francisco Giants
1970
Johnny Bench, catcher, Cincinnati Reds
1971
Joe Torre, third base, St. Louis Cardinals
1972
Johnny Bench, catcher, Cincinnati Reds
1973
Pete Rose, outfield, Cincinnati Reds
1974
Steve Garvey, first base, Los Angeles Dodgers
1975
Joe Morgan, second base, Cincinnati Reds
1976
Joe Morgan, second base, Cincinnati Reds

CY YOUNG AWARD WINNERS FOR PITCHING

1956
Don Newcombe, Brooklyn Dodgers
1957
Warren Spahn, Milwaukee Braves
1958
Bob Turley, New York Yankees
1959
Early Wynn, Chicago White Sox
1960
Vernon Law, Pittsburgh Pirates
1961
Whitey Ford, New York Yankees
1962
Don Drysdale, Los Angeles Dodgers
1963
Sandy Koufax, Los Angeles Dodgers
1964
Dean Chance, Los Angeles Angels
1965
Sandy Koufax, Los Angeles Dodgers
1966
Sandy Koufax, Los Angeles Dodgers
1967
Jim Lonborg, Boston Red Sox (American League)
Mike McCormick, San Francisco Giants (National League)

1968
Dennis McLain, Detroit Tigers
(American League)
Bob Gibson, St. Louis Cardinals
(National League)
1969
Dennis McLain, Detroit Tigers
(American League)
Mike Cuellar, Baltimore Orioles
(American League)
Tom Seaver, New York Mets
(National League)
1970
Jim Perry, Minnesota Twins
(American League)
Bob Gibson, St. Louis Cardinals
(National League)
1971
Vida Blue, Oakland A's (American
League)
Ferguson Jenkins, Chicago Cubs
(National League)
1972
Gaylord Perry, Cleveland Indians
(American League)
Steve Carlton, Philadelphia Phillies
(National League)
1973
Jim Palmer, Baltimore Orioles
(American League)
Tom Seaver, New York Mets
(National League)
1974
Jim (Catfish) Hunter, Oakland A's
(American League)
Mike Marshall, Los Angeles Dodgers
(National League)
1975
Jim Palmer, Baltimore Orioles
(American League)
Tom Seaver, New York Mets
(National League)
1976
Jim Palmer, Baltimore Orioles
(American League)
Randy Jones, San Diego Padres
(National League)

FIREMAN (RELIEF PITCHER OF THE YEAR) THE SPORTING NEWS MAGAZINE

AMERICAN LEAGUE
1960
Mike Fornieles, Boston

1961
Luis Arroyo, New York
1962
Dick Radatz, Boston
1963
Stu Miller, Baltimore
1964
Dick Radatz, Boston
1965
Eddie Fisher, Chicago
1966
Jack Aker, Kansas City
1967
Minnie Rojas, California
1968
Wilbur Wood, Chicago
1969
Ron Perranoski, Minnesota
1970
Ron Perranoski, Minnesota
1971
Ken Sanders, Milwaukee
1972
Sparky Lyle, New York
1973
John Hiller, Detroit
1974
Terry Forster, Chicago
1975
Rich Gossage, Chicago
1976
Bill Campbell, Minnesota

NATIONAL LEAGUE
1960
Lindy McDaniel, St. Louis
1961
Stu Miller, San Francisco
1962
Roy Face, Pittsburgh
1963
Lindy McDaniel, Chicago
1964
Al McBean, Pittsburgh
1965
Ted Abernathy, Chicago
1966
Phil Regan, Los Angeles
1967
Ted Abernathy, Cincinnati
1968
Phil Regan, Los Angeles, Chicago
1969
Wayne Granger, Cincinnati

1970
Wayne Granger, Cincinnati
1971
Dave Giusti, Pittsburgh
1972
Clay Carroll, Cincinnati
1973
Mike Marshall, Montreal
1974
Mike Marshall, Los Angeles
1975
Al Hrabosky, St. Louis
1976
Rawly Eastwick, Cincinnati

**MAJOR LEAGUE PLAYERS OF
THE YEAR—THE SPORTING
NEWS MAGAZINE**
1936
Carl Hubbell, New York (National
League)
1937
Johnny Allen, Cleveland
(American League)
1938
Johnny Vander Meer, Cincinnati
(National League)
1939
Joe DiMaggio, New York
(American League)
1940
Bob Feller, Cleveland (American
League)
1941
Ted Williams, Boston (American
League)
1942
Ted Williams, Boston (American
League)
1943
Spud Chandler, New York
(American League)
1944
Marty Marion, St. Louis (National
League)
1945
Hal Newhouser, Detroit (American
League)
1946
Stan Musial, St. Louis (National
League)
1947
Ted Williams, Boston (American
League)

1948
Lou Boudreau, Cleveland
(American League)
1949
Ted Williams, Boston (American
League)
1950
Phil Rizzuto, New York (American
League)
1951
Stan Musial, St. Louis (National
League)
1952
Robin Roberts, Philadelphia
(National League)
1953
Al Rosen, Cleveland (American
League)
1954
Willie Mays, New York (National
League)
1955
Duke Snider, Brooklyn (National
League)
1956
Mickey Mantle, New York
(American League)
1957
Ted Williams, Boston (American
League)
1958
Bob Turley, New York (American
League)
1959
Early Wynn, Chicago (American
League)
1960
Bill Mazeroski, Pittsburgh
(National League)
1961
Roger Maris, New York (American
League)
1962
Maury Wills, Los Angeles
(National League)
Don Drysdale, Los Angeles
(National League)
1963
Sandy Koufax, Los Angeles
(National League)
1964
Ken Boyer, St. Louis (National
League)

1965
    Sandy Koufax, Los Angeles
    (National League)
1966
    Frank Robinson, Baltimore
    (American League)
1967
    Carl Yastrzemski, Boston
    (American League)
1968
    Denny McLain, Detroit (American
    League)
1969
    Willie McCovey, San Francisco
    (National League)
1970
    Johnny Bench, Cincinnati
    (National League)
1971
    Joe Torre, St. Louis (National
    League)
1972
    Billy Williams, Chicago (National
    League)
1973
    Reggie Jackson, Oakland
    (American League)
1974
    Lou Brock, St. Louis (National
    League)
1975
    Joe Morgan, Cincinnati (National
    League)

BASKETBALL
(Professional)

**NATIONAL BASKETBALL
ASSOCIATION**

Division Winners

Eastern	*Western*
1946–1947	
Washington	Chicago Stags
Capitols	
1947–1948	
Philadelphia	St. Louis
Warriors	Bombers
1948–1949	
Washington	Rochester
Capitols	Royals

1949–1950
| Syracuse Nationals | Indianapolis |
| | Olympians |

Central Division Co-Champions—
Minneapolis-Rochester

1950–1951	
Philadelphia	Minneapolis
Warriors	Lakers
1951–1952	
Syracuse Nationals	Rochester
	Royals
1952–1953	
New York Knicks	Minneapolis
	Lakers
1953–1954	
New York Knicks	Minneapolis
	Lakers
1954–1955	
Syracuse Nationals	Ft. Wayne
	Pistons
1955–1956	
Philadelphia	Ft. Wayne
Warriors	Pistons
1956–1957	
Boston Celtics	St. Louis
	Hawks
1957–1958	
Boston Celtics	St. Louis
	Hawks
1958–1959	
Boston Celtics	St. Louis
	Hawks
1959–1960	
Boston Celtics	St. Louis
	Hawks
1960–1961	
Boston Celtics	St. Louis
	Hawks
1961–62	
Boston Celtics	Los Angeles
	Lakers
1962–1963	
Boston Celtics	Los Angeles
	Lakers
1963–1964	
Boston Celtics	San Francisco
	Warriors
1964–1965	
Boston Celtics	Los Angeles
	Lakers
1965–1966	
Philadelphia 76ers	Los Angeles
	Lakers
1966–1967	
Philadelphia 76ers	San Francisco
	Warriors

1967–1968
  Philadelphia 76ers St. Louis Hawks
1968–1969
  Baltimore Bullets Los Angeles Lakers
1969–1970
  New York Knicks Atlanta Hawks
1970–1971
  Baltimore Bullets Milwaukee Bucks

Starting with the 1970–1971 season the NBA subdivided its two conferences into the Atlantic and Central Divisions in the East and the Midwest and Pacific Divisions in the West. The teams listed below are the winners of the Atlantic and Central Divisions contest versus the Midwest and Pacific winner.

1971–1972
New York Knicks, Los Angeles Lakers
1972–1973
New York Knicks, Los Angeles Lakers
1973–1974
Boston Celtics, Milwaukee Bucks
1974–1975
Washington Bullets, Golden State Warriors
1975–1976
Boston Celtics, Phoenix Suns
1976–1977
Philadelphia 76ers, Portland Trailblazers

Playoff Winner
1946–1947	Philadelphia Warriors
1947–1948	Baltimore Bullets
1948–1949	Minneapolis Lakers
1949–1950	Minneapolis Lakers
1950–1951	Rochester Royals
1951–1952	Minneapolis Lakers
1952–1953	Minneapolis Lakers
1953–1954	Minneapolis Lakers
1954–1955	Syracuse Nationals
1955–1956	Philadelphia Warriors
1956–1957	Boston Celtics
1957–1958	St. Louis Hawks
1958–1959	Boston Celtics
1959–1960	Boston Celtics
1960–1961	Boston Celtics
1961–1962	Boston Celtics
1962–1963	Boston Celtics
1963–1964	Boston Celtics
1964–1965	Boston Celtics
1965–1966	Boston Celtics
1966–1967	Philadelphia 76ers
1967–1968	Boston Celtics
1968–1969	Boston Celtics
1969–1970	New York Knicks
1970–1971	Milwaukee Bucks
1971–1972	Los Angeles Lakers
1972–1973	New York Knicks
1973–1974	Boston Celtics
1974–1975	Golden State Warriors
1975–1976	Boston Celtics
1976–1977	Portland Trailblazers

Rookie of the Year
1952–1953
  Don Meineke, Ft. Wayne Pistons
1953–1954
  Ray Felix, Baltimore Bullets
1954–1955
  Bob Pettit, Milwaukee Bucks
1955–1956
  Maurice Stokes, Rochester Royals
1956–1957
  Tom Heinsohn, Boston Celtics
1957–1958
  Woody Sauldsberry, Philadelphia 76ers
1958–1959
  Elgin Baylor, Minneapolis Lakers
1959–1960
  Wilt Chamberlain, Philadelphia 76ers
1960–1961
  Oscar Robertson, Cincinnati Royals
1961–1962
  Walt Bellamy, Chicago Bulls
1962–1963
  Terry Dischinger, Chicago Bulls
1963–1964
  Jerry Lucas, Cincinnati Royals
1964–1965
  Willis Reed, New York Knicks
1965–1966
  Rick Barry, San Francisco Warriors
1966–1967
  Dave Bing, Detroit Pistons
1967–1968
  Earl Monroe, Baltimore Bullets
1968–1969
  Wes Unseld, Baltimore Bullets
1969–1970
  Lew Alcindor, Milwaukee Bucks
1970–1971
  Dave Cowens, Boston Celtics
  Geoff Petrie, Portland Trailblazers

1971–1972
 Sidney Wicks, Portland Trailblazers
1972–1973
 Bob McAdoo, Buffalo Braves
1973–1974
 Ernie DiGregorio, Buffalo Braves
1974–1975
 Keith Wilkes, Golden State Warriors
1975–1976
 Alvan Adams, Phoenix Suns
1976–1977
 Adrian Dantley, Buffalo Braves

Most Valuable Player (Podoloff Cup)
1955–1956
 Bob Pettit, St. Louis Hawks
1956–1957
 Bob Cousy, Boston Celtics
1957–1958
 Bill Russell, Boston Celtics
1958–1959
 Bob Pettit, St. Louis Hawks
1959–1960
 Wilt Chamberlain, Philadelphia
 76ers
1960–1961
 Bill Russell, Boston Celtics
1961–1962
 Bill Russell, Boston Celtics
1962–1963
 Bill Russell, Boston Celtics
1963–1964
 Oscar Robertson, Cincinnati Royals
1964–1965
 Bill Russell, Boston Celtics
1965–1966
 Wilt Chamberlain, Philadelphia
 76ers
1966–1967
 Wilt Chamberlain, Philadelphia
 76ers
1967–1968
 Wilt Chamberlain, Philadelphia
 76ers
1968–1969
 Wes Unseld, Baltimore Bullets
1969–1970
 Willis Reed, New York Knicks
1970–1971
 Lew Alcindor, Milwaukee Bucks
1971–1972
 Kareem Abdul-Jabbar, Milwaukee
 Bucks
1972–1973
 Dave Cowens, Boston Celtics

1973–1974
 Kareem Abdul-Jabbar, Milwaukee
 Bucks
1974–1975
 Bob McAdoo, Buffalo Braves
1975–1976
 Kareem Abdul-Jabbar, Los Angeles
 Lakers
1976–1977
 Kareem Abdul-Jabbar, Los Angeles
 Lakers

Coach of the Year
1962–1963
 Harry Gallatin, St. Louis Hawks
1963–1964
 Alex Hannum, San Francisco
 Warriors
1964–1965
 Red Auerbach, Boston Celtics
1965–1966
 Dolph Schayes, Philadelphia 76ers
1966–1967
 Johnny Kerr, Chicago Bulls
1967–1968
 Richie Guerin, St. Louis Hawks
1968–1969
 Gene Shue, Baltimore Bullets
1969–1970
 Red Holzman, New York Knicks
1970–1971
 Dick Motta, Chicago Bulls
1971–1972
 Bill Sharman, Los Angeles Lakers
1972–1973
 Tom Heinsohn, Boston Celtics
1973–1974
 Ray Scott, Detroit Pistons
1974–1975
 Phil Johnson, Kansas City-Omaha
 Kings
1975–1976
 Bill Fitch, Cleveland Cavaliers
1976–1977
 Tom Nissalke, Houston Rockets

**AMERICAN BASKETBALL
 ASSOCIATION DIVISION
 CHAMPIONS**

Eastern	*Western*
1967–1968	
Pittsburgh Pipers	New Orleans Buccaneers
1968–1969	
Indiana Pacers	Oakland Oaks

1969–1970
  Indiana Pacers   Denver Rockets
1970–1971
  Virginia Squires   Indiana Pacers
1971–1972
  New York Nets   Indiana Pacers
1972–1973
  Kentucky Colonels   Indiana Pacers
1973–1974
  New York Nets   Utah Stars
1974–1975
  Kentucky Colonels   Indiana Pacers
1975–1976
  New York Nets   Denver
                        Nuggets

Playoff Winners
1967–1968   Pittsburgh Pipers
1968–1969   Oakland Oaks
1969–1970   Indiana Pacers
1970–1971   Utah Stars
1971–1972   Indiana Pacers
1972–1973   Indiana Pacers
1973–1974   New York Nets
1974–1975   Kentucky Colonels
1975–1976   Denver Nuggets

Rookie of the Year
1968
  Mel Daniels, Indiana Pacers
1969
  Warren Armstrong, Oakland Oaks
1970
  Spencer Haywood, Denver Rockets

1971
  Charlie Scott, Virginia Squires
  Dan Issel, Kentucky Colonels
1972
  Artis Gilmore, Kentucky Colonels
1973
  Brian Taylor, New York Nets
1974
  Swen Nater, San Antonio Spurs
1975
  Marvin Barnes, St. Louis
1976
  David Thompson, Denver Nuggets

Most Valuable Player
1968
  Connie Hawkins, Pittsburgh Pipers
1969
  Mel Daniels, Indiana Pacers
1970
  Spencer Haywood, Denver Rockets
1971
  Mel Daniels, Indiana Pacers
1972
  Artis Gilmore, Kentucky Colonels
1973
  Billy Cunningham, Carolina
  Cougars
1974
  Julius Erving, New York Nets
1975
  Julius Erving, New York Nets
  George McGinnis, Indiana Pacers
1976
  Julius Erving, New York Nets

BASKETBALL (COLLEGE)

National Collegiate Athletic Conference

	Regional Winners East Winner	West Winner	Conference Winner
1939	Ohio State	Oregon	Oregon
1940	Indiana	Kansas	Indiana
1941	Wisconsin	Washington	Wisconsin
1942	Dartmouth	Stanford	Stanford
1943	Georgetown	Wyoming	Wyoming
1944	Dartmouth	Utah	Utah
1945	New York University	Oklahoma State	Oklahoma State
1946	North Carolina	Oklahoma State	Oklahoma State
1947	Holy Cross	Oklahoma State	Holy Cross
1948	Kentucky	Baylor	Kentucky
1949	Kentucky	Oklahoma State	Kentucky
1950	CCNY	Bradley	CCNY
1951	Kentucky	Kansas State	Kentucky

	Regional Winners	East Winner	West Winner	Conference Winner
1952	St. John's Illinois Kansas Santa Clara	St. John's	Kansas	Kansas
1953	Indiana Louisiana State Kansas Washington	Indiana	Kansas	Indiana
1954	LaSalle Penn State Bradley Southern California	LaSalle	Bradley	LaSalle
1955	LaSalle Iowa Colorado San Francisco	LaSalle	San Francisco	San Francisco
1956	Temple University Iowa San Francisco Southern Methodist	Iowa	San Francisco	San Francisco
1957	North Carolina Michigan State Kansas San Francisco	North Carolina	Kansas	North Carolina
1958	Temple University Kentucky Kansas State Seattle	Kentucky	Seattle	Kentucky
1959	West Virginia Louisville Cincinnati California	West Virginia	California	California
1960	New York University Ohio State Cincinnati California	Ohio State	California	Ohio State
1961	St. Joseph's (void) Ohio State Cincinnati Utah	Ohio State	Cincinnati	Cincinnati
1962	Wake Forest Ohio State Cincinnati UCLA	Ohio State	Cincinnati	Cincinnati
1963	Duke University Loyola (Ill.) Cincinnati Oregon State	Loyola (Ill.)	Cincinnati	Loyola (Ill.)
1964	Duke University Michigan Kansas State UCLA	Duke University	UCLA	UCLA
1965	Princeton University	Michigan State	UCLA	UCLA

	Regional Winners	East Winner	West Winner	Conference Winner
	Michigan State			
	Wichita State			
	UCLA			
1966	Duke University	Kentucky	Texas-El Paso	Texas-El Paso
	Kentucky			
	Texas-El Paso			
	Utah			
1967	North Carolina	Dayton	UCLA	UCLA
	Dayton			
	Houston			
	UCLA			
1968	North Carolina	North Carolina	UCLA	UCLA
	Ohio State			
	Houston			
	UCLA			
1969	North Carolina	Purdue University	UCLA	UCLA
	Purdue University			
	Drake			
	UCLA			
1970	St. B'venture	Jacksonville	UCLA	UCLA
	Jacksonville			
	UCLA			
	New Mexico State			
1971	Villanova (void)	Villanova (void)	UCLA	UCLA
	Western Kentucky (void)			
	UCLA			
	Kansas State			
1972	North Carolina	Florida State	UCLA	UCLA
	Florida State			
	UCLA			
	Louisville			

	Regional Winners	Semifinal Winners		Conference Winner
1973	UCLA	Memphis State		UCLA
	Providence	UCLA		
	Memphis State			
	Indiana			
1974	North Carolina State	North Carolina State		North Carolina State
	UCLA	Marquette		
	Marquette			
	Kansas State			
1975	Louisville	Kentucky		UCLA
	Kentucky	UCLA		
	Syracuse			
	UCLA			
1976	Michigan State	Michigan State		Indiana
	Indiana	Indiana		
	UCLA			
	Rutgers University			
1977	Marquette	Marquette		Marquette
	North Carolina	North Carolina		
	Las Vegas-Nevada			
	UNC-Charlotte			

NCAA College Division Tournament Winners

1957	Wheaton
1958	South Dakota
1959	Evansville
1960	Evansville
1961	Wittenberg
1962	Mount St. Mary's
1963	South Dakota State
1964	Evansville
1965	Evansville
1966	Kentucky Wesleyan
1967	Winston-Salem
1968	Kentucky Wesleyan
1969	Kentucky Wesleyan
1970	Philadelphia Textile
1971	Evansville
1972	Roanoke
1973	Kentucky Wesleyan
1974	Morgan State
1975	Old Dominion
1976	Puget Sound

National Invitational Tournament Winners

1938	Temple
1939	Long Island
1940	Colorado
1941	Long Island
1942	West Virginia
1943	St. John's
1944	St. John's
1945	De Paul
1946	Kentucky
1947	Utah
1948	St. Louis
1949	San Francisco
1950	CCNY
1951	Brigham Young
1952	LaSalle
1953	Seton Hall
1954	Holy Cross
1955	Duquesne
1956	Louisville
1957	Bradley
1958	Xavier (Ohio)
1959	St. John's
1960	Bradley
1961	Providence
1962	Dayton
1963	Providence
1964	Bradley
1965	St. John's
1966	Brigham Young
1967	Southern Illinois
1968	Dayton
1969	Temple
1970	Marquette
1971	North Carolina
1972	Maryland
1973	Virginia Tech
1974	Purdue
1975	Princeton
1976	Kentucky
1977	St. Bonaventure

A.A.U. BASKETBALL

Women's A.A.U. Tournament Champions

1925–1926	Pasadena A. and C. C.
1928–1929	Schepps Aces, Dallas
1929–1930	Sunoco Oilers, Dallas
1930–1931	Golden Cyclones, Dallas
1931–1932	Durant Cardinals, Oklahoma
1932–1933	Durant Cardinals, Oklahoma
1933–1934	Tulsa Business College
1934–1935	Tulsa Business College
1935–1936	Tulsa Business College
1936–1937	Little Rock Flyers
1937–1938	Galveston, Texas, Anicos
1938–1939	Galveston, Texas, Anicos
1939–1940	Lewis-Norwood Flyers, Arkansas
1940–1941	Lewis-Norwood Flyers, Arkansas
1941–1942	A.I.C. Davenport, Iowa
1942–1943	A.I.C. Davenport, Iowa
1943–1944	Vultee Acft, Nashville
1944–1945	Vultee Acft, Nashville
1945–1946	Nashville Goldblumes
1946–1947	Atlanta Georgia Sports Arena
1947–1948	Nashville Goldblumes
1948–1949	Nashville Goldblumes
1949–1950	Nashville Business College
1950–1951	Hanes Hosiery Mills, North Carolina
1951–1952	Hanes Hosiery Mills, North Carolina
1952–1953	Hanes Hosiery Mills, North Carolina
1953–1954	Wayland College, Plainview, Texas

1954–1955	Wayland College, Plainview, Texas
1955–1956	Wayland College, Plainview, Texas
1956–1957	Wayland College, Plainview, Texas
1957–1958	Nashville Business College
1958–1959	Wayland College, Plainview, Texas
1959–1960	Nashville Business College
1960–1961	Wayland College, Plainview, Texas
1961–1962	Nashville Business College
1962–1963	Nashville Business College
1963–1964	Nashville Business College
1964–1965	Nashville Business College
1965–1966	Nashville Business College
1966–1967	Nashville Business College
1967–1968	Nashville Business College
1968–1969	Nashville Business College
1969–1970	Hutcherson Flying Queens, Texas
1970–1971	Hutcherson Flying Queens, Texas
1971–1972	J. F. Kennedy College, Nebraska
1972–1973	J. F. Kennedy College, Nebraska
1973–1974	Wayland College, Plainview, Texas
1974–1975	Wayland College, Plainview, Texas
1975–1976	National General, Fullerton, California

Men's A.A.U. Tournament Champions

1896–1897	New York 23rd Street YMCA (Round Robin)
1898–1899	New York Knickerbocker YMCA (Round Robin)
1899–1900	New York Knickerbocker YMCA (Round Robin)
1900–1901	Chic. Ravenswood YMCA, Fond du Lac, Wis.
1903–1904	Buffalo Germans (Round Robin)
1909–1910	Company F. Portage, Wis. Premiere Lodgw
1912–1913	Chicago Cornell-Armour (Round Robin)
1913–1914	Chicago Cornell-Armour
1914–1915	San Francisco Olympic C.
1915–1916	Utah University
1916–1917	Illinois Athletic Club
1918–1919	Los Angeles A.C.
1919–1920	New York University
1920–1921	Kansas City A. C.
1921–1922	Kansas City Lowe-Campbell
1922–1923	Kansas City A. C.
1923–1924	Butler University
1924–1925	Washburn College
1925–1926	Kansas City Hillyards
1926–1927	Kansas City Hillyards
1927–1928	Kansas City Cooks
1928–1929	Kansas City Cooks
1929–1930	Wichita Henrys
1930–1931	Wichita Henrys
1931–1932	Wichita Henrys
1932–1933	Tulsa Diamond Oilers
1933–1934	Tulsa Diamond Oilers
1934–1935	Kansas City Stage Lines
1936–1937	Denver Safeways
1937–1938	Kansas City Healeys
1938–1939	Denver Nuggets
1939–1940	Phillips 66ers
1940–1941	20th Century-Fox
1941–1942	Denver Legion
1942–1943	Phillips 66ers
1943–1944	Phillips 66ers
1944–1945	Phillips 66ers
1945–1946	Phillips 66ers
1946–1947	Phillips 66ers
1947–1948	Phillips 66ers
1948–1949	Oakland Bittners
1949–1950	Phillips 66ers
1950–1951	San Francisco Stewarts
1951–1952	Peoria Cats
1952–1953	Peoria Caterpillar Diesels
1953–1954	Peoria Caterpillar Diesels
1954–1955	Phillips 66ers
1955–1956	Seattle Buchan Bakers

1956–1957	Air Force All-Stars	George Grebenstein, Dartmouth
1957–1958	Peoria Caterpillar Diesels	Harold Amberg, Harvard John Schommer, Chicago
1958–1959	Wichita Vickers	Marcus Hurley, Columbia
1959–1960	Peoria Caterpillar Diesels	Eugene Cowell, Williams Ralph Griffiths, Harvard
1960–1961	Cleveland Pipers	Garfield Brown, Minnesota
1961–1962	Phillips 66ers	
1962–1963	Phillips 66ers	
1963–1964	Akrn. Goodyear Wingfoots	
1964–1965	Armed Forces All-Stars	
1965–1966	Ford Mustangs	
1966–1967	Akrn. Goodyear Wingfoots	
1967–1968	Armed Forces All-Stars	
1968–1969	Armed Forces All-Stars	
1969–1970	Armed Forces All-Stars	
1970–1971	Armed Forces All-Stars	
1971–1972	Armed Forces All-Stars	
1972–1973	Lexington Marathon Oil	
1973–1974	Jacksonville	
1974–1975	Capitol Inuslation of L.A.	
1975–1976	Athletes in Action	

COLLEGE BASKETBALL ALL-AMERICA TEAMS and PLAYER OF THE YEAR—Citizens Savings Athletic Foundation.

To select All-America teams back to 1905, this organization began intensive research in 1941. It contacted coaches, athletic directors, sports-information directors, and members of the press for their recollections and advise.

Established 1941.

ALL-AMERICA TEAMS
1905
Chris Steinmetz, Wisconsin
Harry Fisher, Columbia
Gilmore Kinney, Yale
James Ozanne, Chicago
Willard Hyatt, Yale
George Tuck, Minnesota
Marcus Hurley, Columbia
Walter Runge, Colgate
Oliver de G. Vanderbilt, Princeton
C. D. McLees, Wisconsin
1906
George Flint, Pennsylvania
Charles Keinath, Pennsylvania
James McKeag, Chicago

1907
George Flint, Pennsylvania
Charles Keinath, Pennsylvania
Gilmore Kinney, Yale
L. Parson Warren, Williams
John Schommer, Chicago
John Ryan, Columbia
Arthur Frank, Wisconsin
Marcus Hurley, Columbia
Oswald Tower, Williams
Albert Houghton, Chicago
1908
Charles Keinath, Pennsylvania
Helmer Swenholt, Wisconsin
John Pryor, Brown
Ira Streusand, C.C.N.Y.
John Schommer, Chicago
John Ryan, Columbia
Harlan O. Page, Chicago
Hugh Harper, Wisconsin
Julian Hayward, Wesleyan
Haskell Noyes, Yale
1909
Theodore Kiendl, Columbia
Charles Keinath, Pennsylvania
Helmer Swenholt, Wisconsin
Raymond Scanlan, Notre Dame
John Schommer, Chicago
John Ryan, Columbia
Harlan O. Page, Chicago
Biaggio Cerussi, Columbia
Julian Hayward, Wesleyan
Tommy Johnson, Kansas
1910
Theodore Kiendl, Columbia
Ernest Lambert, Oklahoma
Samuel Harman, Rochester
W. Vaughn Lewis, Williams
William Broadhead, New York University
David Charters, Purdue
W. A. Capthorne, Army
Charles Eberle, Swarthmore
Harlan O. Page, Chicago
Leon Campbell, Colgate
1911
Harry Hill, Navy
Theodore Kiendl, Columbia

Frank Lawler, Minnesota
John Keenan, St. John's
A. D. Alexander, Columbia
David Charters, Purdue
Lewis Walton, Pennsylvania
Walter Scoville, Wisconsin
C. A. Clementson, Washington
W. M. Lee, Columbia
1912
R. L. Sisson, Dartmouth
William Turner, Pennsylvania
Otto Stangel, Wisconsin
Alphonse Schumacher, Dayton
Emil Schradieck, Colgate
Lewis Castle, Syracuse
Thomas Canfield, St. Lawrence
Fred Gieg, Swarthmore
Claus Benson, Columbia
E. E. Mensel, Dartmouth
1913
Eddie Calder, St. Lawrence
Hamilton Salmon, Princeton
Alphonse Schumacher, Dayton
Allen Johnson, Wisconsin
W. L. Roberts, Army
Lawrence Teeple, Purdue
George Halstead, Cornell
Laurence Wild, Navy
Sam Carrier, Nebraska
Edward Hayward, Wesleyan
1914
Everett Southwick, C.C.N.Y.
Nelson Norgren, Chicago
Walter Lunden, Cornell
Elmer Oliphant, Purdue
Lewis Castle, Syracuse
Eugene Van Gent, Wisconsin
Dan Meehan, Columbia
Gil Halstead, Cornell
Ernest Houghton, Union
Carl Harper, Wisconsin
1915
Elmer Oliphant, Army
George Levis, Wisconsin
Ralph Sproull, Kansas
Leslie Brown, Cornell
Anthony Savage, Washington
William Strickling, Virginia
W. P. Arnold, Yale
J. Charles Lee, Columbia
Ernest Houghton, Union
Ray Woods, Illinois
1916
George Levis, Wisconsin
Cyril Haas, Princeton

Ade Seiberts, Oregon State
Clyde Littlefield, Texas
William Chandler, Wisconsin
Fred Williams, Missouri
Edward McNichol, Pennsylvania
E. L. Dick Romney, Utah
Ray Woods, Illinois
Roy Bohler, Washington State
1917
Francis Stadsvold, Minnesota
Orson Kinney, Yale
F. I. Reynolds, Kansas State
Harry Young, Washington & Lee
Clyde Alwood, Illinois
George Hjelte, California
Harold Olsen, Wisconsin
Cyril Haas, Princeton
Charles Taft, Yale
Ray Woods, Illinois
1918
George Sweeney, Pennsylvania
Earl Anderson, Illinois
Harold Gillen, Minnesota
Craig Ruby, Missouri
William Chandler, Wisconsin
Joseph Schwarzer, Syracuse
Hubert Peck, Pennsylvania
Eber Simpson, Wisconsin
Gene Vidal, Army
Alfred Sorenson, Washington State
1919
Andrew Stannard, Pennsylvania
Knight Farwell, Navy
Arnold Oss, Minnesota
Craig Ruby, Missouri
George Parrish, V.P.I.
Leon Marcus, Syracuse
Paul "Tony" Hinkle, Chicago
Erling Platou, Minnesota
Daniel McNichol, Pennsylvania
Arthur Lonborg, Kansas
1920
George Sweeney, Pennsylvania
George Gardner, S. W. Kansas
Howard Cann, New York University
Forrest De Bernardi, Westminster
Charles Carney, Illinois
George Williams, Missouri
Paul "Tony" Hinkle, Chicago
Hubert Peck, Pennsylvania
Dan McNichol, Pennsylvania
Irving Cook, Washington
1921
Arnold Oss, Minnesota
Forrest De Bernardi, Westminster

Edward Durno, Oregon
R. D. Birkhoff, Chicago
George Williams, Missouri
Everett Dean, Indiana
Dan McNichol, Pennsylvania
Donald White, Purdue
Herbert Bunker, Missouri
Basil Hayden, Kentucky
1922
Charles Carney, Illinois
Arthur Browning, Missouri
George Gardner, S. W. Kansas
Ira McKee, Navy
William Grave, Pennsylvania
Marshall Hjelte, Oregon State
Herbert Bunker, Missouri
Ray Miller, Purdue
Paul Endacott, Kansas
Arthur Loeb, Princeton
1923
Al Fox, Idaho
Arthur Browning, Missouri
Ira McKee, Navy
James Lovely, Creighton
John Luther, Cornell
Richard Carmichael, North Carolina
Arthur Loeb, Princeton
Paul Endacott, Kansas
Charles Black, Kansas
Herbert Bunker, Missouri
1924
John Cobb, North Carolina
Richard Carmichael, North Carolina
Amory Gill, Oregon State
James Lovely, Creighton
Tusten Ackerman, Kansas
Hugh Latham, Oregon
Harry Kipke, Michigan
Charles Black, Kansas
H. W. Middlesworth, Butler
Abb Curtis, Texas
1925
John Cobb, North Carolina
John Miner, Ohio State
Tusten Ackerman, Kansas
Victor Hanson, Syracuse
Gerald Spohn, Washburn
Earl Mueller, Colorado College
Burgess Carey, Kentucky
Noble Kizer, Notre Dame
Carlos Steele, Oregon State
Emanuel Goldblatt, Pennsylvania
1926
Victor Hanson, Syracuse
George Spradling, Purdue

John Cobb, North Carolina
Gale Gordon, Kansas
Albert Peterson, Kansas
Richard Doyle, Michigan
George Dixon, California
Carl Loeb, Princeton
Samuel Goldblatt, Pennsylvania
Algot Westergren, Oregon
1927
Benjamin Oosterbaan, Michigan
Victor Hanson, Syracuse
Ashworth Thompson, Montana State
Gerald Spohn, Washburn
John Nyikos, Notre Dame
Ross Mc Burney, Wichita
George Dixon, California
John Lorch, Columbia
Harry Wilson, Army
Syd Corenman, Creighton
1928
Benjamin Oosterbaan, Michigan
Charles Hyatt, Pittsburgh
Ernest Simpson, Colorado College
Ashworth Thompson, Montana State
Victor Holt, Oklahoma
Charles Murphy, Purdue
Joseph Schaaf, Pennsylvania
Alfred James, Washington
Sykes Reed, Pittsburgh
Glen Rose, Arkansas
1929
Charles Hyatt, Pittsburgh
Ashworth Thompson, Montana State
Joseph Schaaf, Pennsylvania
Vern Corbin, California
Charles Murphy, Purdue
Frank Ward, Montana State
Carey Spicer, Kentucky
Eugene Lambert, Arkansas
Bruce Drake, Oklahoma
Harlow Rothert, Stanford
1930
Charles Hyatt, Pittsburgh
Branch Mc Cracken, Indiana
Bart Carlton, Ada (Okla.)
Ashworth Thompson, Montana State
Charles Murphy, Purdue
Frank Ward, Montana State
John Wooden, Purdue
John Lehners, Southern California
Paul McBrayer, Kentucky
Marshall Craig, Missouri
1931
Richard Linthicum, U.C.L.A.
Elwood Romney, Brigham Young

Carey Spicer, Kentucky
Bart Carlton, Ada (Okla.)
George Gregory, Columbia
Joseph Reiff, Northwestern
John Wooden, Purdue
Wesley Fesler, Ohio State
Ralph Cairney, Washington
Louis Berger, Maryland
1932
Elwood Romney, Brigham Young
Joseph Kintana, California
Edward Krause, Notre Dame
Les Witte, Wyoming
Forest Sale, Kentucky
Ad Dietzel, Texas Christian
John Wooden, Purdue
Dave Jones, Columbia
Louis Berger, Maryland
Allen Brachen, Providence
1933
Joseph Reiff, Northwestern
Jerome Nemer, Southern California
Les Witte, Wyoming
Ken Fairman, Princeton
Forest Sale, Kentucky
Ed Lewis, Oregon State
Don Smith, Pittsburgh

Frank Baird, Butler
Elliott Loughlin, Navy
Ellis Johnson, Kentucky
1934
Robert Galer, Washington
Les Witte, Wyoming
John De Moisey, Kentucky
Harold Eifert, California
Wesley Bennett, Westminster, Pa.
Lee Guttero, Southern California
Wallace Myers, Texas Christian
Claire Cribbs, Pittsburgh
George Ireland, Notre Dame
Emmett Lowery, Purdue
1935
Wesley Bennett, Westminster, Pa.
Al Donniwell, Dartmouth
Jack Gray, Texas
Glen Roberts, Emory & Henry
Leroy Edwards, Kentucky
Lee Guttero, Southern California
Claire Cribbs, Pittsburgh
William Nash, Columbia
George Ireland, Notre Dame
Omar Browning, Oklahoma
1936
Angelo Luisetti, Stanford

Basketball All-American Angelo "Hank" Luisetti, who dribbled at Stanford University. (Citizens Savings Athletic Foundation)

John Moir, Notre Dame
Robert Kessler, Purdue
Ike Poole, Arkansas
Paul Nowak, Notre Dame
Bill Kinner, Utah
William Nash, Columbia
Vernon Huffman, Indiana
Robert Egge, Washington
Norman Iler, Washington & Lee

1937

Angelo Luisetti, Stanford
Jewell Young, Purdue
John Moir, Notre Dame
John O'Brien, Columbia
Paul Nowak, Notre Dame
Bob Spessard, Washington & Lee
Fred Pralle, Kansas
Jules Bender, Long Island
Francis Murray, Pennsylvania
Merle Rousey, Oklahoma State

1938

Angelo Luisetti, Stanford
Jewell Young, Purdue
John Moir, Notre Dame
Bonnie Graham, Mississippi
Hubert Kirkpatrick, Baylor
Paul Nowak, Notre Dame
Fred Pralle, Kansas
John O'Brien, Columbia
Ignatius Volpi, Manhattan
Meyer Bloom, Temple

1939

Lauren Gale, Oregon
James Hull, Ohio State
Irving Torgoff, Long Island
Gus Broberg, Dartmouth
Chester Jaworski, Rhode Island State
Urgel Wintermute, Oregon
Ernie Andres, Indiana
Jesse Renick, Oklahoma State
John Lobsiger, Missouri
Bobby Moers, Texas

1940

Ralph Vaughn, Southern California
Gus Broberg, Dartmouth
John Dick, Oregon
William Hapac, Illinois
George Glamack, North Carolina
Stan Modzelewski, Rhode Island
Jesse Renick, Oklahoma State
Bobby Moers, Texas
John Lobsiger, Missouri
Fred Beretta, Purdue

1941

Gus Broberg, Dartmouth
John Adams, Arkansas

Howard Engleman, Kansas
Gene Englund, Wisconsin
George Glamack, North Carolina
Stanley Modzelewski, Rhode Island
Lee Huber, Kentucky
Milton Phelps, San Diego State
Walter O'Connor, Drake
Ray Sundquist, Washington State

1942

John Kotz, Wisconsin
Price Brookfield, West Texas State
James Pollard, Stanford
George Munroe, Dartmouth
Stanley Modzelewski, Rhode Island
Bob Kinney, Rice
Scott Hamilton, West Virginia
Ray Evans, Kansas
Bud Millikan, Oklahoma State
Andrew Phillip, Illinois

1943

Robert Bishop, Washington State
Kenneth Sailors, Wyoming
George Senesky, St. Joseph's
Andrew Phillip, Illinois
Gerald Tucker, Oklahoma
Bill Tom Closs, Rice
Raymond Evans, Kansas
William Morris, Washington
Robert Rensberger, Notre Dame
John Mahnken, Georgetown

1944

Dale Hall, Army
Bod Dille, Valparaiso
Arnold Ferrin, Utah
Otto Graham, Northwestern &
Colgate
Audley Brindley, Dartmouth
Robert Brannum, Kentucky
George Mikan, De Paul
Alva Paine, Oklahoma
Robert Kurland, Oklahoma State
Bill Henry, Rice

1945

Bill Henry, Rice
Dale Hall, Army
Howie Schultz, Hamline
Max Morris, Northwestern
George Mikan, De Paul
Vince Hanson, Washington State
Robert Kurland, Oklahoma State
Adrian Back, Jr., Navy
Walton Kirk, Jr., Illinois
Herbert Wilkinson, Iowa

1946

Max Morris, Northwestern
Charles Black, Kansas

Leo Klier, Notre Dame
Tony Lavelli, Yale
Robert Kurland, Oklahoma State
George Mikan, De Paul
Sid Tanenbaum, New York University
Jack Parkinson, Kentucky
Paul Huston, Ohio State
James Jordan, North Carolina
1947
Gerald Tucker, Oklahoma
John Hargis, Texas
George Kaftan, Holy Cross
Ralph Hamilton, Indiana
Don Barksdale, U.C.L.A.
Ed Koffenberger, Duke
Sidney Tanenbaum, New York University
Arnold Ferrin, Utah
Ralph Beard, Kentucky
Leland Byrd, West Virginia

Charles Black, Kansas
William Gabor, Syracuse
Kenneth Shugart, Navy
Paul Hoffman, Purdue
Ephraim Rocha, Oregon State
Alex Groza, Kentucky
Kevin O'Shea, Notre Dame
Herbert Wilkinson, Iowa
David Humerickhouse, Bradley
Daniel Kraus, Georgetown

Ambrose Bennett, Oklahoma State
Tony Lavelli, Yale
James Homer, Alabama
Joseph Lord, Villanova
Clifton McNeely, Texas Wesleyan
Ernest Vandeweghe, Colgate
Jack Smiley, Illinois
Dick McGuire, St. John's
Ed Macauley, St. Louis
Lew Beck, Oregon State
1948
Tony Lavelli, Yale
Murray Wier, Iowa
Richard Dickey, North Carolina State
Duane Klueh, Indiana State
Ed Macauley, St. Louis
Jack Nichols, Washington
Ralph Beard, Kentucky
Kevin O'Shea, Notre Dame
Arnold Ferrin, Utah
Andrew Wolfe, California

Don Ray, Western Kentucky
George Kaftan, Holy Cross
Robert Gale, Cornell
Joseph Nelson, Brigham Young
Alex Groza, Kentucky
James McIntyre, Minnesota
Jackie Robinson, Baylor
Howard Shannon, Kansas State
Peter Elliott, Michigan
Ambrose Bennett, Oklahoma State

Frank Kudelka, St. Mary's
Robert Cope, Montana
Hal Haskins, Hamline
Paul Courty, Oklahoma
Walter Budko, Columbia
Adolph Schayes, New York University
Slater Martin, Texas
Andrew Tonkovich, Marshall
Edward Beach, West Virginia
Edward Mikan, De Paul
1949
Anthony Lavelli, Yale
Ernest Vandeweghe, Colgate
Vince Boryla, Denver
Vern Gardner, Utah
Alex Groza, Kentucky
Ed Macauley, St. Louis
Ralph Beard, Kentucky
Robert Harris, Oklahoma State
William Erickson, Illinois
Slater Martin, Texas

Robert Cousy, Holy Cross
Donald Lofgran, San Francisco
Cliff Crandall, Oregon State
William Sharman, Southern California
Vern Mikkelson, Hamline
Paul Unruh, Bradley
Mac Otten, Bowling Green
J. L. Parks, Oklahoma State
Richard McGuire, St. John's
John Pilch, Wyoming

Harold Haskins, Hamline
Paul Courty, Oklahoma
Richard Schnittker, Ohio State
Fred Schaus, West Virginia
Chester Giermak, William and Mary
Bill Tom, Rice
James McIntyre, Minnesota
John Oldham, Western Kentucky
George Stanich, U.C.L.A.
George Cheek, Davidson

1950
  Robert Cousy, Holy Cross
  Sam Ranzino, North Carolina State
  William Sharman, Southern
  California
  Harold Haskins, Hamline
  Paul Arizin, Villanova
  Don Lofgran, San Francisco
  Paul Unruh, Bradley
  Richard Schnittker, Ohio State
  Irwin Bambrot, C.C.N.Y.
  John Pilch, Wyoming

  Gene Melchiorre, Bradley
  Thomas Hamilton, Texas
  Richard Harman, Kansas State
  Sherman White, Long Island
  Chester Giermak, William and Mary
  Don Rehfeldt, Wisconsin
  Ed Gayda, Washington State
  George Stanich, U.C.L.A.
  Charles Cooper, Duquesne
  Keven O'Shea, Notre Dame

  George Yardley, Stanford
  Richard Dickey, North Carolina
  State
  Billy Joe Adcock, Vanderbilt
  Robert Lavoy, Western Kentucky
  Charles Share, Bowling Green
  Clyde Lovellette, Kansas
  William Spivey, Kentucky
  Robert Zawoluk, St. John's
  Clemens Rzeszewski, Indiana State
  Meyer Skoog, Minnesota
1951
  Dick Groat, Duke
  Sam Ranzino, North Carolina State
  Bill Milkvy, Temple
  Bob Zawoluk, St. John's
  William Spivey, Kentucky
  Clyde Lovellette, Kansas
  Ernie Barrett, Kansas State
  Gale McArthur, Oklahoma State
  Mel Hutchins, Brigham Young
  Gene Melchiorre, Bradley

  John Azary, Columbia
  Jay Handlan, Washington and Lee
  James Slaughter, South Carolina
  Ray Ragelis, Northwestern
  Ernie Beck, Pennsylvania
  Meyer Skoog, Minnesota
  Mark Workman, West Virginia
  Frank Guisness, Washington

  Don Sunderlage, Illinois
  John Kiley, Syracuse

  Bill Garrett, Indiana
  Mel Payton, Tulane
  Zeke Zinicola, Niagara
  Larry Hennessey, Villanova
  Richard Ridgway, U.C.L.A.
  Walter Davis, Texas A & M
  Bill Hagler, California
  Roger Johnson, Arizona
  Don Meineke, Dayton
  Carl McNulty, Purdue
1952
  Ernest Beck, Pennsylvania
  Richard Groat, Duke
  Cliff Hagan, Kentucky
  Dick Hemric, Wake Forest
  Larry Hennessey, Villanova
  Bob Kenney, Kansas
  George McLeod, Texas Christian
  John O'Brien, Seattle
  Bobby Speight, North Carolina State
  Ray Steiner, St. Louis
  Mark Workman, West Virginia

  Jesse Arnelle, Pennsylvania State
  Charles Darling, Iowa
  Walter Dukes, Seton Hall
  Robert Houbregs, Washington
  Clyde Lovellette, Kansas
  Don Meineke, Dayton
  Robert Pettit, Louisiana State
  James Tucker, Duquesne

  James Buchanan, Nebraska
  Rodney Fletcher, Illinois
  Don Johnson, Oklahoma State
  Don Johnson, U.C.L.A.
  Richard Knostman, Kansas State
  Carl McNulty, Purdue
  Bob Peters, Santa Clara
  George Radovich, Wyoming
  Frank Ramsey, Kentucky
  William Stauffer, Missouri
  Robert Zawoluk, St. John's
1953
  Robert Houbregs, Washington
  Robert Pettit, Louisiana State
  John O'Brien, Seattle
  Tom Gola, La Salle
  Don Schlundt, Indiana
  Walter Dukes, Seton Hall
  Richard Knostman, Kansas State
  Ernest Beck, Pennsylvania

B. H. Born, Kansas
Robert Mattick, Oklahoma State

Richard Ricketts, Duquesne
Frank Selvy, Furman
Togo Palazzi, Holy Cross
Gene Shue, Maryland
Paul Ebert, Ohio State
Robert McKeen, California
Robert Leonard, Indiana
Chester Noe, Oregon
Larry Costello, Niagara
Irving Bemoras, Illinois

Joe Richey, Brigham Young
Bobby Speight, North Carolina State
Anthony Morocco, Georgia
Don Lange, Navy
Richard Hemric, Wake Forest
Eugene Schwinger, Rice
Robert Carney, Bradley
Kenneth Flower, Southern
California
Arnold Short, Oklahoma City
Larry Hennessey, Villanova
1954
Tom Gola, La Salle
Cliff Hagan, Kentucky
Togo Palazzi, Holy Cross
Jesse Arnelle, Pennsylvania State
Robert Pettit, Louisiana State
Don Schlundt, Indiana
Robert Carney, Bradley
Richard Rosenthal, Notre Dame
Frank Selvy, Furman
Robert Mattick, Oklahoma State

Richard Ricketts, Duquesne
Richard Hemric, Wake Forest
John Clune, Navy
Gene Shue, Maryland
John Kerr, Illinois
Eugene Schwinger, Rice
Frank Ramsey, Kentucky
Robert Leonard, Indiana
Arnold Short, Oklahoma City
B. H. Born, Kansas

Walter Walowac, Marshall
Tom Marshall, Western Kentucky
Roy Irvin, Southern California
Robert Schafer, Villanova
Paul Ebert, Ohio State
Cleo Littleton, Wichita
Richard Wilkinson, Virginia
Maurice Stokes, St. Francis

Larry Costello, Niagara
Kenneth Sears, Santa Clara
1955
Tom Gola, La Salle
Dick Garmaker, Minnesota
Darrell Floyd, Furman
Edward Conlin, Fordham
Bill Russell, San Francisco
Don Schlundt, Indiana
Dick Hemric, Wake Forest
Richard Wilkinson, Virginia
Jack Stephens, Notre Dame
Richard Ricketts, Duquesne

Robert Patterson, Tulsa
Frank Ehmann, Northwestern
Jesse Arnelle, Pennsylvania State
Richard O'Neal, Texas Christian
Bob Burrow, Kentucky
Wade Halbrook, Oregon State
Cleophus Littleton, Wichita
Denver Brackeen, Mississippi
John Moore, U.C.L.A.
Art Bunte, Utah

Jack Twyman, Cincinnati
Leonard Rosenbluth, North Carolina
John Mahoney, William and Mary
Bob McKeen, California
Jerry Harper, Alabama
Kenneth Sears, Santa Clara
Burdette Haldorson, Colorado
Lester Lane, Oklahoma
Jim Reed, Texas Tech
William Seaberg, Iowa
1956
Bill Russell, San Francisco
Darrell Floyd, Furman
Robin Freeman, Ohio State
Thomas Heinsohn, Holy Cross
Charles Tyra, Louisville
Willie Naulls, U.C.L.A.
Leonard Rosenbluth, North Carolina
Harold Lear, Temple
Sihugo Green, Duquesne
Norman Stewart, Missouri

Bob Burrow, Kentucky
Jerry Harper, Alabama
Richard O'Neal, Texas Christian
Julius McCoy, Michigan State
Raymond Downs, Texas
Joe Holup, George Washington
Rod Hundley, West Virginia
Ron Sobieszczyk, De Paul

Bill Logan, Iowa
Art Bunte, Utah

Ronnie Shavlik, North Carolina State
Roger Sigler, Louisiana State
James Ray, Toledo
Joe Capua, Wyoming
Bill Ebben, Detroit
Chet Forte, Columbia
Jim Krebs, Southern Methodist
William Uhl, Dayton
Lloyd Aubrey, Notre Dame
Paul Judson, Illinois
1957
Leonard Rosenbluth, North Carolina
Grady Wallace, South Carolina
Joseph Gibbon, Mississippi
Chet Forte, Columbia
Wilt Chamberlain, Kansas
Jim Krebs, Southern Methodist
Rod Hundley, West Virginia
Jim Ashmore, Mississippi State
Jack Quiggle, Michigan State
Gary Thompson, Iowa State

Elgin Baylor, Seattle
Charles Tyra, Louisville
Raymond Downs, Texas
Bill Ebben, Detroit
Jack Parr, Kansas State
Archie Dees, Indiana
Bobby Joe Mason, Bradley
Vincent Cohen, Syracuse
Tom Steinke, Brigham Young
Guy Rogers, Temple

Win Wilfond, Memphis State
Johnny Cox, Kentucky
Ted Guzek, Butler
Larry Friend, California
Richard Heise, De Paul
Hubert Reed, Oklahoma City
Dave Gambee, Oregon State
Don Hennon, Pittsburgh
Eugene Brown, San Francisco
Melvin Wright, Oklahoma State
1958
Elgin Baylor, Seattle
Oscar Robertson, Cincinnati
Bob Boozer, Kansas State
Mike Farmer, San Francisco
Wilt Chamberlain, Kansas
Archie Dees, Indiana
Vernon Hatton, Kentucky
Guy Rodgers, Temple

Dom Flora, Washington and Lee
Don Hennon, Pittsburgh

Tom Hawkins, Notre Dame
Pete Brennan, North Carolina
James Cunningham, Fordham
Jerry West, West Virginia
Bailey Howell, Mississippi State
Hubert Reed, Oklahoma City
Jack Kubiszyn, Alabama
Alan Seiden, St. John's
Joe Hobbs, Florida
Henry Stein, Xavier (Ohio)

Dave Gambee, Oregon State
Phillip Murrell, Drake
Arlen Clark, Oklahoma State
Leo Byrd, Marshall
John Green, Michigan State
Wayne Embry, Miami (Ohio)
Tony Windis, Wyoming
Gary Simmons, Idaho
Don Ohl, Illinois
Bob Beckel, Air Force Academy
1959
Bob Boozer, Kansas State
Johnny Cox, Kentucky
Oscar Robertson, Cincinnati
Jerry West, West Virginia
John Green, Michigan State
Bailey Howell, Mississippi State
Don Hennon, Pittsburgh
Lou Pucillo, North Carolina State
Alan Seiden, St. John's
Walter Torrence, U.C.L.A.

Leo Byrd, Marshall
Bob Ferry, St. Louis
Thomas Hawkins, Notre Dame
Rex Frederick, Auburn
Darrall Imhoff, California
Doug Smart, Washington
Bob Beckel, Air Force Academy
Lee Harman, Oregon State
Bill Kennedy, Temple
Willie Merriweather, Purdue

M. C. Burton, Michigan
Don Goldstein, Louisville
Ron Johnson, Minnesota
Calvin Ramsey, New York University
Arlen Clark, Oklahoma State
H. E. Kirchner, Texas Christian
Bobby Joe Mason, Bradley

Jim Rogers, Idaho State
Herschell Turner, Nebraska
Tony Windis, Wyoming
1960
Oscar Robertson, Cincinnati
Tom Sanders, New York University
Jerry West, West Virginia
Tom Stith, St. Bonaventure
Darrall Imhoff, California
Jerry Lucas, Ohio State
Len Wilkens, Providence
James Darrow, Bowling Green
William Kennedy, Temple
Roger Kaiser, Georgia Tech

Tony Jackson, St. John's
Al Butler, Niagara
Lee Shaffer, North Carolina
Jeff Cohen, William and Mary
Terry Dischinger, Purdue
Horace Walker, Michigan State
Henry Hart, Auburn
Max Perry, Utah State
Jay Arnette, Texas
Gary Phillips, Houston

Wayne Hightower, Kansas
Dave DeBusschere, Detroit
John Foley, Holy Cross
Jim Mudd, North Texas State
Walter Bellamy, Indiana
Chester Walker, Bradley
Frank Burgess, Gonzaga
John Arrillage, Stanford
Dick Hickox, Miami (Fla.)
Charles Rask, Oregon
1961
Tom Stith, St. Bonaventure
Bob Wiesenhahn, Cincinnati
John Rudometkin, Southern
California
Tony Jackson, St. John's
Jerry Lucas, Ohio State
Terry Dischinger, Purdue
Roger Kaiser, Georgia Tech
Chet Walker, Bradley
Larry Siegfried, Ohio State
Frank Burgess, Gonzaga

Carroll Broussard, Texas A & M
Jack Foley, Holy Cross
Tom Meschery, St. Mary's
Jack Egan, St. Joseph's
Walt Bellamy, Indiana
Billy McGill, Utah

York Larese, North Carolina
Bill Lickert, Kentucky
Gary Phillips, Houston
John Egan, Providence

Dave DeBusschere, Detroit
Jeff Cohen, William and Mary
Art Heyman, Duke
John Turner, Louisville
Leonard Chappell, Wake Forest
Charles Henke, Missouri
Lee Patrone, West Virginia
John Tidwell, Michigan
Larry Armstrong, Arizona State
Earl Shultz, California
1962
Leonard Chappell, Wake Forest
John Foley, Holy Cross
John Havlicek, Ohio State
Art Heyman, Duke
Terry Dischinger, Purdue
Paul Hogue, Cincinnati
Jerry Lucas, Ohio State
Billy McGill, Utah
John Green, U.C.L.A.
Charles Nash, Kentucky
Rodney Thorn, West Virginia
Chet Walker, Bradley

Dave DeBusschere, Detroit
Cornell Green, Utah State
John Rudometkin, Southern
California
Jerry Smith, Furman
Bill Hanson, Washington
Mike Wroblewski, Kansas State
Eddie Miles, Seattle
Bobby Rascoe, Western Kentucky
Jimmy Rayl, Indiana
Tony Yates, Cincinnati

Don Nelson, Iowa
Paul Silas, Creighton
Charles Warren, Oregon
Garry Roggenburk, Dayton
Le Roy Ellis, St. John's
Harold Hudgens, Texas Tech
Jim Kerwin, Tulane
Robert Duffy, Colgate
Jerry Gardner, Kansas
W. D. Stroud, Mississippi State
1963
Ron Bonham, Cincinnati
William Bradley, Princeton
Joseph Caldwell, Arizona State

Ken Charlton, Colorado
David Downey, Illinois
William Green, Colorado State
Gerald Harkness, Loyola (Chicago)
Arthur Heyman, Duke
Barry Kramer, New York University
William O'Connor, Canisius
David Stallworth, Wichita
Nicholas Werkman, Seton Hall

Gary Bradds, Ohio State
Mel Counts, Oregon State
Thomas Dose, Stanford
Lyle Harger, Houston
Fred Hetzel, Davidson
Nate Thurmond, Bowling Green

Walter Hazzard, U.C.L.A.
Gary Hill, Oklahoma City
James Kerwin, Tulane
Bennie Lenox, Texas A & M
Eddie Miles, Seattle
Charles Nash, Kentucky
James Rayl, Indiana
Flynn Robinson, Wyoming
W. D. Stroud, Mississippi State
Tom Thacker, Cincinnati
Rodney Thorn, West Virginia
Tony Yates, Cincinnati
1964
Rick Barry, Miami (Fla.)
Ron Bonham, Cincinnati
William Bradley, Princeton
Wayne Estes, Utah State
Rick Kaminsky, Yale
Bud Koper, Oklahoma City
Barry Kramer, New York University
Jeffrey Mullins, Duke
Willie Murrell, Kansas State
Charles Nash, Kentucky
David Stallworth, Wichita
Nicholas Werkman, Seton Hall

James Barnes, Texas Western
Gary Bradds, Ohio State
Bill Buntin, Michigan
Mel Counts, Oregon State
Thomas Dose, Stanford
Fred Hetzel, Davidson
Lucious Jackson, Pan American
Ollie Johnson, San Francisco
Willie Reed, Grambling
Kendall Rhine, Rice
Paul Silas, Creighton
John Thompson, Providence

Darel Carrier, Western Kentucky
Rich Falk, Northwestern
Gail Goodrich, U.C.L.A.
Walter Hazzard, U.C.L.A.
Walter Jones, Villanova
Howard Komives, Bowling Green
Bennie Lenox, Texas A & M
Ron Miller, Loyola (Chicago)
Flynn Robinson, Wyoming
Cazzie Russell, Michigan
Levern Tart, Bradley
Stephen Thomas, Xavier (Ohio)
1965
Rick Barry, Miami (Fla.)
William Bradley, Princeton
Bill Cunningham, North Carolina
A. W. Davis, Tennessee
Keith Erickson, U.C.L.A.
Wayne Estes, Utah State
Wilbur Frazier, Grambling
Louis Hudson, Minnesota
Ron Reed, Notre Dame
Dave Schellhase, Purdue
Dave Stallworth, Wichita State
Skip Thoren, Illinois

Bob Andrews, Alabama
John Beasley, Texas A & M
Bill Buntin, Michigan
John Fairfield, Brigham Young
Henry Finkel, Dayton
Fred Hetzel, Davidson
Ollie Johnson, San Francisco
Thomas Kimball, Connecticut
Clyde Lee, Vanderbilt
Mike Silliman, Army
Jim Washington, Villanova
Walter Wesley, Kansas

John Austin, Boston College
David Bing, Syracuse
Gail Goodrich, U.C.L.A.
Jim Jarvis, Oregon State
Robert Leonard, Wake Forest
Kenneth McIntyre, St. John's
John Malaise, Texas Tech
Flynn Robinson, Wyoming
Cazzie Russell, Michigan
William Somerset, Duquesne
Stephen Thomas, Xavier (Ohio)
James Walker, Providence
1966
David Bing, Syracuse
Jerry Chambers, Utah
Norman DeFore, Auburn

Don Freeman, Illinois
Mal Graham, New York University
Bob Lewis, North Carolina
John Marin, Duke
Pat Riley, Kentucky
Dave Schellhase, Purdue
Charles Schmaus, Virginia Military
Dick Snyder, Davidson
Jerry Lee Wells, Oklahoma City

John Beasley, Texas A & M
John Block, Southern California
Melvin Daniels, New Mexico
Lloyd Dove, St. John's
Henry Finkel, Dayton
Elvin Hayes, Houston
Tom Kerwin, Centenary
Clyde Lee, Vanderbilt
David Newmark, Columbia
Austin Robbins, Tennessee
Westley Unseld, Louisville
Walt Wesley, Kansas

Orsten Artis, Texas Western
John Austin, Boston College
James Barnett, Oregon
Louie Dampier, Kentucky
Matthew Guokas, St. Joseph's
Bobby Joe Hill, Texas Western
Robert Leonard, Wake Forest
William Melchionni, Villanova
Dick Nemelka, Brigham Young
Cazzie Russell, Michigan
James Walker, Providence
Charles White, Oregon State
1967
Cliff Anderson, St. Joseph's
Bob Arnzen, Notre Dame
Alfred Beard, Louisville
Wesley Bialosuknia, Connecticut
Lloyd Dove, St. John's
Shaler Halimon, Utah State
Clem Haskins, Western Kentucky
Elvin Hayes, Houston
Donald May, Dayton
Larry Miller, North Carolina
Ron Widby, Tennessee
Sam Williams, Iowa

Lewis Alcindor, U.C.L.A.
Joseph Allen, Bradley
Melvin Daniels, New Mexico
Tom Kondla, Minnesota
David Lattin, Texas Western
Gary Lechman, Gonzaga

Steve Mix, Toledo
Don Sidle, Oklahoma
Don Smith, Iowa State
Jim Tillman, Loyola (Chicago)
Keith Swagerty, Pacific
Westley Unseld, Louisville

Lucius Allen, U.C.L.A.
Jim Burns, Northwestern
Louis Dampier, Kentucky
Mal Graham, New York University
Gary Gray, Oklahoma City
Walter Frazier, Southern Illinois
Harry Hollins, Denver
Bob Lewis, North Carolina
Robert Lloyd, Rutgers
Robert Verga, Duke
James Walker, Providence
Mike Warren, U.C.L.A.
1968
Bob Arnzen, Notre Dame
Shaler Halimon, Utah State
Elvin Hayes, Houston
Bill Hewitt, Southern California
Keith Hochstein, Holy Cross
Bill Hosket, Ohio State
Jim McMillian, Columbia
Don May, Dayton
Pete O'Dea, St. Peter's
Walt Piatkowski, Bowling Green
Robert Portman, Creighton
Sam Williams, Iowa

Lewis Alcindor, U.C.L.A.
Joe Allen, Bradley
Tom Boerwinkle, Tennessee
Bob Lanier, St. Bonaventure
Mike Lewis, Duke
Steve Mix, Toledo
Cliff Parson, Air Force Academy
Dave Scholz, Illinois
Don Sidle, Oklahoma
Don Smith, Iowa State
Westley Unseld, Louisville
Neal Walk, Florida

Lucius Allen, U.C.L.A.
Russell Critchfield, California
Harry Hollines, Denver
Mervin Jackson, Utah
Pete Maravich, Louisiana State
Larry Miller, North Carolina
Rick Mount, Purdue
Calvin Murphy, Niagara
Ron Nelson, New Mexico

Richard Travis, Oklahoma City
Mike Warren, U.C.L.A.
Joseph White, Kansas
1969
Johnny Arthurs, Tulane
John Baum, Temple
Kenneth Durrett, La Salle
Gene Ford, Western Michigan
Jim McMillian, Columbia
Rex Morgan, Jacksonville
Bob Portman, Creighton
Marvin Roberts, Utah State
Charlie Scott, North Carolina
Bobby Smith, Tulsa
Rudy Tomjanovich, Michigan
Elnardo Webster, St. Peter's

Lewis Alcindor, U.C.L.A.
Dennis Awtrey, Santa Clara
Terry Driscoll, Boston College
Spencer Haywood, Detroit
Dan Issel, Kentucky
Bob Lanier, St. Bonaventure
Bob Lienhard, Georgia
Jim Daniels, Western Kentucky
Mike Maloy, Davidson
Dave Scholz, Illinois
Dave Sorenson, Ohio State
Neal Walk, Florida

Butch Beard, Louisville
Don Curnutt, Miami (Fla.)
Dick Esleeck, Furman
Bill Justus, Tennessee
Willie McCarter, Drake
Pete Maravich, Louisiana State
Rick Mount, Purdue
Calvin Murphy, Niagara
John Roche, South Carolina
Robert Tallent, George Washington
Rich Travis, Oklahoma City
Joseph White, Kansas
1970
Kenneth Durrett, La Salle
John Johnson, Iowa
James McMillian, Columbia
Andrew Owens, Florida
Marvin Roberts, Utah State
Curtis Rowe, U.C.L.A.
Charlie Scott, North Carolina
John Sutter, Tulane
Ollie Taylor, Houston
Fred Taylor, Pan American
Rudy Tomjanovich, Michigan
Sidney Wicks, U.C.L.A.

Dennis Awtrey, Santa Clara
Dave Cowens, Florida State
Artis Gilmore, Jacksonville
Dan Issel, Kentucky
Bob Lanier, St. Bonaventure
Robert Lienhard, Georgia
Stan Love, Oregon
James McDaniels, Western Kentucky
Mike Maloy, Davidson
Dave Robisch, Kansas
Dave Sorenson, Ohio State
Rich Yunkus, Georgia Tech

Austin Carr, Notre Dame
Jimmy Collins, New Mexico State
Don Curnutt, Miami (Fla.)
Peter Maravich, Louisiana State
John Mengelt, Auburn
Dean Meminger, Marquette
Rick Mount, Purdue
Calvin Murphy, Niagara
Jim Oxley, Army
John Roche, South Carolina
Ralph Simpson, Michigan State
John Vallely, U.C.L.A.
1971
Kenneth Durrett, La Salle
Julius Irving, Massachusetts
George McGinnis, Indiana
Cliff Meely, Colorado
John Neumann, Mississippi
Howard Porter, Villanova
Marvin Roberts, Utah State
Dave Robisch, Kansas
Curtis Rowe, U.C.L.A.
Henry Wilmore, Michigan
Sidney Wicks, U.C.L.A.
Charles Yelverton, Fordham

Dave Bustion, Denver
William Chatmon, Baylor
Randy Denton, Duke
John Gianelli, Pacific
Artis Gilmore, Jacksonville
Steve Hawes, Washington
Dana Lewis, Tulsa
Willie Long, New Mexico
Stan Love, Oregon
James McDaniels, Western Kentucky
Bill Smith, Syracuse
Rich Yunkus, Georgia Tech

Fred Brown, Iowa
Austin Carr, Notre Dame
James Cleamons, Ohio State

Charlie Davis, Wake Forest
Jimmy England, Tennessee
Dean Meminger, Marquette
John Mengelt, Auburn
Mike Newlin, Utah
John Roche, South Carolina
Clarence Sherrod, Wisconsin
Marvin Stewart, Nebraska
Paul Westphal, Southern California
1972
Allan Bristow, Virginia Tech
Bob Davis, Weber State
Mel Davis, St. John's
Ernie Fleming, Jacksonville
Travis Grant, Kentucky State
Bob Lackey, Marquette
Dwight Lamar, Southwestern
Louisiana
Robert McAdoo, North Carolina
Bob Morse, Pennsylvania
Bud Stallworth, Kansas
Henry Wilmore, Michigan
Dennis Wuycik, North Carolina

Michael Bantom, St. Joseph's
Dave Bustion, Denver
Kresimir Cosic, Brigham Young
Dwight Davis, Houston
John Gianelli, Pacific
Steve Hawes, Washington
Tom McMillen, Maryland
Tom Riker, South Carolina
Hank Siemontkowski, Villanova
Ansley Truitt, California
Mike Stewart, Santa Clara
Bill Walton, U.C.L.A.

Henry Bibby, U.C.L.A.
Fred Boyd, Oregon State
Doug Collins, Illinois State
Richard Fuqua, Oral Roberts
Allan Hornyak, Ohio State
Ron King, Florida State
Greg Kohls, Syracuse
Barry Parkhill, Virginia
Jim Price, Louisville
Ed Ratleff, Long Beach State
Wil Robinson, West Virginia
Brian Taylor, Princeton
1973
Ron Behagen, Minnesota
Allan Bristow, Virginia Tech
John Brown, Missouri
Ozie Edwards, Oklahoma City
Wendell Hudson, Alabama

Dwight Lamar, Southwestern
Louisiana
Bill Schaeffer, St. John's
John Shumate, Notre Dame
Aron Stewart, Richmond
David Thompson, North Carolina
State
Nick Weatherspoon, Illinois
Keith Wilkes, U.C.L.A.

Marvin Barnes, Providence
Mike Bantom, St. Joseph's
Jim Brewer, Minnesota
Tommy Burleson, North Carolina
State
Kresimir Cosic, Brigham Young
Steve Downing, Indiana
Kevin Kunnert, Iowa
Tom McMillen, Maryland
Steve Mitchell, Kansas State
Mike Stewart, Santa Clara
Bill Walton, U.C.L.A.
Kermit Washington, American

Willie Biles, Tulsa
Doug Collins, Illinois State
Ernie Di Gregorio, Providence
Larry Finch, Memphis State
Richard Fuqua, Oral Roberts
Allan Hornyak, Ohio State
Kevin Joyce, South Carolina
Louis Nelson, Washington
Barry Parkhill, Virginia
Ed Ratleff, Long Beach State
Harry Rogers, St. Louis
Martin Terry, Arkansas
1974
Len Elmore, Maryland
Larry Fogle, Canisius
Steve Green, Indiana
Kevin Grevey, Kentucky
Bobby Jones, North Carolina
Frank Kendrick, Purdue
Bill Knight, Pittsburgh
Campy Russell, Michigan
Aron Stewart, Richmond
David Thompson, North Carolina
State
Keith Wilkes, U.C.L.A.
James Williams, Austin Peay

Alvan Adams, Oklahoma
Marvin Barnes, Providence
Tommy Burleson, North Carolina
State

John Garrett, Purdue
Leonard Gray, Long Beach State
Maurice Lucas, Marquette
Tom McMillen, Maryland
Robert Parish, Centenary
Kevin Restani, San Francisco
John Shumate, Notre Dame
Mike Sojourner, Utah
Bill Walton, U.C.L.A.

Dan Anderson, Southern California
Willie Biles, Tulsa
Gary Brokaw, Notre Dame
Dennis Du Val, Syracuse
Tom Henderson, Hawaii
Ronald Lee, Oregon
Sam McCants, Oral Roberts
Frank Oleynick, Seattle
Michael Robinson, Michigan State
Kevin Stacom, Providence
Monte Towe, North Carolina State
Brian Winters, South Carolina
1975
Ulysses Bridgeman, Louisville
Adrian Dantley, Notre Dame
Steve Green, Indiana
Kevin Grevey, Kentucky
Rudy Hackett, Syracuse
Bernard King, Tennessee
Bob McCurdy, Richmond
Scott May, Indiana
Clyde Mayes, Furman
David Meyers, U.C.L.A.
Phil Sellers, Rutgers
David Thompson, North Carolina
State

Alvan Adams, Oklahoma
Kent Benson, Indiana
Leon Douglas, Albama
Bob Elliott, Arizona
John Garrett, Purdue
Rich Kelley, Stanford
Charles Kupec, Michigan
Mitch Kupchak, North Carolina
Joe Meriweather, Southern Illinois
Robert Parish, Centenary
Ruben Rodriguez, Long Island
Richard Washington, U.C.L.A.

Skip Brown, Wake Forest
Luther Burden, Utah
Lionel Hollins, Arizona State
Jim Lee, Syracuse
Ronald Lee, Oregon

John Lucas, Maryland
Walter Luckett, Ohio University
Allen Murphy, Louisville
Frank Oleynick, Seattle
Ricky Sobers, Nevada, Las Vegas
Chuckie Williams, Kansas State
Gus Williams, Southern California
1976
Kenny Carr, North Carolina State
Will Bynum, Virginia Military
Adrian Dantley, Notre Dame
Terry Furlow, Michigan State
Jack Givens, Kentucky
Ernie Grunfeld, Tennessee
Marques Johnson, U.C.L.A.
Bernard King, Tennessee
Scott May, Indiana
Eddie Owens, Nevada, L.V.
Phil Sellers, Rutgers
Richard Washington, U.C.L.A.

Kent Benson, Indiana
Rick Bullock, Texas Tech
Leon Douglas, Alabama
James Edwards, Washington
Bob Elliott, Arizona
Ed Gregg, Utah State
Mitch Kupchak, North Carolina
Dave Kyle, Cleveland State
Marcos Leite, Pepperdine
Cedric Maxwell, North Carolina-
Charlotte
Robert Parish, Centenary
Ira Terrell, Southern Methodist

Quinn Buckner, Indiana
Phil Ford, North Carolina
Rickey Green, Michigan
Hercle Ivy, Iowa State
Ronald Lee, Oregon
John Lucas, Maryland
Marshall Rogers, Pan American
Willie Smith, Missouri
Pat Tallent, George Washington
Earl Tatum, Marquette
Todd Tripucka, Lafayette
Chuckie Williams, Kansas State

PLAYER OF THE YEAR
1905
    Chris Steinmetz, Wisconsin
1906
    George Grebenstein, Dartmouth
1907
    Gilmore Kinney, Yale

1908
  Charles Keinath, Pennyslvania
1909
  John Schommer, Chicago
1910
  Harland Page, Chicago
1911
  Theodore Kiendl, Columbia
1912
  Otto Stangel, Wisconsin
1913
  Eddie Calder, St. Lawrence
1914
  Gil Halstead, Cornell
1915
  Ernest Houghton, Union
1916
  George Levis, Wisconsin
1917
  Ray Woods, Illinois
1918
  William Chandler, Wisconsin
1919
  Erling Platou, Minnesota
1920
  Howard Cann, New York University
1921
  George Williams, Missouri
1922
  Charles Carney, Illinois
1923
  Paul Endacott, Kansas
1924
  Charles Black, Kansas
1925
  Earl Mueller, Colorado College
1926
  John Cobb, North Carolina
1927
  Victor Hanson, Syracuse
1928
  Victor Holt, Oklahoma
1929
  Ashworth Thompson, Montana State
1930
  Charles Hyatt, Pittsburgh
1931
  Bart Carlton, Ada (Okla.)
1932
  John Wooden, Purdue
1933
  Forest Sale, Kentucky
1934
  Wesley Bennett, Westminster, Pa.

1935
  Leroy Edwards, Kentucky
1936
  John Moir, Notre Dame
1937
  Angelo Luisetti, Stanford
1938
  Angelo Luisetti, Stanford
1939
  Chester Jaworski, Rhode Island State
1940
  George Glamack, North Carolina
1941
  George Glamack, North Carolina
1942
  Stanley Modzelewski, Rhode Island
1943
  George Senesky, St. Joseph's
1944
  George Mikan, De Paul
1945
  George Mikan, De Paul
1946
  Robert Kurland, Oklahoma State
1947
  Gerald Tucker, Oklahoma
1948
  Ed Macauley, St. Louis
1949
  Anthony Lavelli, Yale
1950
  Paul Arizin, Villanova
1951
  Dick Groat, Duke
1952
  Clyde Lovellette, Kansas
1953
  Robert Houbregs, Washington
1954
  Tom Gola, La Salle
1955
  Bill Russell, San Franciscso
1956
  Bill Russell, San Francisco
1957
  Leonard Rosenbluth, North Carolina
1958
  Elgin Baylor, Seattle
1959
  Oscar Robertson, Cincinnati
1960
  Oscar Robertson, Cincinnati
1961
  Jerry Lucas, Ohio State

1962
  Paul Hogue, Cincinnati
1963
  Arthur Heyman, Duke
1964
  Walter Hazzard, U.C.L.A.
1965
  William Bradley, Princeton
  Gail Goodrich, U.C.L.A.
1966
  Cazzie Russell, Michigan
1967
  Lewis Alcindor, U.C.L.A.
1968
  Lewis Alcindor, U.C.L.A.
1969
  Lewis Alcindor, U.C.L.A.
1970
  Sidney Wicks, U.C.L.A.
  Peter Maravich, Louisiana State
1971
  Sidney Wicks, U.C.L.A.
  Austin Carr, Notre Dame
1972
  Bill Walton, U.C.L.A.
1973
  Bill Walton, U.C.L.A.
1974
  David Thompson, North Carolina
  State
  Bill Walton, U.C.L.A.
1975
  Kevin Grevey, Kentucky
  David Meyers, U.C.L.A.
1976
  Scott May, Indiana
  Kent Benson, Indiana

HENSHEL AWARD—Amateur Athletic Union
  For the winners of the Men's A.A.U. National Basketball Championship. Established 1963.
  1963   Phillips 66ers
  1964   Goodyear Wingfoots
  1965   Armed Forces All-Stars
  1966   Ford Mustangs
  1967   Akron Goodyear
  1968   Armed Forces All-Stars
  1969   Armed Forces All-Stars
  1970   Armed Forces All-Stars
  1971   Armed Forces All-Stars
  1972   Armed Forces All-Stars
  1973   Marathon Oil
  1974   Jacksonville, Fla., A.A.U.

1975   Capitol Insulation, Los Angeles, Calif.
1976   Atheletes in Action, Tustin, Calif.

BOWLING

Masters Bowling Tournament Winners
  1963   Harry Smith
  1964   Billy Welu
  1965   Billy Welu
  1966   Bob Strampe
  1967   Lou Scalia
  1968   Pete Tountas
  1969   Jim Chestney
  1970   Don Glover
  1971   Jim Godman
  1972   Bill Beach
  1973   Dave Soutar
  1974   Paul Colwell
  1975   Ed Ressler, Jr.
  1976   Nelson Burton, Jr.

Firestone Tournament of Champions Winners
  1965   Billy Hardwick
  1966   Wayne Zahn
  1967   Jim Stefanich
  1968   Dave Davis
  1969   Jim Godman
  1970   Don Johnson
  1971   Johnny Petraglia
  1972   Mike Durbin
  1973   Jim Godman
  1974   Earl Anthony
  1975   Dave Davis
  1976   Marshall Holman

Bowler of the Year Award Winners (Men)
  1942   Johnny Crimmins
  1943   Ned Day
  1944   Ned Day
  1945   Buddy Bomar
  1946   Joe Wilman
  1947   Buddy Bomar
  1948   Andy Varipapa
  1949   Connie Schwoegler
  1950   Junie McMahon
  1951   Lee Jouglard
  1952   Steve Nagy

1953	Don Carter
1954	Don Carter
1955	Steve Nagy
1956	Bill Lilliard
1957	Don Carter
1958	Don Carter
1959	Ed Lubanski
1960	Don Carter
1961	Dick Weber
1962	Don Carter
1963	Dick Weber
1964	Billy Hardwick
1965	Dick Weber
1966	Wayne Zahn
1967	Dave Davis
1968	Jim Stefanich
1969	Billy Hardwick
1970	Nelson Burton, Jr.
1971	Don Johnson
1972	Don Johnson
1973	Don McCune
1974	Earl Anthony
1975	Earl Anthony

All Star/U.S. Open Champions

1941–1942	John Crimmins
1942–1943	Connie Schwoegler
1943–1944	Ned Day
1944–1945	Buddy Bomar
1945–1946	Joe Wilman
1946–1947	Andy Varipapa
1947–1948	Andy Varipapa
1948–1949	Connie Schwoegler
1949–1950	Junie McMahon
1950–1951	Dick Hoover
1951–1952	Junie McMahon
1952–1953	Don Carter
1953–1954	Don Carter
1954–1955	Steve Nagy
1955–1956	Bill Lillard
1956–1957	Don Carter
1957–1958	Don Carter
1959	Billy Welu
1960	Harry Smith
1961	Bill Tucker
1962	Dick Weber
1963	Dick Weber
1964	Bob Strampe
1965	Dick Weber
1966	Dick Weber
1967	Les Schissler
1968	Jim Stefanich
1969	Billy Hardwick
1970	Bobby Cooper
1971	Mike Lemongello
1972	Don Johnson
1973	Mike McGrath
1974	Larry Laub
1975	Steve Neff
1976	

Professional Bowlers Association—National Championship

1960	Don Carter
1961	Dave Soutar
1962	Carmen Salvino
1963	Billy Hardwick
1964	Bob Strampe
1965	Dave Davis
1966	Wayne Zahn
1967	Dave Davis
1968	Wayne Zahn
1969	Mike McGrath
1970	Mike McGrath
1971	Mike Lemongello
1972	Johnny Guenther
1973	Earl Anthony
1974	Earl Anthony
1975	Earl Anthony

Bowler of the Year Award Winners (Women)

1948	Val Mikiel
1949	Val Mikiel
1950	Marion Ladewig
1951	Marion Ladewig
1952	Marion Ladewig
1953	Marion Ladewig
1954	Marion Ladewig
1955	Sylvia Martin
1956	Anita Cantaline
1957	Marion Ladewig
1958	Marion Ladewig
1959	Marion Ladewig
1960	Sylvia Martin
1961	Shirley Garms
1962	Shirley Garms
1963	Marion Ladewig
1964	LaVerne Carter
1965	Betty Kuczynski
1966	Joy Abel
1967	Millie Martorella
1968	Dotty Fothergill
1969	Dotty Fothergill
1970	Mary Baker
1971	Paula Sperber
1972	Patty Costello
1973	Judy Cook
1974	Betty Morris
1975	Judy Soutar

All Star/U.S. Open Champions
(Women)

1949–1950	Marion Ladewig
1950–1951	Marion Ladewig
1951–1952	Marion Ladewig
1952–1953	Marion Ladewig
1953–1954	Marion Ladewig
1954–1955	Sylvia Wene
1955–1956	Anita Cantaline
1956–1957	Marion Ladewig
1957–1958	Merle Matthews
1959	Marion Ladewig
1960	Sylvia Wene
1961	Phyllis Notaro
1962	Shirley Garms
1963	Marion Ladewig
1964	LaVerne Carter
1965	Ann Slattery
1966	Joy Abel
1967	Gloria Bouvia
1968	Dorothy Fothergill
1969	Dorothy Fothergill
1970	Mary Baker
1971	Paula Sperber
1972	Lorrie Koch
1973	Mildred Martorella
1974	Patty Costello
1975	Paula Sperber
1976	Patty Costello

BOXING

HEAVYWEIGHT WINNERS

1882–1892
John L. Sullivan
1892–1897
James J. Corbett
1897–1899
Robert Fitzsimmons
1899–1905
James J. Jeffries
1905–1906
Marvin Hart
1906–1908
Tommy Burns
1908–1915
Jack Johnson
1915–1919
Jess Willard

1919–1926
Jack Dempsey
1926–1928
Gene Tunney
1928–1930
Vacant
1930–1932
Max Schmeling
1932
Jack Sharkey
1933
Primo Carnera
1934
Max Baer
1935–1937
James J. Braddock
1937–1949
Joe Louis
1949–1951
Ezzard Charles
1951–1952
Joe Walcott
1952–1956
Rocky Marciano
1956–1959
Floyd Patterson
1959
Ingemar Johansson
1960–1962
Floyd Patterson
1962–1964
Sonny Liston
1964–1967
Cassius Clay (Muhammad Ali)
1970–1973
Joe Frazier
1973–1974
George Foreman
1974–
Muhammad Ali

LIGHT HEAVYWEIGHT WINNERS

1903
Jack Root, George Gardner
1903–1905
Bob Fitzsimmons
1905–1912
Philadelphia Jack O'Brien
1912–1916
Jack Dillon

Heavyweight Floyd Patterson. (Memory Shop)

1916–1920
  Battling Levinsky
1920–1922
  Georges Carpentier
1922–1923
  Battling Siki
1923–1925
  Mike McTigue
1925
  Paul Berlenbach
1926–1927
  Jack Delaney
1927–1929
  Tommy Loughran
1930–1934
  Maxey Rosenbloom
1934–1935
  Bob Olin
1935–1939
  John Henry Lewis
1939
  Melio Bettina
1939–1940
  Billy Conn
1941
  Anton Christoforidis

1941–1948
  Gus Lesnevich, Freddie Mills
1948–1950
  Freddie Mills
1950–1952
  Joey Maxim
1952–1960
  Archie Moore
1961–1962
  Vacant
1962–1963
  Harold Johnson
1963–1965
  Willie Pastrano
1965–1966
  Jose Torres
1966–1968
  Dick Tiger
1968–
  Bob Foster

MIDDLEWEIGHT WINNERS
1884–1891
  Jack "Nonpareil" Dempsey
1891–1897
  Bob Fitzsimmons

1897–1907
   Tommy Ryan
1907–1908
   Stanley Ketchel, Billy Papke
1908–1910
   Stanley Ketchel
1911–1913
   Vacant
1913
   Frank Klaus, George Chip
1914–1917
   Al McCoy
1917–1920
   Mike O'Dowd
1920–1923
   Johnny Wilson
1923–1926
   Harry Greb
1926–1931
   Tiger Flowers, Mickey Walker
1931–1932
   Gorilla Jones
1932–1937
   Marcel Thil
1938
   Al Hostak, Solly Krieger
1939–1940
   Al Hostak
1941
   Tony Zale
1942–1947
   Tony Zale
1947–1948
   Rocky Graziano
1948
   Tony Zale, Marcel Cerdan
1949
   Marcel Cerdan, Jake LaMotta
1950
   Jake LaMotta
1951
   Ray Robinson, Randy Turpin, Ray
   Robinson
1953–1955
   Carl (Bobo) Olson
1955–1957
   Ray Robinson
1957
   Gene Fullmer, Ray Robinson,
   Carmen Basilio

1958
   Carmen Basilio, Ray Robinson
1959
   Gene Fullmer (NBA). Ray Robinson
   (New York)
1960
   Gene Fullmer (NBA), Paul Pender
   (New York and Massachusetts)
1961
   Gene Fullmer (NBA), Terry Downes
   (New York, Massachusetts, Europe)
1962
   Gene Fullmer, Dick Tiger (NBA),
   Paul Pender (New York and
   Massachusetts)
1963
   Dick Tiger (Universal)
1963–1965
   Joey Giardello
1965–1966
   Dick Tiger
1966–1967
   Emile Griffith
1967
   Nino Benvenuti
1967–1968
   Emile Griffith
1968–1970
   Nino Benvenuti
1970
   Carlos Monzon

WELTERWEIGHT WINNERS
1892–1894
   Mysterious Billy Smith
1894–1896
   Tommy Ryan
1896
   Kid McCoy
1900
   Rube Ferns, Matty Matthews
1901
   Matty Matthews, Rube Ferns
1901–1904
   Joe Walcott
1904–1906
   Dixie Kid, Joe Walcott, Honey
   Mellody
1907–1911
   Mike Sullivan

1911–1915
  Vacant
1915–1919
  Ted Lewis, Jack Britton
1919–1922
  Jack Britton
1922–1926
  Mickey Walker
1926
  Pete Latzo
1927–1929
  Joe Dundee
1929
  Jackie Fields
1930
  Jackie Fields, Jack Thompson,
  Tommy Freeman
1931
  Tommy Freeman, Jack Thompson,
  Lou Brouillard
1932
  Jackie Fields
1933
  Young Corbett, Jimmy McLarnin
1934
  Barney Ross, Jimmy McLarnin
1935–1938
  Barney Ross
1938–1940
  Henry Armstrong
1940
  Fritzie Zivic
1941–1946
  Fred Cochrane
1946
  Marty Servo, Ray Robinson
1946–1950
  Ray Robinson
1951
  Johnny Bratton (NBA), Kid Gavilan
1951–1954
  Kid Gavilan
1954–1955
  Johnny Saxton
1955
  Tony De Marco, Carmen Basilio
1956
  Carmen Basilio, Johnny Saxton,
  Carmen Basilio

1957
  Carmen Basilio
1958–1960
  Virgil Akins, Don Jordan
1960
  Benny Paret
1961
  Emile Griffith, Benny Paret
1962
  Benny Paret, Emile Griffith
1963
  Luis Rodriguez, Emile Griffith
1964–1966
  Emile Griffith
1966–1969
  Curtis Cokes
1969–1970
  Jose Napoles, Billy Backus
1971–1975
  Jose Napoles
1975
  John Stracey

LIGHTWEIGHT WINNERS
1896–1899
  Kid Lavigne
1899–1902
  Frank Erne
1902–1908
  Joe Gans
1908–1910
  Battling Nelson
1910–1912
  Ad Wolgast
1912–1914
  Willie Ritchie
1914–1917
  Freddie Welsh
1917–1925
  Benny Leonard
1925
  Jimmy Goodrich, Rocky Kansas
1926–1930
  Sammy Mandell
1930
  Al Singer, Tony Canzoneri
1930–1933
  Tony Canzoneri
1933–1935
  Barney Ross

1935–1936
Tony Canzoneri
1936–1938
Lou Ambers
1938
Henry Armstrong
1939
Lou Ambers
1940
Lew Jenkins
1941–1943
Sammy Angott
1944
Sammy Angott (NBA), Juan Zurita
1945–1951
Ike Williams (NBA, later universal)
1951–1952
James Carter
1952
Lauro Salas, James Carter
1953–1954
James Carter
1954
Paddy De Marco, James Carter
1955
James Carter, Bud Smith
1956
Bud Smith, Joe Brown
1956–1962
Joe Brown
1962–1965
Carlos Ortiz
1965
Ismael Laguna
1965–1968
Carlos Ortiz
1968–1969
Teo Cruz
1969–1970
Mando Ramos
1970
Ismael Laguna
1970–1972
Ken Buchanan
1972
Roberto Duran

FEATHERWEIGHT WINNERS
1892–1900
George Dixon

1900–1901
Terry McGovern, Young Corbett
1901–1912
Abe Attell
1912–1923
Johnny Kilbane
1923
Eugene Criqui, Johnny Dundee
1923–1925
Johnny Dundee
1925–1927
Kid Kaplan
1927–1928
Benny Bass, Tony Canzoneri
1928–1929
Andre Routis
1929–1932
Battling Battalino
1932–1934
Tommy Paul (NBA)
1933–1936
Freddie Miller
1936–1937
Petey Sarron
1937–1938
Henry Armstrong
1938–1940
Joey Archibald
1938–1941
Petey Scalzo (NBA)
1941
Richard Lemos (NBA)
1941–1943
Jackie Wilson (NBA)
1942–1948
Willie Pep
1943
Jackie Callura (NBA)
1943–1944
Phil Terranova (NBA)
1944–1946
Sal Bartolo (NBA)
1948–1949
Sandy Saddler
1949–1950
Willie Pep
1950–1957
Sandy Saddler
1957–1959
Hogan (Kid) Bassey

1959–1963
  Davey Moore
1963–1964
  Sugar Ramos
1964–1969
  Vicente Saldivar
1969
  John Famechon
1970
  Vicente Saldivar
1970–1972
  Kuniaki Shibata
1972
  Clemente Sanchez
1974
  Ruben Olivares
1975
  Alexis Arguello

BANTAMWEIGHT WINNERS
1890–1892
  George Dixon
1892–1894
  Vacant
1894–1899
  Jimmy Barry
1899–1900
  Terry McGovern
1901–1902
  Harry Harris
1902–1903
  Harry Forbes
1903–1904
  Frankie Neil
1904
  Joe Bowker
1905–1907
  Jimmy Walsh
1907–1910
  Vacant
1910–1914
  Johnny Coulon
1914–1917
  Kid Williams
1917–1920
  Pete Herman
1920–1921
  Joe Lynch
1921
  Pete Herman, Johnny Buff

1922
  Johnny Buff, Joe Lynch
1922–1924
  Joe Lynch
1924
  Abe Goldstein, Eddie Martin
1925
  Eddie Martin, Charley (Phil)
  Rosenberg
1925–1926
  Charley (Phil) Rosenberg
1927–1928
  Bud Taylor (NBA only)
1929–1935
  Al Brown
1935–1936
  Baltazar Sangchili
1936
  Tony Marino, Sixto Escobar
1937
  Sixto Escobar, Harry Jeffra
1938–1940
  Sixto Escobar
1941–1942
  Lou Salica
1942–1947
  Manuel Ortiz
1947
  Harold Dade, Manuel Ortiz
1948–1950
  Manuel Ortiz
1950–1952
  Vic Toweel
1952–1954
  Jimmy Carruthers
1954–1956
  Robert Cohen
1956–1957
  Mario D'Agata
1957–1959
  Alphonse Halimi
1959–1960
  Jose Becerra
1961–1965
  Eder Jofre
1965–1968
  Fighting Harada
1968–1969
  Lionel Rose

1969–1970
Ruben Olivares
1970–1971
Chuchu Castillo
1971–1972
Ruben Olivares
1972
Rafael Herrera
1972–1973
Enrique Pinder
1973
Romero Anaya, Arnold Taylor
1974–1975
Soo Hawn Hong
1975
Alfonso Zamora

FLYWEIGHT CHAMPIONS
1916–1923
Jimmy Wilde
1923–1925
Pancho Villa
1925–1927
Fidel LaBarba
1927–1928
Izzy Schwartz
1928–1929
Frankie Genaro
1929
Emile (Spider) Pladner
1929–1930
Frankie Genaro
1930–1931
Midget Wolgast
1931–1932
Young Perez
1932–1935
Jackie Brown
1935–1938
Benny Lynch
1938–1943
Peter Kane
1943–1948
Jackie Paterson
1948
Rinty Monaghan
1950
Terry Allen
1950–1952
Dado Marino

1952–1954
Yoshio Shirai
1954–1960
Pascual Perez
1960–1962
Pone Kingpetch
1962–1963
Fighting Harada
1963
Pone Kingpetch
1963–1964
Hiroyuki Ebihara
1964–1965
Pone Kingpetch
1965–1966
Salvatore Burruni
1966
Walter McGowan
1966–1969
Chartchai Chionoi
1969–1970
Efren Torres
1970
Chartchai Chionoi
1970–1973
Erbito Salvarria
1973–1975
Venice Borkorsor
1975
Miguel Canto

BOXING HALL OF FAME—Amateur Athletic Union
Presented by the *San Francisco Examiner,* this is awarded to someone who has given outstanding service to amateur boxing.
Established 1967.

1967	John J. "Tam" Sheehan
	Al Sandell
1968	F. X. "Pap" Duffy
1969	Paul Staff
1970	Dr. Ben Becker
1971	Leo Salakin
1972	Roland Schwartz
1973	Bill Downey
1974	no award
1975	Robert J. Surkein
	Clyde Quisenberry

MORSE AWARD—Amateur Athletic Union

Super Bowler Joe Namath, who quarterbacked the New York Jets to the first American Football League victory at the big one. (Memory Shop)

For the amateur boxing coach of the year.

Established 1969.

1969	Pat Nappi
1970	Arrington B. Klice
1971	Tom Johnson
1972	Joe Clough
1973	Bill Cummings
1974	no award
1975	William Cummings, Jr.

FOOTBALL

PROFESSIONAL

Super Bowl Winners

1967	Green Bay Packers
1968	Green Bay Packers
1969	New York Jets
1970	Kansas City Chiefs
1971	Baltimore Colts
1972	Dallas Cowboys
1973	Miami Dolphins
1974	Miami Dolphins
1975	Pittsburgh Steelers
1976	Pittsburgh Steelers
1977	Oakland Raiders

National Football Conference/League Championship Game Winners

1933	Chicago Bears
1934	New York Giants
1935	Detroit Lions
1936	Green Bay Packers
1937	Washington Redskins
1938	New York Giants
1939	Green Bay Packers
1940	Chicago Bears
1941	Chicago Bears
1942	Washington Redskins
1943	Chicago Bears
1944	Green Bay Packers
1945	Cleveland Rams
1946	Chicago Bears
1947	Chicago Cardinals
1948	Philadelphia Eagles
1949	Philadelphia Eagles
1950	Cleveland Browns
1951	Los Angeles Rams

1952	Detroit Lions
1953	Detroit Lions
1954	Cleveland Browns
1955	Cleveland Browns
1956	New York Giants
1957	Detroit Lions
1958	Baltimore Colts
1959	Baltimore Colts
1960	Philadelphia Eagles
1961	Green Bay Packers
1962	Green Bay Packers
1963	Chicago Bears
1964	Cleveland Browns
1965	Green Bay Packers
1966	Green Bay Packers
1967	Green Bay Packers
1968	Baltimore Colts
1969	Minnesota Vikings
1970	Dallas Cowboys
1971	Dallas Cowboys
1972	Washington Redskins
1973	Minnesota Vikings
1974	Minnesota Vikings
1975	Dallas Cowboys
1976	Minnesota Vikings

American Football Conference/ League Championship Game Winners

1960	Houston Oilers
1961	Houston Oilers
1962	Dallas Texans
1963	San Diego Chargers
1964	Buffalo Bills
1965	Buffalo Bills
1966	Kansas City Chiefs
1967	Oakland Raiders
1968	New York Jets
1969	Kansas City Chiefs
1970	Baltimore Colts
1971	Miami Dolphins
1972	Miami Dolphins
1973	Miami Dolphins
1974	Pittsburgh Steelers
1975	Pittsburgh Steelers
1976	Oakland Raiders

Jim Thorpe Trophy Winners—Most Valuable Player

1955
Harlon Hill, Chicago Bears
1956
Frank Gifford, New York Giants
1957
John Unitas, Baltimore Colts

1958
Jim Brown, Cleveland Browns
1959
Charley Conerly, New York Giants
1960
Norm Van Brocklin, Philadelphia Eagles
1961
Y. A. Tittle, New York Giants
1962
Jim Taylor, Green Bay Packers
1963
Jim Brown, Cleveland Browns
Y. A. Tittle, New York Giants
1964
Lenny Moore, Baltimore Colts
1965
Jim Brown, Cleveland Browns
1966
Bart Starr, Green Bay Packers
1967
John Unitas, Baltimore Colts
1968
Earl Morrall, Baltimore Colts
1969
Roman Gabriel, Los Angeles Rams
1970
John Brodie, San Francisco 49ers
1971
Bob Griese, Miami Dolphins
1972
Larry Brown, Washington Redskins
1973
O. J. Simpson, Buffalo Bills
1974
Ken Stabler, Oakland Raiders
1975
Fran Tarkenton, Minnesota Vikings

George Halas Trophy Winners— Outstanding Defensive Player

1966
Larry Wilson, St. Louis Cardinals
1967
Deacon Jones, Los Angeles Rams
1968
Deacon Jones, Los Angeles Rams
1969
Dick Butkus, Chicago Bears
1970
Dick Butkus, Chicago Bears
1971
Carl Eller, Minnesota Vikings
1972
Joe Greene, Pittsburgh Steelers

1973
  Alan Page, Minnesota Vikings
1974
  Joe Greene, Pittsburgh Steelers
1975
  Curley Culp, Houston Oilers

COLLEGE

National ("We're No. One") Champion Winners
(Unofficial title voted by Associated Press and United Press International, some years two teams won)

1936	Minnesota
1937	Pittsburgh
1938	Texas Christian
1939	Texas A & M
1940	Minnesota
1941	Minnesota
1942	Ohio State
1943	Notre Dame
1944	Army
1945	Army
1946	Notre Dame
1947	Notre Dame
1948	Michigan
1949	Notre Dame
1950	Oklahoma
1951	Tennessee
1952	Michigan State
1953	Maryland
1954	Ohio State, UCLA
1955	Oklahoma
1956	Oklahoma
1957	Auburn, Ohio State
1958	Louisiana State
1959	Syracuse
1960	Minnesota
1961	Alabama
1962	Southern California
1963	Texas
1964	Alabama
1965	Alabama, Michigan State
1966	Notre Dame
1967	Southern California
1968	Ohio State
1969	Texas
1970	Nebraska, Texas
1971	Nebraska
1972	Southern California
1973	Notre Dame, Alabama
1974	Oklahoma, Southern California
1975	Oklahoma

1976   Pittsburgh

Rose Bowl Winners—Pasadena

1902	Michigan
1916	Washington State
1917	Oregon
1918–1919	Armed Forces Teams
1920	Harvard
1921	California
1922	Washington, Jefferson, California tied 0-0
1923	Southern California
1924	Navy, Washington tied 14–14
1925	Notre Dame
1926	Alabama
1927	Alabama, Stanford tied 7-7
1928	Stanford
1929	Georgia Tech
1930	Southern California
1931	Alabama
1932	Southern California
1933	Southern California
1934	Columbia
1935	Alabama
1936	Stanford
1937	Pittsburgh
1938	California
1939	Southern California
1940	Southern California
1941	Stanford
1942	Oregon State
1943	Georgia
1944	Southern California
1945	Southern California
1946	Alabama
1947	Illinois
1948	Michigan
1949	Northwestern
1950	Ohio State
1951	Michigan
1952	Illinois
1953	Southern California
1954	Michigan State
1955	Ohio State
1956	Michigan State
1957	Iowa
1958	Ohio State
1959	Iowa
1960	Washington
1961	Washington
1962	Minnesota
1963	Southern California
1964	Illinois
1965	Michigan
1966	UCLA

1967	Purdue
1968	Southern California
1969	Ohio State
1970	Southern California
1971	Stanford
1972	Stanford
1973	Southern California
1974	Ohio State
1975	Southern California
1976	UCLA
1977	

Cotton Bowl Winners—Dallas

1937	TCU
1938	Rice
1939	St. Mary's
1940	Clemson
1941	Texas A & M
1942	Alabama
1943	Texas
1944	Randolph Field, Texas tied 7-7
1945	Oklahoma A & M
1946	Texas
1947	Arkansas, LSU tied 0-0
1948	Southern Methodist, Penn State tied 13-13
1949	Southern Methodist
1950	Rice
1951	Tennessee
1952	Kentucky
1953	Texas
1954	Rice
1955	Georgia Tech
1956	Mississippi
1957	TCU
1958	Navy
1959	TCU, Air Force tied 0-0
1960	Syracuse
1961	Duke
1962	Texas
1963	LSU
1964	Texas
1965	Arkansas
1966	LSU
1967	Georgia
1968	Texas A & M
1969	Texas
1970	Texas
1971	Notre Dame
1972	Penn State
1973	Texas
1974	Nebraska
1975	Penn State
1976	Arkansas

Orange Bowl Winners—Miami

1933	Miami (Fla.)
1934	Duquesne
1935	Bucknell
1936	Catholic University
1937	Duquesne
1938	Auburn
1939	Tennessee
1940	Georgia Tech
1941	Mississippi State
1942	Georgia
1943	Alabama
1944	LSU
1945	Tulsa
1946	Miami (Fla.)
1947	Rice
1948	Georgia Tech
1949	Texas
1950	Santa Clara
1951	Clemson
1952	Georgia Tech
1953	Alabama
1954	Oklahoma
1955	Duke
1956	Oklahoma
1957	Colorado, Clemson tied 21-21
1958	Oklahoma
1959	Oklahoma
1960	Georgia
1961	Missouri
1962	LSU
1963	Alabama
1964	Nebraska
1965	Texas
1966	Alabama
1967	Florida
1968	Oklahoma
1969	Penn State
1970	Penn State
1971	Nebraska
1972	Nebraska
1973	Nebraska
1974	Penn State
1975	Notre Dame
1976	Oklahoma

Sugar Bowl Winners—New Orleans

1935	Tulane
1936	TCU
1937	Santa Clara
1938	Santa Clara
1939	TCU
1940	Texas A & M
1941	Boston College
1942	Fordham

1943	Tennessee
1944	Georgia Tech
1945	Duke
1946	Oklahoma A & M
1947	Georgia
1948	Texas
1949	Oklahoma
1950	Oklahoma
1951	Kentucky
1952	Maryland
1953	Georgia Tech
1954	Georgia Tech
1955	Navy
1956	Georgia Tech
1957	Baylor
1958	Mississippi
1959	LSU
1960	Mississippi
1961	Mississippi
1962	Alabama
1963	Mississippi
1964	Alabama
1965	LSU
1966	Missouri
1967	Alabama
1968	LSU
1969	Arkansas
1970	Mississippi
1971	Tennessee
1972	Oklahoma
1972 Dec.	Oklahoma 14, Penn State 0—Penn State gets game by forfeit
1973	Notre Dame
1974	Nebraska
1975	Alabama

Bluebonnet Bowl Winners—Houston

1959	Clemson
1960	Texas, Alabama tied 3-3
1961	Kansas
1962	Missouri
1963	Baylor
1964	Tulsa
1965	Tennessee
1966	Texas
1967	Colorado
1968	SMU
1969	Houston
1970	Oklahoma, Alabama tied 24-24
1971	Colorado
1972	Tennessee
1973	Houston
1974	North Carolina State, Houston tied 31-31

1975	Texas

Fiesta Bowl Winners—Phoenix

1971	Arizona State
1972	Missouri
1973	Arizona State
1974	Oklahoma State
1975	Arizona State

Gator Bowl Winners—Jacksonville

1946	Wake Forest
1947	Oklahoma
1948	Maryland, Georgia tied 20-20
1949	Clemson
1950	Maryland
1951	Wyoming
1952	Miami (Fla.)
1953	Florida
1954	Texas Tech
1955	Auburn
1956	Vanderbilt
1957	Georgia Tech
1958	Tennessee
1959	Mississippi
1960	Arkansas
1961	Florida
1962	Penn State
1963	Florida
1964	North Carolina
1965	Florida State
1966	Georgia Tech
1967	Tennessee
1968	Penn State, Florida State tied 17-17
1969	Missouri
1969 (Dec. 27)	Florida
1971	Auburn
1972	Georgia
1973	Auburn
1973 (Dec.)	Texas Tech
1974	Auburn
1975	Maryland

Liberty Bowl Winners—Memphis

1959	Penn State
1960	Penn State
1961	Syracuse
1962	Oregon
1963	Mississippi State
1964	Utah
1965	Mississippi
1966	Miami (Fla.)
1967	North Carolina State
1968	Mississippi

1969	Colorado
1970	Tulane
1971	Tennessee
1972	Georgia Tech
1973	North Carolina State
1974	Tennessee
1975	USC

Peach Bowl Winners—Atlanta

1968	LSU
1969	West Virginia
1970	Arizona State
1971	Mississippi
1972	North Carolina State
1973	Georgia
1974	Vanderbilt, Texas Tech tied 6-6
1975	West Virginia
1976	

Sun Bowl Winners—El Paso

1936	Hardin-Simmons, New Mexico State tied 14-14
1937	Hardin-Simmons
1938	West Virginia
1949	Utah
1940	Catholic University, Arizona State tied 0-0
1941	Western Reserve
1942	Tulsa
1943	Second Air Force
1944	Southwestern (Texas)
1945	Southwestern (Texas)
1946	New Mexico
1947	Cincinnati
1948	Miami (Ohio)
1949	West Virginia
1950	Texas Western
1951	West Texas State
1952	Texas Tech
1953	Col. Pacific
1954	Texas Western
1955	Texas Western
1956	Wyoming
1957	George Washington
1958	Louisville
1959	Wyoming
1960	New Mexico State
1961	New Mexico State
1962	Villanova
1963	West Texas State
1964	Oregon
1965	Georgia
1966	Texas Western
1967	Wyoming

1968	Texas-El Paso
1969	Auburn
1969 (Dec. 20)	Nebraska
1970	Georgia Tech
1971	LSU
1972	North Carolina
1973	Missouri
1974	Mississippi State
1975	Pittsburgh

Tangerine Bowl—Orlando

1968	Richmond
1969	Toledo
1970	Toledo
1971	Toledo
1972	Tampa
1973	Miami, Ohio
1974	Miami, Ohio
1975	Miami, Ohio

Heisman Trophy Winners

1935
Jay Berwanger, halfback, Chicago
1936
Larry Kelley, end, Yale
1937
Clinton Frank, halfback, Yale
1938
David O'Brien, quarterback, Texas Christian
1939
Nile Kinnick, quarterback, Iowa
1940
Tom Harmon, halfback, Michigan
1941
Bruce Smith, halfback, Minnesota
1942
Frank Sinkwich, halfback, Georgia
1943
Angelo Bertelli, quarterback, Notre Dame
1944
Leslie Horvath, quarterback, Ohio State
1945
Felix Blanchard, fullback, Army
1946
Glenn Davis, halfback, Army
1947
John Lujack, quarterback, Notre Dame
1948
Doak Walker, halfback, SMU

1949
Leon Hart, end, Notre Dame
1950
Vic Janowicz, halfback, Ohio State
1951
Richard Kazmaier, halfback,
Princeton
1952
Billy Vessels, halfback, Oklahoma
1953
John Lattner, halfback, Notre Dame
1954
Alan Ameche, fullback, Wisconsin
1955
Howard Cassady, halfback, Ohio
State
1956
Paul Hornung, quarterback, Notre
Dame
1957
John Crow, halfback, Texas A & M
1958
Pete Dawkins, halfback, Army
1959
Billy Cannon, halfback, Louisiana
State
1960
Joe Bellino, halfback, Navy
1961
Ernest Davis, halfback, Syracuse
1962
Terry Baker, quarterback, Oregon
State
1963
Roger Staubach, quarterback, Navy
1964
John Huarte, quarterback, Notre
Dame
1965
Mike Garrett, halfback, USC
1966
Steve Spurrier, quarterback, Florida
1967
Gary Beban, quarterback, UCLA
1968
O. J. Simpson, halfback, USC
1969
Steve Owens, fullback, Oklahoma
1970
Jim Plunkett, quarterback, Stanford
1971
Pat Sullivan, quarterback, Auburn
1972
Johnny Rogers, fullback, Nebraska

1973
John Cappelletti, halfback, Penn
State
1974
Archie Griffin, running back, Ohio
State
1975
Archie Griffin, running back, Ohio
State
1976
Tony Dorsett, running back,
Pittsburgh

**Outland Award Winners—
Outstanding Interior Lineman**
1946
George Connor, tackle, Notre Dame
1947
Joe Steffy, guard, Army
1948
Bill Fischer, guard, Notre Dame
1949
Ed Bagdon, guard, Michigan State
1950
Bob Gain, tackle, Kentucky
1951
Jim Weatherall, tackle, Oklahoma
1952
Dick Modzelewski, tackle, Maryland
1953
J. D. Roberts, guard, Oklahoma
1954
Bill Brooks, guard, Arkansas
1955
Calvin Jones, guard, Iowa
1956
Jim Parker, guard, Ohio State
1957
Alex Karras, tackle, Iowa
1958
Zeke Smith, guard, Auburn
1959
Mike McGee, tackle, Duke
1960
Tom Brown, guard, Minnesota
1961
Merlin Olsen, tackle, Utah State
1962
Bobby Bell, tackle, Minnesota
1963
Scott Appleton, tackle, Texas

1964
Steve DeLong, tackle, Tennessee
1965
Tommy Nobis, guard, Texas
1966
Lloyd Phillips, tackle, Arkansas
1967
Ron Yary, tackle, Southern
California
1968
Bill Stanfill, tackle, Georgia
1969
Mike Reid, defensive tackle, Penn
State
1970
Jim Stillwagon, linebacker, Ohio
State
1971
Larry Jacobson, defensive tackle,
Nebraska
1972
Rich Glover, middle guard,
Nebraska
1973
John Hicks, guard, Ohio State
1974
Randy White, defensive end,
Maryland
1975
Leroy Selmon, defensive tackle,
Oklahoma
1976
Ross Browner, defensive tackle,
Notre Dame

**Grantland Rice Trophy—Football
Writers Association of America**
1954   UCLA
1955   Oklahoma
1956   Oklahoma
1957   Ohio State
1958   Iowa
1959   Syracuse
1960   Mississippi
1961   Ohio State
1962   Southern California
1963   Texas
1964   Arkansas
1965   Michigan State, Alabama (tie)
1966   Notre Dame
1967   Southern California
1968   Ohio State
1969   Texas
1970   Nebraska
1971   Nebraska

1972   Southern California
1973   Notre Dame
1974   Southern California
1975   Oklahoma
1976

**Coach Of The Year—Football Writers
Association of America**
1957
Woody Hayes, Ohio State
1958
Paul Dietzel, Louisiana State
1959
Ben Schwartzwalder, Syracuse
1960
Murray Warmath, Minnesota
1961
Darrell Royal, Texas
1962
John McKay, Southern California
1963
Darrell Royal, Texas
1964
Ara Parseghian, Notre Dame
1965
Duffy Daugherty, Michigan State
1966
Tom Cahill, Army
1967
John Pont, Indiana
1968
Woody Hayes, Ohio State
1969
Bo Schembechler, Michigan
1970
Alex Agase, Northwestern
1971
Bob Devaney, Nebraska
1972
John McKay, Southern California
1973
Johnny Majors, Pittsburgh
1974
Grant Teaff, Baylor
1975
Woody Hayes, Ohio State
1976

**ROSE BOWL FOOTBALL PLAYER
OF THE GAME**—Citizens Savings
Athletic Foundation
It's easier to win this award, which is
presented in the locker room right after
the game, if you're on the winning
team. But a few accomplished the near-

impossible: Ernie Nevers in 1925; George Wilson, 1926; Benjamin Lom, 1929; Jack Crabtree, 1958; and Ron VanderKelen, 1963.

Established 1945.

1902
Neil Snow, Michigan
1916
Carl Dietz, Washington State
1917
John Beckett, Oregon
1918
Hollis Huntington, Mare Island
1919
George Halas, Great Lakes
1920
Edward Casey, Harvard
1921
Harold Muller, California
1922
Russell Stein, Washington & Jefferson
1923
Leo Calland, Southern California
1924
Ira McKee, Navy
1925
Elmer Layden, Notre Dame
Ernest Nevers, Stanford
1926
John Mack Brown, Alabama
George Wilson, Washington
1927
Fred Pickhard, Alabama
1928
Clifford Hoffman, Stanford
1929
Benjamin Lom, California
1930
Russell Saunders, Southern California
1931
John Campbell, Alabama
1932
Erny Pinckert, Southern California
1933
Homer Griffith, Southern California
1934
Cliff Montgomery, Columbia
1935
Millard Howell, Alabama
1936
James Moscrip, Stanford
Keith Topping, Stanford

1937
William Daddio, Pittsburgh
1938
Victor Bottari, California
1939
Doyle Nave, Southern California
Alvin Krueger, Southern California
1940
Ambrose Schindler, Southern California
1941
Peter Kmetovic, Stanford
1942
Donald Durdan, Oregon State
1943
Charles Trippi, Georgia
1944
Norman Verry, Southern California
1945
James Hardy, Southern California
1946
Harry Gilmer, Alabama
1947
Claude Young, Illinois
Julius Rykovich, Illinois
1948
Robert Chappius, Michigan
1949
Frank Aschenbrenner, Northwestern
1950
Fred Morrison, Ohio State
1951
Donald Dufek, Michigan
1952
William Tate, Illinois
1953
Rudy Bukich, Southern California
1954
Billy Wells, Michigan State
1955
Dave Leggett, Ohio State
1956
Walter Kowalczyk, Michigan State
1957
Kenneth Ploen, Iowa
1958
Jack Crabtree, Oregon
1959
Bob Jeter, Iowa
1960
Bob Schloredt, Washington
George Fleming, Washington
1961
Bob Schloredt, Washington

1962
   Sandy Stephens, Minnesota
1963
   Pete Beathard, Southern California
   Ron VanderKelen, Wisconsin
1964
   Jim Grabowski, Illinois
1965
   Mel Anthony, Michigan
1966
   Bob Stiles, U.C.L.A.
1967
   John Charles, Purdue
1968
   O. J. Simpson, Southern California
1969
   Rex Kern, Ohio State
1970
   Bob Chandler, Southern California
1971
   Jim Plunkett, Stanford
1972
   Don Bunce, Stanford
1973
   Sam Cunningham, Southern
   California
1974
   Cornelius Greene, Ohio State
1975
   Pat Haden, Southern California
   John McKay, Southern California
1976
   John Sciarra, U.C.L.A.

GOLF

MASTERS TOURNAMENT WINNERS

1935	Gene Sarazen (won playoff)
1936	Horton Smith
1937	Byron Nelson
1938	Henry Picard
1939	Ralph Guldahl
1940	Jimmy Demaret
1941	Craig Wood
1942	Byron Nelson (won playoff)
1943	tournament not held
1944	tournament not held
1945	tournament not held
1946	Herman Keiser
1947	Jimmy Demaret
1948	Claude Harmon
1949	Sam Snead
1950	Jimmy Demaret
1951	Ben Hogan
1952	Sam Snead
1953	Ben Hogan
1954	Sam Snead (won playoff)
1955	Cary Middlecoff
1956	Jack Burke, Jr.
1957	Doug Ford
1958	Arnold Palmer
1959	Art Wall, Jr.
1960	Arnold Palmer
1961	Gary Player
1962	Arnold Palmer (won playoff)
1963	Jack Nicklaus
1964	Arnold Palmer
1965	Jack Nicklaus
1966	Jack Nicklaus (won playoff)
1967	Gay Brewer
1968	Bob Goalby
1969	George Archer
1970	Billy Casper (won playoff)
1971	Charles Coody
1972	Jack Nicklaus
1973	Tommy Aaron
1974	Gary Player
1975	Jack Nicklaus
1976	Ray Floyd

BRITISH OPEN WINNERS

1900	John H. Taylor
1901	James Braid
1902	Alexander Herd
1903	Harry Vardon
1904	Jack White
1905	James Braid
1906	James Braid
1907	Arnaud Massy
1908	James Braid
1909	John H. Taylor
1910	James Braid
1911	Harry Vardon
1912	Edward (Ted) Ray
1913	John T. Taylor
1914	Harry Vardon
1915	tournament not held
1916	tournament not held
1917	tournament not held
1918	tournament not held
1919	tournament not held
1920	George Duncan

1921	Jack Hutchison (won playoff)
1922	Walter Hagen
1923	Arthur G. Havers
1924	Walter Hagen
1925	James M. Barnes
1926	Robert T. Jones, Jr.
1927	Robert T. Jones, Jr.
1928	Walter Hagen
1929	Walter Hagen
1930	Robert T. Jones, Jr.
1931	Tommy D. Armour
1932	Gene Sarazen
1933	Denny Shute (won playoff)
1934	Henry Cotton
1935	Alfred Perry
1936	Alfred Padgham
1937	Henry Cotton
1938	R. A. Whitcombe
1939	Richard Burton
1940	tournament not held
1941	tournament not held
1942	tournament not held
1943	tournament not held
1944	tournament not held
1945	tournament not held
1946	Sam Snead
1947	Fred Daly
1948	Henry Cotton
1949	Bobby Locke (won playoff)
1950	Bobby Locke
1951	Max Faulkner
1952	Bobby Locke
1953	Ben Hogan
1954	Peter Thomson
1955	Peter Thomson
1956	Peter Thomson
1957	Bobby Locke
1958	Peter Thomson (won playoff)
1959	Gary Player
1960	Kel Nagle
1961	Arnold Palmer
1962	Arnold Palmer
1963	Bob Charles (won playoff)
1964	Tony Lema
1965	Peter Thomson
1966	Jack Nicklaus
1967	Roberto de Vicenzo
1968	Gary Player
1969	Tony Jacklin
1970	Jack Nicklaus (won playoff)
1971	Lee Trevino
1972	Lee Trevino
1973	Tom Weiskopf
1974	Gary Player
1975	Thomas Watson

1976	Johnny Miller

UNITED STATES OPEN

1900	Harry Vardon
1901	Willie Anderson (won playoff)
1902	Laurie Auchterlonie
1903	Willie Anderson
1904	Willie Anderson
1905	Willie Anderson
1906	Alex Smith
1907	Alex Ross
1908	Fred McLeod
1909	George Sargent
1910	Alex Smith (won playoff)
1911	John McDermott (won playoff)
1912	John McDermott
1913	Francis Ouimet (won playoff)
1914	Walter Hagen
1915	Jerome D. Travers
1916	Charles Evans, Jr.
1917	tournament not held
1918	tournament not held
1919	Walter Hagen (won playoff)
1920	Edward Ray
1921	Jim Barnes
1922	Gene Sarazen
1923	R. T. Jones, Jr. (won playoff)
1924	Cyril Walker
1925	Willie Macfarlane (won playoff)
1926	R. T. Jones, Jr.
1927	Tommy Armour (won playoff)
1928	Johnny Farrell (won playoff)
1929	R. T. Jones, Jr. (won playoff)
1930	R. T. Jones, Jr.
1931	Billy Burke (won playoff)
1932	Gene Sarazen
1933	John Goodman
1934	Olin Dutra
1935	Sam Parks, Jr.
1936	Tony Manero
1937	Ralph Guldahl
1938	Ralph Guldahl
1939	Byron Nelson (won playoff)
1940	Lawson Little (won playoff)
1941	Craig Wood
1942	tournament not held
1943	tournament not held
1944	tournament not held
1945	tournament not held
1946	Lloyd Mangrum (won playoff)

1947	Lew Worsham (won playoff)
1948	Ben Hogan
1949	Cary Middlecoff
1950	Ben Hogan (won playoff)
1951	Ben Hogan
1952	Julius Boros
1953	Ben Hogan
1954	Ed Furgol
1955	Jack Fleck (won playoff)
1956	Cary Middlecoff
1957	Dick Mayer (won playoff)
1958	Tommy Bolt
1959	Billy Casper, Jr.
1960	Arnold Palmer
1961	Gene Littler
1962	Jack Nicklaus (won playoff)
1963	Julius Boros (won playoff)
1964	Ken Venturi
1965	Gary Player (won playoff)
1966	Billy Casper, Jr. (won playoff)
1967	Jack Nicklaus
1968	Lee Trevino
1969	Orville Moody
1970	Tony Jacklin
1971	Lee Trevino (won playoff)
1972	Jack Nicklaus
1973	Johnny Miller
1974	Hale Irwin
1975	Lou Graham
1976	Jerry Pate

PROFESSIONAL GOLF ASSOCIATION CHAMPIONSHIP TOURNAMENT WINNERS

1919	James M. Barnes
1920	Jock Hutchison
1921	Walter Hagen
1922	Gene Sarazen
1923	Gene Sarazen
1924	Walter Hagen
1925	Walter Hagen
1926	Walter Hagen
1927	Walter Hagen
1928	Leo Diegel
1929	Leo Diegel
1930	Tommy Armour
1931	Tom Creavy
1932	Olin Dutra
1933	Gene Sarazen
1934	Paul Runyan
1935	Johnny Revolta
1936	Denny Shute
1937	Denny Shute

1938	Paul Runyan
1939	Henry Picard
1940	Byron Nelson
1941	Vic Ghezzi
1942	Sam Snead
1943	tournament not held
1944	Bob Hamilton
1945	Byron Nelson
1946	Ben Hogan
1947	Jim Ferrier
1948	Ben Hogan
1949	Sam Snead
1950	Chandler Harper
1951	Sam Snead
1952	Jim Turnesa
1953	Walter Burkemo
1954	Chick Harbert
1955	Doug Ford
1956	Jack Burke, Jr.
1957	Lionel Hebert
1958	Dow Finsterwald
1959	Bob Rosburg
1960	Jay Hebert
1961	Jerry Barber (won playoff)
1962	Gary Player
1963	Jack Nicklaus
1964	Bob Nichols
1965	Dave Marr
1966	Al Geiberger
1967	Don January (won playoff)
1968	Julius Boros
1969	Ray Floyd
1970	Dave Stockton
1971	Jack Nicklaus
1972	Gary Player
1973	Jack Nicklaus
1974	Lee Trevino
1975	Jack Nicklaus
1976	Dave Stockton

YEARLY MONEY WINNERS

1941	Ben Hogan	$18,358
1942	Ben Hogan	13,143
1943	War Bond Prizes	
1944	Byron Nelson	37,967
1945	Byron Nelson	63,335
1946	Ben Hogan	42,556
1947	Jimmy Demaret	27,936
1948	Ben Hogan	32,112
1949	Sam Snead	31,593
1950	Sam Snead	35,758
1951	Lloyd Mangrum	26,088
1952	Julius Boros	37,032
1953	Lew Worsham	34,002

1954	Bob Toski	65,819
1955	Julius Boros	63,121
1956	Ted Kroll	72,835
1957	Dick Mayer	65,835
1958	Arnold Palmer	42,607
1959	Art Wall	53,167
1960	Arnold Palmer	75,262
1961	Gary Player	64,450
1962	Arnold Palmer	81,448
1963	Arnold Palmer	128,230
1964	Jack Nicklaus	113,284
1965	Jack Nicklaus	140,752
1966	Billy Casper	121,944
1967	Jack Nicklaus	188,988
1968	Billy Casper	205,168
1969	Frank Beard	175,223
1970	Lee Trevino	157,037
1971	Jack Nicklaus	244,490
1972	Jack Nicklaus	320,542
1973	Jack Nicklaus	308,362
1974	Johnny Miller	353,021
1975	Jack Nicklaus	298,149

UNITED STATES OPEN—Women

1946	Patty Berg
1947	Betty Jamieson
1948	Babe Zaharias
1949	Louise Suggs
1950	Babe Zaharias
1951	Betsy Rawls
1952	Louise Suggs
1953	Betsy Rawls
1954	Babe Zaharias
1955	Fay Crocker
1956	Kathy Cornelius
1957	Betsy Rawls
1958	Mickey Wright
1959	Mickey Wright
1960	Betsy Rawls
1961	Mickey Wright
1962	Murle Lindstrom
1963	Mary Mills
1964	Mickey Wright
1965	Carol Mann
1966	Sandra Spuzich
1967	Catherine Lacoste (amateur)
1968	Susie Berning
1969	Donna Caponi
1970	Donna Caponi
1971	JoAnne Carner
1972	Susie Berning
1973	Susie Berning
1974	Sandra Haynie
1975	Sandra Palmer

1976	JoAnne Carner

*Amateur

LADIES' PROFESSIONAL GOLFERS ASSOCIATION CHAMPIONS

1955	Beverly Hanson
1956	Marlene Hagge
1957	Louise Suggs
1958	Mickey Wright
1959	Betsy Rawls
1960	Mickey Wright
1961	Mickey Wright
1962	Judy Kimball
1963	Mickey Wright
1964	Mary Mills
1965	Sandra Haynie
1966	Gloria Ehret
1967	Kathy Whitworth
1968	Sandra Post
1969	Betsy Rawls
1970	Shirley Englehorn
1971	Kathy Whitworth
1972	Kathy Ahearn
1973	Mary Mills
1974	Sandra Haynie
1975	Kathy Whitworth
1976	Betty Burfeindt

VARE TROPHY WINNERS

1953	Patty Berg
1954	Babe Zaharias
1955	Patty Berg
1956	Patty Berg
1957	Louise Suggs
1958	Beverly Hansen
1959	Betsy Rawls
1960	Mickey Wright
1961	Mickey Wright
1962	Mickey Wright
1963	Mickey Wright
1964	Mickey Wright
1965	Kathy Whitworth
1966	Kathy Whitworth
1967	Kathy Whitworth
1968	Carol Mann
1969	Kathy Whitworth
1970	Kathy Whitworth
1971	Kathy Whitworth
1972	Kathy Whitworth
1973	Judy Rankin
1974	JoAnne Carner
1975	JoAnne Carner

UNITED STATES NATIONAL AMATEUR CHAMPIONS (Men)

1900	Walter J. Travis
1901	Walter J. Travis
1902	Louis N. James
1903	Walter J. Travis
1904	H. Chandler Egan
1905	H. Chandler Egan
1906	Eban M. Byers
1907	Jerome D. Travers
1908	Jerome D. Travers
1909	Robert A. Gardner
1910	William C. Fownes
1911	Harold H. Hilton
1912	Jerome D. Travers
1913	Jerome D. Travers
1914	Francis Ouimet
1915	Robert A. Gardner
1916	Charles Evans, Jr.
1917–1918	no competition
1919	Davidson Herron
1920	Charles Evans, Jr.
1921	Jesse P. Guilford
1922	Jess W. Sweetser
1923	Max R. Marston
1924	Robert T. Jones, Jr.
1925	Robert T. Jones, Jr.
1926	George Von Elm
1927	Robert T. Jones, Jr.
1928	Robert T. Jones, Jr.
1929	Harrison R. Johnston
1930	Robert T. Jones, Jr.
1931	Francis Ouimet
1932	C. Ross Somerville
1933	George T. Dunlap, Jr.
1934	W. Lawson Little, Jr.
1935	W. Lawson Little, Jr.
1936	John W. Fischer
1937	John G. Goodman
1938	William P. Turnesa
1939	Marvin H. Ward
1940	Richard D. Chapman
1941	Marvin H. Ward
1942–1945	no competition
1946	Stanley E. Bishop
1947	Robert H. Riegel
1948	William P. Turnesa
1949	Charles R. Coe
1950	Sam Urzetta
1951	Billy Maxwell
1952	Jack Westland
1953	Gene A. Littler
1954	Arnold D. Palmer
1955	E. Harvie Ward
1956	E. Harvie Ward
1957	Hillman Robbins
1958	Charles R. Coe
1959	Jack Nicklaus
1960	Deane Beman
1961	Jack Nicklaus
1962	Labron Harris, Jr.
1963	Deane Beman
1964	Bill Campbell
1965	Bob Murphy
1966	Gary Cowan
1967	Bob Dickson
1968	Bruce Fleisher
1969	Steve Melnyk
1970	Lanny Wadkins
1971	Gary Cowan
1972	Vinny Giles
1973	Craig Stadler
1974	Jerry Pate
1975	Fred Ridley
1976	Bill Sander
1977	

WALKER CUP

1922	United States
1923	United States
1924	United States
1926	United States
1928	United States
1930	United States
1932	United States
1934	United States
1936	United States
1938	Great Britain
1940–1946	no competition
1947	United States
1949	United States
1951	United States
1953	United States
1955	United States
1957	United States
1959	United States
1961	United States
1963	United States
1965	United States
1967	United States
1969	United States
1971	Great Britain
1973	United States
1975	United States

UNITED STATES AMATEUR CHAMPIONS (Women)

1900	Frances Griscom
1901	Genevieve Hecker

1902	Genevieve Hecker
1903	Bessie Anthony
1904	Georgianna Bishop
1905	Pauline Mackay
1906	Harriot Curtis
1907	Margaret Curtis
1908	Katherine Harley
1909	Dorothy Campbell
1910	Dorothy Campbell
1911	Margaret Curtis
1912	Margaret Curtis
1913	Gladys Ravenscroft
1914	H. A. Jackson
1915	C. H. Vanderbeck
1916	Alexa Stirling
1917–1918	no competition
1919	Alexa Stirling
1920	Alexa Stirling
1921	Marion Hollins
1922	Glenna Collett
1923	Edith Cummings
1924	Dorothy Hurd
1925	Glenna Collett
1926	G. H. Stetson
1927	M. B. Horn
1928	Glenna Collett
1929	Glenna Collett
1930	Glenna Collett
1931	Helen Hicks
1932	Virginia Van Wie
1933	Virginia Van Wie
1934	Virginia Van Wie
1935	Glenna Vare
1936	Pamela Barton
1937	J. A. Page
1938	Patty Berg
1939	Betty Jameson
1940	Betty Jameson
1941	Mrs. Frank Newell
1942–1945	no competition
1946	Babe Zaharias
1947	Louise Suggs
1948	Grace Lenczyk
1949	Mrs. Mark Porter
1950	Beverly Hanson
1951	Dorothy Kirby
1952	Mrs. Jackie Pung
1953	Mary Lena Faulk
1954	Barbara Romack
1955	Pat Lesser
1956	Marlene Stewart
1957	JoAnne Gunderson
1958	Anne Quast
1959	Barbara McIntire
1960	JoAnne Gunderson
1961	Anne Quast Decker

1962	JoAnne Gunderson
1963	Anne Quast Welts
1964	Barbara McIntire
1965	Jean Ashley
1966	JoAnne Carner
1967	Lou Dill
1968	JoAnne Carner
1969	Catherine Lacoste
1970	Martha Wilkinson
1971	Laura Baugh
1972	Mary Budke
1973	Carol Semple
1974	Cynthia Hill
1975	Beth Daniel
1976	

COLLEGIATE CHAMPIONS—NCAA DIVISION I—TEAM CHAMPIONS

1901	Harvard
1902	Yale (spring)
1902	Harvard (fall)
1903	Harvard
1904	Harvard
1905	Yale
1906	Yale
1907	Yale
1908	Yale
1909	Yale
1910	Yale
1911	Yale
1912	Yale
1913	Yale
1914	Princeton
1915	Yale
1916	Princeton
1917–1918	no competition
1919	Princeton
1920	Princeton
1921	Dartmouth
1922	Princeton
1923	Princeton
1924	Yale
1925	Yale
1926	Yale
1927	Princeton
1928	Princeton
1929	Princeton
1930	Princeton
1931	Yale
1932	Yale
1933	Yale
1934	Michigan
1935	Michigan
1936	Yale

1937	Princeton
1938	Stanford
1939	Stanford
1940	Princeton
	Louisiana State
1941	Stanford
1942	Louisiana State
	Stanford
1943	Yale
1944	Notre Dame
1945	Ohio State
1946	Stanford
1947	Louisiana State
1948	San Jose State
1949	North Texas State
1950	North Texas State
1951	North Texas State
1952	North Texas State
1953	Stanford
1954	Southern Methodist
1955	Louisiana State
1956	Houston
1957	Houston
1958	Houston
1959	Houston
1960	Houston
1961	Purdue
1962	Houston
1963	Oklahoma State
1964	Houston
1965	Houston
1966	Houston
1967	Houston
1968	Florida
1969	Houston
1970	Houston
1971	Texas
1972	Texas
1973	Florida
1974	Wake Forest
1975	Wake Forest
1976	

NCAA DIVISION I—INDIVIDUAL CHAMPIONS

1901
  H. Lindsley, Harvard
1902
  Charles Hitchcock, Jr., Yale (spring)
1903
  Chandler Egan, Harvard (fall)
1903
  F. O. Reinhart, Princeton

1904
  A. L. White, Harvard
1905
  Robert Abbott, Yale
1906
  W. E. Clow, Jr., Yale
1907
  Ellis Knowles, Yale
1908
  H. H. Wilder, Harvard
1909
  Albert Seckel, Princeton
1910
  Robert Hunter, Yale
1911
  George Stanley, Yale
1912
  F. C. Davison, Harvard
1913
  Nathaniel Wheeler, Yale
1914
  Edward Allis, Harvard
1915
  Francis Blossom, Yale
1916
  J. W. Hubbell, Harvard
1917–1918
  no competition
1919
  A. L. Walker, Jr., Columbia
1920
  Jess Sweester, Yale
1921
  Simpson Dean, Princeton
1922
  Pollack Boyd, Dartmouth
1923
  Dexter Cummings, Yale
1924
  Dexter Cummings, Yale
1925
  Fred Lamprecht, Yale
1926
  Fred Lamprecht, Yale
1927
  Watts Gunn, Georgia Tech
1928
  Maurice McCarthy, Georgetown
1929
  Tom Aycock, Yale
1930
  G. T. Dunlap, Jr., Princeton
1931
  G. T. Dunlap, Jr., Princeton

1932
   J. W. Fischer, Michigan
1933
   Walter Emery, Oklahoma
1934
   Charles Yates, Georgia Tech
1935
   Ed White, Texas
1936
   Charles Kocsis, Michigan
1937
   Fred Haas, Jr., Louisiana State
1938
   John Burke, Georgetown
1939
   Vincent D'Antoni, Tulane
1940
   Dixon Brooke, Virginia
1941
   Earl Stewart, Louisiana State
1942
   Frank Tatum, Jr., Stanford
1943
   Wallace Ulrich, Carleton
1944
   Louis Lick, Minnesota
1945
   John Lorms, Ohio State
1946
   George Hamer, Georgia
1947
   Dave Barclay, Michigan
1948
   Bob Harris, San Jose State
1949
   Harvie Ward, North Carolina
1950
   Fred Wampler, Purdue
1951
   Tom Nieporte, Ohio State
1952
   Jim Vickers, Oklahoma
1953
   Earl Moeller, Oklahoma State
1954
   Hillman Robbins, Memphis State
1955
   Joe Campbell, Purdue
1956
   Rick Jones, Ohio State
1957
   Rex Baxter, Jr., Houston
1958
   Phil Rodgers, Houston

1959
   Dick Crawford, Houston
1960
   Dick Crawford, Houston
1961
   Jack Nicklaus, Ohio State
1962
   Kermit Zarley, Houston
1963
   R. H. Sikes, Arkansas
1964
   Terry Small, San Jose State
1965
   Marty Fleckman, Houston
1966
   Bob Murphy, Florida
1967
   Hale Irwin, Colorado
1968
   Grier Jones, Oklahoma State
1969
   Bob Clark, Los Angeles State
1970
   John Mahaffey, Houston
1971
   Ben Crenshaw, Texas
1972
   Ben Crenshaw, Texas
   Tom Kite, Texas
1973
   Ben Crenshaw, Texas
1974
   Curtis Strange, Wake Forest
1975
   Jay Haas, Wake Forest
1976
   Scott Simpson, Southern California
1977

NCAA DIVISION II—TEAM CHAMPIONS

1963	Southwest Missouri
1964	Southern Illinois
1965	Middle Tennessee
1966	Chico State
1967	Lamar
1968	Lamar
1969	Northridge State
1970	Rollins
1971	New Orleans
1972	New Orleans
1973	Northridge State
1974	Northridge State
1975	California-Irvine

NCAA DIVISION II—INDIVIDUAL CHAMPIONS

1963
Gary Head, Middle Tennessee
1964
John Kurzynowski, Aquinas
1965
Larry Gilbert, Middle Tennessee
1966
Bob Smith, Sacramento State
1967
Larry Hinson, Middle Tennessee
1968
Mike Nugent, Lamar
1969
Mike Spang, Portland State
Corky Bassler, Northridge State
1970
Gary McCord, California-Riverside
1971
Stan Stopa, New Orleans
1972
Jim Hilderbrand, Ashland
1973
Paul Wise, Fullerton State
1974
Matt Bloom, California-Riverside
1975
Jerry Wisz, California-Irvine

CHARLIE BARTLETT AWARD—
Golf Writers Association of America

To a playing professional "for unselfish contributions to the betterment of society."
Established 1971.

1971   Billy Casper
1972   Lee Trevino
1973   Gary Player
1974   Chi Chi Rodriguez
1975   Gene Littler

GOLF WRITING AWARD—Brunswick-MacGregor, collected by Golf Writers Association of America.
Established 1965.

1965
News, Bruce Phillips, *Raleigh* (N.C.) *Times*

Feature, Jerry Izenberg, *Newark* (N.J.) *Star-Ledger*
1966
News, Sam Blair, *Dallas Morning News*

Feature, Phil Taylor, *Seattle Post Intelligencer*

Magazine, Gwilym S. Brown, *Sports Illustrated*
1967
News, Art Spander, *San Francisco Chronicle*

Feature, Joe Schwendeman, *Philadelphia Evening Bulletin*

Magazine, Herbert Warren Wind, *Golf Digest*
1968
News, Jim Trinkle, *Fort Worth Star-Telegram*

Feature, Jack Patterson, *Akron* (Ohio) *Beacon-Journal*

Magazine, Cal Brown, *Golf Digest*
1969
News, Gene Roswell, *New York Post* (p.m.)
Jim Trinkle, *Fort Worth Star-Telegram* (a.m.)

Feature, Doug Mintline, *Flint* (Mich.) *Journal*

Magazine, Dan Jenkins, *Sports Illustrated*
1970
News, Blackie Sherrod, *Dallas Times-Herald* (p.m.)
Art Spander, *San Francisco Chronicle* (a.m.)

Feature, Sam Blair, *Dallas Morning News*
Magazine, Dan Jenkins, *Sports Illustrated*
1971
News, Jack Patterson, *Seattle Post* (p.m.)
Phil Taylor, *Akron* (Ohio) *Beacon Journal*

Feature, Maury White, *Des Moines Register*
Magazine, Dan Jenkins, *Sports Illustrated*
1972
News, Fred Russell, *Nashville Banner* (p.m.)
D. L. Stewart, *Dayton Herald-Journal* (a.m.)

Feature, Bill Beck, *St. Louis Post-Dispatch*
Magazine, Lee Mueller, *Golf*

1973
News, Blackie Sherrod, *Dallas Times-Herald* (p.m.)
D. L. Stewart, *Dayton Herald-Journal* (a.m.)
Feature, Dave Nightingale, *Chicago Daily News*
Magazine, Jim Trinkle, *Golf*
1974
News, Bill Beck, *St. Louis Post-Dispatch* (p.m.)
Marv Moss, *Montreal Gazette* (a.m.)
Feature, Blackie Sherrod, *Dallas Times-Herald*
Magazine, Ross Goodner, *Golf*

JOE GRAFFIS AWARD—National Golf Foundation
For contributions to junior golf education.
Established 1970.
1970 Ellen Griffin
1971 Barbara Rotuig
1972 Les Bolstad
1973 no award
1974 Opal Hill
1975 Patty Berg

BEN HOGAN AWARD—Golf Writers Association of America
For someone who has continued to be active in golf despite a physical handicap.
Established 1954.
1954 Babe Zaharias
1955 Ed Furgol
1956 Dwight Eisenhower
1957 Clint Russell
1958 Dale Bourisseau
1959 Charlie Boswell
1960 Skip Alexander
1961 Horton Smith
1962 Jimmy Nichols
1963 Bobby Nichols
1964 Bob Morgan
1965 Ernest Jones
1966 Ken Venturi
1967 Warren Pease
1968 Shirley Englehorn
1969 Curtis Person
1970 Joe Lazaro
1971 Larry Hinson
1972 Ruth Jessen
1973 Gene Littler

1974 Gay Brewer
1975 Patty Berg

BOB JONES AWARD—United States Golf Association
This award "commemorates the vast contributions to the cause of fair play and sportsmanlike conduct made by Bob Jones both during and after his competitive career. While sportsmanlike conduct may be difficult to define, the USGA has in mind the demonstration of personal qualities esteemed in sport: fair play, self control and perhaps self denial, generosity of spirit toward an opponent or toward the game as a whole, and unselfishness." The very award for Ilie Nastase if he had been a golfer instead of a tennis player.
Established 1955.
1955 Francis Ouimet
1956 William C. Campbell
1957 Mrs. Mildred D. Zaharias
1958 Miss Margaret Curtis
1959 Findlay S. Douglas
1960 Charles Evans, Jr.
1961 Joseph B. Carr
1962 Horton Smith
1963 Miss Patty Berg
1964 Charles R. Coe
1965 Mrs. Glenna Collett Vare
1966 Gary Player
1967 Richard S. Tufts
1968 Robert B. Dickson
1969 Gerald H. Micklem
1970 Roberto De Vicenzo
1971 Arnold Palmer
1972 Michael Bonallack
1973 Gene Littler
1974 Byron Nelson
1975 Jack Nicklaus

MOST BEAUTIFUL GOLFER—*Golf Digest* Magazine
So far no male winners. Johnny Miller is kind of cute.
Established 1954.
1954
Dimmie Thompson, Greenville, S.C.
1955
Betty Jane Martinez, San Antonio, Tex.
Paula Ann West, Sacramento, Calif.
1956
Barbara Williams, Richmond, Calif.

1957
Judy Easterbrook, Peoria, Ill.
1958
Sally Bergman Robb, Cleveland, Ohio
1959
Elaine Woodman, Wichita, Kans.
1960
Florence Zupnik, Washington, D.C.
1961
Sue Dobson, Macomb, Ill.
1962
Carol Sorenson, Janesville, Wis.
1963
Nancy Albert, Trenton, N.J.
1964
Marlene Floyd, Fayetteville, N.C.
1965
Laura Anne MacIvor, Fort Walton Beach, Fla.
1966
Sharron Moran, Carlsbad, Calif.
1967
Margo Fletcher Brinkley, Raleigh, N.C.
1968
Carolyn Finley, Huntington Beach, Calif.
1969
Priscilla Sauter Grosch, Switzerland
1970
Jane Fassinger, New Wilmington, Pa.
1971
Laura Baugh, Long Beach, Calif.
1972
Jonya Stapp, Miami, Okla.
1973
Debbie De Agostine, Walkill, N.Y.
1974
Mary Cushing, San Antonio, Tex.
1975
Beth Boozer, Lawrence, Kans.

MOST IMPROVED GOLFERS—
MEN PROS—*Golf Digest* Magazine
Established 1953.

1953	Doug Ford
1954	Bob Toski
1955	Mike Souchak
1956	Dow Finsterwald
1957	Paul Harney
1958	Ernie Vossler
1959	Don Whitt
1960	Don January

1961	Gary Player
1962	Bobby Nichols
1963	Tony Lema
1964	Ken Venturi
1965	Randy Glover
1966	Gay Brewer
1967	Dave Stockton
1968	Bob Lunn
1969	Dave Hill
1970	Dick Lotz
1971	Jerry Heard
1972	Jim Jamieson
1973	Tom Weiskopf
1974	Tom Watson
1975	Pat Fitzsimons

MOST IMPROVED GOLFERS—
WOMEN PROS—*Golf Digest* Magazine
Established 1954.

1954	Beverly Hanson
1955	Fay Crocker
1956	Marlene Hagge
1957	Mickey Wright
1958	Bonnie Randolph
1959	Murle MacKenzie
1960	Kathy Whitworth
1961	Mary Lena Faulk
1962	Kathy Whitworth
1963	Marilynn Smith
1964	Judy Torluemke
1965	Carol Mann
1966	Gloria Ehret
1967	Susie Maxwell
1968	Gerda Whalen
1969	Donna Caponi
1970	Jane Blalock
1971	Jane Blalock
1972	Betty Burfeindt
1973	Mary Mills
1974	JoAnne Carner
1975	JoAnn Washam

BYRON NELSON AWARD—*Golf Digest* Magazine
For the most victories on the Professional Golfers Association tour.
Established 1954.

1955	Cary Middlecoff
1956	Ted Kroll
1957	Arnold Palmer
1958	Ken Venturi
1959	Gene Littler
1960	Arnold Palmer
1961	Arnold Palmer

1962	Arnold Palmer
1963	Arnold Palmer
1964	Jack Nicklaus
1965	Jack Nicklaus
1966	Billy Casper
1967	Jack Nicklaus
1968	Billy Casper
1969	Dave Hill
1970	Billy Casper
1971	Lee Trevino
1972	Jack Nicklaus
1973	Jack Nicklaus
1974	Johnny Miller
1975	Jack Nicklaus

PGA PLAYER OF THE YEAR—The Professional Golfers Association

At one time this award was decided by PGA members and sportswriters around the country. Since 1969 the PGA's executive committee has decided the winner based on playing record, scoring average and "character."

Established 1948.

1948	Ben Hogan
1949	Sam Snead
1950	Ben Hogan
1951	Ben Hogan
1952	Julius Boros
1953	Ben Hogan
1954	Ed Furgol
1955	Doug Ford
1956	Jack Burke, Jr.
1957	Dick Mayer
1958	Dow Finsterwald
1959	Art Wall
1960	Arnold Palmer
1961	Jerry Barber
1962	Arnold Palmer
1963	Julius Boros
1964	Ken Venturi
1965	Dave Marr
1966	Billy Casper
1967	Jack Nicklaus
1968	no award
1969	Orville Moody
1970	Billy Casper
1971	Lee Trevino
1972	Jack Nicklaus
1973	Jack Nicklaus
1974	Johnny Miller
1975	Jack Nicklaus
1976	Jack Nicklaus

PGA PROFESSIONAL OF THE YEAR AWARD—The Professional Golfers Association

To a club professional who, among other things, has promoted junior golf, encouraged ladies' play, shown concern for caddie welfare, and has given service to his club.

Established 1955.

1955
Bill Gordon, Tam O'Shanter Country Club, Chicago, Ill.

1956
Harry Shepard, Mark Twain Community Golf Club, Elmira, N.Y.

1957
Dugan Aycock, Lexington Country Club, Lexington, N.C.

1958
Harry Pezzullo, Mission Hills Golf Club, Northbrook, Ill.

1959
Eddie Duino, San Jose Country Club, San Jose, Calif.

1960
Warren Orlick, Tam O'Shanter Country Club, Orchard Lake, Mich.

1961
Don Padgett, Green Hills Country Club, Selma, Ind.

1962
Tom Lo Presti, Haggin Oaks Golf Club, Sacramento, Calif.

1963
Bruce Herd, Flossmoor Country Club, Flossmoor, Ill.

1964
Lyle Wehrman, Merced Golf and Country Club, Merced, Calif.

1965
Hubby Habjan, Onwentsia Club, Lake Forest, Ill.

1966
Bill Strausbaugh, Jr., Turf Valley Country Club, Ellicott City, Md.

1967
Ernie Vossler, Quail Creek Country Club, Oklahoma City, Okla.

1968
Hardy Loudermilk, Oak Hills Country Club, San Antonio, Tex.

1969
A. Hubert Smith, Arnold Center Country Club, Tullahoma, Tenn.

1969
  Wally Mund, Midland Hills Country
  Club, St. Paul, Minn.
1970
  Grady Shumate, Tanglewood Golf
  Club, Clemmons, N.C.
1971
  Ross Collins, Dallas A.C.C.C.,
  Dallas, Tex.
1972
  Howard Morrette, Twin Lakes
  Country Club, Kent, Ohio
1973
  Warren Smith, Cherry Hills Country
  Club, Englewood, Colo.
1974
  Paul Harney, Paul Harney's Golf
  Club, Hatchville, Mass.
1975
  Walker Inman, Jr., Scioto Country
  Club, Columbus, Ohio
1976
  Ron Letellier, Cold Spring Country
  Club, Cold Spring Harbor, N.Y.

PLAYER OF THE YEAR—Golf Writers Association of America
  Speaks for itself.
  Established 1968.
1968   Billy Casper
1969   Orville Moody
1970   Billy Casper
1971   Lee Trevino
1972   Jack Nicklaus
       Kathy Whitworth
1973   Tom Weiskopf
       Kathy Whitworth
1974   Johnny Miller
       JoAnne Carner
1975   Jack Nicklaus
       Sandra Palmer

RICHARDSON AWARD—Golf Writers Association of America
  For contributions to golf.
  Established 1948.
1948   Robert A. Hudson
1949   Scotty Fessenden
1950   Bing Crosby
1951   Richard Tufts
1952   Chick Evans
1953   Bob Hope
1954   Babe Zaharias
1955   Dwight Eisenhower
1956   George S. May

1957   Francis Ouimet
1958   Bob Jones
1959   Patty Berg
1960   Fred Corcoran
1961   Joseph C. Dey, Jr.
1962   Walter Hagen
1963   Joe and Herb Graffis
1964   Cliff Roberts
1965   Gene Sarazen
1966   Robert E. Harlow
1967   Max Elbin
1968   Charles Bartlett
1969   Arnold Palmer
1970   Roberto de Vicenzo
1971   Lincoln Werden
1972   Leo Fraser
1973   Ben Hogan
1974   Byron Nelson
1975   Gary Player

ROOKIE OF THE YEAR—*Golf Digest* Magazine
  Established 1957.
1957   Ken Venturi
1958   Bob Goalby
1959   Joe Campbell
1960   Mason Rudolph
1961   Jacky Cupit
1962   Jack Nicklaus
1963   Raymond Floyd
1964   R. H. Sikes
1965   Homero Blancas
1966   John Schlee
1967   Lee Trevino
1968   Bob Murphy
1969   Grier Jones
1970   Ted Hayes, Jr.
1971   Hubert Green
1972   Lanny Wadkins
1973   Tom Kite
1974   Ben Crenshaw
1975   Roger Maltbie

HORTON SMITH AWARD—The Professional Golfers Association
  For contributions by a professional to golf education.
  Established 1965.
1965
  Emil Beck, Black River Country
  Club, Port Huron, Mich.
1966
  Gene C. Mason, Columbia-
  Edgewater Country Club, Portland,
  Ore.

1967
Donald E. Fischesser, Evansville
Country Club, Evansville, Ind.
1968
R. William Clarke, Hillendale
Country Club, Phoenix, Md.
1969
Paul Hahn, Miami, Fla.
1970
Joe Walser, Oklahoma City Country
Club, Oklahoma City, Okla.
1971
Irving Schloss, Dunedin, Fla.
1972
John Budd, New Port Richey, Fla.
1973
George Aulbach, Pecan Valley
Country Club, San Antonio, Tex.
1974
Bill Hardy, Chevy Chase Club,
Chevy Chase, Md.
1975
John P. Henrich, Elma Meadows
Golf Club, Elma, N.Y.
1976
Jim Bailey, Adams Country Golf
Course, Brighton, Colo.

VARDON TROPHY AVERAGES—
The Professional Golfers Association
To be eligible, a golfer must compete in eighty official tournament rounds, and must have the lowest strokes-per-round record in the tournament year. Established 1937.

1937	Harry Cooper
1938	Sam Snead
1939	Byron Nelson
1940	Ben Hogan
1941	Ben Hogan
1942	no award
1943	no award
1944	no award
1945	no award
1946	no award
1947	Jimmy Demaret
1948	Ben Hogan
1949	Sam Snead
1950	Sam Snead
1951	Lloyd Mangrum
1952	Jackie Burke
1953	Lloyd Mangrum
1954	Dutch Harrison
1955	Sam Snead
1956	Cary Middlecoff

1957	Dow Finsterwald
1958	Bob Rosburg
1959	Art Wall
1960	Billy Casper
1961	Arnold Palmer
1962	Arnold Palmer
1963	Billy Casper
1964	Arnold Palmer
1965	Billy Casper
1966	Billy Casper
1967	Arnold Palmer
1968	Billy Casper
1969	Dave Hill
1970	Lee Trevino
1971	Lee Trevino
1972	Lee Trevino
1973	Bruce Crampton
1974	Lee Trevino

WOMEN ROOKIES OF THE YEAR
—*Golf Digest* Magazine
Established 1962.

1962	Mary Mills
1963	Cliff. Ann Creed
1964	Susie Maxwell
1965	Margee Masters
1966	Jan Ferraris
1967	Sharron Moran
1968	Sandra Post
1969	Jane Blalock
1970	JoAnne Carner
1971	Sally Little
1972	J. Bourassa
1973	Laura Baugh
1974	Jan Stephenson
1975	Amy Alcott

MICKEY WRIGHT AWARD—*Golf Digest* Magazine
For the most victories on the Ladies Professional Golf Association tour. Established 1955.

1955	Patty Berg
1956	Marlene Hagge
1957	Patty Berg
1958	Mickey Wright
1959	Betsy Rawls
1960	Mickey Wright
1961	Mickey Wright
1962	Mickey Wright
1963	Mickey Wright
1964	Mickey Wright
1965	Kathy Whitworth
1966	Kathy Whitworth
1967	Kathy Whitworth

1968	Kathy Whitworth
1969	Carol Mann
1970	Shirley Englehorn
1971	Kathy Whitworth
1972	Kathy Whitworth
1973	Kathy Whitworth
1974	JoAnne Carner
1975	Sandra Haynie

HORSE RACING

THOROUGHBRED

KENTUCKY DERBY WINNERS

1900	Lieut. Gibson
1901	His Eminence
1902	Alan-a-Dale
1903	Judge Himes
1904	Elwood
1905	Agile
1906	Sir Huon
1907	Pink Star
1908	Stone Street
1909	Wintergreen
1910	Donau
1911	Meridian
1912	Worth
1913	Donerail
1914	Old Rosebud
1915	Regret
1916	George Smith
1917	Omar Khayyam
1918	Exterminator
1919	Sir Barton
1920	Paul Jones
1921	Behave Yourself
1922	Morvich
1923	Zev
1924	Black Gold
1925	Flying Ebony
1926	Bubbling Over
1927	Whiskery
1928	Reigh Count
1929	Clyde Van Dusen
1930	Gallant Fox
1931	Twenty Grand
1932	Burgoo King
1933	Brokers Tip
1934	Cavalcade

1935	Omaha
1936	Bold Venture
1937	War Admiral
1938	Lawrin
1939	Johnstown
1940	Gallahadion
1941	Whirlaway
1942	Shut Out
1943	Count Fleet
1944	Pensive
1945	Hoop, Jr.
1946	Assault
1947	Jet Pilot
1948	Citation
1949	Ponder
1950	Middleground
1951	Count Turf
1952	Hill Gail
1953	Dark Star
1954	Determine
1955	Swaps
1956	Needles
1957	Iron Liege
1958	Tim Tam
1959	Tomy Lee
1960	Venetian Way
1961	Carry Back
1962	Decidedly
1963	Chateaugay
1964	Northern Dancer
1965	Lucky Debonair
1966	Kauai King
1967	Proud Clarion
1968	Forward Pass
1969	Majestic Prince
1970	Dust Commander
1971	Canonero II
1972	Riva Ridge
1973	Secretariat
1974	Cannonade
1975	Foolish Pleasure
1976	Bold Forbes
1977	Seattle Slew

PREAKNESS STAKES WINNERS

1900	Hindus
1901	The Parader
1902	Old England
1903	Flocarline
1904	Bryn Mawr
1905	Cairngorm
1906	Whimsical
1907	Don Enrique
1908	Royal Tourist

1909	Effendi
1910	Layminster
1911	Watervale
1912	Colonel Holloway
1913	Buskin
1914	Holiday
1915	Rhine Maiden
1916	Damrosch
1917	Kalitan
1918	War Cloud
	Jack Hare, Jr.
1919	Sir Barton
1920	Man o' War
1921	Broomspun
1922	Pillory
1923	Vigil
1924	Nellie Morse
1925	Coventry
1926	Display
1927	Bostonian
1928	Victorian
1929	Dr. Freeland
1930	Gallant Fox
1931	Mate
1932	Burgoo King
1933	Head Play
1934	High Quest
1935	Omaha
1936	Bold Venture
1937	War Admiral
1938	Dauber
1939	Challedon
1940	Bimelech
1941	Whirlaway
1942	Alsab
1943	Count Fleet
1944	Pensive
1945	Polynesian
1946	Assault
1947	Faultless
1948	Citation
1949	Capot
1950	Hill Prince
1951	Bold
1952	Blue Man
1953	Native Dancer
1954	Hasty Road
1955	Nashua
1956	Fabius
1957	Bold Ruler
1958	Tim Tam
1959	Royal Orbit
1960	Bally Ache
1961	Carry Back
1962	Greek Money

1963	Candy Spots
1964	Northern Dancer
1965	Tom Rolfe
1966	Kauai King
1967	Damascus
1968	Forward Pass
1969	Majestic Prince
1970	Personality
1971	Canonero II
1972	Bee Bee Bee
1973	Secretariat
1974	Little Current
1975	Master Derby
1976	Elocutionist

BELMONT STAKES WINNERS

1900	Ildrim
1901	Commando
1902	Masterman
1903	Africander
1904	Delhi
1905	Tanya
1906	Burgomaster
1907	Peter Pan
1908	Colin
1909	Joe Madden
1910	Sweep
1913	Prince Eugene
1914	Luke McLuke
1915	The Finn
1916	Friar Rock
1917	Hourless
1918	Johren
1919	Sir Barton
1920	Man o' War
1921	Gray Lag
1922	Pillory
1923	Zev
1924	Mad Play
1925	American Flag
1926	Crusader
1927	Chance Shot
1928	Vito
1929	Blue Larkspur
1930	Gallant Fox
1931	Twenty Grand
1932	Faireno
1933	Hurryoff
1934	Peace Chance
1935	Omaha
1936	Granville
1937	War Admiral
1938	Pasteurized
1939	Johnstown

1940	Bimelech
1941	Whirlaway
1942	Shut Out
1943	Count Fleet
1944	Bounding Home
1945	Pavot
1946	Assault
1947	Phalanx
1948	Citation
1949	Capot
1950	Middleground
1951	Counterpoint
1952	One Count
1953	Native Dancer
1954	High Gun
1955	Nashua
1956	Needles
1957	Gallant Man
1958	Cavan
1959	Sword Dancer
1960	Celtic Ash
1961	Sherluck
1962	Jaipur
1963	Chateaugay
1964	Quadrangle
1965	Hail to All
1966	Amberoid
1967	Damascus
1968	Stage Door Johnny
1969	Arts and Letters
1970	High Echelon
1971	Pass Catcher
1972	Riva Ridge
1973	Secretariat
1974	Little Current
1975	Avatar
1976	Bold Forbes
1977	Seattle Slew

TOP MONEY WINNERS (HORSE)

1920	Man O'War	$166,140
1921	Morvich	115,234
1922	Pillory	95,654
1923	Zev	272,008
1924	Sarazen	95,640
1925	Pompey	121,630
1926	Crusader	166,033
1927	Anita Peabody	111,905
1928	High Strung	153,590
1929	Blue Larkspur	153,450
1930	Gallant Fox	308,275
1931	Top Flight	219,000
1932	Gusto	145,940
1933	Singing Wood	88,050

1934	Cavalcade	111,235
1935	Omaha	142,255
1936	Granville	110,295
1937	Seabiscuit	168,580
1938	Stagehand	189,710
1939	Challedon	184,535
1940	Bimelech	110,005
1941	Whirlaway	272,386
1942	Shut Out	238,872
1943	Count Fleet	174,055
1944	Pavot	179,040
1945	Busher	273,735
1946	Assault	424,195
1947	Armed	376,325
1948	Citation	709,470
1949	Ponder	321,825
1950	Noor	346,940
1951	Counterpoint	250,525
1952	Crafty Admiral	277,225
1953	Native Dancer	513,425
1954	Determine	328,700
1955	Nashua	752,550
1956	Needles	440,850
1957	Round Table	600,383
1958	Round Table	662,780
1959	Sword Dancer	537,004
1960	Bally Ache	455,045
1961	Carry Back	565,349
1962	Never Bend	402,969
1963	Candy Spots	604,481
1964	Gun Bow	580,100
1965	Buckpasser	568,096
1966	Buckpasser	669,078
1967	Damascus	817,941
1968	Forward Pass	546,674
1969	Arts and Letters	555,604
1970	Personality	444,049
1971	Riva Ridge	503,263
1972	Droll Role	471,633
1973	Secretariat	860,404
1974	Chris Evert	551,063
1975	Foolish Pleasure	716,278

TOP MONEY WINNERS (JOCKEY)

1946	Ted Atkinson	$1,036,825
1947	Doug Dodson	1,429,949
1948	Eddie Arcaro	1,686,230
1949	Steve Brooks	1,316,817
1950	Eddie Arcaro	1,410,160
1951	Willie Shoemaker	1,329,890
1952	Eddie Arcaro	1,859,591
1953	Willie Shoemaker	1,784,187
1954	Willie Shoemaker	1,876,760
1955	Eddie Arcaro	1,864,796

1956	Billy Hartack	2,343,955
1957	Billy Hartack	3,060,501
1958	Willie Shoemaker	2,961,693
1959	Willie Shoemaker	2,843,133
1960	Willie Shoemaker	2,123,961
1961	Willie Shoemaker	2,690,819
1962	Willie Shoemaker	2,916,844
1963	Willie Shoemaker	2,526,925
1964	Willie Shoemaker	2,649,553
1965	Braulio Baeza	2,582,702
1966	Braulio Baeza	2,951,022
1967	Braulio Baeza	3,088,888
1968	Braulio Baeza	2,835,108
1969	Jorge Velasquez	2,542,305
1970	Laffit Pincay, Jr.	2,626,526
1971	Laffit Pincay, Jr.	3,784,377
1972	Laffit Pincay, Jr.	3,225,827
1973	Laffit Pincay, Jr.	4,093,492
1974	Laffit Pincay, Jr.	4,251,060
1975	Braulio Baeza	3,695,198

TRIPLE CROWN WINNERS

1919	Sir Barton
1930	Gallant Fox
1935	Omaha
1937	War Admiral
1941	Whirlaway
1943	Count Fleet
1946	Assault
1948	Citation
1973	Secretariat
1977	Seattle Slew

HARNESS RACING

THE HAMBLETONIAN WINNERS

1926	Guy McKinney
1927	Isola's Worthy
1928	Spencer
1929	Walter Dear
1930	Hanover's Bertha
1931	Calumet Butler
1932	The Marchioness
1933	Mary Reynolds
1934	Lord Jim
1935	Greyhound
1936	Rosalind
1937	Shirley Hanover
1938	McLin Hanover
1939	Peter Astra
1940	Spencer Scott
1941	Bill Gallon
1942	The Ambassador

1943	Volo Song
1944	Yankee Maid
1945	Titan Hanover
1946	Chestertown
1947	Hoot Mon
1948	Demon Hanover
1949	Miss Tilly
1950	Lusty Song
1951	Mainliner
1952	Sharp Note
1953	Helicopter
1954	Newport Dream
1955	Scott Frost
1956	The Intruder
1957	Hickory Smoke
1958	Emily's Pride
1959	Diller Hanover
1960	Blaze Hanover
1961	Harlan Dean
1962	A. C.'s Viking
1963	Speedy Scot
1964	Ayres
1965	Egyptian Candor
1966	Kerry Way
1967	Speedy Streak
1968	Nevele Pride
1969	Lindys Pride
1970	Timothy T.
1971	Speedy Crown
1972	Super Bowl
1973	Flirth
1974	Christopher T.
1975	Bonefish
1976	Steve Lobell

KENTUCKY FUTURITY (TROTTERS)

1900	Fereno
1901	Peter Sterling
1902	Nella Jay
1903	Sadie Mac
1904	Grace Bond
1905	Miss Adbell
1906	Siliko
1907	General Watts
1908	The Harvester
1909	Baroness Virginia
1910	Grace
1911	Peter Thompson
1912	Manrico B.
1913	Etawah
1914	Peter Volo
1915	Mary Putney
1916	Volga

1917	The Real Lady
1918	Nella Dillon
1919	Periscope
1920	Arion Guy
1921	Rose Scott
1922	Lee Worthy
1923	Ethelinda
1924	Mr. McElwyn
1925	Aileen Guy
1926	Guy McKinney
1927	Iosola's Worthy
1928	Spencer
1929	Walter Dear
1930	Hanover's Bertha
1931	Protector
1932	The Marchioness
1933	Meda
1934	Princess Peg
1935	Lawrence Hanover
1936	Rosalind
1937	Twilight Song
1938	McLin Hanover
1939	Peter Astra
1940	Spencer Scott
1941	Bill Gallon
1942–1945	no competition
1946	Victory Song
1947	Hoot Mon
1948	Egan Hanover
1949	Bangaway
1950	Star's Pride
1951	Ford Hanover
1952	Sharp Note
1953	Kimberly Kid
1954	Harlan
1955	Scott Frost
1956	Nimble Colby
1957	Cassin Hanover
1958	Emily's Pride
1959	Diller Hanover
1960	Elaine Rodney
1961	Duke Rodney
1962	Safe Mission
1963	Speedy Scot
1964	Ayres
1965	Armbro Flight
1966	Governor Armbro
1967	Speed Model
1968	Nevele Pride
1969	Lindys Pride
1970	Timothy T.
1971	Savoir
1972	Super Bowl
1973	Arnie Almahurst
1974	Waymaker

1975	Noble Rogue

THE YONKERS FUTURITY WINNERS (TROTTERS)

1955	Scott Frost
1956	Add Hanover
1957	Hoot Song
1958	Spunky Hanover
1959	John A. Hanover
1960	Duke of Decatur
1961	Duke Rodney
1962	A. C.'s Viking
1963	Speedy Scot
1964	Ayres
1965	Noble Victory
1966	Polaris
1967	Pomp
1968	Nevele Pride
1969	Lindys Pride
1970	Victory Star
1971	Quick Pride
1972	Super Bowl
1973	Tamerlane
1974	Spitfire Hanover
1975	Surefire Hanover

THE LITTLE BROWN JUG WINNERS (PACERS)

1946	Ensign Hanover
1947	Forbes Chief
1948	Knight Dream
1949	Good Time
1950	Dudley Hanover
1951	Tar Heel
1952	Meadow Rice
1953	Keystoner
1954	Adios Harry
1955	Quick Chief
1956	Noble Adios
1957	Torpid
1958	Shadow Wave
1959	Adios Butler
1960	Bullet Hanover
1961	Henry T. Adios
1962	Lehigh Hanover
1963	Overtrick
1964	Vicar Hanover
1965	Bret Hanover
1966	Romeo Hanover
1967	Best of All
1968	Rum Customer
1969	Laverne Hanover
1970	Most Happy Fella

1971	Nansemond
1972	Strike Out
1973	Melvins Woe
1974	Armbro Omaha
1975	Seatrain

THE WILLIAM H. CANE
FUTURITY WINNERS
(PACERS)

1955	Quick Chief
1956	Noble Adios
1957	Torpid
1958	Raider Frost
1959	Adios Butler
1960	Countess Adios
1961	Cold Front
1962	Ranger Knight
1963	Meadow Skipper
1964	Race Time
1965	Bret Hanover
1966	Romeo Hanover
1967	Meadow Paige
1968	Rum Customer
1969	Kat Byrd
1970	Most Happy Fella
1971	Albatross
1972	Hilarious Way
1973	Smog
1974	Royden Hanover
1975	Nero
1976	Keystone Ore

THE MESSENGER STAKE
WINNERS (PACERS)

1956	Belle Acton
1957	Meadow Lands
1958	O'Brien Hanover
1959	Adios Butler
1960	Countess Adios
1961	Adios Don
1962	Thor Hanover
1963	Overtrick
1964	Race Time
1965	Bret Hanover
1966	Romeo Hanover
1967	Romulus Hanover
1968	Rum Customer
1969	Bye Bye Sam
1970	Most Happy Fella
1971	Albatross
1972	Silent Majority
1973	Valiant Bret
1974	Armbro Omaha

1975	Bret's Champ

LEADING MONEY WINNERS
(TROTTERS)

1946	Victory Song	$43,608
1947	Hoot Mon	56,811
1948	Egan Hanover	67,567
1949	Bangaway	74,439
1950	Proximity	87,175
1951	Pronto Don	80,850
1952	Sharp Note	101,625
1953	Newport Dream	94,933
1954	Katie Key	84,867
1955	Scott Frost	186,101
1956	Scott Frost	85,851
1957	Hoot Song	114,877
1958	Emily's Pride	118,830
1959	Diller Hanover	149,897
1960	Su Mac Lad	159,662
1961	Su Mac Lad	245,750
1962	Duke Rodney	206,113
1963	Speedy Scot	244,403
1964	Speedy Scot	235,710
1965	Dartmouth	252,348
1966	Noble Victory	210,696
1967	Carlisle	231,243
1968	Nevele Pride	427,440
1969	Lindy's Pride	323,997
1970	Fresh Yankee	359,002
1971	Fresh Yankee	293,950
1972	Super Bowl	437,108
1973	Spartan Hanover	262,023
1974	Delmonica Hanover	252,165
1975	Savoir	351,385

LEADING MONEY WINNERS
(PACERS)

1946	Ensign Hanover	$34,368
1947	April Star	51,750
1948	Dr. Stanton	50,550
1949	Good Time	58,766
1950	Scottish Pence	73,387
1951	Tar Heel	66,629
1952	Good Time	110,299
1953	Keystoner	59,131
1954	Red Sails	66,615
1955	Adios Harry	98,900
1956	Adios Harry	129,912
1957	Torpid	113,982
1958	Belle Acton	167,887
1959	Bye Bye Byrd	199,933
1960	Bye Bye Byrd	187,612
1961	Adios Butler	180,250

1962	Henry T. Adios	220,302
1963	Overtrick	208,833
1964	Race Time	199,292
1965	Bret Hanover	341,784
1966	Bret Hanover	407,534
1967	Romulus Hanover	277,636
1968	Rum Customer	355,618
1969	Overcall	373,150
1970	Most Happy Fella	387,239
1971	Albatross	558,009
1972	Albatross	459,921
1973	Sir Dalrae	307,354
1974	Armbro Omaha	345,146
1975	Silk Stockings	336,312

LEADING MONEY WINNERS (DRIVERS)

1949	Clint Hodgins	$184,108
1950	Delvin Miller	306,813
1951	John Simpson, Sr.	333,136
1952	William Haughton	311,728
1953	William Haughton	374,527
1954	William Haughton	415,577
1955	William Haughton	599,455
1956	William Haughton	572,945
1957	William Haughton	586,950
1958	William Haughton	816,659
1959	William Haughton	711,435
1960	Delvin Miller	567,282
1961	Stanley Dancer	674,723
1962	Stanley Dancer	760,343
1963	William Haughton	790,086
1964	Stanley Dancer	1,051,538
1965	William Haughton	889,943
1966	Stanley Dancer	1,218,403
1967	William Haughton	1,305,773
1968	William Haughton	1,654,172
1969	Delmer Insko	1,635,463
1970	Herve Filion	1,647,837
1971	Herve Filion	1,915,945
1972	Herve Filion	2,473,265
1973	Herve Filion	2,233,302
1974	Herve Filion	3,431,366
1975	Carmine Abbatiella	2,275,093

HORSEMAN AWARD—The Horseman & Fair World

In the beginning, which was 1956 until 1969, the only winners of this award for "those who have meant the most to the harness racing world" were drivers and trainers. To give others a shot at the silver Julep Cup set, the subscribers of *Horseman & Fair World,* "the oldest weekly turf publication devoted to the trotting and pacing horse," no longer find drivers and trainers on their ballots. Established 1956.

1956
  Delvin Miller, leading trainer-driver and breeder
1957
  John Simpson, Sr., leading trainer-driver, later president of Hanover Shoe Farms, largest Standardbred farm
1958
  William Haughton, trainer-driver who has won more purse money in career than any other
1959
  Joe O'Brien, trainer-driver most noted for producing speed
1960
  Clint Hodgins, leading trainer-driver and breeder
1961
  Frank Ervin, leading trainer-driver
1962
  Stanley Dancer, leading trainer-driver
1963
  Ralph Baldwin, leading trainer-driver
1964
  Frank Ervin
1965
  Frank Ervin
1966
  Robert Farrington, leading race-winning trainer-driver
1967
  William Haughton
1968
  Stanley Dancer
1969
  Mr. and Mrs. Frederick Van Lennep, owners of Castleton Farm, home of numerous champions since 1793
1970
  Stanley F. Bergstein, executive of Harness Tracks of America and U.S. Trotting Assn., publicity innovator
1971
  William R. Hayes II, head of Du Quoin State Fair, home of trotting's classic, The Hambletonian

1972
Mr. and Mrs. H. Willis Nichols,
owners of Walnut Hall Farm, top
breeding farm, in the same family
since 1892
1973
E. Roland Harriman, co-founder
U.S. Trotting Assn., leading owner
and breeder
1974
Elgin Armstrong, head of Armstrong
Brothers farm in Ontario, one of
sports greatest producing farms
1975
Henry C. Thomson, co-founder of
society that sponsors sport's top
pacing classic, The Little Brown Jug
1976
Norman Woolworth and David
Johnston, co-owners of Stoner Creek
Stud, a farm founded in 1964 but
already home of sport's most
expensive yearlings

ICE HOCKEY

STANLEY CUP WINNERS
1917–1918	Toronto Arenas
1918–1919	tournament not held
1919–1920	Ottawa Senators
1920–1921	Ottawa Senators
1921–1922	Toronto St. Pats
1922–1923	Ottawa Senators
1923–1924	Montreal Canadiens
1924–1925	Victoria Cougars
1925–1926	Montreal Maroons
1926–1927	Ottawa Senators
1927–1928	New York Rangers
1928–1929	Boston Bruins
1929–1930	Montreal Canadiens
1930–1931	Montreal Canadiens
1931–1932	Toronto Maple Leafs
1932–1933	New York Rangers
1933–1934	Chicago Black Hawks
1934–1935	Montreal Maroons
1935–1936	Detroit Red Wings
1936–1937	Detroit Red Wings
1937–1938	Chicago Black Hawks
1938–1939	Boston Bruins
1939–1940	New York Rangers
1940–1941	Boston Bruins
1941–1942	Toronto Maple Leafs
1942–1943	Detroit Red Wings
1943–1944	Montreal Canadiens
1944–1945	Toronto Maple Leafs
1945–1946	Montreal Canadiens
1946–1947	Toronto Maple Leafs
1947–1948	Toronto Maple Leafs
1948–1949	Toronto Maple Leafs
1949–1950	Detroit Red Wings
1950–1951	Toronto Maple Leafs
1951–1952	Detroit Red Wings
1952–1953	Montreal Canadiens
1953–1954	Detroit Red Wings
1954–1955	Detroit Red Wings
1955–1956	Montreal Canadiens
1956–1957	Montreal Canadiens
1957–1958	Montreal Canadiens
1958–1959	Montreal Canadiens
1959–1960	Montreal Canadiens
1960–1961	Chicago Black Hawks
1961–1962	Toronto Maple Leafs
1962–1963	Toronto Maple Leafs
1963–1964	Toronto Maple Leafs
1964–1965	Montreal Canadiens
1965–1966	Montreal Canadiens
1966–1967	Toronto Maple Leafs
1967–1968	Montreal Canadiens
1968–1969	Montreal Canadiens
1969–1970	Boston Bruins
1970–1971	Montreal Canadiens
1971–1972	Boston Bruins
1972–1973	Montreal Canadiens
1973–1974	Philadelphia Flyers
1974–1975	Philadelphia Flyers
1975–1976	Montreal Canadiens
1976–1977	Montreal Canadiens

HART MEMORIAL TROPHY WINNERS—Most Valuable Player
1924
Frank Nighbor, Ottawa Senators
1925
Billy Burch, Hamilton
1926
Nels Stewart, Montreal Maroons
1927
Herb Gardiner, Montreal Canadiens
1928
Howie Morenz Montreal Canadiens
1929
Ray Worters, New York Americans
1930
Nels Stewart, Montreal Maroons
1931
Howie Morenz, Montreal Canadiens

1932
Howie Morenz, Montreal Canadiens
1933
Eddie Shore, Boston Bruins
1934
Aurel Joliat, Montreal Canadiens
1935
Eddie Shore, Boston Bruins
1936
Eddie Shore, Boston Bruins
1937
Babe Siebert, Montreal Canadiens
1938
Eddie Shore, Boston Bruins
1939
Toe Blake, Montreal Canadiens
1940
Ebbie Goodfellow, Detroit Red
Wings
1941
Bill Cowley, Boston Bruins
1942
Tommy Anderson, New York
Americans
1943
Bill Cowley, Boston Bruins
1944
Babe Pratt, Toronto Maple Leafs
1945
Elmer Lach, Montreal Canadiens
1946
Max Bentley, Chicago Black Hawks
1947
Maurice Richard, Montreal
Canadiens
1948
Buddy O'Connor, New York Rangers
1949
Sid Abel, Detroit Red Wings
1950
Chuck Rayner, New York Rangers
1951
Milt Schmidt, Boston Bruins
1952
Gordie Howe, Detroit Red Wings
1953
Gordie Howe, Detroit Red Wings
1954
Al Rollins, Chicago Black Hawks
1955
Ted Kennedy, Toronto Maple Leafs
1956
Jean Beliveau, Montreal Canadiens
1957
Gordie Howe, Detroit Red Wings

1958
Gordie Howe, Detroit Red Wings
1959
Andy Bathgate, New York Rangers
1960
Gordie Howe, Detroit Red Wings
1961
Bernie Geoffrin, Montreal Canadiens
1962
Jacques Plante, Montreal Canadiens
1963
Gordie Howe, Detroit Red Wings
1964
Jean Beliveau, Montreal Canadiens
1965
Bobby Hull, Chicago Black Hawks
1966
Bobby Hull, Chicago Black Hawks
1967
Stan Mikita, Chicago Black Hawks
1968
Stan Mikita, Chicago Black Hawks
1969
Phil Esposito, Boston Bruins
1970
Bobby Orr, Boston Bruins
1971
Bobby Orr, Boston Bruins
1972
Bobby Orr, Boston Bruins
1973
Bobby Clarke, Philadelphia Flyers
1974
Phil Esposito, Boston Bruins
1975
Bobby Clarke, Philadelphia Flyers
1976
Bobby Clarke, Philadelphia Flyers

**CALDER MEMORIAL TROPHY
WINNER**— Rookie of the Year
1949
Pentti Lund, New York Rangers
1950
Jack Gelineau, Boston Bruins
1951
Terry Sawchuk, Detroit Red Wings
1952
Bernie Geoffrion, Montreal
Canadiens
1953
Gump Worsley, New York Rangers
1954
Camille Henry, New York Rangers

1955
Ed Litzenberger, Chicago Black Hawks
1956
Glenn Hall, Detroit Red Wings
1957
Larry Regan, Boston Bruins
1958
Frank Mahovlich, Toronto Maple Leafs
1959
Ralph Backstrom, Montreal Canadiens
1960
Bill Hay, Chicago Black Hawks
1961
Dave Keon, Toronto Maple Leafs
1962
Bobby Rousseau, Montreal Canadiens
1963
Kent Douglas, Toronto Maple Leafs
1964
Jacques Laperriere, Montreal Canadiens
1965
Roger Crozier, Detroit Red Wings
1966
Brit Selby, Toronto Maple Leafs
1967
Bobby Orr, Boston Bruins
1968
Derek Sanderson, Boston Bruins
1969
Danny Grant, Minnesota North Stars
1970
Tony Esposito, Chicago Black Hawks
1971
Gilbert Perreault, Buffalo
1972
Ken Dryden, Montreal Canadiens
1973
Steve Vickers, New York Rangers
1974
Denis Potvin, New York Islanders
1975
Eric Vail, Atlanta
1976
Bryan Trottier, New York Islanders

JAMES NORRIS MEMORIAL TROPHY WINNERS—Best Defenseman
1954
Red Kelly, Detroit Red Wings

1955
Doug Harvey, Montreal Canadiens
1956
Doug Harvey, Montreal Canadiens
1957
Doug Harvey, Montreal Canadiens
1958
Doug Harvey, Montreal Canadiens
1959
Tom Johnson, Montreal Canadiens
1960
Doug Harvey, Montreal Canadiens
1961
Doug Harvey, Montreal Canadiens
1962
Doug Harvey, Montreal Canadiens
1963
Pierre Pilote, Chicago Black Hawks
1964
Pierre Pilote, Chicago Black Hawks
1965
Pierre Pilote, Chicago Black Hawks
1966
Jacques Laperriere, Montreal Canadiens
1967
Harry Howell, New York Rangers
1968
Bobby Orr, Boston Bruins
1969
Bobby Orr, Boston Bruins
1970
Bobby Orr, Boston Bruins
1971
Bobby Orr, Boston Bruins
1972
Bobby Orr, Boston Bruins
1973
Bobby Orr, Boston Bruins
1974
Bobby Orr, Boston Bruins
1975
Bobby Orr, Boston Bruins
1976
Denis Potvin, New York Islanders

VEZINA TROPHY WINNERS—Goaltenders with lowest average of goals scored against them
1949
Bill Durnan, Montreal Canadiens
1950
Bill Durnan, Montreal Canadiens
1951
Al Rollins, Toronto Maple Leafs

1952
Terry Sawchuk, Detroit Red Wings
1953
Terry Sawchuk, Detroit Red Wings
1954
Harry Lumley, Toronto Maple Leafs
1955
Terry Sawchuk, Detroit Red Wings
1956
Jacques Plante, Montreal Canadiens
1957
Jacques Plante, Montreal Canadiens
1958
Jacques Plante, Montreal Canadiens
1959
Jacques Plante, Montreal Canadiens
1960
Jacques Plante, Montreal Canadiens
1961
Johnny Bower, Toronto Maple Leafs
1962
Jacques Plante, Montreal Canadiens
1963
Glenn Hall, Chicago Black Hawks
1964
Charlie Hodge, Montreal Canadiens
1965
Terry Sawchuk, Toronto Maple
Leafs
Johnny Bower, Toronto Maple Leafs
1966
Gump Worsley, Montreal Canadiens
Charlie Hodge, Montreal Canadiens
1967
Glenn Hall, Chicago Black Hawks
Denis DeJordy, Chicago Black
Hawks
1968
Gump Worsley, Montreal Canadiens
Rogatien Vachon, Montreal
Canadiens
1969
Jacques Plante, St. Louis
Glenn Hall, St. Louis
1970
Tony Esposito, Chicago Black
Hawks
1971
Ed Giacomin, New York Rangers
Gilles Villemure, New York Rangers
1972
Tony Esposito, Chicago Black
Hawks
Gary Smith, Chicago Black Hawks

1973
Ken Dryden, Montreal Canadiens
1974
Tony Esposito, Chicago Black
Hawks
Bernie Parent, Philadelphia Flyers
1975
Bernie Parent, Philadelphia Flyers
1976
Ken Dryden, Montreal Canadiens

ART ROSS TROPHY WINNERS—
Top Scorer
1949
Roy Conacher, Chicago Black
Hawks
1950
Ted Lindsay, Detroit Red Wings
1951
Gordie Howe, Detroit Red Wings
1952
Gordie Howe, Detroit Red Wings
1953
Gordie Howe, Detroit Red Wings
1954
Gordie Howe, Detroit Red Wings
1955
Bernie Geoffrion, Montreal
Canadiens
1956
Jean Beliveau, Montreal Canadiens
1957
Gordie Howe, Detroit Red Wings
1958
Dickie Moore, Montreal Canadiens
1959
Dickie Moore, Montreal Canadiens
1960
Bobby Hull, Chicago Black Hawks
1961
Bernie Geoffrion, Montreal
Canadiens
1962
Bobby Hull, Chicago Black Hawks
1963
Gordie Howe, Detroit Red Wings
1964
Stan Mikita, Chicago Black Hawks
1965
Stan Mikita, Chicago Black Hawks
1966
Bobby Hull, Chicago Black Hawks
1967
Stan Mikita, Chicago Black Hawks

1968
Stan Mikita, Chicago Black Hawks
1969
Phil Esposito, Boston Bruins
1970
Bobby Orr, Boston Bruins
1971
Phil Esposito, Boston Bruins
1972
Phil Esposito, Boston Bruins
1973
Phil Esposito, Boston Bruins
1974
Phil Esposito, Boston Bruins
1975
Bobby Orr, Boston Bruins
1976
Guy Lafleur, Montreal Canadiens

LADY BYNG MEMORIAL TROPHY WINNERS—Sportsmanship and outstanding performance
1949
Bill Quackenbush, Detroit Red Wings
1950
Edgar Laprade, New York Rangers
1951
Red Kelly, Detroit Red Wings
1952
Sid Smith, Toronto Maple Leafs
1953
Red Kelly, Detroit Red Wings
1954
Red Kelly, Detroit Red Wings
1955
Sid Smith, Toronto Maple Leafs
1956
Earl Reibel, Detroit Red Wings
1957
Andy Hebenton, New York Rangers
1958
Camille Henry, New York Rangers
1959
Alex Delvecchio, Detroit Red Wings
1960
Don McKenney, Boston Bruins
1961
Red Kelly, Toronto Maple Leafs
1962
Dave Keon, Toronto Maple Leafs
1963
Dave Keon, Toronto Maple Leafs

1964
Ken Wharram, Chicago Black Hawks
1965
Bobby Hull, Chicago Black Hawks
1966
Alex Delvecchio, Detroit Red Wings
1967
Stan Mikita, Chicago Black Hawks
1968
Stan Mikita, Chicago Black Hawks
1969
Alex Delvecchio, Detroit Red Wings
1970
Phil Goyette, St. Louis Blues
1971
Johnny Bucyk, Boston Bruins
1972
Jean Ratelle, New York Rangers
1973
Gilbert Perreault, Buffalo
1974
John Bucyk, Boston Bruins
1975
Marcel Dionne, Detroit Red Wings
1976
Jean Ratelle, Boston Bruins

CONN SMYTHE TROPHY WINNERS—Player most valuable in playoffs
1965
Jean Beliveau, Montreal Canadiens
1966
Roger Crozier, Detroit Red Wings
1967
Dave Keon, Toronto Maple Leafs
1968
Glenn Hall, St. Louis Blues
1969
Serge Savard, Montreal Canadiens
1970
Bobby Orr, Boston Bruins
1971
Ken Dryden, Montreal Canadiens
1972
Bobby Orr, Boston Bruins
1973
Yvan Cournoyer, Montreal Canadiens
1974
Bernie Parent, Philadelphia Flyers
1975
Bernie Parent, Philadelphia Flyers

1976
    Reg Leach, Philadelphia Flyers

BILL MASTERTON MEMORIAL TROPHY WINNERS—Sportsmanship, Dedication and Perseverance
1968
    Claude Provost, Montreal Canadiens
1969
    Ted Hampson, Oakland
1970
    Pit Martin, Chicago Black Hawks
1971
    Jean Ratelle, New York Rangers
1972
    Bobby Clarke, Philadelphia Flyers
1973
    Lowell MacDonald, Pittsburgh
1974
    Henri Richard, Montreal Canadiens

LESTER O. PATRICK TROPHY WINNERS—Service Award

1966	Jack Adams
1967	Gordie Howe
	Charles F. Adams
	James Norris, Sr.
1968	Thomas F. Lockhart
	Walter Brown
	Gen. John R. Kilpatrick
1969	Bobby Hull
	Edward Jeremiah
1970	Eddie Shore
	James Hendy
1971	William M. Jennings
	John B. Sollenberger
	Terry Sawchuk
1972	Clarence S. Campbell
	John Kelley
	Cooney Weiland
1973	Walter L. Bush, Jr.
1974	Alex Delvecchio
	John Murray
	Weston W. Adams, Sr.
	Charles L. Crovat
1975	Tommy Ivan
	Bill Chadwick
	Donald M. Clark
1976	Al Leader
	Stan Mikita
	Bruce A. Norris

PRINCE OF WALES TROPHY WINNERS—East Division Winners

1924–1925	Montreal Canadiens
1925–1926	Montreal Maroons
1926–1927	Ottawa Senators
1927–1928	Boston Bruins
1928–1929	Boston Bruins
1929–1930	Boston Bruins
1930–1931	Boston Bruins
1931–1932	New York Rangers
1932–1933	Boston Bruins
1933–1934	Detroit Red Wings
1934–1935	Boston Bruins
1935–1936	Detroit Red Wings
1936–1937	Detroit Red Wings
1937–1938	Boston Bruins
1938–1939	Boston Bruins
1939–1940	Boston Bruins
1940–1941	Boston Bruins
1941–1942	New York Rangers
1942–1943	Detroit Red Wings
1943–1944	Montreal Canadiens
1944–1945	Montreal Canadiens
1945–1946	Montreal Canadiens
1946–1947	Montreal Canadiens
1947–1948	Toronto Maple Leafs
1948–1949	Detroit Red Wings
1949–1950	Detroit Red Wings
1950–1951	Detroit Red Wings
1951–1952	Detroit Red Wings
1952–1953	Detroit Red Wings
1953–1954	Detroit Red Wings
1954–1955	Detroit Red Wings
1955–1956	Montreal Canadiens
1956–1957	Detroit Red Wings
1957–1958	Montreal Canadiens
1958–1959	Montreal Canadiens
1959–1960	Montreal Canadiens
1960–1961	Montreal Canadiens
1961–1962	Montreal Canadiens
1962–1963	Toronto Maple Leafs
1963–1964	Montreal Canadiens
1964–1965	Detroit Red Wings
1965–1966	Montreal Canadiens
1966–1967	Chicago Black Hawks
1967–1968	Montreal Canadiens
1968–1969	Montreal Canadiens
1969–1970	Chicago Black Hawks
1970–1971	Boston Bruins
1971–1972	Boston Bruins
1972–1973	Montreal Canadiens
1973–1974	Boston Bruins

CLARENCE S. CAMPBELL BOWL WINNERS—West Division Winners

1967–1968	Philadelphia Flyers
1968–1969	St. Louis Blues
1969–1970	St. Louis Blues

1970–1971	Chicago Black Hawks	1908	William Larned
1971–1972	Chicago Black Hawks	1909	William Larned
1972–1973	Chicago Black Hawks	1910	William Larned
1973–1974	Philadelphia Flyers	1911	William Larned
		1912	Maurice McLoughlin

WORLD AMATEUR TOURNA-
MENT WINNERS

1949	Czechoslovakia	1913	Maurice McLoughlin
1950	Canada	1914	Norris Williams
1951	Canada	1915	William Johnston
1952	Canada (Olympics)	1916	Norris Williams
1953	Sweden	1917	Lindley Murray
1954	U.S.S.R.	1918	Lindley Murray
1955	Canada	1919	William Johnston
1956	U.S.S.R. (Olympics)	1920	Bill Tilden
1957	Sweden	1921	Bill Tilden
1958	Canada	1922	Bill Tilden
1959	Canada	1923	Bill Tilden
1960	United States (Olympics)	1924	Bill Tilden
1961	Canada	1925	Bill Tilden
1962	Sweden	1926	Rene Lacoste
1963	U.S.S.R.	1927	Rene Lacoste
1964	U.S.S.R. (Olympics)	1928	Henri Cochet
1965	U.S.S.R.	1929	Bill Tilden
1966	U.S.S.R.	1930	John Doeg
1967	U.S.S.R.	1931	Ellsworth Vines
1968	U.S.S.R. (Olympics)	1932	Ellsworth Vines
1969	U.S.S.R.	1933	Frederick Perry
1970	U.S.S.R.	1934	Frederick Perry
1971	U.S.S.R.	1935	Wilmer Allison
1972	U.S.S.R. (Olympics)	1936	Frederick Perry
1972	Czechoslovakia	1937	Don Budge
1973	U.S.S.R.	1938	Don Budge
1974	U.S.S.R.	1939	Bobby Riggs
1975	U.S.S.R.	1940	Don McNeill
1976	U.S.S.R. (Olympics)	1941	Bobby Riggs
		1942	Fred Schroeder
		1943	Joseph Hunt
		1944	Frank Parker
		1945	Frank Parker

TENNIS

1946	Jack Kramer
1947	Jack Kramer
1948	Pancho Gonzales
1949	Pancho Gonzales
1950	Arthur Larsen

UNITED STATES TENNIS
**   ASSOCIATION CHAMPIONS**

		1951	Frank Sedgman
		1952	Frank Sedgman
		1953	Tony Trabert
Men's Singles		1954	Vic Seixas
1900	Malcolm Whitman	1955	Tony Trabert
1901	William Larned	1956	Ken Rosewall
1902	William Larned	1957	Malcolm Anderson
1903	Hugh Doherty	1958	Ashley Cooper
1904	Holcombe Ward	1959	Neale Fraser
1905	Beals Wright	1960	Neale Fraser
1906	William Clothier	1961	Roy Emerson
1907	William Larned	1962	Rod Laver

1963	Rafael Osuna
1964	Roy Emerson
1965	Manual Santana
1966	Fred Stolle
1967	John Newcombe
1968	Arthur Ashe
1968	Arthur Ashe*
1969	Stan Smith
1969	Rod Laver*
1970	Ken Rosewall*
1971	Stan Smith*
1972	Ilie Nastase*
1973	John Newcombe*
1974	Jimmy Connors*
1975	Manual Orantes*
1976	Jimmy Connors*

*U.S. Open Champion

Men's Doubles

1900	Holcombe Ward-Dwight Davis
1902	Holcombe Ward-Dwight Davis
1902	Reginald Doherty-Hugh Doherty
1903	R. F. Doherty-Hugh Doherty
1904	Holcombe Ward-Beals Wright
1905	Holcombe Ward-Beals Wright
1906	Holcombe Ward-Beals Wright
1907	Harold Hackett-Frederick Alexander
1908	Harold Hackett-Frederick Alexander
1909	Harold Hackett-Frederick Alexander
1910	Harold Hackett-Frederick Alexander
1911	Raymond Little-Gustave Touchard
1912	Maurice McLoughlin-Thomas Bundy
1913	Maurice McLoughlin-Thomas Bundy
1914	Maurice McLoughlin-Thomas Bundy
1915	William Johnston-Clarence Griffin
1916	William Johnston-Clarence Griffin
1917	Frederick Alexander-Harold Throckmorton

1918	Bill Tilden-Vincent Richards
1919	Norman E. Brookes-Gerald Patterson
1920	William Johnston-Clarence Griffin
1921	Bill Tilden-Vincent Richards
1922	Bill Tilden-Vincent Richards
1923	Bill Tilden-Brian Norton
1924	Howard Kinsey-Robert Kinsey
1925	Vincent Richards-Norris Williams
1926	Vincent Richards-Norris Williams
1927	Bill Tilden-Francis Hunter
1928	George Lott-John Hennessey
1929	George Lott-John Doeg
1930	George Lott-John Doeg
1931	Wilmer Allison-John Van Ryn
1932	Ellsworth Vines-Keith Gledhill
1933	George Lott-Lester Stoefen
1934	George Lott-Lester Stoefen
1935	Wilmer Allison-John Van Ryn
1936	Don Budge-Gene Mako
1937	Gottfried von Cramm-Henner Henkel
1938	Don Budge-Gene Mako
1939	Adrian Quist-John Bromwich
1940	Jack Kramer-Fred Schroeder
1941	Jack Kramer-Fred Schroeder
1942	Gardnar Mulloy-Bill Talbert
1943	Jack Kramer-Frank Parker
1944	Don McNeill-Robert Falkenburg
1945	Gardnar Mulloy-Bill Talbert
1946	Gardnar Mulloy-Bill Talbert
1947	Jack Kramer-Fred Schroeder
1948	Gardnar Mulloy-Bill Talbert
1949	John Bromwich-William Sidwell
1950	John Bromwich-Frank Sedgman
1951	Frank Sedgman-Ken McGregor
1952	Vic Seixas-Merv Rose
1953	Rex Hartwig-Merv Rose
1954	Vic Seixas-Tony Trabert
1955	Kosei Kamo-Atsushi Miyagi
1956	Lew Hoad-Ken Rosewall
1957	Ashley Cooper-Neale Fraser
1958	Hamilton Richardson-Alejandro Olmedo
1959	Neale Fraser-Roy Emerson
1960	Neale Fraser-Roy Emerson

1961	Chuck McKinley-Dennis Ralston		1928	Helen Wills
1962	Rafael Osuna-Antonio Palafox		1929	Helen Wills
			1930	Betty Nuthall
			1931	Helen Moody
1963	Chuck McKinley-Dennis Ralston		1932	Helen Jacobs
			1933	Helen Jacobs
1964	Chuck McKinley-Dennis Ralston		1934	Helen Jacobs
			1935	Helen Jacobs
1965	Roy Emerson-Fred Stolle		1936	Alice Marble
1966	Roy Emerson-Fred Stolle		1937	Anita Lizana
1967	John Newcombe-Tony Roche		1938	Alice Marble
1968	Bob Lutz-Stan Smith		1939	Alice Marble
1968	Bob Lutz-Stan Smith*		1940	Alice Marble
1969	Dick Crealy-Alan Stone		1941	Sarah Cooke
1969	Ken Rosewall-Fred Stolle*		1942	Pauline Betz
1970	Pierre Barthes-Nikki Pilic*		1943	Pauline Betz
1971	John Newcombe-Roger Taylor*		1944	Pauline Betz
			1945	Sarah Cooke
1972	Cliff Drysdale-Roger Taylor*		1946	Pauline Betz
1973	John Newcombe-O. Davidson*		1947	Louise Brough
			1948	Margaret du Pont
1974	Bob Lutz-Stan Smith*		1949	Margaret du Pont
1975	Jimmy Connors-Ilie Nastase*		1950	Margaret du Pont
1976	Marty Riessen-Tom Okker*		1951	Maureen Connolly

*U.S. Open Champion

Women's Singles

1900	Myrtle McAteer
1901	Elisabeth Moore
1902	Marion Jones
1903	Elisabeth Moore
1904	May Sutton
1905	Elisabeth Moore
1906	Helen Homans
1907	Evelyn Sears
1908	Maud Bargar-Wallach
1909	Hazel Hotchkiss
1910	Hazel Hotchkiss
1911	Hazel Hotchkiss
1912	Mary Browne
1913	Mary Browne
1914	Mary Browne
1915	Molla Bjurstedt
1916	Molla Bjurstedt
1917	Molla Bjurstedt
1918	Molla Bjurstedt
1919	Hazel Wightman
1920	Molla Mallory
1921	Molla Mallory
1922	Molla Mallory
1923	Helen Wills
1924	Helen Wills
1925	Helen Wills
1926	Molla Mallory
1927	Helen Wills

1952	Maureen Connolly
1953	Maureen Connolly
1954	Doris Hart
1955	Doris Hart
1956	Shirley Fry
1957	Althea Gibson
1958	Althea Gibson
1959	Maria Bueno
1960	Darlene Hard
1961	Darlene Hard
1962	Margaret Smith
1963	Maria Bueno
1964	Maria Bueno
1965	Margaret Smith
1966	Maria Bueno
1967	Billie Jean King
1968	Margaret Court
1968	Virginia Wade*
1969	Margaret Court
1969	Margaret Court*
1970	Margaret Court*
1971	Billie Jean King*
1972	Billie Jean King*
1973	Margaret Court*
1974	Billie Jean King*
1975	Chris Evert*
1976	Chris Evert*

*U.S. Open Champion

Women's Doubles

1900	Edith Parker-Hallie Champlin

1901	Juliette Atkinson-Myrtle McAteer	1940	Sarah Palfrey-Alice Marble
1902	Juliette Atkinson-Marion Jones	1941	Sarah Cooke-Margaret Osborne
1903	Elisabeth Moore-Carrie Neely	1942	Louise Brough-Margaret Osborne
1904	May Sutton-Miriam Hall	1943	Louise Brough-Margaret Osborne
1905	Helen Homans-Carrie Neely	1944	Louise Brough-Margaret Osborne
1906	L. S. Coe-D. S. Platt		
1907	Marie Weimer-Carrie Neely	1945	Louise Brough-Margaret Osborne
1908	Evelyn Sears-Margaret Curtis		
1909	Hazel Hotchkiss-Edith Rotch	1946	Louise Brough-Margaret Osborne
1910	Hazel Hotchkiss-Edith Rotch		
1911	Hazel Hotchkiss-Eleonora Sears	1947	Louise Brough-Margaret Osborne
1912	Dorothy Green-Mary Browne	1948	Louise Brough-Margaret du Pont
1913	Mary Browne-R. H. Williams		
1914	Mary Browne-R. H. Williams	1949	Louise Brough-Margaret du Pont
1915	Hazel Wightman-Eleonora Sears	1950	Louise Brough-Margaret du Pont
1916	Molla Bjurstedt-Eleonora Sears	1951	Doris Hart-Shirley Fry
1917	Molla Bjurstedt-Eleonora Sears	1952	Doris Hart-Shirley Fry
		1953	Doris Hart-Shirley Fry
1918	Marion Zinderstein-Eleanor Goss	1954	Doris Hart-Shirley Fry
		1955	Louise Brough-Margaret du Pont
1919	Marion Zinderstein-Eleanor Goss	1956	Louise Brough-Margaret du Pont
1920	Marion Zinderstein-Eleanor Goss	1957	Louise Brough-Margaret du Pont
1921	Mary Browne-R. H. Williams	1958	Jeanne Arth-Darlene Hard
1922	Marion Jessup-Helen Wills	1959	Jeanne Arth-Darlene Hard
1923	Kathleen McKane-B. C. Covell	1960	Maria Bueno-Darlene Hard
1924	Hazel Wightman-Helen Wills	1961	Darlene Hard-Lesley Turner
1925	Mary Browne-Helen Wills	1962	Maria Bueno-Darlene Hard
1926	Elizabeth Ryan-Eleanor Goss	1963	Robyn Ebbern-Margaret Smith
1927	Kathleen Godfree-Ermyntrude Harvey	1964	Billie Jean Moffitt-Karen Susman
1928	Hazel Wightman-Helen Wills		
1929	Phoebe Watson-Peggy Michell	1965	Carole Graebner-Nancy Richey
1930	Betty Nuthall-Sarah Palfrey	1966	Maria Bueno-Nancy Richey
1931	Betty Nuthall-Eileen Whitingstall	1967	Billie Jean King-Rosemary Casals
1932	Helen Jacobs-Sarah Palfrey	1968	Maria Bueno-Margaret Court
1933	Betty Nuthall-Freda James	1968	Maria Bueno-Margaret Court*
1934	Helen Jacobs-Sarah Palfrey		
1935	Helen Jacobs-Sarah Fabyan	1969	Margaret Court-Virginia Wade
1936	Marjorie Van Ryn-Carolin Babcock	1969	Francoise Durr—Darlene Hard*
1937	Sarah Fabyan-Alice Marble		
1938	Sarah Fabyan-Alice Marble	1970	Margaret Court-Judy Dalton*
1939	Sarah Fabyan-Alice Marble	1971	Rosemary Casals-Judy Dalton*

1972	Francoise Durr-Betty Stove*		1949	Fred Schroeder
1973	Margaret Court-Virginia Wade*		1950	Budge Patty
			1951	Dick Savitt
1974	Billie Jean King-Rosemary Casals*		1952	Frank Sedgman
			1953	Vic Seixas
1975	Margaret Court-Virginia Wade*		1954	Jaroslav Drobny
			1955	Tony Trabert
1976	Linky Boshoff-Llana Kloss*		1956	Lew Hoad
*U.S. Open Champion			1957	Lew Hoad
			1958	Ashley Cooper

INTERNATIONAL CHAMPIONS (WIMBLEDON)

Men's Singles

1900	Reginald Doherty
1901	Arthur Gore
1902	Hugh Doherty
1903	Hugh Doherty
1904	Hugh Doherty
1905	Hugh Doherty
1906	Hugh Doherty
1907	Norman Brookes
1908	Arthur Gore
1909	Arthur Gore
1910	Anthony Wilding
1911	Anthony Wilding
1912	Anthony Wilding
1913	Anthony Wilding
1914	Norman Brookes
1915–1918	no competition
1919	Gerald Patterson
1920	Bill Tilden
1921	Bill Tilden
1922	Gerald Patterson
1923	William Johnston
1924	Jean Borotra
1925	Rene Lacoste
1926	Jean Borotra
1927	Henri Cochet
1928	Rene Lacoste
1929	Henri Cochet
1930	Bill Tilden
1931	Sidney Wood
1932	Ellsworth Vines
1933	John Crawford
1934	Fred Perry
1935	Fred Perry
1936	Fred Perry
1937	Don Budge
1938	Don Budge
1939	Bobby Riggs
1940–1945	no competition
1946	Yvon Petra
1947	Jack Kramer
1948	Robert Falkenburg

1959	Alex Olmedo
1960	Neale Fraser
1961	Rod Laver
1962	Rod Laver
1963	Chuck McKinley
1964	Roy Emerson
1965	Roy Emerson
1966	Manuel Santana
1967	John Newcombe
1968	Rod Laver
1969	Rod Laver
1970	John Newcombe
1971	John Newcombe
1972	Stan Smith
1973	Jan Kodes
1974	Jimmy Connors
1975	Arthur Ashe
1976	Bjorn Borg
1977	Bjorn Borg

Men's Doubles

1900	Reginald Doherty-Hugh Doherty
1901	Reginald Doherty-Hugh Doherty
1902	Sidney Smith-F. L. Risely
1903	Reginald Doherty-Hugh Doherty
1904	Reginald Doherty-Hugh Doherty
1905	Reginald Doherty-Hugh Doherty
1906	Sidney Smith-F. L. Riseley
1907	Norman Brooks-Anthony Wilding
1908	Anthony Wilding-M. J. G. Ritchie
1909	Arthur Gore-H. Roper Barrett
1910	Anthony Wilding-M. J. G. Ritchie
1911	Max Decugis-Andre Gobert
1912	H. Roper Barrett-Charles Dixon
1913	H. Roper Barrett-Charles Dixon

1914	Norman Brooks-Anthony Wilding
1915–1918	no competition
1919	R. V. Thomas-Pat Wood
1920	R. Norris Williams-Charles Garland
1921	Randolph Lycett-M. Woosnam
1922	Randolph Lycett-J. O. Anderson
1923	Randolph Lycett-L. A. Godfree
1924	Vincent Richards-Francis Hunter
1925	Jean Borotra-Rene Lacoste
1926	Henri Cochet-Jacques Brugnon
1927	Bill Tilden-Francis Hunter
1928	Henri Cochet-Jacques Brugnon
1929	Wilmer Allison-John Van Ryn
1930	Wilmer Allison-John Van Ryn
1931	George Lott-John Van Ryn
1932	Jean Borotra-Jacques Brugnon
1933	Jean Borotra-Jacques Brugnon
1934	George Lott-Lester Stoefen
1935	John Crawford-Adrian Quist
1936	Charles Tuckey-George Hughes
1937	Don Budge-Gene Mako
1938	Don Budge-Gene Mako
1939	Bobby Riggs-Elwood Cooke
1940–1945	no competition
1946	Jack Kramer-Thomas Brown
1947	Jack Kramer-Robert Falkenburg
1948	John Bromwich-Frank Sedgman
1949	Frank Parker-Pancho Gonzalez
1950	John Bromwich-Adrian Quist
1951	Frank Sedgman-Ken McGregor
1952	Frank Sedgman-Ken McGregor
1953	Ken Rosewall-Lew Hoad
1954	Rex Hartwig-Merv Rose
1955	Rex Hartwig-Merv Rose
1956	Lew Hoad-Ken Rosewall
1957	Gardnar Mulloy-Budge Patty
1958	Sven Davidson-Ulf Schmidt
1959	Neale Fraser-Roy Emerson
1960	Rafael Osuna-Dennis Ralston

1961	Neale Fraser-Roy Emerson
1962	Fred Stolle-Robert Hewitt
1963	Rafael Osuna-Antonio Palafox
1964	Rex Hewitt-Fred Stolle
1965	John Newcombe-Tony Roche
1966	Ken Fletcher-John Newcombe
1967	Bob Hewitt-Frew McMillan
1968	John Newcombe-Tony Roche
1969	John Newcombe-Tony Roche
1970	John Newcombe-Tony Roche
1971	Rod Laver-Roy Emerson
1972	Bob Hewitt-Frew McMillan
1973	Ilie Nastase-Jimmy Connors
1974	John Newcombe-Tony Roche
1975	Vitas Gerulaitis-Sandy Mayer
1976	Brian Gottfried-Raul Ramirez

Women's Singles

1900	Blanche Hillyard
1901	Charlotte Sterry
1902	M. E. Robb
1903	Dorothy Douglass
1904	Dorothea Douglas
1905	May Sutton
1906	Dorothy Douglass
1907	May Sutton
1908	Charlotte Sterry
1909	Dorothea Boothby
1910	Dorothy Chambers
1911	Dorothy Chambers
1912	Ethel Larcombe
1913	Dorothy Chambers
1914	Dorothy Chambers
1915–1918	no competition
1919	Suzanne Lenglen
1920	Suzanne Lenglen
1921	Suzanne Lenglen
1922	Suzanne Lenglen
1923	Suzanne Lenglen
1924	Kathleen McKane
1925	Suzanne Lenglen
1926	Kathleen Godfree
1927	Helen Wills
1928	Helen Wills
1929	Helen Wills
1930	Helen Moody
1931	Cecile Aussem
1932	Helen Moody
1933	Helen Moody
1934	Dorothy Round
1935	Helen Moody
1936	Helen Jacobs
1937	Dorothy Round

1938	Helen Moody
1939	Alice Marble
1940–1945	no competition
1946	Pauline Betz
1947	Margaret Osborne
1948	Louise Brough
1949	Louise Brough
1950	Louise Brough
1951	Doris Hart
1952	Maureen Connolly
1953	Maureen Connolly
1954	Maureen Connolly
1955	Louise Brough
1956	Shirley Fry
1957	Althea Gibson
1958	Althea Gibson
1959	Maria Bueno
1960	Maria Bueno
1961	Angela Mortimer
1962	Karen Susman
1963	Margaret Smith
1964	Maria Bueno
1965	Margaret Smith
1966	Billie Jean King
1967	Billie Jean King
1968	Billie Jean King
1969	Ann Jones
1970	Margaret Court
1971	Evonne Goolagong
1972	Billie Jean King
1973	Billie Jean King
1974	Chris Evert
1975	Billie Jean King
1976	Chris Evert
1977	Virginia Wade

Women's Doubles

1913	R. J. McNair-Dora Boothby
1914	A. M. Morton-Elizabeth Ryan
1915–1918	no competition
1919	Suzanne Lenglen-Elizabeth Ryan
1920	Suzanne Lenglen-Elizabeth Ryan
1921	Susanne Lenglen-Elizabeth Ryan
1922	Suzanne Lenglen-Elizabeth Ryan
1923	Suzanne Lenglen-Elizabeth Ryan
1924	Hazel Wightman-Helen Wills
1925	Suzanne Lenglen-Elizabeth Ryan
1926	Elizabeth Ryan-Mary Browne
1927	Elizabeth Ryan-Helen Wills

1928	Mrs. H. Watson-Peggy Saunders
1929	Mrs. H. Watson-Peggy Michell
1930	Elizabeth Ryan-Helen Moody
1931	Mrs. D. C. Shepherd-Barron-Phyllis Mudford
1932	D. Metaxa-J. Sigart
1933	Elizabeth Ryan-Rene Mathieu
1934	Elizabeth Ryan-Rene Mathieu
1935	Katherine Stammers-Freda James
1936	Katherine Stammers-Freda James
1937	Rene Mathieu-A. M. Yorke
1938	Alice Marble-Sarah Fab
1939	Alice Marble-Sarah Fab
1940–1945	no competition
1946	Louise Brough-Margaret Osborne
1947	Doris Hart-Patricia Todd
1948	Louise Brough-Margaret du Pont
1949	Louise Brough-Margaret du Pont
1950	Louise Brough-Margaret du Pont
1951	Doris Hart-Shirley Fry
1952	Doris Hart-Shirley Fry
1953	Doris Hart-Shirley Fry
1954	Louise Brough-Margaret du Pont
1955	Angela Mortimer-Anne Shilcock
1956	Angela Buxton-Althea Gibson
1957	Althea Gibson-Darlene Hard
1958	Althea Gibson-Maria Bueno
1959	Jeanne Arth-Darlene Hard
1960	Maria Bueno-Darlene Hard
1961	Karen Hantze-Billie Jean Moffitt
1962	Karen Susman-Billie Jean Moffitt
1963	Maria Bueno-Darlene Hard
1964	Margaret Smith-Lesley Turner
1965	Maria Bueno-Billie Jean Moffitt
1966	Maria Bueno-Nancy Richey
1967	Rosemary Casals-Billie Jean King
1968	Rosemary Casals-Billie Jean King

1969	Margaret Court-Judy Tegart
1970	Billie Jean King-Rosemary Casals
1971	Billie Jean King-Rosemary Casals
1972	Billie Jean King-Betty Stove
1973	Billie Jean King-Rosemary Casals
1974	Peggy Michel-Evonne Goolagong
1975	Ann Kiyomura-Kazuko Sawamatsu
1976	Chris Everet-Martina Navratilova

YACHTING

AMERICA'S CUP
1901
  Columbia, United States
1903
  Reliance, United States
1920
  Resolute, United States
1930
  Enterprise, United States
1934
  Rainbow, United States
1937
  Ranger, United States
1958
  Columbia, United States
1962
  Weatherly, United States
1964
  Constellation, United States
1967
  Intrepid, United States
1970
  Intrepid, United States
1974
  Courageous, United States

MISCELLA-
NEOUS SPORTS

See Journalism, Murray Kramer Award, Boston University

See Olympic Games

THEODORE ROOSEVELT AWARD
—The National Collegiate Athletic Association

Jerry Ford couldn't miss with this award. It is presented to someone of national stature who was involved in collegiate athletics as an undergraduate.

Established 1967.
1967
  Dwight D. Eisenhower, General of the Army, president of the United States
1968
  Leverett Saltonstall, United States senator, governor of Massachusetts
1969
  Byron R. White, United States Supreme Court Justice
1970
  Frederick L. Hovde, president, Purdue University
1971
  Christopher C. Kraft, Jr., National Aeronautics and Space Administration
1972
  Jerome H. Holland, United States ambassador to Sweden
1973
  Omar N. Bradley, General of the Army
1974
  Jesse Owens, Jesse Owens, Inc.
1975
  Gerald R. Ford, House Majority Leader, president of the United States
1976
  Thomas J. Hamilton, Rear Admiral, United States Navy
1977
  Tom Bradley, mayor, city of Los Angeles

TODAY'S TOP FIVE—The National Collegiate Athletic Association

You've got to be a college senior. You've got to be good in athletics. And you've got to be good in the classroom.

Established 1973.

Theodore Roosevelt Award winner Gen. Omar Bradley.

1973
Robert Wesley Ash, Cornell College, football
Bruce Patrick Bannon, Pennsylvania State University, football
Blake Lynn Ferguson, Drexel University, lacrosse
Jerry Alan Heidenreich, Southern Methodist University, swimming
Sidney Allen Sink, Bowling Green State University, track
1974
David A. Bladino, University of Pittsburgh, football
Paul Douglas Collins, Illinois State, basketball
David D. Gallagher, University of Michigan, football
Gary W. Hall, Indiana University, swimming
David J. Wottle, Bowling Green State University, track
1975
John R. Baiorunos, Pennsylvania State University, football
Patrick C. Haden, University of Southern California, football

Randy L. Hall, University of Alabama, football
Jarrett T. Hubbard, University of Michigan, wrestling
Tony G. Waldrop, University of North Carolina, track
1976
Marvin Lawrence Cobb, University of Southern California, baseball and football
Archie Griffin, Ohio State University, football
Bruce Alan Hamming, Augustana College, basketball
Patrick Timothy Moore, Ohio State University, diving
John Michael Sciarra, UCLA, football
1977
Jeffrey Dankworth, UCLA, football
Randolph Dean, Northwestern University, football
Steven Furniss, University of Southern California, swimming
John Hencken, Stanford University, swimming
Gerald Huesken, Susquehanna University, football

SILVER ANNIVERSARY AWARD—

The National Collegiate Athletic Association.

You had to have been an outstanding collegiate athlete. You had to have gotten good grades, done something significant in your post-collegiate career, and have graduated twenty-five years before receiving the award. Established 1973.

1973

Ray R. Evans, University of Kansas, bank president

John Feraro, University of Southern California, city councilman

John D. Hopper, Dickinson College, insurance consultant

Donald G. Mulder, Hope College, surgeon

Stewart L. Udall, University of Arizona, lawyer

1974

Howard H. Callaway, United States Military Academy, secretary of the Army

Robert S. Dorsey, Ohio State University, jet engine expert

Robert B. McCurry, Jr., Michigan State University, vice-president Chrysler Corporation

Dr. Robert J. Robinson, Baylor University, minister

Eugene T. Rossides, Columbia University, lawyer

1975

Robert S. Folsom, Southern Methodist University, investments

Billy M. Jones, Vanderbilt University, president, Memphis State University

William J. Keating, University of Cincinnati, president, Cincinnati Inquirer

Ralph E. O'Brien, Butler University, insurance

Philip J. Ryan, United States Naval Academy, commander in United States Navy

1976

Napolean A. Bell, Mount Union College, attorney

Ernest Jackson Curtis, Vanderbilt University, corporate marketing

H. Samuel Greenawalt, University of Pennsylvania, banking

Ross J. Pritchard, University of Arkansas, president, Arkansas State University

Wade Roger Stinson, University of Kansas, banking

1977

Donald E. Coleman, Michigan State University, minority programs director, College of Osteopathic Medicine, Michigan State University

Richard W. Kazmaier, Princeton University, president, L & R Industries, Inc., and Eastern Sports Sales, Inc.

Vincent George Rhoden, Morgan State University, podiatrist, foot surgeon

William J. Wade, Vanderbilt University, assistant vice-president, Third National Bank

Frederick A. Yonkman, Hope College, executive vice-president and general counsel, American Express Company

AWARD OF VALOR—The National Collegiate Athletic Association

For any current or former varsity letterman who places himself in physical danger—off the battlefield—to avert or minimize a potential catastrophe. Established 1973.

1973

Ursinus College Basketball Team— Robert E. Cattell, William J. Downy, Warren Fry (head coach), Robert Handwerk (assistant coach), George P. Kinek, Jack S. Messenger, Norman Reichenback (trainer), Randy D. Stubits, Thomas E. Sturgeon, Michael C. Weston

Charles C. Driesell, University of Maryland

William Jeffrey Miller, University of Texas, Arlington

1977

Dwayne A. Wright, Saint Mary's of California

SPORTSMAN OF THE YEAR—

Sports Illustrated Magazine

And sometimes it's Sportswoman of the Year. Established 1954.

1954	Roger Bannister
1955	Johnny Podres
1956	Bobby Morrow

1957	Stan Musial
1958	Rafer Johnson
1959	Ingemar Johansson
1960	Arnold Palmer
1961	Jerry Lucas
1962	Terry Baker
1963	Pete Rozelle
1964	Ken Venturi
1965	Sandy Koufax
1966	Jim Ryun
1967	Carl Yastrzemski
1968	Bill Russell
1969	Tom Seaver
1970	Bobby Orr
1971	Lee Trevino
1972	John Wooden
	Billie Jean King
1973	Jackie Stewart
1974	Muhammad Ali
1975	Pete Rose
1976	Chris Evert

SULLIVAN AWARD—Amateur Athletic Union

The biggie of the A.A.U., it goes to the top amateur athlete of the year.

Established 1930.

1930
  Robert T. Jones, golf
1931
  Bernard E. Berlinger, track and field
1932
  James A. Bausch, track and field
1933
  Glenn Cunningham, track and field
1934
  William R. Bonthron, track and field
1935
  W. Lawson Little, Jr., golf
1936
  Glenn Morris, track and field
1937
  J. Donald Budge, tennis
1938
  Donald R. Lash, track and field
1939
  Joseph W. Burk, rowing
1940
  J. Gregory Rice, track and field
1941
  T. Leslie MacMitchell, track and field
1942
  Cornelius Warmerdam, track and field

1943
  Gilbert Dodds, track and field
1944
  Ann Curtis, swimming
1945
  Felix Blanchard, football
1946
  Y. Arnold Tucker, football
1947
  John B. Kelly, Jr., rowing
1948
  Robert B. Mathias, track and field
1949
  Richard T. Button, figure skating
1950
  Fred Wilt, track and field
1951
  Robert E. Richards, track and field
1952
  Horace Ashenfelter, track and field
1953
  Samme Lee, diving
1954
  Malvin G. Whitfield, track and field
1955
  Harrison Dillard, track and field
1956
  Patricia Keller McCormick, diving
1957
  Bobby J. Morrow, track and field
1958
  Glenn Davis, track and field
1959
  Parry O'Brien, track and field
1960
  Rafer Johnson, track and field
1961
  Wilma Rudolph, track and field
1962
  James T. Beatty, track and field
1963
  John Thomas Pennel, track and field
1964
  Don A. Schollander, swimming
1965
  Bill Bradley, basketball
1966
  James R. Ryun, track and field
1967
  Randy Matson, track and field
1968
  Deborah Meyer, swimming
1969
  William Toomey, decathlon

1970
John Kinsella, swimming
1971
Mark Spitz, swimming
1972
Frank Shorter, marathon
1973
Bill Walton, basketball
1974
Rick Wohlhuter, track
1975
Timothy Shaw, swimming
1976
Bruce Jenner, track and field

**WORLD TROPHY AWARDS,
NORTH AMERICA**—Citizens Savings Athletic Foundation
North America's foremost amateur athletes as judged by the foundation. All winners have been American except for the 1928 winner who was Canadian.
Established 1948.
1896
Robert Garrett, track and field
1897
Robert D. Wrenn, tennis
1898
Juliette P. Atkinson, tennis
1899
T. Truxton Hare, football
1900
Alvin C. Kraenzlein, track and field
1901
Charles Daly, football
1902
William A. Larned, tennis
1903
Walter J. Travis, golf
1904
James Lightbody, track and field
1905
May Sutton, tennis
1906
Walter Eckersall, football
1907
Martin J. Sheridan, track and field
1908
Melvin Sheppard, track and field
1909
Charles M. Daniels, swimming
1910
Fred C. Thomson, track and field

1911
Hazel Hotchkiss, tennis
1912
James Thorpe, football, track and field
1913
Maurice McLoughlin, tennis
1914
Francis Ouimet, golf
1915
Jerome D. Travers, golf
1916
J. E. "Ted" Meredith, track and field
1917
Molla Bjurstedt, tennis
1918
Avery Brundage, track and field
1919
William Johnston, tennis
1920
Charles W. Paddock, track and field
1921
William T. Tilden II, tennis
1922
Thomas Hitchcock, Jr., polo
1923
John Weissmuller, swimming
1924
Harold Grange, football
1925
Ernest Nevers, football
1926
Robert T. Jones, golf
1927
Benjamin Oosterbann, football, basketball
1928
Percy Williams, track and field
1929
Helen Wills, tennis
1930
Glenna Collett, golf
1931
Helene Madison, swimming
1932
H. Ellsworth Vines, tennis
1933
Glenn Cunningham, track and field
1934
W. Lawson Little, golf
1935
Jesse Owens, track and field
1936
Glenn Morris, track and field

Olympian Jesse Owens.

1937
J. Donald Budge, tennis
1938
Angelo Luisetti, basketball
1939
Alice Marble, tennis
1940
J. Gregory Rice, track and field
1941
Robert L. Riggs, tennis
1942
Cornelius Warmerdam, track and
field
1943
Gilbert Dodds, track and field
1944
Ann Curtis, swimming
1945
Glenn Davis, football
1946
Pauline Betz, tennis
1947
John A. Kramer, tennis
1948
Robert Mathias, track and field
1949
Melvin Patton, track and field

1950
Richard Attlesey, track and field
1951
Robert Richards, track and field
1952
Horace Ashenfelter, track and field
1953
Malvin Whitfield, track and field
1954
Wes Santee, track and field
1955
Patricia McCormick, diving
1956
Parry O'Brien, track and field
1957
Robert Gutowski, track and field
1958
Rafer Johnson, track and field
1959
Ray Norton, track and field
1960
Wilma Rudolph, track and field
1961
Ralph Boston, track and field
1962
Terry Baker, football

1963
   Brian Sternberg, track and field
1964
   Alfred Oerter, track and field
1965
   Michael Garrett, football
1966
   James Ryun, track and field
1967
   J. Randel Matson, track and field
1968
   Robert Beamon, track and field
1969
   William Toomey, track and field

1970
   Gary Hall, swimming
1971
   Pat Matzdorf, track and field
1972
   Mark Spitz, swimming
1973
   Keena Rothhammer, swimming
1974
   Tim Shaw, swimming
1975
   Shirley Babashoff, swimming

STATE

STATE AWARDS

Some go to favorite sons and daughters; others to someone the state fathers and mothers just happen to like. Established at various times.

HAWAII—ORDER OF THE SPLINTERED PADDLE
1956
   Dwight D. Eisenhower, president of the United States
   Walter F. Dillingham, corporation executive
   Duke P. Kahanamoku, sheriff, city and county of Honolulu
   George Lycurgus, proprietor, Hilo Hotel and Volcano House
1957
   Charles F. Chillingworth, retired legislator, public service worker
   C. K. Ai, treasurer and manager, City Mill Co., Ltd.
   Frank F. Baldwin, president, Hawaiian Commercial and Sugar Co., Ltd.

   Adm. Raymond Ames Spruance, United States Navy (retired)
   Adm. Arthur W. Radford, United States Navy (retired)
1958
   Conrad C. Von Hamm, chairman of the board, Von Hamm-Young Company
   Adm. Felix B. Stump, United States Navy (retired)
   Raymond S. Coll, editor, *Honolulu Advertiser*
1959
   Samuel Wilder King, governor of Hawaii
1960
   Ingram M. Stainback, governor of Hawaii
   Riley H. Allen, editor, *Honolulu Star-Bulletin*
1962
   Leslie A. Hicks, chairman of the board, Hawaiian Electric Company
   William H. Heen, partner, Heen, Kai & Dodge, attorneys-at-law
1963
   Adm. Harry D. Felt, commander-in-chief, Pacific

Oren E. Long, United States senator
1964
Arthur Godfrey, entertainer
1965
Forrest J. Pinkerton, M.D.,
humanitarian
1966
Henry J. Kaiser, industrialist
1969
George H. Lehleitner, philanthropist
and benefactor of statehood for
Hawaii
Dan Liu, retiring chief of police,
Honolulu
1973
Frank E. Midkiff, humaniatrian

MISSOURI—ACADEMY OF MISSOURI SQUIRES

1960
Thomas Hart Benton, Kansas City
James T. Blair, Jr., Jefferson City
Clarence Cannon, Elsberry
Tilghman R. Cloud, Pleasant Hill
Michael Kinney, St. Louis
Stanley Musial, St. Louis
Miss Adah Peckenpaugh, Clinton
Roy Roberts, Kansas City
Francis Smith, St. Joseph
Ethan A. H. Shepley, Jr., St. Louis
Harry S. Truman, Independence
1961
William L. Bradshaw, Columbia
Arthur V. Burrowes, St. Joseph
August A. Busch, Jr., St. Louis
John M. Dalton, Jefferson City
Russell L. Dearmont, St. Louis
Elmer Ellis, Columbia
Don Faurot, Columbia
Albert L. Reeves, Kansas City
Gerald R. Massie, Jefferson City
Floyd C. Shoemaker, Columbia
Stuart Symington, Clayton
1962
Henry S. Caulfield, St. Louis
Forrest C. Donnell, St. Louis
Lloyd C. Stark, Louisiana
Richard H. Amberg, St. Louis
David R. Calhoun, St. Louis
James G. Conzelman, St. Louis
E. L. Dale, Carthage
W. True Davis, Washington, D.C.
Samuel S. Mayerberg, Kansas City
James S. McDonnell, Jr., St. Louis
Joyce C. Hall, Kansas City

Dr. Charles N. Kimball, Kansas City
Sterling Price Reynolds,
Caruthersville
1963
Edwin M. Clark, St. Louis
Howard Cook, Jefferson City
James A. Finch, Jr., Jefferson City
Robert M. Good, Point Lookout
James M. Kemper, Kansas City
Dillard A. Mallory, Buffalo
John I. Rollings, St. Louis
Dr. Ruth Seevers, Osceola
Leif J. Sverdrup, St. Louis
Roy D. Williams, Boonville
1964
L. Mitchell White, Mexico
Rex M. Whitton, Jefferson City
Mrs. Raymond A. Young, Columbia
Frederick A. Middlebush, Columbia
Mrs. G. Baird Fisher, Osgood
James P. Hickok, St. Louis
Laurance M. Hyde, Jefferson City
Edward V. Long, Bowling Green
Morton D. May, St. Louis
J. Wesley McAfee, St. Louis
1965
Gen. Omar N. Bradley, Los Angeles,
Calif.
Frank P. Briggs, Macon
Warren E. Hearnes, Charleston
Dr. Franc L. McCluer, St. Charles
William A. McDonnell, St. Louis
Dr. Charles Allen Thomas, St. Louis
W. Howard Adams, Washington,
D.C.
Lester E. Cox, Springfield
William B. Massey, Bonne Terre
Mrs. Holton R. Price, Jr., Ladue
Homer C. Wadsworth, Cleveland,
Ohio
1966
Sam C. Blair, Jefferson City
Thomas H. Eliot, St. Louis
Miss Jacqueline Grennan, Tenafly,
N.J. (Mrs. Paul J. Wexler)
Fred V. Heinkel, Columbia
William F. James, Clayton
Lue C. Lozier, Moberly
Arthur Mag, Kansas City
Paul C. Reinert, St. Louis
Sidney Salomon, Jr., St. Louis
Clem F. Storckman, Jefferson City
1967
Henry D. Bradley, St. Joseph
Ernest R. Breech, Detroit, Mich.

Richard S. Brownlee, Columbia
Stanley R. Fike, Independence
Edmund I. ("Mike") Hockaday,
Jefferson City
Paul C. Jones, Kennett
Leonard Hall, Caledonia
Theodore D. McNeal, St. Louis
Arthur Clay Magill, Cape Girardeau
Raymond R. Tucker, St. Louis
1968
Proctor N. Carter, Jefferson City
Edward Pope Coleman, Jr., Sikeston
Judge Richard M. Duncan, Kansas
City
Oliver B. Ferguson, Fredericktown
Henry C. Haskell, Kansas City
James C. Kirkpatrick, Jefferson City
Isaac A. Long, St. Louis
Lewis E. Meador, Springfield
Dr. Howard A. Rusk, New York City
Adm. Sidney E. Souers, St. Louis
1969
Maurice R. Chambers, St. Louis
Dr. Earl E. Dawson, Jefferson City
Sen. Thomas F. Eagleton, St. Louis
Harry F. Harrington, St. Louis
Robert Hyland, St. Louis
Judge James H. Meredith, St. Louis
H. Lang Rogers, Joplin
Dr. John W. Schwada, Tempe, Ariz.
Charles W. Schwartz, Jefferson City
Joseph C. Welman, Kennett
1970
Charles L. Bacon, Kansas City
H. Roe Bartle, Kansas City
G. Duncan Bauman, St. Louis
Dan Devine, South Bend, Ind.
A. J. Drinkwater, Jr., Charleston
Richard H. Ichord, Houston
Earle B. Jewell, Forsyth
Jack Matthews, Columbia
Lewis M. Means, Fayette
Jack Stapleton, Sr., Stanberry
Elliot H. Stein, St. Louis
1971
John R. Cauley, Washington, D.C.
D. Howard Doane, Point Lookout
D. W. Gilmore, Kansas City
C. Brice Ratchford, Columbia
Jane Froman Smith, Columbia
Leonor K. Sullivan, St. Louis
Robert M. White II, Mexico
1972
Howard F. Baer, St. Louis
William H. Danforth, St. Louis

Betty Cooper Hearnes, Charleston
Everett Keith, Columbia
M. C. Matthes, St. Louis
Fred R. Weber, Jr., St. Louis
1973
Christopher S. Bond, Mexico
1974
John C. Danforth
Floyd R. Gibson
Roy W. Harper
Clarence M. Kelley
Maurice E. Van Acheren

NEBRASKA—NEBRASKA HALL OF FAME
George W. Norris, U.S. senator
Willa Cather, novelist
Gen. John J. Pershing
Father Edward Joseph Flanagan,
founder of Boys Town
William F. Cody (Buffalo Bill), Army
scout and showman
William Jennings Bryan, national
political figure
Bess Streeter Aldrich, author
John G. Neihardt, Nebraska's Poet
Laureate

NORTH CAROLINA—NORTH CAROLINA AWARDS
1964	John N. Couch
	Inglis Fletcher
	John Motley Morehead
	Clarence Poe
	Frances Speight
1965	Frank P. Graham
	Paul Green
	Gerald W. Johnson
	Hunter Johnson
	Frederick A. Wolf
1966	Bernice Kelly Harris
	Luther H. Hodges
	A. G. Odell, Jr.
	Oscar K. Rice
1967	Albert Coates
	Jonathan Daniels
	Carl W. Gottschalk
	Benjamin F. Swalin
	Hiram Houston Merritt
1968	Robert Lee Humber
	Hobson Pittman
	Vermont C. Royster
	Charles Phillips Russell
	Stanley G. Stephens
1969	Kenneth M. Brinkhous

May Gordon Latham
Kellenberger
Ovid Williams Pierce
Charles W. Stanford, Jr.
1970 Philip Handler
Frances Gray Patton
Henry C. Pearson
Terry Sanford
1971 Guy Owen
James H. Semans
Mary Duke Biddle Trent
Semans
Capus Waynick
James Edwin Webb
1972 Sidney Alderman Blackmer
Edward E. Davis, Jr.
John Ehle
William Dallas Herring
Harold Hotelling
1973 Helen Smith Bevington
Ellis Brevier Cowling
Burke Davis
Sam J. Ervin
Kenneth Ness
1974 William C. Fields
Thad G. Stem, Jr.
Ellen Black Winston
James B. Wyngaarden
1975 Robert Ward
Doris Betts
William C. Friday
John L. Etchells

**NORTH DAKOTA—THE
THEODORE ROOSEVELT
ROUGHRIDER AWARD**
Ivan Dmitri, artist
Eric Sevareid, television commentator
Dorothy Stickney, Broadway actress
Lawrence Welk, entertainer
Dr. Anne H. Carlsen, superintendent of
the Crippled Children's School,
Jamestown, N. Dak.
Dr. Robert H. Bahmer, U.S. archivist
Casper Oimoen, capt. of the U.S.
Olympic Team, skiing, 1936
Bert Gamble, with partner Phil
Skogmo, built Gamble-Skogmo into
the twentieth largest retail store
chain in the country
Louis L'Amour, author and
screenwriter of westerns
Edward K. Thompson, editor of *Life*
magazine, special assistant to the

secretary of state for Far Eastern
affairs
Peggy Lee, motion picture actress and
singer
Gen. Harold K. Johnson, Chief of Staff
of the Army
Roger Maris, major league baseball
player

NEW YORK STATE AWARD—New
York State Council on the Arts
For significant contribution to the
material beauty and artistic life in the
Empire State.
Established 1966.
1966
Binghamton Commission on
Architecture and Urban Design
The Buffalo Festival of the Arts
Today
Citizens Advisory Committee for the
Town and Village of Cazenovia
Corning Community College
Judson Memorial Church, New York
City
The New York State Racing
Association, Jamaica
New York Shakespeare Festival,
New York City
St. James Community Center, New
York City
The Stockade Association,
Schenectady
The Syracuse Savings Bank
Mrs. Albert D. Lasker
1967
American Craftsmen's Council, New
York City
The Carborundum Company,
Niagara Falls
The First Unitarian Church of
Rochester
Historic Pittsford, Inc.
The Jacob Riis Houses Plaza, New
York City
Jazzmobile, Inc., New York City
Kleinhans Music Hall, Buffalo
Lake George Opera Festival, Glens
Falls
The New York City Department of
Parks

Olana Preservation, Inc., Hudson

Saratoga Performing Arts Center, Saratoga Springs

Whitney Museum of American Art, New York City

Ada Louise Huxtable

1968

Albright-Knox Art Gallery, Buffalo

Art on Tour, Scarsdale

Eastern Airlines, New York City

Endo Laboratories Inc., Garden City

The Ford Foundation, New York City

Hudson Valley Philharmonic Society, Poughkeepsie

Lake George Park Commission, Ticonderoga

Paley Park, New York City

Society for the Preservation of Landmarks in Western New York, Rochester

Waterford Historical Museum and Cultural Center

WBAI-FM, New York City

Alfred H. Barr, Jr.

1969

The Air Preheater Company, Inc., Wellsville

The American Museum of Natural History, New York City

Brooklyn Academy of Music

Committee for a Library in the Jefferson Courthouse, New York City

Everson Museum of Art, Syracuse

Geneva Historical Society

Lincoln Center for the Performing Arts, New York City

New York University, New York City

Albert A. List Foundation, New York City

92nd Street Young Men's and Young Women's Hebrew Association, New York City

Rochester Museum and Science Center

State University Construction Fund, Albany

Xerox Corporation, Rochester

1970

The Adirondack Museum, Blue Mountain Lake

Alice Tully Hall, New York City

The Asia Society, New York City

Bedford Lincoln Neighborhood Museum (MUSE), Brooklyn

Children's Television Workshop, New York City

The City Center of Music and Drama, New York City

Erie County and the City of Buffalo

The Metropolitan Museum of Art, New York City

The New York State Conservation Bill of Rights

The Scriven Foundation and the Citizens of Cooperstown

Syracuse University Press

Youtheatre, Rochester

John B. Hightower

1971

Abraham & Straus, Brooklyn

Center of the Creative and Performing Arts in the State University of New York at Buffalo

The James Prendergast Library Association, Jamestown

Lithopinion, New York City

South Mall Riverfront Pumping Station, Albany

Temple Beth Zion, Buffalo

Valley Development Foundation, Binghamton

Carl Carmer

A Special Citation for Henry Allen Moe

1972

The Hudson River Museum, Yonkers

Madison County Historical Society, Oneida

New York City Landmarks Preservation Commission

New York State Bar Association, Albany

Six Nations Indian Museum, Onchiota

Three Village Reconstruction at Stony Brook, Setauket, and Old Field, and Ward and Dorothy Melville

George Balanchine

Joseph Papp

1973
 The Alvin Ailey City Center Dance Theater, New York City
 County of Orange
 Kenan Center, Lockport
 La Mama Experimental Theatre Club, New York City, and Ellen Stewart
 New York Zoological Society, Bronx
 Theatre Development Fund, New York City
 Martha Graham
1974
 Chautauqua Institution
 City of Albany and the Albany Board of Education
 Dance Theatre of Harlem, New York City, and Arthur Mitchell
 International Arts Relations (INTAR), New York City
 The Municipal Art Society of New York, New York City
 The New Yorker, New York City, and William Shawn
 The Paper Bag Players, New York City
 The F. & M. Schaefer Brewing Company, Brooklyn

 Tri-Cities Opera, Binghamton
 Nelson A. Rockefeller
 A Special Tribute to Kenneth Dewey and Donald Harper
1975
 Cayuga County Homesite Development Corporation, Auburn
 The Cooper Union for the Advancement of Science and Art, New York City
 Corning Glass Works Foundation
 Cunningham Dance Foundation, New York City
 Gotham Book Mart, New York City, and Frances Steloff
 The Negro Ensemble Company, New York City
 Rensselaer County Junior Museum, Troy
 South Street Seaport Museum, New York City
 Young Filmaker's Foundation, New York City
 Aaron Copland
 Sheldon and Caroline Keck
 A Special Citation for Seymour H. Knox
1976   no awards

WOMEN

See Achievement, Women of the Year, Ladies Home Journal

BEAUTY PAGEANTS

MISS AMERICA
1921
 Margaret Gorman, Washington, D.C.

1922–1923
 Mary Campbell, Columbus, Ohio
1924
 Ruth Malcolmson, Philadelphia, Pa.
1925
 Fay Lanphier, Oakland, California
1926
 Norma Smallwood, Tulsa, Oklahoma
1927
 Lois Delaner, Joliet, Illinois
1928   no contest
1929   no contest
1930   no contest

*Mary Ann Mobley, showing
the dimples that won her the
1959 Miss America title.
(Memory Shop)*

1931   no contest
1932   no contest
1933
  Marion Bergeron, West Haven,
  Conn.
1934   no contest
1935
  Henrietta Leaver, Pittsburgh, Pa.
1936
  Rose Coyle, Philadelphia, Pa.
1937
  Bette Cooper, Bertrand Island, N.J.
1938
  Marilyn Meseke, Marion, Ohio
1939
  Patricia Donnelly, Detroit, Michigan
1940
  Frances Marie Burke, Philadelphia,
  Pa.
1941
  Rosemary LaPlanche, Los Angeles,
  Calif.
1942
  Jo-Carroll Dennison, Tyler, Texas
1943
  Jean Bartel, Los Angeles, Calif.
1944
  Venus Ramey, Washington, D.C.

1945
  Bess Myerson, New York City, N.Y.
1946
  Marilyn Buferd, Los Angeles, Calif.
1947
  Barbara Walker, Memphis,
  Tennessee
1948
  BeBe Shopp, Hopkins, Minnesota
1949
  Jacque Mercer, Litchfield, Arizona
1950   no contest
1951
  Yolande Betbeze, Mobile, Alabama
1952
  Coleen Kay Hutchins, Salt Lake
  City, Utah
1953
  Neva Jane Langley, Macon, Georgia
1954
  Evelyn Margaret Ay, Ephrata, Pa.
1955
  Lee Meriwether, San Francisco,
  Calif.
1956
  Sharon Ritchie, Denver, Colorado
1957
  Marian McKnight, Manning, S.C.

1958
   Marilyn Van Derbur, Denver,
   Colorado
1959
   Mary Ann Mobley, Brandon, Miss.
1960
   Lynda Lee Mead, Natchez, Miss.
1961
   Nancy Fleming, Montague,
   Michigan
1962
   Maria Fletcher, Asheville, N.C.
1963
   Jacquelyn Mayer, Sandusky, Ohio
1964
   Donna Axum, El Dorado, Arkansas
1965
   Vonda Kay Van Dyke, Phoenix,
   Arizona
1966
   Deborah Irene Bryant, Overland
   Park, Kansas
1967
   Jane Anne Jayroe, Laverne,
   Oklahoma
1968
   Debra Dene Barnes, Moran, Kansas
1969
   Judith Anne Ford, Belvidere, Ill.
1970
   Pamela Anne Eldred, Birmingham,
   Michigan
1971
   Phyllis Ann George, Denton, Texas
1972
   Laurie Lea Schaefer, Columbus,
   Ohio
1973
   Terry Anne Meeuwsen, DePere,
   Wisconsin
1974
   Rebecca Ann King, Denver,
   Colorado
1975
   Shirley Cothran, Fort Worth, Texas
1976
   Tawney Elaine Godin, Yonkers, N.Y.
1977
   Dorothy Kathleen Benham, Edina,
   Minn.

**WOMEN   OF   CONSCIENCE
AWARD**—The National Council of
Women of The United States, Inc.

1963
   Rachel Carson, distinguished author
1964
   Hazel Brannon Smith, Mississippi
   editor
1965
   Virginia Senders, author of the
   Minnesota Plan
1966
   Judge Florence M. Kelley, judge of
   Family Court in New York City
1967
   Ellen Jackson, first Black woman
   cited for creative community
   program
1968
   Dr. Dorothy Ainsworth
   Mrs. Andrew Brown
   Dr. Mary S. Calderone
   Mrs. Edward Carter
   Mme. Marcel De Gallaix
   Mrs. D. Joe Hendrickson
   Mrs. Florence Smith Jacobsen
   Dr. May Hall James
   Mrs. Martin Luther King, Jr.
   Mrs. Dorothy M. Lewis
   Mrs. Margaret Moore
   Mrs. Jan Papenek
   Mrs. Mamie B. Reese
   Mrs. Harold E. Rodden
   Mrs. Dean Rusk
   Mrs. Dorothea W. Sitley
   Miss Hilda Torrop
   Mrs. Raphael Tuorover
   Miss Helen F. Winfield
   Mrs. William Volker
   Lt. Violet Hill Whyte
1969
   Annie May Bankhead, black leader
1970
   Ellen Sulzberger Straus, creator of
   "Call for Action" on a New York
   radio station
1971   No award
1972
   Sister Ruth Dowd, achievements as
   educator with teenagers in Harlem
1973
   Patricia Smith, M.D., heroic hospital
   and medical work in Vietnam
1974
   Mrs. Frances F. Pauley, dedicated
   work in civil rights struggle
1975
   Margaret Mead, internationally

renowned ethnologist and anthropologist

1976
Barbara Jordan, congresswoman from Texas

NATIONAL MOTHER—Awarded Annually by the American Mothers Committee, Inc.

1942
Mrs. William N. Berry, North Carolina

1943
Mrs. Alexander Thomsom, Ohio

1944
Mrs. John W. Phillips, Pennsylvania

1945
Mrs. Harper Sibley, New York

1946
Mrs. Emma C. Clement, Kentucky

1947
Mrs. Fred A. Murray, Iowa

1948
Mrs. Herbert W. Hines, Illinois

1949
Mrs. E. A. Gillis, Texas

1950
Mrs. Henry Roe Cloud, Oregon

1951
Dr. Mary T. Sloop, North Carolina

1952
Mrs. Toy Lee Chin Goon, Maine

1953
Mrs. Ethlyn Wisegarver Bott, Illinois

1954
Mrs. Love Mc.T. Tolbert, Georgia

1955
Mrs. Lavina C. Fugal, Utah

1956
Mrs. Maxwell Pritchard, Michigan

1957
Mrs. Hazel Hempel Abel, South Carolina

1958
Mrs. May Roper Coker, South Carolina

1959
Judge Jennie Loitman Barron, Massachusetts

1960
Mrs. Emerald Barman Arbogast, California

1961
Mrs. Louise Giddings Currey, Tennessee

1962
Mrs. Mary Celeste Weatherly, Alabama

1962
Mrs. Clara Sproat Glenn, Ohio

1963
Mrs. Olga Pearson Engdahl, Nebraska

1964
Mrs. Cora Hjertaas Stavig, South Dakota

1965
Mrs. Lorena Chipman Fletcher, Utah

1966
Mrs. Bertha Holt, Oregon

1967
Mrs. Minnie Knoop Guenther, Arizona

1968
Mrs. Elizabeth Grossman Bodine, North Dakota

1969
Mrs. Evelyn Peterson LeTourneau, Texas

1970
Mrs. Dorothy Lee Wilson, Tennessee

1971
Mrs. Fred H. Zahn, Oklahoma

1972
Mrs. Esther Hunt Moore, North Carolina

1973
Mrs. Ruth Youngdahl Nelson, Minnesota

1974
Mrs. Russell S. Marriott, District of Columbia

1975
Mrs. Josephine Wainam Burson, Tennessee

1976
Mrs. Maxine Grinstaff, New Mexico

See Science, Garvan Medal, American Chemical Society